BEHIND BLUE EYES

Craig Sawyer

BEHIND BLUE EYES

Copyright © 2026 Craig Sawyer
ISBN: 979-8-9947368-0-7

Printed by Kindle Direct Publishing

First printing, 2026

Craig Sawyer Media
Cape Coral, FL
www.CraigSawyerMedia.com

DEDICATION

For the ones who stayed and for the ones I pushed away.
For the ones who had to stand back and watch me learn the hard way.
And mostly for my son, who gives me a reason to keep trying.

Table of Contents

PREFACE

Writing *Behind Blue Eyes* has ended up being one of the most unexpected things I've ever taken on.

When I started, I honestly thought it would be pretty straightforward. Just tell my story. Lay out the big moments, connect the dots, and maybe wrap it up with a little perspective like, "Here's what I learned."

But it hasn't worked like that at all.

The more I write, the more it feels like I'm not just documenting what happened. I'm running into parts of myself I thought I already understood. Old beliefs I didn't realize were still driving me. Assumptions I've carried for so long they started to feel like facts. Stuff I thought I'd moved past, only to realize I'd just packed it away and called it "handled."

And what's surprised me most is how personal it still feels. Like putting it into words forces me to stop dodging the uncomfortable parts, or the messy parts, or the parts that don't fit into a clean "this happened, then this happened, and now I'm better" storyline. It's been more honest than I expected. More emotional. More uncomfortable.

And the title is more than a nod to the color of my eyes. It's about the gap between what people see and what's actually going on inside me.

My eyes have always gotten attention. People comment on how bright they are, how "pretty" they are. I've watched someone lose their train of thought mid-sentence because they got stuck staring at them. It's almost funny sometimes. Until it isn't. Because what they're reacting to is just the surface.

What they don't see is what sits behind them. The pain. The confusion. The quiet torment. The questions I carried for decades without answers. That's why this memoir exists. To let people look behind those blue eyes and finally see the person living there.

When I first started writing, I assumed this would be a book of "big moments." Major turning points. Dramatic decisions. And sure, some of that is in here. But what surprised me was how often those weren't the real defining moments.

It wasn't always the grand forks in the road that changed me. A lot of the time it was the small stuff. The throwaway afternoons. The quiet scenes I never thought I'd remember. The little choices I made on a whim. The subtle looks. One sentence someone said that landed harder than they probably ever meant it to.

For years, I walked around with this idea that I was the architect of my own fate. That if I just made the right choices, I could build the perfect life and avoid blowing anything up too badly.

That's cute, right?

But when you really sit with your own story, you start noticing how much of it wasn't planned. The address your parents picked. The bus route you took. The side of the road your house happened to land on. The random day you ended up standing next to the exact person who would change everything, without either of you realizing it yet. The timing. The accidents. The dumb luck. The stuff you couldn't control if you tried.

At first, seeing it that way made me feel small. Like maybe I wasn't as in charge as I liked to believe. Like I wasn't the "architect" so much as the guy inside the building trying to figure out why the lights keep flickering.

But eventually, it did something else.

It made me grateful.

Not the hashtag-gratitude, "live laugh love" kind of grateful. I mean the kind you feel when you look back at a version of yourself that should've been wrecked by something, and somehow wasn't. Or was, but still got up. Still kept going. Still found a way to keep living even when it didn't look pretty.

I'm grateful for the detours. For the people who drifted in and out and still left their mark. For the relationships that broke in exactly the wrong way at exactly the right time. For the pain I've endured. And yeah, even the pain I've caused.

Some of my most meaningful memories aren't the big life events. They're the small, warm ones. A quiet moment dancing in the living room with my infant son. A brief look of understanding from someone who got it. A laugh that showed up in the middle of a really dark day and reminded me I wasn't completely alone.

Those are the moments I go back to when I need to remember who I am. No one can see those things when they look into my eyes, and most people could never fully understand them. But they built me.

When I was younger, I wanted freedom more than anything. I didn't always know what to do with it, but I wanted it. I chased it through impulsive decisions. I tried to outrun pain with women, with reinvention, with bad decisions that felt like good stories at the time.

I hit the self-destruct button more than once, all in the name of living. Through people I knew weren't right for me. Through places that felt far enough away from whatever I was trying not to deal with.

And maybe in some ways, it really was living. At least it felt like it.

But at some point, you have to stop and ask, honestly, what have I actually learned?

That's where growth starts. Not in the running. In the returning.

Writing this memoir became that pause for me. The deep breath. The long look backward. The chance to ask questions I'd avoided for years. *Who have I become? What matters to me now? What am I still carrying?*

Somewhere between freedom and reflection, between chasing and coming home, that's where we start finding ourselves. That's where we stop pretending we can control every outcome and start taking ownership of the whole ride. The good parts. The broken parts. The confusing parts. The parts we're proud of, and the parts we'd rather never talk about.

It's also where you stop blaming the past and start listening to it. Not romanticizing it. Not rewriting it. Just listening.

And in that space, something shifts. You soften in a way you didn't know you needed to. You stop living like your story is only the highlight reel, and you finally take in the whole game.

That's when change becomes possible. Real change. Not the kind you say out loud to sound mature, but the kind that actually shows up in your choices.

My path has been anything but a straight line. There have been detours, regrets, and more than a few bad decisions. But there's also been unexpected beauty. More than I gave myself credit for at the time. I see it now in the people I've loved, the laughter I've shared, and moments I almost missed but somehow didn't.

Memory, for me, has never been a neat timeline. It's scattered. We like to pretend memory is factual, like we're flipping through a photo album of hard evidence. That's not how it works in my head. I remember through emotion. Through a smell. A song. The way a room felt.

Sometimes my memories even contradict each other. I've told stories I would've sworn were accurate, only to have someone say, "That's not how it happened." Maybe they're right. Maybe I've got details wrong. Maybe I blended two moments together or filled in gaps without realizing it.

But the feeling? The lump in my throat, the shame, the joy, the adrenaline. That part is real to me.

That emotional truth has started to matter more to me than factual precision. So that's what this book is. Not a legal record. Not a court transcript. It's a collection of emotional heartbeats. It's my best attempt to tell the truth of what it felt like to be me inside this particular life.

I'm not here to prove anything or defend myself. I'm not trying to force my life into a neat, polished storyline that wraps up clean at the end. My life hasn't been clean. It's been messy, complicated, and in more than a few places, downright embarrassing.

There are parts I'm not proud of. You'll probably hit moments where you think, *Why would you even admit that?*

Because I already judged myself harder than anyone reading this ever will.

Nobody reading this book is ever going to judge me more harshly than I've already judged myself. I've done that part thoroughly. This is me. All of me. I am who I am.

But I've made peace with the mess. I've started to see the beauty in it. And looking back now, I can honestly say I don't regret it. Not even the painful chapters. Not even the days I didn't think I'd get through.

Each one gave me something. Insight. Resilience. Humility. Compassion. All of it led me here. To *this* page. To *this* version of myself. To *this* moment where I'm finally willing to look in a mirror.

The truth is, a lot of us are hiding behind our own version of blue eyes. We put something shiny, or at least "fine," on the outside while quietly falling apart on the inside. We smile when we want to scream. We crack jokes when we're barely holding it together. We carry invisible burdens and still show up for work, for family, for life like nothing's wrong.

When I step back and look at everything, I see all of us doing the same thing in different ways. Searching. For love. For connection. For identity. For peace.

We don't always know that's what we're doing. Sometimes it looks like rebellion. Sometimes it looks like people-pleasing. Sometimes it looks like ambition, perfectionism, burnout, or just staying busy so we don't have to sit with ourselves for too long.

But underneath it, we want the same things. We want to belong. We want to feel safe. We want to be seen.

For the ones who feel unseen. For the ones who've been told to "get over it" while they were still bleeding on the inside. For the ones carrying more than anyone realizes.

This book is for you. I *see* you. I *am* you.

And I hope my story reminds you that your pain isn't meaningless. Your story matters. Your journey, no matter how tangled or imperfect it looks from the outside, is still worth telling.

Writing *Behind Blue Eyes* gave me a chance to see myself clearly, maybe for the first time. Not as a list of mistakes or achievements, but as a human being doing the best he could with what he had. And sometimes doing the absolute worst with what he had.

If there's anything I've learned that's worth passing on, it's this. Give yourself some grace. Pay attention to the small wins. And don't be afraid to look behind someone's eyes. You might find a whole life hiding there.

Life isn't made in the big, picture-perfect moments. It's made in the ones that slide by quietly. The ones you almost miss. The ones that leave a mark so deep you don't recognize it until years later. Those are the real milestones. And those are the ones worth remembering.

Yes, my blue eyes have turned heads. That's fine. What matters more to me now is what they've witnessed, both beautiful and brutal, and what I've finally found the courage to say out loud.

This memoir isn't a final verdict or some polished version of my life. It's an offering. A crack in the armor. An invitation to see not just through my eyes, but beyond them.

I wish I could tell you it's a neat arc. Boy hurts, boy grows, boy heals, cue inspirational music. It's not that. My growth hasn't been linear. It's more like a heart monitor. Up, down, flatline, up again, down again.

What I can say is this. I've learned to stop editing my story so it looks good from the outside. I've stopped pretending that the version people saw when they complimented my blue eyes was the whole picture.

Underneath every chapter here is the same simple belief. We are all an accumulation of our experiences and our conversations. Not just the big ones, not just the pretty ones, and not just the ones we brag about. *All* of them.

I had a childhood full of simple magic and real struggle, sometimes in the same afternoon. I learned resilience from frozen fingers hauling firewood, empathy from watching my brother get mocked on a sidewalk, and self-awareness lying alone on a gym floor with a cassette player while everyone else played outside.

I also learned how easy it is to look fine on the outside while you're quietly falling apart on the inside.

So this book is for people like that. For the ones who smile through it. The ones who got really good at being "okay" while their chest was on fire. The kids who grew up being told to suck it up, be grateful, move on, and now find themselves in midlife wondering, *What the hell just happened,* and *is this really it?*

If you've ever felt unseen, or misjudged, or like your story didn't matter because it wasn't tragic enough or dramatic enough or tidy enough, I'm talking to you.

I see you.

I don't have all the answers. I don't even have most of them. But I can offer you my story, told as honestly as I know how, with a mix of sarcasm, regret, gratitude, and a stupid amount of detail.

I hope that by the time you step back from these pages, you feel less alone. I hope you feel a little more permission to tell the truth about your own story.

And I hope the next time you look into someone's eyes, blue, brown, green, whatever, you remember there's a whole universe behind them that you know nothing about. And yeah, mine have turned a few heads. But more importantly, they've watched some beautiful, brutal, unbelievable moments I'm finally ready to share.

But I understand that not everyone who was part of my story is ready to tell their own, or have their story told for them. So until they are ready to let you look behind what's hiding behind their eyes, I have changed their names in my story.

What I'm sharing here is true to my memory, the people, the situations, the conversations, and the emotions. I'm not trying to rewrite what happened or make anyone look a certain way. I'm protecting privacy, not changing the point. The characters may have new names, but the experiences behind them are real.

These pages aren't about making myself look good. They're about finally telling the truth about what's been living behind my blue eyes.

These are some of the things they have seen.

Welcome behind the blue.

INTRODUCTION
IMPACT: All of Me, All at Once

I had the top down on my little white MG Midget, black vinyl tucked and folded neatly behind me. To anyone else, it was probably just an old, tiny British car. To me, a sixteen-year-old with a fresh driver's license, it was freedom on four wheels. The engine wasn't powerful, but it had an eager little roar as I accelerated. My hand rested on the leather gear shifter, worn smooth from years of being gripped by somebody who needed escape just as much as I did.

The road stretched out ahead, surrounded on both sides by fields of corn and soybeans slowly giving up their green for rust, gold, and that crispy end-of-season brown. Even at sixteen, with my brain still half-formed and full of hormones, I knew this wasn't just a drive. It was one of those moments that feels ridiculously vivid, like time slows down just enough for you to notice everything and think, *remember this.*

Up ahead, in his blue '86 Nissan pickup, Adam led the way. He was my best friend. My ride-or-die. We were always doing dumb shit, two idiots in old vehicles pretending every back road was some kind of adventure. We weren't drag racing or doing anything stupid. We were just being sixteen-year-old boys on an overpass above I-74 on our way to Lake of the Woods Park to spend a few hours hanging out with the mini-truck club.

Adam crested the overpass first, his tailgate bobbing as he hit the top. I dropped a gear and gunned it, trying to close the gap. The MG answered back, giving everything it had.

But when I hit the top of the hill, my whole life swung in about half a second. Which, let's be honest, wasn't much.

Just up the road, coming straight at me, was a white sedan, and it wasn't on his side of the road. Those old country tar roads didn't have the standard yellow lines painted down the center, but it was still obvious what side you were supposed to drive on.

Driving tip: Straddling the center isn't the correct side.

People talk about time slowing down like it's a cliché, but they're not wrong. My heart froze, but I punched the gas and yanked the wheel to the right, trying not to turn my little MG into a crushed soda can. Gravel spit out from under my tires as I shot onto the shoulder, with the steering wheel bucking under my hands. The MG shuddered and bounced.

The sedan roared past my left side, missing me by inches.

For a half-second, relief hit. I'd done it. I'd avoided the crash.

I eased the wheel left, trying to guide the car back onto the asphalt like they teach you in those driver's ed videos, where the narrator calmly explains how to re-enter the lane and everything works out. But this was real life, not some VHS tape with cheesy background music.

My front passenger tire hit a pothole, deep enough to rip the steering wheel right out of my hands.

My car twisted sideways. Suddenly the ditch bank wasn't off to the side anymore. It was coming straight at me.

The world went into this weird slow-motion blur. Fence posts flashed by. The tall grass in the ditch bent and smeared into streaks of green and yellow. My tires screamed against the pavement, begging for traction.

And then I saw my dad's face.

Not in front of me, not standing on the road, but in my head. That look I'd seen a hundred times before over stupid stuff. Tracking mud in the house. Forgetting chores. A bad grade. Only this time it was twisted metal and broken glass and, *what were you thinking, Craig?*

I saw the damage that hadn't even happened yet.

The crumpled white hood. The shattered windshield. The mess. The bill. The regret.

Shit.

"Ssshhhhiiiiiiiit!" I screamed it this time, out loud, stretched out, like if I made the word longer it could cover everything that was about to go wrong.

And then gravity let go.

My little MG launched. There was no more road, no more ditch, no more sense of up or down. Just weightlessness. My stomach lifted and my body floated and I became this loose thing inside the car, a rag doll getting tossed wherever physics felt like throwing me.

There was no engine noise anymore. No tire squeal. No music. No wind. Just this strange, muffled silence.

I hit something. Or something hit me. Glass, metal, seat belt, doorframe. I couldn't tell. Pain didn't register yet. Just impact. Sensation. Motion. My body slammed, flipped, folded, snapped back. The world somersaulted around me. Sky. Ground. Sky. Ground.

It wasn't like a movie reel of my life playing in perfect, chronological order. It wasn't even organized. It was more like someone grabbed every memory I'd ever had and dumped it all at once into my chest.

Sixteen years, all piled together.

Faces.

Mom. Dad. My sister. My brother. Adam. Teachers. Kids from school.

Moments.

Christmas mornings. Birthday parties. Riding the bus. Playing on the playground. Standing under the kitchen table listening to grown-ups laugh.

Dreams.

Who I thought I might be. The blurry image of "someday" that every kid dreams about.

I felt absolutely everything and somehow nothing at all.

They hit like a flood. Everything at once.

ROUND 1
Crayons, Crushes, and Cassette Tapes

I grew up in rural Central Illinois, in that nowhere space between Champaign and Mahomet. We were about six miles in either direction from each town, which meant we weren't *really* from either place, at least not in the way kids like to claim hometowns. On envelopes, our address said Rural Route 3, Box 59, Champaign, Illinois. I later found out that if our house had been across the road, literally just on the other side, we would've had a Mahomet address instead.

Fifteen feet. That's all it would've taken for me to have a completely different story. Different school, different town, different friends, different everything. A sleepy little place of 2,000 instead of a university city of nearly 60,000 people.

It's wild when you think about it. We act like our lives are shaped by these big, dramatic choices, but sometimes it's just coordinates. A dot on a map. A property line. One side of the road or the other.

That address became one of my first real lessons in perspective. Later in life, it grounded me. It made me grateful for the life I did get, the friends I did have, the memories that still live on in my heart. It also made me more compassionate toward people who grew up just a little differently. Because honestly, a different bus route, a different school, a different neighborhood, and I could've been someone else entirely.

Looking back now, as an adult with way too many bills and not nearly enough naps, I couldn't have asked for a better childhood. I had a close family, loving parents, and a country environment that felt like it was designed specifically for a kid's imagination. Sure, it would've been easier to live in town, closer to friends and bike rides and convenience stores with cheap candy. But the country had its own magic.

Living outside city limits came with its own complications though. Birthday parties and sleepovers weren't just "Hey, can Jason come over?" situations. They required planning. Maps. Gas. Parents committing to a solid 20–30-minute round trip *twice*, once to drop their kid off, once to come get them again. So, no, we weren't the house where kids just wandered in and out all the time. But we still had friends over. We still had birthday parties.

When I played Little League, my parents would invite the whole team out at the end of the season. We'd run wild in the backyard, no neighbors to complain about the noise, no cars flying down the street, no one telling us to keep it down. Just kids, grass, and the kind of freedom you don't realize is rare until you're older and sitting in traffic somewhere, staring at brake lights and missing the sound of crickets.

A lot of my favorite memories are anchored to that house. Even now, though, when I see pictures of it in some old photo album, it doesn't look the same as in my memory. That's one of the hardest things about nostalgia; you eventually realize that your memories have been edited.

You start to wonder: *How much of what I remember is real, and how much did I just… create over time?*

Writing this book has kicked a lot of that dust into the air. I'll start describing something that feels accurate, and then another memory shows up that doesn't quite line up. Contradictions pop up out of nowhere. And I know there will be more of that. That's the price of digging around in your own head.

I heard once that memories are merely memories of each other, not of the actual event itself. You actually only remember the original event once. Every memory after that is just remembering the last time you remembered it. So, you keep remembering what you remembered. So, as time passes, like playing "telephone", a little detail gets lost with each "remember." I don't know if that's true, but it makes sense.

Some of my earliest memories are from that country house, around age four. I remember feeling safe there. Normal. Whatever "normal" is. And even now, I've never wished I'd grown up anywhere else. I loved that place then, and I still do in my head. I miss the house. I miss the land. Mostly, I miss how I *felt* when I was there.

Nostalgia is a weird thing. It's like emotional Instagram filters for your past. I know not everyone had that kind of childhood. I'm not naïve enough to think my experience was universal. We were blessed. And a lot of people weren't.

One of my earliest, clearest snapshots inside that house is me standing under the kitchen table while the grown-ups talked and laughed above me. I must've been three or four. I was always small, still am. At five-foot-three as a grown man, I've simply committed to the part. But back then, I could stand fully upright under that wooden table with room to spare. The legs felt like pillars, and I'd just wander between them like it was my own personal forest, the underside of the tabletop hanging over me like a low, wooden sky.

Down there, I was technically "there" but not really *seen*, and somehow that felt perfect. I could hear the whole soundtrack of adulthood without having to participate. The murmur of voices rolled together into this constant, soothing hum. Every now and then I'd catch one of those sudden bursts of laughter, silverware clinking, coffee cups hitting the table after a quick sip. The air was thick with the smell of coffee and whatever my mom had thrown together for everyone to eat. My aunts and uncles drifted in and out of those nights, along with a few friends from nearby Mahomet. There was always some kind of inside joke floating above my head.

I didn't understand the conversations, not really. I didn't know what bills were, or who was mad at who this week, or what adult life was quietly doing to all of them. But I knew the *feeling* in that room. I knew it was good. I knew it was safe.

Under that table, with all that noise overhead, I felt wrapped up in something solid and warm, like their laughter was this invisible blanket that said, *You're okay.*

Around seven or eight is when my memories start clicking into more solid shapes. That's when the blur turns into actual scenes instead of flashes: riding the bus, walking into school, playing with friends whose names I can still conjure if I sit with it long enough. But even before that, little pieces stand out, like photographs left too long in the sun but still recognizable.

Kindergarten was at Garden Hills Elementary. The school sat right off Route 150, the same road we took every day to get from home into town. That made it feel familiar, like an extension of our rural life rather than some foreign place I got dropped off and abandoned at for the day. It felt like the road just... continued, and school happened to be sitting alongside it.

My teacher was Mrs. Wiggins, a black woman with big round plastic-frame glasses. If I had to guess now, I'd say she was in her mid-thirties, but to five-year-old me she might as well have been a thousand years old. Every teacher was. They were statues with voices, ancient and permanent, like they'd always been there and always would be.

I liked her, though. She had a soft voice and a calm presence that made my little nervous system settle down. Kindergarten wasn't magical or traumatic; it just *was*. Paste, crayons, naps on thin blue mats, the smell of tempera paint and floor cleaner. No big explosions, no disasters, nothing that branded itself as a wound. Just a quiet introduction to the idea that life happens on a schedule. At that age, not hating school is already a win.

First grade brought Mrs. Freehill. What I remember most about that year isn't her personality, exactly, it's the handwriting award. Somewhere along the line, we were told we'd be practicing our letters, all those looped cursive E's and perfectly upright H's, and that there would be an actual certificate for the student with the best handwriting.

And something in me latched onto that like it was oxygen.

I wanted my name on that paper like it proved I belonged there, that I could be *good* at something, that there was a reason for me to take up space in that classroom. So I worked at it in the way only a kid searching for approval can work, tight grip on the pencil, tongue pressed to the corner of my mouth, shoulders hunched, trying to make my letters look like they'd been printed by a machine.

It felt like my first real goal in life: win the handwriting award. Something small I could control in a world where I didn't control very much at all.

And I did.

I still have that certificate in a scrapbook my mom made, mud splatter and all from the bus ride home that day. It's ridiculous and tiny in the grand scheme of things, just a flimsy piece of paper with my name on it, but it still means something to me. It's proof that even as a kid, I needed something to chase, some reason to feel seen. I needed acknowledgement, even if it was just for how neatly I could curl an S.

Second grade was with Mrs. Danneberger. I remember her name, pale complexion, her short white hair, a gentle, older face that never looked particularly thrilled or upset. Just… there. Not much else sticks. It's like that whole year has been filed under "background noise."

Third grade was Mrs. Zimmerman. Same thing, name, a vague impression of a woman in front of a chalkboard, and not many specifics. It's funny which years grab onto you and which just float away into the blur. Sometimes it's not about what happened, but how *you* were feeling when it happened that determines whether it stays.

Fourth grade was when I had Mrs. Peppers, a thin Black woman with a steady presence and a warm smile. I liked her. She made class feel safe and predictable, like nothing was going to explode or surprise me. No frenzy, no raised voices that sent my stomach into a knot, no big drama. Just a solid year on a steady boat. Sometimes "nothing crazy happened" is the best possible description. Sometimes "uneventful" is its own kind of blessing.

Fifth grade, though, that's when the world started expanding in my head.

My teacher was Mrs. O'Dea, an older, heavyset white woman with dark hair streaked with silver. She always smelled overwhelmingly like coffee, with something underneath that might've been cigarettes, might've been just stale breath, I don't know. But I remember that smell. Whenever she leaned over my desk to help with an assignment, I'd hold my breath, eyes glued to the paper, trying not to cringe or make a face that would give me away.

She was a decent teacher, firm but not cruel. The thing that changed that year wasn't really about math or spelling tests anyway. Fifth grade is when my life stopped being just "home and school" and started becoming more about people. When I started noticing who got laughed with and who got laughed at. When crushes started sneaking in and this confusing awareness of certain girls that didn't feel like the innocent "she's nice" stuff from earlier years. It was stronger. More intense.

Fifth grade was where that hunger I'd had for a handwriting certificate started evolving into something bigger and more dangerous: the hunger to be accepted. To be liked. To be chosen. And once that switch flipped, it never really ever flipped back. It just kept getting louder.

My core group of school friends then was Randy, Matt, and Axel. We were always together, laughing, acting out imaginary fight scenes, pretending to be superheroes on the playground or action movie stars with invisible cameras following us. We were invincible in the way kids are before the world of responsibility starts taking over.

Then there were the girls in our circle: Annie, Wynnie, and Dani.

I had a major crush on Annie that entire year. Dani and I rode the same bus, and I liked her too. She was funny and easy to talk to. But Annie… Annie was different. Ten-year-old heart, first full-blown crush that actually hurt a little when she walked away.

She lived close to the school, just a couple blocks away, and walked every day. I can still see her little white ranch house in my mind on Marigold Lane. That address has been sitting in my brain rent-free for over forty years. I can't remember what I ate yesterday, but I could probably still mail her a letter without looking anything up. Same with my childhood phone number: 863-2033. Those things were just engrained into me.

We all ran around together, me, the guys, the girls, playing on the blacktop, chasing each other through the grass, inventing games on the fly that had rules no one fully understood but we all agreed to anyway.

But one memory of Annie burns brighter than the rest: Halloween, fifth grade, 1984.

She came to school dressed as a black cat.

Now, to an adult, it would've looked like a cute kid costume. Innocent, simple. But to ten-year-old me, it was basically the preview version of those "sexy cat" costumes you see at every college party. She wore this snug black leotard with a hood that had little cat ears, whiskers drawn on her cheeks, and a perfect little black circle painted on the tip of her nose.

Nothing about it was inappropriate. It was completely age-appropriate. But to me, it was… electric. My brain and body didn't have the language yet, but they knew something had changed. That was the moment I knew this wasn't just, *She's nice.* This was my first real crush, the kind that makes your stomach drop, your palms sweat, and your brain short-circuit when she looks in your direction and laughs with a cute, light giggle.

She never liked me back that way. Of course she didn't. Why would she? But that didn't stop my heart from sprinting every time she laughed anywhere near me, or from secretly hoping she'd choose to walk next to *me* instead of someone else. It was the beginning of that painful little truth: sometimes your heart runs full speed toward someone who never even notices.

That year was the start of everything getting bigger emotionally. The world outside my own head started to matter more. Friends. Feelings. Tiny relational dramas that felt enormous at the time. Fifth grade is when life started turning from a vague, black-and-white childhood into something more like full color. None of it made sense yet, but I could feel the volume turning up.

Even now, when I think back on that time, I feel this pressure in my chest, this little lump forming in my throat that never quite goes away. It's that strange emotional tightrope between smiling and crying, a mix of sweetness and grief. The kind of ache you get when you realize how simple things used to be, and how quietly they slipped away while you were busy just being a kid.

Garden Hills Elementary, especially that playground just off the basketball courts, was pure joy for me in those early years. It wasn't just a place we went for recess, it was a whole world. Some of my most vivid memories are from that stretch of cracked blacktop and packed dirt. Standing there, breathing in the cold air that burned a little in my lungs, climbing, running, falling, laughing until my sides hurt. That playground didn't feel like "equipment" to me, it felt like its own country, a separate universe where the rules were simple: climb higher, run faster, hang on tighter.

We had this towering tornado slide, monkey bars that might as well have been actual jungle territory, and swings so tall that if you pumped your legs hard enough, it felt like you might actually loop over the top bar and disappear into the sky. For a kid who always felt small, that kind of height felt like power. Like if I just leaned back a little farther, I could actually escape gravity, and maybe a few other things too.

The tornado slide was legendary. Ten feet tall, narrow metal ladder, grated platform at the top where you would stand for a split second, heart hammering hard enough that you could feel it in your throat, fingers gripping the cold metal, before you dropped yourself into the spiral. The slide itself was shiny metal, twisted into about one and a half turns, 540 degrees of, *this is a little frightening, but I'm doing it anyway.* That split second before you let go, that was my favorite feeling. Fear, excitement, defiance, all stacked on top of each other like those kids on the ladder.

On hot days, that metal turned into a skillet. If you went down in shorts, you would rocket through the tunnel, the heat biting into the backs of your thighs so sharply it almost stole your breath, and sometimes you'd catch air at the bottom and bounce off the lip like a rock skipping across a pond. We all had slide scars, those little pink reminders on our legs, but nobody complained. Not really. That was just part of the deal, part of the unspoken agreement we made with childhood.

We get to feel this alive, and in exchange, sometimes it's going to hurt.

They took that slide down years later. Too dangerous. Too risky. Too much liability for a world that is terrified of bruises and scraped knees and the possibility of things not being perfectly safe.

Now, as a parent myself, I get it. Sort of. I can picture my own kid on that overcrowded ladder and feel my stomach seize. We used to cram that thing full, kid after kid, chest to back, clinging to the rungs, stacked like a human Jenga tower. If the kid at the top leaned back too far or got shoved, the whole chain could collapse, everyone tumbling down to the packed dirt below. Broken arms were absolutely on the table. The danger was real, not imagined.

But still… I miss it.

I miss driving past the school and seeing that bright metal spiral standing there like a guard tower over our childhood, this gleaming dare at the edge of the blacktop. I miss knowing that if you stood at the bottom and closed your eyes, just for a second, you could still *hear* the echoes of kids shrieking their way down, that mix of terror and joy that only kids can pull off. Now it's gone, replaced with safer, softer, more "appropriate" equipment. Probably better for bones, sure. But not better for stories. Not better for that wild feeling of being right on the edge of danger and having the time of your life.

There was also a merry-go-round. I hated that thing with a passion.

I've never been able to handle spinning. There is something about that endless circling that makes my stomach revolt, like my insides are trying to escape through my skin. Other kids lived for it. They would pile on, hands gripping the bars so tight their knuckles turned white, and someone would stay on the ground and push, running in tight circles, cranking that thing as fast as humanly possible just to see who could hang on and who would get launched off like a human frisbee. Then they would stumble away, green-faced, laughing or puking or both, and somehow call that a good time.

Not me.

I would watch from the side, feet planted firmly on the ground, feeling queasy just looking at it and thinking, *Yeah… no. Hard pass.* I would rather throw myself down a burning metal tube from ten feet up and take the impact at the bottom than spin slowly in circles and feel my stomach betray me in front of everybody. Even as a kid, humiliation felt worse than pain.

Funny, looking back now, how clear it is: even as a kid, I already had lines I wouldn't cross. I would take the sudden drop, the burn, the quick hit at the bottom, but not the endless, disorienting spin. I could handle pain that came quickly and was over, but not the kind that dragged on.

I think nine or ten was when I stopped feeling like just another kid and started feeling… off. Different. Tilted a few degrees to the side while everyone else seemed to be standing straight. There was no single big trauma moment that flipped a switch, more like a slow, creeping awareness that I felt things deeper and noticed things other people seemed to skim past.

There's one moment from back then that still shows up crystal clear, like it has been laminated in my brain so time can't smudge it. Our school cafeteria doubled as the gym, so it always smelled like this weird mix of sweat, hot food, and industrial cleaner. The floor was that cold, hard tile that echoed every footstep. One day, after lunch, the other kids bolted outside for recess, shouting, shoving, slamming the heavy metal doors behind them like they were escaping prison.

But I stayed.

I had talked my mom into letting me bring my little cassette recorder to school. This little plastic rectangle suddenly felt like a portal. I laid flat on my back in the middle of that empty gym floor, the cool tile pressing into my shoulder blades, the gym lights buzzing above me. The echo of the last voices faded, and for a moment there was this beautiful silence.

I held the recorder close, hit rewind, then play, then rewind again.

"Let's Hear It for the Boy" by Deniece Williams, over and over.

> *"… I just wanna cheer*
> *Let's hear it for the boy…"*

I was determined to learn every word, every little vocal run, every note. I don't even know what I thought I was going to do with it. There was no talent show on the calendar, no performance coming up, no audience waiting to clap. I just knew I needed to sing that song.

It was like I was trying to match something inside myself to something outside myself, to prove I wasn't completely out of tune with the world. I don't know. I couldn't explain it then and I can't explain it now.

While the rest of the kids were outside screaming on the blacktop, burning off sugar and energy, I was inside, alone, with a cassette player pressed to my ear, soaking up that song like it was oxygen. I could have gone outside. I could have joined in the adventure. But my body stayed on that cool tile floor, eyes up at the buzzing lights, humming along, rewinding the same section five times.

I didn't know why I stayed behind; I just knew I *had* to. There was a pull there, stronger than the sound of kids yelling my name through the doors, stronger than the fear of looking weird or different. Something in me already knew that I needed moments like that, those little pockets of silence where I could just feel things without anyone watching.

Looking back, I think that was the first time I truly chose my own company over the crowd. The first time I let myself drift away from what everyone else was doing, not because I'd been pushed out or rejected, but because something inside pulled me somewhere quieter. Somewhere I could turn the volume up on my own thoughts and feelings, even if I didn't have the words for them yet.

That little boy on the gym floor, clutching a cassette player like a lifeline while everybody else ran around outside, that wasn't just some cute, quirky childhood story. That was the beginning of understanding that I was built a little differently. And that difference felt both lonely and oddly comforting at the exact same time. I didn't feel like I fit, but I also didn't want to trade that part of me away.

After school, my siblings and I went to Affi's house. She lived a few blocks from Garden Hills and watched us after school while my dad spent his days driving a cement truck through dusty job sites and my mom worked day shifts at Kmart. Tim, my brother, was in fifth grade, my sister, Allie, was in second, and I was the baby, just starting kindergarten.

Affi always made egg drop soup. That's what sticks with me the most about her. I don't know if she was Asian, or where she learned to make it, or if it came from some family recipe or the back of a soup can, but that soup was everything to me. Warm, salty broth with those delicate ribbons of egg folding over themselves like they were dancing. Simple, but it felt fancy to me. Comfort in a chipped bowl, handed to me by someone who wasn't family but felt close enough.

I haven't had egg drop soup in years, but every time I see it on a menu, I think about her tiny kitchen, the cluttered counters, the smell of broth in the air, and that strange mix of exhaustion and calm that came after school. That feeling of being somewhere safe, even if it wasn't home. Part of me still wants to order it just to see if it hits the same, if it can pull me back to that little table with my legs swinging off the chair.

One afternoon, the three of us were walking to Affi's when a group of older boys started picking on my brother, Tim. Tim was a bigger kid, what people called "husky" back then. Even the word sounded like it was smirking, like it was trying not to just say *fat* out loud, like it was doing him some kind of favor by trying to be polite.

They started in on him, and it happened fast. Teasing at first, then snickering, then those little jabs at his weight. To them, it was just a joke. To him, to me, he was clearly the target of a heartless punchline. It wasn't funny. It was hurtful.

I was only five, but that moment burned itself into me like someone branded it on the inside of my chest. I can still see the sidewalk, the way the sun hit the cracks in the concrete, the sound of gravel under our shoes, all of it wrapped around that one awful exchange like a frame.

I remember looking up at Tim's face and watching it change in real time. A second earlier he had been just... Tim. My big brother. And then, as the words landed, his whole expression transitioned. The way his eyes sank a little, like someone had quietly dimmed the lights inside them. The way his shoulders dropped, as if somebody had just walked up behind him and hung heavy bags of sand from his neck. The way his smile didn't just fade, it *collapsed*, like it was embarrassed for ever having been there.

I swear I could feel his heart sink, even though I couldn't see it.

The words they threw at him felt like they hit me too. Every insult bounced off his body and somehow lodged itself in mine. I could feel my face getting hot, like my skin had turned into a warning light. My fists clenched so tight my nails dug half-moon marks into my palms, this tiny five-year-old body trying to hold an anger way too big for it.

I was furious, and under that fury was something even louder: helplessness.

It was this awful, gut-deep realization that no matter how much I loved him, no matter how hard I clenched my fists or how hot my face got, I couldn't stop their mouths. I couldn't grab the words out of the air and shove them back down their throats. My legs were short, my arms were small, and my voice felt like it was trapped.

I wanted to scream at them. I wanted to shove them, push them back, make them feel even one percent as small as they were trying to make him feel. I wanted to stand in front of him like a shield, this ridiculous little kid daring them to go through me first.

Instead, I froze.

I just stood there and watched my brother's heart take a hit he didn't deserve. Watched him shrink into himself, watched the boys laugh, watched the scene play out like a movie I hated but couldn't walk out of. My voice stayed quiet while everything inside me was on fire.

And that silence did something to me. Even at five, a part of me knew I had failed him, even though logically there was nothing I could have done. That is the twisted thing about empathy. When you feel someone's pain that deeply, you start taking responsibility for it, even when you had no power to stop it.

That was the first time I really felt someone else's pain as if it were my own. And it hurt. Not just in a "that's not nice" kind of way, but in a deep, heavy way that sat in my chest. It was like someone had poured wet concrete over my heart, and every time I thought it might finally crack and fall away, the memory would replay and harden again.

I didn't want him to feel less than. I didn't want him to ever believe, not even for a second, that his value could be measured by the size of his jeans. I didn't have the language yet for "body shaming" or "bullying" or "self-worth," but I felt all of it at once.

I felt the injustice.
I felt the shame that wasn't even mine.
I felt the guilt of not doing more.

And underneath it all, I felt this quiet promise forming, even if I couldn't put it into words yet: that I never wanted to be the one holding the knife in someone else's story. That if I could help it, I would stand next to the person being cut down, even if all I could offer was the simple, fragile act of *not* joining in.

That day on the sidewalk wasn't just about some older boys being mean. It was the moment I realized how quickly a person's joy can be stripped away, and how brutally powerless it feels to stand there and watch it happen to someone you love.

I understood, in the way a five-year-old can understand, that words could devastate people just as much as fists could.

We had another babysitter for a while, at a different house. Those memories aren't clear, they are foggy, out-of-focus snapshots. What I do remember though, is that I didn't like it there. At all.

The whole place had this basement energy, even if we weren't actually in a basement. Dark, heavy, like the air itself didn't want us there. I always felt like I was in the way, like the adults were just tolerating us until it was time for us to leave. No warmth, no laughing at the table, no egg drop soup simmering on the stove. Just existing in someone else's space, trying not to be too loud or too much.

I would count the minutes until my mom showed up. Her walking through that door always felt like a rescue, even if nothing "technically" bad had happened. I didn't know what I needed saving from, exactly. I just knew that when she arrived, my whole body exhaled, like I had been holding my breath the entire time without realizing it.

Books were my escape there. If I could disappear into a story, I didn't have to feel how wrong the room felt. I'd bury my nose in the pages and try to forget everything around me, using other people's made-up stories to drown out my own anxiety. But no matter how good the book was, there was always this low hum under it all, a background noise of feeling misplaced, unwanted, alone.

Mahomet was the opposite of that.

That's where my best friend Adam lived. Our moms had been friends since high school, so I didn't just *meet* Adam, I was basically born into his life. We've known each other literally since I came screaming into the world. He lived about six miles from us, along country roads that smelled like burning leaves and looked like they led to nowhere, and his house felt like a second home in a way a place can only feel when you grow up inside it.

His mom, Louise, watched us sometimes too. She was tough in a solid, maternal way. The kind of woman who didn't mess around, but somehow made you feel safer because of it.

She's the one who taught me how to tie my shoes. I remember sitting on her living room floor, laces in my hands, frustrated out of my mind, cheeks burning, while she kept telling me to try again. I could feel the embarrassment rising, *why is this so hard for me when other kids just seem to get it?* My mom showed up to pick us up, but Louise basically put her hand up and said no without saying no.

"He's going to learn before he leaves."

And I did. Eventually. Angry, stubborn, determined, but I learned.

To this day, people still comment on my weird way of tying shoes, and I always say, "Blame Louise," half joking, half grateful.

She also believed in boiled spinach like it was some kind of religion. Not fresh spinach. Not salads. I'm talking the dark-green, soggy, canned stuff. The sludge Popeye used to squeeze out of a can like it was liquid superpower. All of us kids hated it. She served it anyway. And we ate it. Because Louise didn't play, and because sometimes love looks like making you eat something disgusting because it's "good for you."

Adam and I got into the kind of trouble kids *should* get into. Nothing felony-level, just curiosity, boredom, and country living colliding in the best possible way. We ran through fields that felt like they went on forever, poked at things we probably shouldn't have, old boards, questionable puddles, mystery holes in the ground, built entire worlds out of sticks, dirt, and whatever else we could find, and laughed until our sides hurt and our lungs burned. Those were the kind of days that left you dirty, scraped up, exhausted, and somehow more alive than anything else in your life.

With Adam, I didn't have to perform. I didn't have to be the little brother, the quiet kid, the scared kid, or the kid who felt things too hard. I could just be… me. Loud, weird, dramatic, annoyed, creative, emotional, sarcastic, all of it. He rolled with it. He matched it. Sometimes he even out-weirded me, which was impressive.

He was my first real friend. Not just a kid I played with because our parents threw us in the same room, but the kind of friend that feels like a brother. The kind who sees you at your absolute strangest, the dumb jokes, the meltdowns, the wild ideas, and doesn't blink. He didn't pull away when my emotions ran too deep or when my imagination ran too far. He stayed. There's a quiet kind of safety in that, the kind you don't realize you're standing inside of until much later, when you're older and alone in some apartment or house thinking, *Man, I really had it good back then.*

Even now, with adult life stacked on top of everything, jobs, bills, failed attempts at being a fully functioning grown-up, those memories with him still feel close. We've walked through so much of life together that sometimes it feels like he's my historian.

He doesn't just know my stories; he lived them with me. He was there for the long summer days, the first heartbreaks, the quiet moments where something inside me changed and I didn't have words for it. There is something deeply, almost sacredly comforting in that, in knowing someone else has the same mental footage you do. That when you say, "Do you remember that time…?" he doesn't look at you like you're crazy. He nods. He laughs. He fills in the details you forgot.

There's a special kind of gratitude in having a person who can confirm your life actually happened the way you remember it. That you weren't being dramatic. That the good parts were really that good. That the hard parts were really that hard.

Adam is that person for me. And underneath all the jokes and the stories and the nostalgia, there's this strong, steady appreciation: that I didn't have to grow up alone inside my own head. I had him beside me, getting dirty, getting in trouble, getting through it, all of it, right along with me.

When I think about that version of me back then: the kid lying on the gym floor listening to Deniece Williams while everyone else played tag outside, the little brother watching Tim get torn down by stupid grade school boys, the kid counting seconds at the wrong babysitter's house, the wild friend at Adam's place. I can see it now in a way I couldn't back then.

Back then, it just felt like… me. Now I can see it as the beginning of a split, like two versions of myself starting to form. The me who ran and laughed and tried to keep up with everybody else, and the quieter one who watched everything a little too closely and felt everything a little too deeply. Something really was changing in me, and it wasn't loud or sensational, it was subtle and private, happening just under the surface where nobody could see it but me.

I didn't have the words for it, but what I wanted more than anything that day on the gym floor wasn't just to learn the song. It looked like that on the outside, little kid with a cassette player, trying to nail every lyric. But underneath, I was chasing something else. I wanted to feel something, fully and completely, without having to explain it to anyone. I wanted to lay there in the quiet and let that music move through me, wash over the parts of me that felt confused and alone, and make it all make sense for four and a half minutes.

I wanted a place where my emotions weren't too big or too much, where they could spill out without bumping into anybody else, without hurting anybody. Where nobody rolled their eyes because I was "too sensitive," and nobody told me to "shake it off" or "toughen up." Music didn't tell me I was too much. It just… took me as I was.

That was probably the first time I realized I liked silence. Not the awkward, uncomfortable silence that feels like something is wrong, but the kind that feels like a soft room you can walk into and finally exhale. I needed space to think and feel and be inside my own head, without the noise of other people's expectations. I didn't know how to say, "I need to be alone right now," so I just wandered off into moments like that gym floor.

I wasn't lonely. I was alone on purpose. And that difference matters.

Lonely is when you want someone there and they aren't. Alone on purpose is when you finally admit that sometimes you are the only person who can sit with what you are feeling without trying to fix it or talk you out of it. Even as a kid, I think I knew that about myself, even if I couldn't have explained it to anyone.

The thing with Tim and those boys, that is where empathy really cracked open for me. Not the Hallmark-card kind where you say, *"Aww, that's sad,"* and move on, but the kind where someone gets hit and your own chest aches, your own eyes sting, and you carry that moment with you for decades. I watched their words impact him like punches, and my body reacted as if I had been hit too.

Little by little, I started realizing I don't just see people's emotions, I absorb them. I carry them around like they're my own. I walk into a room and it's like my brain is scanning faces and my heart is taking inventory. Who's angry, who's hurt, who's pretending they're fine when they're clearly not. And yeah, that can be a gift when you want to help people, but it is also heavy as hell. It means words don't just float past you, they land and stick and sometimes bruise, even when you were just standing off to the side.

Those babysitter houses were like emotional training grounds too. One felt wrong. One felt safe. Simple as that. I didn't know anything about "energy" or "vibes" back then, but my body knew when it didn't want to be somewhere. I knew when a room felt like a hug and when it felt like a sign. My gut always knew before my brain did. I would feel that tightness in my chest, that restless feeling in my legs, that sense of counting minutes before being saved.

Even now, I walk into a space and I can tell pretty quickly if it feels like home or like someplace I need to escape. My internal alarm system started forming in those living rooms and kitchens, in those afternoons where I felt welcome in one house and tolerated in another.

And then there was Louise's house and Adam. Places and people where I felt seen, even if I was being force-fed boiled spinach or bullied by shoelaces. Safe doesn't always look pretty, but you feel it in your shoulders, in how they finally drop. You feel it in how loud you laugh and how unafraid you are to be ridiculous. That's what those places gave me.

When you grow up with any kind of emotional awareness, you start building this inner compass. You don't always know what it's called, you just know when something feels right or wrong, safe or unsafe, real or fake. Sometimes you think you are just "picky" about people or places, but really you are listening to a part of yourself that has been paying attention for a long time.

Later, people started calling it "trusting your gut."

For me, that gut started forming around that time. In quiet gyms with cassette players. On sidewalks where kids were cruel to someone I loved. In living rooms that felt heavy in all the wrong ways. In kitchens that smelled like egg drop soup and kindness. All those ordinary little incidents were actually laying down the wiring for who I would become.

That version of me lying on the gym floor and the world shut out wasn't just a weird little kid obsessed with a song. That was me learning how to sit with myself, how to be my own company, how to let music translate feelings I didn't know how to explain. It was me discovering that I could step out of the madness and create my own little island of quiet, even in the middle of a school.

That was the beginning of me becoming someone who notices the kid getting picked on. Someone who can't walk past another person's pain without feeling some of it in my own chest. Someone who knows what it feels like to wait for rescue, and who, one day, would want to be that rescue for other people, even in small ways, a listening ear, a bad joke, a moment of real understanding.

And under all of that, even then, there was music.

Music became the place I could go when I didn't know what I was feeling, but needed to feel *something*. It held my loneliness without calling it lonely. It sat with my anger without telling me to calm down. It wrapped itself around the isolated little kid on the gym floor and said, *You're not crazy. You just feel a lot. And that's okay.*

ROUND 2
Guardian Angels and Guts

Our house sat in the middle of a full acre of open land that, to us kids, might as well have been Disney World. We didn't see the peeling paint or the worn wood the way adults would. We saw endless possibility.

Behind the house, in that big grassy stretch, was this old wooden shed stacked high with bales of hay. Just east of the shed, across the gravel drive, was the pig lot. Our landlord was a pig farmer, so every year, like clockwork, seventy-five to a hundred hogs would show up and move in like they were paying rent. The lot itself was simple. A big concrete slab, metal fencing, metal gates, and a rounded metal dome where the pigs could hide from the weather.

Later, he added a wooden chute. Just an L-shaped ramp that started high, dropped down, and hooked around a sharp corner into the pen. It was built to funnel pigs into the back of a truck. Very practical.

To us, it was more of a wintery roller coaster.

In a Midwest winter, where "sledding hill" usually means "ditch," that wooden chute was everything. After a big snowstorm, the ramp would fill up with fresh powder. We'd pack it down with our boots until it turned into this slick, icy slide. Out came the plastic saucer sleds.

We would climb up to the top, puffing in the cold air, one of us sitting in the sled while the other two waited below or hovered nearby, ready to push.

When it was my turn, I'd grip the sides of the saucer so tight my fingers ached. That was the best part, that split second at the top when everything stood still. The world went quiet, just long enough for the fear and excitement to blur together into this one awesome, electric feeling.

My sister or, if I was really lucky, my older brother would plant his hands square in the middle of my back and shove with all his strength.

That shove was everything. It was basically saying, *Alright, kid, here we go, no turning back now.*

I'd shoot down the ramp, the saucer jerking to life underneath me, picking up speed so fast the air sliced past my ears. The wooden walls of the chute flashed by on either side, and that ninety-degree turn came up like a punch. I'd slam into it, bounce off the side of the chute hard enough to knock the breath half out of me, then keep going, faster and faster, every bump jarring through my spine.

And then: launch.

The sled would finally spit me out into the empty pig pen at the bottom, this wide, open landing zone. I'd spin out, tip over, or just flat-out wipe out, arms and legs flying, landing on my back and staring up at the sky.

Then I'd pop up, snow jammed into my gloves, ice creeping down my sleeves, cold burning my cheeks until they stung. My nose running, eyes watering from the wind, lungs blazing. And I'd be laughing, loud, stupid, uncontrollable laughter that made my cheeks hurt in the best possible way.

Before the laughter even died down, my body already knew the next step. I'd grab the saucer, tuck it under my arm, and start scrambling right back up the ramp, boots slipping, legs shaking, not caring at all. No hesitation, no thinking, just pure determination: *I have got to do that again!*

It wasn't just about the ride. It was about the climb back up, the earning of it. The way your thighs burned and your breath came out in little white clouds, and how none of that mattered because you knew what was waiting at the top: that moment where you sit, grip, breathe, and let someone you trust shove you into the unknown.

Sometimes one of us would be halfway up while someone else was already coming down. There was no "spotter," no coordination, no safety meeting. Just the inevitable *boom* of a sled crashing into shins and a kid tumbling back down the ramp in a tangle of limbs and curses. It hurt like hell, but we thought it was hilarious.

Having pigs in the backyard all summer never seemed weird. It was just part of the scenery, like the trees or sky. They were just... there. Background animals.

When the wind swung and the smell of pigs rolled across the yard, we didn't gag, we barely even noticed. It was this thick, earthy wave that settled over everything, a mix of manure, mud, and hay. It wasn't one smell; it was layers of a heavy musk from their bodies and rot from straw that had been wet too long.

Somehow, all of that blended in with the smell of drying corn from the neighboring fields and freshly cut grass. Sun-baked dirt, gasoline from the mower, hot metal, pig shit, and corn stalks, it sounds like a nightmare candle, but back then, it just smelled like... *outside.*

To this day, some tiny, messed-up part of my brain smells that combination, manure plus warm grass plus dusty air, and thinks, *ahhhh... home.*

The sound of them was part of it too. A constant low backdrop underneath the day. Grunts, snorts, the wet slap of their bodies bumping into each other, the scrape of hooves on concrete. Metal gates rattling. Flies buzzing. You couldn't always see the pigs from inside the house, but you could hear them, like the farm version of white noise.

Every once in a while, though, all hell would break loose.

A sudden spike in noise, sharper squeals, frantic grunts, the clanging of metal on metal. The pigs would somehow unlatch the gate and bust out, sprinting into our yard and then into the cornfields like they'd finally hit their breaking point and gone for it. For animals that looked kind of dumb and slow when they just stood around, they moved fast when they were free. Pink and brown bodies barreling across the grass, hooves tearing up clumps of dirt, ears flapping, sides heaving, their skin slick and shiny in the sun.

I was too young to understand how they escaped or how they eventually got herded back in, but I remember the pandemonium. Adults suddenly yelling in voices I didn't hear any other time. Boots pounding across gravel. Dogs losing their minds, barking, circling, darting in too close and then skittering away. Gates slamming open and shut. The sharp metallic ring of a panel getting hit too hard.

Luckily, it only happened a couple times. But farm life never stayed boring for long.

We always had dogs, too. They were outside dogs, which now feels unthinkable, but back then, it was normal. Princess was our beautiful gray and white Husky, and Bandit, one of her pups, was black and white with eyes that made you feel like he knew all your secrets. He was my favorite.

We only brought them inside when it was brutally cold, like below ten degrees, and even then, sometimes they only made it to the enclosed back porch. I remember going out in the mornings and breaking the top layer of ice off their metal water buckets, fingers stinging in the cold. We'd bring the buckets inside, thaw them in the kitchen sink by turning them upside down and running hot water over the bucket until the chunk of ice dropped to the metal sink, refill them, and carry them back out, slipping across the frozen ground.

It sounds harsh now, I know, but at the time, it was just a normal routine. On the rare occasions they got to come inside and curl up by the wood-burning stove, it felt like Christmas for all of us.

That wood-burning stove was the heart of our house in winter.

It was a black, cast-iron cylinder in the living room that looked like something pulled straight out of a farmhouse catalog, only ours was dented and real and smelled like smoke. At night, Dad would load it up with wood before we went to bed, and it would burn low and steady while we slept.

On really cold, dead-of-Winter mornings, the house would drop into the fifties or low sixties. We'd step out of bed and feel that cold floor bite into our toes, shooting a little electric shock up our legs that woke us up faster than any alarm. You could see your breath if you stood close enough to a window. Your skin would pucker, goosebumps running up your arms.

We didn't complain. Not really. Because what were we going to compare it to? Central heating? Programmable thermostats? That stuff wasn't our world. When you don't know another way, you just assume that's what mornings feel like: teeth-chattering, breath-clouding, wood-stove-or-die kind of mornings.

But underneath that "this is just how it is" mindset, there was this quiet understanding: *If we didn't do our part, it got cold. Period.* Just cause and effect.

My brother and I were part of the prep team for that heat. That sounds official now, but back then it was just chores. Every summer, we'd go out with Dad to cut down trees. The chainsaw noise, the smell of fresh-cut wood in the air, sawdust clinging to our clothes and drifting into our mouths when we breathed in too hard. Tree sap clinging to our fingers like left over super glue from assembling a model airplane.

Then came the wood splitter.

We'd spend hours feeding chunks of wood into the hydraulic splitter, taking turns, learning the rhythm. The machine would slowly push the steel wedge through the wood with this soft, satisfying crack that you could feel in your chest. Split logs would fall away. We'd toss the pieces onto a growing pile, the stack getting bigger, our arms getting heavier, and sweat running down our backs.

There was something weirdly motivating about watching that pile grow. You'd start with nothing but roughly cut tree trunk pieces scattered all over the ground, and by the end of the day you had a wall of wood that silently promised, *You'll be warm this winter because of this.* It wasn't just chores. It was satisfying. You could actually see the results of your work in front of you.

Then came hauling and stacking.

Dad had built a shed about five feet from the back screen door, specifically for the wood. He wasn't stupid. The closer the wood was to the door, the fewer miserable winter trips we'd have to make. We'd stack logs from floor to ceiling, row after row, making sure the ends lined up so the whole thing didn't collapse on us. Then, once the shed filled up, we'd overflow onto the steel rack outside.

It was hot, dirty, exhausting work. My shirt would stick to my back, sweat burning my eyes, little wood splinters working their way into my fingers. My hands would get coated with sticky sap that felt impossible to scrub off. No matter how much you washed, there would still be that faint tackiness, that pine smell that clung to your skin. Sometimes it felt like I spent half the summer trying to get my fingers unstuck.

But there was a rhythm to it. Lift, carry, stack. Repeat. It got into your muscles, into your bones, into your idea of what it meant to "pull your weight."

In winter, one of our daily chores was bringing in that wood we spent the past few months carefully cutting and stacking. My brother and I would bundle up, pulling on layers until we walked like little marshmallow soldiers. We'd step out the back door and feel that slap of cold hit our faces, the kind that steals your breath for a second. Then we'd crunch across the frozen ground and grab as much wood as our arms could carry.

We'd load up until the edges of the logs dug into our forearms and our fingers felt like they couldn't stretch any farther. Inside, we'd stack it by the stove like ammo for a war we knew was coming. Every log we stacked was one less shiver. One more hour of warmth. One more night where we didn't wake up with our teeth knocking together.

We complained a little, sure. We were kids, not saints. We'd roll our eyes, drag our feet, maybe mutter something under our breath when Dad wasn't close enough to hear. But under the sighing and sarcasm, there was this shared understanding: *No wood meant no heat.*

Even at that age, that math was easy to understand. You could complain about it, procrastinate for a few minutes, but at the end of the day, somebody had to carry that wood or everybody froze. It was one of the first times in my life where my effort had a clear, direct line to everybody's comfort. It wasn't abstract. It wasn't, "Do your homework so someday you can get into college." It was, "Carry these logs or your ass is going to be cold tonight."

When I describe all this now, it sounds like some story from the 1800s. Like I should be wearing suspenders and talking about "the harvest" or something. But this was the 1970s and '80s. We weren't pioneers. We were just broke kids in a drafty country house, doing what we had to do to stay warm.

And weirdly, there's a part of me that's grateful for it.

Those cold mornings, those hours out by the woodpile, those sap-sticky hands, they taught me what responsibility *feels* like. They taught me determination long before I ever heard the word. When your knuckles are red from the cold and you're still stacking logs, that's determination. When you want to drop the last armful and quit, but you go back for one more load because you know Dad will be up late feeding that fire, that's responsibility.

And honestly? It was kind of great.

Winter was one of the best parts of my childhood.

My dad had this black snowmobile with a scorpion embossed on the vinyl seat. It was cool in that very '70s way. He'd tie one of our sleds to the back with a thick rope, fire it up, and off we'd go, blasting across the snowy fields.

We'd cling to each other, screaming and laughing as the sled whipped over bumps and ruts. The fields, usually corn or soybeans, were full of uneven rows from being tilled after harvest. If the snow wasn't deep enough, those dirt ridges would stick up like hidden speed bumps. Hit one of those going fast and you'd catch air, your stomach dropping as the sled jumped and slammed back down.

We loved it. We were basically human popcorn, and we thought that was fantastic.

But the real magic came from the snowdrifts.

With nothing but flat land around us, the wind could stack snow into drifts that looked like something out of a snow globe. Some years, the drifts would pile up as high as the roofline. There were times when our doors were completely blocked.

No problem.

We'd climb out the attic window in my brother's upstairs bedroom and slide down the drift to the ground like it was our personal ski resort.

Imagine a wall of snow that started at the roof and sloped all the way down to three feet of powder on the ground. When the drifts were perfect, we used them until our fingers and faces were numb.

We had our uniform: thick gray coveralls, heavy gloves, snow boots, and sometimes ski masks that made us look like tiny bank robbers. The cold was brutal. It stung your face and chewed through any spot your clothes didn't cover.

When we finally trudged back inside, half-frozen, we'd peel off our gear and toss the soaked gloves, hats, and masks onto the cast-iron wood burning stove in the living room. You could hear the sizzle as the ice melted and the steam hissed off the fabric. In seconds, everything was dry and toasty, and we'd gear back up and head out again.

At the time, I had no idea how special that was.

I didn't know we were poor. Nobody sat me down and said, "Hey, just so you know, money's tight." I didn't compare my wood piles and stove-heated mornings to anyone else's central air and plush carpets.

We had chores. We had bitter winters. But we also had laughter, adventure, and a kind of raw, simple joy that didn't know it was supposed to be jealous of anything.

That childhood taught me resilience.

We got knocked around by sleds, thrown off snowdrifts, and smacked in the shins with plastic saucers. We were cold, muddy, bruised, and exhausted… and then we got up and did it again the next day. It taught me resourcefulness. No snow park? Fine. We had a pig chute and a drift that could launch us from the roof. That was plenty.

It taught me the value of hard work in a way that was painfully literal. If we didn't cut and haul wood, we didn't stay warm. No one else was coming to do it for us. Comfort wasn't guaranteed; it was earned. That sticks with you, long after the wood stove has cooled down and the house belongs to someone else.

Maybe the biggest thing it taught me, though, was how to find happiness in simplicity.

I didn't need a lot. I needed my brother behind me, giving me a good solid shove down an icy ramp. I needed the dogs curled up by the stove, the crackle of wood, and snowdrifts big enough to erase the whole front of the house.

You rarely know you're in the "good old days" while you're living them. You just know you're tired and cold and laughing way more than seems logical. Pleasure doesn't need perfection. Magic doesn't need money. And some of the strongest parts of who you are get built while your fingers are frozen, carrying firewood that feels too heavy for your size.

Those years roughed me up in all the right ways.

They taught me it is okay to get knocked around, as long as you keep laughing, keep pushing each other down sled ramps and pulling each other back up.

And then, when the snow melted and winter finally surrendered, summer stepped in like it had been waiting its turn the whole time.

Summers out there were their own kind of magic. You wouldn't think a country kid would ride his bike much, but I basically lived on mine.

The best part was that I never had anywhere I *had* to be. That was the freedom. I'd hop on my bike and just… go. I'd fly down tar and gravel roads, dust kicking up behind me, or cut across fields. I'd ramp over ditches, hit one side, bounce through the bottom, and shoot up the other side, tires skidding as I looped around to do it all over again. Over and over, like I was my own Evel Knievel.

We also had a minibike.

It was basically a tiny steel frame with a cushioned seat and a 5-horsepower motor stolen from some mower. Loud, shaky, and absolutely incredible. I never got to drive it. That was my brother's job. My role was "cargo."

I'd wrap my arms around his waist and hang on while he tore across the fields, hitting ditches with way more speed than anyone's mother would have approved of. Sometimes, I'd lose my grip and get flung off the back, getting tossed into the grassy ditch like a rag doll.

Looking back, yeah, it was dangerous. But at that age, we were immortal. At least we felt that way. The big, bulky black motorcycle helmet I wore probably saved my brain more than once, but back then, I just liked how cool it made me feel.

I can still feel those landings, the shock in my chest as I hit the ground, the sound of the engine purring in my ears, the ache in my ribs from laughing so hard after I wiped out.

Those moments were pure, reckless joy. No filters. No screens. No awareness of how easily it all could've gone wrong.

Just an old rusty minibike, an acre of land, and a couple of kids who thought the whole world existed inside that little slice of Illinois.

But sometimes we actually had somewhere to go. Not often, but sometimes.

We had three main destinations.

The first was the bridge, just a quarter mile from home. It crossed this narrow, winding creek, *crick*, if you grew up where I did, that widened into a lazy little pond under the bridge before squeezing itself thin again and wandering off. Underneath, there was a poured concrete pad, probably meant for drainage or erosion or some other adult word, but to us it was a full-service hangout: fishing spot, swimming hole, dog bath, and mud factory.

The water was disgusting. I'm sure now it was loaded with farm runoff, chemicals, and whatever else central Illinois felt like leaking into it, but at the time, it was just "water." Our dogs would jump in headfirst, roll in the mud, and come home smelling like something that had crawled out of a swamp.

Adam and I would sit on the seats of our bicycles and lean over the galvanized steel guardrail with our lines in the water, baiting hooks with whatever we could steal from the kitchen. Raw breakfast sausage, chunks of Velveeta sliced into golden cubes, gourmet bluegill cuisine. Little fish would dart around in the mirky brown water, and every time we pulled one up, it felt like winning.

We also did things that make me wince now.

Sometimes we'd pop their eyes out. Just to see. Just to find out what would happen. We weren't trying to be cruel, we weren't planning our future as serial killers, we were just reckless kids with too much curiosity and not enough supervision.

Now, if I saw some kid doing that, I'd probably have a whole mental debate about whether to call a therapist or an exorcist. Back then, it was just another afternoon at the crick.

The second destination was the grain elevator, about three-quarters of a mile down the road to the east. It had a red brick office and, more importantly, an old-school horizontal Pepsi machine. The kind where the bottles stand upright inside on a metal track, and you had to slide one over to the opening and lift it out after dropping in a quarter.

If we actually had a quarter, we'd get an ice-cold soda and feel like royalty. If we didn't… well, that's where my brother's genius kicked in.

He found this dusty box in Dad's garage filled with random hardware, nuts, bolts, washers. He realized some of the washers were almost the exact size of a quarter. So we tested it. Dropped one into the Pepsi machine, slid the bottle along the rail until it reached the end, and pulled it right out.

It worked.

That washer dropped like real money, the machine clunked, and we pulled out that frosty glass Pepsi bottle. For an entire summer, we bought sodas with metal washers instead of coins. Every *hiss* of a cap popping off was like a victory parade.

We knew it wouldn't last. Someone was going to open that machine and see a pile of metal washers sitting where the money should've been. But until that day came, we rode that scam like a stolen bike.

The third destination was the fort. But that was just for me and Adam. My brother and sister weren't invited to the fort.

You went the opposite way for that. Quarter mile west, left at the end of our road, then just another hundred feet before you reached the ditch with the weird little crater in it. It was maybe six feet by six feet, a dip carved out by rain or erosion. Whatever made it, we claimed it.

Adam and I made that crater our clubhouse.

A thin, sagging wire fence ran along the field above it, and nearby there was this old green metal fence post lying on the ground. We picked it up and instantly saw its potential.

We invented what we proudly called our "pee chute."

We propped the post up at an angle, one end jammed into the dirt in the cornfield, the other resting on one of the fence wires. It had a V-shape, and that was all we needed. Any time one of us had to pee, we'd stand there like engineers, place our wieners carefully in the groove, and let it flow. The pee would run neatly down the post, through the fence, and out of our fort area and into the dirt clumps of the cornfield. Dry clubhouse. No puddles. We thought we were geniuses.

But what really made the fort feel like forbidden territory was the décor.

Porn.

You'd be amazed how often we found those magazines. Every so often, Adam and I, or even my brother, would wander down to the creek and find a big paper grocery bag stuffed with dirty magazines, dumped like someone was trying to erase a guilty conscience. That's actually how I learned what sex was.

The first time we opened a bag, it was like being hit in the face with a completely different universe.

"Whoa, dude… there are naked people in here."

We said it out loud, but it still didn't sound real. We were shocked. Intrigued. Confused. Turned on. A little scared. And absolutely hooked. We knew we weren't supposed to have them. So, obviously, we took them.

We'd rip out the "best" pictures, jab a hole through the top with a stick, and hang them around the fort like posters in a teenage boy's bedroom, only we were still just kids hiding in a ditch. Those pages flapped in the wind around us: glossy, stolen fragments of a world we didn't understand but were suddenly very aware existed.

I still wonder where those magazines came from.

Maybe some pissed-off wife found her husband's stash and tossed it in the creek. Maybe some guy panicked and decided, *I gotta get rid of these somewhere.* I don't know. I didn't ask questions. I just knew this: it happened at least three different times, and every time, it felt like we'd hit some kind of perverted jackpot.

Penthouse is the one I remember the most.

Those images burned themselves into my kid brain, surrounded by summer heat, the buzz of insects, and the feeling that we'd crossed some invisible line without any idea where it led.

Another thing burned into my memory from those years were the roads themselves.

Out in the country, we didn't have smooth asphalt or polished concrete. Our roads were tar and chip. That's what we called them. They were built by lumbering trucks that looked gigantic to me as a kid.

First, one truck would crawl along, laying down a thick coat of black tar. Behind it, a dump truck would follow and rain white, chalky rock over the top. That was it. That was the road. Sticky tar plus rock. Rough, ugly, perfect.

Every so often, they'd come back and lay more tar, sometimes with more rock, sometimes just another layer of goo over what already existed. In the summer heat, that tar would bubble and blister like it was alive.

I would plop myself down right in the middle of that road and spend hours popping those little tar bubbles with my fingers.

No phone, no screen, no music. Just me, the sun, the road, and little domes of tar making soft *pffft* sounds as they burst under my fingertips. It destroyed my clothes. Tar doesn't come out. Once it stuck to your jeans or T-shirt, that was it. My mom could scrub, soak, threaten, swear, whatever, but those outfits were marked for life.

I didn't care. I was completely hypnotized by that road. By the heat miraging up off it, by the smell of hot tar, by the sensation of squishing those bubbles flat one by one. It was our little country bumpkin version of popping bubble wrap.

Even riding my bike on those roads felt different.

The tires would hit soft tar patches and you'd hear that rhythmic pop-pop-pop-pop as you rolled along. Sometimes the tar was so soft, my tires left tracks behind me, permanent little signatures sealed into the road. Part of me liked knowing I'd leave those marks behind long after I grew up and left.

At the deepest part of our backyard, beyond the hay shed, was another important piece of my childhood map.

There was a concrete pad back there, about twelve by twelve, and most of the time it was buried under a mountain of corn cobs, leftovers from whatever the pigs didn't eat. To us, that pile was pure gold.

Adam and I climbed it like a mountain, sliding down, throwing cobs at each other, inventing games that usually ended with one of us taking a cob to the head and both of us laughing. We would tumble around in it until the farmer finally hauled them away.

Once the cobs were gone, that same concrete pad became the burn pile.

My dad used that area for anything that needed to disappear. Brush. Junk. Old wood. Random garbage that could burn. He'd light it up, and we'd stand there watching it all curl into flame, collapse into glowing coals, then finally crumble into ash and smoke. Things went in as *stuff* and came out as nothing.

Left alone with that fire, Adam and I did exactly what you'd expect two curiosity-fueled boys with underdeveloped frontal lobes to do.

We weaponized it.

It didn't happen all at once. At first, we were just staring. Poking the edges of half-burned boards with long sticks. Testing how close we could get before our shins felt like they were melting. But curiosity has this way of creeping in, of whispering, *Okay… what else can it do?*

So one day we got "creative."

We'd dig through the garage, which already felt like a treasure chest of bad ideas, old spray paint cans, half-empty, rusty, their labels peeling. Stuff nobody cared about anymore, which in our minds meant: fair game. We'd shake them next to our ears, listening for the slosh, judging which ones still had enough in them to be "fun." Then we'd toss them into the fire like grenades.

As soon as the can hit the flames, there was this immediate jump in energy. The fire wrapped around it, like it knew what we were trying to do. We'd sprint to our "safe spot", which was barely safe in any universe, usually behind a piece of warped plywood or a tipped-over wheelbarrow. That plywood might as well have been a superhero shield, the way we believed in it. We'd crouch down, hearts pounding in our throats.

That silence right before the explosion was deafening. The world kind of narrowed down to the crackle of the fire and the tiny ticking sounds from the can heating up. I'd find myself holding my breath without realizing it, eyes locked on the flames, part of me scared and another part thinking, *This is going to be awesome.*

Then: BOOM.

The sound would hit us in the chest, not just our ears. Sometimes the can would launch into the air like a flaming rocket, streaking up through the smoke so fast it disappeared into the sky. Other times it would just blow, sending sparks and little fragments of burning label spinning out into the field.

Every explosion was followed by the same ritual: yelling, jumping, celebrating, high-fiving, shoving each other's shoulders like we'd just survived a war zone instead of almost causing one.

We were absolutely convinced we'd done something brilliant and borderline heroic.

We were idiots. Happy idiots.

It's a miracle none of us took shrapnel to the face or ended up in the ER. Honestly, it's a miracle the garage didn't go up with us. If even one of those cans had burst sideways instead of straight up, the story I'd be telling right now would be a lot shorter and involve more skin grafts.

But at that age, danger didn't register as danger. It registered as possibility. Curiosity. An experiment.

We'd think, *Okay, that worked. What's next?*

And because apparently we were trying to give God and our guardian angels panic attacks, we escalated.

We ran through the fire.

Not metaphorically. Literally.

The burn pile would be going full force, flames flicking up and leaning in whichever direction the wind pushed them, heat pouring off in waves. Ash floated everywhere, these little gray ghosts drifting past our faces. The ground around the pit was blackened and crunchy, dead grass and old coals hiding under a thin layer of dust.

And there we were, a bunch of scrawny kids in dirty jeans and smoke-stained sneakers, standing on one side of the fire, daring each other.

"Bet you won't do it."

"I'll go if you go first."

"No, we'll go at the same time."

Then we'd pick our moment.

We'd wait for the flames to dip just enough, for the wind to shift so the smoke blew slightly off to one side, and then one of us would yell, "Go!"

We bolted.

Those few steps into the fire felt like jumping into another world. One second it was normal, the next it was bright orange and white, the heat slamming into my legs and face all at once, the sound of the fire roaring in my ears. For a heartbeat, everything went silent inside my head, like my brain short-circuited from sheer sensory overload. I could feel the heat clawing at my jeans, the air so hot it almost hurt to breathe.

And then, just like that, I was out the other side.

We'd stumble away, screaming and laughing, waving our arms like we'd just outrun death. My lungs would burn from the smoke, my eyes watering. I'd check my pant legs like, *Am I on fire?* and, once I confirmed I wasn't, the relief and excitement hit like a second explosion.

Adrenaline buzzed in my veins, this wild high that told me: *You did it. You made it through.*

For that split second inside the flames, I felt completely untouchable. Like I'd walked straight through something that should've destroyed me and came out the other side unchanged. There was this tiny, secret belief that if I could outrun fire, maybe nothing else could hurt me either.

So, what's next?

Remember all of those glass Pepsi bottles we paid hard earned metal washers for at the grain elevator?

I think it was my brother Tim who thought it would be super cool to pour about an inch worth of gasoline from the red gas can in the garage into a few of those leftover bottles. Then he'd push an old dirty rag from the garage into the top and light it on fire.

We'd hurl that bottle up into a high arc over the top of that concrete pad, then sprint away as far as we could. We'd turn back just in time to see the bottle explode into a radiant ball of fire as it crashed down onto the concrete.

What's a Molotov Cocktail amongst friends?

Looking back now, the whole list, minibikes through cornfields, popping tar bubbles in the street, exploding paint cans, running through fire, and the occasional Molotov Cocktail, reads like a lawsuit and a child safety pamphlet got drunk and had a baby.

But back then?

It was just summer.

Nobody was standing there with a waiver. No one was giving a TED Talk on risk management. Adults weren't shadowing us with SPF and GPS trackers. They basically just cracked the door, said, "Be home by dark," and trusted the rest to God and whatever guardian angels drew the short straw that day.

Those wild summers didn't just fill up my childhood; they welded together the framework of who I became. At the time, I thought I was just a kid burning daylight, riding my bike to nowhere, messing with tar in the road, building forts out of an old country road ditch, and seeing how close I could get to actual, literal flames without fully catching on fire. It all looked random and stupid from the outside, but underneath it, something was being built.

Riding my bike with no real destination taught me more about being present than any mindfulness book ever has. There was no plan. Just motion. Just the rhythm of pedals, the chain ticking, my breath syncing up with the hum of rubber on gravel. Dust in my teeth, sun on my neck, sweat drying into salt on my skin. That wasn't "wasting time." That was the training ground for understanding that some of the best parts of life really are the in-between moments. The part of the drive between point A and point B. The conversation that happens on the way home. The long walk to nowhere that somehow resets your soul.

Back then, I didn't think, *I'm practicing presence.* I just knew that out there, with no schedule and no destination, I felt more like myself than I did anywhere else.

The fort, the ditch, the pee chute, the creek under the bridge, they were more than just spots on a mental map. Those places were our kingdoms, our classrooms, our confessionals. They didn't belong to us because our names were on a deed or our parents paid property taxes. They belonged to us because we filled them with imagination, stupidity, and laughter until they soaked it in like gasoline.

We built empires out of dirt and trash.

The porn magazines from the creek. God, those soggy, swollen pages, were my first crash course in "adult reality." There was nothing romantic or cinematic about it. No slow music. No dim lighting. Just naked strangers stapled together, water-logged and grainy. It wasn't sexy; it was confusing. It was too much information delivered too fast in the least sacred container possible.

But in its own messed-up way, it was honest.

Life doesn't always hand you age-appropriate intros with thoughtful explanations and gentle transitions. Sometimes it just drops a soggy paper bag of naked strangers at your feet under a bridge and basically says, "Good luck, kid. Figure it out."

Part of me is still annoyed about that, how early exposure can tangle wires that take years to straighten out. But another part of me recognizes that life doesn't care if you're ready. It shows up on its own schedule, not yours. Those magazines were one of a thousand tiny examples of that.

The danger, the minibike wipeouts, the exploding cans, sprinting through actual fire, those weren't just dumb stunts for the sake of being idiots, even though we absolutely were idiots. Underneath, they were my first experiments with risk, thrill, and consequence. There was a wild kind of magic in those summers, this reckless blend of boredom and creativity. We were still kids, but not as innocent as we wanted people to believe.

We didn't have language like "adrenaline" and "coping mechanisms." We just knew that when the world felt too small or too quiet, standing a little too close to danger made us feel alive.

I learned something then that I didn't have words for until decades later: fear isn't the enemy. Going numb is.

Fear meant my body still cared about keeping me alive. It meant my heart could still race, my breath could still catch, my brain could still scream, *This is really stupid and you might die.* Numbness is the opposite. Numbness is when nothing in you reacts anymore, when you can stand in the middle of your own life and feel like a ghost.

The worst thing you can be, as a kid or as an adult, is motionless. Uninterested. So safe that you're basically dead inside.

Freedom, curiosity, and a little bit of chaos were my early teachers. They weren't gentle. They didn't give handouts or review sheets before the exam. They just shoved us into situations and let the lessons bubble up afterward, sometimes through pain, sometimes through laughter, sometimes through the sound of your own blood in your ears while you wait to see if you're hurt or just scared.

Later on, reflection had to walk in and balance it all out.

Reflection is the grown-up part of the story, the voice that comes in years later and says, "Okay, let's unpack that." It's what lets me sit here now and admit that we were lucky. Not smart. Not careful. Lucky. Not everybody hits the ditch, runs through the fire, explodes cans, wipes out a minibike, and walks away with nothing more than a scar and a story.

That era etched itself into me. The scars are mostly invisible now, but I can still feel where they live. They're woven into how I see the world, how I parent, how I manage risk, how I react when my own kid wants to try something that makes my stomach drop and my heart say, "No," while a quieter voice inside me whispers, "Yeah, but that's how he'll learn."

I can look back now and see that behind every stupid stunt was something deeper we were reaching for. We weren't just killing time. We were trying to find the edges of ourselves.

How fast can I go before I wipe out? How far can I jump before I fall? How close can I get to the flames and still sprint through to the other side? How much can I see, learn, feel, know before an adult steps in and slams the door shut?

All of that happened inside this tiny little world of ours: the country roads, the creek, the ditch, the concrete pad, the house, the shed. It wasn't some exotic setting. It was ordinary as hell. But that's part of the wisdom I carry now: you don't need extraordinary places to have defining moments. Most of us are shaped in backyards, side streets, ditches, church basements, and school hallways.

The world doesn't have to look special on the outside to permanently rearrange you on the inside.

When I look back now, I don't just see a highlight reel of reckless boyhood. I see a crude blueprint of my adult wiring: the part of me that still craves freedom, the part that still leans toward risk, the part that resents being over-managed, the part that wants my kid safe but not bubble-wrapped to the point of never knowing what his own body and courage can do.

I see how early turbulence made adulthood both easier and harder.

Easier, because I already knew life wasn't safe, fair, or neatly packaged. Harder, because once you've sprinted through fire, the idea of sitting quietly in a cubicle pretending spreadsheets are the point of existence feels like its own kind of death.

The wisdom didn't show up in the moment. Back then, I was too busy trying not to crash. But reflection lets me zoom out now and see the pattern: we weren't just reckless; we were rehearsing for the bigger risks that would come later, relationships, careers, fatherhood, grief, love, loss.

Those summers were a sandbox for courage and stupidity, and sometimes those two wear the same outfit.

Now, when I sit in the quiet and rewind those moments, I don't just laugh at how insane it all was. I do laugh, sure. But I also feel this deep, strange gratitude. Somehow, out of fire and tar and porn in a creek and rusted metal and country roads and bad ideas… a person emerged.

Me.

And the older I get, the more I realize that kid wasn't just trying to pass time. He was trying to wake up.

ROUND 3:
Built for Wings, Got a Funky Finger

Between that multi-use concrete pad at the back of the yard and our old country house stood a slightly leaning, weather-beaten shed. It had once been white, but most of the paint had peeled away, leaving tired wood exposed. The nails were rusted, the boards warped, and when the wind slipped through the cracks, the whole thing sighed and complained like an old man getting out of a chair.

It wasn't just an old hay shed. It was also a sanctuary.

That's where Princess always chose to have her puppies.

Princess was our gray and white Husky, thick fur and blue eyes. Whenever she was ready to give birth, she'd disappear into that shed and nose through the hay, circling and scratching, pushing it into a shallow nest. She knew what she needed. She knew what her babies would need. Nobody had to teach her.

Hay stacked high along the walls kept the cold out in winter and the worst of the heat off in summer. The air inside the shed always felt different from the rest of the yard, warmer, stiller. Dust floated in the shafts of light that slipped in through gaps in the slats.

Even as a kid, I knew that when Princess was in there with pups, you had to move gently. You couldn't stomp in like you owned the place. You entered like you'd been invited.

Every couple of years, we'd pull open that creaky door, and there she'd be, curled around a pile of new life. Four, sometimes six, tiny bodies pressed tight against her belly, blind and wriggling, little pink noses rooting and bumping their way to warmth and milk. Her tail would give this faint little thump.

I can still smell it if I close my eyes. Dust and hay and that warm, sweet, milky scent of newborn puppies. The smell of dog fur pressed into straw. The faint musty scent of the wind sneaking in under the door. It all layered together into something that felt safe. Grounding.

I'd kneel down beside her, moving slowly, feeling the hay scratch at my knees through my jeans. My hands suddenly had to learn a new kind of careful. I'd slide both hands under one tiny pup and lift, cupping it like a handful of sand.

They were impossibly soft and fragile. Their bellies rose and fell with these tiny breaths, squeaking out little sounds.

That smell, that feeling, it never really leaves. The smell of beginnings. Of innocence. Of something you want to protect for as long as you possibly can, even if you're not sure you know how.

One of those litters gave me Bandit.

He came from what I think was Princess's very first litter of pups. Out of all the dogs that cycled through our yard, working dogs, outside dogs, "not really ours" dogs, Bandit is the only one we kept for real. Black and white, half Husky and half mutt.

Bandit wasn't just a dog. He was *my* dog.

He became my shadow. If I walked across the yard, his paws scuffed in the grass behind me. If I disappeared into the fields, he was there, a black-and-white blur weaving in and out of tall grass and corn stalks.

He was my partner in crime, my lookout, my decoy, my built-in best friend. We had an understanding without ever needing a single word. I'd toss a stick way too far and he'd tear after it, sprinting full-out like the most important job in the world was bringing that stupid stick back to my hand. And he always did. Tongue hanging out, chest heaving, eyes bright with pride, dropping it at my feet.

Bandit was also my audience.

We lived too far away from town to have friends over on a regular basis, so I'd talk to him instead. Half-formed thoughts, worries, questions I didn't have the courage to ask anyone else. Stuff about school. About home. About how my chest could feel too tight even when nothing was "wrong."

He'd just sit there and listen, occasionally tilting his head like he was considering my rambling with the seriousness of a judge in a courtroom. Sometimes he'd nudge my hand with his nose, or lean his whole weight into my leg, grounding me with thirty pounds of dog saying, I'm here.

He never once asked why I needed him close.
He never asked me to explain why I felt the way I felt.
He never told me I was overreacting.

Bandit didn't fix anything. He didn't change the house or the rules or the way life felt too big some days. But he made it bearable in a way nobody else seemed able to. He turned long, empty afternoons into adventures. He turned humid evenings on the porch into shared silence.

Bandit was there for all of it. And in the summers, that usually meant running around the front yard as Mom turned our quiet little patch of nowhere into a retail outlet.

The summertime garage sales.

Every summer, Mom would set up garage sales in our front yard like we lived on some busy highway, not miles out in the country where your closest neighbors were corn, soybeans, and the occasional pissed-off skunk. Our old farmhouse sat way out from Champaign, straight shot down a rural road where the most exciting traffic was a tractor or a beat-up pickup that looked like it had survived three different owners and at least one divorce.

Still, every year, we dragged out folding tables, taped handwritten signs to fence posts, and waited like we were about to be mobbed by bargain hunters desperate for a used crockpot or a box of my sister's worn-out paperbacks.

While Mom sorted old knickknacks and lined up clothes by size and season like a one-woman Kmart, I ran my own little empire beside her.

I wasn't just a kid killing time. I was, in my head anyway, an entrepreneur.

Most years, I set up a lemonade stand, but my real pride and joy was the Pepsi stand.

I had this plastic drink dispenser with the Pepsi logo sticker on the side that we ordered from the Sears catalog. The second that thing showed up, I basically decided I was a franchise owner. Never mind that the stuff inside was never actual Pepsi. It was usually some off-brand special from IGA or Aldi, "Fizz Pop," "Cola Time," whatever was cheapest.

But that blue-and-red logo on the dispenser, that was my license to pretend it was the real deal.

I'd carefully pour the soda from the two-liter bottles into the dispenser, making sure not to spill a drop, then haul everything under the biggest shade tree in the yard. I set up my stack of waxy paper cups, straightened my little station, and mentally prepared for the rush.

Twenty-five cents a cup.

Some days I made a couple of bucks. Some days I sold one or two and drank most of the inventory myself. But I loved it. The serious way adults would dig into their pockets and hand over quarters like I was running something official.

And I think Mom knew it would keep me occupied and out of her hair for the afternoon.

That same overactive imagination, the one that turned a knockoff soda stand into a full-blown corporate operation, also gave me one of the strangest, most stubborn memories of my entire childhood.

One that still lives in this weird space between fantasy and reality.

Because I swear to you, down to the marrow, down to whatever invisible wiring keeps my heart beating, I used to be able to fly.

Not "felt like" I could fly. Not "dreamed" I could fly.

Actually, literally, body-leaving-the-ground, backyard-airborne flying.

Look, I know exactly how that sounds. Ridiculous. Impossible. Like one of those stories people tell at barbecues and everyone laughs and says, "Oh, I had that dream too when I was a kid." But this never lived in the same category as dreams for me. Even now, some stubborn, unreasonable part of me refuses admit it wasn't real.

I was around seven or eight and weighed exactly forty-five pounds, and that number wasn't just some detail. It was the whole equation.

Forty-five was the magic line.

As long as I stayed forty-five or under, I could fly. The moment the scale tipped even one pound higher, the gift would be gone. No negotiations. Simple math, written in invisible ink on my soul.

It felt less like I made that rule up and more like I discovered it, the way you "discover" gravity by dropping something. It was just there. I accepted it with the kind of unquestioning faith only kids and true believers have.

I'd step outside into the backyard like I was clocking into a secret shift at some undercover government operation only I knew about. Everything about it felt intentional. The way I took that first breath, filling my small lungs like I was loading fuel.

I'd stand there, knees soft, arms loose, heart thumping in my chest, not from fear, but from this electrified anticipation.

I wasn't just hoping it would work.

I was expecting it to.

That's the difference between imagination and faith, I think. Imagination says, "Wouldn't that be cool?" Faith says, "Of course it will."

I'd bend my knees, pull in a breath, and jump.

And I swear, I flew.

Not like the cartoons. I wasn't zooming through clouds or circling the earth. It was more like gravity forgot about me for a few seconds. I'd leave the ground and hang there, hovering just above the yard, weightless and suspended in this soft, impossible pause.

It didn't feel like falling. Falling has panic and you're aware you're heading back to the ground whether you like it or not. This was something else. Like the world hit pause and I was the only thing still moving.

I remember drifting around the perimeter of our backyard and from that height, maybe just ten feet up, it all looked different.

I could see the roof of our house, the faded shingles and those sad, bald spots where the tar paper peeked through, like the house was losing its hair. I'd notice patterns in the way the boards overlapped, the shape of water stains, stuff you don't see when you're grounded.

I'd see the wood shed stuffed to the rafters with firewood. I'd see the rusty old well pump we used to fill water buckets for the dogs, the chipped red paint clinging to it like it still remembered being new. The crooked light pole stood off to the side, leaning like a tired old man.

Up there, nothing had changed. Same house. Same yard. Same junk. But the angle transformed everything. It made me feel like I'd found a secret level in a video game before anyone else.

And that's where the euphoria lived, not in some loud, cartoon happiness, but in this deep, quiet bliss. It felt like I was exactly where I was supposed to be. Like this was the version of reality that made sense and everything else, school, dinner, bedtime, was the act. The ground was just where I landed when it was time to pretend to be normal again.

I didn't question why I could fly. I didn't sit there with a tiny eight-year-old clipboard, running calculations. I didn't need proof. I was the proof.

But under that, there was something almost spiritual about it.

Back then, God was this huge, invisible Someone I'd been told about in Sunday school or when I went to church with Adam and his family. A guy in the sky with rules and rewards, apparently. I'd see pictures of angels in children's Bibles, soft white robes, golden wings, holding harps like overdressed birds at a funeral, and I'd think, "That's not it."

Whatever let me float in that backyard, whatever paused gravity for me, didn't feel like a painting hanging in a church hallway. It felt personal.

Intimate. Like Someone noticed me specifically and decided I got this one small loophole.

I didn't have words for it then, but it felt like favor.

Not the big, dramatic "chosen one" kind you see in movies. Just this quiet, secret sense that God, or the universe, or whatever's in charge, reached down and pressed a hidden button inside me and said, "Here. This is yours. Just for a while."

And the crazy part is, I treated it like a responsibility.

If I could fly as long as I stayed forty-five pounds, then it was on me to stay forty-five pounds. That number became this sacred boundary. It wasn't about body image or vanity. I didn't think I was too skinny or too small. I thought I was calibrated.

Forty-five was balanced. Forty-six meant exile.

I'd stand on the scale sometimes and stare at the tiny black line, holding my breath like even that might weigh something. If it hovered just to the left of the forty-five mark, I'd exhale, flooded with relief, like God had renewed my license for another day.

No one told me to think that way. No adult sat me down and said, "Son, at this exact weight, you will possess the ability to lightly hover in the backyard." This was pure eight-year-old theology, cause and effect mixed with fantasy, hammered into faith.

Because every time I stepped out there and jumped, it happened.

One afternoon, I was hovering just above the wood shed, drifting slowly along the roofline like some lazy balloon, when I heard it. It was "99 Red Balloons" by Nena playing on WLRW 94.5 through my little radio.

> *"...Everyone's a superhero*
> *Everyone's a Captain Kirk*
> *With orders to identify*
> *To clarify and classify*
> *Scramble in the summer sky*
> *Ninety-nine red balloons go by..."*

Then the crunch of tires on gravel out front.

That sound was as familiar as my own name. The gravel had its own grind that told you exactly who it was long before you saw the car. My stomach flipped. My mom was turning off the tar road, easing into the driveway.

I panicked.

Not because I thought she'd be mad. Not because I thought I'd get in trouble for breaking the laws of physics. I panicked because some deep part of me knew this wasn't supposed to be witnessed.

I dropped fast behind the shed, heart pounding so hard it felt like it might knock me back into the air. I pressed myself into the shadow of the building, back against the rough boards, splinters catching my shirt, trying to make myself small.

I stood there and waited.

I listened to the engine cut off, the creak of the car door, the slam, the sound of her footsteps on the patio, the squeak of the screen door, then the heavy wooden door closing behind her. Only then did I let myself breathe again.

I didn't want her to see me like that.

I didn't want anyone to.

This wasn't a party trick. I had no desire to run inside yelling, "Mom, look what I can do!" and drag her out to the yard for a demonstration. I didn't want applause. I didn't want validation. I didn't even want witnesses.

It felt secret. Sacred. Fragile.

Some part of me believed that the second someone else saw it, the magic would end. Like belief, in this case, was a limited resource, and if someone else started believing, there wouldn't be enough left for me.

So I protected it.

I protected it by hiding. By not talking about it. By wrapping it in silence like bubble wrap, hoping that would keep it from breaking.

That's the part that still messes with me.

I don't remember what I was wearing. I don't remember if it was a school day or a weekend, or what we had for dinner that night. Those details are gone. But I remember the yard from above with obscene clarity. The angle of the roof, the way the sunlight bounced off the metal well pump, the shadow of the light pole dragging across the grass.

I remember the air on my face, softer up there, somehow. I remember the way the ground looked smaller but not less dangerous. I remember the precise moment that innocence felt like evidence.

If it was only imagination, why does it sit in my memory with the same weight and structure as real things? Why does it feel more solid than the birthdays, the report cards, the school pictures?

Some people would say, "Well, that's how powerful imagination is." And they're not wrong. A kid's mind can build whole universes out of boredom and backyard dirt. But I think there's a thin, blurry line between imagination and faith, and I lived right on that line.

Imagination let me picture it.

Faith let me trust it.

Faith is what made me step back outside the next day and test it again. And again. And again. It's what made me treat that scale like an altar. It's what made me duck behind the shed like a thief hiding stolen light.

Maybe it was some kid-version of lucid dreaming, some trick of the brain layered over micro-moments of time when my body just happened to be in the air. Maybe it was a glitch in the way memory forms, a loop I rewound so many times it hardened into something that feels like fact.

But here's the thing. There's also a quieter possibility I can't quite bring myself to throw away.

Maybe, for a brief slice of childhood, the world bent a little for me.

Maybe it was a mercy. Maybe it was an early love language from a God I didn't really know yet. Maybe it was the universe whispering, "You're going to feel heavy for most of your life. Here's a preview of what it feels like when you're not."

All I know is this: somewhere between the wood shed and the crooked light pole, between forty-four and forty-five pounds, between imagination and physics, I learned how to believe in something I couldn't explain and couldn't prove.

And a small, stubborn part of me still believes that, once upon a time, in a tired backyard behind a weathered house, I actually flew.

Not all my early "adventures" were mystical though. Some were just painful.

Mom did her weekly grocery shopping at Kroger. I was four, which meant I went wherever she went, along with my brother and sister. I don't remember most things about that store. It was just aisles and fluorescent lights and cold air. But one day carved itself into my memory and never left.

We did the usual route, weaving through aisles, loading up on cereal, bread, canned stuff, all the milk three kids could destroy in a week. I remember the shock of cold every time we hit the refrigerated section. I'd be sitting in the cart's child seat, legs dangling through the metal bars, watching the world roll by at Mom's push.

Then we got to the checkout.

That's when I saw it.

The rubber conveyor belt had a tear in it. Not huge, just a jagged slit torn out of the edge closest to us. But to my four-year-old brain, it was fascinating. The tear would surface on my end, ride forward, disappear under the metal counter, then come back around again. Over and over like a little magic trick.

I locked onto it.

I leaned over the side of the cart, reaching as far as my little arms could stretch. I tried to time it just right, waiting for the tear to come around again and again. Almost. Missed it. Okay, next time.

Then, finally, I got it.

My index finger slipped perfectly into that moving slit like it had been waiting for me. For a second, it felt amazing. I was part of the belt, riding along like some tiny human conveyor accessory.

Then reality snapped back.

The belt carried my finger forward into the place where the rubber disappeared under the counter, and that innocent little slit turned into a trap. My finger got wedged between the moving belt and the hard metal edge.

Small, soft skin versus machine.

The machine won.

Everything that happened next plays in my head like a jumpy film. Fast, bright, loud.

People shouting. Someone hitting the stop button. Mom's face going pale. Blue paper towels, those thin, scratchy rolls you see in gas station bathrooms, being pulled out, wrapped around my hand. The blue turning darker, quickly, until it was more red than anything else.

I remember sitting in the cart, stunned, watching adults scramble around my tiny, bleeding hand like it was the center of the universe.

Mom didn't stroll at that point. She flew down those aisles, pushing the cart like a battering ram toward the restrooms in the back corner. My memory cuts in and out there. I don't remember if they ran it under water or just swapped bloody towels for fresh ones. All I remember is confusion, voices, and those blue paper towels.

The next clear scene is the car.

This was 1979. No one was strapping a four-year-old into a car seat. I was standing on the front passenger seat, clutching a wad of bloody paper towels around my hand while Mom sped to Burnham City Hospital. In my version of the story, I didn't cry. I stood there stoic and brave, like a tiny warrior who'd just lost a finger in battle and was nobly accepting his fate.

My mom, however, probably remembers it differently. But this is my book, so I'm going with stoic.

What actually happened mechanically was simple. My finger went where fingers are not meant to go, and when the belt kept moving, it essentially shaved the tip off. Whether anybody ever fished that little fingertip out of the inner guts of the machine, I have no idea.

The doctors at Burnham managed to save most of it. They grafted skin from my wrist to rebuild the end of the finger.

To this day, the scar is still there. The finger is now blunt at the tip, the nail is weird and misshapen. My wife likes to tease me and call it my "funky finger."

But to me, it's more than a weird trivia fact about my hand. It's a reminder of that day when curiosity, risk, and pain all collided in a grocery store checkout lane. One second I was playing with a little rip in a rubber belt. The next, I was bleeding all over a Kroger grocery store and being rushed to the ER.

Life comes at you fast, even when you're four.

When I read over these memories, the shed, the puppies, the Pepsi stand, the flying, the conveyor belt accident, I can see the thread running through all of it.

That old hay shed, the one Princess chose for her litters, wasn't just a storage building. It was a refuge. Warmth and safety in the simplest, most unassuming way. Walls of hay, old wood, dust in the air, and a circle of squirming puppies.

That's where I learned what it feels like to protect something small and helpless. To be gentle. To be invited into something fragile and new and treat it with the care it deserves.

Bandit came from one of those litters, and he didn't just become a pet. He became my soft place to land. His loyalty and quiet presence taught me more about unconditional love than any lecture ever could. Those moments with him and Princess, tucked into that leaning shed, are still where my brain goes when I need to remember what safety feels like.

The lemonade and soda stands in the middle of nowhere were my first sparks of ambition. No business plan, no mentor, no big speech. Just a kid setting something up and feeling proud when a stranger stopped and handed over a quarter. Even surrounded by cornfields and gravel roads, I could build something, even if it was small.

And the flying.

Whether it was real or not almost doesn't matter anymore. What matters is that at eight years old I believed, fully, that I could rise above the ordinary. That I could lift off, even if only for a little while, and see my world from a different angle.

That belief stayed in me.

Every time I've taken a leap later in life, every time I've gone after something that didn't make sense to anyone else, I can feel a faint echo of that backyard hover. That quiet voice that says, *Take the leap.*

And the finger, the funky finger I earned at Kroger, is the scar that reminds me there are always costs. Curiosity isn't free. Taking risks sometimes hurts. You can be brave and stupid at the same time. But most of the time, I'd still rather reach and get bitten than sit perfectly still and stay "safe."

Living out in the country meant waking up wrapped in the kind of quiet most people pay money to escape to on weekends. Out there, the sky went on forever. At night, the stars looked like somebody had spilled glitter across the universe. Everything felt big and slow.

Except for 6:00 a.m.

That came crashing in like a tidal wave.

Most weekdays started the same. Groggy, stiff, breathing out fog in the chilly air as I forced myself out of bed. We didn't have a shower for most of the years in that old farmhouse. We were a bathtub family. Nighttime baths were required, and ours always started with a step no one ever puts in commercials.

Cricket removal.

Living in the middle of cornfields meant black crickets were just there. Everywhere. Part of the décor. Before we could plug the tub with the rubber stopper and run the warm water, we had to rinse a few of them down the drain. It was like some messed-up country version of baptism. "In the name of cleanliness, we send you to the pipes."

Morning wasn't luxury. It was routine and survival.

Breakfast was cereal from a bulk box, almost always off-brand. No bright cartoon mascots, just bags of "crunchy oat circles" or "frosted wheat squares" in generic packaging, eaten under the dull glow of the kitchen light. A small kerosene heater usually sat in the middle of the kitchen floor, flame flickering behind its little grate, trying its best to push back the cold.

Winters out there were mean. Wind didn't just blow, it sliced. It skimmed across the empty fields, slid through the old drafty windows, and found every crack in that house.

By 6:45 a.m., we were in the living room, layered up and watching the road for the bus.

One of the perks of living on flat farmland was the view. After harvest, with the corn gone and the trees stripped bare, you could see almost everything coming for you, including your daily doom in the form of a yellow school bus. We'd spot it early, this tiny blur turning off Route 150 onto Rising Road, then again as it turned right at the grain elevator about three-quarters of a mile from our house. Watching it crawl toward us gave us an extra two or three minutes to scramble for gloves, grab our backpacks or Trapper Keepers, and sprint down the gravel driveway.

Then came the familiar rumble of the diesel engine and the hiss of the brakes as the bus stopped at the end of the driveway in front of our house.

We were always one of the first stops, which meant the bus was nearly empty in the mornings. Just a couple of other farm kids looking the same kind of half-awake. The morning ride to school was usually quiet and calm. Maybe a soft hum of conversation, the growl of the engine, windows fogging up around us.

Afternoons were different. By the time we were dropped off, we were one of the last stops, and the sun was leaning hard toward the west, throwing long shadows across the fields.

The real magic, though, lived in the back of the bus.

The last two rows were legendary. That was where the brave and the borderline stupid sat. The county wasn't big on filling potholes, so those rural roads were full of dips and ruts that turned the back of the bus into a discount amusement ride. Sitting behind the rear axle was like having a season pass.

We learned every bump. Every hidden dip that would lift us clean off the seat. Hit it at the right speed and you'd slam your head into the ceiling, and land back on the vinyl laughing so hard your stomach hurt. I swear our bus driver knew exactly what she was doing.

Her name was Patty.

She wore pitch-black aviator sunglasses like she was about to join a biker gang and had thick brown hair pulled back into a practical ponytail. She had this quiet, cool energy. She never tried to be the "fun adult," but somehow ended up being one of the coolest people in my life.

In the mornings, when we were quiet and sleepy, she'd chat with us like we were real people, not just noisy cargo. In the afternoons, when we were wired and full of stories, she listened. My brother, sister, and I would sometimes sit in the front seat right behind her just because we wanted to, not because we had to.

She never shushed us. Never brushed us off.

She talked to us like we mattered.

That's why I am still convinced she hit those bumps on purpose. She knew we loved it. And I have a feeling she got her own kick out of hearing our bodies thump off the seats and our laughter explode in the back.

The bus became our neighborhood on wheels.

Out there, our closest neighbors were a mile away in any direction. There were no cul-de-sacs full of kids riding bikes in circles. But twice a day, every day, we crammed into that rolling yellow capsule and created our own little community. Quiet nods turned into inside jokes. Strangers turned into seatmates.

At some point, we even gave ourselves superhero names.

That was Chet's idea. He was a few years older, one of my brother's friends, with a sketchbook that never left his side. His sister, Joanie, was close with mine, so we were kind of a bundled set. One afternoon, he passed around hand-drawn cartoons of each of us as superheroes.

Mine was "Mighty Mouth." Apparently I have always had a lot to say.

It was a play on Mighty Mouse, and honestly, I loved it. There was something about being turned into a character, given a name and a power, that made me feel seen in a way teachers and classmates didn't.

My sister's alter ego was "Thunder Thighs."

I don't think Chet meant anything cruel by it, but it landed differently for her. Maybe that was one of the first times I saw how labels can sting. How something meant as a joke can latch onto someone and leave a mark.

Still, we had our own bus-universe. Heroes, villains, back-row daredevils, front-row chatterers, and Patty at the wheel, sunglasses on, taking us over potholes like Evel Knievel.

It's funny how a school bus, something so loud and completely unglamorous, can become a landmark in your life. Just a long yellow box that smelled like vinyl, dirt, and whatever the kid in front of you had for breakfast.

But ours did become a landmark.

It was freedom and structure, boredom and excitement, dread and relief, all jammed together and painted school-bus yellow.

Those mornings started in the cold kitchen, before my brain had any interest in joining the day. The air would bite a little, the linoleum was frigid under our feet, and everything had this gray, sleepy tone to it. There was nothing glamorous about it. No one was giving a motivational speech at the table. It was just, wake up, get dressed, try not to miss the bus.

The race against the bus every morning was its own kind of ritual. It taught me that life doesn't always wait for you to be ready. That ugly yellow beast would barrel down the road at the same time whether I'd eaten breakfast or not, whether I'd found my other shoe or not, whether I was emotionally prepared for third-grade math or not.

There was no "Are we there yet?" because there was no shortcut. You got there when the route decided you got there. Period.

Buried inside all that "have to" was a quiet, early understanding. Life isn't built for your convenience. And if you keep waiting for conditions to feel perfect, you're going to miss a lot of rides.

The bus also taught me connection, though I wouldn't have called it that then. We were just a bunch of kids from scattered houses and isolated farms, miles apart and living separate lives. But on that bus, twice a day, we were crammed into the same narrow aisle, breathing the same recycled air, feeling the same potholes, laughing at the same dumb jokes.

You can build a community anywhere.

And then there was Patty.

She didn't try to be our friend, but she didn't treat us like a burden either. She listened. She remembered who sat where, who liked who, who was having a rough morning.

She'd ask simple questions that felt small at the time and enormous looking back.

"How'd that test go?"

"You get that bike fixed?"

"You doing okay today?"

Tiny check-ins that said, "I see you," without making a big performance out of it.

Her leadership didn't look like speeches. It looked like steady hands on the wheel while we lived out our little dramas behind her. It looked like letting us tell terrible jokes and occasionally laughing at them, not because they were funny, but because we needed to be heard. It looked like tapping the brakes or hitting a bump a little harder when she knew we needed a small thrill.

That bus was a moving lab where I learned how people work.

I learned the "in-between" parts of life aren't empty. The going-to and coming-from moments aren't filler. They're where so much of the real stuff happens.

We like to think the defining moments are the big ones. Graduations, weddings, funerals, job offers, hospital rooms. And sure, those moments matter. But the bus taught me that your life is mostly made out of the parts you're tempted to sleepwalk through. The commute. The waiting. The routine.

That's where your character gets built.

And maybe the deepest part of it is this.

No matter how bumpy the ride got, I always knew where we were headed.

The bus might lurch, kids might scream, books might scatter, someone might cry. Under all of it was a simple, solid truth.

This route goes home.

I didn't understand then how much that sense of direction would matter later, when life stopped giving me neat routes and familiar roads. When home stopped being a driveway and started being something I had to build inside myself.

But those rides planted something in me. A quiet, steady compass.

To this day, when things get loud or disorienting, I can still feel some version of that bus rhythm in my bones. Even if the road is cracked and uneven, even if you're taking the long way around, even if you're tired and staring out the window wondering when it's going to get easier.

You're still moving.

You're still on the route.

And somewhere out there, even if you can't see it yet, there's a place that feels like home.

ROUND 4:
First Chair, Last to be Seen

For sixth, seventh, and eighth grade, I went to Edison Middle School. Same place my older brother and sister had gone, which you'd think would make things easier. Familiar halls, familiar teachers, a last name they already recognized.

In reality, it just meant expectations.

I walked in already being "someone's little brother." There were invisible standards I didn't know how to meet. Whatever people had liked about them didn't automatically transfer to me. If anything, it made me feel like I was already behind, like I was failing at a race I didn't even know I was running.

I don't say this lightly. Those three years were the darkest of my life emotionally.

No contest.

When I say "dark," I don't mean slow-motion hallway encounters with bullies shoving books out of my hands. It was more subtle than that. More pathetic, in a way. It was the kind of darkness that seeps in slowly, day after day, until one morning you wake up and realize you don't actually remember what it feels like to be okay.

I was depressed. I was bullied. I was lonely, ignored, and quietly crushed under the weight of questions I didn't know how to ask out loud.

What did I do wrong?
Why me?
Why am I so different?

What made it worse was that nobody had actually handed me those questions. I came up with them myself. That's the twisted logic of a kid in pain. If something feels this bad, it must be your fault. There has to be a reason, and the easiest target is your own reflection.

Even now, decades later, I can still feel that dull ache in my chest when I think about those days, weeks, months, and years at Edison. It's not as raw anymore. It's not fresh. It's like an old bruise you forgot about until you bump it on the corner of a table. A little shock of, *Oh yeah. That's still there.*

There's a part of me that wants to skip this chapter entirely. Just jump over it, pretend it never happened. Go straight from "funny childhood" to "adult redemption" and leave the middle school hellscape on the cutting-room floor.

Because loneliness like that is embarrassing.

Not just painful. Embarrassing.

There's shame baked into it. Shame that you weren't liked. Shame that you didn't know how to fix it. Shame that you cared so much.

I remember walking into that building and feeling like I'd landed on the wrong planet, but somehow everyone else had the instructions. They moved in little currents and clusters, flowing around lockers and down hallways, and I was always half a step off. Wrong timing. Wrong clothes. Wrong jokes. Wrong everything.

Loneliness isn't just about being alone. Half the time I wasn't physically alone at all. I was surrounded by kids, crowded hallways, full classrooms, loud lunchrooms. That was the worst part. Being unseen in front of people.

It's easier to be invisible when no one's around. It's brutal to feel invisible while someone is looking right through you.

I remember the way the lunchroom sounded. Loud but somehow far away. Trays clattering, kids laughing, that weird echo of voices bouncing off hard walls and tile floors. I'd stand there with my brown paper bag lunch, pretending I was just "looking for a seat," when really I was scanning the room for anywhere I wouldn't be obviously unwanted.

Sometimes I'd find a spot at the end of a table and try to slide in like I belonged there. Sometimes nobody said anything. They didn't tell me to leave, but they didn't talk to me either. I'd sit there, nodding along like I was part of the group, while conversations happened over and around me.

Other days, I'd retreat to some quieter corner, eat fast, and stare at the clock like it was a lifeline. Just make it to the bell. Then make it to the next one. Then the next.

Depression, for me, didn't show up as dramatic sobbing fits in the bathroom. It arrived as this slow erosion of color. The things I used to care about started to feel pointless.

When you're hurting that much and you don't know how to say, "I'm not okay," you start sending out these sad little signals instead. You hope someone will notice the way you hang back, the way your shoulders curve in, the way your eyes look away. You hope some adult, or honestly, anyone, will pull you aside and say, "Hey, something's wrong, isn't it?"

No one did.

And I don't say that to blame anyone, exactly. Most adults are just trying to keep their own lives from falling apart. Teachers saw a quiet kid who did his work. They didn't see the kid lying awake at night replaying every awkward social interaction like a courtroom cross-examination.

I was angry about that for a long time. Angry that no one saw. Angry that I didn't know how to scream loud enough without actually screaming.

Those years changed me.

And trying to write about them now has made me realize something ugly and unfair. I can't pull the memories up the way I want to. It's like walking into a room you know you lived in for years and finding all the furniture missing, just the outline of where it used to sit.

I know things happened. I know there were comments that cut deep. Moments in classrooms. Hallway encounters. Bus rides home with my stomach in knots. I can feel the residue of all of it, like sludge at the bottom of a lake. But when I reach for specifics, they slip away.

That's one of the cruelest tricks of trauma. Not always the big, obvious events, but that slow grind of repeated hurt. Your brain, at some point, decides: *We're done replaying this. Shut it down.* And just starts locking doors.

There are a few sharp moments I can still see, but I know there are dozens, maybe even hundreds more buried deep, sealed in compartments I locked up a long time ago.

A phrase here. A laugh there. The look on someone's face. A day I went home and decided not to tell anyone how bad it felt because I didn't want to sound pathetic or cause trouble or be "dramatic." So I swallowed it. Again. And again. And again.

I pushed those moments down so they wouldn't keep hurting me. That was the only tool I had.

Now that I want them back, to make sense of them, to give them a voice, they won't come. They stay blurred, just out of reach, like I'm trying to watch a movie through fogged glass.

So if this part feels incomplete… it is.

The feelings are still there. The darkness is still there. But the stories that created it? Some of them might stay at the bottom of that ocean forever. Like a battered warship, rusting in the deep.

And maybe that's its own kind of heartbreak. Knowing there are chapters of your life you can feel but not fully see. Whole days and weeks and months that shaped who you became, but exist now only as heaviness, as vague outlines.

But here's the thing I'm only just starting to accept.

Loneliness isn't less real just because the details are blurry.

Those years taught me what it feels like to be isolated even in a crowd, to sit in a room full of people and feel like a hologram. They taught me how dangerous it is to believe that your pain is an inconvenience to everyone else. They taught me what happens when you start to believe you're the problem, instead of recognizing you're just a person in pain.

They also taught me what I never wanted anyone else, especially my own kid, to feel.

So when I say those three years were the darkest of my life, I don't mean nothing good ever happened during them. I mean the loneliness built a shadow that swallowed almost everything else.

And yet, here I am, trying to write about it anyway. Reaching into murky water, knowing I might only pull up a few pieces.

Maybe that's enough.

Maybe the point isn't to remember every incident with perfect clarity, but to honor the kid who survived them, even if he can't tell the whole story.

I have always been small. Not "Oh, he's kind of short," but small in a way that other people seemed to notice before they noticed anything else about me. Before my name, before my personality, before anything I might've been good at, there was my height… or lack thereof, I should say.

Even as a grown man, I stand at only five foot three and hover around 145 pounds. In sixth grade, I was basically action-figure sized. While other boys shot up over one summer, coming back to school with new voices and new height and this weird new confidence, I stayed compact. Easy to shove, easy to grab, easy to pick on.

Middle school kids don't need a good reason to be cruel. My size just made me convenient.

And then came the glasses.

I started wearing them in fifth grade. Thick, plastic, brown-rimmed frames that swallowed half my face. These weren't cool, retro, fashionable glasses like people pretend to wear now. They were cheap. Practical. Ugly. We couldn't afford anything else.

My clothes were off-brand specials from the blue-light clearance racks at Kmart. Shirts that never quite fit right, jeans that were either a little too short or a little too baggy. My haircut came courtesy of students at the local cosmetology school, still learning, still practicing, and it showed. My hair was hacked short, full of cowlicks that refused to behave.

And I had a gap between my front teeth that felt about three miles wide.

Put it all together and I looked like the billboard for "obvious target for bullies."

Sixth grade hit hard.

The teasing ramped up immediately. I don't remember anything like that happening in elementary school. Back then, we were all still learning how to be people. We were small together. Awkward together. We were just kids with backpacks, trying to figure out how to write in cursive and not pee our pants during recess.

But something changed during that one short summer.

The same kids came back taller and more cruel, with new words and new ways to hurt each other. Suddenly there was a social ladder, and everyone knew exactly where they stood on it, except me. I just knew I was somewhere near the bottom, in the part of the chart nobody bothered to look at unless they needed someone to laugh at.

They had figured out how to turn their own insecurities into weapons.

I never stood a chance.

But the worst part wasn't the jokes or the shoves. It wasn't even the names, though I heard plenty of those. Four-eyes. Shrimp. Midget. Gap-tooth. Half of them weren't even creative. They were just lazy observations shouted with enough volume to get a laugh.

The worst part was how alone I felt inside all of it.

Isolation isn't just about walking the halls by yourself. It's the feeling that even when you're surrounded by people, you're not really with them. You're near them. Parallel to them. But not one of them.

I remember stepping off the bus in the morning and feeling like I was entering someone else's story. Kids moved in groups, clustered around lockers, collecting in doorways, filling the hallways in loud, moving crowds. There was an energy there, this messy middle-school ecosystem full of inside jokes and shared stories and nods and eye-rolls that meant something.

I was outside of all of it.

I'd walk down the hall with my head tilted just slightly down. Not enough to look completely defeated, but low enough to avoid eye contact. I got very good at looking like I was on my way somewhere important, even when I wasn't. Like I had someone to meet, something to do, some reason to walk with purpose.

That was part of the isolation too. The constant performance.

If I looked lost, people noticed.
If I looked like I had a destination, they mostly ignored me.

So I faked having a destination a lot.

In classrooms, isolation took on a different shape. I'd sit down at a desk and feel, immediately, how every other desk seemed to belong to somebody. The kid who always had the answer. The kid who always had the joke. The kid who always had the attention. My desk felt like a folding chair someone had dragged in at the last minute.

Teachers saw a quiet kid, maybe a little awkward, but not a problem. I wasn't acting out. I wasn't failing. I wasn't drawing attention, and that, in a middle-school classroom, is often enough to pass you off as "fine."

But inside, I didn't feel fine.

I felt like someone who'd been invited to a party but wasn't allowed to talk to anyone.

Every environment had its own version of the same message. *You don't fit.*

In the locker room, it was obvious. Bigger boys, louder boys, the ones with muscles starting to form and voices starting to drop, they took up all the oxygen. I tried to change as fast as possible, eyes down, hoping no one would notice that my body felt like it was still stuck in the "before" section of everyone else's transformation montage.

In the lunchroom, the isolation was more obvious. You feel it when you're standing there, scanning the room. Nobody waves you over. Nobody says, "Sit here." You're left doing this pathetic social math in your head. *Which table will make me look the least desperate? Where can I sit where I won't get told it's "taken"? Where can I blend just enough to not be obvious?*

Even when I did sit down, conversation flowed around me like I was a rock in the middle of a stream.

They'd talk over me, next to me, around me. I'd laugh at the right times, nod when it seemed appropriate, trying to stitch myself into their world with these tiny, invisible threads. But the whole time, I felt like an extra standing just out of focus in the back of the scene.

That's the special cruelty of middle-school isolation. You're not truly invisible. You're just not seen for anything you actually are.

They saw the height. The glasses. The cheap clothes. The bad haircut. The teeth. They saw the surface and decided that was the whole story. They treated me like a caricature of a kid instead of an actual person in a body that he didn't get to custom-order.

And because I was young, and lonely, and already questioning myself, I started to believe them.

That's how isolation really gets its hooks in. Not just when other people keep you out, but when you start locking the door from the inside too.

I stopped volunteering answers even when I knew them. I stopped trying to crack jokes even when I thought of something funny. I stopped asking, "Can I sit here?" because I already knew what it felt like to hear, "We're saving that." I stopped trying to make new friends after a couple of attempts fizzled into nothing.

I started doing the emotional equivalent of shrinking my shoulders, pulling everything inward and hoping if I took up less space, I'd attract less pain.

On the outside, it looked like I was just a quiet kid.

On the inside, I was screaming as I disappeared in slow motion.

And the thing about being small is, it's easy to disappear. You start to wonder if anyone would notice if you did. You start to question if they'd be relieved, actually. One less target. One less weird kid hanging around.

Middle school kids are experts in sniffing out difference, and they weaponize it without thinking. My size, my glasses, my clothes, my hair, my teeth, they were all different enough to make me stand out but not special enough to make me admired. I wasn't unique. I was just wrong.

So I lived in this strange space where I was too visible and completely unseen at the same time.

Too visible to avoid being picked on.
Too unseen to be protected.

That's isolation at its worst. Being noticed only when it hurts.

Looking back now, I almost want to reach into that chapter and grab my own shoulders, shake that tiny version of me, and say, "You're not the problem. You're not broken. You're just outnumbered."

But at the time, none of that wisdom existed. There was just the grind. Day after day of walking into a building that felt like it had already made up its mind about me.

And the more the outside world treated me like a punchline, the more I retreated into my own head. I built whole inner worlds where I wasn't small, where my body matched my sense of self, where I was fast or strong or charming or invisible by choice, not by neglect.

Those inner worlds kept me company in a way real people didn't.

Which is its own kind of loneliness.

Because at the end of the day, no matter how elaborate your imagination is, you still have to walk back into the cafeteria. You still have to put your tray down somewhere. You still have to feel your feet hit the floor of a place where you know you're not wanted.

Sixth grade didn't just hit hard.

It taught me that being different makes you vulnerable. It taught me that kids can be ruthless long before they're old enough to understand why. It taught me how easy it is for a person to become a role, "the small kid," "the weird kid," "the one we mess with," and how hard it is to break out of that once people decide that's who you are.

Mostly, though, it taught me what isolation really feels like.

Not just being alone.
Being outside.

Edison itself didn't help.

The building used to be a high school, back when Champaign was smaller. By the time I got there, it had been demoted to a middle school, but it felt institutional.

Cold stone floors. Echoing stairwells. Narrow hallways that funneled sound and made everything louder and more abrasive. The red-brick exterior looked more like a prison than a place for kids, and the eight-foot chain-link fence around the back playground might as well have had razor wire to complete the picture.

In my mind, it's always gray there. Always cold.

But then this blue drum kit showed up in our living room like a spaceship.

My parents gave it to my brother for his fifteenth birthday in November of 1985. A full five-piece set in this loud, shimmering blue with chrome hardware that caught every bit of light. The second I saw it, I was hooked. It was nothing like the violin I'd been dragging to school since third grade. The violin felt delicate and proper, like it needed good posture and straight backs.

The drums were pure mayhem.

They were loud, heavy, physical. You didn't just play them. You attacked them. I was obsessed.

I started sneaking into my brother's room whenever he was gone. I'd drag his oversized Koss studio headphones across the carpet, plug them into his stereo, and sit behind that kit like it belonged to me. I'd cue up a cassette, hit play, and spend hours trying to match every snare hit, every kick, every little fill.

The first song I figured out was "Small Town" by John Mellencamp.

I must have played it a hundred times that summer between fifth and sixth grade. That song became my private anthem long before I realized how much the lyrics matched my life. All I knew then was that when the drums kicked in, my arms and chest and ribs vibrated with every beat, and for those three minutes and forty-five seconds, nothing else existed.

> *"Well, I was born in a small town*
> *And I live in a small town…"*

By the time sixth grade rolled around, I'd had enough of strings. Enough of dragging that squeaky little violin case around like a plastic coffin.

So I packed up the violin, walked away from the squeaky bows, and joined percussion.

From the outside, it was just an elective switch. Violin to drums. One instrument for another. But inside, it felt way bigger, like I was quietly defecting from one version of myself to another.

The band room felt like home in a way nothing else in that school did.

Out in the hallways, I walked around like a target with legs. Too small, too dorky, too "other." Every step between classes felt like crossing an open field in a war movie. Eyes forward. Shoulders tight. Hoping no one decided they were bored enough to use me for entertainment.

But the second I stepped through that band room door, the air changed.

It smelled different in there. Valve oil, old sheet music, and that dusty-metal scent of music stands that had been dragged around for a decade.

And there was noise, but not the chaotic, weaponized kind that filled the hallways. This was organized noise. Scales. Warm-ups. Someone in the brass section trying to nail a high note and failing spectacularly. Random honks and taps and squeaks all mixed together into something that felt alive instead of dangerous.

Mr. Johnson, our band director, was tall and serious and had a presence that shut up even the loud kids. He didn't have to yell. He just existed with this controlled intensity that said, *I will absolutely end you musically if you screw around in here.*

He ran his class tight. No nonsense. No slack.

Which, of course, meant I had to test him.

In band class, I could finally relax and be myself without constantly feeling on edge like I did in the hallways or the cafeteria. In there, I was bold, talkative, confident. Honestly, I was kind of a pain in the ass. Mouthy, restless, always running my mouth when I should've been counting rests.

The band room brought out this version of me that felt real, like I wasn't bracing for impact every second.

That's what made middle school so confusing. It felt like there were two versions of me. The band-room me, and the "every other part of the day" me.

I picked up drum notation fast.

All of a sudden, the lines and dots on the page didn't feel like a language I was faking my way through like it did with the violin. Rhythms made sense to me in a way melody never had. I learned snare, bass drum, all the little auxiliary toys. The triangle, tambourine, crash cymbals. If it made noise when you hit it, I wanted to figure it out.

Within a short time, I climbed my way to first chair.

That spot mattered more than I let on.

Out in the hallways, there was no ranking system for kids like me, just social hierarchies I had already lost. But in here? There was an actual seat, an actual role, with my name attached to it. First chair on snare meant something. It meant I wasn't just the short kid or the punchline.

It was like that handwriting award back in first grade. Proof that I could be the best at something in a room full of kids trying to.

First chair on snare meant I was the lead voice.

The one driving the beat.

The one no one could ignore.

For forty-five minutes a day, I wasn't the kid getting torn apart in the hallways.

I was the best drummer in the room.

And that feeling, that contrast, was like stepping out of a storm and into a room where people suddenly cared what you had to say.

The xylophone? Absolutely not. Too many notes. Too much like the violin I was trying to leave in the dust. Melody had betrayed me once already. Hours of practice for a sound that still felt flimsy and apologetic. I didn't want delicate. I didn't want pretty.

I needed impact.

I wanted sticks in my hands and sound that punched through the air. I needed to hit something and have the room respond. I wanted each note to feel like a small declaration. *I am here. You will hear me.*

And honestly, I was good.

That sounds arrogant, but it's the truth. I was the best drummer in the band every year. And yeah, I acted like it. That room, with that instrument, was the only time I had confidence, and I took full advantage of that feeling.

Out there, I was small.
In here, I was loud.
Out there, I tried to disappear.
In here, I wanted every eye.

I was cocky, I talked too much, and I drove Mr. Johnson up the wall. We butted heads constantly, me pushing boundaries, him snapping them back into place like a tight snare head. But under all that friction there was this strange, unspoken respect.

He knew I cared.
I knew he did too.

Because if he didn't, he wouldn't have pushed me. He wouldn't have stopped the whole band to call me out when my sticking was sloppy or I got lazy with a roll. He wouldn't have made me play parts alone in front of everyone just to prove I could do it.

And as much as I wanted to roll my eyes or crack a joke when he did that, the truth is, I loved it.

Being singled out for being good was such a bizarre feeling compared to the rest of my day. Same school, same building, same kid. In one hallway I was the easiest target, and in this room, I was the standard.

The band room became this weird little pocket of safety inside a school that otherwise felt like enemy territory.

In English class, my heart would pound because I didn't want to be called on. In band, my heart pounded because I knew I would be.

In the lunchroom, my brain raced trying to figure out where to sit so I wouldn't look pathetic. In band, I knew exactly where I belonged. Back row, percussion section, hands on sticks, eyes on the page.

Outside, my size made me easy to push around.

In here, my timing made me impossible to ignore.

There's this moment that happens in band, right after everyone tunes, right before the first note, when the room goes still. All the instruments ready, all the eyes up front, everyone waiting for the downbeat. For most kids, that moment was about the conductor.

For me, it was about the drum.

Because when Mr. Johnson dropped that baton and it was my part leading the charge, snare snapping in on beat one, clean and sharp, that was the sound of me taking up space on purpose.

I didn't have the language for it then, but looking back, band was the first place I learned that identity isn't one thing. You can be invisible in one room and indispensable in another, all in the same day, wearing the same stupid off-brand clothes.

Sixth grade was still a train wreck for me emotionally. I still felt my stomach knot up at the sight of certain kids, still stood in front of my locker some mornings feeling like I'd been dropped into the wrong life.

But in that room, behind that drum, something clicked.

I mattered.

Not because anyone gave me a pity seat. Not because someone was "being nice." But because I was good at something objective. The notes were either right or wrong. The rhythm was either locked in or it wasn't. And I could make it lock.

Out there, I was the small kid with glasses and clearance-rack clothes, trying to dodge comments and pretend I wasn't hurting.

In here, I was first chair.
In here, I was the beat everyone followed.
In here, for forty-five minutes a day, I didn't feel alone.

But there's one day in particular that never left me.

It doesn't show up as a full scene, like a movie. It's more like a series of still frames, overexposed snapshots burned into my brain. The kind your mind goes back to when it wants to remind you exactly when the ground shifted under your feet.

My homeroom teacher was Mrs. Alexis.

She had strong features, short blond hair, and eyes that could cut through chatter like a knife. Some adults might have described her as attractive, "put together," "professional," all those adult words. To me, she was terrifying. Not horror-movie terrifying. Just that constant dread of never knowing when you were about to be singled out.

I could never seem to stay off her radar.

I was the kid who had too many words and nowhere good to put them. I'd try to crack jokes, whisper comments, say something at the wrong time, and like clockwork, her eyes would snap to me. That quick, laser look that made you feel five inches tall.

With other teachers, getting in trouble felt like getting in trouble. You broke a rule, they called it out, you dealt with it. It sucked, but it felt connected to behavior. With her, the punishment didn't just feel like discipline. It felt personal. Like she wasn't correcting what I did. She was annoyed by who I was.

In my eleven-year-old brain, I connected the dots in the most painful way possible.

She doesn't just dislike what I'm doing. She dislikes me.

I was convinced she hated me.

Maybe she didn't. Maybe she was just strict and overworked and exhausted and had her own invisible pile of shit waiting at home. But to an eleven-year-old already drowning in self-doubt, she felt like one more adult who had decided I wasn't worth the effort. One more person silently agreeing with the bullies. *Yeah, this kid is a problem.*

That day, she'd had enough.

I don't remember what I said. I don't remember the joke, or the comment, or if I even meant to be funny. I just remember her voice. Sharp, clipped, final.

"Go sit on the stairs," she snapped.

Not the office.
Not detention.
Not even moving my seat to the front of the room.

Just out.

And somehow that felt worse. Like the message wasn't "You crossed a line." It was "I'm done with you."

The room went quiet and I felt the embarrassment burn hot in my face as I stood up. I could feel all the eyes on me without seeing them. The scrape of my chair against the floor sounded way too loud.

I shuffled out into the hallway and let the door close behind me.

Instantly, the sound changed. Inside the classroom, the noise was muffled, voices turned to a low hum behind the wall. Out in the hall, everything was echoey and cold.

The staircase to the second floor sat just a few feet outside her classroom door.

Marble steps. Hard. Slick. Impersonal. I climbed a few steps up and sat somewhere around the middle between the landing and the floor. Halfway up, halfway down. That about summed it up. Not really in class, not really out of school. Just parked in some emotional waiting room no one else could see.

From where I sat, and with the door closed, I couldn't see into the classroom, but I could still hear it. The occasional burst of laughter. The rise and fall of her voice. The scrape of chairs. Life went on without me. That's what isolation feels like at that age. Realizing the world doesn't pause because you're hurting. It just keeps going, and you're the one edited out of the scene.

I had my notebook with me.

In it lived two cartoon characters I had created, Koozie Cat and Doogie Dog. They were ridiculous little things. Simple, silly, over-exaggerated animals with big eyes and goofy expressions. They weren't high art. They were escape routes.

Drawing them was my exit hatch. My way out of rooms I couldn't physically leave.

So I did what I always did when I felt cornered. I flipped open the notebook and started sketching. My hands moved on autopilot, like they already knew the shapes. Oval faces. Little whiskers. Dumb smiles.

Only this time, I pressed the pencil harder than I needed to. Lines dug into the paper, carving grooves like I was trying to scratch my way through to another universe. I focused on the details with a kind of desperation. If I could just perfect this curve, this expression, maybe I wouldn't have to feel what was happening inside my chest.

Because somewhere in that moment, something in me broke.

I actually felt it.

Not like a snap. Not a clean break. More like a crack slowly spreading in glass you've been pushing on for too long. The tight knot in my chest pulled tighter, then sagged, like it had given up. My shoulders slumped under a weight that had nothing to do with my backpack and everything to do with the realization that I didn't belong. Not here. Not with them. Not anywhere in that building.

The heat behind my eyes swelled, that sting that means tears are coming, but they never quite spilled over. I held them back like my life depended on it. Crying would've felt like admitting defeat. It would've made everything too real.

So instead, I redirected the hate.

I hated my school. I hated the kids who laughed at me. I hated my teacher and her sharp voice and her sharper eyes and the way she could exile me with one sentence.

But mostly, I hated myself.

I hated myself for being the kid who got singled out. For not knowing how to be normal. For always saying the wrong thing, or being too loud, or too much, or just off. I hated that I couldn't fix it. I hated that I couldn't stop caring. I hated that I was sitting on those stairs trying to draw cartoons like it could save me, and it wasn't saving me. It was just keeping me quiet.

And the hardest part to admit is that somewhere in that moment, I didn't just feel embarrassed.

I felt defective.

Like there was something about me that made people want to push me away, and I didn't even know what it was, which meant I couldn't defend myself from it. I couldn't explain it. I couldn't correct it. I could only feel it.

So I sat there, halfway up the stairs, trying to disappear without actually leaving. Trying to be invisible. Trying to be tough. Trying not to cry. Meanwhile the class kept going on behind the door like I had never existed at all.

That's the sick twist of isolation as a kid. Other people hurt you, and you turn the knife on yourself. I sat there on those cold steps thinking, *If I were different, this wouldn't be happening. If I weren't so annoying. If I weren't so weird. If I weren't so… me.*

No one came out and found me sobbing. There was no big outburst, no thrown books, no concerned adult kneeling down to say, "Hey, buddy, what's going on? Talk to me." It was quiet. Ordinary. Just another day for everyone else.

But inside me, a line got crossed.

Up until then, I'd been able to joke my way through most things. Humor was my shield, my distraction, my bargaining chip. If I could make people laugh, maybe they'd like me. Or at least they wouldn't hit me as hard.

Sitting there alone on those stone steps with a notebook full of make-believe animals, I realized my usual tricks weren't cutting it anymore.

That was the day I started pretending I was okay.

Not the casual kind of pretending, either. Not the "I'm fine" you toss out when you're just mildly annoyed. This was a full-time job. A performance. A mask that slowly fused to my face.

I learned how to smile on the outside and drown on the inside.

I started rehearsing my reactions before they happened. What I'd say if someone teased me. How I'd laugh it off. How I'd shrug like I didn't care. I started editing myself in real time. Don't say that. Don't ask that. Don't let them see that it hurt.

Because somewhere deep down, I'd absorbed the belief that if I showed how much it bothered me, it would only get worse.

Sitting there, I couldn't keep joking my way out of how I felt. I couldn't keep brushing off the comments, laughing like it didn't matter.

Because it did.
It mattered.

I wasn't okay.
I. Wasn't. Okay.

I knew it in my bones that day. I knew it in the ache in my chest, in the way the staircase suddenly felt like the safest and loneliest place in the world at the same time. I knew it in the way my hand kept drawing big smiling cartoon faces while my own face felt like it might crack.

And the worst part was, I had no idea how to tell anyone.

Who was I supposed to go to? The teacher who sent me out there? The kids who laughed at me? My parents, who already had enough to worry about, who might say, "Just ignore them," like that was a real solution?

I didn't know if anyone would even care if I did tell them.

So I didn't.

I just filed that moment away somewhere deep and got very, very good at acting like I was fine.

The rest of that year is gone.

That is the last clear memory I have of sixth grade.

After those stairs, everything goes dark. The rest of the school year and the summer that followed feel like they were erased. Not neatly, more like taped over. Static where there used to be experiences.

But that one image remains.

A small boy on cold stone steps.
A cheap notebook.
Two goofy cartoon animals grinning up from the page.

And a kid who finally realized he was completely, utterly alone, and decided, right then, to never let anyone see it.

What I do remember from that blank stretch is the music.

Sad songs. Depressing love ballads by Chicago, Journey, Heart, and Mr Mister that wrapped themselves around my heart and stayed there. I'd play them over and over, sinking into lyrics and melodies like they were a warm bath instead of a slow flood.

> *"...Reach the stars*
> *Fly a fantasy*
> *Dream a dream..."*
>
> "Never Ending Story" by Lamahl

I let those songs say what I couldn't.

Those three years at Edison weren't just "a rough patch." They were a turning point. The beginning of my depression. The start of me splitting into two versions of myself.

The one the world saw.

And the one sitting alone on a staircase, drawing cartoon animals and wondering why he hurt so much.

Seventh grade didn't suddenly turn everything into a feel-good movie, but it wasn't as pitch-black as sixth. The days were still heavy more often than not, and I still carried that same quiet sadness in my chest, but here and there, small lights started to cut through.

Most of those lights were people.
Most of those people were in band.

Music had always been there, long before the blue drum kit. I started violin in third grade with tiny hands and squeaky notes, and somehow, every year at competitions, I took first place. Three years in a row.

For a while, those medals were everything. They made me feel like I had a superpower. I wore them like a badge of honor.

But by fifth grade, I was still winning, still playing, but the joy had leaked out. I was going through the motions, playing the notes perfectly, and feeling absolutely nothing. That last first-place medal felt heavy in the wrong way. I set the violin down one day and just never picked it back up.

To this day, I barely remember how to hold the bow.

By seventh grade, percussion and the band kids had become my tribe. We were, for the most part, the outsiders, but we were outsiders together.

We were the kids with calloused fingers and weird senses of humor. The ones who didn't quite fit the usual categories of jocks, preps, popular, whatever. We were the background noise of school concerts and pep rallies, but in that little corner of the building, we were the main event.

And then there was Shelby.

Shelby wasn't loud. She wasn't over the top. She didn't walk into a room demanding attention. She was the opposite of all that, and somehow she stood out more because of it.

She was one of those people you just immediately relax around.

There wasn't a big moment where we "became friends." No dramatic cafeteria rescue, no group project that forced us to talk. We just fit. Like we'd been orbiting near each other and finally snapped into the same gravity.

She was funny in this laid-back way. Under-her-breath comments that made you choke on your drink because they were so perfectly timed. She was calm without being boring, chill without being checked out. And she was genuinely cool without trying, which, in middle school, is like spotting a unicorn.

Our friendship deepened through eighth grade and into high school, not because we had some formal Best Friend Agreement, but because we just kept showing up in each other's days.

Same band room.
Same sections of the hallway.
Same casual, "Hey, what's up?" that slowly turned into routine comfort.

She became one of the only constants in a time when everything else felt shaky.

And yes, of course I had a crush on her.

How could I not?

When most of your school day feels like dodging landmines, bullies, teachers who don't get you, classes where you feel two steps behind, someone like Shelby becomes more than just "nice." She becomes oxygen.

She was the bright spot in the school day, the person I scanned the room for without even realizing I was doing it. I'd walk into a classroom and my eyes would automatically go: door, whiteboard, teacher… Shelby.

If I saw her, I could breathe.

It sounds dramatic, but it's true. Her presence dialed everything down a notch. The anxiety didn't vanish, but it loosened its grip. My brain, which was usually running worst-case scenarios, could rest for a second because there, in that desk or that chair or that seat in the band room, was proof that not everything in my world was hostile.

I don't think she ever fully understood how much she held me together just by being there.

We never dated.

We never had the big dramatic "So… what are we?" talk.

I always wanted to. God, did I want to. There were a hundred moments where I thought, *This is it. This is when I tell her.* Walking next to her after band. Sitting near her on the bus for a field trip. Standing in the hallway between classes, both of us leaning against lockers as we complained about something dumb.

I'd feel the words building in my chest. *I like you. More than just as a friend.* And then, like clockwork, fear would slam the emergency brake.

Because here's the thing: when someone is one of the only good, steady things in your life, risking that feels like standing on the edge of a cliff and tossing your parachute over just to see if it opens.

I think she knew how I felt, though.

There was this quiet mutual awareness, this unspoken I-see-you-more-than-you-think thing between us. The way she'd look at me when I made a joke. The way she'd roll her eyes at something dumb someone else said, then glance my way to see if I caught it too. The way she stuck by me through years when other people drifted off.

For whatever reason, that quiet, unspoken understanding was enough.

There's a picture of us in the eighth-grade yearbook, both of us laughing like nothing in the world is wrong and trying not to get yelled at by the teacher across from us. It's not a posed, stiff smile. It's mid-laugh, eyes crinkled, mouths open, totally unguarded. One of those rare, honest snapshots where you can see that, at least for a second, we were free.

When I flip to those pages now, I don't think of the bullying, or the hallway dread, or the nights I fell asleep to sad songs because I didn't have the language for "depressed" yet.

I think of her.

I think of standing in the band room, drumsticks in my hands, her holding her trumpet on her lap, catching her eye across the noise and trading some small, stupid grin that made the whole day feel less heavy.

I think of walking out of school after a rough day and hearing her call my name, her voice cutting through the noise, and realizing I wasn't leaving that building completely alone.

I think of all the conversations that didn't seem monumental at the time. Complaining about assignments, talking about music, joking about teachers, sharing tiny bits of our lives. How those little, ordinary moments stacked up into something huge.

Proof that I wasn't invisible.
Proof that I wasn't unlovable.
Proof that at least one person at that school genuinely liked me for who I was.

She made the worst years of my life feel survivable.

Not by swooping in to rescue me. Not by grand gestures. Just by sitting next to me. By laughing with me. By letting me exist beside her without making me feel like I had to audition for the privilege.

In a world that had mostly taught me to brace for impact, Shelby was one of the first people who taught me what it felt like to just rest. To be myself without constantly checking the room for danger.

And if that's not something to be deeply, permanently grateful for, I don't know what is.

Seventh grade was also when I started to push back. Not in a healthy, mature, therapist-approved way. More like a cornered animal that had finally had enough.

I slowly started the struggle of growing a spine and being heard. I wanted to stop being the kid who just swallowed every insult and cried in his room later. I started snapping back. Sometimes with words. Sometimes with fists. I would love to say I was calm and calculated, but no. I was reactionary and angry and tired of being a target.

One night at a school dance, all of that collided.

We were in the gym, lights dimmed, music echoing off the walls, trying to be romantic in a place that usually smelled like sweat and floor cleaner.

The hardwood floor was packed with clumps of kids swaying awkwardly to whatever was popular that month. Teachers lined the walls like bored security guards, arms crossed, pretending not to watch too closely.

I don't even remember what the other kid said to me. That's how small it probably was. But I remember my part. I remember the way my mouth moved before my brain caught up. I shot back with some smartass comment, because that's what I did. Sarcasm was the only tool I had that made me feel bigger than I was.

And then suddenly we were chest to chest in the middle of the gym.

I remember how fast it happened. One second, just words. The next, that strange tightening in the air around us, like everyone nearby could sense something was about to happen and quietly shifted their attention just enough to catch it.

He shoved me. Hard.

I stumbled backward and hit the floor flat on my back, the impact slamming all the air out of me. For a second, all I could see were the gym lights above me, blurred at the edges. It felt like the whole room exhaled at once but I couldn't breathe at all.

It wasn't the pain. That part I could've handled. I'd wiped out on bikes, crashed minibikes, run through fire. Pain and I had an understanding. Pain was familiar.

This was something else.

This was exposure.

For a second, I just lay there, not from pain so much as shock. Shock that it happened. Shock at how fast it happened. Shock that no one stepped in before, during, or after. It felt like the whole world had been watching, waiting to see what the short kid with the big mouth would do.

And here's what I did.

Nothing.

I didn't yell.
I didn't get up swinging.
I didn't cry.

I got up slowly, brushed off my clothes with shaking hands, turned my back to the crowd, and walked off the dance floor.

And then I sat down on the bleachers.

Alone.

That's the part that still hits hardest. Not the shove, not the fall, but the walk afterward. The way it felt like I was on a lit stage while everyone else faded into the shadows. I knew people had seen me go down. That's the kind of thing middle school eyes are trained for.

Nobody followed me to the bleachers.
Nobody came over and said, "Hey, you okay?"
Nobody even sat near me, like getting too close might make the embarrassment contagious.

And underneath the humiliation, there was this nagging voice in my head. *Why did you open your mouth? Why didn't you just let it go?*

Because here's the thing. I had a plan for that night.

I had planned on asking Shelby to dance when "Always" by Atlantic Starr played. That song was my shot, my tiny little movie moment. I'd built a whole scene in my head. The song would start, I'd spot her across the gym, heart pounding, palms sweaty, but I'd walk over anyway. I'd ask. She'd say yes, maybe surprised, maybe not, and we'd walk out to the middle of the floor.

> *"Girl, you are to me*
> *All that a woman should be…*
>
> *… And I will love you so*
> *For always…"*

We'd sway under the dimmed lights, my hands on her waist, her hands on my shoulders, both of us pretending we knew how to slow dance. For a few minutes, I'd get to feel like the main character in my own life instead of the extra who gets shoved into the background.

That was the fantasy.

Reality was me on the bleachers, staring at the same floor I'd just been knocked onto.

I remember how cold the wood bleachers felt under me, even through my slacks. I remember my heart pounding so hard it felt like it was trying to escape my chest. My back hurt a little, sure, but what hurt more was the realization that the night was over for me, even though the dance wasn't.

When "Always" finally came on, it didn't feel like some romantic anthem. It felt like a taunt. The opening notes floated out across the gym, and instead of standing up and walking toward Shelby like I'd pictured a hundred times, I stayed seated.

Frozen.

Regret settled in fast and heavy. Regret about everything I wasn't doing in that moment. I wasn't apologizing. I wasn't walking across the floor to the one person who made school bearable. I wasn't doing anything.

I was just sitting.

My chest ached, but not from the impact. It was the humiliation. The exposure. The knowledge that everyone saw me hit the floor and no one saw me get back up. It's a special kind of lonely when your worst moments are public and your attempts to recover are private.

That moment branded itself into me.

Not because I "lost a fight." There barely was a fight. One shove. One fall. End of story. No, it stuck because of what it confirmed in my twelve-year-old brain.

You're unprotected.

No one stepped in front of me. No one stood beside me. No one sat next to me afterward and cracked a joke to take the edge off. Not a teacher, not a friend, not even the kid who'd pushed me. He just went back to the dance, back into the blur of bodies and music, while I sat there on the bleachers.

The isolation in that moment wasn't just being physically alone on the bleachers. It was the realization that no one saw me in the way that mattered. They saw the fall. They saw the humiliation. But they didn't see the kid sitting there afterward, replaying everything in his head and quietly deciding he deserved it.

Regret dug in deeper with every couple that stepped onto the floor.

I watched kids sway under the same lights I'd stared up at from the ground. I watched hands link, heads lean together, smiles flash. Somewhere in that crowd, I knew Shelby was out there. Maybe dancing. Maybe laughing. Maybe wondering where I'd gone.

I could have gotten up.
I could have walked over.
I could have still asked.

But I didn't.

Shame pinned me to that bleacher harder than his shove ever could have pinned me to the floor. I felt small, stupid, exposed, like the whole gym had silently agreed on who I was. The kid who gets pushed down and stays there, even when he stands back up.

That dance ended with me still sitting there, watching other kids slow dance while I waited for my parents to pick me up.

The walk out to the car afterward might've been one of the longest of my life. I climbed into the car, buckled up, and when my parents asked the casual, "So, how was it?" I did what I'd learned to do.

I shrugged. "It was fine," I said.

Because how was I supposed to explain that, in the span of a few seconds, I'd gone from potential main character to background extra in my own story?

That night wasn't just about a dance, or a shove, or a missed slow song. It was one more notch in the belt of isolation, one more piece of evidence that I didn't belong and my own mind telling me, *See? This is who you are.*

And the regret isn't just that I got knocked down.

It's that I stayed seated long after I could've stood back up.

ROUND 5:
Loud When it Counts

Seventh grade wasn't all punches to the gut.

There were a few people who made the days bearable, and one of them was my science teacher, Mr. Cabutti.

He was young in teacher years, early thirties maybe, with this kind of charismatic energy that made you want to listen even when you didn't care. My sister had him years earlier and always said, "Just wait, he's the best." She wasn't wrong.

He made science feel like it was happening *to* us, not just *around* us.

One of his projects involved pretending we were TV meteorologists. He brought in an actual camcorder, which in the late '80s was basically like bringing a spaceship into the classroom. This wasn't a phone-in-your-pocket world. Cameras were rare, heavy, and important. If something was being filmed, it meant it mattered.

We wrote weather forecasts. Highs, lows, temperature swings, storm fronts. Then we took turns standing in front of the camera, explaining it all like we were on the evening news.

Because our presentations were scheduled alphabetically by our last names, I was to be one of the last few kids to give my weather forecast.

Last meant I got to watch everyone else go first. It meant more time to prepare, which really just meant more time to overthink.

The thing is, this should've been my moment.

I liked performing. I liked being funny. I liked attention when I could control it. I was a drummer who loved being loud. I cracked jokes in class. I could talk. If you'd asked anyone, "Who's going to ham it up for the camera?" my name would've been near the top of that list.

And honestly, part of me wanted that. I pictured myself standing there, nailing the lines, getting laughs, maybe even impressing the teacher. Another little shot at being the main character, on my own terms.

I was ready for it. Nervous, but ready.

But underneath the "ready" was something else. Something ugly.

Fear.

Not the normal "Oh man, I'm nervous" fear before a test or a performance. This was deeper. It wasn't just fear of messing up. I'd messed up in front of people plenty of times. I knew I could survive that.

This was fear of being captured.

The idea of being recorded, of my face and voice getting frozen on tape, hit something raw in me. Live attention I could handle. If I said something stupid in class, the moment passed. People laughed, I shrugged, we all moved on. Even getting shoved at the dance, as humiliating as it was, happened and then ended.

But video? Video meant it could be rewound.

Paused.
Replayed.
Shared.

My brain didn't think in those exact words at the time, but that was the dread humming underneath. If I looked weird, sounded weird, moved weird, if I looked as small and awkward as I felt, it wouldn't just be a moment. It would be evidence.

Evidence they could watch again. Evidence I couldn't outrun. Evidence I couldn't control.

So while everyone else took their turn, walking up to the front with their notebook forecasts and nervous smiles, I sat there stewing. I watched each kid on the tiny TV screen and clocked everything, how they looked, how they sounded.

And slowly, this horrible question started circling:

What if I look worse than all of them?

Not just, *What if I mess up my forecast?*
Not just, *What if I stutter?*

What if I finally get to see myself the way everyone else already sees me, and I can't unsee it?

Because by that point, I didn't trust my own reflection.

Mirrors already felt like liars. Some days I'd look and think, *Maybe I'm not that bad.* Other days I saw nothing but the short kid with the glasses and the bad hair and the gap teeth and the cheap clothes. I had no stable image of myself. Just fragments.

The idea of a camera stepping in and saying, *Here. This is you, all at once,* was terrifying.

It wasn't just stage fright. Stage fright is about failing in the moment. This was about confirmation. About getting all my worst suspicions played back to me while the whole class watched.

So when the day came for my forecast and my name was on that list, it wasn't the sky I was worried about predicting.

It was the reaction.

I imagined kids laughing at how my voice sounded. Too high? Too soft? Too weird?
Laughing at how I stood. Too stiff? Too fidgety?
Laughing at my face on a screen that big. Too small? Too awkward? Too me?

I knew what they could do with a weak spot. I'd seen it. Lived it. One stumble, one visible crack, and middle school would turn it into a running joke that lasted for months, maybe years.

So my brain did what it always did when it sensed danger. It started making backup plans.

Maybe I can go really fast so they don't see me for long.
Maybe I can make it funny so they focus on the jokes, not on me.
Maybe I can... not be there.

That last thought came in quiet, almost like a relief.

I could just not be there.

Was I sick? Maybe. That's what I told people. That's the story I settled on because it was convenient and believable. Kids get sick. Things happen. No big deal.

But if I'm honest, I think I panicked.

Not the visible kind. No hyperventilating, no meltdown, no begging my parents not to make me go. It was subtler. The kind that slides in overnight and whispers, *You don't have to do this. You can just disappear.*

The idea of being recorded, of everyone watching me, of seeing myself on a screen later, ripped open the same vulnerable spot I'd felt in the gym at the dance.

That gym floor moment wasn't just about the shove. It was about being seen at my most powerless. And here I was again, staring down another situation where I could be frozen in that powerlessness, except this time it could be replayed on demand.

So my body did what my mouth couldn't.

It opted out.

That's the part that haunts me a little. How my fear learned to speak for me without words. I didn't advocate for myself. I didn't say, "Hey, this scares me," or "I don't think I can handle this." I didn't give anyone the chance to help me or push me through it or stand beside me.

I just vanished from the moment.

From the outside, it was nothing. A kid missed a project. He'll make it up later. Life goes on.

But on the inside, that absence meant something.

It meant fear got to call the shots.

It meant avoidance won.

And the internal story that formed underneath was brutal:

When it really counts, you bail.
When the spotlight shows up, you disappear.
You're not built for being seen.

The saddest part is that I might have been great at it. I might have nailed the forecast, made the class laugh in a good way, impressed the teacher, and walked away with one more little piece of proof that I was more than the kid people mocked in the hallways.

But I'll never know.
Because fear didn't just keep me from doing the project.
It kept me from finding out who I could be on that tape.

That summer, between seventh and eighth grade, everything transitioned again.

We moved.

We traded in that quiet country sanctuary for the faster rhythm of Champaign. Suddenly, I wasn't miles away from everything. I was *in* it. Closer to school, closer to friends, closer to basketball courts, closer to the mall.

It felt like someone flipped a switch labeled "options."

Saturday mornings were my first real taste of independence. Not the dramatic kind where you "find yourself," or whatever. More like the kind where you learn that money doesn't magically appear in your pocket, and you have to sweat for it. Sometimes you even bleed a little if you're stupid with a weed whacker.

Once we moved into town, we actually had neighbors. That meant lawns, which meant opportunity. My dad and I worked out this deal where he'd toss the push mower in the back of the truck on Saturdays and drive me around so I could mow yards and make my own money.

That became our routine for the next few years. Mid-May to mid-October, like clockwork. He'd load the mower in the bed, throw in the red five-gallon gas can and the weed whacker, and we'd hit four or five houses every weekend. I usually made five bucks a yard, sometimes ten if the yard was bigger, which felt like I'd just signed a professional athlete contract. Ten dollars. Are you kidding?

I'd push that mower back and forth until the grass looked neat, like those light-green and dark-green stripes you see on a golf course. I'd keep an eye out for dog toys and random rocks because nothing ruins your day like realizing you're one small rock away from buying someone a new window.

After twenty or thirty minutes, the mowing part would be done, and I'd switch to the weed whacker to clean up the edges so it looked "professional."

Here's the part that gets me now. Back then, I didn't thank my dad for any of it. Not once.

Every Saturday, for months, he spent half his day driving me around town so I could earn spending money, and he never complained. He'd sit there watching me sweat, probably thinking about the list of stuff at our own house that needed to get done, and he still just did it. Like it was nothing. And I never once stopped to think, *Why is he doing this? What's he getting out of it?*

Because that's what kids do. They assume the world is built to support them, and dads are just part of the structure.

Now I'm a father, and I know exactly what he sacrificed. Time is the one thing you never have enough of. There's always something to fix, something to clean, something to handle, something that needs you. So the fact that he gave up those Saturdays, over and over, just so I could feel a little proud handing someone a freshly cut yard and taking their five dollars. That hits different now. It's huge.

So, Dad, I never said it then, but I'm saying it now.

Thank you. For the truck rides, the gas can, the mower in the bed, the patient silence, the time. Thank you for teaching me responsibility without making it some cheesy lecture. Thank you for showing me what sacrifice looks like without needing credit for it.

You were a better role model than I ever admitted. You deserved more gratitude than you got. And you've always been amazing for all of us, even when I was too young, too cocky, or too distracted to notice.

One of the biggest changes that came with moving into town was transportation. I traded the familiar yellow school bus for city bus transportation, which made me feel both older and more lost at the same time.

The school gave us a book of paper tickets as "transfer passes" because we had to take two separate buses to get to and from school each day. One bus would pick me up a few blocks from our house, drive its route, and end at the exchange terminal downtown. I'd get off there, clutching my backpack and trying to look like I knew what I was doing, then climb onto the next bus, hand the driver my ticket like a ride at the county fair, and watch him drop the ticket into this cloudy plastic container.

That second bus would take me the rest of the way to school.

It all felt very official and adult and absolutely not built for someone who already felt small, but there was one part of the whole routine that made everything else worth it.

Waiting at the bus stop with Regan.

She lived a block away from the stop, in our neighborhood, and she might as well have been from another universe.

Regan had these big, crystal blue eyes. Long, spiraled brown hair that bounced when she walked. Bright white smile with metallic braces that somehow made her look even cuter, like the universe handed her the one version of orthodontia that actually enhanced a person instead of destroying them.

And she had a laugh.

God, that laugh.

Not the loud, performative kind some girls did when the popular boys were around. Hers started low, like she was trying to hold it in, and then spilled out and made you feel like you'd actually said something funny, not just something she was being polite about. And for reasons I still don't fully understand, I actually felt like she liked me.

Not "wanted to marry me" liked me. Not "write our initials in a notebook" liked me. But liked being around me. She didn't seem annoyed by my jokes. She didn't look past me while I was talking, scanning for someone cooler. When we stood at that corner of Neil Street and Arcadia Drive waiting for the bus, her body was pointed toward me, like I had her full attention.

That was rare currency in my world.

We'd talk for a few minutes while we waited. Nothing epic. No soul-baring confessions. Just little slices of conversation, homework, teachers, random neighborhood stuff, music, whatever stupid thing I could bring up that might get her to smile in my direction.

Every day on my four-block walk through the neighborhood to get to the bus stop, I looked forward to seeing if she was already there.

That walk became its own ritual.

I'd rehearse possible opening lines in my head.

Ask about the test.
Ask if she watched that show last night.

Don't say something stupid. Don't say something stupid. Don't. Say. Something. Stupid.

I'd pretend to be casual, kicking at leaves on the sidewalk, but inside I was on high alert for that first glimpse of her white jacket, her hair, her backpack. On days when I turned the corner and she was already there, it felt like the sun came up twice. On days when she wasn't, the whole block felt muted.

I would fantasize about sitting together on the bus, our shoulders brushing. Our hands accidentally touching and not moving away. And maybe, somehow, eventually, holding hands on purpose.

I imagined sneaking a kiss.
Feeling the softness of her lips on mine.
Her breath warm on my cheek.

I built whole scenes in my head. The bus would be half-full, somehow quiet. The world outside the window would blur, and inside that blur, we'd be in our own little secret universe. She'd look at me just a second too long, and I'd know. I'd lean in, she'd meet me halfway, and there it would be. Validation. Magic. Proof that I wasn't just some background character in my own life.

I created so many of those moments in my head, I could've story-boarded them.

Reality was simpler.

The only feelings I actually had out there were the flutter in my chest and the cold October air blowing in my face.

The flutter was relentless. I'd feel it as soon as I saw her, this little stutter in my heartbeat. My hands would suddenly feel too big and too clumsy. I'd become hyper-aware of dumb stuff, how I was standing, whether my backpack strap was twisted, if there was a huge pimple on my face.

Meanwhile, the October air didn't care about my internal romantic saga. It just slapped me in the cheeks and made my nose run while I tried to act chill in front of the prettiest girl I'd ever spoken to at close range.

Sure, she entertained me with conversation. Maybe even a little light flirtation, those joking nudges, the way she'd sometimes laugh and touch my arm for a second longer than necessary. But it was nothing like what I ran in my head.

There were no romantic runaways in our future. No running off the bus at the same stop just to walk each other home. No dramatic confessions on the sidewalk.

But that didn't stop me from building an entire alternate timeline where all of that happened.

In my head, we had a whole life together.

We walked home from school holding hands.
We lay in the grass somewhere, talking about life like we were older than we were.
I introduced her to the parts of me nobody else cared about, my drawings, my weird thoughts, the music I liked.

She told me secrets she'd never told anyone else.

In those mental movies, I was taller. I was still me, but a version of me smoothed out and upgraded for romance.

The real me was shorter, nervous, and trying not to trip over a curb while Regan's ponytail bounced in my peripheral vision.

Crushes like that are sacred when you're that age. Nothing has happened, nothing probably *will* happen, but the possibility alone keeps you going. In a life where a lot of things felt heavy and gray, Regan was this bright, impossible color only I could see.

Those mornings didn't fix my self-esteem or magically heal all my middle-school wounds. But they did something gentler, something quieter. They gave me a reason to straighten my shoulders. To keep walking those four blocks even on the days I wanted to disappear.

Because if there was even a tiny chance I'd get three minutes of Regan's blue eyes and that ridiculous, brilliant smile, it was worth it.

Looking back now, I can see how innocent it all was. How wildly disproportionate my inner drama was to the actual facts. But I don't roll my eyes at that kid. I get him.

When you feel invisible in most of your life, a crush isn't just about wanting someone. It's about wanting to be seen by someone who feels like light.

Regan never became my girlfriend. We never shared that bus-seat kiss. Those scenes stayed in my head, on repeat.

But she was the girl at the corner of Neil and Arcadia who made my heart beat too fast and my brain race with possibilities before the bus ever came into view.

And in those years, that alone was enough to keep me writing love stories in my mind, even if they never made it onto the page of real life.

Eventually, I started riding my bike to school. From our house on Winding Lane to Edison Middle School was a little over two miles each way.

To most people now that probably sounds like a punishment, but to me, it was freedom.

The first morning I decided to ride instead of taking the bus, it felt like I was stepping out of one version of my life and into another. No waiting on a corner. No climbing onto a city bus full of strangers and stale air. No shuffling down an aisle trying to guess which seat made me look the least pathetic.

Just me, my bike, and the road. And it took less than half the time to ride than it did to take two city buses.

I'd hop on in the morning, feel the cool air hit my face, and pedal down State Street. The neighborhood looked different from the bike seat. Houses I'd passed a hundred times suddenly had details, cracked walkways, crooked porch railings, wind chimes, dogs watching me from behind chain-link fences.

By the time I got to school, I was awake in a way I never felt by riding the bus.

The bus woke my body up enough to exist. The bike woke me up enough to feel alive. My lungs would be open, my legs would be buzzing, and my mind, usually spinning on all the ways the day could go wrong, would be quiet for once. Just the rhythm of pedal, breathe, pedal, breathe.

I'd lock my bike, walk into the building, and feel this tiny spark of independence.

It wasn't dramatic. No one was standing there handing out medals for "Most Self-Sufficient Eighth Grader." Nobody cared how I got there. There was no applause waiting at the door. But I knew. I knew I had carried myself there. Under my own power. On my own terms.

After school, I did it all over again.

Two miles back. Legs pumping, brain unwinding, the weight of the day slowly sliding off my shoulders with each rotation of the tires. Whatever had happened in the building, awkward moments, quiet humiliations, class boredom, near-misses with bullies, stayed there while I coasted away.

I rode that bike everywhere.

It stopped being just "transportation" and became a passport. Not just to and from school, but across town, into Urbana, down streets I had no business being on, just to see what was there.

There was a special kind of thrill in that, rolling past corners no adult had specifically pointed to and said, "You can go here." No supervision. No permission slip. Just two wheels and curiosity.

One of my favorite routes took me along Neil Street, across to University Avenue, through downtown Champaign, and eventually into Urbana past Carle Hospital.

In total, I'd cruise for about two and a half miles until I reached Durst Cycle, our local bike shop. Pushing open that shop door felt like entering a temple built for people like me. No one cared how short I was, or what brand my clothes came from, or whether I looked like an easy punchline. All that mattered in there was the bike you rode and how much you loved it.

Half the time, I didn't even buy anything.

I just walked the aisles, fingertips grazing handlebar grips and brake levers, staring at decals and gadgets I didn't need but desperately wanted. Seats that looked like they belonged on racing bikes. Tires with more aggressive treads than mine. Every part felt like an upgrade not just to the bike, but to the life riding it.

Most of my lawn-mowing money wound up there eventually, and I don't regret a single dollar.

And then I'd climb back on my own not-perfect, not-brand-new Redline bicycle, and ride home.

Those quiet little trips, just me and my bike and the road, became my therapy.

No one called it that, of course. This wasn't an era of "emotional check-ins" or "mental health days." You were expected to cope, usually in silence, and if you couldn't, you were "too sensitive." My coping mechanism just happened to have two wheels and a chain.

On those rides, I wasn't the kid getting shoved in gyms and ignored at dances. I wasn't the boy on the stairs drawing cartoon animals to keep from falling apart. I wasn't the small, awkward kid with the off-brand clothes and the gap teeth and the glasses that never quite sat right on my face.

I was someone moving forward, literally and figuratively, one pedal at a time. Nobody could stop me mid-ride to tell me who I was or wasn't. No one could turn my existence into a joke if they couldn't catch me.

I set my own pace.
I chose my own route.

If I wanted to detour, I did. If I wanted to push harder, I could. If I wanted to coast, I coasted.

There's a kind of fierce joy in knowing that, for at least a slice of your day, nothing is expected of you except to keep moving. No grades. No social rules. No performance. Just road and breath and the sound of your own tires on the pavement.

Sometimes, I'd use that time to rehearse things I wanted to say but was too scared to say out loud. Conversations with teachers. Comebacks to bullies. Jokes I might tell Shelby or Regan. On the bike, in my head, I was bolder. Funnier. Braver.

Other times, I wouldn't think at all.
I'd just ride.
Let the wind strip the noise out of my head. Let my body do the work while my brain finally shut up for five minutes.

Independence, for me, wasn't about breaking away from everyone forever. It was about proving to myself, in small ways, that I was capable. That I could get myself from point A to point B without falling apart. That I could choose my path, even if it was just which turn to take on a Tuesday afternoon.

That bike gave me something no classroom, no bus, no teacher had ever really given me: a sense of control over my own movement in the world.

And for a kid who felt powerless in almost every other area of his life, that feeling was everything.

That period between seventh and eighth grade felt like a clumsy but important bridge. I wasn't suddenly confident or healed or anything dramatic. But the world felt a little less hostile, and I was learning how to navigate it.

I also started to figure out my survival strategy.

Up to that point, I had been the kid people made fun of in hallways, in whispers. The scrawny one, the one with too-tight jeans, the one with the ugly glasses and the gap between his teeth.

I realized something simple and brutal: if I got there first, they had less power.

So I became the funny guy.

I leaned into self-deprecation before they could. I laughed at myself. I took their jokes and flipped them, turned them into bits, made other people laugh *with* me, instead of *at* me. On the outside, it looked like confidence. Like I didn't care.

On the inside, it still hurt every single time.

But pretending it didn't hurt helped me survive.

And then there was the day I finally snapped in front of everybody.

Up to that point, most of my "standing up for myself" moments lived in fantasy. In my head, I always had the perfect comeback, the perfectly timed joke, the cinematic moment where the bully got put in his place and everyone clapped. In real life, I usually just swallowed it. Took the hit. Laughed it off.

But not that day.

My jeans were always too tight. Not "fashionably slim." Just wrong. They were whatever was on sale, not what actually fit. I wish I could tell you they were tight because I was hiding some massive secret down there, but no. I was just an average eighth-grade boy with extremely unfortunate pants.

Somewhere along the way, the popular kids decided I stuffed my pants with socks.

Middle school logic: if something on your body draws even the tiniest bit of attention, it must be turned into a joke. It became this running bit, whispered in corners, snickered about behind my back. I'd catch fragments of it in hallways, hear my name followed by laughter.

Nobody ever had the guts to say it straight to my face.

Until Shane did.

Shane was loud and cocky and lived to roast people. He was that kid who treated the classroom like his personal comedy club, always "on," always performing, always punching downward because it was easy and got a guaranteed laugh.

Right before first period one morning, I walked into class and felt it. That weird almost-silence where the noise doesn't stop, but it changes.

Shane decided it was time to put on a show.

He made the joke.
He said the thing about the sock.

And this time, he said it loud enough for everyone to hear, and the room laughed on cue.

For a second, everything slowed down. I could feel the heat crawling up my neck, the familiar humiliation rising, the old script ready to cue up: *laugh it off, look away, pretend you didn't hear it, wait for the moment to pass, add it to the pile.*

But something in me snapped. Today is the day.

I didn't think. I didn't weigh the pros and cons. I didn't consider the fact that this might be a really bad idea in a school setting. I just reacted.

In the middle of the classroom, in front of everyone, I stopped. Turned to face him. Felt this weird calm drop over me like a weighted blanket. My hands moved before my brain caught up.

I calmly unbuttoned my jeans and yanked the zipper down.

I pulled the fly wide open, exposing my bright white underwear to the entire room, looked him dead in the eyes and said, "Does this look like a sock to you?"

Silence.

The kind of silence you almost never get in a middle-school classroom. Even the class clown's friends didn't know what to do with that.

And then absolute chaos.

The class lost their damn minds. People were laughing, yelling, slamming their hands on desks.

But this time, the laughter wasn't *at* me. It was *for* me. I'd hijacked the joke, grabbed the wheel, and driven it straight off the cliff.

The energy flipped completely. Shane, for once, had nothing to say. His face turned this deep, uncomfortable shade that matched exactly what I'd felt in a hundred other moments.

And in that split second, watching him look away from me, I felt something I wasn't used to feeling at school.

Power.

Not the cruel kind he'd been throwing around. Not the "I can hurt you and everyone will laugh with me" kind. Just this grounded sense that for once, I wasn't the one being pushed down. I was the one drawing the line.

I zipped my jeans back up, buttoned them, adjusted my shirt, and walked to my seat like nothing had happened.

Inside, adrenaline was doing backflips. I half-expected a teacher to materialize out of the ceiling tiles and drag me to the office. I half-expected the class to turn on me, someone to yell, "Gross!" or "You're disgusting!" and reset the social order.

None of that happened.

Shane never said another word to me about it.

Did he still talk behind my back? Probably. I'm not naïve. But after that morning, he didn't come at me directly again. He didn't make me the easy target. He didn't throw the sock joke in my face. It was like that moment redrew the boundary lines, and even *he* knew better than to cross them.

Was I proud of myself?

Fuck yes, I was!

And not just in the quick, shallow way of, *Ha, I got him.* It went deeper than that. It was the first time I stood up for myself in a way that everyone could see. The first time I didn't shrink and wait for the moment to pass. The first time I made it clear, publicly, that I wasn't going to be their punching bag anymore.

For a kid who'd spent years feeling small and powerless and humiliated in a thousand little ways, that was huge.

In the hallway afterward, I walked a little differently. Same height, same clothes, same body, but there was a new weight under my feet. I'd proven something to myself that no one could take away.

If you push me hard enough, I will push back.

And yeah, my method was wildly inappropriate by school standards. If a kid did that today, there'd probably be a SWAT team and a board meeting about it. But back then, in that room, in that life, it felt like a necessary overcorrection. I'd been pushed so far down for so long that the only way I knew to stand up was to blow the roof off.

That moment felt like a win. A big one.

I carried it with me like a trophy.

Not something I bragged about to adults. Not something I framed as my "empowerment moment" in some classroom reflection essay. Just this quiet, internal plaque I could touch when things got rough. *You didn't just take it. You didn't stay silent. You did something.*

It didn't fix everything. Bullies didn't suddenly become kind. My self-esteem didn't magically repair itself. But from that day on, when someone came for me, they had to factor in the possibility that I might do something unexpected.

And more importantly, I had proof that I was capable of surprising even myself.

That's what real confidence feels like at that age. Not constant swagger or unshakable belief, but a growing stack of moments where you didn't abandon yourself.

That day in the classroom, with my fly open and my underwear out and my voice steady, was one of the first times I chose me. And once you feel that, even just once, it's hard to go back to being the kid who always stays quiet.

Unfortunately, that small victory was about to be overshadowed by something much heavier.

It was late December, right before winter break, when I heard about the crash.

Just another piece of hallway gossip at first. Norman, a kid in a few of my classes, was flying to Tennessee with his family for Christmas. Not some big commercial flight with peanuts and safety cards in the seatbacks. A small private plane, six or seven family members packed in together, heading off for the holidays.

It sounded almost glamorous to me. Private plane. Christmas trip. Family all together. Like something out of a primetime TV soap opera.

They never made it.

"The plane went down."

That's how it was said. Simple. Blunt. Like someone was reporting the weather. Not, *A boy you know just had his entire world ripped apart.* Just, "The plane went down."

At that age, you don't really have a file folder for "plane crash that kills almost everyone," so your brain just kind of stalls. There's no emotional software update for that.

I remember hearing that Norman was the only survivor.

That word hits different when you're a kid: survivor. You learn it in history books, in stories about wars or shipwrecks or some distant tragedy that happened to other people, long ago. Suddenly it was attached to a boy who sat two rows over in Social Studies.

They said he was rushed to the hospital, hooked up to machines, placed on life support while doctors tried to figure out whether there was anything left to save.

I didn't understand what that really meant, but I understood enough to feel the bottom drop out of my stomach.

Life support.

The phrase sounded both hopeful and horrible at the same time. "Support" sounded like help. "Life" sounded like something you could still grab onto. But underneath the adult phrasing, I could feel what they weren't saying. *His body is here, but we don't know if _he_ is.*

Days went by and nothing improved.

No brain activity.

I didn't fully understand the biology, but I understood the verdict. It meant that even if his heart was still beating, even if machines were doing the breathing for him, the part that made him Norman, was gone.

Norman died on New Year's Eve, 1988.

New Year's Eve is supposed to be this glittery, hopeful thing with confetti, countdowns, and resolutions. A big symbolic reset. But for me, that date became something else: the night a boy my age slipped out of the world while the rest of us were yelling, "Happy New Year."

We weren't best friends.

We didn't hang out after school. We didn't have sleepovers, we didn't trade secrets, there were no inside jokes carved into a desk somewhere. We didn't have that kind of story.

But he was in several of my classes, and he stood out.

Taller than most of us. A little more grown-looking. Always in that same black Guns N' Roses T-shirt, like it was his personal uniform. He wore it so often it felt like part of his identity.

Back then, I didn't even know who Guns N' Roses were. I just knew he loved that shirt.

I can still see it in my head, washed black, cracked logo, sleeves that didn't quite fit his arms anymore because he was growing faster than his clothes could keep up. I didn't know the songs, but that shirt told me he belonged to some world of music and attitude I hadn't reached yet.

What mattered more to me than his music taste was this:

Norman never made fun of me.

In a time when people lined up for their turn to take a shot at my glasses, my clothes, my size, my everything, he never joined in. He could have. He had the social standing for it.

But he didn't.

He didn't roll his eyes at me when I answered questions.
He didn't whisper about my jeans.
He didn't pile on with the rest of the crowd when someone else decided I was the joke of the day.

There was this kind of silence from him I'll never forget. Not the silence of ignoring me, but the silence of opting out. When other kids laughed, when they made comments, when they mimed my tight pants or my glasses, he didn't add his voice to the chorus.

He didn't step in front of them. He wasn't that guy. But he also didn't twist the knife.

He treated me like a human being.

And at that point in my life, that counted as friendship.

So when he died, it hit someplace raw inside me.

It wasn't the hurricane of grief you see in movies when someone loses their best friend. It was quieter and more confusing. I didn't feel entitled to be as sad as I was. I wasn't "his person." I didn't know his middle name. I couldn't tell you his favorite food or his birthday.

But I knew this: in a world that mostly felt hostile, he was safe.

And suddenly, he was gone.

There's a special kind of grief reserved for people who entered your life through kindness and left it through tragedy. You don't just miss them. You miss what they represented.

For me, Norman represented this simple, radical idea: *not everyone is against you.*

When you're a kid who's used to being targeted, your radar is always scanning for threat. You learn to brace around certain people, certain corners, certain times of day. You start expecting the worst from everyone because it hurts less if you see it coming.

Norman disrupted that pattern just enough to prove it wasn't universal. He didn't go out of his way to protect me, but he also refused to throw me to the wolves.

And then life threw him out of the sky.

I remember sitting in class after the news sank in, staring at his empty seat and feeling this heavy mixture of sadness, fear, and something uglier I didn't want to admit: guilt.

Guilt that I hadn't known him better.
Guilt that I hadn't said thank you.
Guilt that I was still here and he wasn't.

Survivor's guilt doesn't care how close you were. It just cares that you're alive and they're not. My brain didn't have the maturity to process all of that, so it came out in fragments.

He was just here.
He wore that shirt.
He raised his hand in class.
He walked the same halls I did.

And now… he doesn't exist anymore?

I'd lie in bed at night and picture that plane, tiny in a huge sky, full of people talking, joking, maybe passing snacks around. Just a family going to spend Christmas together. Then I'd picture what I thought a crash looked like: noise, flames, metal, confusion.

It was too much for my brain to handle, so it did what it always did when something hurt too much. It blurred the details and left the feeling.

The feeling that the world was even less safe than I already thought it was.

Up until then, my threats had been local: bullies, teachers, social humiliation, my own reflection. Now, suddenly, I had to consider that the sky itself could decide to drop you. That you could do nothing wrong, wear your favorite band shirt, sit in class, make jokes, be decent to the weird kid, and still end up as a name whispered through hallways. *Did you hear? Norman…*

Grief, for me, showed up sideways. I didn't cry in front of anyone. I didn't talk about it. There was no group processing session. This was the late '80s, you just "dealt with it," which really meant you swallowed it and hoped it didn't choke you on the way down.

But I carried him.

Every time I saw a band T-shirt after that, especially a GNR one, something inside me shattered. Every time a teacher read off a roster and skipped over a name like it had never been there, my stomach knotted. Every time people casually said, "See you after break," I remembered that sometimes… well… sometimes you don't.

Norman became this quiet, permanent marker in my timeline. Before the plane crash. After the plane crash.

Before: the world was cruel in petty, human ways.

After: the world was also cruel in big, random ways.

And somehow, in the middle of all that, what stood out to me most wasn't the drama of the tragedy, but the simplicity of what he'd given me before he was gone.

He let me exist without making me pay for it.

It sounds small. It wasn't.

When you're drowning in mockery and isolation, the kid who chooses not to push your head under again, even if he just stands on his own island and lets you swim near it, becomes a kind of lifeline.

So no, we weren't best friends. We didn't have matching bracelets or pages of inside jokes.

But I grieved him just the same.

Because in a time when I felt disposable, Norman's quiet refusal to treat me like a joke made me feel, in his own wordless way, like maybe I wasn't.

When we came back from winter break, the air in the building felt wrong.

It was January-cold outside, but that wasn't it. Kids still joked in the halls, lockers still slammed, bells still rang, but underneath all of that there was this heaviness. Like the whole school had taken a breath and never fully let it out.

Then they called an assembly in the auditorium to honor him.

We filed in, row by row, shuffling into those hard, squeaky seats that made every movement sound louder than it was. I remember the stage lights feeling too bright for such a dark occasion. I don't remember who spoke first or what the principal said. I'm sure there were carefully chosen words about tragedy and loss and "taken too soon."

What I remember is when they opened the floor.

"If anyone would like to come up and share something about Norman…"

And then, somehow, kids started to move.

One. Two. A handful of us. Seven or eight in total.

Somehow, I was one of them.

Me, the kid who panicked at the thought of being on camera for a fake weather report. The kid who planned out every joke before telling it so it wouldn't land wrong. The kid who usually hated standing in front of people so much that just imagining it tied my stomach in knots.

But that day was different.

I wasn't thinking about my voice shaking or my face turning red. I wasn't picturing myself from the outside, like I usually did. I wasn't rehearsing what people might say about me later.

I wasn't thinking about myself at all.

I just knew I needed to say something for the one person who had quietly chosen not to hurt me.

Norman and I weren't close in the way yearbooks like to document, but he'd given me something way more valuable. He'd given me the gift of not piling on. Of seeing me and deciding I didn't deserve extra pain.

In a season of my life when I felt like I had a target painted on me, that kind of neutrality felt like kindness. Like grace.

So when they asked for people to speak, my body made the decision before my brain could talk me out of it. My legs pushed me up, my hands brushed my jeans, my feet walked me down the aisle toward the stage.

I hadn't written anything down. No notes. No practice runs in the mirror. I had nothing prepared except the weight in my chest and the sense that silence would be worse than saying the wrong thing.

I remember walking up to the microphone and feeling how tall it was, how the metal stand looked too grown-up for the kid standing behind it. My heart was banging around in my ribcage, but my voice, when it came out, was surprisingly steady.

I said the only sentence that felt true enough to matter.

"Some of us knew him as Norman, some of us knew him as 'T,' but we all knew him as our friend."

That was it. One line.

No story. No long tribute. No attempt to sum up a whole life in three minutes. Just that one sentence that somehow held all of it, the formal version of him, the nickname version, and the way he belonged to all of us in different ways.

And then I stepped back.

But that line stuck.

I didn't know that in the moment. In the moment, I just felt this mix of heartbreak and relief. Heartbreak that this was how we were saying goodbye. Relief that I'd gotten the words out without collapsing into a mess.

Later, I found out how much it stuck.

The school turned it into a plaque that hung in the front hallway of Edison Middle School. On it were the words: The Norman "T" Tyler Award.

Underneath, my line.
My tribute.

Every year, they gave that award to one male and one female student who showed kindness and character, the way Norman had. The way he had, without even realizing he'd become this lifeline for a kid like me who just needed one person not to join the mob.

My words, that one unplanned line, became part of that.

I was proud of that.

Still am.

It wasn't the chest-puffed-out "Look what I did" kind of pride. It was the kind you feel when you've managed, just once, to say the right thing at the right time for the right person.

The school, a place that had been the backdrop for some of my worst humiliation, now also held this tiny piece of proof that I wasn't just background noise. That my voice could do more than crack jokes or get me into trouble.

It could honor someone.

At some point, years later, the plaque disappeared.

Schools change. Walls get repainted. Hallways get modernized with fresher colors. Old trophies and plaques get shuffled into closets and storage rooms, buried behind broken desks and bent music stands and forgotten banners from long-ago sports seasons.

I imagine it now, sitting somewhere in the dark, collecting dust. Another artifact from a time most people have moved on from.

But for me, it's still there.

Physically, it might be gone. Spiritually, it's still bolted to that wall. When I think of Edison, I don't see the lockers first or the classrooms or even the gym where I hit the floor. I see that plaque. My appreciation. His name.

After the assembly, those of us who had spoken stayed onstage to sing "When the Children Cry" by White Lion.

We didn't pick an upbeat song. We could have chosen something hopeful, something comforting. We picked that one.

A song that isn't subtle. A song that goes straight for the throat.

We stood there, surrounded by classmates in hard wooden chairs, and tried to sing through this weird mix of grief and disbelief. The lyrics felt bigger than us, older than us, but somehow they fit what we were carrying.

Pain too big for our age.
Loss too big for our vocabulary.

Every line felt like it was being pulled straight out of something deep in our chests and turned into sound.

My voice trembled more on that song than it had at the microphone. I remember trying not to look directly at anyone because if I did, something in me might crack. My eyes burned. My throat tightened. The words came out, thin but determined.

> *"Little child*
> *Dry your crying eyes*
> *How can I explain*
> *The fear you feel inside?...*
>
> *... When the children cry*
> *Let them know we tried..."*

To this day, if that song comes on, I'm right back on that stage. Too-bright lights. The smell of the auditorium, dust, old fabric, adolescent nerves, all wrapped around me. I can hear the wobble in our voices. I can feel how every kid in that room is trying to figure out what to do with this much sadness packed into one space.

And layered over all that is this weird double thing inside me.

Heartbroken.
And proud.

Heartbroken that someone like Norman, who did something as simple and almost sacred as not hurting people he could've easily hurt, was gone before he ever got to grow into the kind of man he seemed like he might become.

Proud that when it mattered, when the adults said, "Does anyone want to speak?" I didn't stay in my seat.

Proud that the kid who disappeared on weather-report day and sat alone on gym bleachers found the courage, just once, to stand up. Not for himself, but for someone else.

Proud that my words got to hitch a ride with his name into whatever version of "legacy" a middle school can offer.

So yeah, the plaque might be stuffed in some forgotten closet now. The award might've been discontinued. New kids walk those halls with no idea who Norman was or what my statement really meant.

But for me, that moment is permanent.

I can still feel the mic in my hand.

I can still hear my own voice saying, "Some of us knew him as Norman, some of us knew him as 'T,' but we all knew him as our friend."

It was one line.
But it was honest.
And it was enough.

That was middle school for me.

Not just homework, locker combinations, and who-sat-by-who at lunch, but plane crashes, memorial assemblies, and an award named after a kid who never got the chance to grow old. It was fragile friendships and invisible wounds. A thousand little cuts from growing up too fast in a place that didn't know what to do with a kid like me.

When I look back at that sixth-grade version of me, small for my age, awkward, feelings spilling over with nowhere to put them, I feel it in my chest. Like an actual ache. I want to walk into that hallway, grab that kid by the shoulders, and pull him into a hug he would've pretended not to need.

He was trying so hard to disappear.

He tried to blend in, but his whole life kept dragging him into spotlights he didn't ask for. The blue eyes people complimented. The way teachers noticed him. The way trouble seemed to follow him around like a stray dog looking for scraps. He wanted to be background noise, and instead he kept getting turned up to full volume.

So when he couldn't disappear, he compensated.

He drew.
He drummed.
He cracked jokes.
He got in trouble.

You know that feeling when you don't know who you are yet, so you try on personalities like outfits, waiting to see which one doesn't get laughed at? That was me. If I could make someone laugh, I wasn't a target for a second. If I could draw something cool, I mattered for more than my mistakes. If I could tap out a rhythm on a desk, I wasn't that kid who felt like crying in the middle of math class for no obvious reason.

That's what you do when you don't know where you fit. You start building your own little corner out of whatever scraps you can grab. A cartoon character. A drumstick. A sarcastic comment. You take anything that makes you feel even a little less invisible and you guard it like it's life support.

Because, in a way, it is.

That day on the staircase with my notebook, that quiet moment nobody else saw, that was a fault line. Something under the surface shifted, and after that, nothing felt quite the same.

I was sitting there with Koozie Cat and Doogie Dog in my notebook, banished from class yet again, pretending I didn't care. My back against the cool cinderblock wall. The smell of floor cleaner and sweaty gym shoes. The buzz of fluorescent lights overhead. Kids' voices echoing faintly down the stairwell. Lockers slamming somewhere far away.

On the inside, I was coming apart.

And it finally landed, clean and heavy, like a sentence dropped into my brain and refused to move.

I'm not okay.

Not "having a bad day."
Not "a little upset."
Not "just sensitive."

I was not okay.

And once you let yourself say that, even silently, even just once, you can't really un-say it. The world doesn't rearrange itself. The bullies don't stop. Teachers don't suddenly get it. But something in you shifts. You stop arguing with your own pain. You stop doing that thing where you tell yourself, *Come on, it's not that bad,* while your chest is basically begging for help.

I remember staring at that page, pencil hovering over the half-finished outline of a cartoon dog, and realizing my drawings weren't just drawings. They were exits. They were proof I existed as more than the kid getting sent into hallways and stairwells. More than the kid who kept showing up in rooms where grief and tragedy lived.

Edison taught me something I didn't have words for then, but I do now. Sometimes survival is small and stubborn. It's hanging on to one tiny thing that makes you feel real and refusing to let go.

For me, survival looked like a drumstick in my hand, feeling the vibration travel up my arm. A cartoon character on a page, with big eyes and a dumb grin that made me smile back. A friend like Shelby, whose presence made the air feel a few degrees lighter. A kid like Norman, who chose kindness instead of cruelty before life yanked him away from us.

From those small, ordinary things, I started building a sense of self. One shaky brick at a time. It wasn't pretty. It wasn't neat. Some days it looked more like rubble than progress. But it was my story.

And somewhere in the middle of all that, something else started to register. Back then, I couldn't have explained it. I just felt it, like a low hum in the background whenever someone shoved me in the gym or made a joke about me in the hallway.

The kids who hurt me were hurting too.

That doesn't excuse anything. It doesn't make the shove softer or the laughter any quieter. It doesn't erase the stomach-drop when you hear your name followed by a punchline.

But it gave me a kind of clarity I didn't have before.

Hurt people hurt people.

I know. It sounds like a cliché now, like something slapped over a sunset photo. But for me, back then, it clicked. Because if hurt people hurt people, then maybe the chain isn't unbreakable. Maybe somebody, somewhere, can decide, I'm not passing this on.

That didn't turn me into some saint. I still made bad jokes at other people's expense. I still lashed out. I still tried to get my laughs in first so nobody could use me as the punchline. I was hurt, and I hurt people too.

But something got planted in that stairwell.

If there's any real wisdom I dragged out of those dark years at Edison, it's this:

You don't have to be big to matter.
You don't have to be loud to be heard.
You don't have to be healed to keep going.

But you keep going anyway.

You show up to school with your stomach in knots. You sit through class while your mind spins. You draw cats and dogs in the margins. You laugh too loudly at dumb jokes. You get sent to the hallway again. You sit on a cold stair with your back against a wall and your heart in your throat, and you admit, *I'm not okay.* Then you breathe.

That kid on the staircase, pencil in hand and heart sinking, didn't know any of this yet. He didn't know that one day he'd look back and see a bigger pattern, not just random misery. He didn't know that beneath those blue eyes he'd spend most of his life trying to hide behind, something solid was already forming in the cracks.

He thought he was broken.
He thought he was the problem.
He thought if he could just be quieter, better, less him, everything would hurt less.

But he wasn't broken.

He was learning how to hold pain in one hand and a pencil in the other.
He was learning that surviving doesn't always look heroic.
He was learning that feeling too much isn't a defect.
He was learning that he is not the end result.

He was just beginning.

ROUND 6:
Freshman Year on Fast-Forward

That summer after eighth grade, everything in my life felt like it was slowly, awkwardly shifting. And I got one thing I'd wanted for a long time.

My eyes.

I got rid of the glasses. Those thick, brown, plastic-rimmed monsters had been my trademark for years, and not in a cool, "this is my look" kind of way. They were the physical embodiment of every insecurity I had.

Contacts changed everything.

The first time I put them in, it felt like I'd finally joined the human race. No more frames swallowing my face. No more smudged lenses between me and the world. For the first time, people could actually see my eyes, these blue eyes I'd secretly always loved. They were the single feature I didn't hate.

Those glasses hadn't just changed how people looked at me. They changed how *I* looked at me. With contacts, I felt lighter. A little more confident. A little less like the sad, easy punchline of the room.

That summer wasn't just a makeover, though.

I spent hours every day with my headphones on and drumsticks in my hands, pounding along to anything I could get my hands on. John Mellencamp, Loverboy, Stryper, Chicago. During middle school, my soundtrack had been full of slow, aching songs, the kind of stuff you put on when you feel broken and want the music to agree with you.

But something shifted that summer.

Without really deciding to, I started leaning toward more upbeat songs. More energy. Motley Crue, Alice Cooper, Bon Jovi. Maybe it was the contacts. Maybe it was the idea of a fresh start. Maybe I was just tired of feeling like a walking raincloud. Whatever it was, something inside me started to lift, one song at a time.

Then came the first day of high school.

Walking into that building as an actual student felt nothing like sitting in the audience for my sisters' concerts. Everything looked bigger. The hallways stretched farther. The noise level felt like standing inside a beehive.

I'd "graduated" from middle school, whatever that meant, and now high school loomed ahead as this massive, echoing building full of people who all seemed bigger, louder, and more put-together than I could ever imagine being.

Seniors, especially.

They weren't just older kids to me. They were basically adults with car keys and timecards. They walked the halls like they'd built the place, leaning against lockers, laughing with this lazy confidence, jangling their keys like some kind of status symbol. Meanwhile, I was about to enter as a freshman, the lowest in the food chain. I already lived life closer to people's armpits than their eyes, and the idea of trying to navigate this sea of giant humans made my stomach twist.

Technically, it was only three floors. But seniors had this long-running joke where they'd tell clueless freshmen who asked for directions to their biology class to go find the "fourth floor." When someone tried it on me, I laughed like I was in on it, but inside I was thinking, *Please, God, don't let me be the butt of a seniors stupid prank..*

The surprising thing?

Freshman year was better than I expected.

I made friends. Quickly, actually. People laughed at my jokes. I wasn't the invisible, bullied kid I'd been at Edison. I started to feel like I had a place. And yeah, a dark part of me wondered if it was because of the contacts.

Did swapping two little pieces of plastic on my eyeballs really make that much of a difference?

Honestly? I think it did.

It sounds shallow, but when you've spent years hiding behind something that magnifies everything you hate about yourself, taking it off can feel like stepping out of a costume you never wanted to wear.

It wasn't just the glasses, either.

I'd use the money I made on weekends mowing yards and ride my bike to a little strip mall and buy T-shirts with actual brand name: T&C Surf Designs, Vuarnet, Ocean Pacific. Shirts I'd only seen on the cool kids before. Then I bought my first real pair of name-brand shoes: Lottos. Almost a hundred bucks. That was a small fortune to me, and every penny of it came from my own sweat.

People say money doesn't buy happiness, and they're right. But it does buy the ability to blend in.

I couldn't change my height, but I could change how I showed up. And once I did, something else changed.

I walked a little taller, even though my body had only added an inch.
I spoke a little louder, even if my voice still trembled sometimes.
I looked in the mirror and, for the first time, didn't immediately look away.

High school became my reset button.

After three brutal years at Edison, I finally felt like I had more than just a front-row seat to my own misery. I had a shot at something better.

That summer between eighth grade and freshman year was a lot more than new clothes and contacts. It was me stepping up and putting my hands on the steering wheel of my own story.

Up until then, I'd been letting other people drive. Letting bullies, teachers, circumstances, and old glasses decide who I was. That summer, I let myself be seen. And once I did, the dominoes started falling.

I started choosing music that made me feel alive instead of leaking sadness.

I started dressing like I had something to say.
I started entertaining the idea that maybe, just maybe, I belonged here.

Change didn't hit like a lightning bolt. It came in tiny, almost forgettable choices. A shirt. A job. A pair of contacts. A drumbeat.

But they added up.

Transformation doesn't always look like a Hollywood movie trailer. Sometimes it looks like brushing lawn clippings off your sneakers, buying the shirt you actually like, and daring to make eye contact with the world.

Freshman year came at me fast, like somebody hit fast-forward on my life. One minute I was just trying to survive middle school trauma and acne, the next I was in high school, collecting "firsts" like they were trading cards.

Some of those firsts were cringey.

Some were incredible.

All of them are still lodged somewhere in my nervous system, firing off every now and then when a song, a smell, or a random memory decides to sneak-attack me.

One of my biggest firsts had a name:

Rachael.

She was my first real girlfriend. Not the "we held hands once during recess" type of girlfriend. A real one. We started dating in January, and like most high school relationships, it escalated at warp speed, because we were fourteen and had absolutely no concept of pacing. Emotional seatbelts? Never heard of 'em.

Rachael lived on stage. If there was a school play, musical, or any excuse to dim the lights and raise a curtain, she was in it. So, naturally, after every show, there was a cast party on closing night. Drama kids throwing drama parties, what could possibly go wrong?

Since she was in the cast and I was the boyfriend, I got the golden ticket.

The first cast party I ever walked into felt like stepping into an underground society. Like I'd stumbled into a secret level of high school no one tells you about.

The house belonged to one of the actresses. Big place, quiet neighborhood, the kind of house that made you think, *Yeah, these people definitely have more than one kind of cereal in their pantry.* Down in the basement, twenty-five or thirty kids were crammed together, still buzzing off the high of performing. Laughter ricocheted off the walls. Music leaked from a boombox in the corner. It was chaotic, sweaty, and loud.

Everyone seemed to know everyone.

Rachael stayed close to me, which helped. She'd squeeze my hand, lean into me, introduce me to people whose names I forgot instantly. I was the outsider in their little tribe, the plus-one in a room full of seasoned cast members who already had history, inside jokes, and memories I wasn't part of.

You know that feeling when you walk into a room and immediately think, *They've all done this a hundred times, and I'm the new kid who doesn't know where the cups are?* That was me.

Then, somewhere through the noise, I heard it. Live guitar.

Not clumsy power chords or someone butchering "Stairway to Heaven." This was the kind of sound that cuts through conversation and makes people turn their heads.

I leaned over to Rachael.

"Who's playing that?"

She shrugged, way too casual about it.

"Oh, that's Zeke. You haven't met him yet?"

"No," I said. "But I want to."

She smiled and pulled me upstairs.

We walked into one of the bedrooms, and there he was.

Zeke.

He sat on the edge of the bed, curly hair bouncing slightly as he nodded along with what he was playing. Black electric guitar plugged into this vintage-looking golden amp at his feet. His fingers flew over the fretboard like it was nothing, like he was just talking and the guitar was his voice. He didn't even look up when we came in.

The sound coming out of that amp was ridiculous. Crunchy. Distorted. Soulful. No wasted notes. No "look at me" sloppiness. Just confidence.

And something in me snapped into focus.

This. I want to do… this.

Not kinda, not maybe, not someday. Some internal switch flipped from drummer who plays alone in his room to maybe I belong with people like this.

When he finally stopped playing, Rachael introduced us.

Zeke had that quiet-cool thing down. Not loud, not trying to dominate the room, but the second he picked up the guitar, it was obvious who the star was.

"I play drums," I told him.

His face brightened just a little, like he was trying not to look too excited.

"No way," he said. "I've got a buddy. Miles, he plays too. Lately he's been more into singing, though. We mess around sometimes. If he's cool with it, you could play drums, he could sing… and then we'd just need a bassist."

I didn't even have to think.

"Oh, I've got one," I said. "Beau. He's in jazz band with me. Dude's nasty, like, wild slap bass, super funky."

He laughed. "Okay, alright."

"I'm serious," I said. "I'll talk to him."

Just like that, the idea existed. Out loud.

Not just a fantasy in my head, not just something I thought about while practicing alone. It was in the air between us, real enough to grab.

Sure, every high school kid talks about starting a band. Most of it ends with a name, a logo, and zero rehearsals. But this didn't feel like that. This felt like the first time all the random, jagged pieces of me might actually fit with someone else's.

Like maybe I wasn't just a kid pounding drums in his basement to drown out his own thoughts. Maybe I was a drummer. In a band. With other people. People who understood what it felt like when music lit up your insides.

Of course, it wasn't just a night of musical destiny and emotional breakthroughs.

It was still a high school cast party.

Which meant alcohol.

Somebody's older sibling had "a keg guy." Because there is always an older sibling with a keg guy. It's basically an adolescent law of physics. One minute you're downstairs eating chips and trying to look like you belong, and the next a keg shows up like some illegal fairy godmother and suddenly everyone's acting like they've been drinking IPAs since birth.

Red Solo cups appeared out of nowhere, stacked by the sink like we were in a frat house instead of a basement full of fourteen- and fifteen-year-olds who still had algebra homework. Kids wandered around swirling warm beer like it was a Cabernet. Tiny little careful sips. Big tough faces. Immediate regret. Nobody wanted to be the first one to admit it tasted like ass water.

The basement smelled like hops, sweat, Polo cologne, and that weird "freedom" feeling you only get when you're doing something you're not supposed to be doing. It felt huge and electric right then, and looking back, it also feels like it could've gone bad in about twelve different ways.

For a while, it was fun.

Music was loud. People were yelling over it. Someone kept trying to hijack the playlist. Bodies bumping into each other in that awkward almost-dancing way where nobody knows what to do with their hands. I remember laughing, actually laughing, and feeling lighter than I had in a long time, like maybe I'd finally cracked the code to being a normal kid doing normal, dumb high school stuff.

And then the night took one of those sharp turns that happens so fast you don't even understand you're in trouble until you're already standing in it.

The room changed in about half a second. The music cut off mid-song. Somebody near the stereo hissed, "Shh!" and the entire room obeyed, which never happens with drama kids unless something is seriously wrong.

And then we saw it, flashing red and blue through the windows.

If you want to see pure panic, that's the recipe: underage kids, alcohol, red and blue lights.

Panic spread fast. Wide eyes. Anxious whispers. Everyone suddenly sober. Everyone suddenly remembering they have a future.

A bunch of us bolted upstairs and flew down a hallway like we were in some low-budget heist movie. Somebody yanked open the door to a walk-in closet and we all piled in like we were being smuggled out of the country in a heap of winter coats.

It was dark and hot. Shoulder-to-shoulder. Clothes brushing your face. Somebody's elbow in your ribs. The air was thick with cologne, deodorant, and straight-up fear. You could hear breathing and soft whispers of, *oh fuck!*

Then footsteps. Heavy. Coming up the stairs and then down the hall.

That silence in the closet was unreal. Not peaceful silence, terrified silence. The kind where you can feel everyone thinking the same thing: *Please don't open this door. Please don't open this door.*

Then the door flew open.

A flashlight hit us right in the face. That harsh white circle that makes you feel guilty even if you're not sure what you did.

"Welcome to the world of the police," the officer said.

Dry. Almost amused. Like we were a mildly interesting detour in his night.

Somewhere in the back of my brain, N.W.A.'s "Fuck tha Police" started playing on a loop, and I had this brief, stupid urge to smirk, like I was in a movie and this was my big moment. Luckily, the part of my brain that wanted to keep living tackled that idea and choked it out. This was not the time to test my comedic timing with law enforcement.

They herded us out. Questions. Ages. Who lives here. Whose parents are home. The whole routine. Nobody got cuffed. Nobody made a run for it. We just stood there blinking like guilty deer in headlights, trying to look innocent.

And then came the worst part.

They made us call our parents.

There's a specific kind of dread that settles in when you're holding a phone, staring at the numbers, knowing you're about to wreck whatever "good kid" image your parents have been hanging onto. Even if you didn't drink. Even if you barely touched the keg. Doesn't matter. The facts don't get a vote. The story is already written:

Party. Police. My kid was there.

When I saw my dad's car pull up, my stomach dropped so hard it felt like it hit the pavement. I wanted to vanish. Crawl under the porch. Reverse time. Do literally anything other than get into that car.

I got in, bracing for the yelling. The explosion. The speech about choices and consequences and, *what were you thinking?* I already had half a defense prepared, because that's what you do when you're fourteen and scared. You build a little courtroom in your head.

None of that happened.

He didn't yell.
He didn't explode.
He didn't give some dramatic lecture.

He just sat there with both hands on the wheel, jaw tight, eyes forward. And then he looked at me, just once, with that disappointed expression parents come factory-installed with. Just that look that slices right through whatever teenage swagger you thought you had.

The *"I expected better from you"* face.

You know… that one.

It was so much worse than yelling. Yelling would've at least been loud. This was quiet. Heavy. Personal.

"I wasn't drinking," I said. The classic teenage defense. The verbal equivalent of tossing a Band-Aid onto a car crash.

Now that I'm a parent, I can tell you with full confidence: he did not believe me for a second. I can see it now, from his side of the car. The silence, the stare, the internal eye roll he didn't even bother to hide.

But still.

No breathalyzer. No ticket. No charges.

Just a stern lecture later, an awkward ride home, and the kind of shame that sticks to you because it almost became a real disaster, but didn't.

My first real high school party.
My first time getting busted.
Two rites of passage in one night.

Underneath all of that, the music, the adrenaline, the fear, the humiliation, something else was happening too. That night stitched together a few more pieces of who I was becoming:

A kid who wanted to belong.
A kid who could feel his life tilt every time music filled a room.
A kid who was already learning that sometimes, the best and worst parts of growing up happen in the same exact moment.

But the real turning point wasn't the beer, or the band idea, or even the cops.

It was Rachael.

She was my first love. The first girl I ever felt truly close to, emotionally, physically, all of it wrapped together in this messy, intense, teenage way.

There's one afternoon though that will forever sit in its own little glass case in my memory.

It was early May. Warm enough that the air felt soft. My parents were gone and I had a jazz band concert later that night, one of those three-night events we did every year where the school acted like we were the second coming of Duke Ellington.

Rachael came over.

We'd fooled around before, in that clumsy, exploratory way you do when you're young and trying to figure out both your own body and someone else's at the same time. She was often the more confident one, which, at that age, was equal parts intimidating and reassuring.

But that day felt different.

There wasn't some big speech. No "Are we ready?" conversation where we sat across from each other like adults in a movie. It was quieter than that. Just this unspoken understanding hanging in the air, heavy, obvious, like we'd both finally stopped circling the subject and were standing at the edge of it.

So we crossed it.

Not gracefully. Not like people pretend it happens. It wasn't some perfectly timed moment where the lighting is soft and everyone knows exactly what to do. It was two nervous kids who cared about each other, trying to be brave at the same time, trying not to show how shaky we felt inside.

It was tender. And awkward. And real.

And afterward, we just stayed there, close, skin against skin, staring at the ceiling like the world had turned the volume down. I can still smell the Chanel No 5 softly radiating from the soft skin of her neck. My heart was still doing that stupid fast thing, like it didn't get the memo that everything was over now.

For a few minutes, it was calm. The kind where you don't have to talk yet. Where you're both still here. Where nothing outside that room can reach you.

Then I looked over at the clock and reality came rushing back in. Jazz band didn't care one bit about my sexual milestones.

Rachael slipped into the bathroom, and I pulled myself together, climbing out of that full-size bed to get dressed. Black slacks, white button-down shirt, thin red tie. I stood in the hallway mirror, wrestling with the knot on that tie.

When I finally looked up at my reflection in the hallway mirror, I didn't quite recognize myself.

Something felt heavier in my chest. Different in my face. I felt older, fast. Like I'd aged five years in thirty minutes. Taller. More mature.

Not necessarily better. Not necessarily worse. Just different.

That date, May 5th, 1990, stuck.

Later that night, I grabbed the calendar above my nightstand and marked the square with a bold letter "S." It was my secret code, a ridiculous little system where I'd use letters instead of words to track certain "milestones." Only I knew what they meant. To anyone else, it looked like random graffiti.

To me, it was a record.

I don't think my parents ever cracked the code. Maybe they really didn't know. Maybe they did and just chose not to bring it up. Parents have a way of knowing more than we think they do.

Looking back now, that whole stretch of time, new contacts, new clothes, new friends, new love, new mistakes, wasn't just "freshman year."

It was the beginning of me learning how to show up in my own life.

Not as a background character.
Not as the punchline.
Not as the invisible kid hiding on the stairs.

But as someone who could stand in front of a mirror, tie slightly crooked, and say, *Okay. This is me now. Let's see where this goes.*

A few weeks after that magical milestone before the jazz band concert, we were parked outside some little Italian restaurant downtown, her mom and brother still inside paying the check. It was one of those rare teenage moments where the universe hands you unsupervised time on a silver platter. Five minutes. Maybe less. The kind of window where you're supposed to steal kisses, run your fingers through her hair, whisper stupid things that feel profound when you are fourteen and full of hormones.

Instead, she leaned in, and before I even knew what was happening, her hand slipped down the front of my pants.

And I froze.

I wasn't feeling it. My brain went straight to the worst-case scenario: her mom yanking the van door open, her little brother climbing in, me caught half-zipped, red-faced, busted. Every part of it felt rushed and mechanical, like we skipped the feeling and went straight to the act.

It didn't feel romantic. It didn't feel special. It felt like she was chasing something physical while I was craving something emotional.

So the next day, I did what I thought was "mature."

I broke up with her.

I told myself I was doing the right thing. Standing up for what I believed in. Refusing to be reduced to a body, a fix, a prop in somebody else's show. The truth? I was just a confused kid who didn't know how to say, "Hey, this doesn't feel good to me," without nuking the entire relationship.

Instead of talking about it, I walked away.

And it destroyed me.

I was heartbroken for months. I wanted her back so badly my chest physically ached, but she never gave me another chance, and honestly, I don't blame her. I hurt her, and she did the healthy thing. She moved on. I stayed stuck, replaying that stupid choice over and over in my head like a bad song I couldn't turn off.

During that same week, life did what it always does when your heart is shattered. It kept going.

I started my first job at this little hot dog joint called Wiener Lose on the corner of Neil St and John St. Classy name, I know. The kind of place where the sign out front was a little too bright, the letters a little too crooked, and the smell of onions hit you half a block before you got there.

I'd ride my bike to work, pull into the parking lot already sweating through my shirt, hop off, and lean my bike against the faded brick wall. Lock up. Deep breath. Clock in.

Inside, it was always loud.

Orders being shouted over the sizzle of the flat top. The soft, constant *shhhh* of the fryer dropping baskets of fries into oil that probably had a longer history than some of the employees. The clack of tongs on metal. The obnoxious buzz of the neon sign in the window.

The work was fast and repetitive. Grabbing buns, wrapping dogs, refilling napkins, wiping down counters that never stayed clean for more than thirty seconds. My shoes stuck to the floor half the time from layers of who-knows-what, and my shirt always smelled like a tragic love triangle between mustard, grease, and sweat.

And honestly? It was exactly what I needed.

Wiener Lose gave my hands something to do while my heart was busy falling apart.

I kept a small picture of Rachael tucked inside my wallet. Her freshman photo. Green shirt. Dark hair curling just right around her face. That soft, almost shy smile. The background was that cheap school-photo blue, but my brain blurred it out every time. All I saw was her.

I took that picture with me everywhere.

It lived behind a couple of crumpled dollar bills, but it might as well have been pressed straight into my chest. Every time I opened my wallet, even if I was just grabbing a few singles for lunch, I'd catch a tiny flash and feel the sting.

Not a stab. Not a full-body heartbreak every time. Just a sting.

The kind of sting that says, *You did this. Remember?*

It wasn't just sadness. Sadness is heavy, sure, but it's simple. Regret is heavier and it comes with Polaroids. Every time I looked at that picture, my brain replayed the moment I shut down instead of explaining what was actually going on inside me. I couldn't look at her face without also seeing every version of myself that screwed it up.

On slow shifts, when the lunch rush died down and the grill went from pandemonium to a low simmer, I'd take a quick bathroom break. It was this tiny, off-to-the-side room with a flickering light and a mirror that somehow made you look worse than reality, which is hard to do when you're already wearing a hot dog joint uniform.

I'd lock the door, lean over the sink, and stare at myself.

Grease-smeared apron. Hair matted down from heat and sweat. Hands smelling like onions and dish soap. Eyes. Yeah. The eyes told the truth.

It was all sitting there, just under the surface. The way they looked tired in a way that had nothing to do with being fifteen years old and working a part-time job. That dull, slightly hollow gaze you get when you've been pretending to be "fine" for so long you could probably win an award for it, but you know you're lying.

If I stared long enough, I could see it clearly. I wasn't just hurt. I was guilty.

Not guilty of some huge betrayal, but guilty of all the small, stupid things that slowly pull two people apart. The careless comments. The times I rolled my eyes instead of listening. The times she needed me to be present and I was somewhere else in my head, stuck in my own anxiety.

Then I'd pull out that little photo. Slide it from behind the plastic like it was some hidden file I wasn't supposed to access. I'd stare at her face and feel that same punch of regret and longing hit again. Missing her, missing us, missing the version of myself that existed when I still believed first love could actually work out, and that I was capable of not screwing it up.

Because here is the ugly part about regret that nobody really advertises: it's not just about what you lost. It's about what you did.

Every time I looked at her, the questions started.

Why didn't you just tell her how scared you were?
Why didn't you just talk to her?

I could pretend I was just unlucky, just a victim of timing and teenage confusion, but the mirror and that photo together told a different story. Somewhere in there, I had choices. And I didn't always make good ones.

How many times did I do that bathroom ritual?

Fifty? A hundred? A thousand?

It felt endless, like clockwork.

Take order. Wrap hot dog. Smile at customer. Laugh at their dumb joke. Toss trash. Wipe table. Nod at coworker like everything was normal. Slip into the bathroom. Lock the door. Look at my own eyes. Pull out her picture. Try not to fall apart.

Repeat.

I wasn't just missing a girlfriend. I was grieving my first shot at real love, and the part I played in losing it.

There's a difference.

Losing a girlfriend is breakups and sad songs. Losing the first person you really believed in, believed with, hits in a different place, especially when you know most of the blame sits quietly in your own hands.

It's not just them you lose. It's the future your brain had quietly started building with them in it. The imagined holidays. The shared inside jokes ten years down the road. The idea that this one might be the one who doesn't leave.

Regret makes losing all of that feel like your fault, even if reality is more complicated.

Freshman year was like that. One long free fall of firsts.

My first real relationship.
My first heartbreak.
My first band.
My first busted party.

My first time having sex.

It all came tumbling in on top of me faster than I could process it. Like somebody was rapid-firing milestones at my head and I was ducking as best I could, but still catching a few straight to the face anyway.

On the outside, I played it cool, because that's the rule in high school.

Don't flinch.
Don't crack.
Don't let anybody see how much anything actually matters to you.

So I did the whole act. Sarcasm. Jokes. *I'm fine, it's whatever.*

Inside, I was barely keeping up. Regret had moved in and started rearranging furniture in my chest.

I was this kid in a greasy apron, standing behind a counter at Wiener Lose, handing out hot dogs with a practiced smile, while quietly trying to figure out how the hell I'm supposed to move on from my first big everything without leaving parts of myself scattered behind me.

So I did the only thing I knew how to do at the time.

I worked.

I smiled.
I joked around with customers.
I mopped floors until the tiles squeaked under my shoes.

And every now and then, I locked myself in that bad-lit bathroom, pulled out a wallet-worn picture of a girl in a green shirt, and let all the regret and what-ifs and *you did this* thoughts show up in my eyes for just a minute.

Then I'd shove it all back down, slide the photo behind the plastic again, wash my hands, unlock the door, and go flip another burger like nothing was wrong.

Looking back, that year taught me one of the hardest lessons I've ever learned: what real regret feels like.

Breaking up with Rachael wasn't just some teenage drama. It was the first time I truly hurt someone who didn't deserve it. Not because I didn't care about her, but because I had no idea how to express my own discomfort without lighting the whole thing on fire. I didn't know how to say, *I need something different,* without turning it into, *I need you to be gone.*

I didn't understand yet that boundaries aren't breakups. They're conversations.

I thought love was supposed to magically understand you without you having to say anything. That if it was "real," it would just know. So when something felt off, I didn't speak up. I stayed silent, pretended I was fine, right up until I wasn't, and then I detonated the whole thing.

Rachael taught me that, without ever trying to.

She showed me that intimacy without honesty will eventually fall apart. That you can care deeply about someone and still fail them completely if you're too afraid to speak the truth when it matters.

Young love is fragile. It cuts deep when it breaks, even if the world thinks it's just puppy love.

I thought about her for years. Not in the obsessive "I'll win her back" way, but more like a song that catches in your chest every time you hear the first note. That photo stayed in my wallet long after we ended. She became a symbol of that first real everything. And of how easily I let fear and silence take it away.

Rachael had made me a cassette with her talking to me and a playlist of a few of her favorite songs when she was grounded somewhere around the middle of our five-month relationship. And one of those songs was "Eternal Flame" by The Bangles.

> *"Close your eyes, give me your hand, darling*
> *Do you feel my heart beating?...*
>
> *Do you feel the same? Am I only dreaming?*
> *Or is this burning an eternal flame?..."*

If I had to put the lesson into one line, it would be this:

Don't confuse silence with strength.

Speak up.
Say what you want.
Say what you need.
Say when something feels wrong.

Especially when it's awkward. Especially when your voice shakes. Especially when your heart is on the line.

Back then, I thought maturity meant handling everything alone. Not needing help. Swallowing your feelings like pills. Now I know better. Real maturity is telling the truth, even when it risks discomfort, because that's the only way you get a real shot at connection.

Rachael, wherever you are, I hope life has treated you with the love and appreciation you deserved back then and still deserve now. You were my first real everything. I was too young to understand what that meant. But you changed me. I'm better for it.

I'm sorry.

Wiener Lose was greasy, ridiculous, and somehow one of the best classrooms I ever had.

I started there at fourteen, just a couple of weeks shy of turning fifteen, still more kid than anything else. Most people picture a teenager at a fast-food place working the register, handing out napkins, trying not to screw up the change while some manager hovers over their shoulder.

Not me.

I was in the kitchen. And not in a "we'll let him help with the easy stuff" kind of way.

I was the prep guy.
I was the fry guy.
I was the grill cook.
Some days, I was all three at once.

Saturday afternoons were pure mayhem. The lobby would fill up with impatient customers, their voices blending into this constant hum made of complaints and ketchup packets. The kitchen had its own weather, a storm of sizzling meat, fryer hiss, and thick greasy air that stuck to your skin and clothes and followed you home.

If someone called in sick, which happened way more than it should have, I was the one running the entire backline by myself.

If it was on the menu, I cooked it. Hamburgers. Pork tenderloin sandwiches. Mozzarella sticks. French fries. Onion rings. If it went into a basket or onto a bun, it went through my hands.

Orders came through a crackly little speaker, shouted in from whoever was working the register. No printed tickets, no POS system, nothing organized or modern. Just noise and speed.

They would yell, "Two burgers, one with everything, one with ketchup and mustard only, fries, tenderloin, no pickle, extra onion!"

We'd scribble on a whiteboard with a greasy hand and a half-dead marker, already dropping fries and flipping patties before the sentence even finished. One wrong move, one second too slow, and you were buried under a pile of backed-up orders and angry customers staring holes through the counter.

It was insane. And I loved it.

There was something addictive about the rhythm of it, the way the kitchen moved in this messy, frantic kind of harmony. The fryers. The grease popping and jumping out to burn your forearms. The sizzle of burgers hitting the flat-top. The burst of new orders shouted from the front. I'd be sweating, exhausted, half-starved because I kept forgetting to eat, and somehow it felt good.

For the first time in my life, people were relying on me for something other than a punchline or a group project.

My favorite prep job was cutting fries.

We had this industrial potato cutter bolted to the wall by the sink, one of those old metal beasts that looked like it had survived the 1950s and just refused to die. You'd shove a whole potato into the cradle, grab the handle with both hands, and slam it downward with your full body weight.

The potato exploded into perfect fry strips, shooting straight down into the stainless-steel sink below like a tiny starch waterfall.

The sink was filled with cold water to keep them from browning, the potatoes floating around like pale little rafts. When it was full, we'd scoop the fries into five-gallon buckets, top them off with water, salt the hell out of them, and slide them into the walk-in cooler to soak.

Later, when those fries came out of the fryer, they were perfect. Crispy on the outside, soft on the inside, just enough salt to make you reach for another handful without even thinking about it. They were the kind of fries you still think about twenty years later, and if that sounds dramatic, you have clearly never tasted them.

The dining room had its own personality. Instead of normal fast-food tile flooring, Wiener Lose had artificial turf that used to be under the University of Illinois football team inside Memorial Stadium. When the stadium remodeled, somehow the owners got their hands on the old turf and laid it down in the restaurant. They even added padding underneath, so walking across the lobby felt like standing on a football field to order a hot dog. It was bizarre and brilliant at the same time.

The walls were covered in University of Illinois memorabilia, orange and blue everywhere, the menu was full of hot dogs, and the name Wiener Lose, their little pun on "win or lose," was just goofy enough to work. You don't forget a place like that. It had character, even if that character smelled like grease and chili.

And then, one day, it was gone.

No warning. No "we're closing next month." No handwritten sign taped to the door thanking customers for their business. Just gone.

It was a Saturday like any other. I rode my bike there, chain clicking, sun on my back, brain already shifting into work mode. I pulled into the parking lot, hopped off, and knew something was wrong. The windows were dark. I walked up and tried the handle anyway, because that's what hope does. It makes you check doors you already know are locked.

Inside, I could see it was already stripped. The fryers were gone. The grill was gone. The turf was gone. Everything was gone.

No phone call. No explanation. No "thanks for your hard work, kid." No last shift. No goodbye.

One day I had a job, a place where I felt important, where I knew what I was doing and people counted on me. The next day, I was standing there staring through dusty glass at an empty building that used to smell like grease and ketchup and overcooked cheeseburgers, and it hit me harder than I expected.

It wasn't just the paycheck, although losing that sucked. It was losing that first taste of being trusted. That feeling of, If I don't show up, this place falls apart a little bit. That mattered to me. A lot.

I still don't know what happened. Bankruptcy, bad business decisions, shady dealings, a landlord pulling the plug. I have no idea. One day there was a kitchen and a turf floor and a kid learning how to handle pressure behind the grill, and the next day it was nothing. Just silence and a For Lease sign.

As much as they worked me, as exhausted as I was, as many times as I went home smelling like fryer oil and onions, I kind of loved it. Wiener Lose was ridiculous. It was greasy. It was loud and chaotic and strange. But it was also the first place that taught me what it felt like to be relied on, to be in the middle of the storm and realize, *I can do this.*

For a kid who spent a lot of time feeling out of place everywhere else, that little hot dog joint on the corner of Neil and John was one of the first places I ever felt like I actually mattered. It was the first time in my life I felt capable in a way that had nothing to do with grades or music or trying to impress anyone.

No test score. No solo. No adult patting me on the head for being "such a smart kid." Just me, a flat-top grill, a wall of orders, and a line of hungry people who didn't give a damn about my GPA.

I was a fifteen-year-old kid holding down a kitchen in the middle of a lunch rush. Burgers popping, fries dropping, grease snapping at my arms, and still, I kept up. I didn't fall apart. I didn't walk out. People were depending on me, even if they never said it out loud.

Nobody came back and said, "Hey, Craig, if you don't show up today we're screwed." But you feel it. You feel it when the orders are flying in and you're the one moving your hands fast enough to keep the whole thing from collapsing.

In there, I learned how to prioritize under pressure: whose order hits the grill first, what you can drop in the fryer and forget for a minute versus what you have to watch like a hawk, when to ignore the lady at the counter tapping her foot because the patties on the grill are more important than her impatience. I learned how to think three steps ahead without even realizing that's what I was doing.

If I drop these fries now, they'll be done when the burgers come off. If I start the tenderloin first, I can throw down the onions halfway through and they'll finish together. It was like this greasy little chess game, and somehow, I was actually good at it.

And underneath all that movement, all that noise, there was this quiet, surprising thought forming: *maybe I'm not just a screwup. Maybe I can handle more than I think.*

I learned how to keep going when everything felt like too much, because sometimes it did. Orders stacked, shirt soaked with sweat, head pounding from the heat and the constant noise, slip-ups piling up in my brain like evidence in a trial. *You burned that one. You're behind. That lady's mad. You forgot extra pickles.*

But there wasn't time to spiral. You couldn't sit down and have a feelings meeting about it. You just moved. One more burger. One more drop of fries. One more order up.

Looking back, that kitchen wasn't just teaching me how to cook. It was teaching me how to function inside chaos.

And when it vanished without so much as a goodbye, I learned something else: effort does not guarantee stability. That lesson slid in under the door and settled in my bones before I even had language for it. All I knew in the moment was this: I showed up, I worked my ass off, I did everything right, and it still disappeared. No warning. Just a locked door and an empty building where my life had been happening two days a week.

You tell yourself that if you just try hard enough, be good enough, show up enough, you'll earn safety. Security. Some kind of guarantee that things will stay. Wiener Lose quietly called bullshit on that.

I hadn't done anything wrong. No epic failure, no screwup that got me fired. One day I was on the schedule, the next day there was no schedule, no restaurant, no job. Just me and my bike and a dark window reflecting my own confused face back at me.

That hit me harder than I admitted. Back then, I shrugged it off like, *Well, that sucks. Guess I need a new job.* But it wasn't just about losing a job. It was realizing life can take things away even when you haven't messed up, even when you've done everything you were supposed to do.

That the things you love, the places you feel important, the routines that feel permanent, can all just disappear.

No drama. No goodbye. Just you standing there trying to figure out why everything feels different.

It planted this seed in me: nothing is guaranteed. Not the job you're good at. Not the person you're in love with. Not the version of your life you've quietly rehearsed in your head. And once you see that, you can't unsee it.

Part of me started holding things a little differently after that. Not always consciously, not all at once, but looking back, I can feel it. This slight hesitation. This tiny emotional shield. Like, *Yeah, this is good. How long until it's gone?*

It's funny, the places that teach you the big stuff. You think it's going to be some mentor or a big inspirational speech or a near-death experience. Sometimes, sure. But sometimes it's a hot dog joint with turf on the floor and a stupid pun for a name, closing overnight without a goodbye.

And yet you start again. You put your bike back on the road. You find another way to make money. You walk into some new place, fill out an application with the same shaky teenage handwriting, and hope they see something in you. You start again in a world that has already shown you it owes you nothing.

That's the quiet resilience nobody clapped for back then. Not the "bounce back" you see in movies where the underdog lands an even better job. Just a kid who keeps showing up after his first little corner of competence gets ripped away.

At fifteen, I didn't have the words for any of this but now, looking back, I can see it more clearly: that kitchen gave me my first taste of feeling capable, and losing it gave me my first taste of how fragile everything is.

Both of those truths have been riding shotgun with me ever since.

ROUND 7:
Cymbals, Snares, and Small Cars

While Wiener Lose was quietly evaporating out from under me, the band was finally starting to feel real. Zeke on guitar. Miles on vocals. Beau on bass. Me on drums.

It didn't happen in one big dramatic "we're a band now" moment. It was more like trying to assemble a jigsaw puzzle while half the pieces were still under somebody's couch. We were fifteen. No cars. Strict parents. Homework. Curfews. A million obstacles for four kids who just wanted to play loud music together. Somehow, we made it work.

Most of our practices happened in my basement. The acoustics were terrible. The ceilings were low. Every sound ricocheted. My kit took up half the space, amps took up the rest, and my mom took up the role of unofficial noise police. Every thirty minutes or so, she'd come downstairs and say, "Boys, you need to turn it down," and we'd nod politely and keep doing the exact opposite.

We weren't turning it down. We were finally doing something that felt like ours. That basement was our first stage.

Sometimes we'd move the whole circus over to Miles's house at the corner of Prospect Avenue and Green Street. His garage was a disaster zone. Tools piled in corners. Old boxes stacked wherever they'd fit. Oil stains on the floor. But it felt like a venue to us. On warm days we'd open the garage door and let the sound spill out toward Prospect Avenue. Cars passed. People glanced over. Every time someone slowed down, my stomach tightened, waiting for a cop to pull in and shut us down.

They never did.

The spaces were small and cramped and nowhere near glamorous, but they were electric. There is nothing like playing with people who love it as much as you do.

For a few minutes at a time, the world finally shuts up and actually makes sense. You're not thinking about homework, or parents, or who's mad at you, or who you lost, or what you said wrong. You're just there, right then, riding the sound.

Those basements and garages and loud, sweaty, imperfect practices are where I started to understand passion. Concrete floors. Mismatched rugs. Amps buzzing even when nobody touched them. Cables snaked across the room like tripwires. Someone's mom yelling down the stairs to keep it down, which of course we never did. Air thick with dust and teenage deodorant. Walls vibrating just enough to make you wonder if something might actually fall. It wasn't glamorous, but it was real.

In those cramped, echoing rooms, I could feel things I couldn't always put into words. Anger. Loss. Frustration. Hope. All of it coming out through my hands instead of my mouth. I could say things with a snare hit and a crash cymbal that I couldn't say to another human face-to-face.

Wiener Lose and the band feel like two separate stories, but in my head they're tied together. Two sides of the same coin. The hot dog place gave me pressure, responsibility, the experience of getting thrown into the fire and realizing I could handle it. In that kitchen, the stakes were simple and immediate: orders, timing, not burning the food, keeping up when everything hit at once. Survival in a very practical, grease-stained way. You show up. You move fast. You figure it out.

The band gave me passion, expression, and somewhere to put all of my emotions that I couldn't say out loud, wrapped up in drum fills and crash cymbals. In that basement, the stakes were emotional. Every song felt like a confession I could hide behind volume. Every rehearsal was a tiny escape hatch from everything I didn't know how to fix. I could take all the noise in my head and turn it into a different kind of noise. Beautiful noise. Music.

When Wiener Lose vanished, the band was still there. When my heart was still cracked from losing Rachael, the band was still there. When life knocked out one support beam, another one quietly held. It didn't announce itself. It didn't say, *Hey, we're your emotional support system now.* It just kept showing up. One more practice. One more song. One more night of playing until my arms ached and my ears rang.

Looking back, I can see it. That weird little restaurant taught me that jobs, places, even stability itself can disappear without warning. You can do everything right and life can still shrug and say, *Thanks, we're done here.*

The band taught me you can build something, even from nothing. Find a guitar player, a bassist, a singer, a basement that smells like old laundry, and suddenly there's a new thing in the world that wasn't there before.

And together they shaped this part of me that knows how to work under pressure, how to start over, how to find satisfaction in disorder and loud guitars.

Life is messy. Things close overnight. People leave. Feelings get tangled. First loves end in parked minivans and silent regrets you carry in your wallet until the picture wears thin. But if you're lucky, you also get a few friends in a basement, a pair of drumsticks in your hands, and just enough stubbornness to keep going when everything else says stop.

Sophomore year didn't exactly explode into my life. It didn't show up with fireworks or a grand entrance. It just sort of crept in. One minute I was pretending summer would last forever, and the next I was standing on a blazing hot football field in a sweat-soaked T-shirt with a snare drum strapped to my ribcage like medieval armor.

Band camp.

The harness was this clunky metal contraption that felt like someone had taken a car bumper, bent it into shape, and decided, *Yeah, let's hang that off a fifteen-year-old dwarf.* It dug into my shoulders and cinched across my stomach so tight it felt like it was trying to fold me in half. We'd march for hours in the sun, learning drill sets, cleaning formations, stopping and starting at the bark of a whistle, over and over and over. Forward eight. Back eight. Left slide. Right slide. Reset. Do it again.

My shirt would be drenched, sticking to my back like wet plastic. Sweat ran into my eyes until everything blurred. My lower back screamed. By the end of each day, my shoulders were bruised, my calves were toast, and I'd discovered new muscles in my neck I didn't know existed. It was miserable. It was exhausting. And I kind of loved it. Not in a "this is so fun way." In a "this hurts like hell but I'm still here" way.

There's a moment, somewhere around hour two or three in that heat, where your body starts negotiating with you. *You could quit, you know. You could fake being sick. You could "accidentally" twist an ankle and sit the rest out.* And honestly, nobody would blame you. It was band camp, not boot camp. Nobody was handing out medals. But something in me refused. Every time my brain started whispering, *You can't do this,* something deeper pushed back.

Watch me.

So I kept marking time. Kept locking my eyes on the drum major. Kept dragging that stupid harness around the field like it wasn't slowly sawing into my shoulders. I'd shift the weight, roll my neck, take one more deep breath that barely felt like enough, and move to the next set. I wasn't out there to be heroic. I wasn't trying to prove anything to anyone else. Half the time, I wasn't even sure anyone noticed if I nailed my part or not.

But *I* noticed.

Every time I finished a rep I didn't think I had in me, something small and stubborn inside me got stronger. By the end of each day, my body was demolished. My shoulders were purple with strap marks, my calves burned, and my hands buzzed from hours of sticking patterns. I'd drag myself home, collapse on the couch, and swear I was going to die. Then I'd wake up the next morning and do it again.

That was grit in its baby form. Just showing up when everything in you is voting for nope.

Once school actually started, the intensity backed off. Practices got shorter, the harness didn't feel quite as murderous, and band went from survival training to something closer to normal. Halftime shows on Friday nights. Pep band tunes in the stands. The steady rhythm of high school life kicking back in.

But even when it got easier, I could still feel what that field had carved into me. Because grit isn't getting through the hard thing once. It's what you build in yourself by repetitiously not quitting.

Those weeks under that sun, with that drum strapped to my ribs, taught me something simple.

I could be uncomfortable and keep going.
I could hurt and still stay in step.
I could want to quit and decide not to.

Later, when life started handing me bigger, messier kinds of pain, breakups, vanished jobs, empty restaurants, grief that didn't clock out at the end of a shift, that same muscle kicked in.

You've felt this before, it would say. *Not this exact thing, but this same feeling.*

Tired. Overwhelmed. Done.

Keep marching anyway.

Sophomore year wasn't explosive. No giant scandals. No movie-level drama. But it did have one huge perk. I had the same lunch period as my sister, Allie.

That changed everything.

Our high school had open lunch, which sounds glamorous until you remember most freshmen and sophomores didn't have cars. If you wanted food beyond the cafeteria mystery meat, your options were: walk to Colonial Pantry, a convenience store that was basically the unofficial second lunchroom, or know somebody with a car.

Colonial Pantry was a zoo at lunchtime. They actually had to limit how many students could be inside at once because it was wall-to-wall teenagers shoving cheap snacks into their faces and maybe, just maybe, into their pockets. I went a few times, shuffled through that packed little store, but I usually had something better.

I had Allie.

Allie wasn't the kind of older sister who pretended she didn't know me once we stepped onto school property. She was cool. She let me tag along.

Her car was a fire-engine red Renault Fuego. Five-speed manual. Gray trim along the bottom. A canvas moonroof that folded all the way back. To most adults, it was probably just a weird little eighties car. To us, it was a rocket ship. I've never seen another one since.

At lunch, we'd bolt out the doors, pile into the Fuego, roll the windows down, and crank the music. Prospect Avenue was our track.

KFC was the go-to. Chicken Littles were thirty-nine cents back then, which meant for two bucks you could eat like royalty. Other days we'd hit Daddy O's, this double drive-thru with no indoor seating. You ordered from your car at one of two windows, got your food, and either ate in the parking lot or on the road. Their battered fries were legendary. Thick, crispy, dusted in this orange seasoning that clung to your fingers and stayed in your mouth all afternoon. Daddy O's was a splurge spot, usually reserved for paydays or Fridays.

We only had forty minutes for lunch, and it always felt like a heist. Sprint to the car. Race to the drive-thru. Eat too fast. Pray you didn't spill anything on your clothes. Park somewhere along a random side street, because there was no student lot. Then hustle back before the bell.

Those lunches were more than just food runs, though. They were a little daily reset. A chance to breathe, to laugh, to be seen. I didn't know it then, but Allie letting her awkward, drum-obsessed little brother pile into the Fuego with her and her friends was one of the quiet kindnesses that kept me afloat.

Beyond that, sophomore year slid by in a blur. Classes. Hallways. The usual high school background noise. Then football season hit full swing and the drumline took center stage again, and Allie was this steady presence through it all. Our lunch drives in the Fuego. The shared playlists. The casual way she always made space for me. Those little, ordinary acts were louder than most of the adult stuff going on around me.

The summer before junior year showed up as long days, late nights, and this quiet sense that something inside me was shifting.

I turned sixteen in June. The magic age. The one that screams freedom in every teen movie. Except in my case, freedom got delayed. My behind-the-wheel sessions got pushed back, so while some of my friends were already cruising around town, I was stuck in summer driver's ed. Me, a cranky instructor who smelled like coffee and exhaustion, and a white station wagon that could probably house a small army. It wasn't glamorous, but it was necessary.

Two extra weeks later than planned, I passed the test. They snapped my picture, printed my license, and handed me that flimsy little card that said: *you are officially allowed to drive.* Sliding it into my wallet felt like something clicking into place. I didn't know where I was going yet, but now I could.

By that point, I was already on my third car. Yeah. Third. While other kids were saving for video games or shoes, I was elbows-deep in old metal.

At fourteen, I fell in love with a 1957 Morris Minor Woody Wagon. If you've never seen one, picture a tiny British car someone halfway turned into furniture. Wooden frame. Weird proportions. It looked like it should be delivering bread in some little European village, not driving around Champaign, Illinois, which is exactly why I wanted it. It wasn't cool in the everyone-wants-one way. It was cool in the "what the hell is that?" way. I didn't want normal. I wanted character. I wanted something that made people stop and stare.

Tom, one of my dad's friends who owned a dry cleaner downtown, was into restoring old cars. Behind the dry cleaners, he had this big garage and workshop stuffed with parts, tools, and half-finished automotive corpses. That's where the Morris was.

We made a deal. I'd pay it off in sweat. Hours and hours of sanding down one of his new project cars in exchange for that ridiculous little Woody. So that big dusty garage became my second home, and when the debt was finally paid, the Morris officially became mine and the real work started.

For a year, that car lived in our garage as a side project, but it didn't stay a side project in my head. Between school, band, work, and whatever social life I was pretending to have, I'd carve out time to go out there with my dad and chip away at it.

It wasn't some big heart-to-heart thing. We weren't the type to sit at the kitchen table and talk about feelings. The garage was how we did it.

Some nights we barely said much. He'd just be there in his old clothes, leaning over the fender. I'd hand him tools. Hold a light. Sweep up the grit. Try not to screw up whatever he'd just told me to do. Other nights he'd get going on a story about when he was my age, or some job he had, or some dumb thing he did, and I'd catch myself smiling.

I needed that more than I knew.

We stripped it down, swapped in bucket seats from a junkyard, and laid new carpet. Then came the bodywork. We sanded every panel down to bare metal, peeling away old paint, rust, and whatever questionable choices previous owners had made. The air would get thick with dust. It stuck to our arms and our faces and the inside of my nose. My hands would cramp up from the block sander, and my shoulders would burn, and my dad would just keep going like pain was a normal part of the process.

Sometimes he'd glance over and say, "You good?"

And I'd lie. "Yeah."

Because I didn't want to be the kid who quit. Not out there. Not with him.

We filled, smoothed, and shaped the body until it looked almost new. When we'd step back to check a panel, he'd squint and run his hand over the metal and go, "Nope. Not yet." And we'd go right back to it. I'd get frustrated. He'd get quiet. Then he'd show me some small trick, how to angle the paper, how to feel the high spot, how to slow down and stop fighting it. Stuff that sounded like it was about car repair, but it hit deeper than that.

Those nights in the garage felt like borrowed time. Like I was getting a version of him I didn't always get inside the house. No distractions. No bullshit. Just work and radio noise and the sound of sandpaper doing its slow job. I didn't have to perform. I didn't have to talk much. I could just be there, shoulder to shoulder with him, and for whatever reason, that made me feel steady.

The wood was a whole different beast. It was cracked, dried out, splintered. We patched it with glue and sawdust, the two of us hunched over it like surgeons. Then sanded. Stained. Sealed. Slowly, it went from  gray and tired to warm and golden, framing the glossy white paint we sprayed on the rest of the car.

I remember the smell of that stain. Pungent and sweet at the same time. It got into everything. Our hands, our clothes, the whole garage. My dad would wipe his fingers on a rag and look at the wood like he was proud of it, but he'd never say that. He'd just nod, almost like, *Okay. That'll do.*

And it did.

The day we finally rolled it out into the sunlight, I stepped back and thought, *Damn. That is a cool little car.*

But what hit me harder was seeing my dad stand there with it. Quiet. Hands on his hips. Looking at it like it was more than a car.

I wanted to tell him how much that year mattered to me. How those nights in the garage felt like the safest part of my life. How I'd remember that time long after I forgot half my classes and all the dumb high school drama.

I didn't say any of that.

I just stood there next to him, squinting into the sun, pretending I was only admiring the paint.

Then reality tapped me on the shoulder. *Is this really the car I want to pull up to a movie theater in with my girlfriend? The car I want to roll through the parking lot of a Friday night football game in?*

I loved the project. I loved the process. I loved what it meant between me and my dad. But I didn't want to be the kid in the wooden surf wagon every day.

So I sold it.

Car number two was a red Renault Alliance. Four doors. Practical. Normal-adjacent. I drove it while I had my learner's permit, white-knuckling turns while my dad gripped the door handle like he was praying without words. It was fine.

Until the head gasket blew.

The mechanic mentioned it had already been replaced once, which was basically him telling me, *This thing is going to break your heart _and_ your wallet.* So we fixed it. And then I sold that one too.

Then came the car that felt like fate. A 1973 MG Midget convertible. British again. Two seats. Comically small. It looked like something you'd find in the toy aisle, not sitting in a real driveway with plates on it.

The paint had once been red, but it had faded into this tired rust-orange. The lower panels had rust holes. The black interior baked under the sun and threw heat like a stovetop turned to medium. But none of that mattered. It was a convertible.

And it was mine.

That word meant something different now. Not my parents' car I could borrow if I begged hard enough. Not the family sedan that smelled like old French fries. This was my car. My name on the insurance. My hands on the wheel. My problem when something rattled, squeaked, or broke.

When I slid into that low seat, wrapped my hands around that skinny steering wheel, and looked over that short hood, I didn't feel like a kid pretending. I felt like me.

The car wasn't fast. Let's be honest. The acceleration was more "determined lawnmower" than sports car. Getting up to highway speed felt less like launching and more like Flintstone peddling. But it didn't need to be fast. It just needed to be alive.

And it was.

The steering was tight and twitchy in that old-car way. Every tiny movement in my hands went straight to the tires. The engine had this throaty little growl that came up through the wheel and into my chest. No computers. No screens. Just metal, gas, and noise.

People turned their heads when I drove by, not because it was fancy, but because it was different. This wasn't the shiny new Mustangs the rich kids' parents bought them. It wasn't a minivan. It wasn't my dad's old work truck.

It was me.

Small. Different. A little rough around the edges, but full of spirit. For once, that didn't feel like an insult. It felt like a match.

That was the car I had when my license finally slid into my wallet.

My first solo drive with the top down was everything teenage movies promise, and more. The sun warmed my arms. The wind tugged at my hair. The single sad little speaker in the dash tried its best to blast whatever cassette I'd jammed in, distorting at anything above a polite volume. The seat was low, the horizon wide, and for the first time there was no adult in the passenger seat. No instructor sighing. No parent white-knuckling the handle. No one telling me when to turn, when to brake, when I was too close to the line.

Just me.

Sixteen years old, in a car barely bigger than a go-kart, and the world suddenly felt wide open.

And here's where the pride comes in. Not the loud, braggy kind. Not "look at me in my tiny British clown car" pride. This was quieter. Deeper. I was proud because I'd earned it. Proud I survived driver's ed. Proud I worked crappy jobs. Proud I cared enough to keep that ridiculous little car running. Proud I was trusted, by the state and by my parents, with real keys, and real consequences.

Proud that when I turned the key and that little engine coughed to life, it was because I'd done what it took to get there.

You know that feeling when you realize nobody else is going to steer for you anymore? It's terrifying. But under that fear there's also another voice.

I'm really doing this.

Every mile in that MG felt like proof. Proof I could handle a clutch on a hill without rolling back into the car behind me. Proof I could navigate side streets and stoplights and lane changes without someone narrating my every move. Proof that maybe I wasn't just the kid who screwed things up and apologized later.

I can still see it. The road stretching out ahead. Fields on either side. The sky wide open above me. My left arm resting on the door, my right hand on the wheel, music barely audible over the wind and engine noise.

That wasn't just a car. That was freedom. That was identity. That was proof I could move under my own power.

And for a kid who'd spent so much time feeling stuck, in houses he didn't choose, in hallways he didn't fit in, in feelings he couldn't express, that little faded red convertible was more than metal and bolts. It was me out in the world, finally going somewhere of my own choosing.

And for the first time, I was genuinely, quietly proud of myself.

Of course, freedom and disaster like to share the same roads.

A few weeks before school started, we were in one of our final summer marching band practices. Same blazing field. Same harness digging into my shoulders. Same sweat trickling down my back. I'd parked my MG along the curb like always, lined up with the other cars, feeling that familiar little swell of pride when I shut the door and glanced back as I walked away.

Practice was brutal. Hot. Loud. Endless. But the thought of that drive home kept me going. When practice finally ended, I slung my towel over my shoulder and headed toward the parking lot, already imagining dropping the top, cranking the music, letting the breeze clear my mind.

But when I got back to the curb after practice, my car wasn't quite how I'd left it.

Seth, one of our trumpet players, drove this massive, boxy white cargo van. The kind of vehicle that looks like it should be used for moving furniture or kidnapping people. At some point while we were out on the field sweating through formations, he tossed his trumpet case in the front seat, threw the van in reverse, and backed straight into my MG.

From his seat, he probably barely felt it. Van versus Midget is not a fair fight. But standing there on the curb, staring at my crumpled little car, I felt it in my teeth.

At first glance, it didn't look that bad. A dent here. A twist there. I told myself it was fixable. A bruise, not a break. I tried to stay calm. Tried to believe this was going to be one of those *no big deal, hammer it out* situations.

It wasn't.

When the insurance adjuster showed up with his clipboard, he took one look and basically pronounced it dead. Too much damage for what the car was "worth." Totaled. That was the word. I hated that word.

To me, that MG was freedom. To him, it was a low-value line item that didn't justify the repair costs. Numbers on a page. Scrap with a VIN.

Losing that car felt like someone yanked the training wheels off my independence and then kicked the bike into a ditch. It wasn't just metal and paint. It was the first thing in my life that felt like mine, and now it was folded up against the back end of Seth's giant white box on wheels.

What I didn't see right away, in the middle of all that dread and teenage devastation, was the one thing the adjuster brought with him that wasn't terrible: the check.

The payout ended up being just enough to buy another MG Midget. Same make and model, just a year older. Instead of a 1973, I got a 1972. On paper that sounded like a downgrade.

In reality, it wasn't.

This one was white. Clean white. And running from the front fenders all the way to the rear were thick black racing stripes, with a second vertical stripe just behind each door. It sounds a little ridiculous, like someone tried to turn a British go-kart into a race car, but somehow it worked. Those stripes made it look faster, meaner. Like it wasn't just a quirky toy.

And the best part was it was in better shape than my first MG. No rust curling up at the bottom. No cancer creeping along the doors. No old scars from past accidents. In this weird sideways way, it felt like I'd leveled up.

MG 2.0.

All of this went down in early August, right before junior year. The weather was still hot, the days still long, and for a little while it felt like maybe this was how life worked. Something breaks, something better replaces it. Destroy, upgrade, repeat. A little bad luck with a little fate sprinkled on top.

Six weeks later, on October 11th, I would take my last ride in that car.

I didn't know it then, of course. That's the thing about lasts. They don't always introduce themselves.

Those first two years of high school didn't change me in some big cinematic explosion. There was no single moment where everything finally made sense. They changed me in smaller ways, quiet ways, the kind you don't notice until you look back and realize you became someone else while you were busy just trying to get through the day.

Through grease under my fingernails and marching band sweat-soaked shirts. Through delayed licenses and late nights in the garage with my dad. Through getting hired, then abandoned, by a weird hot dog joint with turf for flooring.

By the time the leaves started turning at the beginning of junior year, I wasn't the same kid. Same body. Same blue eyes. Same sarcasm. But something under the skin had shifted.

That 1957 Morris Minor was the first thing I ever really built. Not just fixed. Built. Piece by piece. Panel by panel. Mistake by mistake. It was old and odd and not remotely mainstream. While other kids drooled over Camaros and Mustangs, I was in the driveway with an old British woody wagon that looked like it wandered out of the wrong decade and decided to stay.

It didn't look like anyone else's idea of cool, which is probably why I loved it so much. It matched something in me.

That beat-up Morris taught me I'm drawn to the overlooked stuff, the weird stuff, the things most people pass without a second glance. I didn't want what everyone else wanted. I wanted something that felt like mine, even if nobody understood why.

Especially if nobody understood why.

There was pride in that, standing next to this strange little car other people side-eyed and thinking, *Yeah, I know you don't get it. But I do.*

I put in the hours. I sanded the metal. I breathed in way too much dust and paint. I swore when bolts wouldn't budge, then felt that dumb, perfect satisfaction when they finally did. That car wasn't just a project. It was a mirror.

And yeah, I sold it. That part still stings a little when I think about it, but selling it didn't erase what it taught me. If anything, it made the lesson clearer.

Sometimes the joy is in the creation, not the keeping.

You can pour yourself into something, love the process, feel every small win in your bones, and still outgrow the result. That doesn't make it less meaningful. It just means its job in your life is done.

Then came the red Renault. Then the MG. Then the second MG. Each one showed up with a new little lesson tucked under the hood.

The Renault taught me about practicality, and about walking away when something is going to cost you more than it's worth. Not just money. Time, energy, sanity. Sometimes "I can fix this" quietly becomes "I *shouldn't* fix this."

The first MG taught me what it feels like when something finally fits. Not because it's perfect, but because when you're inside it, you feel like yourself. Like the outside world and the inside world line up for a second.

And when Seth's white van crumpled that first MG and the insurance money dropped a second, better one into my life, I learned something else.

Sometimes life doesn't give back what it took. Sometimes it gives you something else instead. Not a replacement. Not a consolation prize. Something different. Sometimes better. Sometimes not. But you only see it if you loosen your grip on what you were clinging to.

Getting my license wasn't just about legally being allowed to drive. It was about taking up space.

That first solo drive in the MG, top down, music bleeding out of the dash speaker, no adult in the passenger seat, that was my quiet graduation. No cap, no gown. Just a kid and a car and a stretch of open road saying, *Okay. Let's see who you are now.*

That drive taught me something I didn't expect. I liked my own company.

I could be alone without feeling lonely. I could sit behind the wheel with no one to impress, no one to entertain, no one to protect, and still feel solid. No audience. No witness. Just me and the road and a small engine doing its best.

And when the first MG got crushed and the second MG rolled into my life like some odd little cosmic upgrade, I started to understand resilience. Not as some heroic, movie-ready thing, but as a simple stubborn willingness to adapt.

Okay, that one's gone. What now?
Okay, that broke. What can I build next?

I was learning that you don't always get a vote in what life takes. But you do get a say in what you do after.

That summer between sophomore and junior year, the cars, the crashes, the long days of marching and sweating and sanding metal in the garage with my dad, that was my training ground in letting go and shifting gears.

Letting go of what I thought things were supposed to look like. Shifting into what they actually were.

I didn't know what was coming. I didn't know October 11th was going to take everything I'd been learning and set it on fire.

All I knew was this: if I kept showing up, to the field, to the garage, to the driver's seat, something good usually met me there. A cleaner drill set. A smoother coat of paint. A car that started on the first try.

And it did. Over and over again.

Until it didn't.

ROUND 8:
Don't Cry

It was mid-October in central Illinois, the kind of stolen, golden day that feels like it got slipped into the calendar by accident. The sun sat low and soft. Cirrus clouds smeared thin across the sky. Sixty-five degrees. Just enough chill to remind you summer was over, not enough to make you put the top up.

So I didn't.

The black vinyl roof of my white '72 MG Midget was folded neatly behind me, snapped down like a blanket. The little four-cylinder hummed in front of me, that low, buzzy sound that always felt more like a heartbeat than an engine. One hand on the wheel, the other on the gearshift, wind sliding past my ears, air smelling like dry leaves and harvested corn.

If you've never driven an underpowered British tin can down a two-lane country road with the top down on a perfect fall day, it's hard to explain. Every sense is turned up. Late-season cornstalks were yellow and brittle, soybeans rusted out to a deep orange-brown, and the whole world looked like it had been dipped in honey. The tach hovered around 3,000 RPM. Fifty-five miles an hour. Just fast enough to feel free, not fast enough to feel reckless.

I knew even then this was one of those days, the kind your brain quietly files under *Do Not Erase*. I felt wide awake. Alive. Like life and I were finally on the same page.

Adam was just ahead of me, leading the way in his beat-up blue '86 Nissan pickup. We were headed over the I-74 overpass, just another little hill on another little county road. But when you're sixteen with your best friend in front of you, everything is an excuse to race. I watched his taillights crest the hill and disappear, and of course, I did the most responsible thing a teenage boy could do.

I floored it.

The MG answered with everything it had, which wasn't much, but it tried. The engine revved, the nose lifted a little, and we climbed. For a second, it was just road, sky, and possibility.

Then I saw it.

The white sedan barreling down the road ahead of me. For half a second my brain tagged it as normal, just another car on a quiet country road. Then the next detail snapped into focus and my stomach dropped.

It wasn't in its lane.

It was coming straight down the center, maybe even nudging into mine, and all the charm of my little MG evaporated. A second earlier it felt like a toy, a go-kart for adults. Now it felt like a soda can with headlights, small enough to be erased by a real car without the driver even realizing what they'd done.

The road gave me nothing. No shoulder. Just sun-baked chip-and-tar, cracked and crumbling at the edges into loose gravel that would happily swallow a light car if you drifted into it. To my right, a steel guardrail, bright, silver, and absolute. Not protective. Not comforting. It looked like the kind of barrier you slam into in a video game right before the screen goes black.

There was nowhere to go. No margin. No easy out.

My chest tightened like something cinched from the inside, and my thoughts stopped forming sentences. Everything turned into raw, panicked electricity.

My foot hit the gas.

Even now, I can't tell you it was a smart decision. It wasn't a plan. It was instinct. Fight instead of flight. This desperate, stupid hope that if I could just get past the guardrail, I could bail right and avoid a head-on collision. Outrun steel. That was my whole strategy, and it wasn't even a strategy so much as a prayer with a gas pedal.

The sedan didn't slow. It didn't drift politely back into its lane. No hesitation, no correction, no "oh my God" moment I could read through a windshield. It just kept coming, bullet-straight.

And then, finally, the guardrail curved away and ended, like someone remembered to add an exit at the last second. I didn't think. I yanked the wheel hard right.

The MG hopped off the asphalt with a violent jolt and dropped onto the gravel. The steering wheel twitched and fought me. The whole car bucked and rattled. Stones spit out behind me, and I felt the sedan tear past so close it felt like it stole air with it. Inches from my door.

For half a second, there was a flicker of relief. Long enough for my body to go, *I did it! I got away!*

I started easing the wheel back left, trying to slide back onto the road, and that's when one of the front tires found a pothole hidden in the gravel. Deep. Jagged. Perfectly placed, like it had been waiting on me.

The wheel ripped out of my hands. The car snapped sideways, skidding across the lane like a hockey puck on new ice. And in that quick, horrifying instant, I had the one thought that still makes my stomach turn.

I'm not driving anymore. I'm just along for the ride.

I reacted on reflex, cranking the wheel back right. But the tires screamed and then quit. All four lost grip at once. The back end whipped around hard and fast. In less than a heartbeat I'd done a full 180, staring back down the road I'd just come from, like the car decided the only solution was to turn me around and send me back.

Time didn't slow down the way people always say. It broke. It turned into frames. Little snapshots that still don't play in order.

The ditch rushing up. Tall weeds bowing. Crooked fence posts leaning like drunks. My hands locked on the wheel like squeezing harder could bring control back. The wheel was basically a prop at that point, but I held it like it mattered because what else do you grab when you're about to lose everything?

My life didn't flash before my eyes. Not yet.

My dad's face did.

Just calm and disappointed and already tired, like he could see the whole thing from wherever he was and all he had to offer was that familiar sigh. I could almost hear him: "You've gotta take care of your car, Craig," like this was just another dumb mess I'd made and would have to explain.

"Shiiit!" I yelled, deep and primal.

Then the car slammed sideways into the far edge of the ditch, driver's side first. Bone-jarring. No warning. Just impact, hard enough to scramble everything inside me. And after that, the MG did something I didn't even know cars could do.

It lifted.

Suddenly I wasn't driving. I was flying.

Nothing at all like the floating when I was eight years old in the backyard of my childhood home. Not weightless like a roller coaster. The motion was violent, and the sound got distant, like it was happening in another room. I got tossed around inside the cabin like a rag doll in a metal tumbler. Shoulder smashing the door. Knees cracking into the dash. My head snapping forward.

At some point, my head went through the windshield.

I didn't watch it happen like a movie scene. I didn't see glass exploding in slow motion. I didn't feel impacts. I just felt… movement.

And then, just as suddenly, it was over.

When the car finally landed, it did it with quiet finality. No dramatic bounce, no skid. Just done. The MG lay there like a wounded animal, front wheels near the broken edge of the asphalt, rear wheels sunk into tall, uncut grass.

And somehow, I wasn't in it anymore.

That part is missing. I don't remember unbuckling. I don't remember crawling out. I don't remember anything that would make that transition make sense. One second I was inside the car, and the next I was standing in the ditch looking at it, like I'd been placed there by an invisible hand.

Dust hung in the air in slow, lazy clouds. I took a step through the grass toward the road and my legs felt rubbery, borrowed. My jeans were smeared with red. My mouth felt gritty and dry, like I'd been chewing gravel.

Then I felt it on my scalp, this cold sensation, like a breeze moving over wet skin. I lifted my right hand up to the top of my head, slow and careful, like I was afraid of what I'd find.

Warm.
Slick.
Wet.

I pulled my hand down and stared at my palm. Blood. So much blood it didn't look real at first. Four, maybe five separate streams running down my forehead, collecting into my hand like little rivers, dark and shiny.

That's when the panic actually hit, late but loud.

My heart was pounding so hard I could hear it in my ears. Everything sounded far away and underwater. I was breathing fast and shallow, but it didn't feel like oxygen was doing anything useful. My body just moved on its own, pushing me toward the road because some part of me believed the road meant help. People. Phones. Answers. Anything besides standing in a ditch, bleeding like this, trying to guess what to do next.

My vision kept collapsing in on itself until it felt like I was looking through a paper towel tube. Behind me, the MG sat cockeyed in the ditch, the engine still sputtering like it was confused, like it couldn't process how we'd gone from "driving to the park" to "crumpled metal" in a handful of seconds.

And I just kept walking. One shaky step after another. Not because I had a plan, but because stopping felt like the same thing as giving up.

"Adam…"

I tried to call out, but what came out barely counted as a sound. It was more like air leaking through a throat that felt shredded. I swallowed and tasted metal, and I forced it again.

"Adam!" I rasped, louder this time.

The word scraped its way out tangled up with blood and grit and whatever else was in my mouth. I still couldn't really hear my own voice. I only knew I'd made noise because I felt my throat vibrate.

I didn't even know where he was or if he'd already driven off. I just knew saying his name was the only thing that made sense. If I could get one familiar person back into my sightline, maybe the whole thing would stop feeling like a bad dream.

I lifted my right arm to wave and it felt like trying to raise a cement beam.

Help. Please. I'm still here.

Then, far up the road, maybe a hundred yards, I saw it. Adam's blue Nissan pulled over to the left, turning around wide and slow, circling back. Through the dust and the red haze in my vision, I watched the front of his truck swing toward me, and then lunge forward. He must've seen me standing there, because the truck suddenly accelerated and the distance between us started shrinking.

My arm dropped because it finally ran out of strength. My knees did this ugly wobble that scared me more than the blood did, because it made me realize I might not be as upright as I thought. Tears mixed with whatever was running down into my eyes, and everything turned into a smeared, red-tinted mess.

The world felt slippery, like I could slide right out of it at any second. For a few long, awful beats, he still looked too far away.

Then, finally, he was there.

His truck barreled toward me and dove into the brakes. The front end dipped, the tires skidded, and I smelled burnt rubber before my brain fully caught up to the fact that he'd stopped. Dust exploded around us. The truck came to a halt only a few feet in front of me.

And that's when sound came roaring back.

It started with a couple soft pops in my ears, like surfacing after being underwater, and then the world crashed in all at once. October wind. Gravel snapping under tires. My own ragged breathing. Somewhere behind us, the MG's engine still idling like nothing had happened.

Underneath all of it was this weird, unsettling quiet inside my body. Because even with blood pouring down my face and my vision swimming, I didn't feel pain. Just vibration. Confusion. And this heavy, sick certainty that something enormous had happened, something I wasn't going to be able to undo.

Adam's door flew open and he jumped out, moving fast, running toward me with a look I'd never seen on him before. No joke. No smirk. No "holy shit, dude." Just panic and focus and forward motion.

For a suspended second everything felt frozen. Dust hanging in the low light. My little MG humming quietly in the ditch. Blood dripping off my chin. Adam sprinting at me like I was the only thing on that road that mattered.

My life split right there, whether I understood it or not. Before the flip, and everything after.

He got to me, white as a ghost, eyes huge like he'd just watched me die.

"You're fucked up, man! We gotta get you to a hospital!"

No "Are you okay?" No easing into it. Straight truth, Adam-style. And honestly, it was oddly comforting. It meant he was real. It meant this wasn't a hallucination.

"Do you have anything to stop this bleeding?" I asked, calmer than I should've been.

He yanked open the truck and dug around behind the seat, then came up with an old sleeping bag, the one he and his girlfriend, Lani, had probably left in there after some park date the weekend before. When he shoved it into my hands, the first thing I noticed was how soft it was. Silky. Familiar. Which made absolutely no sense in that moment, but my brain clung to it anyway, like it was hunting for anything normal.

My fingers sank into the fabric and it triggered this stupid little flashback to my childhood security blanket, the one I used to rub between my fingers on sleepless nights. That blanket had been blood red too. Funny how details like that don't matter until you're covered in the real thing.

Only this wasn't comfort. This was survival.

I dragged the heavy sleeping bag up toward my head with clumsy hands, everything slick with blood. I sucked in a breath and pressed the fabric hard against the right side of my head. My hand shook while I held it there, trying to keep pressure, trying to believe pressure was enough. My heartbeat roared so loud it swallowed everything else.

The bleeding will stop. It has to stop.

Out of the corner of my eye I saw Adam watching me, his face locked into something I couldn't quite read. Fear, shock, guilt, all of it piled together. I couldn't untangle it. I just knew this stupid sleeping bag was suddenly the only thing between me and whatever was happening with my head.

His hands were shaking too as he grabbed my left arm and the small of my back and steered me toward the passenger side. His touch was firm but frantic, like he was trying to hold more than my body together, like if he let go, everything would fall apart.

My knees buckled when we reached the door. I stared at the seat, trying to convince my legs to keep doing their job, and then I didn't sit so much as collapse into it, my right hand still glued to my head.

The sleeping bag was already soaking through. I could feel the fabric turning heavy and slick under my fingers. The blood just kept coming, warm and relentless, down my neck, into my ears, into my eyes.

It felt like my life was literally leaking out, and for some reason that made me angry. Like, really angry. Not just scared. Pissed off at the unfairness of it, the mess of it, the fact that my body was doing this to me.

Adam fought with the tail end of the sleeping bag hanging out of the door, this long red-streaked strip dragging onto the asphalt like some pathetic flag of surrender. He yanked it, cursed under his breath, and finally whipped it inside and shoved it down by my feet.

"Just hold on," he snapped.

His voice cracked on the last word. His eyes locked with mine for half a second, pure desperation, and then he slammed the door. I felt the vibration of it through my whole body, but I barely heard it. My ears were doing that thing again, sound fading in and out like a busted radio.

Inside the cab, the air felt too warm. Too tight. I kept taking these short, shallow pulls of breath while I pressed harder into the fabric, watching the dark stain spread like ink on paper.

Then the smell hit me. Sweat, blood, musty cloth seats. It was disgusting and, weirdly, grounding. Like, *Okay. This is real. This is happening.*

I watched Adam cut across the front of the truck, his body briefly outlined in the orange smear of the lowering sun. Every second felt stretched, delayed, like the world was buffering. When he finally climbed into the driver's seat, he looked even worse up close. Drained, scared, pale.

"I've got you," he muttered, but it sounded more like he was trying to convince himself than reassure me.

His hands clamped onto the steering wheel and the truck lurched forward. We shot out like we were trying to outrun death itself. Every gear shift jolted me, forward, back, making my head bounce. I watched him out of the corner of my eye, jaw locked, breathing fast, eyes glued to the road.

And the strangest part was I kept thinking, *Why is he freaking out so much? I'm not even in pain.*

It was true. I didn't hurt. Not yet. I was just sticky and wet and furious about it, the warm blood crawling down my neck, pooling in my ears, sliding into the corners of my eyes. Uncomfortable, disgusting, terrifying in a logical way, but not sharp pain.

Adam looked like *he* was the one dying.

We barreled back up the overpass. Outside the windshield the world smeared into streaks of color and light. Inside the cab everything felt too crisp, too loud, too permanent, like the moment was carving itself into my brain.

As we hit the crest, the truck went briefly weightless, like gravity got turned off for a second, and time stretched thin. It reminded me of that rollercoaster moment at the top when you hang there for a breath, knowing the drop is coming, knowing you can't stop it.

Then the drop came.

We slammed back down and the whole truck shuddered. The impact jerked me forward and snapped me back hard enough to make my teeth click. Exhaust seeped into the cab, hot and dirty, mixing with the metallic tang of my own blood, and for a second it felt like I was breathing inside a closed garage.

And then, randomly, absurdly, sound punched through in a different way. Underneath the chaos, I could make out the radio. Guns N' Roses, "Don't Cry," bleeding softly through the speakers.

That's what my brain grabbed. Not the blood. Not the speed. Not the fact that my head was apparently trying to fall apart.

The song.

It didn't fit at all, which is probably why it stuck. The wrong song at the worst possible time, like the universe had a warped sense of humor.

> *"...I'll still be thinking of you*
> *And the times we had, baby...*
>
> *Don't you cry tonight*
> *There's a heaven above you, baby*
> *And don't you cry tonight..."*

And my brain, being my brain, latched onto it and welded it to the memory so tight I still hear it when I think about that drive. For a few seconds, maybe longer, I honestly don't know, I felt suspended between two worlds. Gravity and free fall. Panic and this strange, quiet acceptance.

Up ahead and to the left, the high school came into view. Big. Familiar. The kind of place that usually meant normal life: lockers, gossip, football games, crappy cafeteria pizza. Routine. Structure. The boring stuff that made sense. It looked like safety.

Adam didn't even slow down.

His hands cinched tighter around the wheel until his knuckles went washed-out white, and the truck kept pushing forward like he had one mission and one mission only. We hit the three-way stop, the T-intersection where you're supposed to at least pretend you're considering your options, and he barely glanced at it. Tires screeched, the wheel cranked hard right, and we whipped around the corner.

My body lurched sideways. My left hand slammed down on the seat to brace myself while my right stayed glued to my head.

The neighborhoods flew past. Houses, trees, mailboxes, driveways. One long smear of almost-places we could've stopped. Every driveway looked like an option. A porch we could run to. A door we could pound on. A phone someone could hand us so we could call 9-1-1.

But Adam had tunnel vision. Eyes locked on the road, jaw clenched, and his whole body set like he'd already decided the only destination he trusted. Common sense got dragged under the tires back at that intersection.

Seconds stretched into an endless loop of, *what the hell is happening?* I wanted to scream. I wanted to tell him to pull over, to stop the truck, to do something that made sense.

When my voice finally clawed its way up, it came out loud and raw.

"Where are we going?!" I yelled.

"Lani's," he shot back, like that explained everything.

Lani's? My heart kicked harder, not from fear this time, but from frustration and disbelief. "I don't need your girlfriend," I shouted. "I need a fucking hospital!"

He didn't even look at me. He didn't argue. He just kept driving.

The road rose and fell ahead of us, one long gray ribbon that refused to offer any mercy. I bit my tongue, partly from exhaustion and partly because fighting him felt pointless, and I stared out at the horizon while trying not to think about how slick my hand felt against my head. Like it could slide right off if I loosened my grip.

Finally, he jerked the wheel left and we cut into a white gravel driveway at the bottom of a small hill. He yanked the handbrake and the truck skidded sideways, rocks pinging off the undercarriage like hail. With one last jolt, we stopped with the front tires half-buried in loose stone.

Before the truck even fully settled, Adam was already moving. He flung the door open and jumped out, shoes crunching into the gravel as he sprinted toward the house.

And just like that, everything went quiet.

The engine ticked softly. The driveway sat still. The house looked almost offensively peaceful, pale blue siding catching the last of the daylight, yard neat and tidy, like it had no idea what kind of wreckage had just slid into it. Inside the cab, the silence pressed down heavy, but my brain wouldn't shut up for even a second.

Was any of this real? What actually happened to me?

Then another thought shoved everything else aside, loud and immediate. *Why does my head feel so... weird? Slick.*

I moved my hand just a little and my fingertips slid across my scalp and came away warm and wet. More blood. That part didn't surprise me. What surprised me was the texture, the way my fingers glided over something that didn't feel like it was supposed to be there. Like I was touching a version of myself that wasn't meant to be accessible. Not ever.

I needed to know. Because my brain was starting to feel like a bad narrator.

The sleeping bag slipped off my head and shoulder, the silky fabric clinging for a second before it slid down and pooled in my lap. I felt detached, like my body was making choices while my mind hovered a few inches above it, watching.

With my left hand I reached forward and grabbed the rearview mirror. My fingers smeared red across the glass as I tilted it down toward my face, and the mirror resisted just enough to make the whole moment slower. Crueler.

What stared back at me almost stopped my heart.

It was my face, technically, but it didn't feel like mine. My skin looked gray and waxy, like the color had been drained out. My eyes were too wide, pupils blown out. My hair was matted and clumped with dried blood. The coppery smell filled the cab, thick and metallic.

I lifted my left hand, shaking, and touched the right side of my head. At first my brain tried to bargain. Maybe my hair was just plastered down. Maybe it was stuck. Maybe it only felt weird because I was in shock and my nerves were lying to me.

But as my hand moved higher, my fingers found something that didn't make sense.

There was no hair. Not even stubble.

I froze, swallowed hard, and tried again, slower, like moving carefully could somehow rewrite reality. My fingertips slid over a surface that was smooth and hard and slick. For one desperate second I tried to convince myself it was swollen skin pulled tight. Something temporary.

But the longer I traced it, the less my brain could hold the lie together.

It wasn't skin.

It was bone.

My skull.

You are literally touching your skull.

Panic surged up from my chest and even though I didn't want to, my fingers moved again. They skimmed over the exposed bone, and dipped into the sticky edges where blood and tissue met.

You can't unfeel that. You can't unknow what your own skull feels like under your fingertips. It felt like rubbing motor oil over glass.

I wanted to close my eyes. I wanted to shove the mirror back up and go back to that numb, underwater place where none of it felt fully real. But my eyes stayed locked on the reflection, horrified, and my thoughts started sprinting.

How much blood have I already lost? How much more can I lose before everything just goes... black?

I glanced down at the sleeping bag in my lap, now fully transformed into a soaked, heavy red clump. My heart was hammering so hard it felt like it might crack my ribs, but that pounding was the only proof I had that I was still on the alive side of this thing.

As it turned out, Adam hadn't completely lost his mind. The second he crashed through Lani's front door, wild-eyed, shaking, barely able to get words out, he did the first logical thing he'd done since he found me on the road.

He called 9-1-1.

What neither of us knew, and what very easily could've been the difference between my heart still beating or not, was that fate had basically parked a lifeline next door. A paramedic lived beside Lani, one of those guys who keeps a scanner within reach and his instincts even closer. He heard the call come over and bolted out his front door.

He reached the truck in what felt like no time. He took one look at me and his whole posture changed. Work mode. His voice cut through the fog, sharp and solid, the kind of voice that doesn't ask. It tells.

"Fill the bathtub with hot water," he barked. "As hot as you can. Grab every clean towel you've got."

They scattered immediately, and he turned back to me like everyone else in the world had stopped mattering. I watched his hands, steady, fast, practiced, and it felt surreal that a stranger had just walked out of the house next door and taken over my survival like this was just a routine Friday.

The first steaming towel he wrapped around my head made me flinch so hard my whole body tried to recoil. The heat slammed into the raw right side of my scalp like someone pressed fire against it. Up until then it had been shock and adrenaline and numb disbelief, but that hot towel dragged pain into the cab and introduced itself to all the exposed nerves on my head.

And now that I knew what was under there, I couldn't unknow it.

Every time he tightened the towel, my brain replayed that sensation under my fingertips. The flesh that should've been smooth and attached wasn't. My scalp had been sliced through and slid downward toward my ear, folding over itself in thick, bloody layers. The towel wasn't just a towel. It was a clamp. A bandage. A last-ditch attempt to keep my head assembled.

The surface pain was sharp and stinging, but underneath it was this deep, throbbing ache. Each squeeze sparked a new wave, higher, brighter, meaner, like white-hot needles being shoved behind my eyes.

For the first time since the accident, agony finally caught up with me, and it showed up angry.

This is my head. This is my skull. This is my life being held together by hot towels and a stranger's hands..

Then the thought landed with its full weight.

I might actually die..

He didn't waste energy on comfort or reassurance, and honestly, I didn't need it. Not from him. He wasn't there to soothe me. He was there to keep me from bleeding out. It was just pressure. More pressure. Towels and steam and his hands.

Even in the middle of all that, something stupid and small kept nagging at me. My right ear. Blood was trickling into it in this slow, maddening drip.

"Please," I managed, my voice shaking. "Get the blood out of my ear."

"I'm not worried about your ear," he snapped back without even looking at me.

Instant parental scolding. Message received. I shut up.

My eyes drifted forward toward the front of the truck, and that's when I saw Adam. He was standing there in the gravel driveway, just a few feet in front of the truck, with Lani and her sister. Shoulders caved in. Tears running down his face. He leaned into Lani like his legs might give out, like the adrenaline had drained and left him with nothing but the reality of what he'd just seen.

Something in my chest twisted. For a second, the fire in my head dimmed, not because it got better, but because watching your best friend break like that does something to you. It rearranges things. Even in the middle of your own emergency.

"Tell him not to cry," I whispered to the paramedic, because my brain was still doing the one thing it knew how to do when things got scary. Manage someone else's emotions.

"Tell him… Don't Cry."

He didn't answer. He just kept working.

His hands moved with this calm, almost unreal precision. The towels, ordinary, boring towels that probably spent their lives drying hair and hands, turned into weapons against the blood pouring out of my head. Steam rolled off each one as he wrapped, pressed, adjusted, building a barrier layer by layer, trying to keep my blood where it belonged. Inside me.

He moved fast, but he wasn't frantic. He was focused. Grounded. Like the only adult in a driveway full of terrified kids.

And that's what it felt like. We were kids. Adam, Lani, me. All of us suddenly shoved into a situation none of us were remotely qualified to handle. The only actual grown-up was this stranger with a scanner and a decent set of instincts.

This guy doesn't even know me, I kept thinking. *And he's the one keeping me alive.*

Those steaming towels became a line in the sand. Despair on one side, survival on the other. Between "this is it" and "maybe you get another shot."

But the mercy never lasted. Every time a towel soaked through and he shifted it or replaced it, the nightmare came roaring right back. The squeeze of mangled skin and exposed nerves being pressed back against bone.

Minutes dragged into small eternities. And then, finally, the wail of the ambulance cut through the neighborhood, sirens slicing the quiet, red and white lights splintering across the gravel driveway.

More than twenty minutes had passed, but somehow his presence made it feel survivable. Not less painful. Not less insane. Just barely bearable.

By the time the other paramedics piled out and took over, the bleeding had slowed. Not stopped, but slowed enough to matter. Slowed enough to give me something I hadn't really had up to that point.

A fighting chance.

What came after that isn't one smooth memory. It's broken glass. Snapshots. Fragments. Little scenes scattered across my brain like Polaroids tossed on the floor, none of them in order.

The first one I can grab onto clearly is the bright yellow of the backboard. They rolled me onto it and my body shook uncontrollably, muscles firing in sharp, jerking spasms.

My arms were pinned at my sides, my chest rising and falling too fast, like I was strapped to a board in a walk-in freezer. The October air that had felt mild earlier now bit through everything. The warmth was gone.

The hard plastic collar jammed against my throat, making each swallow feel like a struggle.

Where is Adam?

The question looped on repeat. I tried to ask. At least, I think I did. My throat wouldn't cooperate. My lips wouldn't form words. My eyes darted around instead, searching for him, panicked, stuck to this goddamn board like some science experiment.

I blinked.

And suddenly, I was somewhere else.

Now there's an off-white ceiling above me, textured and ugly. A man's face leans into view. Dark hair. Serious eyes. His mouth moves and I can tell he's talking, but the words are muffled, like he's on the other side of a wall. Still, his eyes are focused and locked on me.

He started asking questions.

"What day is it?"

"Friday," I breathed.

He nodded, his face lighting up with this weird mix of relief and excitement, like I'd just remembered his birthday.

"What's today's date?"

Time felt meaningless at that point. Everything was sliding around, out of order. But one number rose to the surface.

"Eleventh," I whispered.

"Yes!" he said, like he was genuinely proud of me for remembering a number on a calendar.

Then he smiled, warming up for the next one.

"Who's the President?"

"Bush."

"Good," he nodded, then grinned. "Alright, here's a hard one: do you know who…?"

Whatever came next never made it into my brain. His words got swallowed by the same creeping gray haze that kept sliding over everything. I squinted like seeing him clearer would help me hear better, but his face was already starting to blur at the edges, fading into shadow.

"I don't know," I mumbled, embarrassed and exhausted.

He laughed. A real laugh. Warm. Light.

"That's okay," he said. "I don't either."

It was ridiculous. Completely absurd. And somehow, that made it perfect.

A tiny, fragile laugh broke loose from somewhere inside me. I was lying there with my head busted open, my skull exposed, and we were joking about not knowing some random person.

I was dying, and I laughed.

Then the whole scene vanished.

Next frame: a hallway ceiling sliding past in pieces. Rectangles of fluorescent light drift into view one after another as if I'm being reeled along under them. Each one appears above my head, hangs there for a second, then floats away, replaced by the next.

I'm on a gurney. I know I am, but I can't really feel my body. I can feel the motion, the gliding, the little jolts, but it's like it's happening to someone else.

The walls are that pale hospital blue and white, cold and judgmental in that way hospitals can be. Every bump in the floor vibrates straight through my spine.

Voices float around me, hollow and blurred, like they're echoing down cardboard tubes. I can't make out words, just the rhythm of them, the quick back-and-forth of people who are used to rushing and fixing and not panicking.

The hum of the lights and the squeak of the wheels start to feel hypnotic, and underneath it all is my own heartbeat thudding along.

Still here. Still here. Still here.

Where is Adam?

And then it all dissolves again. The ceiling, the walls, the fluorescent glare, everything slips into that thick gray fog. It's soft and suffocating at the same time. For a beat, I feel weightless. Outside of sound, outside of light, like someone hit pause on life.

I could've stayed there. I wanted to.

But reality doesn't care what you want.

The scene tears open and drops me into another room. The fog still clings to the edges, but I can hear more clearly now. Voices weaving together into something strangely beautiful and out of place, like the world accidentally left a window cracked open.

I focus on the hands near my head. Blue gloves moving confidently under bright, glowing lights. The antiseptic smell hits me hard, intense and chemical, nothing like the musty, blood-soaked air in Adam's truck.

And then the pain surges back, reborn. This time it isn't just sharp. It's relentless. My skull feels like it's in a vise, pressure squeezing from every side. Nausea rolls in with it and I want to throw up but I'm locked inside my own body.

I can see. I can hear. I can smell. I can feel every damn thing.

I just can't respond.

I'm too tired. Bone-deep, soul-deep tired.

"Can you hear me?" a man asks, his voice closer than the rest.

I try to nod. I think I do. The attempt sends waves of pain crashing down my neck and across my shoulders.

"Stay with me," he says, firm, but not unkind.

Those words grab hold of me like an anchor. Because everything in me wants to let go. To shut my eyes and slip back into that gray place where nothing hurts, where none of this is happening. I'm so tired I can barely tolerate being conscious.

I just want to sleep. Just for a minute. Just let me sleep.

Machines beep steadily around me, keeping an obnoxious little beat. The low hum of the room becomes a soundtrack of its own, and through that blur I catch scraps of conversation drifting over me like they're talking about a different person.

"Severe laceration…"
"Scalp injury…"
"Exposed cranium…"
"Hemorrhage…"
"Potential concussion…"
"Lucky he's alive…"

Lucky.

That word sticks, lodged in my head like a splinter.

Where is Adam?

When the fog peeled back again, I dropped into another one of those weirdly vivid moments.

My left arm was stretched out beside me, palm up, and for a second it didn't feel like mine. It looked like an object. Like a prop. I stared at my own hand with this detached curiosity, tracing the shape of my fingers, the pale skin, the tiny tremor that kept insisting on being there no matter how hard I tried to will it away.

One hand held a small curved needle. The other supported the underside of my palm like it was something delicate, like it could crumble if they didn't hold it just right.

I watched the needle go in, the sharp tip disappearing into my skin, then come back out again, dragging a dark thread behind it. I felt the pain, but it was dull and far away. More pressure than sharpness. More tugging than screaming.

The doctor moved fast, but not careless. Quick, practiced, efficient. Stitch after stitch, those little black lines started to appear, closing up the jagged tear in my palm, pulling me back together one loop at a time.

It reminded me of watching someone sew up a ripped seam, only this seam was me.

Part of me wanted to look away. To shut my eyes and not watch my own body being stitched like a torn shirt. But another part of me couldn't stop staring. It was gross and fascinating at the same time, and honestly, it felt like the only real thing I had. Everything else was fog and drifting and disappearing.

My eyelids kept trying to drop. Heavy and stubborn, like they'd been replaced with bricks. I fought them, because I didn't want to slip under again. The clarity felt rare, like if I blinked too long, I'd lose it and wake up somewhere else, or… not wake up at all.

That's when I noticed the marks near the wound. Numbers. Little inked notes along the edges of my palm. At first my brain didn't know what it was looking at, but then it clicked.

Are they labeling me? Counting damage?

It was such a strange thought, and even in that condition I had this flash of dark humor about it, like I was a piece of luggage at the airport with a tag on it. *This one's got a cut here, a problem there, don't lose him.*

The doctor rotated my hand, turning my arm slightly to get a better angle. In his right hand he held a pen, and I watched him draw a line through one of the numbers and write a new one in its place. Slow. Calm. Like he was correcting a grocery list.

"13"

It just sat there on my skin, simple and ridiculous. Thirteen stitches. That's what my brain latched onto, because it needed something it could hold. Something concrete. I wanted to read the other numbers too, to add them up, to figure out what they meant, to make it all fit into some kind of explanation that didn't feel insane.

But the gray fog started creeping back in, curling around the edges of my vision like it had been waiting patiently for its turn. My hand, the stitches, the ink, the doctor, everything blurred, softened, faded, and then slid away like I'd been dropped back under water.

As it swallowed me again, one last thought floated through the haze.

Thirteen stitches.

Then came the quiet.

Not actual silence. Machines still hummed, air still moved. But the kind of heavy quiet that settles inside your skull, like someone threw a weighted blanket over your thoughts. I didn't know where I was anymore, or how much time had passed. I just lay there, feeling the faint vibration of the world against my body while my mind drifted around like loose paper. Scattered. Disordered. Refusing to land anywhere for long.

Eventually, small details started breaking through again.

The smell hit first. Intense and sterile. Rubbing alcohol and bleach and something else that made my nose sting. And weirdly, that smell cleared my head just enough for the obvious to finally appear.

Hospital.

Then I heard the beeping. Steady. A heart monitor calmly tracking my life, one tiny electronic chirp at a time.

I tried to move and nothing happened. Not even a real pain response yet. My body had decided it was done cooperating. Heavy. Distant. Unresponsive.

The only thing that still seemed to remember its job, was my lungs. Still breathing.

So I held onto that. I focused on the simplest, most basic proof that I was still here.

Inhale.

Exhale.

Okay. Still here.

Shapes drifted in and out at the edges of my vision until one finally came into focus. A nurse leaned over me, her face soft but all business. She had the kind of eyes that said you're going to be okay without moving her mouth.

"Welcome back," she said, light and warm, like I'd just woken up from a nap instead of almost dying. "You've been through quite an ordeal."

I tried to answer, but my throat felt like it had been sandblasted. She saw it before I could even choke on the thought and slid a straw to my lips. I took the smallest sip of water and it felt like I was pouring relief straight into my soul.

"Where's Adam?" I rasped. My voice sounded like it had been dragged across gravel.

She smiled. "Your friend is in the waiting room. He's been here the whole time. You're very lucky to have someone like him."

Lucky.

There's that word again.

It echoed in my head. Lucky to be in a hospital bed instead of a morgue. Lucky to have a friend who didn't bail. Lucky to get another shot at this whole life thing. It should have felt comforting, but in that moment it sat on my chest like a cinder block.

The days and weeks after that weren't a clear story. They were a mosaic, bright shards separated by big black gaps. I'd surface in the hospital bed, then sink again. Pain and meds blurred everything around the edges.

The antiseptic smell never left, that acidic whisper of chemicals lingering under everything. It mixed with latex and the faint metallic scent of old blood. Machines kept up their background chorus, beeping and chiming, marking time in a place where time didn't matter.

Sometimes a nurse would lean over me, bare hands cool on my forehead or wrist as she adjusted an IV line. The slightest tilt of my head sent a bolt of pain screaming from deep inside my skull, a pounding ache that felt like my brain was knocking from the inside, trying to beat its way out.

I didn't look in a mirror. I didn't need to. People's faces did the job for me.

If I had looked, I would've seen a stranger. My head shaved, the right side of my skull turned into a roadmap of disaster. One hundred thirty-one stitches ran from my right temple back across my head, neat little train tracks holding me together. My right eye was swollen shut, puffy and purple, with stitches forming a crooked V across my brow and down toward the outer corner. My left ear was held together at the top by five small stitches.

Through the small window of my room, I could see the hallway. Kids from school, family members, people from town. They walked past, slowed, and peeked in. Their eyes stuck to me for a second, then flinched away. Some froze, visibly shaken, before they hurried on.

They didn't recognize me.

My back was its own separate hell. Skin scraped raw from the small of my back up and over my right shoulder blade, one massive scab that screamed every time I adjusted even a little. A physical reminder of getting thrown from a car and reacquainted with the ground in all the worst ways.

Clear vinyl tubes snaked out from the back of my head, quietly draining blood and fluid to keep the swelling down. If the room was quiet enough,

I could almost hear the faint trickle. It was gross and fascinating at the same time.

My hair, what little I had left, stuck in clumps with dried blood and dirt. I was wired, stitched, tubed, taped. A patchwork experiment in pain and recovery. Teenage Frankenstein.

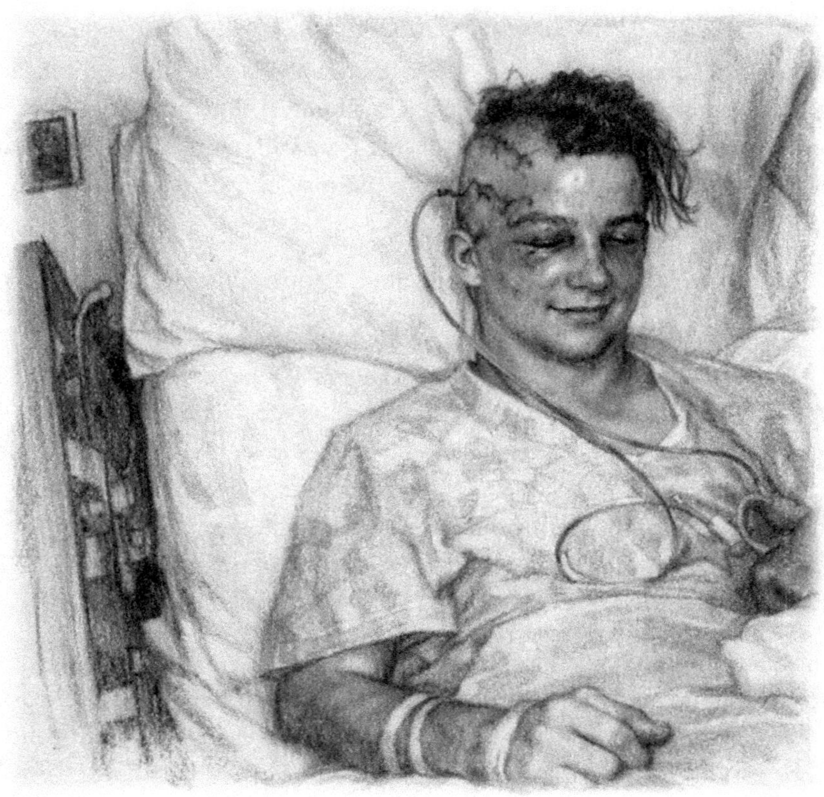

Whenever someone worked up the courage to walk into my room instead of just glancing in, they didn't get the version of me they remembered. They got the ghost version. The in-between version. I drifted in and out, never fully rooted in the moment.

Conversations swirled over me like fog. I caught phrases, laughs, a name here and there, then disappeared again.

I remember flashes.

Opening my eyes and seeing a friend from school standing by the bed, eyes wide and unsure, voice soft like they were afraid they might break me just by speaking too loud. Blink. The picture reoriented. Now there were three relatives standing there, their voices a low hum of worry and love. I couldn't tell you if they'd been there for five minutes or five hours.

Time stretched and snapped and folded on itself. It stopped caring about things like minutes and days.

The visits came as snapshots. A hand sliding over mine. Someone saying my name, carefully. The warmth of a body in the room even after they walked out.

Every person brought a wave of something. Love, fear, guilt, hope. It washed over me whether I was conscious enough to catch it or not.

On the days when my mouth and brain managed to line up for a second, I tried to force out the only words that felt right.

"Thank you… for coming to see me."

It sounded small even as it left my lips, but it was everything I had. Every time someone leaned in closer to hear me, squeezed my fingers, nodded through their own tears, I could feel something unspoken pass between us.

You are not alone.

Little by little, between their stories and the fragments in my own head, I started stitching together what had actually happened. The crash. The overpass. The sleeping bag. The detour to Lani's house that made no sense until it did. The paramedic next door who happened to be home, who happened to hear the call, who happened to… save my life.

None of it felt random anymore. It felt like a web, every thread tied to another, all of it barely holding me together.

Then there was another snapshot that still lives in my mind like a photograph.

Adam, standing at the foot of my bed.

He looked like somebody had scooped out the middle of him. Face pale, eyes red and glassy, the confident kid I knew replaced by a guy staring straight at his best friend's mortality and realizing he had no control over anything.

He came every day. Sat in the room even when I was half out of it. He was quieter than I'd ever seen him, his usual smart-ass comments muted under the weight of what almost happened. A few times, I caught him just staring at me, eyes unfocused, like he was watching the crash again and again inside his head.

One afternoon when my voice was finally a little stronger, I looked at him and said, "Hey. Stop beating yourself up. I'm still here because of you."

He opened his mouth like he wanted to fight me on that, then thought better of it. His jaw worked for a second and then he just nodded.

"I thought I lost you," he said, and his voice broke right in the middle of the sentence.

"You didn't," I told him. "I'm still here."

That's when the tears came harder. He reached for my hand and held it. That driveway image flashed back in my mind, the first time I saw him cry like that. This was only the second. Both times hurt in a way no red-hot nerve could touch.

The doctors started calling it a miracle, and they didn't say it like a headline. They said it like people who've seen enough worst-case scenarios to know exactly what they're looking at. They'd stand in the doorway or at the foot of the bed and talk in those low, careful voices about how much blood I'd lost, how close it was, how razor-thin the timing had been.

Words like "exposed cranium" and "critical window" floated into the room, and every now and then someone would let the end of a sentence hang there.

"If he had arrived even a few minutes later…"

I nodded along because that's what you do when adults in scrubs explain your own survival to you. But inside, it still felt distant. Like they were describing a scene from a movie I hadn't watched yet, but somehow I was the main character.

The full weight of it didn't hit all at once. It came later. Sometimes years later, in the middle of something normal, when a stray thought would hit me like a cold hand on the back of my neck.

That could've been it.

What hit me sooner, faster, deeper, was Adam.

He wasn't just my best friend anymore. He was my brother, and I don't mean that in the casual, throwaway way people say it. I mean it in the way you mean it when you've watched someone choose you in the ugliest, most terrifying moment of your life. Not by blood, but by instinct. By loyalty. By whatever part of a person kicks in when there isn't time to think.

His choice that day, the split-second decision to blow past every driveway and head for that one specific blue house, saved my life. I replay that drive more often than I'll ever admit out loud. The screaming engine. His hands locked on the wheel. The way he must've been doing the math without even knowing he was doing it. *Where's help? Who's close? What's fastest?*

The skid into the gravel, the door flying open, him launching out of the truck.

That house became my emergency exit from death because Adam's panic still had enough logic left in it to get me there. Not the hospital twenty minutes away. Not a random neighbor. No "maybe we should." Just that house. That choice. That one turn that changed everything.

And the thirty years after that accident haven't been some neat, inspirational montage where the music swells and the hero learns a lesson and then everything is meaningful forever. It's been real life. Messy. Loud. Beautiful in places, brutal in others. A kaleidoscope of wins and disasters.

I walked across stages and graduated. I stood tall as a United States Marine. I wrote music that held pieces of my soul. I married. I divorced. I fell in love. I hurt people and got hurt back. I watched my son come into the world and felt my entire definition of important get rearranged in one breath. I stood on the Atlantic coast and then the Pacific. I stood inside the rage of a category five hurricane and learned, again, how small I actually am. I tasted failure that burned going down, and I tasted successes that felt almost too bright to look at for too long.

None of that happens without that afternoon. None of it happens without Adam.

His panic, his tears, his refusal to quit on me bought every one of those moments. He handed me a second chance I didn't earn, and I've been spending it ever since. Sometimes wisely, sometimes like an idiot, but always aware, in the background, that the credit for it doesn't start with me.

The image of him crying in that gravel driveway still haunts me. Not as a nightmare. More like a checkpoint my brain drags me back to when I start getting too cocky or too numb. A reminder of how fragile everything is. A reminder of what real friendship looks like when the tough-guy mask gets ripped off and there's no audience and no filter and no way to pretend you're fine.

He didn't save me because he was fearless. He saved me because he was stubborn as hell and refused to let go.

People talk about love like it's easy, like it's mostly movie kisses in the rain and perfectly timed apologies and romantic speeches. That day taught me what it looks like when love shows up in real life. It looks like shaking hands and bad decisions that somehow turn into the right ones. It looks like ugly crying in somebody's driveway. It looks like doing the terrifying thing, even while you're scared out of your mind.

That stretch in the hospital, those long days and even longer nights between beeping machines and whispered conversations, broke me open in a way I didn't know was possible. But it also rewired me. Not into the old version of myself, not back into who I was before, but into someone who saw everything a little brighter, a little more honestly.

Before the accident, life was just something you did. You went to school, you chased laughs, you chased attention, you chased the next story you could tell later. I didn't think about how thin the line was between here and gone.

Life isn't a guarantee. It isn't a permanent lease. It's a fragile little rental, minute by minute, loaned out by God with no promise of renewal.

When you get your face pressed that close to the edge, when you feel how easy it would be to slip off, something moves inside you. The everyday stuff that used to feel optional starts to feel sacred. Sitting with someone you love. Hearing them laugh. Saying the thing you normally swallow because it's awkward or vulnerable or you don't want to look weak.

Gratitude stops being a cute word on a coffee mug.

Later, once a little maturity got stirred into the mix, my life started to feel more vivid. Not easier. Just more awake. The highs hit higher, the lows hit deeper, but at least I understood the price of admission. At least I understood you don't get to coast through a life you almost didn't get to have.

And the thing that changed me more than the pain, more than the scars, more than the fear, was Adam.

He chose me, over and over, after the moment passed, when it would've been easier to run from the guilt and the horror and the responsibility. He kept showing up. He kept sitting in plastic chairs and watching monitors and holding my hand. He didn't do it because he wanted a medal. He did it because that's who he was to me. That's who he decided to be.

That's what real love looks like. Not the easy kind. The gritty, terrified, desperate kind. The kind that saves your life when it would be simpler to look away.

I carry that with me every day. Not just in scars and foggy memories, but in how I see people now. My life isn't just mine. It belongs, at least partly, to the ones who fought like hell to keep me here.

So here's what I know now, and what I wish I'd known before I ever saw my own skull.

Don't wait for trauma to teach you how fragile all of this is. Don't wait until you're lying in a bed with tubes and stitches to say what needs to be said. Tell the people who matter that they matter. A lot. Tell them again when it feels unnecessary. Tell them when you're busy. Tell them when you're annoyed. Tell them when you're proud.

Tell them while you still can.

Love hard. Love stupid. Love without pride.

Be someone else's lifeline when you can, because one day you might need one too.

And if you ever get a second chance like I did, don't treat it like it's infinite. Hold on with both hands. Live like you remember what it cost. And never, ever let go of the people who helped you get it.

ROUND 9:
Scars, Snacks, and Songs

Teenage resilience is a funny thing. Your body can get split open, stitched back together like a clearance-rack Frankenstein, and then somehow you just keep going. Not healed. Not really. Just moving, because moving is easier than feeling.

A few weeks after the accident, the right side of my head was still a roadmap of pink scars, tight and tender every time I smiled or tried to raise an eyebrow. Speaking of eyebrows, I couldn't raise my right one anymore. One of the nerves that controlled that little bit of facial expression had been severed, which pretty much shut down half my forehead for good. No wrinkles for me. Well, at least not on that side. So if you're into crazy, lopsided expressions, I've got a whole catalog.

I could barely look at myself in the mirror without flinching. Every time I did, it didn't feel like my reflection looked the same as before.

So, naturally, I decided it was time to focus on what really mattered at sixteen. I got a job. At a movie theater.

Market Place Cinemas sat behind the mall like somebody had dropped it there as an afterthought, a little box with four GKC screens, stained red carpet, and that permanent scent of fake butter. To an adult, it was nothing special. To me, at sixteen, it might as well have been Hollywood.

I still remember walking in for that interview. I had my blue Boston cap on backward, pulled down just low enough to cover the worst of the scar line.

I climbed cold concrete stairs, down the narrow back stairway, winding through a maze of offices and storage closets that felt like the backstage of some tiny, low-budget production. When I finally found the manager's office, I stepped inside and watched her take me in, her eyes scrolling up and down like she was grading me.

One look and I felt it. That subtle tightening around her eyes. Backward hat, casual clothes, too much loose-limbed attitude for someone begging for minimum wage. She didn't have to actually say it, because her face said it all.

So I did what any responsible, emotionally mature young man would do. I played the sympathy card.

"I was in a pretty bad car accident a few weeks ago," I said, and slid the cap off my head.

Her eyes went straight to the mess along the right side of my head. Fresh pink scars. The jagged line running through my hair where they'd shaved and stitched and hoped for the best. I watched it happen, the way her whole demeanor shifted half a notch.

Yeah. That's right. I am both tragic *and* employable.

I got the job.

Once they handed me that nametag, red vest, and blue bow tie, I threw myself into that theater with more energy than I ever gave to school, home, or pretty much anything that involved actual adult supervision. That building, dim lights, stale carpet, buttery air, ended up shaping the next couple of years more than I could've known at the time.

I stayed more than two and a half years. For a high school kid, that was legit. Sure, I missed some Friday and Saturday nights. I skipped parties, turned down the "you should come over later" invitations, and clocked out at midnight with stale popcorn in my shoes and Coke syrup trying to glue my fingers together.

But I never really felt like I was missing out.

I was still in the mix. Still drinking too much sometimes, still chasing girls who were bad for me, still collecting dents on my heart like they were punch cards. I was just doing it from a different place than most kids my age.

The perks didn't hurt though. Unlimited popcorn, free movie passes, the ability to watch any movie we played as many times as I wanted. But it was never really about the snacks or the free seats. It was the vibe.

Most nights I was stationed at the ticket podium, that lonely little island wedged between the lobby and the hallway that led to the theaters. People rushed in with coats and kids and candy, holding out their tickets like boarding passes. I'd take the ticket, rip it clean down the middle, hand them the stub, and drop the other half through the slot in the podium where it fell into a locked metal bin. Every time it hit the bottom, it made the same hollow clink. Over and over. Clink after clink after clink.

And for the next six to eight hours, I wasn't the kid who flipped a car and carved his head open on the side of the road. I wasn't the story people whispered about, or the "holy crap, that's him" glance. I was just a worker. A nametag. Part of this strange, popcorn-scented alternate reality where the biggest emergency was whether or not the movie sucked.

The theater itself was pretty small, four screens arranged around this open square hallway. If I stood in the right spot in the middle, I could see all four entrances at once.

On slow nights, when the place went quiet and the air hummed with projector noise more than people, I'd wander into an almost empty theater with my dustpan and broom. Technically, I was "checking for messes." Realistically, I was hiding.

I'd plant myself at the top of the aisle, beside the trash bin, pretending to scan the rows for spilled popcorn, submerged in the glow of the flickering screen. If no one needed me, I let "a couple minutes" stretch into long enough that my body stopped bracing for the next bad thought. Long enough to forget, just for a second, what it felt like to be a walking reminder of that horrific, face-altering October day.

The rules there were loose, and everyone knew it. Show your face when someone called your name, don't steal from the register, and try not to burn the popcorn. Everything else was more like suggestions than rules. It was one of the few places in my life where that looseness didn't feel like dysfunction. It felt like mercy.

Concessions was a whole different animal. Loud and sticky and nonstop. Popcorn scoops scraping metal, soda fountains hissing and sputtering, customers barking for extra butter. The floor was basically a permanent glaze of butter and spilled Pepsi.

But even the wildness of concessions had a repetitive rhythm. Scoop. Bag. Pass. Fill. Lid. Slide. Punch the buttons. Smile. Repeat. Over time it turned into this mindless little dance that let my body stay busy while my brain drifted somewhere else. Like my hands could keep working while my thoughts went and sat down in the back row.

For a kid stitched together after a near-death car wreck, that little theater behind the mall became exactly what I didn't know I was looking for. Somewhere to stand, somewhere to move, somewhere I could be everything I was and still, for a few hours, not feel like a walking reminder of what almost killed me.

And no matter where I was working in that theater, one constant was always there. Grace.

Grace was my assistant manager. Petite. Pale. Fiery red hair that practically glowed under the dull theater lights. She wore the official GKC managers uniform, gray blazer, white shirt, black ribbon tie. On most people it looked like a punishment. On her, it somehow looked right. Like the uniform was lucky to be on her.

She wasn't loud. She didn't try to be the center of attention. She didn't have to. She had this quiet confidence, this calm intelligence, like she was always three moves ahead of everyone else, even when the rest of us were just trying to survive the rush.

The general manager might as well have been a ghost. I rarely saw her, and when I did, she felt like a visitor. In my head, it wasn't her theater. It was Grace's. And I liked it that way.

I also liked her. A lot.

We worked together almost every shift, and at first it stayed in that harmless lane. Teasing behind the counter, little side comments in the hallway, stupid jokes I was way too proud of because I was sixteen, almost seventeen, and fully convinced I was charming. She laughed at my jokes more than they deserved, rolled her eyes, and then hit me back with comebacks that somehow always landed better than mine did.

It was just innocent flirting. Just coworkers messing around. That's what I told myself, anyway. Back then I was great at calling things "innocent" when they made my mind too loud or my chest feel too heavy.

Then one night, our version of "innocent" got real loud. Literally.

It was early December, the kind of cold that stings your lungs if you inhale too fast. The windchill was in the single digits, and the front windows of the theater looked like they could crack with the slightest breeze. Most of the movies had already started, so the lobby was dead. Just me and Grace in this quiet, echoey space that felt too big when it was empty.

We were messing around the way we always did. Jokes, shoulder bumps, those dumb little flirty shoves that are supposed to mean nothing and somehow mean everything when you're that age. I nudged her, she nudged me back. I said something stupid. She smirked.

Then I pushed her.

Not hard. Not angry. Just a quick, careless little shove. But I forgot about the bench right behind her. She hit the edge of it, her balance went, and she stumbled backward.

Straight into the giant front window.

The glass didn't just crack. It didn't slowly spiderweb the way glass does in movies. It exploded. It sounded like the whole building shattered, this violent, breathtaking crash that echoed through the empty lobby and turned my blood cold in an instant. My heart dropped so hard it felt like it landed in my shoes.

For a split second, I was absolutely sure I had just killed her. Or at least seriously maimed her. My brain went straight to blood. To sirens. To me trying to explain it and no one believing I "didn't mean it."

I sprinted to her, already bracing for the worst.

And I found her laughing.

Not fake laughing. Not "I'm fine" laughing. Real laughter. Eyes wide, cheeks flushed, breath showing in the air because now the entire front of the building had basically opened up to December. Her red hair was whipping around like it had its own personality, and she was squatting on the back edge of the bench in a sea of broken glass.

For a second I just stared at her, trying to make sense of it. My whole body was numb with panic and relief at the same time. And then, because I was a teenage idiot and the emotional regulation department of my brain was still under construction, I started laughing too.

It wasn't because it was funny. Not really. It was shock. Relief. Disbelief. That stupid, naive teenage feeling that nothing bad can happen.

We spent the rest of the night waiting for a local window company to show up and slap plywood over what used to be the front window of the theater. Just the two of us in this frozen lobby, cleaning up glass, talking, joking, trying not to picture what could've happened if a single thing had gone a little differently.

Every time we exhaled, our breath hung in the air like smoke.

That moment etched itself into my memory. Her laugh in the cold. The jagged hole where a window was supposed to be. The way it felt like the world cracked open for a second. The real story behind that shattered plate glass window would forever remain our little secret.

Honestly, that whole year felt like that window. Dangerous in a way you don't fully respect when you're living it. Ridiculous. Messy as hell. Absolutely not OSHA-approved.

But God, does it make a good story.

Back at school, I was still staying busy with all the various forms of band activities. Band kids had a reputation, sure. "Band nerds." "Dorks." All that. But the drumline? Different animal.

We weren't the kids quietly counting measures in the back row. We were the loud ones. The heartbeat. The swagger.

And I was first chair snare.

I played in everything: Concert band, Symphonic band, Jazz I, Jazz II, Pep band, Pit for the school musicals, Marching band. If there was a reason to hit something with sticks, I was there. I even lettered in band, which sounds like the setup to a joke, but it was actually rare.

The funny part? I wasn't a music theory guy. I didn't obsess over the ink on the page. Especially in pep band. I mostly played by ear. I'd listen once, lock onto the groove, and then improvise beats and fills I thought sounded cooler than what was written. It made the crowds happy. It made me happy.

It made Mr. Anderson insane.

Mr. Anderson was our high school band director. Saying we didn't get along is like saying the ocean is a little damp. Technically true, but wildly understated.

Before my freshman year, the school had this legendary director everyone worshipped. The guy was loved, respected, practically immortal. Marching band Jesus. But then he moved on to another school somewhere.

Enter Mr. Anderson.

He walked into a program full of kids who adored his predecessor, desperate to keep everything the same, and right on cue, here I came, mouthy and opinionated. From day one, we were gasoline and a lit match.

He didn't like my attitude. I didn't like his... everything.

And because the universe has a twisted sense of humor, the only four years he directed band at Central High School were the exact same four years I was there. We were stuck with each other like an arranged marriage.

For a while, it just simmered. Glares across the room. Snippy comments. Power struggles and stupid little control issues. He'd lay down a rule, I'd push back. Over and over. Death by a thousand petty cuts.

Then, in the spring of my junior year, it finally boiled over.

We had a concert coming up, which meant extra rehearsals after school. These were not part of the official school day. That mattered to me. Once the final bell rang, I was on my time. Not his.

On this particular Thursday evening, I walked into the extra-curricular rehearsal in my standard non-school uniform: jeans, flannel shirt, blue baseball cap, backward. He saw me, raised his hand, and tapped his head. Universal sign for: take it off.

I shook my head. "This isn't school hours," I said. "I don't have to."

He told me again. I refused again.

It was such a stupid standoff when I look at it now, two stubborn males locked in a tug-of-war over a hat. A hat. But in that moment, it felt like every fight we'd ever had about respect and control and who actually owned my time and my identity.

Finally, he snapped. "Get out!" and pointed to the door.

So I did.

The next morning, I walked into band class like nothing had happened, sat down behind my drum, and he immediately sent me to the office like a judge handing down a sentence to a career criminal.

The decision came within the first few minutes in my dean's office. I was kicked out of band for the rest of the year. My schedule was changed and they plugged me into a teacher's aide slot.

And just like that, five and a half years of being the drummer, middle school, high school, all of it, were over. All because of a backward baseball cap.

At first, I was furious. It felt petty and vindictive, like he'd finally found the technicality he needed to get rid of the kid who'd been a thorn in his side since day one. He couldn't control me, so he erased me.

But the longer I sat with it, something unexpected crept in. I didn't want to go back.

I could have swallowed my pride, apologized, begged my way back in for senior year, played the good little band kid one more time. But I didn't. I was done.

Three years of violin. Three years of fighting with Mr. Johnson at Edison. Almost three more locking horns with Mr. Anderson. I was tired. Tired of arguing. Tired of needing their approval to do the thing I loved. Tired of adults pretending my talent lived and died by their permission slips.

Besides, I had my own band now. My music wasn't trapped inside a marching uniform or buried in some concert program anymore. It lived in basements and garages, in cheap amps and original songs and nights that actually felt like my life.

So I let band go.

Senior year, I sat in the bleachers during football games for the first time, surrounded by all my friends, eating junk food, yelling at refs like an idiot, just being a normal high school kid doing normal high school kid things. No wool uniform. No drill charts. No Mr. Anderson hovering over my shoulder.

And the shocking part? I didn't miss it. Not even a little.

Getting kicked out of band should have wrecked me. Being the drummer had been my whole identity. It separated me from being just "the short kid," and gave me something that felt like mine.

But instead of collapsing, something in me finally exhaled. It felt like I'd been holding my breath for years, and somebody finally cracked a window.

I could breathe. And for once, Mr. Anderson didn't get to conduct that.

What I remember most from that time isn't rage or bitterness. It's relief.

Relief that I didn't have to keep proving myself to someone who'd already decided who I was. Relief that I had somewhere else to pour my music. Relief that I could finally just be a teenage kid without a clipboard adult watching my every move.

Meanwhile, my band was starting to become something real.

I hesitate to even call what we did "rehearsing," because that word makes it sound like we had structure. Planning. Discipline. Like we showed up with clipboards and good posture and somebody saying, "Alright guys, from the top."

We had none of that.

What we did have was chemistry. We were usually just crammed into a room with amps plugged in, drums set up wherever they'd fit, and cables snaking across the floor like booby traps. We'd start playing and the walls would shake, and hours would disappear into this loud, sweaty haze. Somewhere in the middle of the commotion, something that vaguely resembled a song would crawl out.

It wasn't about perfection. It was about the feeling. That's what I loved about us. Nothing felt forced. No one stood there with charts or rules. We didn't announce, "We're going to write a song now," like we were clocking into a job. We just started playing, and somehow the music decided where it wanted to go, and we followed it like cats chasing a laser.

Zeke usually kicked things off. He'd roll in with a riff he'd been messing with at home, something raw and gritty. Pure Zeke. Loud, grungy, and dirty. He'd sink into it with his eyes half-closed, like he'd already stepped into whatever little world that sound came from, and the rest of us had to figure out how to follow him in.

That's when Beau would slide in and drop this funky, dirty bass line underneath it, something that shouldn't have fit, but somehow did. He had this way of making the whole thing tilt sideways in the best way. And for whatever reason, it always worked.

My job was simple in theory: find the beat and hold it. In reality, Zeke's phrasing was about as predictable as a drunk squirrel. But once I found the pocket and locked into it, the whole room would click. The noise would start to organize itself. We'd go from random kids making a racket to "This is actually something pretty fucking cool!"

Sometimes we'd ride the same groove for an hour. No breaks, no talking, no plan. Just playing. That's when the real magic showed up, when we stopped thinking about what we were doing and it started feeling like the song was using us instead of the other way around.

We'd stretch chords, add tiny variations, change the dynamics inch by inch, like we were sneaking up on a song instead of building it. And sure, sometimes it fell apart completely. We'd all stop at once, annoyed and laughing.

Other times, though, it felt like we were on fire. Like we'd stumbled into the one combination that made the whole universe make sense for a few minutes.

Most of the time it was somewhere in between, which is probably where real bands live most of the time. But after forty-five minutes, an hour, however long it took, we usually had something become real. Not just noise. Not just jamming because we didn't know what else to do with ourselves. An actual song, born out of repetition and instinct and that stubborn refusal to quit until the thing finally took shape.

Eventually we didn't even have to talk about changes. Nobody would say, "Okay, now go to the bridge." One of us would shift into something new, half a turn, a subtle change, a different feel, and the rest would follow like it had been planned from the start. It hadn't. We just knew. That was the weird part. The best part. The chemistry part.

Zeke and I both wrote lyrics, which is a generous way of saying we walked around with messy feelings, notebooks, and this unhealthy need to turn everything into music.

I'd show up with scraps, lines from old poems, verses scribbled on whatever paper I could find, half-hooks, random images, emotional vomit that made perfect sense to me at 2 a.m. and barely any sense in daylight. My notebooks looked like they'd survived a war: beer stains, smudged pencil, pages bent and torn, cigarette burns eating little moons into the corners. And somehow I didn't even realize how much of me was in there until I started handing those pages over like it was no big deal.

I also didn't realize, at least not right away, that alcohol had a way of loosening the knot in my chest. It didn't make me smarter or deeper or any of that. It just made me less guarded. Like it turned the volume down on the part of my brain that was always second-guessing every word, and turned the volume up on whatever was actually happening inside me.

I could get closer to the emotion. I could find better language for the pain instead of skirting around it.

Later on, I'd do it on purpose. I'd grab a six-pack of Zima, sit down on the living room floor with a notebook and a pencil like it was some kind of ritual, and start dumping myself onto the page. Somewhere around the fourth bottle, the words would start coming out like a faucet. Half the time I didn't even know what I was writing. I just knew I couldn't stop. And I definitely didn't always remember it the next day.

But then I'd flip back through some of those pages later, and every once in a while I'd hit a line that made me pause. I'd exhale and close my eyes, not because it was brilliant, but because it was true. Finally, something that could at least kind of describe what was going on in my head and in my heart without me having to translate it into normal-people language.

Zeke would take some of my lines and reshape them, tighten them up, stitch them into something that sounded more song-like. Or he'd pull out his own stuff and we'd mash it together until it felt like it came from the same place, even if it started in different notebooks.

Half the time I didn't even care who wrote what. I just cared that the feeling made it through, that something inside me got out without me having to stand there and explain myself like I was in a therapist's office, or a courtroom, or a kitchen table interrogation.

I had notebooks full of words just waiting for a chance to be heard, like they were tapping on the inside of my ribs. And if you think about it, a song really is just poetry with a pulse. I was a teenage kid trying to turn pain and hormones into something that didn't embarrass me. Something that could pass for art. Something that could feel like it mattered.

Now that we had a sound, we needed a name.

Zeke came up with Caines Fabel.

At first, I hated it. It felt too obscure, like it required a twenty-minute explanation and a black turtleneck. But the more I sat with it, the more I started to like it.

I dug into the idea. Cain, the first murderer in the Bible. "Fabel," like "fable," a story. "A murderer's tale." Dark. Twisted. Mysterious. It started to make sense, and it had that vibe where people might assume we were cooler than we actually were, which, honestly, is half the job when you're sixteen and seventeen.

That night I sat down and sketched out a rough logo. It was messy and raw and probably looked like something you'd find carved into a desk in detention, but it felt like us. Perfectly imperfect.

Word got around school pretty fast that we had something going. Suddenly we weren't just getting invited to house parties, we were getting invited as the entertainment. Translation: free beer, no cover, and an audience that didn't really have a choice once we started playing.

We weren't rock stars. Not even close. But in that little high school universe, wedged between algebra tests, football games, and whatever social hierarchy everyone acted like they didn't care about, we kind of felt like we were. For a couple hours in somebody's living room with the amps turned up and the floor vibrating under our feet, it felt like we mattered in a way that never showed up on report cards.

One Friday night in particular still replays in my head like an old favorite movie: Shelby's party.

Shelby and I went all the way back to middle school. She lived in this big two-story house, the kind of place you absolutely should not leave unsupervised if you own anything you're emotionally attached to. And of course her dad was out of town, which might as well be an engraved invitation for teenage mischief.

I swear she invited half the school. There was a keg parked on the back porch, red Solo cups multiplying on every flat surface, and music already pumping from the stereo before we even got our gear inside.

Caines Fabel got crammed into the dining room, which had magically transformed from formal eating space to makeshift rock venue. We hauled in the amps and my drum kit and wedged ourselves into a corner by the window.

We played for about an hour and a half, and the house was packed, shoulder to shoulder, wall to wall. People were yelling, dancing, screaming lyrics they didn't really know, sloshing beer onto the floor, onto each other, onto us. The wood floor shook. The air was hot and damp and smelled like Milwaukees Best beer, Drakkar cologne, sweat, and teenage freedom.

It was messy and loud and unhinged, and it felt incredible.

Those kids weren't just listening. They were part of our story. For that little slice of time, in that overheated dining room, we weren't just high school kids from central Illinois. We were a band. Their band. And they were our fans.

After the set, the party didn't wind down.

It detonated.

Even though we were done playing, apparently my drums didn't get a break. I'd been smart enough to hide my drumsticks, but drunk teenagers are a dangerous mix of creative and clueless, so they did what drunk teenagers always do. They improvised.

They raided the silverware drawer.

Butter knives. Forks. Whatever metal object they could get their hands on. Suddenly my drum kit turned into this community percussion experiment from hell. They went at it like toddlers with pots and pans, no rhythm, no restraint, just pure mayhem.

By the end of the night, my drumheads were shredded. Ruined.

I was pissed. Deeply, personally offended pissed. But what was I going to do? Stand in the middle of a packed, sweaty house party and deliver a TED Talk on proper drum etiquette? The timing for righteous indignation was not exactly ideal.

And then came the prank.

Some twenty-year-old genius, older, out of high school, but still lingering around the teen party scene, decided he wanted to stir things up. He knew one of my buddies through his brother, which is how he landed there in the first place. He showed up uninvited, along with his bad ideas and props.

Including a red-and-blue police light.

He drove slowly past the front of the house with that thing spinning on his dashboard like it was a B-movie cop chase. From inside, all we saw was the flicker of red and blue sliding across the front windows.

Somebody yelled, "COPS!"

And that's all it took.

Fifteen-, sixteen-, seventeen-year-old kids exploded in every direction at once like someone had lit a fuse. People charged up the stairs, dove into bedrooms, slammed closet doors, piled into bathrooms. Others flooded out the back door and tore through the yard, launching themselves through bushes and over fences like we'd all been drafted into basic training.

Out back, a bunch of them tried to jump the wooden fence at the same time. Slats snapped. Boards cracked. Whole sections lost their structural integrity. By the time the panic finally cooled off, a solid chunk of that fence was missing or hanging at these sad broken angles like it had been in a bar fight.

And somehow, that still wasn't even the worst part.

Earlier in the night, some other genius had decided setting off firecrackers in the upstairs bathroom was a great idea. Spoiler: it was not. One of them caught a rug on fire. Small fire, sure, nothing that made the news, but still fire inside a house. Somebody stomped it out before it spread, but the rug was done.

Shelby spent the entire weekend trying to fix what we'd destroyed, and the next morning the daylight put a bright spotlight on all the evidence. Empty cups everywhere. Beer-soaked carpet. Cigarette burns. Mud tracked through the house. Broken fence. Blackened rug. It looked like a midwestern tornado had ripped through and then stopped to shotgun a beer on the way out.

She and a few friends rented carpet shampooers, scrubbed until their arms ached, lit candles, sprayed Febreze like holy water, doing everything they could to make it look normal again. But you can't Febreze a burned rug back to life. You can't pretend a busted fence never existed. Some damage just tells on you.

On Sunday evening, when her dad walked in, he probably smelled it before he saw it. Something off in the air that doesn't belong in a clean house. He didn't need a detective. The place told the whole story.

Shelby got grounded into another lifetime, and honestly, I felt bad for her. It wasn't all on her. It was on all of us. Our collective teenage stupidity, the way we treated someone else's home like it was disposable because we were too young to understand what things cost.

Still, that night carved itself into our history. Not because it wasn't serious. It was. But because somehow, despite everything, we all walked away. No one went to the hospital. No one got arrested. The music was loud, the party was insane, the house survived just enough to be repaired, and we ended up with one of those stories that, decades later, still makes you smile and shake your head.

Man. What a night.

Junior year was one of those years that never really fades. It was the year everything felt like it was turning into something bigger. We weren't just playing friends' basements anymore. We started getting booked at real bars. On campus. Places where people could actually order drinks legally.

For a bunch of kids from high school, that jump felt huge. Like we'd crossed some invisible line and landed on the other side as something else.

At the time, Shelby's party just felt like typical teen havoc wrapped in adrenaline and cheap beer. The kind of night you survive, laugh about, and file under "crazy high school memories." Looking back, though, that night meant a lot more.

It was when I felt, for real, how powerful music could be. Not just as sound. Not just as noise we made in the basement. As energy. As presence. As identity.

Before that night, our music was mostly ours. Personal. Something we did because it felt good and because it made sense to us. We weren't chasing a status. We were chasing a feeling.

And that night, we caught it. And *the* weird part is that it didn't just hit us. It hit almost everyone in that house, too.

We turned a friend's dining room into a stage, and that crowd didn't just hear us. They piled into it. They screamed. They danced. They were in it with us.

But the flip side was just as loud. My drumheads got shredded. A friend's house got trashed. A fence got destroyed. A rug caught fire. What started as pure rhythm and electricity ended in smoke and splinters and one very grounded girl with a ruined weekend.

Music can build something beautiful, or it can help burn something down. The sound isn't the only thing that matters. The container matters too. The space. The people. The choices.

You can have all the passion in the world, but without any awareness of consequences, it turns into noise. That's true behind a drum kit. It's true in a crowded party. And it's true in life.

That night, in Shelby's dining room with broken drums and destroyed fences and music still echoing in our heads, Caines Fabel became real.

And so did I.

Our "big break" didn't start with a record exec in a suit, or some magical A&R scout in the back of a smoky room. It started with Zeke and another guy named Curtis.

Curtis played in a local band called, You Understood. They were already doing the thing we were only pretending to do. Regular gigs, real crowds, an actual name on flyers that people recognized. They were campus-famous, which, in our world, might as well have been worldwide.

We were still just kids playing in garages and basements, chasing feedback and feelings.

One night, Curtis' band had a show booked at Mabel's.

Mabel's wasn't just a bar. It was *the* bar. Right on Green Street in the heart of the University of Illinois campus, Mabel's was one of those buildings where legends were made.

REO Speedwagon cut their teeth there before they went global. In the '80s and '90s, Mabel's stage had carried half the soundtrack of alternative rock: *Smashing Pumpkins, They Might Be Giants, Flaming Lips, Living Colour, Jane's Addiction, Pixies, Alice in Chains, Soul Asylum, Cheap Trick, Iggy Pop, Poster Children, Urge Overkill, Faith No More, Soundgarden, White Zombie, Joan Jett,* and a whole lot of other big names that really meant something in the music world.

That's the kind of history Mabel's had. For us, it wasn't just a venue. It was a shrine.

And then one night, their opening act bailed. Just like that.

Curtis reached out to Zeke.

"Hey, you guys want the slot?"

I swear my heart stopped for a second, then fired back up at double speed like it was trying to sprint out of my chest.

We'd never played a real bar. Our résumé at that point was basically high school parties, a couple of random events where the amps were stacked next to empty pizza boxes, and a whole lot of big talk and bigger dreams.

Our biggest gig was a benefit concert we hosted at our high school. The school was planning a renovation of our "Little Theater" and came up with a brilliant idea: let us use the whole thing as an excuse to get our name out there. We put on a concert on our home turf, in front of all of our friends, the Friday night before Junior Prom in April, 1992.

Another band made up of friends from school was on the line-up, along with two other local, campus-famous bands, so it wasn't just us carrying the night. It turned into a pretty bad-ass night. It was a great way to raise money for the theater renovation and show off our talent at the same time.

This was different.

This was Mabel's.

We said yes before he even finished the question.

We only had a few days to get ready, but it didn't matter. I wasn't sleeping anyway. My brain ran on a continuous loop: setlists, drum fills, whether my poor, beat-up kit was going to hold together under actual stage lights.

In my head, we'd already leveled up. We weren't just kids jamming in a basement anymore. We were on our way somewhere. Somewhere with lights and sound guys and drink specials written in neon. I kept picturing the stage, the way my drums would look under those lights, the sound bouncing off the walls, the crowd, even if it was just five people, standing there while we played. It felt like the beginning of everything.

The night of the show, I stood just offstage, and it honestly felt like a thousand tiny metal butterflies were slam dancing in my stomach. My palms were soaked. My heart was pounding against my ribs. The crowd wasn't even big. The place wasn't half full, which, looking back, was probably a gift. If that bar had been packed, I might've ended up throwing up into my floor tom and calling it performance art.

But when I climbed onto that stage, sat down behind my kit, and looked out over that room, something clicked into place.

We had made it. Not made it like money or fame. Not even close. Made it like: *We are actually doing this.*

The set itself? Nothing legendary. I'm sure we sounded exactly like what we were, high school kids pretending to be rock stars, white-knuckling our instruments and praying the monitors wouldn't squeal at the worst possible moment. But that night, that stage, that room. Yeah. That part dug in and never left.

After Mabel's, things started to move. Not fast. But they moved. We picked up more campus bar gigs. We played benefit nights at coffeehouses and church basements, youth centers, anywhere someone would let us plug into an outlet and turn the volume up too loud. We almost never made more than fifty bucks a show.

Four guys. Fifty dollars. Twelve-fifty each. You'd think we were cashing stadium checks.

After every show, we'd lug our gear back into cars, arms rubbery and backs sore, then drive straight to Merry Ann's Diner, a 24/7 grease palace on the corner of Neil Street and Kirby Ave packed with college kids and night owls. At two in the morning, we'd slide into a sticky booth, ears still ringing, hair still damp with sweat, and blow our "winnings" on pancakes and fries. That was our version of the rockstar life. Syrup. Salt. Exhaustion. And this amazingly magic feeling in our chests.

Because honestly, that's what those nights really were. Magic.

Because we were only sixteen or seventeen, there was one tiny catch. To even be in those bars legally, we had to bring a parent with us. They would sit at a little table off to the side, nursing a drink. Eventually they formed their own little support group in the back of the room, sitting at a round table under neon beer signs, watching us like they were at some slightly inappropriate PTA meeting. They'd clap after every song, cheer way louder than the college kids, and share stories while we stumbled through our set.

Looking back now, I can see how much they gave up so we could play. My parents, sure, but my mom especially. At the time, I was grateful in that lazy teenage way. The "Cool, thanks, Mom" kind of gratitude. I thought saying thank you and not slamming my bedroom door too hard counted as appreciation.

I didn't get it. I didn't understand what it meant to drag yourself through a full workday, come home, maybe get an hour to breathe, and then head back out into the night just to sit in some smoky bar while your kid made a lot of very loud noise for very little money. I didn't understand the late nights. The quiet worry. The bone-deep exhaustion. I didn't understand what it meant to sit there, surrounded by strangers and spilled beer, watching your teenager chase something that might turn into his life, or might turn into nothing.

She never complained. Not once. She just showed up. Waited through soundchecks. Sat through sets where we were still figuring it out. Smiled from the back of the room like I was playing Madison Square Garden instead of some small stage with sticky floors.

At the time, I thought that was normal. Moms come to shows. Moms wait in parking lots. Moms are just there.

Now I know better.

If I didn't say it enough back then, and I know I didn't: Thank you, Mom. You were incredible.

Meanwhile, my drum kit was quietly falling apart. Cymbal stands would buckle mid-song if I hit too hard, which, let's be honest, was every time I picked up sticks. My bass pedal would either stick or slide out from under me, turning what should've been a simple, steady beat into a full-blown derailment. Every now and then, a drumhead would give up entirely with a loud POP right in the middle of a chorus, like it was announcing to the room, "He has no idea what he's doing!"

Sometimes Miles, Beau or Zeke would rush over during a song, trying to hold a stand upright with one hand while still playing with the other. We turned technical difficulties into a team sport. The crowd probably thought it was part of the act. I knew better.

I was sixteen. My entire income was minimum-wage movie theater shifts, paid mostly in crumpled bills and the smell of popcorn butter. There was no budget for shiny new gear. I was out there night after night trying to keep a rock band alive with stripped screws, duct tape, and teenage optimism. Looking back, it's kind of endearing. At the time, it was mortifying.

There I was, a teenage kid behind a beat-up kit, trying to look like I belonged under stage lights instead of in somebody's basement.

What hits me is the cost other people quietly paid so we could chase that feeling. We couldn't even be in those bars without a parent posted up like an undercover chaperone, and my mom did it without turning it into a burden. She worked all day, came home, then got back in the car and sat in smoky rooms full of strangers while I tried to keep time on hardware that was one hard hit away from collapsing.

The gigs were important, sure. But so was the table in the back of the room where she sat, believing in us harder than we believed in ourselves.

I didn't understand that kind of love then.

I do now.

ROUND 10:
The Summer I Didn't Deserve

The summer of 1992, between junior and senior year, was the summer I met Belle.

Petite. Italian. Quiet in a way that didn't beg for attention. She had this natural beauty that made everything around her look a little muted by comparison. Long dark hair just past her shoulders, and big, deep brown eyes that could pull the noise out of your head and leave you standing there a little too vulnerable.

Most days she wore her hair down. But on Fridays, game days, when the cheerleaders wore their uniforms, she'd pull it into this tight ponytail that somehow made her even harder to ignore. It wasn't fair. Everything about her was stunningly perfect, even when she was just in jeans and a T-shirt.

I'd seen her around plenty. She was best friends with Shayla, who was dating Zeke, so Belle was always somewhere nearby. But she wasn't really Belle to *me* until that afternoon at Dana's house.

Dana had this above-ground four-foot pool in her backyard and it was one of those brutal summer days where the air sits on your shoulders like wet towels. Zeke invited me over, and looking back now, I'm pretty sure it was a setup from the start. The cheerleaders were absolutely plotting.

The second Belle and I started playfully splashing each other in that pool, something snapped into place. It wasn't just, *oh, she's cute.* It hit lower than that. Like my body figured it out before my brain could throw up its usual bullshit defenses.

Every look, every little shove, every "accidental" bump sent this nervous electricity buzzing under my skin. I could feel myself trying to act normal but completely failing. My face probably looked calm, but inside I was ten again, except with hormones and zero self-control. I wanted to be closer. Closer than made sense for a guy who'd basically just shared pool water with her for the first time.

When we finally climbed out and went inside, my brain kept pretending to be casual while my body did the opposite. I kept finding reasons to end up near her. Leaning where she leaned. Sitting where she sat. Like if I stayed close enough, I could keep whatever magic that was happening between us from evaporating the second I walked out the door.

I didn't want the day to end. I wasn't thinking about senior year, college, or any version of the future. I was stuck on right now. Her voice. The way she looked at me when she talked. I was scared that if I left, whatever this was would slide back into "I've seen her around" and that would be it. Just another almost.

But she didn't seem to mind that I stuck close. If anything, she leaned into it.

We ended up on the couch next to each other, talking with everyone else like we'd been in the same friend group for years instead of only a few hours. I don't remember every word we said, but I remember how easy it felt. How my hand found hers like it already knew where it belonged. How my stomach kept flipping every time our fingers interlocked.

At some point, either Dana or Shayla snapped a photo of us on that couch holding hands. I still have that picture. Back then, I remember looking at it and thinking, *This is the photo I'm going to show our kids someday.*

We started dating almost immediately. No strategic "wait three days to call," no games. We just were. Summer slid into senior year, and that spark didn't fade. It stayed lit, bright and jittery and new, like I'd been walking around half-asleep until she showed up and everything inside me finally turned on, all at once.

Her world became mine. Mine became hers.

I used to call her my Georgia Peach. She had family there, and her house even had a room she called "the Peach Room." Walls painted a warm shade of peach, a little couch, and an old TV against the wall.

That room became our hideout. Our little bubble where everything else, school, parents, expectations, the future, blurred out, and it was just the two of us, sitting in that soft light, hoping that feeling would never go away.

That summer did more than give me a girlfriend. It flipped a switch inside me.

Up to that point, a lot of what I chased was surface-level. Attention. Flirtation. The rush of being wanted. But something about Belle changed the shape of what I needed. I started craving connection more than conquest.

Being with her made everything else fade for a bit. The noise. The performance. The constant need to be "on." With her, I wanted to be real, honest, and present.

What stuck with me most from that time was how easy it felt. We didn't overthink it. We didn't turn it into some weird chess match. It just happened. Love, or whatever version of it a seventeen-year-old can feel, didn't have to be a dramatic, complicated puzzle. It could be simple and still make a real impact.

We had our bumps, sure. Miscommunications. Insecurities. Teenagers are basically walking bags of hormones and unresolved issues, so it wasn't perfect. But I learned that something doesn't have to be perfect to be meaningful. Sometimes the imperfections are the whole point.

Life is full of distractions. People pass in and out of your life constantly. It's easy to chase novelty, to get hooked by the next shiny thing. But every once in a while, you find someone who hits you in a different place. Someone that feels like home.

Then, one afternoon, right before she left for a week to visit family in Georgia, Belle and I crossed a line together. Not in some movie way. No candles, no Kenny G song playing in the background. Just two kids alone in a quiet moment, nervous and steady at the same time, both of us feeling how real and intimate it was.

What mattered most wasn't the act itself so much as what it meant. She trusted me, fully, with something she didn't hand out casually. That kind of trust has weight.

Afterward, she looked at me and I looked back like we were both trying to memorize each other's faces. We both smiled that small, stunned smile, like you do when something between you permanently changes and there's no undoing it. It wasn't about bragging rights or hormones or any of the dumb stuff teenage boys pretend it's about. It felt bigger than that. Like we'd stepped into a new room of the relationship and the door clicked shut behind us.

The next morning she left for Georgia, and the second she was gone I missed her so hard it hurt. This was pre-cell phone, pre-texting, pre-"I'll just FaceTime you later." Long-distance wasn't romantic back then. It was inconvenient.

By the night before she was supposed to come home, my brain was running laps. I couldn't settle. Every worst-case scenario ran through my mind, over and over. *What if something happened on the drive back? What if I never saw her again? What if the last time I'd been with her was actually the last time, period?*

So, naturally, I handled it the mature way.

I went to a party and got annihilated.

Zeke and I went over to Dylan's place and I started drinking like the tequila was going to crawl inside my body and shut the panic off. Zeke, Milo, and Dylan turned it into a game. Counting shots. Laughing. Keeping score like it was an Olympic event. I lost track after eight shots, and that's not even counting the beers.

I was five-foot-three and maybe 110 pounds soaking wet. By all accounts, I should've been face-down in a yard somewhere or waking up under fluorescent lights with a nurse asking me my name. Instead, I just floated through the night in this sloppy, half-conscious haze where the only thing that made sense was the next drink.

I wasn't trying to party. I was trying to shut my mind off. I didn't have the language for anxiety back then. I just knew I couldn't stand the feeling of caring about someone that much and not being able to do a damn thing about it.

Around midnight, somebody finally told me she'd made it home. Rain had slowed them down, that was all. She was fine. Alive. Breathing. The relief hit so hard it almost made me sick, like my body didn't know what to do with the adrenaline once it didn't have anywhere to go.

When the night started to die out, I stumbled into the passenger seat of Zeke's massive old convertible and he drove me toward his house. On the way, we passed Belle's place, and I insisted he stop. Not a "pull over for a second" stop. Full-on drunk determination like it was urgent and sacred and I might not survive if he didn't.

I got out, wobbled up to her driveway, and put my hand on the hood of her mom's car.

It was still warm.

It was proof. Proof she'd actually come home. Proof she'd been there, minutes ago, living a normal life while I was out trying to drown my fear in liquor like an idiot. I didn't need to see her face right then. I didn't need a conversation or a kiss. I just needed one stupid, quiet piece of evidence that she was back in the world where she was safe.

Back at Zeke's place, I barely made it up the back steps. Crawled is probably more accurate. His mom opened the door, looked down at me, this pathetic drunk mess sprawled across her doormat, and instead of lecturing me, she smiled.

"Want a cup of coffee?" she asked.

That woman was a saint.

I passed out on the basement couch and didn't resurface until morning. The hangover was brutal.

One of my favorite memories with Belle came a few weeks later, right at the start of senior year. Homecoming.

The cheerleaders had choreographed a dance routine and decided they wanted their boyfriends to join them for a surprise performance at the pep rally. Instead of being horrified like a normal teenage boy, I jumped at the chance to make a complete ass of myself in front of the entire school. Performing in front of people didn't scare me anymore. I'd been on stages, under bar lights, in front of strangers. A gym full of high school kids? That just felt like a party with mandatory attendance.

All week we practiced early in the mornings before class, half-awake and tripping over our own feet. We stumbled through the routine, bumped into each other, spun the wrong way, then burst out laughing when we screwed it up. Every once in a while we'd nail a sequence perfectly and high-five like we'd just won the Super Bowl or something.

Then Friday came. The Homecoming pep rally.

The cheerleaders did their usual routine first. Everyone knew what to expect. Then suddenly, as if it was all completely unplanned, they called us out of the bleachers.

Nobody saw it coming.

The gym erupted. Screaming, cheering, that wild adolescent roar that makes the bleachers shake. The music kicked in and we launched into our routine. I'm sure I looked ridiculous, more "confused drummer trying to dance on dry land" than "polished backup dancer." But I didn't care. Not even a little. It felt like flying.

There I was, front and center next to my Georgia Peach in her cheer uniform, under the bright gym lights, surrounded by all of our friends. For a few minutes, it really did feel like we were writing one of the best chapters of our youth right there on that worn-out gym floor.

At that moment, we were absolutely on top of the world.

Over the next few months, I never stopped loving Belle. She never stopped being absolutely, painfully beautiful. But my teenage brain did what teenage brains do.

It wandered.

As much as I adored her, my hormones were often louder than my heart. I started noticing other girls, in passing, at school, at work. Little glances that lasted a beat too long. Just enough to poke at my conscience. Just enough to remind me that even when you're holding something good, you are still absolutely capable of screwing it up.

I wish I had a good explanation. I wish I could say it was stress, or the band, or my accident, or something about planets being out of alignment.

The truth is much uglier than that.

There was a freshman girl in my PE class. Soft brown hair, big blue eyes, braces that made her smile look awkward and sweet at the same time. She wasn't the kind of stunning that Belle was. She wasn't my world. But she was new. And she looked at me like I was something.

She lingered a little too long. Laughed at my jokes like they were funnier than they really were. She flirted, shy and obvious all at once, and of course I responded. I wish I could say I didn't, but I did.

It started small. Quick conversations. Little jokes. Folded notes traded in the hallway.

One day she invited me over. The single match that would cause an explosion.

We both knew what that meant. We'd already said enough with our eyes, with the way we stood too close, with all the innuendo that hung in the air between us. There was no confusion. She knew I had a girlfriend. I knew I had a girlfriend.

And yet still, I went.

Her house was only a few blocks from Belle's, which added this extra layer of danger that my stupid teenage brain translated as exciting instead of what it actually was: horrific. I parked on the road behind hers, heart pounding as I walked up to the front door. She answered almost immediately, like she'd been standing there listening for my footsteps.

"I've got the house to myself for a few hours," she said.

We went straight upstairs.

The second her bedroom door clicked shut, we were on each other, kissing, breathing heavy, hands everywhere, hearts racing. For weeks, I'd imagined that moment. What she'd feel like, what she'd taste like, the way her body would look beneath my hands. And then there she was, lying back on the edge of the bed, eyes locked on mine, inviting me closer.

But underneath the rush, something darker was moving. Guilt. Shame. This sick, heavy pressure pressing down on my chest. I was betraying the girl I thought I might marry someday.

And then my body joined the protest.

Despite all the wanting, all the build-up, all the fantasy, when it came down to it, my body just shut down. The desire was there, burning hot, but my guilt was louder. It drowned everything else out. We tried. Nothing happened. My body simply refused to cooperate.

We didn't have sex. But that didn't save me.

I had already crossed the line. The damage wasn't in what we technically did or didn't do. It was in the fact that I walked into that house at all. That I climbed those stairs. That I closed that door.

I left that room different than I walked in. Not because of anything physical, but because I had just met the ugliest parts of myself up close. My selfishness. My immaturity. My need to be wanted by everyone instead of being committed to someone.

I didn't blame her. I didn't blame my hormones, even though they were in full riot mode. The blame was mine. Belle had given me something pure, and I treated it like it was temporary. Optional. Replaceable.

But temptation doesn't care how good your relationship is. It cares how strong your boundaries are.

I had none.

That day didn't immediately end things with Belle, but it cracked something between us. Even if she didn't know the details, the fracture was there. Trust doesn't always break with a loud snap. Sometimes it just starts to crumble quietly, one tiny piece at a time.

Love deserves better than someone who only realizes its value when it's already sliding out of their hands.

Back then, I thought I was just messing up a little. Now I know I was playing roulette with something sacred.

Around that same time, my car died.

A 1976 Triumph TR7, hard top, bright Kermit-the-Frog green with a black strip along the bottom. It looked like someone had taken a wedge of lime, added wheels, and created something quirky and completely impractical. Everything about it fit me a little too well.

I loved that car. I loved driving it, working on it, and especially showing off in it.

One afternoon after school, a group of kids were walking along the sidewalk in front of the building. I saw an opportunity to be impressive, which was always dangerous. I revved the engine, popped the clutch, and tried to get the tires to squeal to make some kind of statement.

Instead, something in the back end exploded.

There was a loud bang, followed by a nasty grinding sound that felt like it traveled straight up my spine. I'd blown the rear end. Shattered the gears. Just like that, the Triumph was dead.

My dad and I decided we'd use the downtime to really fix it up and repaint it. It seemed like a great plan, but in reality, it meant months of me ripping movie tickets and smelling like popcorn butter to fund this little resurrection project.

In the meantime, I still had to get to school. And work. And everywhere else a teenage boy thinks he absolutely must be.

Belle didn't even hesitate.

"You can just drive my car," she said. "As long as you pick me up and drop me off."

And then she handed me her keys like it was the most normal thing in the world.

Who does that? Who willingly gives up their car so their boyfriend doesn't have to bum rides and beg for favors?

Belle did.

That's who she was. Selfless. Better than I deserved. And I took it for granted more than I like admitting.

She drove a burgundy colored four-door Ford Taurus. Not flashy. Not something anyone would turn their head to watch drive by. But it was solid. Reliable. The exact opposite of my temperamental little British disasters.

While my car sat half-disassembled in my parents' garage, I spent afternoons and weekends with my dad, sanding the body down, grinding out rust spots, filling dents, sanding again until the metal felt smooth under my palms. Eventually, we got it into primer, then laid down the black paint, glossy, deep, with a silver stripe running along the base. I added a new Triumph decal above the front bumper like a final signature.

When it was finished, it looked fast even when it wasn't moving. Sleek. A little dangerous. Like the car version of the person I thought I was becoming.

It took three months to bring it back. And for those three months, I was living on Belle's kindness, driving her Taurus every day like it was mine, her trust sitting in my hands every time I turned the key.

One cold late February afternoon, Belle told me she had a doctor's appointment but would be back with her car before I got out of school at 11:30.

"I'll leave the keys on the front seat," she said. "I'll let you know where it's parked."

No big deal. Just another day. Just another errand.

When I walked out of school, kids were streaming back from first lunch, the street humming with that constant teenage white noise of laughter and swearing. I spotted the Taurus right where she said it would be. Door unlocked.

I opened it and leaned in to grab the keys, already thinking about whatever dumb thing I was supposed to do the rest of that afternoon, and then I froze.

Sitting on the front seat next to the keys was a baby spoon. One of those tiny metal ones with the white rubber-coated tip. There was a white ribbon tied around the handle, neat and deliberate, like she'd taken her time with it. Like she'd been trying to make this feel gentle.

My hands felt huge all of a sudden. Clumsy. I picked it up slowly, like it might burn me, and unfolded the note. In her handwriting it said:

"Oh yeah. Six weeks. Sorry."

The words were just there, pencil on cheap paper. Like a note you'd pass in class. Like a joke. Like something that couldn't possibly be what it was.

Six weeks.

Then it hit, hard enough that I swear my throat went dry.

That doctor's appointment hadn't been just a routine check-up. It hadn't been a random errand. It had been a pregnancy test.

Belle was pregnant.

My heart did this weird double-punch. One part of me shot up into this stunned, breathless, almost-joy, like, *We made a life.* And the other part dropped straight through the floor, like, *We made a life.* Same sentence, two completely different meanings depending on which part of me you listened to.

It wasn't a single feeling. It wasn't one emotion. It was a violent tangle. Pride that made me want to laugh. Terror that made my hands shake. This thick, nauseating sense of responsibility landing on my shoulders like a wet blanket. I could feel my own pulse in my fingertips. I could feel the inside of my chest tightening like somebody was cinching a strap.

I stood there half in and half out of the car, one foot still on the pavement, keys in one hand, note in the other, staring at that spoon.

Around me, nothing stopped. Kids kept yelling and laughing, car doors slammed, somebody honked, somebody shouted something stupid. The world stayed normal while my whole life tilted, like someone bumped the table and everything I thought I knew slid a few inches out of place.

My stomach dropped so hard I thought I might throw up right there on the asphalt. My breath got shallow. My mind started sprinting in a dozen directions at once.

I'm seventeen. We're still in school. What are we going to do? Can we even do this? What if I ruin everything? What if she hates me? What if our parents destroy us? What if we can't be who we were anymore?

And there was another layer under the panic, the part that made me feel guilty. Not because I was happy, exactly. I didn't even know what happy meant here. But there was this strange, warm spark in the middle of all the fear. This stupid, impossible tenderness. Like my heart was already attached to the idea. Like something inside me had already started picturing her belly, picturing a tiny face, picturing a future that didn't belong to a seventeen-year-old kid who still had homework.

That was the part that messed me up. The fact that the thought of it being real made me feel both sick and excited at the exact same time.

I got in, closed the door, and just sat there for a second and stared at that ribbon.

Then I started the car and drove off.

I couldn't tell you where I went. I honestly don't remember streets or turns or stoplights. That part is static now, like an old TV channel with no signal.

But I remember the spoon. I remember the ribbon. I remember her handwriting.

Bliss and fear, tangled together on the front seat of a Taurus.

Over the next week, it played on a loop in my head. The spoon. The note. The way my stomach had dropped. The way my brain kept trying to plan a future life. Suddenly everything had consequences. Not like "you're grounded" consequences. Real ones. Big ones. The kind that doesn't end after a weekend.

Eventually, withing a week or so, we told our parents. I went into it braced for yelling, punishment, lectures, that whole storm. I expected doors to slam. I expected my life to get ripped to pieces.

But they were calm. Serious. Steady. More focused on what came next than on how we got there.

And somehow that was almost scarier, because it made it feel real in a way panic never could. Calm meant nobody was pretending. Calm meant adults were already rearranging the future in their heads. For the first time, the consequences of my choices were bigger than me. Bigger than us.

But two weeks later, she miscarried.

Just like that. Something that had barely started existing was already gone.

The whiplash of it messed me up. One minute we were standing at the edge of a life-altering future, trying to picture what we couldn't possibly picture, and the next minute we were standing in this quiet, empty space where that future had been. The air felt different. The room felt different. Like the universe had opened a door, let us look inside for a second, and then slammed it shut.

She blamed herself. Of course she did. She decided it had to be the cheerleading, the jumping, the stunts, the constant motion. Something she did. Something she didn't do. Something she should've done differently. She kept trying to find a lever she could pull in her mind that would rewind it, fix it, make it make sense.

I didn't believe it was her fault. Maybe it was random. Maybe it was biology. Maybe it was God. Maybe the universe stepped in and said, *Not yet.*

I don't know. I still don't.

But she carried the guilt like an invisible bruise, the kind you keep pressing even though it only hurts you. I told her it wasn't her fault, over and over, in every way I knew how. But it felt like my words hit the surface and slid off, while the shame stayed hooked deep inside her where I couldn't reach it.

A few weeks later, we broke up.

The air was cool that day, early spring pretending it was warm because the sun was out, but the wind cut through your bones. The kind that sneaks into your ears and down your collar.

I pulled into the gravel lot at Hessel Park and sat there for a second with my hands on the steering wheel. My palms were damp. My throat felt packed with cotton. I kept telling myself, *just get out of the car, just walk over there.*

She was already there.

Standing near one of those old wooden picnic tables, not pacing, not fidgeting, just waiting. That alone should've told me something. I shut the door, walked toward her, and kept my eyes on hers like it was an anchor, like if I could just hold her gaze long enough, the day would change its mind.

She looked away.

We sat down across from each other, the table between us suddenly feeling less like a place to sit and more like a divider. I tried to read her face, tried to find the version of her that used to soften when she saw me, but it wasn't there. She looked tired in a way that wasn't about sleep, like she'd already spent whatever emotion she had left before I even showed up.

"I think we need to break up," she said.

Just like that. No warm-up. No "this is hard for me." No long speech. Her voice wasn't angry, and it wasn't shaky either. It was calm. Flat. Final. Like she'd already said it a hundred times in her head and all that was left was to say it out loud so it would be real.

Panic rushed up like heat. My chest felt hollow and my heart started racing. I started talking immediately, like I could outrun the sentence if I kept moving.

"Don't do this. Please don't do this." I could hear how desperate it sounded as it was coming out of my mouth. "We're better than this. There's so much more to us. We can fix it. We can get through this."

I meant every word. I also meant the parts I didn't say. We already survived something huge. We're not supposed to end like this. Not now. Not after everything. I wanted her to look at me and crack, even a little, to give me anything I could grab onto. A sigh. A tear. An "I don't know." Anything.

But nothing moved in her face. Her eyes didn't soften. She didn't argue. She didn't even flinch like she was tempted. She just stared past me, somewhere over my shoulder, like she was trying to keep herself from getting pulled back in.

Her shoulders hunched forward and hands clinched in her lap, trying to stay warm.

That's the part I remember most clearly. How still she was. Like she had already made peace with it, and I was the only one still fighting. She'd already left. I was just finally catching up to the fact that she was gone.

And it hit me in this ugly, physical way. Like my insides dropped out. My mouth went dry and my eyes burned, but I couldn't let myself cry in front of her. I also couldn't stop my voice from doing that shaky thing. I felt like I was sitting there trying to negotiate with a door that was already shut.

I kept looking for the smallest sign that she was still in there with me. The tiniest crack in the wall. But all I got was distance.

After a beat, she stood up. No hug. No "I'm sorry." No last touch to make it feel humane. She just turned and walked back toward her car. I watched her shoes crunch through the gravel, each step sounding like punctuation.

She got in, started the engine, and drove off.

And that was it. Just her taillights getting smaller until there was nothing left to look at.

I sat there like an idiot, staring at the empty space where her car had been, like my eyes could rewind time if I didn't blink. My hands were still on the table. I could hear kids playing somewhere else in the park, normal life happening, and it made me want to scream. *How was the world still doing its thing when mine just got ripped in half?*

When I finally stood up, I walked back to my car and got in, and for a second I just sat there again, because I didn't know what to do with myself. I didn't know where to put the energy, the love, the pain, all of it. It didn't disappear. It just had nowhere to go.

Driving home felt like driving through fog. I don't even remember the route, just the way everything looked so gray and misty. My chest kept tightening like I was going to throw up, then it would loosen and I'd feel hollow, then it would slam shut again. I'd catch myself reaching for the radio, then stop, because it felt wrong to have music. Like silence was my punishment.

When I got home, it didn't get better. It got louder. The quiet inside the house made it worse, because there was nothing to distract me from the replay. Her voice. The way she looked past me. I kept going over what I said, what I should've said, what I could've done differently, like there was some hidden combination that would unlock the outcome I wanted.

There wasn't.

I remember sitting on my bed, fully dressed, shoes still on, just staring at the wall. My stomach felt like it was full of rocks. My throat kept tightening and my eyes would fill up, and I'd swallow it back down like I could choke the feeling into submission. Every few minutes I'd get this stupid burst of hope, like maybe she'd call, maybe she'd change her mind, maybe this was a test. But then it would die again and leave me even worse than before.

That breakup didn't feel like two people deciding to separate. It felt like someone unplugged me and walked away. And I hated myself for how much it devastated me, because part of me wanted to be tougher than that. Part of me wanted to be the guy who shrugs and moves on.

But I wasn't that guy. Not then. Maybe not ever.

All I knew was the girl I'd built my whole emotional world around had driven away, and I had to learn how to exist in the space she left behind.

And "Wicked Game" by Chris Isaak played in my head over and over.

> *"The world was on fire and no one could save me but you*
> *It's strange what desire will make foolish people do…*
>
> *… I'd never dreamed that I'd meet somebody like you*
> *And I'd never dreamed that I'd lose somebody like you…"*

That was the end of Craig and Belle.

Six weeks before senior prom.

I still think about that spoon sometimes. That stupid little ribbon. How careful she was with it. How young we were. How fast life can hand you something sacred and terrifying in the same breath, and how fast it can take it right back.

It wasn't just the baby. It wasn't just the cheating. It was all of it stacked together. The betrayal. The grief. The weight of something we were never truly ready for. She had never fully forgiven me, not in the place that actually matters. Losing the baby, after she'd finally made peace with the idea of having one, was too much to set on top of everything else. We were kids trying to carry grown-up consequences.

The storm was bigger than us.

And we didn't survive it.

When I look back, I can see how much I lost in those months. I lost a girl who loved me with everything she had. I lost a version of myself that still believed I was innocent. And I hurt someone who never, not once, deserved it.

That truth still sits with me. It doesn't scream the way it used to. It's not this dramatic, daily punishment anymore. It's quieter than that. It's a low whisper in the background, like a song you can't turn off, reminding you: *you don't get to rewrite what you did just because you eventually learned from it.*

That time with Belle was a turning point. It forced me to look at myself without the filter. No charm. No excuses. No "yeah, but." Just me, standing there with the consequences of my choices.

With her, things clicked in a way I'd never experienced. She showed me what genuine connection could feel like, what it feels like when someone shows up for you again and again, not because they *have* to, but because they *want* to.

And then I showed myself what I was capable of when I stopped paying attention to the person I kept claiming I wanted to be.

When I cheated, I tried to frame it like harmless curiosity. Like it didn't count because it didn't mean anything. Like I could step outside the relationship for a second and step back in like nothing happened. But the moment I crossed that line, the illusion shattered. It showed me how fragile trust actually is, and how fast you can take something beautiful and grind it into dust with one selfish decision you convinced yourself you deserved.

Then Belle's pregnancy hit like a completely different kind of reality check. Suddenly, I had to think past my own skin. Past my band, my friends, my plans, my teenage sense of immortality. There was a real possibility of becoming a father when I was still trying to figure out how to be a halfway-decent boyfriend.

I remember how time felt during that stretch. Everything was too fast and painfully slow at the same time. Like life had me by the collar saying, *Pay attention.*

And then, just as suddenly as that possibility showed up, it vanished.

We weren't ready. We told ourselves we could handle it because we loved each other. But love alone doesn't pay for anything. It doesn't erase fear. It doesn't undo bad decisions or make you mature overnight. It doesn't rewind the part where you broke someone's trust and then asked them to carry something enormous on top of it.

I wish I'd been more present. More awake to what I actually had in front of me instead of chasing whatever shiny thing I didn't. I wish I'd understood that "I didn't mean to" doesn't protect the people you hurt.

And I hate that the lessons came the way they did, through loss and pain and regret. But they did change me. Eventually.

They would eventually teach me that trust is fragile. That love isn't just a feeling you fall into. It's a responsibility, a commitment you have to renew with every decision, especially the ones no one sees. The private decisions. The "nobody will know" decisions. Those are the ones that tell the truth.

You don't get to coast through life assuming things will work out because your intentions were good. Intentions don't build boundaries. They don't keep promises. You have to decide who you are before you're tested, because when the test comes, you don't rise to your ideals. You fall to your habits.

That year with Belle didn't end the way teenage me wanted. There was no big romantic reunion. No prom-night redemption. No movie scene where everything gets cleaned up with a slow song and a kiss and a fresh start. There was pain. Then distance. Then silence. The kind of silence that doesn't feel peaceful.

But it left me with the understanding that some of the hardest, ugliest moments in your life become the clearest mirrors. Not to shame you forever, but to show you who you are when nobody's clapping for you. And if you're willing to actually look, really look, they also show you who you still have the chance to become.

Then came Senior Spring Break, 1993. My band had a gig booked at Bradley's, a two-level bar on the other side of town that usually leaned hard into country. Neon beer signs, line-dancing regulars, the whole thing. But on Sunday nights? "Sunday Night Mass." That was their rock night. Guitars instead of fiddles. Distortion instead of twang. One night a week where the place traded in heartbreak ballads for power chords. And this Sunday? This was our shot to prove we belonged there.

That night changed everything.

After our set, while I was still buzzing and half-deaf, this guy walked up to us. Tom. He was older, early twenties maybe, and carried himself with that easy, unbothered confidence of someone who'd been around the block a few times and didn't need to posture about it. He introduced himself, told us he was a senior at Duke, about to finish his degree, and planning to start an independent record label in Champaign.

Then he dropped the sentence that flipped my whole world on its head.

"I want to sign you guys as my first band."

I almost dropped my drumsticks right there onto the beer soaked floor.

We were just kids. No fancy gear. No polished sound. Just four teenagers who loved playing too loud and getting completely lost inside a song. We barely knew what we were doing half the time. And now somebody wanted to sign us?

We didn't hesitate. We said yes before he could rethink it.

That summer, after junior year ended, we met up with Tom downtown. He'd leased an office on the third floor of this old brick building that overlooked the street. Tall windows, creaky wood floors, the faint smell of dust and coffee, exactly the kind of space you picture when you think indie label in one of those low-budget music movies. This was *Hammerhead Records*. And we were the flagship band.

Caines Fabel, officially on a label. In our heads, that was it. We'd crossed some invisible border from kids with a band to actual musicians. The line between pretending and becoming had slid a little closer.

A few months earlier, we'd scraped together just enough cash to record four songs at *Clubhouse Records*, this small recording studio that looked exactly like the name implied, a converted shack with a loft. Cramped. The kind of place where you could feel every note bouncing off the walls. Out of those four tracks, we picked the two that felt the most like us. Two songs, "Drop It," and "N-Yor-I."

Tom's plan was to press them onto a 45 RPM vinyl. One song on each side. A real record. Something you could hold, scratch, file away in a milk crate, leave sitting on a turntable like a trophy.

When the first shipment came in, we tore downtown like little kids on Christmas morning. Tom opened the boxes and there they were. Our records.

I picked up that glossy black disc and just stared at it. It felt heavy, like it was carrying more than plastic and grooves. It felt like proof that all those late-night practices, half-empty shows, broken drum hardware, and beat-up cars had somehow created an actual physical thing. We'd pulled sound out of the air and trapped it in a circle of vinyl.

For the next few weeks, we basically ran a tiny sweatshop out of Tom's office. We set up this assembly line. One guy stamped the copyright. Another slid the record into a paper sleeve. Another slid that into a plastic cover. Then we stacked them in boxes. Over and over. A thousand times.

Eventually, Tom signed another band to Hammerhead: *Third Stone*. They were older, early to mid-twenties, and you could hear every year of that maturity gap. Their sound was tight, layered, fully formed. They had a real following, real presence. They walked in like they already belonged on every stage they touched.

They were the real deal. We were still in progress.

They went on to do more with the label. We didn't. We made one record. One amazing, flawed, beautiful little slice of vinyl.

And yet, even now, when I think about that time, Bradley's on a Sunday night, Tom's office with its cracked floors and stacked boxes, the weight of that first record in my hands, it doesn't feel like a failure or a dead end. It feels like a doorway we got to walk through, even if just for a while. For a kid with a busted drum kit and a head full of noise, that one record was proof that, for a brief, bright moment, we were exactly who we dreamed we could be.

Within two years, Caines Fabel was gone. But that doesn't erase what we were.

For this stretch of time that lives permanently in the back of my mind, we were the band. Not just a band. *The* band. At least in our little corner of the world. We were the ones onstage. The ones in the studio. The ones hunched over stacks of vinyl in a third-floor office, literally putting our fingerprints on every copy like some tiny, chaotic quality-control department.

That matters.

What stands out to me now isn't the rockstar fantasy we wrapped around it. It's the simple, quiet reality that we got to perform at all. We had no money. Our gear was half-broken and held together by hope and hardware store duct tape. Our songs were rough around the edges, full of missed notes and messy transitions. But we were on stage. We were being loud in public, and somehow someone was paying us for it, even if the payment showed up as pancakes at two in the morning.

Those tiny paydays. Those late-night pilgrimages to Merry Ann's Diner. The shared glances after a good set, the kind that said, *Did we just actually pull that off?* The exhausted laughter after a bad one, where everything went sideways and all you could do was laugh because at least you survived it.

That was our gold.

It was never really about money or fame. It was about believing, for a little while, that we were actually doing something that mattered to us. That we were allowed to want more than just clocking in and out somewhere, watching our lives happen from the break room.

And then came Tom. And that record. It was insane and humbling at the same time. We were a band that couldn't keep a cymbal stand upright for an entire set, and yet someone believed in us enough to press our songs onto vinyl.

We didn't know what we were doing. We didn't know what questions to ask, what steps to take, what doors we should be knocking on. All we knew was that it felt like validation. Like maybe we weren't completely ridiculous for dreaming as big as we did.

If there's a lesson buried in all of that, it's this: success isn't always permanent. Sometimes it's not even the point. Caines Fabel didn't blow up. The record didn't make us famous. The band didn't last.

But the growth did. The nights did. The memories did.

Those moments where we felt truly alive, shoulder to shoulder in some crappy bar, sweat in our eyes, hearts pounding, playing something that came from inside us. That's what stayed.

If I could go back and talk to that kid in the backward cap, I'd tell him: Dream big. Seriously. Let it be ridiculous. But don't judge the value of the dream by how long it lasts.

You're going to fail. A lot. That's not a defect. It's part of the design. Just make sure you fail forward. Collect the lessons. Collect the people. Collect the stories.

Those are the things you'll still be carrying long after the amps go quiet.

I had every intention of going to senior prom with Belle. In my head, that night was already scripted: tux, corsage, slow dance, "Set Adrift On Memory Bliss" by P.M. Dawn playing while we swayed under paper streamers and rented lights.

It was supposed to be ours. Romantic. A little awkward. The kind of memory we'd look back on years later and smile at. Maybe even tell our kids about someday.

But life had other plans. We were done. And suddenly I had two options: skip prom and sulk at home like some tragic cliché, or ask someone else.

So I asked my sister's fiancé's sister.

Yeah. That's a mouthful.

She said yes. She was kind, easy to talk to, and honestly, it turned into a good night. We laughed, we danced, we did the whole pose-awkwardly-for-photos-you'll-hate-in-ten-years thing. On the surface, it worked. It was fun.

But the whole time, underneath the smiles and small talk, there was this hollow spot. This constant whisper in the back of my mind: *This was supposed to be Belle.*

I had a date. But I didn't have *her*.

After the breakup, Belle changed.

Fast.

At first, I told myself it was just normal post-breakup whiplash. Of course she needed space. Of course things were going to be weird. You don't go from *we almost had a baby together* to *hey, want to be best friends?* in a week.

But this wasn't just distance. It felt like a full-blown transformation, like somebody flipped a switch and the version of her I knew simply evaporated. She didn't just step away from me. She stepped away from everything that used to be hers. Her friends. Her energy. That softness she wore like a warm blanket. It all disappeared like it had never existed.

And then she slid into a completely different crowd so fast it made my head spin, like some invisible line had been crossed and she wasn't allowed back on her old side anymore.

The first thing I noticed was her voice. That light, sweet tone that used to make everything feel a little safer was gone. In its place was something harder. Rough slang. Even rougher edges. Like every sentence came wrapped in barbed wire.

It wasn't just new vocabulary. It was like she was trying on a whole new skin, and she was determined to make it fit. And it wasn't that cute, performative rebellion some kids do when they're bored and want a story.

That's what messed with me the most. It wasn't just that I didn't recognize her. It was that it felt like the girl I loved had been erased and replaced with someone wearing her face.

I wasn't even mad at her at first. Not exactly. I was mad at the loss. I was mad at the silence. I was mad at how grief doesn't only show up at funerals. It shows up in hallways and lunchrooms and in those little empty pockets where someone used to laugh.

I kept catching myself looking for her without meaning to. Like maybe if I turned the corner at the right time, I'd see my Georgia Peach again and everything would snap back into place.

But she didn't sound like my Georgia Peach anymore. She sounded like she belonged on the South Side of Chicago, not curled up with me in the Peach Room at her parents' house like we were the only two people in the world.

She had this invisible armor on. And I didn't know what she was trying to protect herself from, but I had this gut-level feeling it was darker than I would understand. Drugs? Maybe. Bad choices? Definitely. A version of herself she didn't know how to live with? Probably.

Whatever it was, it had her locked up from the inside, and I couldn't reach her without getting cut.

And that's when it really hit me. There was no going back. Not the way I wanted. Not the way I kept secretly bargaining for.

One day between classes, I walked past her locker. She was there, leaned in with her new crew, laughing that new laugh. She didn't even look at me. Didn't waver. Didn't even do that quick little sideways glance she used to do when she could feel me nearby.

Nothing.

Like I was a stranger. Like I was air.

I kept walking, jaw clenched so hard my teeth hurt, and it all hit at once. Guilt, love, regret, confusion, anger. Everything stacked together until I felt like I was going to explode right there in the hallway.

So I did the only thing my seventeen-year-old brain could think to do with that much pain and nowhere to put it.

I spun around, wound up, and slammed my fist into her metal locker.

The sound cracked down the hallway like a gunshot. Heads snapped around. Conversations died mid-sentence. When I pulled my hand back, there was a dent right where my knuckles had been, and my skin was already starting to swell.

It was stupid. Pointless. Childish. I knew that even as it was happening.

But it was also honest.

My anger and frustration were the only things I had left that still felt like they belonged to me, because she wouldn't talk to me, and I had a thousand questions and zero answers. I still loved her. I would still love her for years, in that quiet, stubborn way you don't admit out loud because it makes you sound pathetic.

I just didn't have anywhere to put it anymore.

Senior year is one of those stretches of time that doesn't feel real until it's already gone. When you're living it, it feels endless. Lunch bells, passing periods, Friday night games, rehearsals, shifts at work. It all smears together into this long blur where you genuinely believe the future is something that happens to other people. Not you. Not yet.

Because you think you have time. Time to clean up your messes. Time to fix what you broke. Time to figure out who you are. Time to say the thing you keep rehearsing in your head.

And then one day you look up and the girl you thought you'd spend your life with walks past you in a hallway like you're just another face she used to recognize. No pause. No flicker of warmth. Not even the courtesy of eye contact. Just gone.

Then graduation hits. You throw your cap into the air and, in the same instant, everything that felt permanent starts cracking apart. The future shows up without knocking, and suddenly you're standing there in a gown that doesn't fit right, shaking hands with adults who keep saying "congratulations" like that word can actually prepare you for what's next.

That last year was a messy cocktail of freedom, laughter, heartbreak, and the kind of reckless stupidity that only looks charming when you're far enough away from it. In the moment, it just felt like if I kept moving fast enough, nothing could catch me.

Then came graduation night.

God, that night.

Walking across that stage, hearing my name echo through the arena, feeling the diploma in my hand. I swear it felt like I'd just been promoted into a new version of myself. Like I wasn't just some kid lingering in hallways anymore. For a few shining hours, I felt untouchable. Not mature necessarily. Just free.

The future looked wide open and for once, I wasn't thinking about the wreckage behind me. Or maybe I was, and that's why I was so determined to drown it out with noise and bodies and beer. That feeling of standing on the edge of something new, with everyone cheering and clapping like you'd earned a clean slate. You start believing it. You start acting like you deserve to do whatever you want because you survived high school and nobody can tell you shit anymore.

Me, Zeke, and Miles had sublet this third-floor campus apartment at First St and Springfield Ave. Beat-up place. Thin walls. Just enough room to pretend we were adults. A bunch of our friends had spots nearby, and that night the whole campus area lit up like a circuit board. Parties in every direction.

We decided our place would be the final stop. The after-after party. The place everyone ends up when they're too drunk to go home but too wired to let the night die.

So we bounced from one apartment to another, fueled by cheap beer and that dumb teenage sense that we were invincible because we were young. Time got slippery. Rooms blurred. The music never stopped. Faces kept appearing and disappearing, and everyone was laughing like nothing had consequences.

I remember feeling lit from the inside. It wasn't confidence exactly. It was more like desperation dressed up as swagger. Like if I could stay loud enough, wanted enough, touched enough, I wouldn't have to sit still long enough to feel anything else.

At some point in that hazy night, I slept with three different girls. Rachael, the first girl I'd ever been with, the one I lost my virginity to back in freshman year. Jenna, an eighth-grade girlfriend, a familiar face from a previous version of my life. And Kelsey, the girl I'd started casually hooking up with a few weeks after Belle and I broke up.

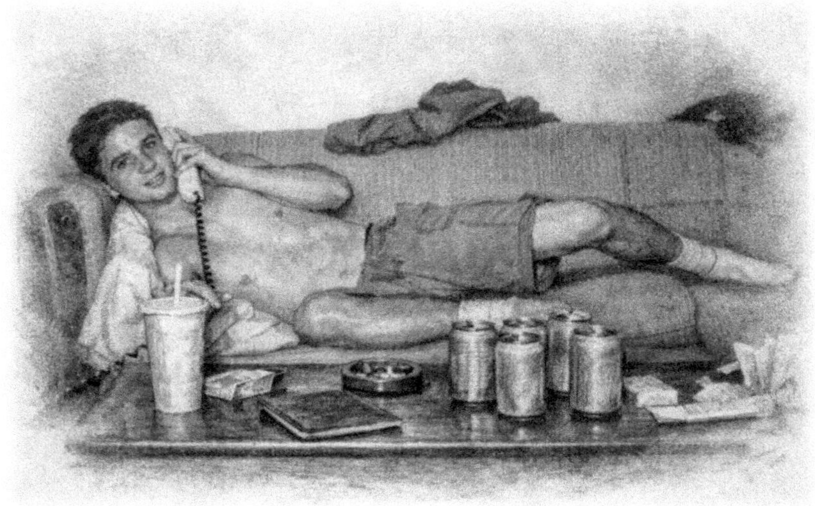

Saying it out loud makes it sound like I was some legend. I wasn't. I was seventeen, only a few days away from eighteen, wasted and wired, ping-ponging from room to room, bed to bed, ego to ego. It wasn't romantic. It wasn't meaningful. It was opportunistic and sloppy and powered by a selfish need to feel desired, to feel in control, to feel like I could rewrite who I was by just stacking up proof that someone wanted me.

I don't remember the order. I don't remember the words. I don't remember how one moment became the next. I remember flashes: a face turning toward mine, a hand on my arm, a kiss in a doorway, laughter echoing down a hallway, music bleeding through the walls. The stupid rush of thinking I was somebody. The way each hookup felt like another stamp on my own perverted version of a sexual passport.

That night I felt like a player, a gigolo, like I'd cracked some code. Like the guy who gets the girls is the guy who wins. Like sex was a scoreboard and I sunk one from the three-point line.

But underneath all of that, I was just a kid trying to outrun how worthless I felt.

Three girls in one night didn't fix anything. It didn't replace any missing pieces. It just turned the volume down for a few hours, like throwing a blanket over a speaker.

It muffled the noise, until the noise came right back the second the night wore off.

ROUND 11:
Cinnamon Schnapps & Coming of Age

The summer after graduation was just clutter. Emotional clutter. Financial clutter. Sexual clutter. Everything everywhere.

It should've been perfect. No school. More freedom. The band. The apartment. Girls. Parties. Late nights turning into early mornings. The kind of summer movies sell you like it's the prize for surviving childhood.

But emotionally, I was unraveling.

No matter what I did, who I was with, what party I went to, how loud the music was, every mental road I took curved back to the same person. Belle. The one I truly loved. The one I'd screwed up. The one I almost had a baby with. The one who wouldn't even look at me anymore.

And the baby part haunted me in a way nothing else did. We almost changed the entire trajectory of our lives without the slightest clue what we were doing. I'd lie awake on that lumpy mattress, staring at the ceiling, running ghost versions of my life in my mind. *What kind of father would I have been? Would we have made it? What would our kid have looked like?*

Questions with no responses. No resolution. Just replay. Just me, stuck in my own head, trying to make sense of something that couldn't be fixed.

Because she was gone.

Radio silence. No calls. No notes slipped under doors. No accidental run-ins that turned into conversations. No "hey" that opened a door. Just absence. Total and complete, like she'd deleted me from her life.

And it was its own kind of hell. The quiet kind. The kind that hides in the background of everything, an ache that settles into your bones. The kind that makes you laugh at a joke and feel guilty two seconds later because how dare you feel normal when your heart still hurts like that.

On the surface, that summer looked like freedom. Underneath, it felt more like drifting. Floating just above the wreckage.

When I finally turned eighteen in June of 1993, just a few days after that crazy graduation night, it felt like almost everything in my life took a hard swing. Between the campus apartment, the wild graduation-night escapades with three different girls, the absence of Belle, and officially reaching "adulthood," I was stuck in a whirlwind of moving parts and emotions.

I guess it was inevitable that the line Grace and I had been dancing on for over a year didn't just get crossed. It disappeared.

Grace was twenty-eight and my assistant manager at the theater. Petite. Pale. Fiery red hair crusted with Aqua-Net hairspray. We'd been flirting forever. Nothing blatant. Nothing you could point to and say, *that's the moment.* Just this steady drip of teasing at the ticket counter, lingering looks in the hallway, a little extra laughter that didn't need to be there. The constant back-and-forth of *are we* and *we're not,* except somehow we always were.

When I was sixteen and seventeen, there was still a line. Unspoken, but still a line. Teachers, bosses, grown women, off limits. You could joke. You could fantasize. But you still knew where the boundary was.

Then my eighteenth birthday hit, and the fence turned into fog.

The touches lasted a little longer. A hand on my arm that didn't move away quite as fast. The glances that said more than they used to.

The turning point came a few days after graduation. Thursday night. We'd just closed the theater. Last show gone. Popcorn machines off. Soda fountains wiped down. The carpet still smelled like butter and spilled Pepsi no matter how much you scrubbed it. The lobby was dim.

It was just the two of us. I was behind the ticket podium emptying those little metal bins of torn ticket halves. Grace was in the upstairs office finishing paperwork. Outside, the parking lot was mostly empty under the orange streetlights, and the night had that humid late-spring heaviness where the air just sticks to your skin.

She finally came out, with her purse tucked under her left arm.

"You want to follow me back to my place for a beer?" she asked.

Just like that. Like she was asking if I wanted to help carry groceries to her car.

I remember trying to keep my face neutral, like I wasn't an eighteen-year-old who suddenly couldn't feel his face.

"Yeah," I said, too casual. "Sure."

We locked up, did the final sweep, and then I followed her out. She drove a small, sensible car and I climbed into my Mustang. Yeah, I finally traded in the Triumph for a beautiful light blue 1979 Mustang coupe. I turned the key, and followed her through town. We passed the same streets I'd driven a hundred times, but that night everything looked a little different somehow.

Her apartment was a small upstairs unit in an older building near downtown. Brick exterior. Creaky stairwell. That faint smell in the hallway of old wood and someone else's cooking. She unlocked the door and let me in, and the second I stepped across the threshold I felt it. This wasn't a friend's basement, or somebody's parents' house, or a teenage bedroom pretending to be a "space." This was an adult's place.

It looked exactly like what I imagined a twenty-eight-year-old woman's apartment would look like. Small but cozy. An actual couch. A low coffee table. Framed prints instead of band posters. A bookshelf with real books. A candle that smelled faintly like vanilla. Dishes drying neatly in a rack by the sink. It had that lived-in feeling that was instantly comfortable.

She handed me a cold Bud Light, sat on the couch, and patted the spot next to her, inviting me to join her. We talked about work, movies, dumb customers, the usual theater complaints. The radio played in the background. And that was the weird part. For a while it felt normal, like this was just two people winding down after a shift. No pressure. Relaxed.

About forty-five minutes in, she got up, disappeared into the kitchen, and came back holding two glasses in one hand and a bottle of Firewater, cinnamon schnapps, by the bottleneck in the other.

She twisted off the cap and gave me this little smile that felt like a question and an answer at the same time.

"Ever had this?" she asked.

I shook my head, and she poured shots into mismatched glasses like she'd done it a hundred times. The first one burned. The second one burned less. A few in, and that space, the one we'd been carefully keeping for over eighteen months, started to shrink without either of us saying a word.

There must have been more than just cinnamon in that bottle because I somehow mustered up the courage to make a move. I leaned in, half expecting her to pull back at the last second and crack a joke to reset everything. She didn't. She slowly leaned toward me.

Her kiss was soft but confident. Not tentative. Not confused. More like she'd made up her mind hours ago and was only now letting me in on it. She tasted like cinnamon, beer, and Marlboro Lights, and I could smell that same perfume she always wore at the theater. Her skin felt cool and smooth under my hands in a way that made my brain glitch for a second, like I couldn't comprehend how familiar she'd been for so long with how suddenly intimate she was now.

She stood up slowly, still kissing me, fingers curling around mine as she guided me down the short hallway toward her bedroom. The lamp in there cast a warm, low light over everything. Bed slightly unmade. Clothes in a basket on the floor. Real life scattered around. And my heart was pounding.

We slept together that night.

And I don't say that like it was some wild teenage conquest, because it didn't feel like that at all. It wasn't clumsy first-time fumbling, and it wasn't a drunken free-for-all either. It felt different. Calmer. Almost strangely grounded.

Grace was confident and experienced. She moved like she knew what she wanted, and I followed, trying to keep up, trying to stay present, trying not to think too hard about what any of it meant once the buzz wore off and the sun came up.

I was eighteen. She was twenty-eight. Those numbers mattered, even then, even if I tried to act like they didn't. We knew what it looked like. We knew what people would say if they ever got the full story. But what I felt wasn't just lust. It was something better: being chosen.

Not tolerated. Not humored. Not "cute for a kid." Chosen. I wasn't just a warm body filling time.

After that, it turned into a rhythm. We closed together more often than not. Late-night theater cleanup slid into early-morning drives home with the sky just starting to lighten, the world quiet in that exhausted, silent way it gets before sunrise.

Sometimes we'd watch TV and half doze on her couch. Sometimes we'd talk. Her family. My band. Her past. My future. Everything tangled together like we were trying to pretend the gap between our lives wasn't there.

And it wasn't just sex. There were jokes that felt easy. Comfortable silences that didn't need filling. Small arguments that were stupid and domestic, like we were playing at adulthood and bumping into real feelings. It had this strange mix of impulse and routine. We were both hooked on the secrecy, but also strangely comforted by the consistency.

With her, I felt seen. Respected. Wanted. I'm not proud of how much I needed that, but I'm not going to lie about it either. At eighteen, I was still a mess in a lot of ways. Still trying to figure out what kind of man I was supposed to be. Still dragging around old insecurities.

Being with Grace didn't fix any of that, but it quieted it for a while. It gave me this temporary, addictive sense of worth.

That's why I'll never forget her.

Not because she was older. Not because of whatever scandal the outside world would sketch if they lined up our ages and job titles and shook their heads. I remember her because of who I was when I was with her. A mess, absolutely, but a mess who, for once, didn't feel like he was begging to be loved. I felt like I belonged in the room.

That stretch of time, graduation, the band, the late shows at the theater, those nights at Grace's apartment, was messy. It sits in my memory like a blur: streetlights, drumsticks, movie tickets, her red hair on my chest, cinnamon schnapps.

But it's strange how a blur can still be crystal clear when you close your eyes.

Meanwhile, Belle kept drifting further into a life I didn't recognize, and I was stuck watching her slide farther away.

She started dating Axel.

Axel was someone I'd known since grade school. At one point he wasn't "Axel the problem." He was just Axel. Recess buddy. I tried to keep the memory of the harmless grade school version, but somewhere along the way he veered into a different lane, and by senior year it was obvious he'd built a whole identity out of being unpredictable.

And now Belle was with him.

I remember hearing it and just blinking, like my brain couldn't make the words fit together. Belle and Axel. My Georgia Peach with a guy whose whole vibe was tattoos and guns. It didn't make sense. Not because Belle was perfect, none of us were, but because she had always felt soft. Like her default setting was warmth. Like she carried this gentleness that made the world feel less callous, and I'd built a whole part of myself around believing that meant something.

Then came the tattoos.

Not the kind people get when they're eighteen and bored. Tiny hearts. Little symbols. Something you laugh about later. These were heavy, dark, prison-style tattoos.

One of them was an Uzi on her leg. An actual gun. Inked into the same body I used to curl up with in the Peach Room. The same girl whose hands used to smell like Cucumber Melon lotion from Bath & Body Works. I know how that sounds, like I'm worshipping the old version of her, but that's honestly how it hit me. The contrast wasn't subtle. It was a punch to the throat.

And I was left standing there holding memories of a person who doesn't exist anymore.

Then came the news.

On the night of July 7th, 1993, Axel was outside a house party with a cigarette hanging off his lips like always. Newport, soft pack.

Another guy came outside for a smoke and asked Axel for one.

Axel said no.

The guy thought he was joking, because who says no to a cigarette at a party? He reached into Axel's shirt pocket to grab one anyway, probably thinking it was nothing. Just messing around.

Axel shoved him back, pulled out a .22 pistol, and when the guy turned to run, Axel shot him twice in the back.

Twice. In the back.

Then he walked up and fired a third shot while the guy was crawling on the sidewalk.

That last shot killed him.

I don't have a softer way to say it, and I don't want one. It was three bullets and one stupid decision, and a kid at a party didn't get to go home. No do-over. No "I didn't mean it." No rewind. A life ended over a cigarette. Over ego and impulse and whatever was already broken in Axel long before anyone stepped onto that sidewalk.

When I heard about it, it didn't feel real. It sounded like something that happens in other towns to other people. People you don't know. People whose names you don't recognize from childhood. Not a guy I'd known since grade school. Not outside the kind of party I could've ended up at on a different night if my life had tilted one degree. The closeness of it was the worst part.

Axel was arrested and eventually sentenced to 25 years to life.

Twenty-five years to life for a Newport, a snap decision, and a chain of choices that probably started years earlier.

That should've been the end of the story for me. A clean break. Someone I used to know did something unforgivable, and the world moved on without him.

But it wasn't that simple.

He made bond before the trial, and while he waited to find out what the rest of his life was going to look like, he was still out. Still around. Still walking the same streets like he didn't steal someone's son from them.

And I reached out.

Even writing that makes me sick, because I still don't have a clear explanation. Maybe I wanted closure in the dumbest place possible. Maybe it was morbid curiosity, this need to look him in the face and confirm he used to be a person. Maybe my brain couldn't separate "Axel from grade school" from "Axel who killed someone," and it kept trying to stitch those versions together like understanding it would make it less disgusting.

Or maybe, if I'm being honest, I thought touching the edge of that world might pull Belle back into view. Like if I got close enough, I'd find the version of her I remembered still in there somewhere.

I don't know. I just know I did it. And I know I can still feel the weight of it now: the confusion, the shame, the weird loyalty to memories that didn't deserve loyalty anymore, and the sick truth that sometimes the people you lose don't disappear. They just change shape until you're staring at them and you can't even recognize what you're seeing.

Axel mentioned a party out on Route 150 on the way to Mahomet, about two miles from my old childhood home. He told me to meet him at the Farm & Fleet parking lot in Urbana and we'd ride over together like it was just another Friday night plan. Casual. Normal. Like we weren't dragging a lit match toward gasoline.

So I pulled into the lot in my Mustang, and Axel rolled in next to me in his mom's teal Mazda MX-3.

Belle was in the passenger seat.

Seeing her sitting there beside him felt wrong in a way I still can't fully explain. It wasn't jealousy in the simple teenage sense. It was more like my brain rejected the picture. Two pieces that didn't belong together jammed into the same frame.

I gave her the guy nod, this weak little "hey," and then I climbed into the backseat like this was totally fine and I wasn't swallowing broken glass.

I don't remember the ride. At all. It's just gone, like my brain took one look at that stretch of time and deleted it.

We pulled up a long gravel driveway to a white farmhouse. Cars lined both sides, headlights off, just silhouettes under the dark sky. Bass thumped from somewhere deep inside the house, that low vibration you feel in your chest before you even open the door. The party was already in full swing. The air heavy with cigarette smoke, stale beer, and sweat.

So I did what I'd been doing all year.

I started drinking.

And I didn't stop.

After that, everything gets sloppy. Walking became a project. Talking became optional. I floated from room to room with a beer in my hand and my emotions spilling out of me. I told anyone who'd stand still long enough how much I still loved Belle. People I didn't even know. I told them that when Axel went to prison, I'd be there for her. That we'd pick up where we left off. That she and I weren't done.

I'm pretty sure I told her that to her face more than once that night.

At some point Axel got into an argument with another guy, a cocktail of alcohol, ego, anger, and something unhinged simmering under his skin. It escalated fast. He reached up over the fireplace, grabbed a decorative sword off the wall, and started waving it at some poor drunk kid like he was about to take his head off in the living room.

The guy who owned the house rushed in, grabbed the sword, ripped it out of Axel's hands, and dragged him outside to cool off.

You'd think that would've been the peak of the night.

It wasn't.

Maybe twenty minutes later, maybe less, maybe more, time was already smearing, someone told Axel what I'd been saying about Belle. I didn't hear it. I didn't see who said it or how.

Axel flipped.

Not a slow build. Not an argument. Not the usual drunk posturing where guys puff up and talk loud first. It was immediate.

I was in the living room, half-slumped on this little footstool that wasn't meant to hold a full human being, let alone one drinking like he was trying to erase himself. My eyes were glazed, unfocused, locked on the demo screen of a Sega game someone had running on the TV. Pixelated characters looping the same motion over and over, bright colors, repetitive music, the same fake fight restarting every thirty seconds.

That's where I was mentally too. Stuck. Looping.

I remember thinking, drunk and detached, *This is so stupid. Look at me. Look at what my life is.* But even that thought felt far away, like it belonged to somebody watching from the ceiling.

The room itself was a blur of bodies and noise. Beer breath. Cigarette smoke. Bass still thumping somewhere deeper in the house. People laughing too loud. Somebody arguing in the kitchen. That party energy that feels fun right up until it turns.

I didn't even see Axel coming. I don't remember footsteps. I don't remember anyone warning me. If someone noticed him moving across the room with that look in his eyes, they froze or decided it wasn't their problem.

The first thing I remember clearly is the feeling of someone right behind me. Not something you sense and turn toward. More like your body knew but there wasn't enough time for it to react.

He grabbed me hard, not by the shoulder like "hey, man," but like he was yanking something out of the ground. He ripped me off the stool so fast that I didn't even get a chance to react. One second I was staring at the Sega screen, the next I was on my back on the floor.

I hit hard. Hard enough that it punched the air out of me in one ugly rush, that involuntary sound you make when your lungs try to inhale and they can't.

It wasn't pain at first. It was shock. Confusion.

What the fuck?

Before I could get a full thought to the front of my mind, he stomped on my chest.

A stomp. Full weight. A deliberate, violent drop like he was trying to crush the life out of me.

And whatever was left in me, breath, fight, sense, just disappeared.

Everything went black.

It's strange how quick it is when you lose consciousness. No slow fade like the movies. More like someone unplugged you. One second you're there, the next you're gone.

What I found out later is that it didn't stop there. While I was out, he kicked me in the side of the head several times with his black combat boots. That detail sticks because it means there was time. More than one chance to stop. More than one chance for someone else to step in faster. More than one moment where the night could've taken a different turn, and it didn't.

Someone finally tackled him into the couch. I picture it now like a shaky home video. Bodies crashing, people yelling, furniture scraping, that Sega demo still chirping in the background.

And that contrast still makes me sick. The fact that in the same room where someone could've died, a stupid little loop of pixelated characters kept restarting like the world was harmless.

That's what messes with me. Not just the violence. Not just the humiliation. The randomness. The casualness. The way it could've ended my life in a farmhouse living room, with strangers around me and a video game demo acting like a soundtrack.

That's how close it was. That's what's hard to live with: not only that it happened, but that it could've ended everything, and nobody in that room, including me, treated it like the life-or-death moment it actually was.

When I came to, I didn't come back all at once. My body powered on before my brain did. The room was loud but muffled at the same time, like cotton stuffed inside my ears. The ceiling lights seemed too bright, then too dim. I had that sour, metallic taste in my mouth like I'd bitten my tongue.

And I had no clue what had actually happened.

That blank space still pisses me off. Not even at Axel, not at the party, not at the idiots who let it happen. I'm mad at the missing footage. I woke up into confusion. Into noise. Into adrenaline with no context.

I stumbled to my feet on instinct alone, swaying like I was on a boat. People were looking at me like I'd crawled out of a wreck. Someone said my name, maybe once, maybe twice, but I barely noticed. All I knew was I felt humiliated, threatened, and exposed.

So I did what drunk eighteen-year-olds do when their pride is bleeding.

I got loud.

I started shouting. Demanding to know what the hell his problem was. Calling him out like this was just some stupid fight between guys who'd be fine tomorrow. Like we'd laugh about it later.

What I didn't know, because I hadn't seen it, was that the tread from his boot was literally imprinted on my chest. I didn't know I had a concussion. I didn't know the way my thoughts were lagging behind my eyes wasn't just drunken fog. I didn't know the dizziness and confusion and that constant sideways feeling were side effects.

And I didn't know how close I'd come to having the same word attached to me that he'd already attached to someone else.

Victim.

That word wasn't in my head yet in any serious way. Victim was for crime shows and courtrooms and newspaper headlines. It wasn't supposed to belong to me. I was still living in that young-man fantasy where you're invincible… until you're not.

Eventually the hysteria burned out the way it always does when there's nothing left to feed it. Voices dropped. The energy in the house shifted from chaos to this low, ugly simmer. People avoided eye contact. They acted like it was over. Like he hadn't crossed a line that couldn't be uncrossed. Somebody finally said what everyone else was thinking but didn't want to be responsible for: "Get him out of here."

It should've been, "Call an ambulance." Or, "Call the cops." Or, "Get Belle away from him." Or, "Don't let that man drive."

But it wasn't.

It was just, *get him out.*

And somehow, because life has a sick sense of humor, Axel ended up driving me back to Urbana to pick my car up at Farm & Fleet. The same guy who had just stomped his boot on my chest and his rage in my skull was suddenly behind the wheel like we were buddies leaving together after a bar fight.

The ride was a blur of headlights and silence. Every bump in the road sent a fresh pulse of pain through my ribs. My chest ached every time I tried to pull in a full breath. I kept swallowing, trying to keep the nausea down, trying to keep my vision steady, trying to piece together what had happened.

But if I pieced together the worst version of what could have happened, the one where nobody tackles him, the one where he kicks a little harder, or my head hits the wrong angle, where I don't wake up, then I'd have to face how thin the line actually was. How easily that night could've ended with sirens and a sheet and my mom getting a phone call that would've split her life in half.

So I stared out the window instead and played tough. Played numb. Played anything but scared.

When we pulled into Farm & Fleet, the parking lot was isolated and vacant. Quiet like a church after everyone leaves. Belle opened the door, pulled her seat forward, and I struggled to climb out. I stood there for a second, bent slightly at the waist, trying to get my body fully upright.

But before I shut the door, I looked directly at Belle.

Just for a second.

She was still in the passenger seat, still close enough to touch, but she felt a thousand miles away. Our eyes met, and everything we'd been busted open in that tiny space between us. Every laugh. Every fight. Every almost. Every never-again. No words. Just one last raw look, like we were both holding our breath over a grave we didn't want to admit was ours.

I know what my eyes said. I know because I can still feel it.

I still love you.
I always will.

Axel, a kid I'd once shared classrooms and playgrounds with, had killed someone over a cigarette. And now he was the one with Belle. Belle. The same girl I used to hold in the Peach Room. The girl who left her car for me when mine was dead. The girl who trusted me with her first time and almost had a baby with me. Now she was riding shotgun next to a guy who was going to spend a big chunk of his life behind bars, and she looked committed to that path in a way I couldn't fix with love or memories or loyalty.

That's when it started to really sink in: the version of me that used to make her feel safe wasn't even on her radar anymore. She wasn't holding onto "us." I was clinging to a memory she'd already buried and walked away from, and I kept calling it devotion because admitting it was desperation would've killed me.

I had to drop the fantasy that loyalty and stubbornness could resurrect what we'd had. That if I just held on long enough, she'd come back. That my persistence was love, not fear.

Because that's what it was.

Fear of change. Fear of being alone. Fear of admitting something beautiful had turned toxic and it was all my fault. Fear of accepting that sometimes people don't just drift away from you. They also drift away from themselves, and you can't love them back into who they used to be.

I started seeing the difference between holding on out of love and holding on because you can't handle the ending. Holding on because you want a rewrite. Holding on because letting go means admitting the story you were living in is over.

I learned something else too: you don't always get the conversation you want. There's no big speech where the person explains themselves and everything falls into place. No confession moment where the puzzle clicks together and you walk away healed.

Sometimes closure is just you stopping. You stop chasing. You stop decoding. You stop trying to make sense of someone else's fall and you turn your attention back to your own life and all of the parts you've been neglecting.

Sometimes it's as small as getting out of the car, shutting the door, and admitting the life you were fighting for isn't coming back, at least not in the form you remember.

I stopped asking what broke her. I stopped trying to read her choices like they were a message meant for me.

Sometimes the bravest thing you'll ever do is walk away from a fire when the person you love is still standing in it.

You don't prove devotion by burning with them.
You prove it by surviving.
And somehow… I did.

I drove home in silence.

No music. No radio. Not even that mindless scan through stations people do just to feel less alone. I kept both hands locked on the wheel like the steering column was the only thing tethering me to reality. Headlights. Asphalt. The faint moan of the tires. That was it. Everything else sat behind a thick wall in my brain. I kept repeating: *stay between the lines, don't drift, don't close your eyes.*

By that time, our campus apartment sublet lease had expired, and I was back where I swore I wouldn't be, living in my parents' house. By the time I pulled into their driveway, I was running on fumes.

I don't remember deciding to sleep. I remember the room spinning, my stomach churning, and then the drop into nothing.

Later, I'd find out I had a concussion.

At the time, I didn't think in terms like "lucky" or "close call." I thought: hide it, sleep it off, don't make it a thing. That was my specialty back then, turning trauma into inconvenience. I didn't end up going to the doctor because I was responsible or self-aware. I went because of Kelsey.

Kelsey was the girl I'd started seeing a month or two after Belle and I broke up. She was stunning. Big blue eyes. Long brown hair. This soft, slow way of kissing that made the rest of the world go silent. More importantly, she was kind. She didn't play games. She listened. She had this steady warmth that should've been comforting.

And it was.

The problem was, I wasn't available for it.

Because even when I was sitting across from Kelsey, smiling, making plans, pretending I was moving forward, my heart was still somewhere else. Still stuck in the Peach Room. Still stuck on Belle.

The next morning, Kelsey called, and I tried to talk like everything was normal. I tried to turn it into a story, like something crazy that happened at a party, like I could laugh it off and she'd laugh too and we'd move on. But the words came out wrong. My voice sounded thin. I kept losing my place mid-sentence. I'd start a thought and then stop because I couldn't remember what I was saying. My chest hurt every time I took a full breath. My head felt like it was full of wet cement.

So I told her. Not like a story with a beginning and end. Just the ugly facts in a jumbled mess. Axel. The party. The stomp to my chest. The boots to my head. The blackout. Waking up disoriented and furious, not even sure what happened until the pain started talking louder than my ego.

I told her my head was pounding, my chest hurt, I felt sick, and something felt off.

She didn't hesitate.

"Go to the doctor," she said. "Please."

So I did.

I wrestled myself out of bed enough to take a quick shower and get the stale funk of cigarette smoke and beer out of my hair and got dressed. Kelsey came by to pick me up and drove me straight to urgent care.

Sitting in that doctors office, I remember answering questions and realizing halfway through that I didn't trust my own timeline. Like my memory had holes and I was trying to patch them with guesses.

The doctor confirmed it: mild concussion, no internal bleeding, no broken ribs. It could've been worse. A lot worse.

Then I thought of Kelsey still sitting out in the waiting room.

Kelsey deserved a version of me that was actually there. A boyfriend who wasn't half-present, with the other half still living inside a relationship that had already died, still stumbling through late nights and irresponsible choices. She deserved someone who could accept love without turning it into a weakness. Someone who could love her back in the same way she was loving me.

I couldn't do that. Not yet.

The truth is, it took me years to fully let go of Belle. I held on way longer than I should have. Not even to the real person anymore, mostly to memory, mostly to longing, mostly to the story I kept on replay. I was holding onto what she used to represent to me.

Your first real love doesn't pack its bags and just slip out the back door quietly. It lingers. It keeps showing up in dumb places. Songs on the radio. A random smell. A phrase. You'll be fine for weeks and then one detail hits and you're right back there, emotionally, like an idiot who can't stop time-traveling.

It breaks your heart twice: once when you lose them, and again when you finally admit to yourself that they're not coming back.

But being alone has never felt neutral to me.

It has never been "me time" or "space to grow" or any of those polished phrases people toss around now like solitude is a luxury item. For me, being alone always felt like punishment. Like I'd done something wrong and the world had quietly decided I wasn't invited.

Alone was middle school. Alone was walking those halls and feeling like furniture, present but not part of anything. Not a friend. Not a boyfriend. Not even someone people remembered to mention when they were recapping their day. I was just background.

And when you're that young, you don't have the tools to challenge the story your brain starts writing. You just absorb it. Being alone whispered lies and I swallowed every one of them: *you're unlovable, you're forgettable, you don't matter.*

So when attention from girls finally showed up, I clung to it like it was oxygen. Any attention. A flirt in the hallway. A smile that lasted a beat too long. A kiss. An invite to hang out. Suddenly I wasn't invisible anymore. I was wanted. I was seen. And that feeling hit me harder than it should have, because it wasn't just excitement. It was confirmation. *Thank God, I exist to somebody.*

That's how Kelsey and I started.

She was a junior and I was a senior, weeks from graduation. We started talking the way teenagers do: little conversations that kept stretching longer, little excuses to be in the same place at the same time. We circled each other in that awkward, hopeful way, acting casual.

Eventually we started sleeping together. Clumsy, nervous, wide-eyed teenage sex. Nothing romantic though, really. Just two kids trying to figure it out.

But if I'm being honest, that relationship wasn't about deep connection for me.

It was about not being alone.

I told myself I was grieving Belle, like that gave me a free pass. Like heartbreak excused using someone else as emotional padding between me and my pain. But that wasn't all of it. I wasn't only mourning a breakup. I was grieving a whole version of my life that evaporated. The version where I felt chosen, where I had a "home base," where I wasn't constantly looking for signs that I was about to be left again.

Underneath all of that, there was this even uglier truth that I didn't know how to be okay with myself. I didn't know how to sit alone in a room without feeling like I was disappearing all over again. Silence didn't feel peaceful. It felt like confirmation I wasn't worth anyone's attention.

So I filled it with people. And when people weren't enough, I filled it with alcohol. Not because I was a hardcore drinker, but because it worked fast and made my shame feel less intense.

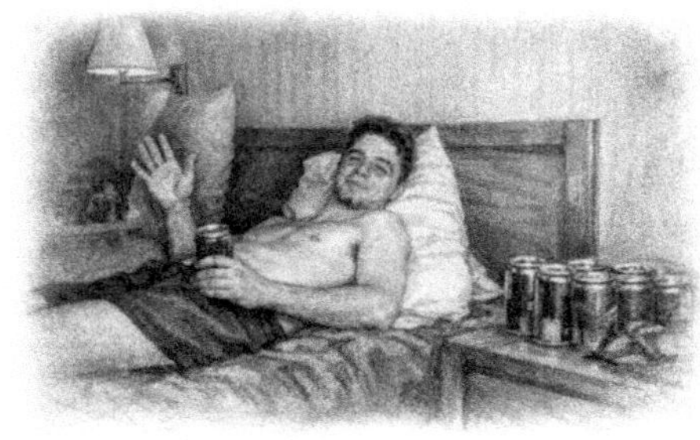

When you don't heal from the past, you don't leave it behind. You haul it into every new relationship like luggage you refuse to unpack. You think it's just "memories," but it's sharp, and sooner or later somebody reaches in and gets cut.

Kelsey never really had a chance.

I couldn't give her what she deserved because I was still tied to a memory. Playing boyfriend while emotionally clinging to someone who had already walked away. I wasn't whole. I wasn't even close. I was there physically, but mentally I was split into pieces. Part of me chasing comfort. Part of me stuck in the past. Part of me numb. Part of me angry. Part of me terrified that if I stopped moving for even a second, loneliness would catch up and swallow me whole.

Now, with years between me and that summer, I can see how backwards I had it. I needed time alone more than I needed anything, or anyone, else. I needed to learn that being alone doesn't automatically mean being abandoned. It doesn't mean you're unworthy or forgotten. Sometimes it just means you finally have enough space to hear yourself.

Because the person you are when nobody's there to clap for you, or text you back, or crawl into bed with you, that's the person you either avoid for years or you finally face.

If I could pull my eighteen-year-old self aside and look him in those bright, clueless blue eyes, I'd tell him this: *stop running from the quiet.*

Not because it's easy. Not because it feels good. Because the quiet is where the truth shows up. That's where you learn the difference between *wanting* love and *needing* it.

You don't need a relationship to prove you're worthy.
You need to be able to look in the mirror and not turn away.

But I didn't know any of that then.

Back then, life felt like it had my head underwater, and all I knew how to do was thrash and grab whoever was closest.

When I wasn't thinking about Belle, or replaying that farmhouse and the fight, or getting drunk enough to shut my brain off, there were really only two other constants in my life that summer: the movie theater and Grace.

The theater was the one place where everything made sense. Show up, clock in, sweep popcorn out of aisles, tear tickets, wipe down counters. Nobody asked how you were doing in any real way. You could hide behind a name tag, a bow tie, and a fake smile.

And then there was Grace, this secret life running parallel to everything else. A second version of me that only existed in dim hallways and after-hours silence.

We were still seeing each other, still wrapped up in that little whirlwind that felt private and dangerous and addictive. It wasn't just the sex, although that was incredible. It was the feeling of being pulled into someone's adult world when I still didn't feel like I belonged in my own skin half the time. It gave me something to focus on that wasn't Belle, wasn't the wreckage, wasn't the guilt.

Every once in a while, in between the bad decisions and the heavy thoughts, there were nights that still stand out. One of those nights started like most of them did: me, Grace, a couch, and way too much Firewater.

The difference this time was Adam came with me.

Adam had met Grace a handful of times already. He worked across the parking lot at the mall in a shoe store, so he'd pop into the theater sometimes with no real reason, just "I was in the area," which was his way of saying, *I'm checking on you without making it weird.* Grace liked him. She thought he was easygoing and funny, and she'd talked to him enough at work that it didn't feel strange to have him around. I had told her the story of the car wreck and how he saved my life, so she knew Adam and I were tight.

By then, Adam had heard all of the stories about Grace, probably in more detail than any best friend ever needs, but he wasn't trying to wedge himself into anything. He wasn't that guy. He was just curious. This older woman I couldn't stop talking about, the one with the red hair and that unbothered energy. Of course he wanted to see what she was like outside the theater lights and the little work conversations.

It really did feel like just three friends unwinding after work. Back at her place, we threw on whatever was on TV, half watched it, half talked over it. Adam was perched on the couch like he always was, comfortable in any room, like he could make himself at home in a dentist office if you gave him five minutes. Grace had that calm, older confidence I'd gotten used to but still didn't fully understand. And I was still basically a kid wearing a grown-up's confidence like a borrowed jacket.

We cracked open beers, the normal stuff. Then came the Firewater. That cinnamon burn had basically become part of the ritual, like the night didn't officially start until your throat hated you a little.

Between the three of us, we knocked back almost two bottles. Not "a few shots." Not "a little buzz." Full-on reckless drinking. The buzz hit fast and heavy with that warm floaty feeling where everything is funny and you start believing you're charming instead of shit-faced drunk.

Eventually, like someone offstage whispered the cue, Grace reached for my hand and led me down the short hallway to her bedroom. That had become our routine. Once the words began to slur, she'd take my hand and lead me to her bedroom. Adam stayed out in the living room, completely unbothered. It felt oddly casual.

Grace was completely naked and already under the covers before I even got my shoes off.

As I peeled off my shirt and started stumbling toward the bed, my stomach dropped. Hard. That unmistakable surge rolled through me.

I bolted.

I flew back down the hall past Adam with my hand clamped over my mouth like that was going to stop the apocalypse, and I barely made it to the bathroom. I hit my knees in front of the toilet and emptied my Firewater-flavored soul into porcelain. It burned coming up just as bad as it had going down, forcing me to recall every dumb choice I'd made in the last hour.

But the relief afterward was instant. That sick pressure vanished. I sat there for a second, breathing like I'd run a mile, then stood up and splashed cold water on my face. I rinsed my mouth, stared at myself in the mirror, and there I was: a drunk, red-eyed kid trying so hard to be grown that he didn't even notice how young he looked.

On my way back through the living room, I saw a half-empty beer on the coffee table. Without a single mature brain cell firing, I grabbed it, took a swig, swished it around like mouthwash, swallowed, and kept walking.

When I got back to the bedroom, Grace was still there, propped up on one elbow, watching the doorway with this half-amused, half "you-absolute-idiot" smile. Not angry. Not disgusted. Just entertained.

And just like that, the night kept going.

Looking back, it's such a small, stupid story, but it still makes me smile. Not because it was glamorous, and definitely not because it was healthy. It makes me smile because for a few hours, the world wasn't the farmhouse. It wasn't Belle. It wasn't shame and regret and that loop in my head. It was just me and Adam and Grace in a tiny apartment. Bad liquor. Loud laughter. That weird feeling you only get when you're young enough to think you're indestructible and old enough to start learning you're not.

It was messy. It was reckless. But it was real.

Maybe that's why it stayed locked into my memory. Even in the most brutal season of my life, there were still little pockets where I could breathe. Where I could forget who I was becoming for a second and just be a kid pretending he had a handle on anything.

But if there's one story from that time that still cracks me up every time it wanders through my brain, it's what I've come to call "The Rocky Horror Night."

There was this tiny indie theater downtown, single screen, old-school marquee out front with missing letters, the kind of place that looked like it had been open since the invention of popcorn. The air inside had a permanent smell of butter, dust, and old upholstery. The carpet was sticky. The seats creaked. Honestly, the place already felt like a time warp before The Rocky Horror Picture Show ever started.

Shane, one of my co-workers from Market Place Cinemas, pulled us into it. He was a U of I student and a full-on theater kid in the best and most exhausting way: loud, high-energy, always doing impressions in the lobby while the rest of us tried to look like responsible employees. He told us he and his friends were doing a live performance of Rocky Horror while the movie played behind them.

I nodded like I understood.

I did not.

Grace and I weren't exactly counting down the days to a midnight showing of anything, but we liked Shane, and it felt like the right thing to do. Show up. Support him. Be those "cool" work friends who actually follow through. Plus, it was something that wasn't a house party or a bar or me alone with my thoughts.

Grace suggested a pre-show "warm-up," which, translated out of Grace-speak, meant shots of Firewater at her apartment and a couple of beers tucked into her purse for later. We sat at her little kitchen table, the cinnamon burning its way down, laughing and just genuinely enjoying each others company. I remember thinking, *This is what adulthood is? Getting tipsy in a kitchen drinking something that tastes like a spicy candle before heading out to watch a movie?*

By the time we got to the theater, I had a good buzz going. Warm. Loose. That sweet spot where you feel like you could talk to anyone and nothing embarrassing could ever happen, which is always the last thought you have before something embarrassing absolutely happens. It was a cool night too, the kind where the air nips your nose but you can get away with just a jacket. We bought our tickets, shuffled into the auditorium, and of course chose the front row, dead center, so Shane could see that we showed up for him.

That's when I understood we were not among our people.

The place was packed with people who clearly knew what they were doing. Fishnets. Corsets. Eyeliner. Props in bags like they were heading to a sporting event. We showed up dressed like normal humans to an event that apparently required wardrobe, make-up, and props.

The movie started and the crowd was already wired. It wasn't even like watching a film. It was like being dropped into a cheerful, organized riot. Props started flying. Rice. Toast. Cards. People yelling callbacks I didn't understand like they'd rehearsed them in the car. Every other line got interrupted by a shout or a perfectly timed insult. Absolute, coordinated chaos.

And I loved it.

Maybe it was the buzz. Maybe it was the energy in that room. Maybe it was just that my brain wasn't dragging me back to Belle for once. Whatever it was, I remember sitting there thinking, *This is what it feels like to be part of something.* Even if I didn't know the rules, I could feel the excitement. Like everyone in that place had agreed to let go for a while and just be ridiculous together.

Then came the moment.

On screen, Rocky is having a steamy scene with Janet. On stage, the actress playing Janet scanned the front row, and for some reason she locked onto me.

Not a glance. Not a quick "random audience member." She chose me with her whole face.

Before I could even process it, she decided I was going to be her Rocky.

She stepped right up to the edge of the makeshift stage in her bra and panties, reached down, and took my hand like this was a normal thing to do to a stranger. I turned my head toward Grace like, *Are you seeing this?* and she just giggled, uncontrollably, and slouched down in her seat in embarrassment.

And maybe it was the Firewater. Maybe it was the little performer part of me, because even back then a piece of me liked that attention. Or maybe it was my ongoing lack of self-preservation. But whatever fear I might've had evaporated. One second I was sitting next to Grace with a smuggled beer. The next I was being yanked up onto the stage.

Oh, and apparently, this performance had a dress code.

Because suddenly hands were on me, quick and confident and casual, and I realized they weren't just pulling me up. They were undressing me.

Next thing I knew, I was standing under those stage lights in nothing but my boxers and socks. My clothes were in a pile near a speaker off to the side of the stage. The floor was freezing against my feet. That detail is burned in my brain because it was the one thing that made me go, *Okay. This is real.*

The crowd lost their minds.

Cheering, whistling, clapping like I'd just won an award for "Most Likely to Regret This." My heart was pounding and my ears rang from the noise. I looked out and everything was a blur of faces and laughter. In the front row, Grace was absolutely embarrassed, and selfishly excited, because I had been targeted and she got front-row seats.

Then, in perfect Rocky Horror fashion, Janet took my hands and placed them on her breasts.

"Toucha, toucha, toucha, touch me…"

She grinned like she knew how I'd react.

And I, eighteen-year-old, buzzed, half-naked, trying not to die on the spot, gave the world's most respectful, barely-there squeeze. Not even a squeeze. More like a cautious confirmation that yes, those were breasts and yes, my hands were on them and also yes, I would like to remain alive.

The theater exploded.

It felt like the walls shook. People howled. Somebody wolf-whistled so loud it sounded like a car alarm. The stage lights felt hot and my face felt like it was on fire. And at the same time, there was this stupid, electric feeling in my chest: *Oh my God. Best night ever!*

Three minutes later the scene ended, the crowd roared, and I scrambled back into my clothes and dropped back into my seat. My heart was still racing. I couldn't decide if I wanted to laugh, cry, or melt into the sticky carpet forever.

Grace was laughing so hard she had tears running down her face. Mascara smudged just enough to prove she wasn't faking it. She looked at me like she didn't know whether to be proud of me or worried about me, but either way it was hilarious.

Even now, if Rocky Horror pops up somewhere, or if I catch that smell of old theater carpet and stale popcorn, I can still see it. That tiny stage. Those lights. My socks on that cold floor. Grace doubled over in the front row.

That night ended back at her place, because that was our rhythm back then. One more story. One more memory. One more little reminder that even in the messiest season of my life, I could still feel light sometimes.

Not long after, the Grace chapter started winding down.

She met someone else. Someone her age and with more relatable life experiences. Our late-night closings stopped turning into mornings together. The electricity between us dimmed. The line that had been blurred for months slowly became a line again.

We stayed friends. Comfortable. Familiar. But the dynamic shifted. She went back to being my assistant manager who wore the gray GKC suit and ribbon tie, and I went back to being the kid ripping tickets at the podium.

But man… what a run it was.

Looking back, I can see how much that stretch would shape me. It wasn't only the sex or the sneaking around or the stories you could tell at a party and watch people's eyes widen. That stuff happened, sure, but it wasn't the center.

The center was how Grace made me feel at a time when I didn't have a solid relationship with myself yet.

I was eighteen, technically an adult, legally allowed to vote and sign papers and pretend I knew what I was doing, but emotionally I was still half a kid. Fresh out of high school, stuck in that weird limbo where everyone expects you to have a plan and you're just trying to fill your gas tank without over drafting your account. I was standing at the doorway of adulthood with no roadmap and no real confidence, always waiting to be exposed as someone who didn't belong in the "real world" yet.

Then Grace. Twenty-eight. Older in all the ways that mattered back then. Not just age, but the way she moved through rooms like she'd already paid the dues. She had her own place, her routines, this calm competence that made me feel like I'd been living in pencil and she wrote in ink.

The thing is, she didn't treat me like some cute high school kid playing dress-up. She didn't pat me on the head or act like she was doing charity work by paying attention to me. She treated me like I really mattered. Like I really mattered to *her*.

Not because I was smooth. God, I wasn't. I had sarcasm. I had jokes. I had loud ambition that was mostly just dressed up insecurities. But she liked *me*. The *real* me. The version trying to be funny because I didn't know what else to do with my nerves. The version that wanted to be taken seriously so badly it probably leaked out of my pores. She'd look at me like I was already someone worth knowing.

She made me feel like I didn't have to beg for space in the room. I could just take it. For a little while, she helped me step into a version of myself that stood up straighter and believed his own words for once.

The complicated part is that I also loved how effortless it felt with her compared to people my age. With girls my age, everything felt like a test. A performance. Who texts first, who cares less, who's allowed to want more. With Grace, it wasn't like that. It was direct. Private. A mix of comfort and adrenaline. Reckless, sure, but inside that recklessness there was a softness I didn't know I needed. A look. A hand on my chest. The way she'd say my name.

That's why it stuck. Not because it was "cool." It stuck because it hit the soft part in me. My need to be seen. My need to feel chosen, respected, desired, without having to contort myself into somebody else.

I know now people come into your life for seasons. Grace was a season. A big one. We were never meant to be forever, but we were meant to be something. She helped me grow, even if I didn't understand what was happening while it was happening.

When she moved on, things changed. The friendship that survived wasn't the same friendship we had before, because it couldn't be. Once you cross certain lines with someone, you don't just walk back to the old version like it's still waiting for you. There was a distance. An awkwardness.

But the impact stayed.

That period taught me self-awareness in a way nothing else had. It taught me you can have fun, make bad choices, and still pull something real out of it if you're willing to look at yourself honestly afterward, without rewriting it so you're either the hero or the victim. It taught me confidence doesn't always look like the loudest guy in the room. Sometimes it's quiet. It's presence. It's a calm voice. The way someone holds eye contact with you and doesn't look away first.

Wherever she is now, a part of me will always say it, quietly, without needing anything back:

Thank you, Grace.

That summer, on the nights when my head wasn't spinning around Belle and I wasn't out drinking with Grace, I was with Kelsey.

And I hate how honest this is, but even that felt hollow.

We'd end up in the same handful of places. Somebody's worn-out couch with a fan rattling in the corner. Parked in my car somewhere quiet with the windows cracked just enough to let the warm air in. We'd drink, talk a little, laugh at the right moments like we were following a script. On the outside it probably looked normal. Two kids killing time.

Inside, it wasn't.

It was surface-level. At least it was for me. It wasn't that Kelsey wasn't kind. She was. That's the part that makes it worse.

A lot of those nights were distraction dressed up as connection. Noise so I didn't have to hear what was screaming underneath. We'd talk about music, friends, gossip, whatever movie someone rented, and I'd nod and play along. Meanwhile my mind was somewhere else.

Half of me still chasing Belle, replaying old moments, bargaining with reality like thinking hard enough could undo what already happened.

The other half of me would be replaying and reliving the last night I spent with Grace. How comfortable it was. How relaxed we always were. How calming she was. But also the sexual tension and attraction we had. The way her skin felt so smooth and her lips felt so soft on my neck.

But there I sat with Kelsey, pretending I wasn't doing any of that.

I drank a lot during that time. Not because I was in love with alcohol. I drank because it turned the volume down. It wrapped those deafening thoughts in cotton for a few hours.

I've never thought of myself as having an addictive personality. I like control too much. I like knowing where I am, how I'm coming across, what I'm doing next. But that summer I finally understood how people slide. How it starts as "this helps." A couple drinks to take the edge off, to make the night easier, to make yourself feel less like you're walking around with exposed nerve endings. But then it slowly becomes "I need this to get through the night." You don't always notice exactly when it flips, but one day you're reaching for it like a reflex.

For a while, drinking made things quieter. It helped me fake okay. It helped me act like I wasn't a mess. Like I wasn't waking up with that heavy ache in my chest and spending the rest of the day trying to outrun it.

But I wasn't okay. Not even close.

I was eighteen. Heartbroken. Broke. Drunk more nights than not. Still chasing the echo of a girl who was gone, like an idiot who can't stop yelling into an empty room just to hear something come back.

And standing close to all of that was Kelsey.

She didn't ask to be there. She didn't deserve to be there. She walked into my life while I was still living in the wreckage of another one, and instead of warning her, instead of backing away and doing the decent thing, I let her get close enough to get hurt.

I didn't want to hurt her. I wasn't plotting it. I wasn't some villain. I was just too lost to see how much of my pain I was bleeding onto everyone around me, especially her.

So Kelsey, if you ever somehow read this, know this much: *I'm sorry.*

You offered me something kind and real. You showed up with softness and patience and a willingness to sit with me even when I didn't deserve it. The best I gave back was fragments. Half-presence. A version of me that was physically there but emotionally stuck in another story, still trying to rewrite an ending that wasn't mine to rewrite.

You deserved someone fully there. Someone who could look at you and actually see you, not someone who kept drifting away mid-conversation because his heart was wrapped in razor wire on the couch in a Peach Room.

I wasn't that person.

And it wasn't because you weren't enough. It was because I didn't know how to be enough for myself.

Graduation night and that whole wild stretch of summer after it felt like the universe handed me a Diploma in one hand, cheap beer in the other, and this inflated confidence that I was an adult now. Like surviving high school earned me control.

But control wasn't what was happening.

I was spinning. I acted like I had it together, but underneath I was just trying to stay in front of my own head.

Back then, I confused mayhem with masculinity. I thought drinking until I drowned my feelings made me tough. I thought sleeping around made me a man. I thought bouncing from girl to girl meant I had options, not a wound I refused to bandage. It sounds gross when I say it now, because it was. At the time it felt like validation. Like if someone wanted me, even for a night, then I couldn't be as worthless as that old middle-school voice kept insisting I was.

And that voice was loud that summer.

The shooting. Axel pulling the trigger over a cigarette like life was that empty. Belle choosing him. The farmhouse. The stomp. The kicks. The aftermath. It shook me more than I wanted anyone to know. I walked around with rage under my skin like a fever. Furious at him. Furious at her. Furious at myself. Furious at how stupid love can make you. How it can keep you loyal while you watch someone walk toward a cliff.

I couldn't make peace between the girl I remembered and the girl in front of me. The soft Georgia Peach in my head versus this armored stranger with prison tattoos. It wasn't only that she changed. It was that she changed into someone I didn't recognize, and I didn't know what that said about me for still wanting her. For still missing her.

So I did what I knew.

I drank.

Not cute, social drinking. Not "a couple beers with the guys." I mean drinking like I was trying to erase myself. Drinking until my thoughts slowed down. Drinking until I could laugh without it sounding fake. Drinking until I could sleep without replaying the same scenes.

Then I chased distraction like it was a job. Parties. Noise. Bodies. Any girl willing to make me feel wanted for an hour so I didn't have to sit alone with the broken parts of myself. I used people who deserved better. I used their affection like medicine. I used their attention like a bandage.

And I called it coping.
I called it living.
I called it getting over it.

In hindsight, that whole era was one long lesson in how empty "validation" can be. You can do everything you think is supposed to make you feel powerful and still feel hollow the moment you're alone. Being busy isn't being okay. Being desired isn't being loved. And real love, the kind that doesn't require you to perform, was something I didn't even know how to accept.

Because the truth was, I didn't know who I was. Not under the jokes. Not under the bravado. Not under the stories I told to sound cooler, tougher, less affected. I kept trying to build myself out of other people's approval. Parties, hookups, fake laughter. Attention and affection like bricks I could stack into a personality.

I tried to assemble an identity from the outside in.

It took years to see the real problem wasn't that I didn't know how to be in a relationship.

The problem was I didn't know how to be with myself.

I didn't know how to sit in silence without feeling punished. I didn't know how to feel sadness without panicking. I didn't know how to feel shame without sprinting away from it. I didn't know how to admit, "Yeah, I'm hurt," without trying to prove I wasn't.

Numbing pain doesn't heal it. It just delays it.

You can't outrun your demons if you keep feeding them and calling it a good time.

And you can't build your identity on anything outside of you, because the second it leaves, or changes, or disappoints you, the whole thing collapses and you're right back at zero. Only now you're hungover.

At some point you have to stop running.

You have to sit in the quiet and let it suck. Not for five minutes while you scroll your phone. I mean really sit there. No audience. No distractions. Let the feelings show up like they've been trying to all along.

Let the sadness rise instead of drowning it.
Let the shame speak instead of choking it out.
Let the anger exist without turning it into your whole personality.

Look at the parts of yourself you'd rather hide, the needy parts, the scared parts, the parts that still feel like that kid in the hallway, and stop treating them like an enemy.

Then, slowly, painfully, sometimes beautifully, you learn how to be okay there.

So if you're standing at some crossroads, lost, hurting, grabbing for anything so you don't have to sit with yourself, here's what I'd tell you from the other side of that summer:

Don't be afraid of alone.

Alone is where the real work happens. It's where you stop performing and finally hear your own voice again, not the one you use to impress people, but the one that tells you the truth underneath the noise.

Alone is where you stop auditioning and start being honest.

You're still the author, even when the story takes a hard turn. Even when something knocks the pen out of your hand for a while.

And sometimes the bravest thing you'll ever do isn't chasing after someone who's slipping away.

It's staying.
Right where you are.
With yourself.

And learning, slowly and honestly…

that you are enough.

ROUND 12:
Disqualified by Spine

By August, now living in my parents' house again, I had also enrolled in community college at Parkland College just across town.

Parkland wasn't the "college experience" I'd imagined. No dorms. No new city. Just an organized collection of brick buildings on the west side of Champaign and a bedroom in the basement of the same house I'd grown up in, reoccupied out of financial necessity. I told myself it was the smart move. Responsible. Practical.

But if I'm honest, it felt like swallowing pride by the handful.

Parkland didn't feel like college. It felt like high school with multiple buildings, a bigger campus, and more parking lots. Same town, same weather, same routines, just older versions of the same faces I'd grown up with. Kids I'd sat next to in fourth period. People I'd passed in the hallway for years. The ones who stayed. The ones who didn't have the money or home life that made leaving feel possible.

It wasn't that Parkland was bad. It was that it didn't feel like moving forward. It felt like the world had taken a step and I'd been left standing on the same square.

Still, technically, I was a "college guy" now. I remember saying it out loud for the first time. *I'm in college now.* As if the words alone could upgrade my life. As if there was a switch that flipped the moment you registered for classes and suddenly you're confident and not carrying a bunch of old baggage like it's strapped to your back.

But the truth was, it wasn't confidence. It was survival.

I learned early that if I could be entertaining enough, likable enough, funny enough, maybe people wouldn't look too closely at what was happening underneath.

I chose Public Relations and Advertising as my major. I thought it made sense. I'd always been the kid who talked too much, and I thought Public Relations was just "professional bullshitting," so I figured I'd found my lane. And honestly, yeah, I could sell a story. I could read a room and adjust my personality like a radio dial until I got the reaction I wanted. I was good at that.

Advertising sounded like creativity with a paycheck. A way to be clever and loud and still be considered "successful," because now it would come with a salary and benefits.

But underneath all of the enrollment excitement and fabricated confidence, I was sinking into a depression that had been lurking in the background for years. It didn't just hang around anymore. It took the wheel.

I started feeling restless in this itchy, trapped way, like my own skin was too tight. I was angry at people who hadn't even done anything, and then I'd feel guilty for it, and then I'd get angry at myself for being guilty, and the whole thing just looped.

I was tired of feeling small. Tired of feeling weak. Tired of feeling like I could be erased from a room and nobody would even notice.

And Parkland, this "new chapter," wasn't going to fix that. A major wasn't going to fix that. A new schedule and a student ID and a campus bookstore weren't going to rewrite whatever was wrong inside me. I didn't want a different school. I didn't even really want a different major.

I wanted a different life.

Not the polite version people say when they mean, "I'm ready to grow." I mean the desperate version. The version where you look around at your own existence and feel this panic in your chest because it's starting to look permanent. The version where you realize you're not just unhappy, you're terrified that this is all you're ever going to be. That you're going to keep circling the same streets, seeing the same faces, telling the same jokes, pretending you're fine.

That's what pulled me through the door of the Marine Corps recruiting office. Not some heroic, flag-waving calling. Not a childhood dream of camo and ceremony. I walked in there because I was exhausted.

Exhausted with myself, exhausted with the version of me that felt small and easy to dismiss. I didn't want people to look at me and see "that kid." I wanted them to see me and think, *there goes someone. Someone with weight. Someone with a spine. Someone who couldn't be shoved to the edge of the room like background noise.*

I thought about the Air Force for maybe ten minutes, the same way you think about taking the elevator instead of the stairs. Everyone said it was "easier." Better food, less misery, fewer horror stories. People said it like it was a perk, like comfort was the point. But the second I pictured myself in that uniform, something in me pushed back hard. Not because there's anything wrong with the Air Force. It just wasn't the fix I needed. I could already hear the voice in my own head later, on the nights I couldn't sleep, telling me I'd taken the safe route. That I'd dodged the hard thing again.

I didn't need an easier life. I needed one that meant something.

What I wanted, what I thought I wanted, was a do-over. I didn't consciously think that at the time, but that's what it was. I wanted someone to put me through a process so definitive that it would burn off whatever weakness I believed was baked into me. The Marine Corps, in my mind, wasn't just a branch of the military. It was an identity you earned. A transformation you survived.

So I walked into the recruiting office and told them I wanted in.

They did the whole thing, of course. Posters on the walls with guys in impossible poses, pamphlets spread out like a menu, the rehearsed "few good men" speech that made it sound like you were signing up to take a post at the Pearly Gates. But they didn't have to sell me. They hadn't hunted me down at the mall. They hadn't talked me into it. I showed up already hungry and my mind made up.

When they slid the paperwork across the desk, I didn't hesitate. I signed like I was signing my name on a new life. Like the person I'd been up to that point was already gone.

A few weeks later, they put me on a bus to St. Louis for MEPS, the Military Entrance Processing Station. That place is all lines and clipboards and being shuffled through stations like a factory production line and you're an item moving down a conveyor belt. Bloodwork. Vision tests. Hearing tests. The ASVAB. People barking instructions like we were already property.

I scored high on the ASVAB. Something measurable. Proof that I wasn't dumb, even if my life decisions sometimes made it look like I was. In that moment, it felt like the universe was tossing me a bone. *See? You're not a lost cause.*

Then came the physical.

They had us bend and twist and squat, duck-walking down a strip of tape on the floor like some humiliating audition. The first time, I didn't think anything of it. It was just part of the process. The second time, I felt that little flicker of doubt. The third time, I knew I was getting flagged.

A doctor kept calling me back. More bending. More twisting. More hands pressing along my spine while someone asked, "Does this hurt?" in a voice that didn't really care if it did. And every time I said no, I thought that should be the end of it. No pain. No problem. Right?

Guys around me finished and drifted out in loose groups, pulling their clothes back on, joking to cover their nerves, complaining about the waiting. The room slowly emptied until it was mostly just me, sitting in a cold plastic chair.

I remember looking around and realizing I was alone. This isn't normal.

Finally, a doctor walked in with a clipboard and called my name.

I stood up and walked over, trying to read his face on the way, trying to catch some hint, anything, about what was coming. He gave me nothing. Just a flat, professional expression.

He stared at the paper and asked, without even looking up, "What's this about a history of back problems?"

I almost laughed, because in my head it wasn't "history of back problems." It was a chiropractor. A couple visits. A minor thing at the end senior year. Shoulder pain. They'd told me I had a slight scoliosis in my lower back, the kind of thing a lot of people have and never even know about. A few adjustments, some stretching, end of story. It was a footnote. A technicality. Nothing really.

So I shrugged and said, "Senior year I went to a chiropractor with some shoulder pain. They said I had a slight scoliosis in my lower back. I had them do a few adjustments and was fine. Haven't had any issues since."

I said it like it was reasonable. Like the truth would clear it up.

He still didn't look up.

"I can't OK this with a history of back problems," he said, and I watched him circle something with a red pen like he was marking an answer wrong on a quiz.

Then he yanked the paper off the clipboard and handed it to me like it was no more personal than a receipt.

Two words were circled in red.

Disqualified. Permanently.

For a second I didn't understand what I was looking at. My brain got stuck on the word "permanently." Permanently from what? This branch? The Marines?

And then the rest of it hit. Not just Marines. Not just today. Not just for now. It was all of it. Every branch. Every door. Closed. Forever.

I walked back to the chair in a daze, holding that paper like it weighed fifty pounds. Permanently. Over a slight curve in my spine I couldn't even feel. A shape on an X-ray. A note in a file. A technicality big enough to erase the only plan I'd had that felt like it could save me.

The bus ride back to Champaign felt endless. I sat with my forehead against the glass watching fields smear by. I remember thinking how stupid it was that the world looked so normal. The sky didn't change. People still drove to work and stopped for gas and ate lunch, and I was sitting there trying to swallow the fact that my escape hatch had just vanished.

Not because I quit.
Not because I wasn't smart enough.
Not because I wasn't strong enough.

Because my backbone wasn't straight enough.

Literally.

Once we arrived at the bus station, the recruiter drove me back to the recruiting office, doing his version of damage control, tossing out motivational lines like life preservers.

"Try again in a couple years. They only keep these records for two years. After that, you'll have a clean slate."

Two years?

Those words punched me in the gut. Two years might as well have been a lifetime. I didn't want a theoretical second chance. I wanted this one. I wanted now.

I had walked into that recruiting office with a match in my hand, ready to burn my old life down and start over, and in a fluorescent-lit room in St. Louis, someone had snuffed it out with a red pen.

And the part that hurt the most wasn't even the disqualification. It was what it meant to me in that moment. The story I immediately wrote around it.

See? Even this doesn't want you. Even here, you don't make the cut. Even your "reset button" rejects you.

I had to face it. I had to pivot, not because I wanted to, but because I had to. Because there's only so long you can stand in front of a locked door before you either break your hand pounding on it or you turn around and walk away.

The dream of becoming a Marine died in red ink.

And just like that, I was dropped back into the same life I'd been trying to escape, only now it felt worse, because I'd tasted the idea of a way out. I'd walked right up to the edge of a new identity and had it taken from me with two words circled in red ink.

It felt like a verdict. Like the world had looked at me and stamped a label across my chest.

Not wanted.

I kept going to Parkland.

That part still surprises me when I look back on it, because everything in my life at the time felt like it was either cracking or already shattered. But somehow I kept showing up. I kept driving there, sitting in rooms with people who actually still believed the world made sense.

From the outside, it just looked like I was doing what you're supposed to do when you're "moving forward." In reality, I was just trying not to get swallowed by my own thoughts.

Academically, I did fine when I felt like it. That's the thing about me. I can turn it on. I can cram the night before, memorize enough to look impressive, walk in calm, and do just fine on the test. I can smile when the grade hits, let it buy me a little confidence, and then flip the switch back off and go right back to not giving a shit.

Because I've never really loved the school part of school. The lectures, the assignments, the fake enthusiasm, the way people talk like the syllabus is holy scripture. Most of the time, it all just blended into this steady white noise that my brain learned to tune out. If my body was in the chair, that counted as attendance, right?

The part I've always loved, the part that's actually held my attention, has been watching people. Who sits near the door like they need an escape plan. Who always takes the aisle seat like they don't want to be trapped. Who acts bored but never misses a word. Who laughs too loud, who doesn't laugh at all, who leans into someone when they're talking and who keeps their whole body angled away like they're already halfway gone.

You can learn more from a classroom seating chart than half the textbooks they're charging you for.

I'd take notes just to keep my hands busy, stare at the clock, count ceiling tiles, do that thing where you suddenly realize you have no idea what the last five minutes were about.

But one class stuck. Intro to Psychology. Psych 101.

It felt like a little flashback to seventh grade and Mr. Cabutti, one of the rare teachers who made me want to pay attention instead of just survive the hour. Maybe it was the subject matter, because psychology felt like someone was finally handing me a manual for the parts of life that never came with instructions. Maybe it was because Jonah, one of my old high school buddies, was in the class with me, so it didn't feel like I was alone in this new chapter. Or maybe it was my ego, honestly, because Psych gave my brain a place to play. A place where all that people-watching suddenly felt like it had a name and a reason.

Probably all three.

Jonah and I always sat together, front row, dead center. Not because I was trying to win Teacher's Pet of the Year, but because it was strategy. If I put myself right in front of the professor, I had fewer escape routes. It was harder to drift. Harder to hide.

Of course, sitting in the front row and being physically incapable of not talking made me stand out. I'm not some towering presence. I'm small, animated, talk with my hands, and when I'm interested in something I ask a lot of questions. Professors tend to love that combo.

Before long, he started using me as his interactive prop, calling on me constantly, making me a walking example for half the concepts he taught, like I was a volunteer assistant. He even gave me a nickname. Watson. Not sure why. Maybe all of my curiosity reminded him of Sherlock Holmes.

And then came the day that burned itself into my memory forever.

We were covering the psychology of lying, what it does to your brain, how your body leaks the truth even when your mouth doesn't, the whole performance of it. The professor walked in with this little digital lie detector from Radio Shack. Two wires, a cheap plastic box, and five little lights that ran from green to red.

He asked for a volunteer, but it wasn't really a question. His eyes were already on me.

So I got up and walked to the front with that mix of confidence and dread you only get when you know you're about to be used for "a demonstration." The class leaned forward the way they do when they smell entertainment.

He clipped the cold, plastic sensors onto my fingertips and started with baseline questions.

"Is your name Craig?"

"Yes."

"Are you a student at Parkland?"

"Yes."

The machine hummed quietly, one little green light flickering.

Then I watched him glance over my shoulder toward Jonah.

And Jonah, traitor that he is, met his eyes and flashed this grin that was way too satisfied. The professor's face lit up with that same conspiratorial look, like they were sharing a joke.

And in that split second, I knew. I was about to get set up.

The professor turned back to me, eyes bright with mischief, and asked, loud enough for the back row to hear:

"Did you have sex with your assistant manager at the movie theater?"

The machine screamed.

All five lights slammed into red at once like a slot machine hitting the jackpot, and the little box started shrieking, a high-pitched squeal. It felt like Radio Shack had built this thing specifically to humiliate me in public.

The room exploded.

Laughter ricocheted off the walls. People slapped desks. Someone actually yelled, "OH MY GOD!" Jonah was doubled over, crying laughing, and I'm standing there at the front of the room with my fingers clipped to a plastic truth-tattler, realizing that I'm the punchline.

My face went full nuclear. Not just red. Hot. I could feel the embarrassment climb up my neck and bloom in my cheeks. But I couldn't even be mad. I just shook my head and laughed, because what else was I going to do? Deny it? The machine had already testified under oath.

We eventually moved on with the lesson, polygraphs, body cues, whatever else we were supposed to be learning, but the damage was done. For the rest of the semester, I wasn't just Craig.

I was Watson.

And the funny thing is, I kind of loved it.

Not the embarrassment, exactly. Not the oversharing moment sponsored by Radio Shack. But the fact that for a few minutes, I wasn't invisible. I wasn't background noise. I wasn't the guy quietly holding his life together with duct tape while pretending everything was normal. I was Psych 101 famous.

That moment summed up what I actually liked about school. Not the lectures, not the assignments, but the randomness. The little surprises that pop up out of nowhere and stay with you longer than anything in the textbook.

Psych 101 didn't just teach me about psychology. It reminded me that I could still show up in a room and make something happen, even when my life outside that room felt like a wreck.

And somewhere in all of that, between MEPS and Psych 101 and the quiet stretches where I tried to convince myself I was "fine," something started to click into place.

The Marines weren't going to fix me.

School wasn't going to fix me.

Nothing external was ever going to hand me the feeling I was chasing.

Because the thing I wanted, peace, confidence, some kind of reliable internal truce, wasn't going to come from a uniform, or a diploma, or a new identity I could wear. It wasn't going to come from anyone else clapping for me, or laughing with me, or picking me to be the example at the front of the room.

If I was going to stop feeling like I was running from myself, it was going to have to start inside the part of me I kept trying to outrun.

That moment at MEPS, sitting alone on that plastic chair while everyone else moved forward, watching my "transformation" evaporate with the stroke of a red pen, changed me. Not in some inspirational phoenix-rising-from-the-ashes way. It didn't make me stronger.

At first, it just made me furious. Ashamed.

I'd wanted the Marine Corps to rebuild me into someone I could finally respect. Someone tougher. Someone worth noticing. I thought discipline, structure, and a uniform would hand me a new identity.

Instead, I got a red circle around the word *disqualified*.

And then I had to do the thing I'd been avoiding my entire life.

Sit with myself.

That was the beginning of a lesson I wouldn't fully understand for years to come. There is no shortcut to self-worth. There isn't a boot camp, a job title, or a relationship that can install it in you like new software.

Growth doesn't come from escape.

It comes from staying.

From waking up in the same teenage bedroom when you'd rather be anywhere else. From trying to find some shred of dignity in days that look nothing like the life you'd imagined.

That period of my life stripped me bare.

But it also handed me the first real tools to start rebuilding on my own terms. It taught me that reinvention doesn't always come dressed in dress blues and medals. Sometimes it shows up in the shape of a hard plastic chair, a community college lecture hall, and a lie detector screaming your secrets while everyone laughs.

Because in that Psych 101 classroom, wires clipped to my fingers, my private life suddenly turned into public comedy, I realized something I hadn't felt in a long time.

I wasn't invisible.

People saw me. They knew my name. They laughed with me, not just at me. I wasn't a Marine. I wasn't some hardened warrior.

But I was someone.

You don't have to leave town, put on a uniform, or earn a title to prove you matter. Sometimes the bravest thing you can do is stay standing when the plan falls apart and learn to like the person who's still there when the dust settles.

And just when I started to settle into that strange, uncomfortable reality of community college, movie theater nights, Psych 101 mornings, she walked through the front doors of Market Place Cinemas and everything was flipped on its head.

It was mid-December, the kind of cold that makes everyone move faster, stiffer. People half-jogged from the parking lot with their shoulders up around their ears, breath fogging the glass as they yanked the doors open. Inside the theater, it was warmer but still had that winter draft creeping along the floor.

I was at my usual post behind the wooden ticket podium, doing what I always did, tearing tickets and pretending my brain was fully online.

Tear. Hand back the stub. Drop the other half into the metal slot.

Clink.

It wasn't a bad job, but it was repetitive in a way that made you feel like you could do it in your sleep. Most nights I basically did. I'd watch the same kinds of people come in, couples holding hands, groups of kids too loud, parents dragging along bored teenagers, and I'd be there like part of the furniture, a warm body in a blue bow tie and red vest.

Then two girls walked in.

They came through the glass doors laughing, already in the middle of a conversation. I noticed them right away because I'd been standing behind that wooden ticket podium on autopilot, and they were the first thing that felt even a little exciting all night.

They were young. Sixteen, maybe. One of them was taller with dark hair, the quieter one. Not shy, just calmer. The kind of girl who can stand half a step back from her friend and still feel like she's running the show. Her friend was the opposite. Blonde. Bright. Animated. Loud in the best way.

She had on these tight green jeans that made it hard for an eighteen-year-old guy stuck at a ticket podium to keep his eyes where they were supposed to be. I noticed the detail and immediately felt guilty, like I should've been more mature about it.

But I wasn't. I was eighteen. I was basically hormones with a name tag, trying to look professional while my brain kept drifting right back to those green jeans.

Still, it wasn't only that. It was her confidence, the way she talked, the way she smiled. She didn't just walk into the lobby. She took it over. You could tell she was the one people naturally followed without even thinking about it.

And then our eyes met.

Not the quick, awkward kind where you both look away and pretend nothing happened. This was a held second. A real moment. My stomach dropped, my hands got warm, my heart picked up speed. One second I'm tearing tickets and doing my fake customer-service smile, and the next I'm suddenly aware of my posture, my face, and the fact that I'd been half-asleep and now I was wide awake.

The weirdest part was I could tell she felt it too. She didn't blush or get shy. She just looked at me like she was waiting to see what I'd do, and she wasn't going to look away first.

So I said something. Some dumb flirty line that probably sounded smoother in my head than it did out loud. I can't even remember the exact words, which is probably for the best. I just remember taking a shot and hoping I didn't instantly regret it.

And I remember waiting for her to crush me.

She didn't.

She laughed, like a real laugh, not a polite one. Her face changed, her eyes lit up, and the second she gave me that, something inside me relaxed. After that, the conversation just felt natural. We traded quick jokes, little digs, that playful back-and-forth people do when they're flirting but don't want to call it flirting.

It felt easy in a way that surprised me. Like we didn't have to force it. Like I didn't have to try so hard to be interesting. I wasn't tired and numb for those few minutes.

Her name was Katarina.

And right away it wasn't just, *she's cute*, or *I should get her number.* I pictured her laughing again. I pictured seeing her the next day. I pictured dumb little things that had nothing to do with a movie theater. Driving around. Sitting too close somewhere.

It was butterflies, but not the cheesy kind. More like a tight knot in my chest that wouldn't go away. More like I was suddenly nervous about saying the wrong thing because I didn't want that moment to end. That part sounds dramatic when you say it out loud, but it's true.

Not long after that, she wasn't just the blonde girl who came into my theater.

We were a thing.

And for the next two and a half years, Katarina and I were basically inseparable, one of those couples people either found adorable or exhausting depending on how long they had to be around us. We didn't just date. We were always together, always talking, always in our own little bubble. Like we'd built a private world and everyone else just lived outside the white picket fence.

What surprised me was how mature she was for someone still in high school. Not the fake-grown kind where you act older because you think that's what being interesting looks like. The real kind. The kind that comes from responsibility.

She lived in Tolono, that small-town stretch just south of Champaign, and a few nights a week after school she helped her mom clean doctor's offices in the old train station building downtown. Vacuuming. Wiping down counters. Emptying trash. The kind of work nobody brags about, but it gave her independence. She wasn't waiting for her life to start. She was already moving.

Sometimes she'd ask me to come with her, and I always said yes. Part of it was obvious. I wanted to be around her like a magnet wants to stick to metal. But it was more than that. It felt good being invited into the unglamorous parts of her life. Not just the fun stuff, movies, flirting, weekends, but the tired hours. The work. Real life.

Being there made me feel like I wasn't just her boyfriend when it was cute and convenient, but her boyfriend when it was boring and just routine.

We'd hang out beforehand, grab something to eat, mess around, flirt, that restless teenage energy where everything feels like a big deal because everything is still so new. Then we'd go clean side by side, turning it into a team thing. A weird little preview of adulthood, like we were play-acting "real life" with mops and trash bags and keys to places we didn't actually own.

And yeah, those empty offices weren't always just for cleaning. There were nights we found privacy where we could. Making out in quiet hallways, whisper-laughing like we were committing some huge crime.

It was reckless and tender and stupid and perfect in the way young love is perfect, because it doesn't know enough yet to be careful. It doesn't have the bruises of experience.

But the first time we slept together was different.

That happened in my parents' basement, my "bedroom," if you could even call it that. No bed frame. No headboard. No real attempt at décor. Just a mattress on bare concrete, a small dresser, and a makeshift nightstand.

At eighteen, I told myself it looked edgy. Minimalist. Artistic. Like I was some tortured musician choosing simplicity on purpose.

It didn't. It looked exactly like what it was.

That afternoon I'd gotten a fresh shipment of CDs in the mail, one of those ridiculous "12 albums for a penny" deals that felt like winning the lottery when you were broke. But it was also the first purchase I'd made with my own credit card, so I felt like I'd just financed a house.

I opened that package like it was Christmas morning. The plastic wrap. The liner notes. That new-CD smell. I slid one into the boom box on my dresser and hit shuffle without thinking.

And then it happened. We crossed that line.

It was awkward in small ways and sweet in bigger ones. That mix of excitement and fear where you realize you're not just doing something physical, you're giving away a piece of yourself you can't get back. It wasn't just sex. It was a moment you could feel permanently engraving itself into your memory while it was happening.

The song that came on in the background was this slow, aching power ballad. "I Want to Know What Love Is" by Foreigner.

The kind of song that should've felt cheesy. The kind of song you'd normally mock if it came on in a car with your friends. But down there, in that basement, on that sad mattress, with Katarina, it fit the moment in this almost embarrassing way.

And somehow, it worked.

Because right then, I *did* want to know what love was.
I was touching it.
I'd found it.

That became our song.

> *"...In my life, there's been heartache and pain*
> *I don't know if I can face it again*
> *I can't stop now, I've travelled so far*
> *To change this lonely life*
>
> *I wanna know what love is..."*

Even now, if I hear it, I'm right back there. Eighteen years old, lying on that mattress on the cement floor with Katarina in my arms. The basement light is off. The air is cool against our skin. The rest of the world is held at bay by nothing more than drywall, shadows, and a cheap boom box on the dresser playing soft rock.

For a few minutes, everything was calm.

Her hair on my chest. Her breath against my neck. The quiet little bubble we built between us in that basement. It felt fragile and sacred, like we'd made something you weren't supposed to be able to make at that age.

Like we'd pressed pause on real life and found a pocket where nothing could get in.

Right then, it felt like we had all the time in the world. And for a kid like me, someone who didn't always feel chosen, someone who'd spent a lot of years feeling like life happened around him instead of to him, that feeling was the closest thing I'd ever known to forever. Not a promise. Not a plan. Just a body-level certainty that this was real, that I was real, that I mattered to somebody in a way I wasn't used to.

After that, we were together constantly. I still don't know how we managed it with her school, my shifts, her work, her family, my family. But somehow we always found a way. Hanging out in stolen hours. Falling asleep on the phone. Driving nowhere just to be in the same car. Making the most of whatever scraps of time we could get, like time was infinite and consequences were just a problem for older people.

When you're that age, time stretches. Sleep is optional. Love is fuel. And it feels so good you don't even realize you're burning through something you can't replace.

For the first six to eight months, Belle floated through my mind more than she should have. Not because I wanted her back, not because Katarina wasn't enough, but because grief and trauma don't just somehow vanish just because someone new walks in with green eyes and a laugh that makes you melt. It had only been nine months since Belle and I broke up, and what we went through wasn't the kind of thing you just "get over." It was the kind of thing you carry until you can finally learn how to pack it away.

Katarina knew all of this. We talked about it. I didn't lie to her, because I didn't want to build something new on top of a secret wound. I told her the truth. Belle had been a big piece of my life, and you don't just unplug from something like that overnight. I wasn't trapped in the past anymore, but I was still learning where it belonged.

Katarina didn't love it. No girl wants to feel like she's competing with a shadow. But she understood. Or she tried to. She was more patient with my demons than I deserved, more gentle with the parts of me that were still bleeding. She didn't demand I be "fully healed" before she loved me. She just stood there and let me be complicated.

I didn't see it then, but that kind of patience is its own kind of love. Like someone saying, without words, *I'm not scared of your shadows. Just don't make me live in them.*

Her family was straight out of a country song, the kind that starts sweet and then you realize it's going somewhere dark.

Two older brothers, both former Navy, both big enough to fold me in half without breaking a sweat. They worked as bouncers at Bradley's, the country bar where my band used to play on Sunday nights. Her dad was shorter but built like a cinder block, with a stern face and a glass eye that made it hard to know which one to look into when he talked to me. Her mom was outspoken but nurturing, the firm anchor holding the whole storm system together.

They lived in this tall white farmhouse out on a country road, wrapped in fields that seemed to go on forever. It reminded me of the old country house I grew up in. But inside, instead of a cozy wood burning stove, there was a gun collection hung proudly on the living room wall. The kind of house that says, *We love each other, but we also believe in a well-stocked Plan B.*

I really felt that part one night.

Sometimes I'd drive out to Katarina's in the middle of the night just to lay next to her. People assume that means one thing, like I was some hormone-driven idiot on a mission, but honestly, most nights it wasn't even about sex. It was about the simplest, dumbest comfort in the world. Just being close enough to hear her breathe in the dark, to feel her stir in her sleep.

Her room was upstairs, down the hall from her parents' room and her sister's. The whole house had that old farmhouse layout, creaky in the places you didn't want it to be, loud in the exact spots your heart begged it to stay quiet. Sneaking in felt like playing house and Mission: Impossible at the same time. High-risk romance. The kind you swear is romantic when you're young.

When I got to her place, I'd turn off the gravel drive before the house, cut through the backyard, and park behind the barn so her parents wouldn't see my car. Then I'd cross the yard in the dark with my heart already thumping too fast. The cold would bite at my face, the grass would crunch under my shoes, and every little sound felt louder than it should. I'd slip in through the back door, ease it shut like I was defusing a bomb, and go up the short flight of steps to the main floor.

After that came the second staircase, the one that led to the upstairs hallway where the stakes suddenly felt higher. Her parents' bedroom was right there at the top of those stairs, the door usually cracked open just a little. I'd make a hard right, pass her sister's room, and move down the hall to the very end, to Katarina's door, where she'd be waiting in the dark.

She'd have that half-smile on her face that always looked like she was happy to see me and mildly entertained by how far I was willing to push my luck. I'd strip down to boxers and a T-shirt, slide into bed, and feel her curl into me like it was the most natural thing in the world. And the world would shrink down to one room, one girl, and one soft breath in the dark.

For a while, the danger made it sweeter. The whispering. The muffled laughs when we almost made noise. The way my pulse would spike every time the house settled or a floorboard popped somewhere in the distance. It felt like something we'd joke about later.

God, we were so stupid.

Until one night. Early morning, really, when the world came crashing back in.

We were dead asleep when someone started pounding on her bedroom door. Not knocking. Pounding. The kind of pounding that delivers consequences.

Her dad's voice came through the door like thunder. "I know he's in there! If he's not downstairs in five minutes, he won't need the stairs to get down!"

My blood turned to ice so fast I swear I felt it move. That wasn't a bluff voice. That wasn't a stern father voice. That was a man who meant every word, and my brain immediately ran through every ending at once. Me getting dragged down the stairs. Me getting put through a wall. Me getting thrown from her bedroom window.

He knew.

Later we'd figure out what gave me away. The frost on the grass. My tire tracks from the driveway to the barn left a dark trail, plain as day in the morning light. Turns out nature itself had snitched on me.

I had five minutes. Maybe.

I scrambled out of bed so fast I couldn't even feel my own body. My hands were shaking hard enough that simple things, pants, shoes, a belt, felt like advanced math. My brain was screaming worst-case scenarios at full volume while I tried to move quietly.

Katarina and I locked eyes for a second. Hers were wide and glassy. Mine were probably pale and blank. And in that one look we had a silent, terrified conversation. *Is your dad about to kill me?*

Then I was out the door.

I moved down the hall like I was walking through a minefield, trying not to breathe too loud, trying not to let a floorboard creak, trying not to picture his face waiting at the bottom of the stairs. Every step sounded like a drum in my chest.

At the bottom, the back entrance had that weird split-level setup. Five stairs down to the back door, a small landing, then another five steps down to the basement where her oldest brother Kevin's room was.

Her dad was standing there on that small landing, blocking the back door, talking to Kevin like this was just another morning conversation. I stopped halfway down, eyes glued to the floorboards like they were the only safe place to look. I couldn't bring myself to meet his face. Not with the gun wall still fresh in my memory, not with that threat still ringing in my ears.

Finally, he turned toward me. What scared me almost as much as the threat was how calm he sounded. Calm in that way that says, I don't need to yell. Yelling is for people who aren't in control.

"You know what you did."

"Yes, sir," I managed, and even that felt like it came out of somebody else's mouth.

"Don't do it again."

"Yes, sir."

He let a pause sit in the air. Then he finished it, blunt and final, like a door slamming.

"Now get the fuck off my property!"

"Yes, sir."

That was it. No lecture. Just a final command.

I slid past him and out the back door like I'd been granted parole. I didn't run. I don't even think I could've without falling apart, but I moved fast. Across the yard. Into the barn. Into my car.

My hands shook as I turned the key, and the engine sounded like a chainsaw in the cold morning air.

The twenty-minute drive home felt like hours. My heart pounding the entire time. My face burned with embarrassment and fear, and with the sudden realization of how thin the line is between "romantic" and "stupid." My chest felt hollow, like I'd left some piece of myself back there on that staircase. Some version of me that still thought love had to be dangerous to be real.

And the weird part, looking back, is how bittersweet it feels. I can still taste the terror. I can still remember my hands shaking, the cold air, that calm voice telling me to get the fuck off the property. But I can also remember the intensity of being that young, being that convinced that closeness was worth any risk, that falling asleep next to a girl you loved was worth sneaking through frost-covered grass like a criminal.

But I never snuck into her house again.

That version of me, young, stupid, terrified, and completely gone over a girl, still lives somewhere in those memories. Creeping down that hallway in the dark, trying not to breathe too loud, learning that love doesn't always feel like safety, even when it's the only thing in your life that feels like home.

Looking back, those nights, slipping through back doors, creeping down hallways, whispering under blankets while the whole house slept, were reckless and stupid. We thought we were writing some epic teenage love story. Really, we were just two kids gambling with other people's patience and property lines. At the time, I told myself I was being romantic and bold, like some bargain-bin Romeo with a knock-off sports car and a big ego.

But when her dad pounded on that door, reality didn't just knock. It kicked the damn hinges off.

That was the first time it really hit me that my choices didn't stay trapped inside this cozy little bubble between me and a girl. I wasn't just in a relationship with her. I was stepping into her whole world, her parents, her brothers, her family history, their rules, their fears, the way they protected their own. I'd been moving through life like feelings were enough, like as long as my heart was in the right place, the rest would magically work itself out.

It doesn't.

That night taught me that love isn't supposed to live in shadows. It's not meant to sneak through back doors and hide under blankets, hoping no one notices the extra pair of shoes by the bed. Real love can stand under actual light, even when it's uncomfortable, even when it means facing an angry father, a wall full of guns, and your own reflection in the middle of all that.

Being with someone, really being with them, means you earn your place in their life. You don't break into it like a burglar in the dead of night.

That pounding on the door wasn't just an angry dad ready to throw me off the second floor. It was life, telling me to grow the hell up and stop pretending my feelings exempted me from consequences.

But messages from life don't automatically change you. You can hear them loud and clear and still shrug them off. You can feel your heart racing, promise yourself you'll do better, and then keep right on doing the same dumb shit you've always done, hoping you'll get away with it.

Still, when I think back on those nights now, the gravel under my tires, the cold air on my face, her half-smile in the dark, I feel this weird mix of gratitude and disbelief. I'm grateful I got to feel that kind of reckless, all-in teenage devotion. Grateful I learned from it, even if it took me way too long. But more importantly, grateful I didn't meet the business end of any of those guns on her living room wall.

In the spring of 1994, a few months before my nineteenth birthday, I landed my first real management job.

On the outside, it was a step up. Respectable. A "real" job. In reality, it was another chaotic chapter I didn't know I needed, and one I'm oddly proud of now.

It also meant giving my notice at the movie theater, a place that had been home base for almost three years. My Thursday, Friday, and Saturday nights since I was sixteen had all lived under those humming fluorescent lobby lights and the smell of popcorn butter that never washed out of my clothes. Walking away from that place, and from Grace, felt like shutting the door on an entire version of myself.

End of an era.

New beginnings are supposed to feel exciting. This did, but it was excitement wrapped tight in anxiety.

My dad had always been obsessed with classic cars. Every decent-weather weekend, he'd be at a show somewhere, weaving through rows of polished chrome and candy-colored fenders, trading stories with other guys from the local car club. Friday or Saturday nights often ended in a parking lot. Steak 'n Shake, some little diner, wherever. Hoods up, headlights glowing, exhaust hanging in the air like gasoline scented cologne.

Around that time, a new locally owned burger joint opened in town. Lickity's. It wasn't a full retro diner, but it flirted with the idea with just enough throwback to feel cool without sliding into cheesy. The owner, Stu, was a local accountant with a very specific vision, and Lickity's quickly became the hangout for the car guys. On weekend nights, the parking lot turned into an unofficial car show. Servers ran food out to people sitting in their cars, burgers, fries, shakes. Like a drive-in scene from 1963, just viewed through a 1994 lens.

One night, my dad was there under the lights with his buddies, talking engines and carburetors like usual. He struck up a conversation with Stu, and at some point Stu started venting about how hard it was to find someone energetic and dependable to help his general manager run the place.

Casually, my dad mentioned me. Said I was responsible, hardworking, smart, and looking for more than just an hourly job. That was my dad. Not a big emotional speech guy, but when it came to me, he'd quietly slide a good word across the table. And now that I decided not to enroll for Spring classes at Parkland, I had even more time on my hands. And historically speaking, that wasn't good for my mind.

Stu agreed to interview me as an assistant manager.

I still remember walking in that first day to meet him. Stu was laid-back but sharp, the kind of guy who could talk small-town gossip one minute and mentally balance a spreadsheet the next. He asked direct questions. I gave honest answers. I didn't try to be anything I wasn't. Whatever I said must've hit the right chord, because by the end of the conversation he looked at me and just handed me the job.

Just like that, I was management. Not yet nineteen and suddenly one of the guys in charge.

The general manager was a guy named Bob. Within a few months, we were calling him "Drywalling Bob" because of the fine white powder that always seemed to be hanging around under his nose. When someone finally asked about it, he swore he'd been remodeling and doing some drywall work at home. Sure, Bob. We all definitely bought that story. At some point the nickname evolved into "Bob the Drywalling Clown," which might've been a little harsh, but not exactly inaccurate.

After wrapping up my time at the theater, I dove headfirst into Lickity's.

It was a standard greasy spoon, clean enough to pass inspection, dirty enough that the food actually had flavor. The kitchen felt familiar. My very first job had been at a hot dog and burger joint, and I already knew my way around a fryer and a grill, so I gravitated to the back of the house without even thinking about it. I liked the pace, the heat, the rhythm. Tickets roll in, burgers drop, orders build, plates fly out. There's something honest about kitchen work. You can't fake your way through a lunch rush.

Within a week or two, I'd found my groove. Efficiency and cleanliness came naturally to me. I cared about systems, even though I didn't have the explanation or terminology for it yet. I just knew when something felt clunky or stupid, and I couldn't stop myself from trying to fix it.

Lickity's had one big problem. Everything was cooked to order. Great for quality, terrible for speed.

Food took about fifteen minutes from ticket to tray. For a relaxed dinner, fine. For lunch, a train wreck. When a wave of high school kids flooded in during their short lunch period, they needed food fast. They had maybe twenty, twenty-five minutes, tops. We couldn't keep up. Orders piled up. Kids got pissed. It was a mess.

So I started experimenting.

I began pre-cooking burger patties just shy of done, leaving them about a minute short, and setting them in a metal pan on the grill with a thin layer of water. The water kept them warm and moist without drying out. When an order came in, we'd finish the patty by popping it back on the grill for a minute, slap it on a bun, dress it, wrap it, and send it.

Instead of drowning when twenty kids hit the counter at once, we could crank out ten or twelve orders back-to-back and barely break a sweat. The burgers were still good. Juicy, hot, not overcooked. It wasn't by the book, but it worked.

And for the first time in my working life, I wasn't just clocking in and following instructions. I was building something. I'd found a problem, worked on it, and fixed it. I watched the lunch rush go from chaos to controlled. Watched kids get their food on time. Watched the line move instead of stall. And I knew I'd done that.

That's when I started realizing I wasn't just a kid punching a timecard. I could walk into a system, see what was broken, and make it better. It was messy, it was loud, it smelled like grease and raw onions, but it was the start of me learning I could actually lead, not just show up.

And I'm still proud of that.

I stopped thinking like an employee and started thinking like an owner. Not legally, obviously. Stu still signed the checks. But mentally, I was all in. I began scanning for inefficiencies, watching for bottlenecks, spotting anything that could trip us up, and rearranging it in my head before it happened. It became a game. *Where's the weak point? How do I fix it?*

I didn't know it then, but that instinct, to sniff out problems and build systems around them, would eventually become the core of how I work, no matter what job I took.

I stayed at Lickity's for close to a year. Most of the time, I truly enjoyed it. I've always had a weird affection for jobs that require long hours, low pay, and strenuous physical effort. There's an honesty to it. You sweat, you hustle, you go home exhausted, and you know you earned every penny in your pocket.

But eventually, I started seeing cracks.

Bob's performance slid from questionable, to concerning, to catastrophic. He showed up late. He looked rough. His decision-making was erratic. Stu was getting more and more frustrated. The stress of running a restaurant on top of his accounting business was grinding him down. You could see it in the way he sighed, in the way he rubbed his temples, in the way his eyes drifted when we talked.

It felt unstable. Deja vu.

I remembered what it felt like when Wiener Lose closed suddenly and left all of us scrambling. I wasn't about to get blindsided like that again. So I started looking, quietly, for my next move.

I was going on twenty, but realistically I was still a kid with a car payment and a half-formed prefrontal cortex. That year at Lickity's was the first time I ever fully showed up somewhere and decided, *This is mine to improve. I'm going to make this better.* Not just, "I work here", but, "I have a say in how this place runs."

Before that, I'd always been just another pair of hands. Do the job. Do it well. Go home. Repeat. I took pride in working hard, but it stopped with the time clock. Then someone hands me keys, calls me "manager," and whether they knew it or not, they were handing me something else too.

Responsibility. Ownership. The chance to actually change things instead of just complaining about them in the break room.

And something in me rose to meet that challenge.

Problems stopped feeling like annoyances and started feeling like puzzles. That pre-cooked burger system I came up with? On paper, it sounds small. A footnote. But standing there in that hot kitchen, realizing I'd turned the lunch rush from chaos into something we could actually handle, that was a rush. That was pride. Not the loud, chest-thumping kind. The quieter kind that just whispers, _you did that._

It was never really about burgers. It was about resourcefulness. About trusting my gut. About realizing that work didn't always have to be something you just suffered through until your shift ended.

Work could be something you shaped.

Looking back, I can see that the job isn't always the lesson. The way you show up for the job is. You don't need a dream career or the perfect workplace to start becoming the person you're meant to be. Sometimes that growth happens behind a greasy flat-top, under flickering lights, with a guy named Drywalling Bob disappearing out the back door while orders pile up and you're the one holding everything together.

That little place gave me confidence. It gave me foresight. When I saw the writing on the wall, I didn't panic. I started planning. Even then, on some basic instinct level, I understood that momentum matters. You don't wait for the roof to cave in before you start looking for another kind of shelter.

Lickity's taught me to move forward before things fall apart.

And it taught me something else too. You can find purpose, and even a real, quiet pride, in the unglamorous stuff. You just have to be willing to see it.

As fate would have it, my Uncle Stanley called one day with a potential lifeline.

He told me there was an opening in Minneapolis for a merchandiser. Nothing glamorous, nothing you'd brag about at a party, but it was steady. It came with a schedule, a paycheck, and that quiet little promise adults love to say like it's sacred: "room to grow." And if I took it, I could stay with my cousin and her fiancé until I got on my feet.

It felt like the universe tossing me a rope, finally. Like, *Here's your chance. Here's a way out of the loop.* But even with that rush of relief, there was this other feeling underneath it. That rope came with a pair of scissors behind its back.

Because the offer wasn't just a job. It was a choice. A fork in the road. The second I pictured Minneapolis, I also pictured everything I'd have to leave behind to go there.

One version of my life was staying in Champaign. Same streets, same people, same jobs that were always "for now," except "for now" was starting to look like it might turn into forever. Same routine where you tell yourself you're figuring it out, but really you're circling the same block and calling it progress. If I stayed, I stayed close to Katarina. Close to my friends. Close to everything predictable. Close to the version of me that didn't have to risk anything new.

The other version was Minneapolis. Snow. Strangers. A city that didn't know me and didn't care about my history or my excuses. A job that wasn't exciting, but it was legit. A chance to build a life that didn't feel temporary. And if I'm being brutally honest, it was also a chance to find out if I could stand on my own.

That's what made it hard. It wasn't "girlfriend versus job." It was comfort versus growth. Familiar pain versus unfamiliar effort. The easy choice versus the one that came with fear of the unknown.

I was torn. Part of me wanted to cling to what I knew, Katarina, my friends, my routines, the comfort of predictability. I didn't have to love my life for it to feel safe. At least it was familiar. At least I knew how to survive it.

But there was another part of me that was tired of feeling like the "almost" version of a person. Almost going somewhere. Almost becoming somebody. That part kept whispering the same thing over and over, like it was trying to push me out the door. *You can do more than this.*

Underneath all of it was this thin thread of hope. The kind you don't want to admit you have because if it snaps, it's going to hurt. Hope that maybe this is how you become who you're supposed to be. Not by reinventing yourself overnight, but by making one uncomfortable decision at a time. By choosing the harder option and finding out if you can handle it.

So with my stomach in knots and my head full of what-ifs, I chose to leap.

I didn't feel brave. That's what people assume later, that you must've felt empowered or confident. I didn't. I felt sick. Guilty. Scared. My stomach stayed in knots because I could already sense the ripple effect of what "yes" would mean. I could already hear the conversations coming, the goodbyes, the disappointment, the possibility that I'd be the bad guy in someone else's story even if I didn't mean to be.

But I also knew that if I didn't go, I'd spend the next year telling myself I still should have. Another doorway I stood in front of and never walked through.

So I told myself the only thing I could honestly promise. *I don't know what I'm walking into, but I'm done standing still.*

I'd never really left Champaign before. Not for real. I talked like I was ready to get out, like I was itching for change, but underneath that talk was this quiet, gnawing terror. The Marine Corps dream had gone up in flames. I wasn't in college anymore. I was floating somewhere between "teenager" and "adult," with nothing solid to stand on and no clear idea what I was supposed to become.

So even a mind-numbing job sounded like a chance to become someone else. Or at least someone else somewhere else.

In the dead of winter, barely into '95, I packed a bag and got on an Amtrak train headed north.

The ride from Champaign to Minneapolis took about twelve hours. Inside the train it was warm enough, but I never really relaxed. My nerves bounced around inside my chest like loose change in a dryer. I kept my Marlboro Mediums tucked in the inside pocket of my black leather coat and made regular trips to the smoking car, which for some reason stayed at a permanent fifty-five degrees.

I'd sit there shivering and chain-smoking two or three at a time, trying to breathe my anxiety out and watch it disappear into the haze against the window. The whole time, I'd have these little flashes of confidence. *Look at you. You're doing it. You're leaving. You're brave.* Then five minutes later I'd be staring at my reflection in the glass thinking, *Who do you think you are?*

When I got to Minnesota, my cousin and her fiancé took me in. They were kind in that easy Midwestern way that doesn't make you feel like a charity case. She even loaned me a car, a small, white sporty two-seater that made me feel cool and successful.

For a minute, it almost worked. For a minute, I felt like I'd pulled it off. Like I'd stepped into a new version of myself and all I had to do now was keep walking forward.

I found out pretty quickly that "merchandiser" is just corporate-speak for "bottom rung." On the surface it sounded decent enough. Steady job. Legit company. Early start so you're done early. A chance to stack a few paychecks and build something resembling a life.

In reality, it was the kind of work that makes you understand why people say, "It builds character," like that's supposed to make you feel better.

My alarm went off at 3:00 AM every morning. The world outside was dead quiet, that eerie hour where even the streetlights look tired. I'd drag myself into clothes that still smelled faintly of soda syrup and cardboard, slam some caffeine, and drive through streets that felt abandoned. By 4:30 I was in the first grocery store.

The job itself was simple but relentless. Stock shelves. Rotate inventory. Build displays. Make the soda aisle look like it belonged in a glossy ad. Six to eight stores a day, depending on the route and whether something blew up, figuratively or literally. It was just lifting, stacking, squatting, stretching, hauling cases, adjusting and re-adjusting until the labels all faced forward and everything lined up "just right."

You'd think there'd be some satisfaction in it. Like, *look, I made something neat and orderly in a chaotic world.* Maybe the first few times there was. But after the fiftieth display, perfection stops feeling like pride and starts feeling like punishment.

And the physical part was rough, my back aching, my hands cracked and sore, knees snapping every time I crouched. But the real thing that got to me was the repetition. Same aisles. Same faint music overhead. Same sticky-sweet smell of syrup, cardboard, dust, and whatever disinfectant they used on the floors. Same internal loop running in my head at an hour when the rest of civilization was still asleep. *Is this it? Is this what adulthood is?*

They sold it as "early start, early finish." Most days I was supposed to be done around 2 PM, which sounds great if you're imagining afternoons full of freedom. Like you'd get off work and still have this whole day left to be a person.

But I didn't come home with normal tired. I came home completely exhausted. I'd eat something without tasting it, blankly stare at the TV, and fall into bed knowing I was just hitting the reset button on each day.

Groundhog Day. Every day.

And underneath all of that was this homesickness I didn't know how to admit without feeling weak. Not the cute kind. Not the "I miss my bed and my favorite food" kind. A deeper one. Like I'd ripped myself out of my own life and my body was quietly panicking, asking, *What are you doing? Who are you trying to prove this to?*

I'd moved on purpose, for a reason, but there were mornings I'd be driving to the first store and it felt like I'd made a mistake I couldn't unmake. Like I'd stepped off the edge of everything familiar and just assumed there'd be a net.

And then there was Katarina.

I missed her more than I wanted to admit before I left, and the distance didn't kill us quickly. It did something worse. That slow, quiet thing where the relationship is technically still breathing, but it's not really alive. Calls that started with energy and ended in silence. Conversations where we were both trying not to say the real thing. *I don't know how we do this.*

And Michael Bolton would come on the radio and sing right to me. And it felt like "How Am I Supposed to Live Without You" somehow became an anthem that winter.

Every night felt like we were inching toward the end without saying it. And because we weren't saying it, it felt like watching something you love fade out, unable to stop it.

Then Minnesota winter really showed up.

I thought I knew cold. I grew up in Illinois. I'd done blizzards, ice storms, those below-zero days where your lungs burn when you breathe in and your face goes numb before you've even scraped the windshield.

But Minnesota cold is different.

That January, the high hovered around -25. Some mornings dipped to -30. The kind of cold that doesn't just bite your skin. It gets into your bones and squeezes.

The soda literally exploded.

Bottles would burst on the trucks before they even made it to the stores. Entire pallets ruined, sticky ice crystallizing around shattered plastic. Sometimes they'd just turn the trucks around and bring them straight back to the warehouse like, *Nope. Not today.*

And you'd stand there watching it happen, knowing the work didn't disappear just because the product did. It just shifted to cleaning and sorting and dealing with supervisors and paperwork.

Inside the warehouse it smelled like diesel exhaust and frozen sugar. Everything echoed off those smooth concrete floors. The ceiling disappeared into darkness above the warehouse lights. Forklifts beeped in reverse, pallets clapped down onto the ground, someone yelled a name from across the warehouse, and it all bounced around like you were living inside a cold metal drum.

Even now, if I catch that exact smell, diesel in winter air, it's a time machine. I'm back there for a second. Back in that warehouse. Back in that brutal cold. Back watching shards of busted bottles roll across the floor.

And the worst part wasn't even that the job was hard. It was that it was hard in a way that didn't feel like it was building anything. It didn't feel like progress. It felt like surviving. Like I'd traded my entire life for a paycheck and a cold warehouse and a relationship slowly slipping through my fingers, and I couldn't tell if I was being brave or just stupid.

I'd lie there at night in a room that wasn't mine, body aching, mind racing, staring at the ceiling and trying to convince myself this was temporary. That this was the grind before the breakthrough. That everyone goes through a chapter like this.

But deep down, in the quiet part of me I didn't want to listen to, something was starting to change. A slow, uncomfortable awareness creeping in. I hadn't just moved states. I'd stepped into a version of my life that didn't fit me, and the longer I stayed in it, the more I could feel myself disappearing.

It didn't take long for the weight of it all to crush the fantasy.

I was twenty years old. Alone. Out of my element and out of my depth. The toughness I thought I had was starting to feel thin.

And I started to admit something I didn't want to admit. I hadn't come to Minnesota for the job. Not really. I'd come to escape my own life. To outrun that sinking feeling in my chest that kept telling me I wasn't becoming anything.

But Minnesota, frozen warehouses, endless aisles of cola, bleached white fields outside store windows, wasn't the salvation I imagined. It was just a new place to be depressed.

And the worst part was how clear it became. *This wasn't me. It was never going to be me.*

When I finally admitted I wanted to go home, it didn't feel like a simple change of plans. It felt like defeat. Not "this job isn't working out" defeat.

A deeper kind. Like I'd failed at becoming someone new, and now I had to crawl back to who I was before, empty-handed.

Right before I left, I walked into a tattoo shop.

I'd been flirting with the idea for a while, imagining something bold on my arm that would scream, *I'm changing. I'm different now.* Some permanent proof that this whole mess meant something.

The funniest part is where the idea even came from. I was in a grocery store and saw a Looney Tunes coloring book, one of those cheap ones near the magazines. I picked it up, flipped through it, and there he was. Animal. The unhinged drummer from The Muppets. Hair everywhere, eyes wild, mouth open like he was mid-yell.

And it hit me in this very direct way. *That's what I feel like right now. Not cool. Not deep. Just chaotic, loud on the inside, and desperate to feel like I belonged somewhere, anywhere.*

So I took that page in and asked the artist if he could make it work as a tattoo. He didn't laugh, which I appreciated. He just did what tattoo artists do, asked a few questions, cleaned it up, and sketched a version big enough to cover my upper left arm.

It was actually well done. That's what made it more dangerous. It wasn't some scribbly joke. It looked legit.

We got all the way there. The stencil went on. We checked the placement in the mirror. He had the needle ready. And I remember laying there with my arm out, trying to act casual, like this wasn't me making a decision out of panic. My heart was doing that stupid fluttery thing it does when you're about to do something you already know you might regret, but you're hoping the adrenaline will carry you through it.

Then I really looked at it. Not the idea of it. Not the story I was going to tell myself about it. The actual thing. Animal, frozen in that manic expression, about to be on my body for the rest of my life.

And I could suddenly see how it would play out. Me walking around years later with a puppet drummer on my arm. Me having to explain it to people who didn't know the context, or worse, people who did. Me trying to defend it with some speech about symbolism when the truth was simpler.

I was spiraling and wanted something to make the moment feel real.

And then the practical thoughts showed up, which is almost embarrassing to admit because they should've been there first. I thought about the train ticket I still needed to buy. I thought about what my bank account looked like. I thought about going home broke with this fresh tattoo and trying to pretend it was a smart move.

So I told him I couldn't do it.

There was a pause, because once you've gone that far, backing out is kind of a dick move. He didn't guilt me, though. He just nodded, wiped the stencil off, and that was that. I paid whatever the shop policy was for the drawing and walked out with my arm untouched.

I remember the feeling when I stepped outside. Like I'd avoided adding one more problem to the pile. No Animal. No permanent reminder of how lost I was. Just me, leaving a tattoo shop unmarked because for once I chose the boring, practical option over the dramatic one.

But to this day, I'm grateful I didn't let twenty-year-old me follow through. Even in the middle of regret and homesickness and that feeling of failure sitting on my chest, I at least protected my future self from carrying that decision around forever.

When I got back to Champaign, my parents were not exactly rolling out a welcome-home banner. My dad was quiet about it in that way dads can be, where you can feel the disappointment without a single word. My mom didn't bother with subtle. She was upset, and more than that, she was hurt, like my coming home meant something had gone wrong with me, not just the plan.

In her version of the story, the whole thing traced back to Katarina. She was convinced I'd run back because of her. She blamed Katarina for the move, for the return, for me hating the job, for the fact that I looked tired and worn down and not at all like someone who'd "gone out into the world." It was like she needed a clear villain, and Katarina was convenient. Blaming a girl was easier than sitting with the messier truth that her son had taken a swing at something and came back without the big payoff everyone hoped for.

But it wasn't Katarina's fault.

It was my choice to go. My choice to come back. Nobody dragged me to Minnesota, and nobody forced me to leave it. I wanted to try something different. I wanted to feel like I was actually doing something with my life, like I wasn't just stuck in the same places with the same people watching me spin my wheels.

And I did try. I gave it an honest shot. I just found out pretty fast that waking up at 3:00 AM to spend my days hauling cases of soda around in the cold, dealing with frozen and busted product, and getting treated like part of the store fixtures was not my calling. It wasn't even close.

What I didn't realize going in was how much the job would mess with my head. The physical part sucked, sure, but the bigger thing was the way every day felt like a copy of the last one. Wake up in the dark. Drive in silence. Work until you're running on fumes. Come "home" exhausted, try to eat something, and do it again. I wasn't building a life. I was just surviving a schedule.

And when you're twenty and already walking around with that pressure to prove you're not wasting your life, a grind like that doesn't toughen you up. It just makes you question what you're doing and why you thought this would fix anything.

So coming back wasn't some romantic surrender to a girlfriend or some dramatic retreat. It was me admitting, out loud, that I'd chased a version of "responsible" that didn't fit me at all. That was a hard thing to say in a house where "stick it out" was basically a religion.

Those first days back, I remember feeling a weird pile of emotions. Relief, because I could breathe again. Shame, because I could tell what everyone was thinking even when they weren't saying it. Anger, because my mom seemed determined to rewrite my whole decision-making process into a simple story where I got "distracted" by a girl. And underneath all of it, there was this fear that maybe she was right about the part that mattered. That I'd failed.

But I hadn't failed. Not really.

That trip taught me something I didn't have the maturity to explain at the time, especially not in a kitchen conversation with my mom. Trying and not making it is still movement. It still counts. Turning around doesn't erase the fact that I went.

I wasn't some washed-up guy limping home after a lifetime of bad decisions. I was a twenty-year-old kid making real choices in real time, with no map, no blueprint, and an inner voice that treated every mistake like a final judgment.

I didn't last long in Minnesota. That's true. But I went. I tried. I learned. And that mattered. At least to me. Because over time, I started to see the difference between running from something and moving toward something better.

ROUND 13:
Luck Is Not a Life Plan

Back in Champaign, licking my wounds and trying not to look as lost as I felt, I went back to work.

I applied for an assistant manager position at the local Arby's on Springfield Avenue, hoping the corporate logo on the sign would translate to a little more stability than the mom-and-pop joints I'd been bouncing between. A national franchise felt legitimate, like maybe there'd be better pay, consistent hours, actual systems already in place, maybe even a real career path if I stuck around long enough.

Thanks to my time at Lickity's, they actually took me seriously. I had "management experience" on my resume now. Keys, scheduling, food costs. It sounded impressive on paper, at least. I went in for the interview, answered their questions as honestly as I could, and a short time later, I got the call. I had the job.

It felt like a win, but not a glamorous, fireworks kind of win. I mean, it was still just a fast-food job. It was more like the kind where you start to think, *maybe I'm not a complete screw up after all.*

Arby's ended up being a smart move. It gave me chain-restaurant experience, something future employers might recognize, but more than that, it introduced me to an actual system. Not the usual "we'll figure it out when we get there" approach I'd seen in other places, where the plan changed every five minutes depending on who was Manager on Duty that day.

At Arby's, everything had a process. Drive-thru timing. Food safety. Cleaning schedules. Prep lists. Inventory. Labor percentages. Metrics and routines that kept the whole thing running. I used to act like I was too independent for structure, but the truth is I needed it more than I wanted to admit.

And I got good at it fast. I learned the flow of the store, where people slowed down, what caused backups, what made the line spiral, what happened when someone didn't stock what they were supposed to stock. I could usually tell within the first ten minutes whether a shift was going to be smooth or turn into a long, loud disaster.

I also learned how to keep a crew moving together, not just doing their jobs, but actually functioning like a unit. Some problems were simple. You fix them with a checklist, a reminder, a better routine. Other problems had nothing to do with work. They were attitude, ego, someone having a bad day, or feeling disrespected. Those took a different kind of attention. Sometimes all it took was just pulling someone aside and talking to them like a human.

There was this satisfaction in it that surprised me. It wasn't a glamorous job. It was roast beef sandwiches, curly fries, the same questions from customers, and the same beeping timers. But when things ran smoothly, I felt proud.

Arby's wasn't a dream job, and it didn't need to be. It was a step, another place where I proved to myself I could function in a world that expected consistency. And somewhere in the middle of all those shifts, closing late, opening early, counting drawers, wiping down stainless steel, and hearing the same drive-thru headset chatter over and over, I started to believe that maybe all these little steps weren't random. Maybe they were building something. Even if I didn't know what the final picture looked like yet, I could feel that the shape of a real life was starting to form, piece by piece.

Arby's was also where I met Malik.

He was a few years older than me. Taller, decent-looking, always wearing that half-smile like he knew something you didn't. Not full-on cocky, but close.

Malik became my closest friend there pretty quickly. When we were scheduled together, the hours didn't drag the same way. There was always something to laugh at, some comment under his breath, some running joke that turned a boring shift into something that actually resembled fun.

He lived with one foot planted in the "adult" world and the other foot firmly in "let's see how much trouble we can get into." He drank, smoked weed, and treated partying like a real responsibility, like if there was an opportunity to turn a normal night into a story, he was going to take it.

Sometimes he'd even get high at work. He'd disappear into the bathroom for a minute, come back with red eyes and that lazy grin, and act like it was the most normal thing in the world to be making sandwiches while half-baked.

He also swore he had a genius trick for not getting caught. According to Malik, he'd blow the smoke down into a sink full of water so it "wouldn't smell." He said it like he'd cracked a code. I never bought it. Even then I was thinking, *man, there is no universe where that works the way you say it works.* But Malik had confidence in his own nonsense. Who was I to argue with Malik's Laws of Weed Smoking Physics.

Despite the long hours, I didn't mind the work. We closed at eleven on weeknights and midnight on weekends, and closing didn't mean "lock the doors and leave." It meant scrubbing fryers, wiping everything down, wrapping meat, finishing prep, cleaning the dining room, counting out whatever needed counting, and trying to make the place look like new for the next business day.

By the time we were done, it was usually after one in the morning, sometimes closer to one-thirty. You'd step outside and the air felt different. Quiet. Empty. Like the rest of the world had been asleep for hours and you were the only one still awake.

On some of those nights, we'd end up going out with coworkers or meeting up with Malik's friends. Beer, loud talk, a lot of bullshit, whatever people did to feel like they weren't wasting their lives working late shifts at a fast-food place. Sometimes a joint would make its way around and I'd try to join in to understand what everybody else seemed to get from it.

Most of the time, I felt nothing. I'd watch other people get loose and giggly and relaxed, and I'd be sitting there wondering why I felt slower and sadder instead of lighter.

But there was one night I'll never forget.

We weren't working that evening, so we went over to a friend's place early. Cards on the table, music in the background, cheap beer. Everybody was comfortable and settled in, and I was tired of being the guy who smoked and "didn't feel anything." I was tired of not understanding why I wasn't having the same experience.

So when the joint started going around, I decided to stop half-assing it. *If I'm going to do this, I'm going to <u>really</u> do it.*

When it got passed to me, I took deep pulls, the kind that burn your chest and make your eyes water. I didn't do the polite little inhale-and-pass. I went all in. Five, six trips around the table, and I didn't hold back once.

And then it hit.

Adam and I used to call it "creeper weed," the kind that lays low for a while and then shows up all at once when you're not expecting it. But this wasn't funny-high. This wasn't "everything is hilarious" high. This felt like getting poisoned, like that heavy, sick feeling you get after one too many shots of cheap tequila.

The room started to spin in that slow, nauseating way. I remember thinking, *I need this shit out of me, right now,* and then realizing there's no emergency eject button with weed. You can't just throw up. You can't sober up with coffee. You just have to sit there and take your punishment.

So I rode it out, miserably, trying not to make it obvious. I sat there quiet, forcing my face to look normal while my body felt like it was moving through mud and my brain asking, *why did I do that, why did I do that, why did I do that?*

Arby's was also where I met Sami.

She was a high school senior. Petite, tan, dark hair, warm brown eyes. She wasn't the kind of girl who stopped a room when she walked in, but there was something about her that just did a little something for me. Well, at least for my hormones and libido.

When she talked to me, she'd lean in just a little closer than she needed to, with that flirtatious smile and soft giggle. Sometimes she'd brush against me at the front counter. Maybe it didn't mean anything to her, but to me, at that point in my life, the smallest hint that something could turn physical was all I needed to start trying to turn the fantasies in my head into something real.

That sounds pathetic when I say it out loud, but it's the truth.

The problem was obvious. I was still with Katarina. Not just with her, but in love with her.

This is one of those chapters I'm not proud of, and there's no way to tell it where I come out looking noble. I wasn't confused. I wasn't "finding myself." I was making stupid choices, fully aware of what they meant, and I was still making them.

After work, I'd offer Sami a ride home. It sounds innocent written like that, like I was just being nice, but I knew what I was doing. And so did she. I wouldn't pull up to her house and let her hop out under the porch light like a normal person. I'd park a couple houses down instead, giving us the privacy the moment required.

We'd sit in the front seat of my Eclipse with the windows fogging over, talking in that quiet, half-whispered way people do when they're pretending they aren't about to do what they're about to do. Then the talking would stop, and our hands would start wandering, and we'd go at it, right there in the front seat of my car.

It only happened a few times. Three, maybe. But even just once was too much.

It wasn't love. I was still completely in love with Katarina, which makes it worse. This was something smaller and uglier. Thrill. Ego. Desire. Curiosity. The cheap rush of getting that kind of attention from someone new. That hit of being wanted. And if I'm being honest, part of me liked that I could cross a line and still feel like I was in control, like I could do something reckless and come out untouched.

I wasn't untouched.

The guilt hit immediately, right there in the car, right after the last kiss as she opened the door to walk the rest of the way to her house. The silence would settle back in, and it would stop feeling exciting and start feeling wrong.

I'd stare through the windshield, trying to act normal, but my stomach would be turning because I knew exactly what I was doing to someone who didn't deserve it.

I wanted to confess. I wanted to throw it all on the table, take the consequences, and get it over with. But telling Katarina meant losing her, and I wasn't ready to lose her. So instead, I did what cowardly people do. I carried it quietly and kept pretending I was still the same guy. Then, I'd do it all over again the next weekend.

Katarina was everything I wasn't. Steady. Loyal. Grounded. She made me feel safe, and I knew how rare that was even then. She was better than me in almost every way that mattered, and I knew that too.

That might've been the worst part. Not ignorance, not immaturity, not "I didn't realize." I realized. I just kept doing it anyway.

And because apparently I wasn't done trying to sabotage the best thing I'd ever had, there was Melanie.

Melanie was Katarina's best friend, the one who was with her the night we first met at the movie theater. Taller than me, which, given my height, isn't exactly rare. She had this quirky sense of humor, quick with the comebacks, the kind of person who could make you laugh even when you weren't in the mood.

From the beginning there was attraction there, and it wasn't subtle. We joked a little too easily, stood a little too close, held eye contact a little too long. That constant, low-level sexual tension that never fully goes away once it's there.

Katarina saw it. She wasn't stupid.

One day, fed up with the tension and innuendos, she called us out on it. And in a move I still don't fully understand, she gave us what she called a "hall pass." She told us she'd be out of town for the weekend and said we should "get it out of our system."

Even now, writing that, it makes me shake my head in disbelief. I don't know if she thought crossing the line once would kill the tension, if she wanted proof she wasn't imagining it, or if she was testing both of us to see if we'd actually go through with it. Maybe it was all of that. Whatever her reasons were, it doesn't change what happened next.

Because we treated it like a golden ticket.

That's on us.

When Friday came, after Katarina left, Melanie and I hung out together. On the surface it felt like any other time. Drinks, jokes, that easy friendship familiarity. But the difference was obvious right away. The one person who always anchored the room wasn't there. No Katarina.

Eventually we ended up at Mattis Lake, which calling it a lake is generous. It's basically a glorified pond tucked behind strip malls and parking lots. We parked, grabbed a blanket, and found a quiet spot where you could see the stars. It felt forced, like we were trying to manufacture a "moment."

We talked for a while, and then I leaned in, just to see if this was even a possibility, and kissed her. If she pulled back, we'd know. We could pass the whole idea off as a stupid idea and just move on.

But she didn't pull back.

It was fine. Not bad. Not electric. Just fine.

And that's what still stands out when I think about it. There was no spark. No surge. No feeling like, *oh, this is what I've been missing.* Nothing even close to what I felt with Katarina. This wasn't some inevitable thing we couldn't resist. It was two young people taking something that worked better as unspoken tension and trying to force it into reality.

That should've been the lesson right there. A kiss, a quick laugh, a mutual recognition of, *yeah, this doesn't feel right.* We could've stopped. We could've gone home, let it die, and let the awkwardness fade with time.

But we were young, reckless, and already halfway committed to the mistake, so we kept going.

Clothes slowly came off, piece by piece, and we had sex right there in the grass by the water. It was quick. Forgettable. The kind of thing that, in the long arc of my life, means nothing, and yet says everything about who I was back then. Not because it was some wild scandal, but because it showed how easily I could shut off the weight of what I was doing in the moment, and then pick it back up later like a cinder block and act surprised it was heavy.

When Katarina got back, she asked if we'd gone through with it.

I told her the truth.

She nodded once. "Good," she said. "You only get the one time. That's it."

Was she okay with it? Of course not. How could she be? She loved me, and I had just slept with her best friend, even if she'd technically signed off on it beforehand. Permission doesn't magically turn betrayal into something else.

I wish I could say that was the turning point. That the emptiness of that night at the lake snapped something into place. That I finally understood what I was risking and stopped playing games with people's hearts like it was all just normal everyday teenage drama.

But that would be a lie.

The truth is, this was part of a pattern I was building. Bad decisions stacked on top of bad decisions while I tried to outrun the parts of myself I didn't want to face. The broken kid who couldn't stand the idea of being alone. The guy who needed constant validation. The version of me who treated love like something you test instead of something you protect.

That's who I was then. And I carry the shame of that with me, whether anyone else sees it or not. Not as a performance, not as a "look how hard I'm being on myself," but as truth. I hurt someone who deserved better. I had something real and I still went looking for cheap validation like it could fill whatever hole I still had inside myself.

And the hardest part is knowing I understood enough to know it was wrong, and I did it anyway.

There were other mistakes, more than I want to admit, more than I can defend.

Eventually, after time to reflect on all of those terrible things I did to the people who cared about me the most, I learned that the value of your worth isn't connected to the number of people who want you. Your worth shows up when you stop needing their attention to believe you matter.

Back then? I wasn't there yet. Not even close.

One of the worst mistakes I made back then involved one of Malik's ex-girlfriends.

She was tall. Like 6'1" tall. And I'm 5'3" on a good day, so standing next to her felt like standing next to a different species. She wasn't "silver screen perfect," but she had that kind of presence where people automatically assume she's out of your league. And if we're being honest, they probably would've been right.

She carried herself like she knew it, too. Confident. Comfortable in her own skin. Not performing for anyone.

A few times, we'd hang out together with another couple Malik knew, usually at this cramped little place off Church Street. The living room always smelled like old beer and burnt microwave dinners. The couch sagged in the middle. It was the kind of place where bad choices were just expected.

One night, her and Malik got into it. Not a normal couples argument where you can tell it's going to burn out and they'll talk it out tomorrow. This was the kind where everyone in the room starts looking at the floor and trying to become invisible.

At some point Malik stormed out mid-fight, and suddenly it was just me, her, the roommate, and the roommate's girlfriend sitting there in awkward silence.

For twenty, maybe thirty minutes, we just sat with it. It started as awkward silence and slowly turned into forced jokes and half laughs. Nobody was relaxed, but nobody wanted to be the one to say, "So, what now?" And then, without any real conversation, we decided to head out for the night.

She drove this white Ford Eddie Bauer Edition SUV. Big and boxy, like it took up its own zip code. I still had my Mitsubishi Eclipse, and I told her to follow me.

I didn't have some plan. I just drove. Out of town, onto back roads I knew without thinking, and eventually to the empty lot where my childhood home used to be.

The house had been torn down years earlier, but the bare plot of land was still there. An empty acre, surrounded by corn fields. No neighbors close by, no streetlights, no anything. Just quiet and open space and that feeling of being far away from consequences and judgement.

I pulled into the grass toward the middle of the lot and she parked behind me.

I walked over, climbed into the passenger seat of her SUV, and we did that pointless small talk people do when they're stalling. We both acted like we didn't know why we were there, like we were just two adults having a totally normal conversation in the middle of nowhere at night. It was nothing meaningful. Just words filling the space until we ran out of patience for pretending.

Then, as if right on cue, we climbed into the back seat. Clothes came off fast and clumsy, like we were trying not to give our conscience time to catch up. And we had raw, passionate, primal sex.

I don't remember every detail, but I remember it was good. Better than I expected. I remember lying there afterward, staring up at the ceiling of that SUV, and feeling two things at the same time that didn't belong together. Pride and shame.

Pride because part of me felt like I'd just pulled off something I didn't think I could. Shame because I knew exactly what it said about me.

She was older. Mid-twenties, maybe twenty-six. Attractive, confident, comfortable in her skin. The kind of woman who took charge.

I was twenty, approaching twenty-one, an assistant manager at Arby's, still living with my parents, walking around like having keys and a title meant I had my life figured out. I remember thinking, really clearly, *what is a woman like her doing with a guy like me?*

And because my brain has always tried to cover panic with humor, that's also the night I told one of the dumbest jokes I've ever said out loud. I told her, "I'm so short, when I do a 69, I get a mouthful of belly button."

It was obscene and stupid. But it was also, unfortunately, accurate. That night I learned the math on that joke wasn't just theoretical.

At the time, it felt like one more reckless decision in a growing pile. Something that would turn into a story later, filed away under *well, that happened*, and then fade out.

I had no idea it was the one that would come back and put my whole future in a chokehold.

About a month later, I heard that the guy she'd dated after Malik was in prison, and that he had been diagnosed with AIDS. I didn't know the details. I didn't know the timeline. I just heard enough for my stomach to drop straight through the floor.

Because if he had it, she might have it.

And if she had it, I might have it.

I began to began immediately. My brain was moving a hundred miles an hour, spinning in every direction. Every dumb decision I'd made filled my head.

I scheduled an HIV test right away, and sitting in that clinic filling out paperwork felt like waiting for a death sentence. Like my whole life was about to be reduced to a phone call and a piece of paper.

When the first test came back negative, I exhaled so hard it felt like my body collapsed in on itself.

For about five minutes.

Then my brain stepped in and ruined it. *What if it was too early? What if the timing is wrong? What if they missed something? What if you're the guy who doesn't know and passes it on?*

For the next two or three years after that, I kept getting tested every six months. Not because anyone told me I had to, but because my mind wouldn't let me leave it alone. Every sore throat, every clammy sweat, every random ache, my brain went straight to, *this is it. This is how it starts.*

It took a long time for me to believe what the doctors kept telling me. *You're fine.*

But the medical fear wasn't the only fallout.

She and I agreed we weren't telling Malik. There was no reason to. It was a one-time thing. Heat-of-the-moment. He wasn't even with her anymore. That was the story we told ourselves, and for a while it held up.

Until it didn't.

Somehow, during another one of their usual fights, whether she was trying to hurt him, or she wanted to blow things up, or she just didn't care, she told him.

I was back at the Church Street house again. Same crew. Beer in my hand and mid-conversation when Malik got a phone call. I casually watched through the screen door as he paced on the sidewalk outside with the phone pressed to his ear. His voice got louder with every lap. I couldn't hear the words, but I didn't need to. You can read rage without hearing it.

He hung up.

The front door flew open and he blew into the house like a storm. No yelling. No questions. No "Is this true?" No chance to explain or deny anything.

He just cocked his left arm and swung.

His fist hit the right side of my face so hard I dropped straight back onto the couch. My ears rang and my eyes began to water instantly. And before I could catch up to what was happening, he was already coming at me again.

The roommate tackled him over the back of the couch and pinned him on the floor.

I didn't stay to see how all of that ended.

I bolted out the door, down the steps, and into my car. My hands were shaking on the steering wheel. My eye throbbed with every heartbeat. My mind was pure static with one thought cutting through it on a loop. *What the hell just happened?*

I got home and went straight to the full-length mirror in my parents' hallway because I needed to see it. I needed to know that I wasn't imagining the whole thing.

Under my right eye was this swollen lump, round and raised, like someone had tucked a ping-pong ball under my skin. No cut. No blood. Just a sore reminder of a night gone wrong.

And I got furious.

At him. At her. At myself. At the entire stupid chain of decisions that kept landing me in situations like this.

And in the way only a twenty-year-old can be, half ego, half adrenaline, I decided the right move was to drive right back.

Not because I wanted to fight. I'm not a fighter, and Malik was bigger than me. I wasn't going back to "win." I wanted answers. I wanted to yell. I wanted to demand how he thought he had the right to rearrange my face over a girl he wasn't even with anymore.

I hopped back in my car and drove back over to that house. But the second I turned the corner near the house, I saw his black Fiero at the intersection, facing my direction.

We spotted each other at the same time, and something in my gut flipped hard. The fantasy of "going back to talk" evaporated.

He gunned it.

He pulled out and got on my bumper so close it felt like he was trying to push my car with his. And suddenly it was a full-on chase through neighborhoods. Nothing but raw rage, adrenaline, and alcohol accelerating those cars through side streets at 1:00 in the morning.

I flew through streets in my Eclipse, shifting gears, cutting corners hard, trying to lose him without wrapping my car around a tree or a parked truck.

He stayed right behind me, that Fiero locked on me like it had only one purpose: make sure I couldn't get away from what I'd done.

I turned onto Fair Street and saw the only move I had. It dead-ended at a "T." I drove all the way down, hit the end, yanked a U-turn, and killed my headlights as I tucked in behind another parked car and sat there, barely breathing, with my hands locked on the steering wheel.

From where I was, I could see him at the top of the block, across the other side of Church Street, at the stop sign. He paused at the intersection, looking straight down the street.

For a second I thought he could see me but I couldn't tell for sure. I just stared, waiting for his headlights to dart toward me.

But then he miraculously turned left and sped away.

I waited longer than I probably needed to, just to make sure he didn't swing back around. My heart was pounding and it was difficult for me to catch my breath. When I finally pulled out from behind that parked car that was keeping me hidden, I drove home and decided it would be best to just stay there this time.

Of course, as fate would have it, we worked the same shift together at Arby's the next day, which is the part people who didn't grow up in small towns don't always understand. You can't just delete someone from your life because they punched you in the face.

You still have to clock in. You still have to stand shoulder to shoulder on the line. You still have to hand them bags of curly fries like they didn't try to chase you down the street and kill you the night before.

And because we were guys, and pride, alcohol and immaturity is a brutal combo, we had to just laugh it off.

He was drunk. He felt betrayed. She told him in the worst possible way and he snapped. I crossed a line with someone he used to care about. And apparently still did.

And as much as I hated admitting it, I couldn't completely blame him.

We never really talked it out in any real way. No real apology. No moment where somebody owned anything and meant it. Guys are like that. We just kept moving. Clocked in. Clocked out. Made orders. Cracked jokes. Acted like it was over.

But it wasn't over for me.

Because that night didn't just leave me with a swollen eye and a story. It left me with fear that stuck with me for years to come. Fear about what disease I might've caught. Fear about what I might've ruined. Fear about how fast your life can turn when you follow the wrong person out the door and tell yourself it doesn't matter.

It does matter.

That night, the SUV, the scare, the punch, the chase, none of it just happened to me. It left a scar. It followed me around as a quiet reminder that I wasn't as decent as I liked to think I was.

It wasn't only because it was such a dramatic experience. It was what it revealed about me as a person. I was a kid who kept walking straight into situations that required a level of emotional maturity I didn't have. And I didn't just stumble into them once. I kept choosing them. I kept stepping into the same messes, knowing it would cost me something, or everything, and acting surprised every time it did.

When I zoom out and look at that whole Arby's stretch now, the weed, the late-night shifts, the parties with Malik, the front seat with Sami, the lake with Melanie, the empty lot with Malik's ex, I don't see some funny season of "youthful mistakes." I see a self-destructive pattern. And I see myself right in the middle of it, acting like I'm just along for the ride when I'm the one driving most of it.

Something broke in me during that time, and it wasn't poetic. It wasn't enlightening. It was ugly and uncomfortable. You catch a clear glimpse of what's underneath, and you don't like it.

Up until then, I had a story I told myself that sounded innocent enough. *I'm just trying to figure it out. I'm doing my best.* I wanted that to be the truth, but the reality was more harsh. I refused to stand still long enough to take responsibility for who I was becoming, so I stayed in motion on purpose.

I kept busy, distracted, and chasing whatever made me feel wanted for five minutes, because if I stopped, I'd have to feel the weight of what I was doing, and who I was doing it to.

Getting that position at Arby's felt like a win at first. A title, a paycheck, a path that made it look like I was stepping into adulthood. From the outside, it probably looked like I was getting it together, but I wasn't there building a future. I was building a disguise. I was trying to create a version of myself I could hide inside. Something that looked grown-up, while on the inside I stayed insecure, selfish, and emotionally paralyzed.

Malik made it easier to keep lying to myself. He was like a walking permission slip for everything I didn't want to examine too closely. Party, laugh, smoke, repeat. He carried himself with this effortless, detached confidence, or at least it looked like confidence, and I wanted to borrow that energy. I followed him into the haze because it felt better than being alone with my thoughts, and I mistook his "nothing touches me" attitude for strength.

But where he floated, I sank.

Weed never really did for me what other people said it did for them, and I get why now. I wasn't trying to escape reality as much as I was trying to escape myself. I wanted to feel something real, but I didn't know how to sit with any emotion for more than a few seconds without reaching for something, anything, anyone, to interrupt it.

So instead of substances, I reached for people. For attention. For that quick hit of being wanted that could drown out the quieter voice in my head asking what the hell I was doing.

And then there were the women. Sami in the front seat of my car, Melanie on a blanket by the water, Malik's ex in the back of that SUV parked on the dirt where my childhood home used to be.

That list alone is enough to make me cringe, but the part that still lands the hardest is that Katarina was always there too. She was the ghost I dragged into every situation. Even when she wasn't physically present, she was standing in the doorway of my conscience, watching me betray her in real time, and I knew it. I felt it. I still did it anyway.

That's the part that's hard to write without cringing, because it wasn't just bad timing or confusion or being "young and dumb." It was emotional cowardice.

I kept telling myself I wasn't trying to hurt anyone, as if intent somehow made the impact softer. But intent is an excuse that only works in your own head. It doesn't change what it feels like to be lied to, or what it does to someone when they realize the person they trusted was living a double life right in front of them.

And I didn't cheat because I didn't care about Katarina. I cheated because I was weak.

I chased new attention because being fully seen by someone who already loved me made me anxious. Steady made me feel exposed, like there was nowhere to hide, so I did what I was good at back then. I sabotaged the thing that was solid because solid meant I had to show up as myself, and I didn't believe that version of me deserved what I had.

It's embarrassing to admit how much of it was me trying to prove my own worst beliefs.

I needed to prove I was unlovable, and then when everything blew up, I could point at the wreckage and say, "See? I told you so." Like predicting the disaster made the fact that I'm the one who caused it seem somehow less pathetic.

I wanted to be the one to burn it down so I wouldn't have to sit with the fear of losing it on someone else's terms. I told myself that was power when it was really just panic.

Sometimes you have to watch yourself become the villain in someone else's story before you admit you need to change. And even then it feels disgusting.

Getting punched in the face that night wasn't a heroic turning point. It was just the physical version of what had already been happening. Life had been trying to get my attention for a while, and that night made it louder because it forced me to see the common denominator in all of it.

The job, the weed, the parties, the women, the lying. The thread running through every mess was me.

Those things didn't define me, but they revealed me. I was a kid playing dress-up in a grown-up world, hoping the uniform, the title, the stories, the notches on the bedpost would magically turn me into a man.

They didn't.

What actually started shaping me were the things I wanted most to hide. The mistakes, the shame, the nights I lay awake replaying scenes I couldn't undo. I'd feel my stomach twist imagining the look on Katarina's face if she ever knew all of it. Every detail. Every betrayal. Every time I chose my own insecurity over her trust.

It took years for those lessons to really land. Years before I could look back without minimizing it, justifying it, or turning it into a joke and calling it "stupid kid stuff" like that would erase the damage.

Years before I could admit that what I called "living" was often just me avoiding myself. Avoiding guilt. Avoiding the truth. Avoiding the quiet moment where I'd have to sit with who I was and decide whether I even liked him.

You can keep running, you can keep rewriting the story so you don't feel as bad, or you can turn around, look it in the eye, and admit what you did, who you were, and how many people you hurt while you were pretending it wasn't that serious.

Only then do you get to decide who you're going to be from here.

And facing that part, facing me, has always been the hardest part.

Another night, Katarina, Melanie, Adam, and I were hanging out at my parents' house while they were out of town. It started like it always started. Cards, drinks, that little agreement that we were just going to keep it chill.

We never kept it chill.

By midnight we'd been playing loud, aggressive euchre for hours and drinking way too much gin and juice. At some point Adam and I landed on the kind of drunk conclusion that feels like a law of nature. We needed Taco Bell.

"You don't need Taco Bell that bad," Katarina said, giving us that look, half concerned, half already annoyed because she knew where this kind of logic usually ended up.

She was right. But drunk logic doesn't have ears.

So Adam and I piled into his little Bronco II and took off. We headed down Neil Street, over the I-74 overpass like we'd done a hundred times. The mall straight ahead and Taco Bell off to the right in the strip mall. Just a simple ten minute taco run.

Except when we pulled in, it was closed. No glowing sign. No drive-thru lights. No cars. Just an empty lot and two idiots sitting there, staring at a dark building.

We sat for a second letting it sink in. No tacos. Just the realization we were going back to the house empty-handed and probably catching hell for it.

So Adam swung around to Anthony Drive, a short frontage road, and then cut over to Market Street where it dips back under the interstate. Then we cut right onto Kenyon Road, which runs alongside the interstate, with loose gravel on the shoulder and a chain-link fence separating the road from a deep grassy ditch.

I remember noticing it because it hit this old nerve in me. There was something about that stretch of road that reminded me too much of the accident I'd been in a few years earlier.

You'd think that would've been the moment I got serious and said, "Hey, slow down." I didn't. I was drunk, I was riding shotgun, and I was still in that mindset where consequences were something that happened to other people.

Adam didn't ease into the curve. He came in fast and loose, like he was driving on a video game track he'd already beaten.

The tires slipped off the pavement onto the gravel and my stomach dropped immediately. An all-to-familiar feeling being replayed in real time.

The truck fishtailed hard, sliding deeper onto the shoulder, drifting toward the fence. The front end dipped and the Bronco lurched sideways.

Then the chain-link started tearing along the passenger side, my side, with that high ripping metal sound.

And then we rolled.

Once, and then another weird half-roll that ended with the Bronco on its side, passenger door pinned against the ground.

I was pressed into that door and Adam was basically on top of me, his weight crushed into me. And yeah, his ass was somewhere near my face.

Neither of us had seat belts on, which is insane to say out loud now, but at the time it was just what we did.

For a second there was nothing. No talking, no movement. Just that heavy pause where you're checking your body without moving it, trying to figure out what's broken and what still works.

Then I heard myself.

"You good?" I groaned.

"Yeah," Adam muttered. "You?"

"Yeah. Now get your ass outta my face."

We both laughed, but it wasn't because it was funny. It was pure relief. The kind of laughter that happens when you know you should not be alive right now, but you are, and don't know what else to do.

We climbed out through the driver's side window, which had become our escape hatch, and dropped down onto the grass. I remember the weird, almost unreal feeling of my feet hitting the ground.

And then we looked up and realized we weren't alone.

There were people lined up along the road watching us. Like an audience. Perkins, a 24-hour restaurant, was up the way and apparently half the place had wandered outside when they heard the crash.

I'm sure it sounded like a dump truck dropping a load of gravel on the road. People were just standing there, staring at this Bronco on its side like it was the late-night entertainment.

The cops showed up pretty fast. Before I'd even fully processed what had actually happened, red and blue lights were bouncing off the brick building and the exposed underside of the truck.

They put Adam through the whole sobriety routine. Walk the line, heel to toe, turn, come back, follow the pen, stand on one foot, touch your nose.

I watched thinking there is no chance he passes this. They can probably smell the gin in the air around us. But somehow he kept nailing it. Walking straight, hitting the marks, pulling it together like he wanted no part of a jail cell.

Meanwhile I'm on the curb. Underage, drunk, clearly involved, trying to be invisible. But I wasn't driving, and in a college town underage drinking wasn't exactly an uncommon occurrence. A rolled truck was an actual problem.

At some point Adam came back and sat next to me and leaned in.

"Hey man," he whispered, low, "I've got a bag of weed in the glove box."

I just stared at him like my brain had to reboot.

"What?" I whispered. "Are you serious?"

So now the situation escalated. Two drunk underage idiots. A truck on its side. A crowd. A bunch of cops. And weed sitting in the glove box of a vehicle that was about to be towed away.

My mind went straight to worst-case. Cops find it. Parents get called. Charges. Criminal records.

Adam, somehow, still had a brilliant plan.

"We need to go get it," he said.

That was the plan. Just go get it.

I told him I wasn't touching it. Not even a little. I wasn't about to add possession to the list of things I was already trying to avoid. We went back and forth in whispers, me basically saying, "I'm not going down for your glove box goodies," and him acting like it was no big deal.

Then he stood up and walked to one of the officers and said, way too casually, something like, "Hey, I know it's going to be impounded, but I've got personal stuff in the glove box. Wallet and things. Is it cool if I grab it before it gets towed?"

It was smooth. I'll give him that.

The cop looked at the Bronco on its side and shrugged. Told him he could, but it was at his own risk. Basically, *I'm not climbing on that thing, buddy. If you want to, that's on you.*

I swear I swallowed a rock. This was the moment everything should've gone sideways. In any other version of this night, the cop says, "Hold up, I'll get it," climbs up, opens the glove box, and suddenly the whole night turns into something we can't take back.

But he didn't.

Adam climbed onto the Bronco, slid back through the driver's side window, popped the glove box, grabbed the weed, stuffed it in his pocket, and crawled back out like he'd just simply retrieved his wallet.

He came back, sat next to me, and whispered, "Since I was driving, they'll probably focus on me more. Take this."

My answer came out immediately.

"Hell no!"

I wasn't doing it. Friendship has limits, and "hold my weed while we're sitting next to cops after rolling a truck" is a pretty easy line for me.

"Keep that shit in your own pocket," I told him, still watching the officers, trying to figure out if they were watching us closer than we realized.

Even though nobody was arresting us, they weren't just going to leave us standing there. Our house was only a couple blocks away, about a ten-minute walk. If we'd had any sense at all, we would've walked to Taco Bell in the first place, or walked home once we saw it was closed.

Instead, they loaded us into the back of the squad car. Two half-drunk idiots in the backseat, trying to act normal while my heart was doing gymnastics.

We started down the road and headed toward Neil Street. When we got to the stop sign, the officer got a call over the radio, and you could feel the shift immediately. His posture changed. His tone changed. Like whatever came through was suddenly more important than babysitting us.

He cut across Neil Street and pulled into the Mobile gas station on the corner, and turned around to look at us.

"How much farther is your house?" he asked.

"It's just a couple blocks," I said. "Right up there."

He nodded once. "Alright. I've gotta take this call."

And then he let us out.

Just like that. No lecture. No threats. No "you boys are lucky tonight." Just an open door, a quick release, and then the squad car peeled out of the lot and disappeared toward somebody else's emergency.

Adam and I just stood there for a second watching the taillights fade away, both of us quiet, like we couldn't believe what just happened.

"Man," Adam said finally, "that was un-fucking-believable."

He wasn't wrong. It felt like we'd been inches away from disaster in about six different directions and somehow none of it touched us.

We went into the gas station and bought a fresh pack of Marlboros and started the short walk home. The air felt colder than it had earlier as the adrenaline wore off.

By the time we came through the back door, the next wave hit. Reality.

The girls were furious. Not just annoyed. Scared, angry, shaken. We'd been gone over an hour and a half for what was supposed to be a quick Taco Bell run. No food. No Bronco in the driveway. Just the two of us walking in smelling like cigarettes, dirt, and leftover fear.

They thought we'd crashed.

And they were right.

When we told them what happened, it didn't calm anything down. If anything, it made it worse, because it wasn't one bad decision. It was a chain of them.

"We rolled the truck."

"The cops picked us up."

"There was weed."

"But it's fine now."

None of that sounded like "fine" to anyone with a sober brain. Or a human one.

They could've lost us that night.

My parents could've gotten a call no parent should ever get. One cop making one different choice could've changed my whole life. One of those wrong place, wrong time moments that turns into a record and a reputation.

Instead, we walked away with bruises, a wrecked truck, and a story. No one dead. No one in handcuffs. No hospital. No phone call to my parents.

And that's what has stayed with me all these years later. Not the "crazy night" version of it. The truth under the story. The quiet, crushing feeling that we were just lucky. Ridiculously, undeservingly lucky. And even if I didn't say it out loud then, a part of me was quietly, deeply grateful that we got to walk back into that house at all.

Back then, I thought I understood consequences. I really did. I thought I knew where the line was, how far I could push without falling. But that night showed me how thin that line really is. How fast "we're just getting tacos" can turn into "we could've died."

No seat belts. A rollover. A fence. A crowd. A bag of weed in the glove box. A cop car. And somehow, no real injuries, no charges, no parents awakened by a phone call that begins with, "There's been an accident."

We walked away with bruises, a wrecked truck, two furious girlfriends, and a story that still doesn't sound real unless you were there.

But the turning point for me wasn't the crash. It was the curb. It was sitting there watching Adam blow through a sobriety test he shouldn't have passed. It was that split second when he tried to hand me his weed and something in me finally said no.

Not this. Not for anyone.

That "no" came from some newly forming place inside me. A boundary I didn't know I even had, let alone could enforce. It was the first time I really understood that loyalty isn't the same thing as self-destruction. That being a good friend doesn't mean carrying someone else's risk just because you happen to be sitting next to them on a curb when everything goes sideways.

Sometimes life hands you a second chance way before you've earned it. And when that happens, the worst thing you can do is treat it like you're bulletproof. Like, "See? I can do whatever I want and still land on my feet."

A second chance is supposed to change something. Not a dramatic overnight transformation where you become a different person, but real change. Small at first. The kind where you start paying attention. Where you understand that walking away in one piece doesn't mean you were untouchable.

It means you got lucky. And luck is a terrible plan to build a life on.

Hopefully, if you get just enough humility to pair with the luck, you do the one thing you should've done all along.

You use it and keep moving forward.

My career at Arby's didn't keep moving forward.

It didn't end with some theatrical two-weeks' notice speech or even an unexpected promotion. It ended the simple, brutal way a lot of fast-food jobs end. I got fired.

It happened after a closing shift with this married couple I worked with, both of them eighteen. Eighteen and married. That fact alone still messes with my head. I was a few years older and could barely commit to a haircut for more than a month, and they were already sharing a last name and paying bills like real adults.

We were actually a good crew, too. Usually we worked well together, got things done, didn't create problems. But that night was one of those shifts where everything that can go wrong does.

Closing at Arby's was this whole routine you had to follow. Restock, scrub, prep, sanitize, count everything, and then weigh the meat. The roast beef was tracked like it was gold. You weighed it when it came in, you weighed it as you sliced, and you weighed what was left at the end of the night. Every number had to match, because that was the whole point. Inventory control. Corporate oversight. Making sure nobody was walking out with half the store stuffed in a backpack.

That night the numbers didn't just not match. They were insane.

We were "missing" almost fifty pounds of roast beef.

Fifty pounds.

At first we thought it had to be a mistake with the scale or the logs. Then we thought maybe we were reading something wrong. Then it turned into this panicked, sleep-deprived scavenger hunt where we double and triple checked, re-weighed, re-counted, re-read the paperwork like the answer was going to magically appear if we stared at it longer. We opened trash bags. We dug through boxes. We tore through the walk-in like we were going to find some hidden stack of meat shoved behind the pickles.

Nothing.

By around 2:30 in the morning, we were wiped out and running on fumes, and we finally figured it out.

It wasn't theft. It wasn't someone trying to screw us over. It wasn't some weird "Arby's conspiracy" where roast beef just evaporates. It was a clerical error.

Somebody misread the delivery slip. Wrong column, wrong line, wrong number. One small mistake earlier that morning that snowballed into a full-blown meltdown. And because we were the ones closing, we were the ones trying to fix it while the clock kept moving and our patience disappearing.

Once we corrected the paperwork and everything finally made sense, we still had to finish closing. Clean the last surfaces, put everything back, lock up.

By the time we were done, we weren't just tired. We were fried. The kind of tired where you get punchy and your brain starts suggesting things that are clearly not smart.

And that's when I remembered I had water balloons in the trunk of my car.

It wasn't even a plan. It was just this random thought that hit me like, *you know what would make this night feel less miserable?*

So we filled them up at the back sink, giggling like children. Then we went outside into the parking lot under those harsh orange lights and just started throwing them.

We were soaked, laughing so hard we couldn't breathe, running around like idiots. Not employees. Not "closers." Not the people who just spent hours solving some stupid inventory crisis. Just three tired kids acting like three tired kids, trying to shake off the whole night before we went home and passed out.

When we stopped, we picked up the big balloon scraps, did a quick look around, and basically decided that was good enough. At the time, it felt harmless. Like, whatever. Water dries. We grabbed what we saw and called it a night.

The next morning, my manager pulled into the lot and saw leftover pieces of colored latex scattered around. To her, it wasn't "three exhausted employees blowing off steam." It was disrespectful. It was irresponsible. It was a mess she had to deal with, and she was already the type who didn't need much to get set off.

A few hours later, I got the call.

No warning. No "What were you thinking?" No "Don't ever do that again." No chance to explain that we'd stayed late, fixed a major screw-up, and still closed the store the right way.

Just: you're fired.

Fired over a water-balloon fight.

And it wasn't just losing the job. It was how fast it happened. How it didn't matter that we'd handled the fifty-pound roast beef disaster. It didn't matter that we'd stayed hours past when we should've been out of there.

It didn't matter that it was her mistake that caused the situation in the first place. She was the one who received the shipment and recorded the wrong weight in the log.

None of that counted.

The only thing that mattered was the parking lot the next morning, and me being the easiest person to make an example out of.

I remember sitting with that afterward, feeling stupid and pissed and embarrassed all at once. Like, of course it was a dumb idea. But it was also this really clear lesson. You can do ten things right, and it might not matter if the one thing people see is the thing they can punish.

That's how Arby's ended for me. Not with a promotion, but with puddles and balloon fragments.

And the thing is, I still wouldn't take any of it back.

Not because getting fired was fun. It wasn't. It sucked. It was embarrassing.

But that night taught me something I probably needed to learn early. The rules aren't as clean as everyone pretends they are.

Work loves clean lines. Do this. Don't do that. Follow the process. Be perfect.

Life doesn't care. You can do everything "right" and still get tossed. You can handle something the "wrong" way, and still be the only one in the room who did anything that felt remotely human.

I learned you can get punished for trying to do the right thing, just because you didn't do it in the approved, neat, corporate way. And even if that costs you a job, it doesn't automatically mean you were wrong.

Sometimes you're better for it, even if it doesn't look like it in the moment.

ROUND 14:
Semper Nope & Six-Inch Lessons

I was twenty, and I was back in that in-between stage. Everything felt like it was supposed to be wide open, like adulthood was waiting to start any second, but my life also felt completely stalled. I wasn't a kid anymore. Nobody lets you hide behind that at twenty. But I also wasn't anywhere close to feeling like a real adult. If someone asked me what I was doing with my life, I could barely answer without wanting to laugh or panic.

I had no job. No plan. Nothing pushing me forward.

Just this weird limbo where the days started blending together, and nagging questions creeping in when I was alone too much.

What now? What the hell am I doing? Who am I? Who do I want to become? Where do I want to go?

It had been exactly two years since the Marine Corps disqualified me.

Two years since I'd sat alone at that MEPS station in St. Louis, waiting to raise my right hand and step into a different version of myself. Two years since I'd walked out with a folder full of paperwork and this empty, quiet ache where my future was supposed to be.

Back then, the recruiter tried to smooth it over like it was a minor detour. He told me they would only keep my records for two years and after that I could try again. At the time, two years sounded like a whole lifetime. I remember thinking, *There's no way I'll even be the same person by then.* I pictured myself having moved on, built something else, found a career, gotten locked into adult life, and not even having the option to go back

354

and try again. I said it out loud to myself: *two years is too long. Life will be different by then.*

But when those two years actually passed, life wasn't different the way I'd imagined. I was still broke. I was still drifting. And underneath all of it was this shame that I hadn't done much with the time except get older and more disappointed in myself. So when that line came back to me, *You can try again,* it didn't just feel hopeful. It felt like a challenge. Like something I owed myself.

So I went back.

Walking into that recruiting office again felt surreal, like I'd wandered back into the same episode of my life. Same scripted friendliness. Same posters of square-jawed Marines staring into some heroic distance. Same energy that made it feel like, the second you walked in, you were supposed to want this more than anything.

And I did want it. Not just because I wanted to be a Marine, but because I wanted what it represented. Structure. Respect. A reset. An honorable identity that was earned. I just knew I was sick of feeling like I was floating through my own life, waiting for something to fix me.

We did everything again: ASVAB, paperwork, the run-through of my history like it was a checklist that could turn into a green light if I answered the right way. And then they bussed me back to MEPS in St. Louis, to the same beige hallways and stale air, the same bored, tired faces behind government desks who looked at you like just another faceless file sliding across the counter.

I tried to tell myself it would be different this time. I tried to act calm, like I wasn't hanging everything on one decision made by strangers in uniforms in a concrete building.

The physical turned into the same slow-motion dread as before. Once again, they zeroed in on my back. Same history of chiropractic visits when I was seventeen. Same questions, same notes being written down, the same look on someone's face when they decide they've already seen enough. I sat there watching it happen and thought, *I've seen this episode before.*

I tried to explain it the best I could. Tried to make it sound small and manageable. Tried not to sound defensive. None of it mattered. The concern about the scoliosis came up again. The red flags came back. And the red ink came back.

And the result was the same.

Disqualified. Again.

There wasn't a motivational speech. Nobody pulled me aside and told me I'd find my path somewhere else. It was quiet and administrative, like a door closing with a soft click. A stamp. A decision. A shrug from the system. The kind of no that doesn't feel personal until you realize how personal you made it in your own head.

The bus ride back to Champaign felt like déjà vu, except now I didn't have that first-time innocence to cushion the hit. I stared out the window and replayed it, trying to figure out what I'd expected. I couldn't decide which part hurt more: that they'd said no again, or that I'd actually believed, even a little, that this time it might go differently. I'd walked in hoping for a clean slate, like the two-year thing meant I could start fresh.

It didn't. That clean slate was just me setting myself up for another failure.

Somewhere on that ride, the reality finally settled in. This wasn't bad luck. This wasn't timing. This wasn't me being one step away from the life I wanted. This was a closed door, and it wasn't going to open just because I wanted it so much.

I'd built this whole story in my head about becoming the disciplined one, the strong one, the guy who finally earned his place. Now it was obvious the Marine Corps wasn't going to be the place where I proved any of that.

I went home with the same body, the same spine they didn't trust, and this heavy, quiet sense that I'd come up short again. Not just in their eyes. But also in my own.

Back home, I started job hunting again, but that's not what I remember when I think about that stretch. What I remember is how split everything felt. Like I was living two lives at the same time, and neither one fully made sense.

I was still with Katarina, and the summer of '96 turned into this weird in-between season. I'd just turned 21, finally old enough to drink legally in all the places I'd already been drinking since I was nineteen, and she had just graduated high school. Even typing that out now, it's obvious how different our timelines were. I don't think either of us had really acknowledged what was happening, but we could feel it. Like we were moving in different directions and pretending we weren't. The seam was starting to pull, and we both knew it. We just stayed inside the parts that still felt good because that was easier than saying the inevitable out loud.

I was renting this old place on Washington Street near downtown, one of those houses that had clearly been around forever. Built sometime in the '30s or '40s, chopped up into crooked little apartments that didn't quite sit level. Everything creaked. The floors had soft spots. The paint was chipped, the windows were drafty, and the heater had commitment issues, working just enough to keep you from freezing, but only if it felt like it.

It was the kind of place you didn't bother decorating. It didn't feel worth it. Also, you sort of assumed you wouldn't be there long. But it was cheap and it was mine. And that's what mattered.

That apartment became the friend group hub, almost by accident. My high school crew, Zeke, Shayla, Miles, Kade, would drift in and out like they lived there. Someone would show up with a case of Milwaukee's Best because it was the cheapest, and someone else would kick their shoes off and sprawl on the couch like they owned the place.

There wasn't some official plan most nights. It was just the usual rhythm, hanging out, talking, messing around, acting like we had all the time in the world. Conversations would bounce from total nonsense to something weirdly serious and deep, then right back to nonsense again, because that's how we were.

We watched every Bulls game that summer of '96 while Jordan chased another ring. My living room basically turned into low-budget box seats. Jordan on the TV, beer on the coffee table, a bunch of us yelling at calls like the ref could actually hear us through the screen. We'd argue about plays, quote commentators, talk trash, laugh way too hard at dumb stuff, and for a few hours the rest of life didn't exist. No job pressure. No questions about what I was doing with myself. No relationship tension. Just the game, the noise, and the comfort of good friends

When we went out, we usually ended up at Fat City Saloon on Chestnut Street, just a few short blocks off the main campus strip. It wasn't flashy. No club vibe, no loud look-at-me energy that made me feel like I had to perform. It was dartboards, pool tables, dim lighting, and a bunch of calmer, more reserved college kids who mostly kept to themselves. You didn't have to dress a certain way or impress anyone. Nobody was spilling beer on your shoes on a crowded dance floor. The only thing that mattered was whose turn it was to throw darts, whether you were going to keep playing, and who was buying the next round. That was my speed.

That stretch of time is one of the last periods I remember feeling something close to steady. Not, *I've got my life all figured out,* steady. More like, *I know what tonight looks like steady.* It was more about a consistent routine that I could depend on than it was about a future I could vision. A small crooked apartment. A girl I loved, but was starting to outgrow. My friends piled onto mismatched furniture, Bulls games on the TV.

For all the confusion swirling around who I was and what I was supposed to become, there was this pocket of life that felt familiar and safe.

It was definitely messy and Imperfect. But it was consistent.

And I'm still grateful for it, which feels strange to say, because I know what I did to people in that era. I know how I mishandled things. I know how much damage I was capable of when I got to deep in my own head. But those nights with my friends, that little apartment, that routine, it kept me from completely unraveling.

Then one weekend my old high school friend, Janelle, invited me up to visit her at UIC in Chicago. I hadn't seen her in a long time, and the idea of getting out of town for a weekend sounded perfect. New scenery. New energy. A reason to stop staring at my own life for a minute. Just a weekend away where I could pretend I wasn't stuck.

There was one catch, though: I'd be staying with her in her dorm.

Katarina didn't love that detail, and she had every reason not to. With my history, the things I'd already done, the lines I'd already crossed, her jealousy wasn't exactly irrational. It was actually completely justified. It was her listening to the part of herself that knew I wasn't safe with her heart, even if she still wanted to believe I could be.

But I was too selfish, and honestly too emotionally checked out, to care the way I should've. I did what I always did when someone held up a mirror I didn't want to look into. I got defensive. I told myself she was overreacting. I told myself it was harmless. I told myself it was just a visit, just a friend, just a weekend.

And underneath all that, I knew the truth. I was making a decision that would hurt her. And I knew it.

We fought about it that morning at my place and it escalated fast. Her questions hit the same old sore spots and my answers came out dismissive and insulting. The old wounds showed up, the new insecurities piled on top, and before long we were shouting.

Then I snapped.

I grabbed my entertainment center and slammed it to the floor. TV, stereo, speakers, everything crashing down at once. Plastic cracking, wood splitting, glass shattering. It was stupid. Utterly childish. It was me throwing a tantrum in a grown man's body and just adding another disaster to the list. Like if I broke something big enough, it would drown out whatever was going on in my head.

And the look on her face when it happened. God. I can still see it. It wasn't just anger back at me. It wasn't even really shock. It was stunned hurt and fear. Like she realized, in that moment, that the person she loved could also be the person she was scared of. That the guy she kept hoping would grow up wasn't just immature. He was unsafe.

That's when something broke for good. Not just the TV and the stereo. Something between us that could never fully come back.

Me going to stay with another woman for the weekend, although an old friend from high school, after that kind of fight wasn't just a bad decision. It was me walking away from us, from her, and from any real chance I had at fixing what I'd already damaged. That was the point where our two-and-a-half-year relationship stopped being complicated and became plainly, painfully over.

And I knew it.

I knew it when I grabbed my keys.
I knew it when I walked out the door.
And I knew it the whole drive to Chicago.

But I drove there anyway. Because in that moment, my need to get away from my own guilt was louder than her pain.

That's what still hurts the most when I look back. Not just that I lost her, but that when it really counted, when she needed me to choose us, I chose to run instead.

The drive up I-57 and onto I-94 took about two and a half hours, and somewhere near the southern suburbs, something happened that still lives in the back of my mind on a loop.

I was cruising in one of the middle lanes with "Changes" by 2Pac turned up,

> *"...We gotta make a change...*
> *... let's change the way we treat each other*
> *You see, the old way wasn't workin'*
> *So it's on us to do what we gotta do to survive..."*

My head wasn't on the road. I was still stuck in those last awful minutes at my apartment, replaying them like maybe there was some hidden detail that could change what happened or some magic combination of words that would smooth it all over once I got back home. I just stared straight ahead.

That's when I saw him.

To my right, a car came flying up the on-ramp. Not the normal "I'm trying to merge and match traffic" kind of speed. Most people come on at sixty, maybe sixty-five. This guy had to be doing eighty, maybe more. He shot onto the interstate like he'd been launched, and with complete disregard of all of the other cars already speeding down each lane.

Before I could fully process it, he cut across the lanes and kept going, fast and aggressive. And it wasn't just one lane. He sliced across all six, missing bumpers by inches. It was the kind of driving you usually see for a second and think, *What an idiot,* and then they disappear up the road.

Except he didn't disappear.

About fifty yards in front of me, he slammed straight into the concrete barrier.

No brake lights. No skid. No attempt to avoid it. Just full speed into the wall.

The sound was violent. Not just loud, but crushing, the kind of noise you feel in your chest. The highway instantly turned into a frenzy. Cars slammed brakes, people swerved, horns started blaring, tires squealed, and for a few seconds it felt like the wreck was going to turn into ten more.

Somehow I threaded through it and got over to the shoulder behind a car that had already stopped just behind the impact.

My hands were shaking before I even opened my door. I didn't even think about it. I just got out of my car as quick as I could to help.

I ran up toward the car, and the closer I got, the worse it looked. The driver's side was pressed against the concrete barrier so hard it was basically fused to it. The whole front end was destroyed, metal folded and compacted in a way that didn't seem possible when you're used to cars being, you know, car-shaped.

I grabbed the driver's handle and yanked like I could muscle it open. It didn't move at all. I pulled again, harder, like maybe I hadn't tried hard enough the first time.

Nothing. Refer back to the whole *driver's side was pressed against the concrete barrier* detail I already mentioned.

I hopped back and tried the window. I kicked at it with my boot, trying to hop over the concrete barrier at the same time. Once, then again, then again, every kick sending a jolt up my leg. All I accomplished was scuffing the window and hurting my foot, and I remember having this stupid flash of frustration like I was failing some basic human test. *Get the window open. Help the guy. Do something.*

Then another guy appeared on the passenger side. You know, the side that *isn't* blocked by a concrete wall, and moved fast like he already knew what he was going to do. He had something in his hand, maybe a big flashlight or some heavy tool, and without hesitating he swung it into the passenger window.

The glass exploded, cutting his arm from the flying fragments. I saw blood immediately, but he didn't stop. He didn't even look. He reached in through the broken glass, fumbled with the lock, and pulled the passenger door open.

Everything sped up after that. People were converging from different cars, running up from behind us, pulling over wherever they could. I moved around to the back of the car and by the time I got there, the other guy was already pulling the driver out through the passenger side.

The driver had slid off the seat, folded down into the footwell under the steering wheel and he was limp. There was white foam at corners his mouth. It didn't look like a person you could talk to or shake awake.

And then the smell hit.

The strong, bitter scent of alcohol poured out of that car like walking into a bar at closing time. It rolled over all of us, and it made me feel sick, because it explained too much about what has just happened.

People formed this rough circle, ten or twelve strangers suddenly acting like a team even though nobody knew each other. Someone yelled to call 9-1-1. Someone else asked if anybody knew CPR. Another person stood there with their hands on their head, frozen, like they were trying to keep their thoughts from spilling out. The guy with the cut arm kept doing what he could to try to wake the guy up as he laid him down on his side on the pavement. I remember hearing voices but not being able to catch a full sentence.

For a second, I just stood there with my heart pounding so hard it felt like it was shaking my ribs. I watched it all unfold like it wasn't really happening in front of me. Like it was a dream or TV show.

Then I stepped back. Not because I didn't care. I just froze. I'm not a medic. I don't know CPR. I can't do anything. I just tried to kick a window in and couldn't. I'm standing here in thin leather boots with a bruised foot and trembling hands and no idea what to do next.

And underneath all that was the stress of everything else I had already been through that day. I was already overwhelmed from what happened earlier that morning before I even got on the highway. This was one more shock stacked on top of the first one, and I felt myself hit a limit.

So my body did what bodies do when they don't know how to hold everything . It went into survival mode. I drifted back toward my car. One foot in front of the other, like I was being pulled. I got in, shut the door, and quietly drove away.

The rest of the drive to Janelle's dorm didn't feel real. The highway signs, the exits, the steady flow of cars, it all looked normal, but it didn't register like normal. It felt like I was watching my own life from the other side of the glass, like the world was happening on a screen and I was somewhere behind my eyes, just observing while my hands stayed on the wheel.

My brain kept circling the same thoughts, over and over.

He could've hit me.
He could've taken out an entire lane of cars.
He went across six lanes and nobody got hurt except him. How does that happen?
Did he aim for the wall? Did he choose it?
Or was he so gone he didn't aim at anything?

Maybe he was already checked out before the car ever hit. Maybe the impact was just the last part of something that had already ended.

I don't know. I still don't.

What I do know is the uneasiness didn't fade when I got off the highway. It didn't fade when I parked. It didn't fade when I finally made it to Janelle's dorm. It just settled into me, muted and heavy, and it stayed there. Because it wasn't only about him. It was about how close everything felt to collapsing at any second, and how powerless I realized I was to stop it.

That weekend at UIC was muddy. Janelle and I bar-hopped, laughed, and pretended life was lighter than it really was. But it felt amazing to spend time with her again. We'd been really close friends throughout high school, and I'd missed her ridiculous sense of humor and that obnoxious laugh.

Her roommate looked exactly like Sandra Bullock. Like, exactly. So yeah, I still tell people I made out with Sandra Bullock one weekend in Chicago. Nobody believes me. Which is fair.

Nothing serious happened, but we got close enough for it to count as another wedge between who I thought I was and the guy I was actually being. On the drive home, everything caught up to me at once. Katarina was gone. The second shot at the Marines was dead. And that car crash replayed in my head in a nauseating loop.

I slid straight back into depression. Just like after Rachael. Just like after Belle.

My apartment turned into a cave again, and music became the soundtrack to my self-loathing. I put Toby Keith's "Blue Moon" on repeat like I was trying to punish myself through my own stereo.

> *"Day by day*
> *We let love just walk away…"*

I sat there alone, picking up every mistake, every argument, every missed opportunity like rocks off the ground, turning them over and over in my hands until my fingers ached. That Tim McGraw album playing "Can't Be Really Gone" over and over.

> *"Her book is lying on the bed*
> *The two of hearts to mark her page*
> *Now who could ever walk away at chapter twenty one*
> *So she can't be really gone…"*

I started as a General Manager at Subway.

This particular Subway was near the mall just off Prospect Avenue and Marketview Drive, one of the rare ones with a drive-thru. It was constant orders, beeping headsets, and the same requests over and over: "just a little more lettuce," "extra pickles." I learned the rhythm fast. Take the order, build the sandwich, wrap it, smile, move on. It wasn't some meaningful chapter of my life, but it was a job. It was money. That was the whole deal.

But I wasn't just the sandwich guy. I was Jon's fixer.

Jon was the franchisee who owned five Subways in the Champaign-Urbana area, and somehow I turned into the director of his cleanup crew. When one of his stores started slipping, he didn't call in a consultant or sit down to write a plan. He'd call me and basically say, "Go over there and make this not suck."

So I did.

I wasn't the guy who showed up, did the bare minimum, and then complained about how bad it was. I watched everything. I paid attention to what customers saw the second they walked in, what they smelled when the door opened, what the staff did when they thought nobody was looking. I watched the line setup, the prep habits, the speed, the way people talked to each other, the way they talked to customers. The stuff that sounds small is never small. Small stuff becomes the reputation.

The Rantoul store was the worst one by a mile. The lighting was dim, the walls looked like they hadn't been properly wiped down in forever, and the floors had that sticky, stained look that tells you mopping is more of a rumor than a routine. The walk-in had this smell that hit you immediately: old onions, wet cardboard, and some other unidentifiable funk.

The staff matched the building. Not busy and overwhelmed. Not short-staffed and trying. Just completely checked out. They moved slow, cut corners like it was standard procedure, and the vibe was this quiet, resigned why-bother energy. Nobody was openly rebelling, but nobody was doing the job either. They were clocking in because they needed a paycheck. That was the end of the commitment.

I spent a few hours doing what I always did at first. I didn't come in swinging. I just watched and listened. I asked questions like I was just there to help for a day or two. I wanted to see whether the problem was training, leadership, morale, or just straight-up laziness.

By the end of that first shift, it was obvious. The store wasn't the real problem. The people running it were.

So I fired the entire shift.

Every single one of them. Same day.

Even now, I can admit that was extreme. I could've taken a week, done some evaluations, tried to salvage one or two, slowly reset expectations. That's what a calmer, more polished manager might do. In that moment, I wasn't interested in easing into anything. That store had gone too far, and I needed the message to be unmistakable. Not, "hey guys, let's tighten up." Not, "we're going to work on some improvements." It was this: *this version of how we operate ends today.*

Word traveled fast, like it always does in places like that. Suddenly everyone who still had a job got very motivated to figure out what the job actually was. People started showing up on time. Surfaces started getting wiped without being asked. Sandwiches got made the way they were supposed to be made. The attitude shifted because it had to.

They realized quickly I wasn't there to be the cool manager or the buddy manager. I wasn't there to keep the peace. I was there to rebuild it or gut it, and I wasn't afraid of either option.

Over the next few weeks, I started rebuilding the team on purpose. I brought in new people and I actually trained them. Not that lazy, half-explained handoff where someone points at the bread oven and goes, "You'll figure it out." I taught them how to set up their station so they weren't constantly reaching, searching, wasting steps. I ran the line with them. I showed them how to move with urgency without acting panicked, how to keep things clean as you go instead of letting the mess build up until closing.

And I didn't hide in the back pretending I was managing. I was in it with them. On my knees scrubbing the floor. Pulling gross stuff out from behind equipment. Swapping out ceiling tiles that looked like they'd survived a flood. Cleaning inside fridges, wiping walls, dealing with the stuff nobody wants to touch because it's not glamorous and it doesn't feel like management work.

I've never been able to respect a manager whose shoes are cleaner than mine, and I wasn't going to be that guy.

As the new team started clicking, I phased out the old guard. The ones who stayed bitter. The ones who kept whispering about how much better things were before, like the store had been some golden era instead of a rundown mess.

They weren't just negative. They were contagious. I'd seen it before. One person who wants to drag everything back to the old way can wreck the people who are actually trying. I wasn't going to let resentment poison the progress, especially when I finally had people who cared enough to learn.

Within a few months the store didn't just look different, it felt different. It was brighter. It smelled clean. The line wasn't sticky. The lobby didn't look like a modern fast-food dungeon. Customers stopped walking in with that cautious, skeptical look and started acting like they expected the place to be decent. We went from "avoid that one" to "oh yeah, they turned that place around."

People actually smiled when they walked in. Customers and staff.

That Rantoul Subway location gave me something no job title ever did: Proof I could walk into a mess, take responsibility for it, and leave it better than I found it. Not because I was some kind of genius, but because I was willing to care when other people had stopped caring, and I was willing to do the work that needed to be done.

After seeing the before and after success with that store location, Jon moved me to his downtown Urbana location. That store was in better shape from the start. Cleaner, friendlier, mostly serving doctors and nurses from the hospital a few blocks away. It didn't require that same triage as the last location. It just needed a little fine-tuning. Keeping things consistent, tightening up the flow, making sure the place ran the same way no matter who was on shift. Fewer fires, more precision.

And then he sent me to the mothership: the Daniel Street Subway, right on the University of Illinois campus. On Daniel Street, between 6th Street and Wright Street, stuck between the two busiest bars on campus: C.O. Daniels and Kam's.

That store was a machine. Every weekday, for over three solid hours, the line was out the door and stretched down the sidewalk. No breaks. No catching your breath. Just a constant stream of college kids, grad students, professors, campus staff, everyone trying to squeeze lunch into a tight window and already annoyed before they even got to the counter.

We ran that line like choreography. One person on bread. One on meat and cheese. One on veggies. One on cash. One always in the lobby cleaning tables and taking out the trash. Nobody freelanced. Nobody decided to switch it up because they felt like it. You stayed in your lane, you did your part fast, and you trusted the next person to do theirs.

If someone tried to improvise, it didn't make them look talented. It slowed everything down and jammed up the whole system. But when everyone did it right, it was smooth and relentless. The same questions, the same motions, the same pace, over and over, and it worked.

That's where it really sank in for me that the job isn't always the point. The job is just the place where you find out how you operate. How you show up teaches you who you are.

I wasn't passionate about Subway. I didn't go home dreaming about cold cuts and bread ovens. But I was passionate about fixing broken systems, pulling people out of autopilot, and building something that worked better today than it did yesterday.

I didn't learn that in a classroom. I learned it from greasy walls in Rantoul and the lunch rush on Daniel Street, where you either got better or you got exposed.

It was at the Daniel Street Subway where I met Amber.

When I first transferred in, she was already a gear in the machine. Moving on auto-pilot like she'd done it a thousand times. She ran through the motions like clockwork. I was astonished at how efficient their process was in that location and how everyone played their part to perfection. And Amber was just another perfect piece in the puzzle.

And then there was Kayla.

Kayla was the kind of girl you noticed before you even had a chance to pretend you weren't noticing. Tall, five-nine, five-ten, athletic, ex-cheerleader energy, long brown hair, confident posture, the whole thing. She was a college student grabbing part-time hours for extra cash. She had this confident energy in everything she did. Not in an arrogant way, just comfortable.

So yeah, of course I flirted with her. A lot. I'd be behind the line pretending to focus on bread counts or toppings, and then she'd say something, or brush past me in that tight Subway workspace, and my brain would turn into static. I was twenty-one and still convinced that charming people was the same thing as having a personality.

Amber was different.

She was smaller, maybe five-four. Brunette. Big blue eyes. Eyeliner that looked like it came from the Hot Topic School of Cosmetology. She had this tough-girl presentation and came off a little trashy to me back then, if I'm being honest, but it was also a weird turn-on. Like she was trying to sell you on the idea that nothing could touch her, while also being the easiest person in the room to read once you really paid attention.

She was eighteen. Tiny. Maybe a hundred and ten pounds soaking wet. And even with the whole "don't mess with me" act, she was easy to be around in a way Kayla wasn't. Kayla was fun but high-energy. Amber was more like: *sit down next to me, talk some shit, laugh at dumb things, and don't try to make this deeper than it actually is.*

She hadn't graduated high school. I think she made it to tenth or eleventh grade before she quit. And I'm not saying that to be cruel, I'm saying it because it mattered to how I saw her then. She didn't come across as particularly bright at the time. Conversations could feel clunky, like we'd start somewhere and then lose the thought, or she'd contradict herself halfway through a story and not even notice.

I've always been drawn to people you can just talk to. Not deep or philosophical necessarily, just easy. Comfortable. The kind of back-and-forth that doesn't feel like work.

With Amber, at first, it wasn't like that. Not in that way.

But we still had fun.

We worked nights together a lot, and once I started doing the schedule, I made sure we worked together even more. And yeah, if I'm being honest, there was something convenient about being in a position where I could stack the deck. "Perks of management," right? Most nights I arranged it so it was me, Amber, and Kayla closing together. It wasn't even subtle. In my head it was practical: people I trusted, good chemistry, fast closers. In reality, it was also me curating my own little world.

C.O. Daniels, a bar next door, and us had this whole system. We'd hook the bartenders up with free sandwiches, and they'd send over mixed drinks in Subway paper cups we brought over to them. At closing time, we'd lock the doors, flip the sign, crank the music up, and go into our closing routine. Scrub the line, wipe everything down, restock, prep for the next day, while sipping whatever mystery drink showed up. Rum and Coke. Tequila Sunrise. Vodka something. Didn't really matter.

After a while, closing didn't feel like closing. It felt like hanging out in this weird in-between space where work is technically over, but nobody's ready to go home yet. Like the night didn't really even start until the customers were all gone.

With Amber, it started as flirting. Nothing extraordinary, just little comments, little looks, the occasional brush of her hand when she reached past me. The occasional inappropriate sexual innuendo. Then it turned into drinking. And then somewhere along the way it slipped into sex, like it was the most natural next step in the world. And for me, it was.

And the sex was good. Really good.

Not romantic. Not soft-focus movie type stuff. But just two young people, both a little messed up in our own way, using each other as a distraction. It was purely physical and straightforward, which was probably the biggest selling point. No big talks. No expectations. No "Where is this going?" Just passion and that temporary relief of the dopamine rush that comes along with sexual escapades.

I didn't see Amber as "relationship material." That was literally the phrase in my head back then, like I was interviewing applicants and deciding who got the job. She was fun. She made me feel wanted. And she satisfied my libido. That was the whole equation as far as I was concerned.

I wasn't thinking about long-term anything. I was thinking about nights, and attention, and not feeling alone in my own head, sitting in a dark bedroom listening to Toby Keith and Tim McGraw on repeat.

But the part nobody really tells you when you're young and convinced you're in control is that if you spend enough time sleeping with someone, something else starts to form in the background. Even if they annoy you. Even if you don't respect them. Even if you keep telling yourself it's "just fun."

Sometimes connection just shows up through repetition. Through routines. Through being the person you see when the nights end. Through the way you start expecting them to be there. Through the way your mood shifts when they're not.

That's exactly what happened with me and Amber.

I didn't wake up one day and decide, *I care about her now*. It was quieter. Slower. Almost annoying, because it didn't match the story I was telling myself about what it was. I thought I was keeping it casual.

What I didn't see at the time was that casual, repeated closeness turns into something real whether you were seeking it out or not.

Kayla was still technically in the picture. She had a long-term boyfriend, and even though she flirted with me like it was a hobby, it never really crossed the line. That's the part I hate admitting out loud: if she'd opened that door even a crack, I would've walked straight through it without pausing to ask myself what kind of person that made me.

I didn't have a strong moral argument ready. I had a crush, an ego, and a huge libido

So when she invited Amber and me over to her place, I didn't hesitate.

She pitched it like it was nothing. Just a casual hangout. A few drinks. Maybe some poker. She mentioned her boyfriend would be there too, and we'd already met a few times before. And honestly, I liked the guy. He was easygoing, friendly, not territorial. The kind of dude who makes you relax because he doesn't act like everything is a competition. He and I got along great, so it sounded like it would be a really fun night out.

Amber and I showed up at Kayla's apartment on John Street, just off First Street, and the night was already in motion. Beers were open. Music was low. Her apartment had that lived-in, college dorm, slightly messy comfort to it. Cups on tables. Someone's hoodie tossed over a chair. A faint scent of her perfume.

Oh, man, her perfume.

It felt like one of those nights that was supposed to be harmless. The kind that starts with "we'll just have a couple" and ends with one of us squinting at the clock, realizing more time passed than we thought.

At some point, Kayla pulled out a deck of cards and said, like she was suggesting we play Go Fish, "Let's play strip poker."

I don't care how chill you think you are. Tell a 21-year-old guy "strip poker" and his brain doesn't go to strategy or rules or boundaries. It goes straight to adolescent sexual excitement. Bulging cartoon eyes, an "Ahh-ooohhh-gaaa" horn blaring, and thoughts of boobies. I tried to act like I wasn't suddenly hyperaware of where everybody was sitting and how close I may soon be Kayla's naked body.

Kayla's boyfriend and I looked at each other with that half-laugh, half *are you serious right now?* expression. Not because we were confused about what it meant, but because it felt like the universe was offering us naked girls on a silver platter and we didn't want to jinx it by saying it out loud.

We sat on the floor in a loose circle. Cards in hand and the burn of the alcohol warm in our faces. The poker part was almost irrelevant. Nobody was doing math. Nobody was reading tells. The whole point was watching the pile of clothes grow and pretending it was an actual serious game.

Shoes went first. Then socks. Then shirts. Then jeans. It sped up fast, like everyone had already agreed, silently, that we weren't here to drag this out. I remember trying to keep my expression neutral while my brain was basically yelling, *Don't be weird. Don't stare. Don't act like this is the greatest thing that's ever happened to you.*

And then suddenly it wasn't just flirting and cards. Both girls were completely butt naked, sitting there on the floor in front of us, almost daring one of us to make the first move. Kayla's boyfriend and I were down to boxers and socks, which is not a look anyone wears with any real confidence. It's the uniform of guys who are pretending they're cool while their minds are racing.

Then Amber and Kayla, sitting shoulder to shoulder, looked at each other, then at us, and leaned in and kissed each other.

Not a goofy little peck. Not some performative "watch this" moment. It was slow and real. Comfortable. Familiar in a way that made my stomach drop a little, because it didn't feel spontaneous. It felt like something they'd imagined before. Talked about before. Maybe even done before.

I remember having this split-second reaction where part of me was stunned and thrilled, and part of me was trying to figure out what I was actually watching. Like I couldn't decide if I should feel lucky or nervous.

Kayla's boyfriend and I locked eyes again, but this time there wasn't a question in it. It was more like, *Okay. It's on now.*

After a bit, Kayla turned toward her boyfriend and kissed him, and she kept one hand on Amber like she didn't want to fully let go of that connection. Amber leaned toward me and planted her lips on mine.

The room shifted from "party game" to something else entirely, and I could feel the air change. Like the night had taken an erotic turn and there was no going back to inside jokes or a silly poker game.

At some point, Kayla and her boyfriend moved to the futon against the wall. It was already laid flat, which should've registered as a detail worth noticing, but I wasn't thinking like a detective. I was thinking like a kid who'd never been in a situation like this and didn't want to let my inexperience be too obvious.

Kayla laid back on the futon, fully exposed, beckoning her boyfriend, and my wandering eyes. Amber and I followed like it was the next obvious step. It felt like everybody had received the "how-to" instructions except me. Four bodies, close together, hands everywhere, the whole thing feeling surreal. Like a dream.

Amber reached for my waistband and pulled my boxers down, and I stepped out of them like I was trying not to trip over my own feet. She went down on me, and for a few seconds I honestly thought, *This is it. This is the night you'll remember forever.*

And I did remember it forever. Just not for the reason I wanted.

Because when it was time for me to actually do what my ego had been bragging it could do, my body completely betrayed me. I was more turned on than I'd ever been in my life, and at the same time I was locked up with nerves. Pressure. Self-consciousness. That stupid internal voice that shows up at the worst possible time, narrating everything and making it worse.

Come on. Seriously? Don't do this. Not now. What is wrong with you?

The more I thought about it, the more it got in my way. And I could feel the panic creeping in, not just "this is awkward," but that deeper, humiliating fear that I was about to ruin the whole moment and everyone would remember me as the guy who couldn't handle it.

So I had to adapt. And quickly.

I stopped trying to force it and tried to stay present instead. I focused on Amber, on touching her, staying close, making her feel wanted, keeping things intimate without turning it into a spotlight on what I couldn't do. I wasn't thinking about being some porn version of myself. I was thinking, *Don't collapse. Don't make her feel rejected. Don't let this turn into silence and embarrassment.*

And honestly, Amber was cool about it. There wasn't mocking or impatience. She stayed with me. She didn't make it a thing, which somehow made me feel worse and better at the same time. Worse because I wanted to impress her. Better because she wasn't punishing me for being human.

Eventually Kayla and her boyfriend disappeared into the bedroom and shut the door. Amber and I stayed out there together, tangled up, buzzed and trying to ride out the weird mix of erotic intimacy and passionate exploration. I don't remember exactly how it ended, if we fell asleep, if we talked, if we just drifted into that half-awake silence people get when they've been drinking and the adrenaline finally fades.

But I remember one thing with uncomfortable clarity: even the next morning, even after everything, I still wanted Kayla. More than ever.

And that's where the honesty gets ugly. Because Amber was right there. Amber had been willing. Amber had stayed with me when my confidence fell apart. But I still had that stupid, stubborn fixation on Kayla, like the night hadn't changed anything except making it more obvious how infatuated I was. I had already experienced Amber. But Kayla? She was still unexplored. She was something new. And that's what turned me on.

On the drive home, with the early light coming in through the windshield, Amber told me the truth.

She said she and Kayla had planned it. Not just the strip poker. The whole night.

She said it started at work, closing the store together, tired, slap-happy, talking about fantasies the way people do when they're exhausted and wired and a little too honest with each other. The conversation drifted into "what would it be like" territory, and instead of it staying a drunk idea, it turned into an actual plan.

They planned the alcohol. The poker. The setup.

And then Amber said the last part, like it was just another detail on the checklist.

The camcorder.

There'd been a tripod sitting in the corner with a camera on it. I remember noticing it when we all sat on the floor in that circle before the night went on a sexual bender. Someone tossed out a casual line like, "We're just gonna record us being dumb and drunk, it'll be funny later." And I bought it. Just a quick mental shrug and a laugh like, *sure, whatever.*

But that wasn't the real plan. The real plan was to film the whole thing. Not a quick clip, not a joke. The whole night.

It was two couples, in the same room, at the same time. And it wasn't this chaotic free-for-all like people imagine when they hear the story. It was controlled. It was structured. It had rules. Boundaries were laid out like a checklist before anything even started. No swapping. No crossover. No me touching Kayla. No Kayla's boyfriend touching Amber. Nothing blurry beyond whatever they'd already decided counted as "safe." They knew exactly what they wanted the night to be.

The strange thing is, I didn't feel used. I didn't feel tricked. I wasn't sitting there thinking, *wait a minute, this is messed up.* At the time, I mostly just thought it was insane in the way "insane" can feel exciting when you're young and numb and you don't have a lot of self-respect to protect.

It felt like one of those nights you file away as just another crazy story that somehow proved you've lived a little. Something you'll tell later with a half-laugh, like, "You won't believe what happened," and people will react the way you expect them to.

Back then, it was just a story. It was adrenaline. It was validation. It was complete freedom.

What I didn't know yet was that nights like that don't just disappear after the hangover wears off. They do something to you. They shape what you think you're supposed to want. They teach you what "connection" looks like, even if it's a broken version of it.

And the people involved? They don't just stay in the past as characters in an old story. They get into your head and quietly start rearranging your priorities, your boundaries, and your idea of what "normal" is.

Looking back now, it's obvious there was more going on with me than I admitted at the time. I wasn't just chasing sex. I was chasing distraction. I wanted to feel desirable without having to be emotionally exposed. I wanted excitement without risk. I wanted something intense that didn't require me to actually show up as a real person with feelings, needs, and fear of rejection.

Sex didn't ask questions. Sex didn't require me to say what I actually wanted or admit what hurt. Sex didn't make me sit in the uncomfortable truth that I didn't feel like enough on a normal day.

In that room, it was easier to focus on bodies and rules and what came next than it was to face the big quiet hole in me that wanted to be seen and cared about.

And that's the part that sticks with me now, the emotional emptiness of it. It was chemistry and impulse and performance, and I didn't even realize how much of it was performance until much later. At the time, I probably would've told you it felt freeing, or wild, or exciting.

But if I strip away the ego and the story I wanted it to be, what it really was was lonely. Just a different kind of lonely than the one I was used to.

It took me a long time to understand that intimacy isn't just being naked in the same room. It's being honest in the same room. Intimacy is trust. It's care. It's the ability to be a full human being in front of someone else and not feel like you're about to get exposed for having needs.

I didn't have that capacity yet. And Amber didn't either.

We were both operating from the same place. Trying not to feel alone, trying to feel wanted, trying to grab onto anything that looked like connection without risking the kind of vulnerability that could actually change us.

We were chasing moments that could pass for closeness, but they didn't reach the parts of us that needed it most. And at the time, we didn't even recognize that. We just knew how to keep moving, keep numbing, keep collecting nights we could call "wild" so we didn't have to call them what they really were.

After that night, things were different between us. We never had the "Are we official?" talk. There was no anniversary date or label. But slowly, without either of us saying it out loud, we became exclusive.

If she'd slept with someone else, I'd have been crushed. If I'd been with someone else, she would've been furious. That's a relationship, whether you give it a tite or not.

The funny part is, it didn't look like one from the outside. We didn't go on dates. No dinner reservations, no movie nights, no weekend getaways. We didn't talk about the future. There were no plans, no "someday we should…" conversations.

It was drinking and sex.
Then more drinking.
Then more sex.

We saw each other constantly. After work. On our days off. At my place. At hers. On couches, in beds, half-watching movies we never remembered.

It was reckless and messy and absolutely unsustainable.

But for a while, it was comfortable. Dependable even. We were two people who didn't know how to love ourselves, trying to lose that problem in each other. And if we couldn't find real peace, at least we could find a warm body and a foggy memory.

In its own twisted way, that time bonded us. Not because it was healthy. Not because it was pure. But because sometimes two broken people recognize the same fracture line in each other and cling to it like a sick kind of proof they aren't completely alone.

And that's what Amber and I were for a time. Two people holding on, thinking passion and proximity would eventually turn into something deeper.

It wouldn't.
Not really.
But I wouldn't understand that fully until much later.

One quiet Saturday afternoon, I stopped by Amber's new apartment. Sunlight leaked through the blinds, TV murmuring in the background. That lazy kind of day with a sense of relaxed calm and peacefulness.

I hadn't been there ten minutes when someone tried to knock the front door off the hinges.

Not a tap. Not a "hey, are you home?" This was pounding. Full fist, full rage, every hit vibrating through the walls.

"AMBER!" a man's voice barked through the door. Deep. Angry. Possessive in that way that makes your spine go cold.

I watched the color drain out of her face so fast it was like someone pulled a plug. One second she was fine, the next she looked like a statue. Her eyes shot to mine, wide and panicked.

She didn't say a word. Just stabbed her finger toward the bedroom and silently mouthed: *Hide.*

When a woman tells you to hide, you don't ask follow-up questions. I bolted down the hallway, slipped into her bedroom, and eased the door shut with that careful, pointless "quiet closing" people do when the entire situation is already on fire.

I scanned the room. First instinct: closet.

Then my brain replayed every bad movie I'd ever seen in about half a second. The guy always hides in the closet. The guy always gets found in the closet. The guy usually ends up in the ER, on the news, or both.

I wasn't going to be that cliché.

The room was small enough that there weren't many options. Panic started to crawl up the back of my neck when I saw it: her waterbed.

If you've never had one, they sit inside this hard, wooden frame, with a little trench between the curved edge of the vinyl mattress and the frame. Just enough space for someone my size who is both desperate and apparently terrible at life choices.

I slid under the blankets and wiggled myself into that gap like a human credit card getting swallowed by a chip reader. I quickly pulled the covers up over my head, flattened my arms to my sides, and tried to melt into the frame.

He won't see me, I told myself. Which was a lie. A stupid one.

Voices exploded in the living room. His, harsh and pissed. Hers, trying to sound calm and landing somewhere between shaky and doomed.

Footsteps started down the hallway, each one landing heavier than the last.

The bedroom door flew open.

My heart just stopped. I didn't breathe. Didn't move. Even my thoughts tried to hold still. I could hear him walk in, boots hitting the floor in slow, deliberate thuds.

Closet door. Yanked open.

"Aha!" he barked.

For a second, my soul packed a bag and left my body. But he'd gone for the obvious move, the closet. I stayed stone-still in my little waterbed coffin.

He slammed the closet door shut, muttered something under his breath, and paused.

I could feel him looking around the room.

Then, in one clean motion, he ripped the covers off the bed.

"Aha."

There I was. Flattened into the side of a waterbed like a terrified squirrel pressed into a crack in the pavement, blinking up at him from the trench between the mattress and the frame. We locked eyes.

There was only one thing I could think to say.

"…What's up?"

Guy head nod included.

He didn't laugh.

He also wasn't the monster I'd built in my head. Not six-foot-four, covered in prison tattoos, veins popping out of his neck. He was maybe 5'6", 140 pounds. But when you're the idiot hiding in someone else's girlfriend's bed, everyone looks dangerous.

He squinted at me. "Don't I know you?"

I shook my head. "I don't think so, man."

The fear in my chest was trying to claw its way out through my ribs. I was already picturing punches, yelling, furniture flying, maybe a police report with my name spelled wrong.

Instead, he just stared for another beat, then turned and walked out.

No yelling. No swinging. No "get the hell out of here." Just left the room.

I lay there for another few seconds, listening to the sound of my own pulse in my ears. Amber's voice met his in the hallway, quiet and tense, too low to make out any details.

I didn't really even try. I didn't want details. I just wanted a clear exit and two working legs.

For half a second, I thought about the bedroom window. We were on the second floor. Jumping out crossed my mind, then immediately crossed back out. If I was going to break my neck, it sure as hell wasn't going to be for this mess.

Then I heard the front door slam.

I exhaled, and it felt like the air started in my toes and had to fight its way all the way out. My whole body went weak in that post-adrenaline, shaky way.

Amber came back into the bedroom as I peeked through the blinds. He was in the parking lot, opening his car door. My heart rate spiked all over again.

"What the hell was that?!?" I demanded, turning to her.

She gave me the vaguest nonsense she could come up with. Something about it "not being a big deal" and "nothing to worry about," which is exactly what you don't want to hear about a man who just tried to Kool-Aid Man through your front door and rip the covers off the bed you were hiding in.

We walked back to the living room, me still interrogating, her still dodging.

Then there was another knock.

This one was polite. Civilized. Like a neighbor borrowing sugar, not a guy who had just been ready to blow the door in.

Same guy.

His car wouldn't start. He was already half an hour late for his shift at a grocery store.

You know that moment when your brain just glitches?

One minute I'm the secret guy hiding from the angry boyfriend, the next minute we're troubleshooting his starter issues like we're on the same team.

I still don't know exactly how it happened, but ten minutes later, I was driving him to work.

The same man who had just ripped the covers off the bed I was hiding in, the same man who had caught me wedged into his girlfriend's waterbed like a guilty rodent, was now sitting in the passenger seat of my car, making small talk, while I chauffeured him to his job.

The drive was about ten minutes. I don't remember what we talked about. Weather. Work. Schedule. Something neutral and stupid that didn't match the fact that twenty minutes earlier I had been silently planning for my own funeral.

All I know is that somehow, between that day and now, we managed not to become enemies. No big showdowns. No revenge plots. Twenty-eight years later, we still occasionally like each other's Facebook posts and ask about each other's kids.

Fear in the moment, irony in the rearview.

Life's funny like that.

With Amber, everything felt like that. Crooked. Off-center. Never quite "normal."

We never did the normal relationship stuff. No anniversaries circled on calendars, no big romantic gestures, no late-night talks about where we'd be in five years.

What we had were fragments. Moments. Nights that smeared together. Fights that lit up quick and burned out just as fast. Long stretches of laughter, sex, inside jokes, and shared hangovers.

It wasn't healthy. But it was real. It was tangible. It was dependable. And more importantly, it occupied my time.

Looking back now, I can see it more clearly than I did when I was the idiot hiding inside that waterbed, adrenaline racing through my veins. That day was the first time I really understood that intimacy doesn't always show up dressed like romance.

Sometimes it arrives as a whirlwind. Sometimes it's you holding your breath in the dark while your almost-girlfriend's other somewhat boyfriend storms through the house. Sometimes it's the two of you sitting on a couch, not having the words for what you are to each other, but feeling something anyway.

Back then, I didn't have any kind of real understanding of vulnerability. I thought it meant crying on someone's shoulder or making some big, dramatic confession at the perfect moment.

But that day nudged me toward the truth that vulnerability can also be admitting you have zero control, walking straight into someone else's storm, and for reasons you don't fully understand, you put on a raincoat and choose to stay.

And then there was the part that still makes me shake my head: driving the guy who had just found me in his girlfriend's bed to his job like some low-budget, unpaid Uber.

Life kept handing me these utterly uncomfortable little tests, and I kept answering them with this strange mix of panic, sarcasm, and something that almost looked like uncoordinated grace if you squinted hard enough.

I wouldn't say I handled it well, but I was learning. Slowly. Quietly. In my own backwards way.

I was learning that you don't always get to control how you look in your own story. Sometimes you're the hero. Sometimes you're the idiot pressed into the side of a waterbed.

By Christmas of 1996, Amber and I were whatever we were, and we decided to spend a few days at her mom and stepdad's place for the holiday.

Her stepdad, Ralph, came in like he'd been practicing for an audience his whole life. The kind of guy who takes up space on purpose. On the surface, he was the "fun one." Loud jokes, big laugh, always a drink in his hand.

He talked the way some people perform. Half story, half sales pitch. Everything was about what he made, what he bought, what he owned, what he was "working on." I didn't know what was real and what was bullshit, but the house was nice, the furniture was nice, there were expensive-looking things everywhere, and he moved through it all like he was giving a tour of his own greatness.

For the first day or so, it was easy to get pulled into the charm. There was food everywhere, snacks out all day, big meals that started early and somehow lasted until midnight. The usual holiday soundtrack was on in the background. But even in the middle of all that, something felt wrong.

You could feel it in the way the room would tense up when Ralph walked in. In the way people would get quieter for a second and then overcorrect with more talking. In the way Amber would glance at her sister Taylor, like she was checking on her without making it obvious. It didn't take some special emotional intelligence to notice there was tension sitting right there with us at the table.

Taylor and I had hung out as a trio with Amber many times before, and I genuinely liked her. She was funny and friendly, the type who can make you laugh in a normal, human way, not the forced "holiday fun" way. But she also had that worn-down look, like life had already asked too much of her and she'd been left to figure out how to power through it on her own.

She wasn't fragile. It was more like she'd been bruised enough times that you could tell she was constantly bracing for the next hit, even when she was smiling.

That weekend, the tension between her and Ralph was building the whole time. Little comments. Side looks. The kind of stuff that doesn't sound like a big deal, but you can feel the power game underneath it. Taylor would say something and Ralph would correct her, or mock it, or turn it into a joke at her expense. He'd talk to her like she was a problem he had to manage, not a person.

And nobody challenged him. They just walked around it, like avoiding a pothole on a road they drove every day. I wanted to say something, but it wasn't my place.

That night, I was in a back bedroom when I heard voices from across the house. At first it was just raised, like an argument that might burn out on its own. Then it got more aggressive.

I couldn't make out every word, but I heard enough. Ralph was tearing into her. Criticizing her choices. Talking down to her. That slow, ugly kind of belittling where someone keeps pushing and pushing until the other person either breaks or explodes, then they get to act like the victim either way.

His tone was what got under my skin the most. Not just anger. That smug edge. Like he believed he had the right to judge her, lecture her, make her feel small, because he had money and a house and a loud voice. Like his paycheck made him superior.

Then it hit a peak.

There was a sharp crack, loud enough that it cut through the whole house. It wasn't a slammed door. It wasn't something falling.

A slap.

Then Taylor came down the hallway fast, crying so hard it looked like she couldn't catch her breath. She stumbled into the bedroom I was in, slammed the door behind her, and just collapsed on the bed.

No words at first. Just sobbing, trying to breathe, wiping her face.

I remember standing there feeling my whole system flip. That hot, instant rage. Because everything that had been "holiday" two minutes earlier was now completely gone. Every forced smile, every polite conversation, every "maybe it'll be fine" story we were telling ourselves, done.

What Ralph just did showed exactly what he was. A man who needed control, and when he didn't get it, he used his hands.

And the part that hit me right after that was the expectation. The unspoken rule in families that you're supposed to just accept it. Sit back down. Don't make a scene. Call it "drama." Pretend it didn't happen. Let him cool off and then act like nothing's wrong because it's Christmas and everyone wants the photos and the dinner and the illusion. Like his behavior was just "how he is."

No. Absolutely fucking not.

There are a lot of things people try to explain away when they don't want to deal with them. "He's had a lot to drink." "He's under stress." "He didn't mean it." But hitting someone isn't a misunderstanding. It's a decision. If you put your hands on someone, you don't get to come back from that with excuses.

Within minutes, something unspoken passed between me, Amber, and Taylor. It wasn't a big discussion. Nobody needed to make a speech about boundaries or respect. It was just this clear, simple agreement: we were not doing this. Not tonight. Not ever.

There wasn't going to be a tearful meeting in the living room. No forced reconciliation. No "let's all calm down." We weren't going to help glue the mask back on his face so everyone else could feel comfortable.

We packed our bags with shaky hands and got out of there. Taylor took her car. Amber and I took mine.

We didn't stage it or try to be quiet about it, but we moved fast, like the house had turned unsafe in a way you can't ignore.

And I remember the feeling as we left. Disgust mixed with clarity. Like something had been confirmed in the worst way, and now there was no pretending we didn't know what we knew.

We drove away from that nice house and that fake holiday atmosphere and that man's loud, polished act, and I remember thinking: *this is what it costs to tell the truth.*

You don't get to keep the comfort and keep your integrity at the same time. You pick one. And that night, we picked Taylor.

On the way back home, Amber asked me to pull into a Walgreens. I figured she needed makeup, aspirin, something to erase the night from her face.

I stayed in the car with the engine running, hands on the wheel, trying to look calm while my head replayed the whole night. She slipped inside without looking at me much, and I watched the automatic doors open and close behind her.

When she came back out a few minutes later, something was off. She climbed in, clicked her seat belt, and turned toward the window like she needed distance from me, from the car, from everything.

We pulled back onto the road and the holiday lights were everywhere. Houses glowing, traffic steady, people out doing normal December stuff. All I could think about was Ralph standing in that nice house, surrounded by decorations and family photos and presents, and still managing to poison the entire room with one outburst.

One slap and everything changed.

Taylor's face, red and wet with tears. Amber going quiet. Me feeling useless and angry, stuck between wanting to do something and not even knowing what "something" looked like.

Back at my apartment, she walked in and went straight to the bathroom without saying much. No dramatic breakdown. No big speech. No "can you believe that?" She just moved with this weird focus, like her brain had latched onto one task and nothing was going to pull her off it.

I carried the bags into my bedroom and started unpacking. Not because it mattered, but because it gave my hands something to do. I folded shirts. I moved things around. I stared at the wall and pretended I was organizing, while my mind was still back in that house, watching the whole holiday go off the rails.

About ten minutes later, the bathroom door opened. Amber came down the hallway slowly. She had something in her hand but she didn't say a word.

She walked right up to me like she'd rehearsed it, reached for my arm, turned my hand palm-up, and set it there.

A pregnancy test with a big, unmistakable blue plus sign.

For a second, my brain didn't process it. I just stared at it, like if I stared long enough the symbol would change, or I'd realize I was reading it wrong.

Everything we'd been doing up to that point, late nights, drinking, flirting like it was a sport, the whole "we'll figure it out later" approach, suddenly didn't feel like a fun mess anymore. It felt irresponsible, like we'd been playing adult with training wheels and now the wheels were gone.

This wasn't one of those conversations you joke about but never think you'll have to actually face. It was sitting in my hand, and it was very, very real.

And because I was who I was back then, the first thing that came out of my mouth was, "I guess you know what this means."

What I meant was marriage. Instantly. Automatically. No pause to breathe, no questions, no conversation about what she wanted or what we were or whether we were even remotely ready. In my head, that was it. That's how the world worked. That's what you did.

The part that's hard to explain is that I actually had always wanted kids. I really had. Somewhere in the quieter part of me, under the ego, under the partying, under the dumb decisions, there was this real picture of a life I wanted. Holidays as a family. A table with more than two chairs. Little bikes in the driveway. Bedtime routines. The kind of home that feels full in a good way.

I always assumed I'd get there later. When I was older, when I had my act together, when I wasn't basically held together by bad sleep, cheap alcohol, and whatever thrill I was chasing that particular week.

I never pictured my first kid coming out of a relationship that was mostly built on booze, sex, and a lot of unspoken stuff neither of us knew how to deal with.

Amber and I knew how to drink together. We knew how to sleep together. We knew how to flirt and laugh and act like everything was fine. What we didn't know was how we handled stress. We didn't know each other's real fears, or what we believed about commitment beyond whatever sounded good in the moment.

We hadn't talked about money. Family dynamics. Parenting. Faith. Any of the stuff that stops being abstract the second there's a kid involved. We skipped the foundation and went straight to the "well, this is what grown-ups do" part.

But the idea of not marrying her wasn't even a consideration. Not once. There wasn't a debate. There wasn't a fork with five different options. There was one script, and it had been handed to me long before Amber ever walked into my life: you get a girl pregnant, you step up. You marry her. You do the right thing. You become the man you're supposed to be.

Even if you aren't ready. Especially if you aren't ready.

So six weeks later, that's exactly what we did.

For a narcissistic jerk, Ralph put together one hell of a wedding. This was the same guy who'd slapped his stepdaughter a week before Christmas, then somehow flipped a switch and delivered this beautiful, almost unreal day like he'd been planning it all his life.

I've gone back and forth in my head about why. Maybe it was guilt. Maybe it was image. Maybe it was that thing some people do where they screw up badly, then try to "fix it" with something big and flashy so nobody talks about what happened right before it. Whatever the motive was, at the time I didn't have the perspective, or the energy, to analyze him. I was just grateful. Amber was too.

We got married in the same church where my parents and my sister had gotten married. Same aisle, same altar, the same smell that churches always have. When those doors opened and everybody turned their heads, I felt that familiar hush settle over the room. It was comforting in a weird way.

I'm not going to pretend I was some calm, grounded groom with my head on straight. Under the tux, I was still a mess in a lot of ways, running on denial, good intentions, and that stubborn kind of optimism you have when you don't know what you don't know yet. I wanted so badly for this to be the clean start, the turning point, the thing that made everything make sense. I remember looking at Amber and thinking, *This is it. This is where it all lines up.*

We stood at the front of a church saying words that sounded huge coming out of our mouths, making promises that felt both serious and surreal. I believed it was the right thing. I wasn't playing games about it. I meant it.

The reception was at C.O. Daniels, the campus bar right next to the Subway where we worked. That part still gets me, because it was so perfectly us at that age. Not some fancy ballroom or country club. A bar we knew by heart, next to the place we clocked in and out of, where our real lives happened every day.

They shut the whole place down for us for four hours on a Saturday afternoon, and at the time that felt like the coolest thing in the world. Like we were important.

My brother DJ'ed, which made it more personal, and it was fun. He ran through all the classics that somehow become mandatory at weddings. "YMCA," "Chicken Dance," "Macarena." Those songs nobody admits they like until they're in a room full of people doing the same goofy moves and suddenly it doesn't matter.

People were laughing, sweating, loosening their ties, yelling over each other to be heard. Drinks were flowing. Cameras were everywhere. Disposable ones, cheap flashes, people shouting, "Get in this one!" and "Wait, do it again!"

And we were genuinely happy.

Amber looked beautiful. I remember that clearly, even if some of the details around it blur together now. I remember the way she smiled when she caught me staring, like she knew I was trying to lock the whole thing into my brain. I remember thinking, *This is my wife,* and feeling proud of it in a way that's hard to describe without sounding corny. But it was real and it was intense.

People clapped for us, toasted us, told us we were going to be great, told us they could "just tell" we were meant for each other. We ate, we drank, we danced, we took pictures we thought we'd frame forever. From the outside looking in, we looked exactly like what we were supposed to look like. A young married couple starting their life, surrounded by friends and family, full of plans and promise.

If someone had stopped me that day and asked, "Are you in love with her?" I wouldn't have hesitated. I would've said yes without even thinking about it. I would've sworn on everything I had that it was the real deal.

And if you ask me now, I still think it was real, at least for that day. Not because we had everything figured out, and not because we were solid and healthy and ready for what marriage actually demands. It was real because I meant it. I was standing there giving myself over to the idea of us as fully as I knew how at twenty-one. I wasn't pretending. I wasn't acting. I was hopeful. I was committed. I was trying.

I can see now that love doesn't automatically come with a foundation. Sometimes it's just a moment you stand in before you understand what it takes to keep standing there when the music stops, the room empties out, and it's just the two of you, alone, with real life waiting. That day felt like validation that things could be good. And for a few hours, they were. Really good.

I wish I could tell you love rushed in and made it all make sense. I wish I could say we instantly became this steady, responsible couple who knew how to communicate and support each other and build a life without tripping over our own baggage. But that's not what happened. Life doesn't work like that.

I chose responsibility before I chose honesty. I chose the image of being a man before I understood what it actually took to become one. From the outside, it looked like I did everything right. In my head, I was still trying to catch up to the decision I'd already made.

But here's what I can see now that I couldn't see then. Even inside all that fear and stubbornness and "this is what a good man does," something real did start to grow.

Not movie love. Not fireworks. Just these small, normal moments that actually matter more in real life than the dramatic stuff does. Late-night talks in crappy apartments. Laughing at something stupid on TV. Her head on my shoulder while we sat there quiet. The baby kicking between us like a reminder that this wasn't theoretical anymore.

We were clumsy. We were unprepared. We got a lot wrong. But we were trying, and there was love inside that trying.

I didn't marry Amber because I was swept away by some romantic story. I married her because a baby meant responsibility, and I had a rigid idea of what responsibility looked like. Marriage, to me back then, was mostly about showing up, providing, and not running away.

I didn't understand that it was also about compatibility, communication, forgiveness, and the willingness to grow together instead of just standing next to each other and hoping time would do the work for you. I honestly thought if I just decided to be a good husband and father, the rest would fall into place.

It didn't.

But I can admit this now without trying to rewrite history. Even with the wrong reasons up front, there were real feelings in there. Imperfect and unfinished, sometimes buried under obligation and fear, but real.

And the part of the story where I start learning what love actually is, the work part, the honest part, the painful part, that came after this. This was just the moment the script got handed to me and I agreed before fully understanding the terms.

ROUND 16:
Cutting the Cord

A few months after the wedding, we moved out of the cramped apartment I'd shared with Zeke and into a small rental house about a mile from my parents. Nothing fancy. Small yard. Basic rooms. But it was ours, and there was something sweet about it. It felt like a starting line. A little place that said, *Alright. Let's give this whole married, family life thing a shot.*

We had about six months to figure out how to be married before the baby arrived. We tried. We really did. Outside of the fun stuff, we weren't exactly a natural fit, but we found a rhythm. Shared dinners. TV on in the background. Little routines that start to feel like a life.

There were arguments, of course. I never minded those much. I've always liked arguments. Arguments are where you actually learn who someone is. Fights are just yelling and doors slamming and nobody hearing a thing. Arguments? Arguments are where you grow. I could live with arguments.

What I didn't see then, but can see clearly now, is how much that whole period exposed my blind spots about love and responsibility. Back then, I thought being "responsible" meant following the script. Marry the girl. Set up the nursery. Keep the lights on. I didn't get that responsibility also meant knowing yourself well enough to be honest, with yourself and with the person in front of you. I skipped that part.

Real love, real commitment, takes time. It's not just a rush on a wedding day or a plus sign on a stick. It's a choice you keep making, over and over, especially when the emotion turns messy. Back then, I mixed up "stepping up" with "rushing in," like urgency and sacrifice automatically meant maturity.

They don't. I know that now.

But in that little house, with our mismatched furniture and our borrowed sense of adulthood, I did the only thing I really knew how to do. I tried to make things better. And for a while, in its own imperfect way, it almost felt like we were getting there.

One of my first big "I'm going to be a dad" projects was the living room wall from hell. It was covered in dark wood paneling and square mirror tiles, like someone had tried to recreate a 1970s nightclub in a small Midwestern rental.

Through the eyes of a soon-to-be father, all I could see was a future trip to the ER. I kept picturing one of those mirrors popping loose, falling, and shattering a little too close to a baby who didn't even exist outside our own imagination yet. So I tore it all down.

The mirrors came off, the paneling came out, and I swapped it for something lighter, softer, safer. It wasn't HGTV-level design, but it also didn't look like Studio 54 anymore, so in my book, that was a win. It felt like the first real step toward turning that little rental into a place a family could actually live.

The bigger project, though, was the nursery.

Both bedrooms came in that standard rental white. Walls, trim, doors. All painted in the same bland shade of We Don't Care. But this was our first child. I didn't want our baby's first room to feel like a leftover space from a landlord's checklist. I wanted it to feel like us.

We picked the middle bedroom for the nursery. We didn't know if we were having a boy or a girl yet, so we kept it neutral. We found some baby Mickey Mouse decorations, little cardboard cutouts and wall decals, and decided that would be the theme. Classic. Simple. Happy.

We kept the walls white, but we decided to paint the baseboards and the door trim in soft pink, teal, and light green to match the Mickey colors. Looking back, it's kind of funny how serious we got about it. Like paint on trim was going to decide whether we were doing this right. But at the time, the details mattered.

We stood in the aisle staring at paint samples like we were making a life-altering decision, holding them up to the light, debating which shade looked more "baby" and which one looked like it belonged in a clown house.

The diaper pail ended up being white with pink and green accents too, an accident that matched perfectly. Back then, that felt meaningful, like we were getting one small win from the universe.

We assembled the crib and put a wooden rocking chair next to it, making the room feel comfortable, like this wasn't just a project anymore. It was a space someone very important was actually going to live in. Near the changing table, we put up shelves and started stocking them with all the stuff you're supposed to have: tiny diapers, baby powder, baby oil, wipes, little lotions. We organized it all like we were prepping for an inspection, like a nurse was going to show up and judge our inventory.

And every night before bed, I'd end up standing in the doorway and just look at it.

I'd stare at the crib and try to picture an actual baby in it instead of an empty mattress. I'd picture Amber in that rocking chair at two in the morning, exhausted, hair a mess, swaying with a crying baby tucked against her shoulder. I'd imagine myself at the dresser we'd turned into a changing table, half-asleep and fumbling with wipes, trying to snap a onesie closed in the dark while silently begging the kid not to go full meltdown.

Standing there, I felt like I was practicing. Like I was rehearsing it in my head. I hadn't held my son, hadn't heard his actual voice, hadn't done a single real father thing, but in that doorway, night after night, I was already stepping into it. I could feel the weight of it coming, and I didn't know if I was ready or just acting ready.

Somewhere in all that sanding and painting and arranging, that place started to feel like home. Not because of the address or the deed, but because we cared enough to make choices. We were building something on purpose. Together. With this stubborn need to make it better than what we'd been handed.

Everyone acts like your life changes because of the big moments, the day you find out you're pregnant, the day you bring the baby home, the big "welcome to parenthood" milestone. But a lot of the change slips in quietly. It happens while you're tearing down mirror tiles and cleaning up dust. It happens while you're arguing about paint colors and tightening screws on a crib. It happens while you're folding these absurdly small socks and realizing there's going to be a whole person attached to them.

As the nursery came together, time did this weird thing where it felt slow and fast at the same time. The room got more complete, more real, more ready. Amber got bigger, more uncomfortable, and understandably more impatient. Her due date was September 5th, and I was convinced she'd go early. I had it in my head it would be September 2nd, maybe the 3rd, like I'd cracked the code just because I had a gut feeling.

Those dates came and went. Then the 4th. Then the 5th. Then the 6th.

Still pregnant. Still cranky. And I was starting to think this kid wasn't "overdue," he was just… comfortable. Like he'd signed a lease and had no intention of leaving. Amber was miserable, I was helpless, and every "any day now" comment from other people made me want to snap, because it wasn't their body and it wasn't their nerves.

So we did the only thing we actually could do. We waited.

We lived in that in-between space with the nursery ready, shelves stocked, crib waiting, and this half-finished life we were excited to step into, even though we had no idea what we were doing. And the closer it got, the more I realized excitement and fear weren't separate feelings. They were basically the same thing, just pointed in different directions.

On Sunday, September 7th, we had a casual end-of-summer cookout with my parents at a family friend's place. The backyard was full of quiet conversation and the hiss of hot dogs and burgers hitting the grill. Folding chairs circled a fire pit. Older folks balanced paper plates on their laps while telling stories they'd told a hundred times before.

Amber, two days past due and radiating that "I'm so done" energy, settled into a lawn chair with her plate resting on top of her belly like a makeshift table. She leaned back and laughed when she had the energy.

People kept sneaking glances at her like she might go into labor right there. She just kept eating chips.

After the cookout, we went home to check on the newest member of our little family, a tiny kitten, white with a few brown spots, that we'd adopted the week before. He was crazy, into everything, chasing shadows, climbing legs, attacking shoelaces. We fed him, did a quick damage inspection, and decided the house had survived him for another day.

Exhausted, we changed into comfortable clothes, turned off the lights, and climbed into bed. I didn't realize how wiped out I was until my head hit the pillow. The house settled into that late-night quiet. And for a moment, it was just another night.

I went out like a light.

A few hours later, around 1:00 a.m., Amber shook me awake.

"I think it's time," she said.

Her voice wasn't dramatic or panicked. It was calm and steady, but it still changed the whole room.

I sat up slow, blinking, still half stuck in that fuzzy space between sleep and reality. I'd pictured this a hundred different ways: me launching out of bed, scrambling for shoes, barking orders, doing the whole "oh my God, it's happening" routine like some sitcom version of a first-time dad.

Instead, I felt strangely calm. Not brave-calm. More like sluggish, surprised calm, like my brain was taking its sweet time flipping the switch. We'd been waiting so long, and she'd been uncomfortable for so long, that part of me honestly wondered if this was going to be a false alarm and we'd end up back home embarrassed and exhausted, trying to laugh it off. Another "not yet," another night where we'd stare at the ceiling and pretend we weren't disappointed.

But Amber was already moving like she knew. She had the bag in her hand and this serious-but-excited look on her face, like she'd crossed a line internally and was already in the next phase. She wasn't spiraling. She wasn't overthinking. She was just ready.

I got dressed in jeans, a worn blue shirt, and tennis shoes. Nothing special, just whatever my hands could find without me having to think too hard. That's what I remember most: how normal it all felt in the middle of something that definitely wasn't normal. My life was about to change forever, and I'm getting dressed like I'm going to the grocery store. My hands even fumbled like they always did in the dark, except this time it wasn't just grogginess. It was nerves trying to stay invisible.

I locked up the house and took one last glance around our little place, like I was mentally checking the room: keys, lights, did we forget anything. But underneath that, I knew what I was really doing. I was taking a final look at the version of us that lived there, because the next time we walked back through that door, we weren't going to be the same people. The house looked exactly the same, and that almost pissed me off. Like the walls had no idea what was about to happen.

Then we stepped outside into the quiet night.

The streets were empty, everything washed in that orange streetlight glow. No traffic. No noise. No one out. Just us in the car, heading toward the hospital. It felt private in a way I didn't expect, like the world had backed off and given us this narrow little tunnel to drive through.

The whole drive felt strange, like we were crossing some invisible line and there was no way to uncross it. We didn't talk a ton. Amber was focused on breathing through the contractions, and I was focused on her. I kept glancing over like I could read the situation better by looking at her face, like I could calculate how close we were based on her expression. Every time her jaw tightened, my stomach tightened with it. Every time she exhaled, I tried to exhale too, like that would help her somehow.

I was trying to be steady, trying to be present, trying not to make it about me, but my mind kept bouncing between "we're really doing this" and "I have no idea what I'm doing." I wanted to be the guy who knew what to say, who could make her feel safe just by being there. Mostly I was just hoping my face wasn't giving away how scared I was.

And somewhere in the middle of that drive, it hit me. Not with tears or some big moment, just this deep, steady thud in my chest. I thought about the crib. The tiny clothes folded in a drawer. The name we'd said out loud and then said again, just to make sure it still felt real.

The next time we came home, it wasn't going to be just the two of us anymore. We weren't going to be two clueless kids playing house, acting like we were adults because we had bills and a crib and a diaper pail that matched the trim.

We were going to be parents.

Ready or not.

We checked in at the hospital around two in the morning. The halls were quiet and half-lit, with that tired hospital feel: dimmed lights, soft voices, machines humming in the background.

They got Amber into a room, hooked her up to the monitor, and a nurse came in to check her. She did it like she'd done it a thousand times, calm and casual, then looked up and said, "Two centimeters."

To me, that sounded like progress. Two down, eight to go. In my head, it was basically a checklist: arrive at hospital, get monitored, confirm labor, have baby. Simple. Linear. The kind of thing my brain likes.

The nurses gently shut that down. They told us it could be a while. They even suggested we might want to go back home, sleep in our own bed, and come back later. Apparently, two centimeters at two in the morning didn't mean "baby incoming." It meant "you could be here all day."

I couldn't fully explain it, but I had this gut feeling that if we left, we'd just end up doing the exact same drive again a couple hours later, only more tired, more stressed, and more scrambled.

We decided to stay.

The morning dragged. Nurses came in and out, adjusted things, checked numbers, asked questions. We tried to rest, but it's hard to rest when you're overflowing with the excitement of becoming a mom and dad for the very first time. And under that excitement, there was this other thing building in me: this tight, restless energy that had nowhere to go.

Real contractions kicked in early that afternoon, and they hit hard and fast. Amber gripped the bedrails, knuckles white, eyes squeezed shut, her whole body tensing with each contraction. I rubbed her lower back, held her hand, tried to stay close and be useful.

I kept saying the standard things. "It's going to be okay." "You've got this." "I'm right here." And I meant every word. I meant them so much it almost made me angry that words were the only thing I had to offer. Every time she cringed or sucked in that sharp breath, I felt it in my chest like a punch. I wanted to do something useful. Something helpful. Not just talk. Not stand just there. Not just watch.

I'm a fixer. Give me a problem and I'll analyze it, break it down, figure out what to do, and start doing it. That's how my brain works.

But this wasn't a problem to solve. This was something happening inside her body that I couldn't manage, couldn't take over, couldn't share. I couldn't trade places for even ten minutes so she could breathe. I was just watching the person I loved get hit by pain over and over, and there was absolutely nothing I could do to take even a small piece of it away.

That helplessness almost hurt more than the fear, because fear at least has somewhere to go. Helplessness just sits there and makes you watch. It made me feel trapped in my own skin, like I was standing in the corner of my own life, hands full of air.

Thank God Taylor was there.

She'd had a baby the year before, so she knew the language. She knew what mattered and what didn't. She knew when to talk and when to shut up. When to crack a joke to break the tension, and when to just stand close and breathe with Amber.

There's something primal about women in those moments. They drop into this instinctive rhythm together, like they've got a secret code. I used to imagine labor as this intimate thing, just Amber and me, holding hands, locking eyes, some romance movie version of love and support. But standing there, watching Taylor steady her, translate for her, be with her in a way I simply couldn't, didn't upset me. I wasn't disappointed. I wasn't jealous.

I was relieved. I was grateful. I was thankful that Amber had someone there who knew how to stand in that fire with her, because I was still trying to figure it all out. I was still standing there doing math in my head, watching the clock, watching the monitor, trying to pretend I wasn't scared, trying not to let Amber see how helpless I felt.

Eventually they gave Amber another epidural and this time it worked almost too well. It didn't just dull the pain. It wiped it out. She couldn't feel anything. Not even the contractions.

The only way we knew they were still happening was by watching the monitor. That little needle started drawing jagged mountains across the page with spikes so high they looked like they were trying to run off the top of the screen. Her body was doing all this work, rolling through these huge contractions, and Amber was sitting there chewing ice chips and talking like we were on the couch at home.

It was surreal. Like someone had flipped the channel from "medical emergency" to "casual afternoon hangout." One minute it felt intense and scary and serious, and the next it felt almost normal, except for the fact that a machine next to her was quietly screaming, in graph form, that her body was still in full labor.

But eventually we hit the part where "numb" wasn't going to work anymore. She had to be able to feel enough to push. So they let the epidural wear off, little by little, and you could see the shift as the pain started creeping back in. Her face changed. Her voice changed. Her whole body got tense again, like it instantly remembered exactly what it had been temporarily spared.

By then, she'd been dealing with this for hours, and I'd been standing beside her the entire time, feeling like dead weight. I'd hold her hand and try to be steady, but inside I was just hoping I could survive watching it. Hoping she could survive feeling it.

But we were past the point of no return. The baby was coming. Ready or not.

That's when everything went sideways.

The baby's heart rate started to drop. I watched the numbers on the monitor dip lower and lower, and my stomach followed them. The energy in the room flipped instantly. Nurses who had been moving at an easy, practiced pace suddenly snapped into high gear. Their usually calm, reassuring voices were replaced with firm, commanding directions.

I just stood there, useless again, watching people who actually knew what they were doing move fast around the woman I loved and the child I hadn't met yet.

And then, like my brain hated me and decided to pick the worst song possible, Tim McGraw's "Don't Take the Girl" started playing on a loop in my head like a broken jukebox I couldn't turn off.

Don't take her. Don't take Amber. Don't take the baby. Please, God, don't take them.

> *"Take the very breath you gave me*
> *Take the heart from my chest*
> *I'll gladly take her place if you'll let me*
> *Make this my last request*
> *Take me out of this world*
> *but God, please, don't take the girl..."*

The nurses cranked the bed so Amber's head was lower than her feet, tipping her almost upside down. I remember her hair falling back, her face flushed, the cords and tubes swinging a little with the sudden movement.

Time turned into sludge. Maybe a minute passed. That's what the clock would probably say if I could go back and check. But standing there, it felt like I was dropping through an endless, silent elevator shaft made of fear. *How long can a heart keep dropping before it doesn't climb back up? How many seconds do you get before "it's okay" turns into "it's too late"?*

And then slowly, mercifully, the numbers on the monitor started creeping back up as his heart rate steadied.

The tension in the room loosened just enough to breathe again. Shoulders dropped. Voices softened. The invisible fist around my heart let go.

I didn't cry, not right then. I just stood there next to Amber, my hand wrapped around hers, completely overwhelmed by the fact that we were still in this. That he was still in this.

Looking back, I can see it plain as day. That was the first time I really understood how fragile and enormous this whole "being a dad" thing was going to be. One minute you're counting centimeters and making jokes about ice chips. The next minute you're quietly bargaining with God over a tiny heartbeat on a screen.

And somehow, inside all that fear, there was a quiet, stubborn thread of hope. My life was already changing, long before I ever saw his face.

My whole life, I'd treated big milestones like progress bars. Two centimeters down, eight to go. High school: check. First job: check. Marriage: check. Baby: loading… loading… loading. Like there was some invisible system keeping score and eventually you'd get what you'd "earned."

Watching my son's heartbeat drop on that monitor destroyed that story in about three seconds. There wasn't a checklist in the world that could fix that moment. No amount of "stepping up" or being a "good man" could control those numbers on the screen. I wasn't the hero in that room. I wasn't the strong, steady rock I always pictured I'd be. I was just another terrified human being standing in the background, hoping the people in scrubs knew what they were doing.

I'd spent so much of my life chasing these loud, flashy versions of love. The dramatic kind. The drunk, reckless kind. The "watch me prove I'm worth something" kind. The stuff that looks great in stories and awful in the rearview mirror. That day taught me a much quieter version.

Love is sitting in a dark hospital room at two in the morning, holding a plastic cup of ice chips for someone who can barely breathe through the pain. Love is rubbing a lower back that's already sore from hours of contractions, even though you know it isn't really doing much except saying, *I'm here. I'm not leaving.* Love is stepping aside while another woman, your wife's sister, her friend, whoever, takes the lead because she's the one who knows what to do. And instead of feeling replaced, you feel thankful she's there. Love is watching a monitor like it's the only window into the future you give a damn about, and bargaining with a God you're not even sure you believe in.

You don't become a parent the second your child is born. That's the part people take pictures of. You become a parent when you realize you are not in control anymore.

That day, I walked into that delivery room thinking responsibility meant saying "I do," painting nurseries, putting cribs together, and showing up to the hospital on time. It was all task-based, like being a grown-up was just a series of projects you finished so you could pat yourself on the back. I walked out understanding that real responsibility meant staying present when you are terrified, helpless, and completely unequipped.

The baby would come. The diapers, the sleepless nights, the long days where every hour feels like three. All of that was waiting for us. But the real change, the part that lives behind my blue eyes, started right there in that room, before I ever heard him cry.

The version of me that walked into that hospital was not the same one who walked out.

Finally, the nurse turned to Amber and said, "We're going to call the doctor now."

Call the doctor… now?

We'd been there since two in the morning. We'd watched the sun rise, crawl across the sky, and start to fade again. We'd waited through centimeters and contractions, fear and false starts, heart rate dips and false alarms, and we're just now calling the guy whose name was on all the paperwork?

I didn't say it out loud, but inside I was yelling, *What have we been doing all day, rehearsing?*

Thankfully, he showed up within ten or fifteen minutes. Calm. Unrushed. Like this was just another Monday for him. No big life-changing event, just another delivery on the schedule. The nurses huddled around him like they'd done this a thousand times, pulling out equipment, unwrapping sterile instruments, wheeling in the incubator and parking it in the corner of the room. You could tell they could've done it in their sleep.

And just like that, after all the waiting, the moment was suddenly here.

I stood by Amber's side, holding her hand, trying to look like some version of strong and steady. Taylor was in the corner with the camcorder, bouncing from one side of the room to the other, filming everything like an over-caffeinated hummingbird.

I'd always imagined I'd be the devoted, locked-in partner. The husband brushing hair back from her forehead, whispering, "You're doing amazing, I'm so proud of you," staying fully present with her. And I did all of that. But my eyes kept drifting to the medical team. The monitors. The doctor's face. Every time he said something I didn't understand, my stomach clenched. Every beep, every adjustment, every quiet order sent my brain into overdrive.

Is that normal? Is that normal? Are we okay? Is he okay?

My body was next to Amber, but my mind kept splitting in two. Her, and the tiny life we still hadn't seen. Concern sat on my chest like a weight, but so did this fierce little sense of duty. I was going to stand beside her and stay there, no matter how scared I was.

And then, somewhere in the shuffle and the soft, focused commands, a nurse said the words I didn't even realize I'd been holding my breath for:

"He's here."

Time didn't slow down. It just went away.

My chest filled up with something too big for my body. My smile actually hurt. I saw him, my son, and my life split cleanly in two. Before him and after him.

They asked if I wanted to cut the cord. I'd always pictured it as this ceremonial, gentle little snip, like cutting a ribbon at a grand opening. No one tells you that cord fights back. It took three determined chops before it finally gave way. My hands weren't exactly steady, but I did it.

I cut him free.

They rushed him over to the incubator and started working on him, suctioning his nose and mouth, checking his breathing, rubbing his back. His first sounds weren't the dramatic cries you expect, just these soft, half-hearted little squeaks like he wasn't totally convinced about this whole "being born" thing yet. I watched, frozen, my heart slamming against my ribs like it was trying to get closer to him.

The nurses moved fast but calm, hands sure and practiced. They didn't look worried, but I was terrified anyway. I stayed beside Amber, stroking her hair, telling her everything was okay, while my eyes stayed locked on that tiny, squirming body across the room.

And then it came. That long, beautiful newborn wail that split the air wide open.

Relief hit me so hard it made me lightheaded. He was breathing. He was crying. He was here.

Cole was born at 4:39 p.m. on September 8th, 1997. Seven pounds, fourteen ounces. A full head of dark hair.

The longest, most surreal day of my life ended with this tiny stranger lying under bright hospital lights, and somehow he already owned my entire heart. Looking back now, I can still feel the concern and the absolute devotion, that quiet, stunned promise I made without saying a word:

I'm yours. I don't know what I'm doing yet, but I'm here. And I'm not going anywhere.

Amber, though, didn't look how I'd imagined she would. There was no glowing smile, no tearful "I can't believe he's here." She just looked exhausted. Wiped out. And underneath that, something else I couldn't quite characterize. Disappointment?

She'd desperately wanted a girl. Her sister had just had one, and I knew she'd pictured matching cousins, little dresses, shared milestones. No one said the word "disappointed," but I felt it hanging there, heavy in the room. I tried to tell myself it was just the exhaustion, the hormones, the sheer weight of what she'd just been through.

I still tell myself that.

At some point, I wandered out to the waiting room to tell my parents they were grandparents to a beautiful baby boy. The words felt almost wrong in my mouth, like I was reading somebody else's line.

I was twenty-two years old, five-foot-three on a good day, maybe 110 pounds soaking wet. My jeans looked like they belonged to someone bigger, someone more prepared for that kind of statement. Standing there in front of my mom and dad, telling them their son now had a son, I felt impossibly young and suddenly ancient at the same time.

It felt like I'd been shoved, ready or not, across some invisible line between boy and man. One sentence, one moment, and my whole identity was modified.

Up until then, I thought strength was loud. I thought it meant being composed, saying the right things, having answers. I had this picture in my head that "strong" meant you stayed calm, stayed in control, and kept everyone else steady just by being steady yourself. Like if you didn't fall apart, you were doing your job.

But in that delivery room, watching Amber do something I could never do in a million years while I stood there basically helpless, I finally understood how wrong that definition was.

Real strength doesn't always make a scene. Sometimes it's quiet. Sometimes it looks like pain and grit and focus. Sometimes it's staying in the unknown when every part of you wants to bolt. It's standing there, breathing through your own panic, even when you have absolutely no control over what happens next.

And then they handed me Cole.

The first time they placed him in my arms, my chest did this strange thing where it felt like it stretched too far, too fast. Not heartbreak. Nothing like that. More like my body was trying to make room for something it didn't know how to hold yet. Like the space inside me needed to be bigger, and there was no gentle way to get there.

I didn't know you could love someone that quickly. I didn't know you could feel that attached to a person you'd just met, whose eyes you hadn't even seen yet, whose voice you'd only heard in those raw, broken cries. He was warm and squirmy and brand new, wrapped up tight like a little burrito, and he felt impossibly fragile.

I remember looking down at him and feeling it settle in: there was nothing I wouldn't do for him. No hesitation. No debate. Just a promise.

Cutting the cord wasn't just some medical step on a checklist. Even then, I felt the weight of what it meant. The first thing I ever did for him was separate him, literally cut him loose from the only home he'd ever known. It hit me later that parenthood is basically a long series of smaller versions of that. Tiny separations. Letting go inch by inch as they learn to breathe without you, walk without you, go to school without you, drive away without you. And eventually, even live without you.

But right then, I wasn't thinking about the future. I wasn't thinking about first steps or school buses or keys to a car. I was just standing there holding him, trying to understand how I could be the same person I'd been earlier that morning, when I clearly wasn't.

All I felt was this simple, overwhelming truth settling into my bones:

I wasn't just somebody's child anymore.

I was somebody's father.

That night I must've passed out in the chair next to Amber's bed, because the next thing I remember, morning light was seeping in around the curtains in the hospital room.

Amber was in the same hospital bed, propped up, trying to get Cole to latch. Her skin was pale, her eyes heavy, her arms cradling him with this tenderness that looked shaky and unsure. She glanced over at me, then back at him, and gently touched his arm.

"He's cold," she whispered.

Her voice was so soft, like she wasn't sure she was allowed to say it out loud. I tried to sound calm and reassuring, even though I had no idea what "normal" was for a newborn. Maybe babies were supposed to feel that way. Maybe the room was too cold. Maybe everything was fine.

He was bundled in a hospital blanket with that little striped knit hat they slap on every newborn. His cheeks were puffy, his eyes barely slits, his face still swollen from the trip. Honestly, he looked a little alien. But he was my alien. My son. And every tiny movement he made felt like an earthquake.

By that evening, we'd crossed the twenty-four-hour mark, and the hospital cleared us to go home. Amber was wheeled downstairs in sweatpants and an oversized T-shirt, holding Cole like he was made of blown glass. I had borrowed my parents' old Ford Crown Victoria, a giant tank of a car that felt like the safest thing on four wheels.

I'd installed the car seat days earlier and checked it obsessively. Now I checked it again. And again. And then one more time, pressing on the base, tugging the straps, making sure nothing moved. Amber placed him into the seat and gently buckled him in.

I have never driven that carefully in my life.

I watched every car with suspicion. Every lane change felt personal. Didn't these people know what I was transporting? Didn't they understand there was a brand-new human being in my back seat who had been on this planet for barely 24 hours? I wanted to roll down the window and shout, BACK OFF. I JUST BECAME A DAD.

When we finally pulled into our driveway, I exhaled for what felt like the first time since we'd left the hospital. I jumped out, unlocked the front door, turned on the lights, and held it open as Amber stepped over the threshold with Cole in her arms.

"Welcome home, buddy," I said.

Three words. But they lodged in my throat in a way I'll never forget and my voice cracked a little. I don't know if Amber noticed.

It was, without question, the best day of my life.

From that point on, every decision, every sacrifice, every long shift and side hustle, every argument I tried not to have in front of him, whether I nailed it or completely screwed it up, got run through one central filter: What does this mean for him?

Up until then, I thought responsibility was bills and jobs and showing up on time. I thought being "responsible" meant marrying the girl when you got her pregnant, painting the nursery, tightening the car seat straps until your fingers hurt.

But standing there in that tiny living room, watching Amber lower our son into his crib for the first time, I understood responsibility was so much bigger than that. It wasn't just doing what you were supposed to do. It was becoming someone your kid could someday look at and think, *Yeah. That's my dad. I'm proud of that guy.*

Love stopped being abstract that day. It stopped being this feeling I chased from girl to girl, bar to bar, bed to bed. It stopped being about butterflies and drama and whether someone texted back.

It became active. Concrete.

Love became staying up all night, not because it was fun, but because a seven-pound human couldn't breathe right unless he was upright on your chest. Love became triple-checking the locks and peeking in on a sleeping baby just to make sure you could see his chest rise and fall. Love became trying to wipe the panic off Amber's face while doing everything you could to keep your own from giving you away.

Real love isn't convenient. It isn't simple. It doesn't come with a script or a guarantee you'll get it right.

Real love is messy and terrifying and holy, all at the same time.

That was the day I became a father. Not just on a certificate. Not just biologically. In the ways that actually matter. That was the day I stopped being the main character in my own story and willingly handed the spotlight to a tiny, dark-haired kid who had no idea how much space he'd just taken up in my heart.

ROUND 17:
Shattered

About a year into our marriage, Amber made plans to go out with her sister, Taylor, one evening. Nothing unusual. Just a bar, a few drinks, and a chance for her to feel human again after nine months of pregnancy, swelling, waddling, and the last few months of being stuck in mom mode, not sleeping longer than twenty minutes at a time.

She left sometime after dinner. I don't remember the exact time, just the snapshot: me standing at the front door, Cole in his bouncy seat behind me, Amber adjusting her earrings in the bedroom mirror, grabbing her purse, giving me a quick kiss like it was any other night out, and then stepping into the dark.

I fed Cole, got him to bed, flipped through channels for a while, and crashed around 11:00. When I noticed she still wasn't home, I didn't think much of it. She and Taylor had a long history of closing places down and then hitting whatever all-night grease pit was open. I trusted her. I really did.

Then I opened my eyes at 5:45 a.m. and rolled over.

Her side of the bed was cold. Empty. Untouched.

That's when the worry hit. Not the slow, creeping kind. The kind that punches you straight in the gut and steals your breath before your brain is even fully online.

I shot out of bed, grabbed the cordless phone from the living room, and called Taylor. She answered, groggy and confused.

"She's not home," I said.

There was this beat of silence, and then, like her brain was buffering, "She's not at home?"

If she were home, I wouldn't be calling at six in the damn morning.

I asked when she'd last seen Amber, if she knew where she might've gone. Taylor hesitated, then said she "might have an idea" and would call me back.

Might have an idea.

I clung to that line like it was a life preserver, set the phone back in its cradle, and headed for the shower. Cole was still asleep, and I figured I could at least start getting ready for work while I waited for answers that, at that point, I was still dumb enough to think could be normal.

By the time I got out, hair dripping, towel around my waist, the phone was still quietly sitting there in its little plastic cradle. So I called Taylor again.

This time it just rang. No answer. No voicemail. Just that dead, endless ringing that gives your imagination room to play. My brain flipped into full disaster mode: car accident. DUI. Date rape drug. Some guy's apartment. Passed out in a parking lot. Lying in a ditch. You name it, my brain cast her in it. When you love someone and they just vanish, you find out how fast your mind can turn into a horror movie.

I got dressed in record time, woke Cole, changed him, fed him, and started packing his diaper bag so I could drop him at my parents' before work. No matter what the hell was going on, I couldn't lose my job. That was the one line I wouldn't cross back then. I could be falling apart, but I couldn't be unemployed.

I was zipping the diaper bag when the front door finally creaked open and Amber stepped inside. She was a mess. Pale. Eyes glassy. Makeup smeared like she'd put it on with her thumbs. Hair a tangled mess. And the sour stench of cheap liquor and stale bar air.

Relief and fury slammed into each other in my chest so hard I honestly didn't know whether to hug her or shake her.

"Where have you been? Are you okay?" I asked.

She barely looked at me. "I'm fine," she muttered, like I'd asked if she checked the mail.

That tone, flat and annoyed, hit harder than the empty bed had. I'd spent the whole morning mentally replaying worst-case scenarios, and she was acting like I was being dramatic for no reason.

"Why didn't you come home?" I pressed. "Why didn't Taylor know where you were? And… where's the car?"

She brushed past me, still dodging my eyes, and finally muttered that her stepmom, Brandi, had dropped her off.

Brandi. Not Taylor. Not a friend from the bar. Not a cab driver. Her stepmother. And no car. None of it made sense. The math wasn't mathing.

She wouldn't say where she'd been. Wouldn't explain how Brandi got involved. Every answer was clipped, vague, defensive, like the real problem here was me giving a shit.

One thing was suddenly, painfully obvious: I wasn't leaving our son alone with her like that. I scooped Cole out of his exer-saucer, grabbed my bag, and headed for the door.

Amber stepped in front of me, arms crossed.

"Where do you think you're going?" she demanded.

"To work. I have to go," I said.

"And where are you taking him?"

"To my parents'. I'm not leaving him here with you like this."

"You're not going anywhere without me."

I just stared at her.

She repeated it, firmer this time, like it was a rule. "You're not going anywhere without me."

I looked at her hard. The truth landed in my face: I had no idea what happened in the last ten hours. Who she'd been with. What she'd done.

How drunk, or worse, she still was. All I knew was there was no way in hell I was putting our son's safety in her hands in that state.

I set Cole back in the exer-saucer, ran my hands through my hair, trying to find some version of this that didn't feel like insanity. We argued, me asking questions, her dodging them like I was a detective and she was mid-interrogation. No answers. Just resistance and attitude.

Finally, I snapped.

I stormed out the front door, yelling, shaking. I had no real plan beyond get to work, get distance. Maybe I'd call my mom to come pick up Cole. Maybe she could help untangle whatever the hell this was.

Our white Dodge Caravan sat neatly parked along the curb. I beelined for the driver's side, keys in hand. Before I could climb in, I heard footsteps behind me.

Amber was marching toward the passenger door, eyes locked on me.

"What are you doing?" I asked.

"You're not going anywhere without me," she repeated.

"Our son is alone in the house right now," I said, feeling the anger finally catching up to the fear. "Do you even realize that?"

"You're not going anywhere without me," she said again, like some broken, drunk mantra.

That was it.

I slammed the van door so hard the frame shuddered, and stormed back up the sidewalk and into the house. No more arguing in the yard. No more giving the neighbors a free show. I went straight to the front door, stepped inside, and locked it behind me.

Inside, Cole was still in his exer-saucer, maybe ten feet from the door. He looked up at me with big, trusting eyes, legs bouncing, completely oblivious to the grenade that had just gone off in his life.

I stood there between him and the door, trying to breathe, trying to think, trying not to lose my shit completely.

Then it happened.

A loud, metallic grind, followed by an explosion of sound.

Amber had ripped the metal mailbox clean off the side of the house and punched it through the glass panel on the front door. The window shattered inward, in a violent spray of glass blasting across the entryway, over the floor and the exer-saucer.

Cole screamed. A high, piercing sound I had never heard from him before. Not an "I'm hungry" cry. Not a "change me" cry. It sounded like pure fear.

I froze.

For a split second, my brain just stopped. How do you process your wife ripping fixtures off your house and throwing them through windows with your baby ten feet away?

Amber reached through the jagged hole, flipped the deadbolt, and stepped into the house. She didn't look at me. Didn't look at Cole. She walked straight past both of us, across a floor covered in broken glass, picked up the cordless phone, and dialed.

"What are you doing?" I yelled, panic cracking my voice.

"Calling the cops," she snapped.

"On me? For what, trying to go to work?" I exploded. "Are you serious right now?"

She was. Dead serious. Strangely calm now. She told them it was a domestic violence situation. Of course she did.

I rushed over to Cole, still shrieking, his tiny body shaking. When I lifted him out of the exer-saucer, little shards of glass fell from his clothes and hair, tinkling onto the hardwood. His seat was sprinkled with glittering slivers of what used to be our front door.

I held him tight against my chest, rubbing his back, whispering, "You're okay, buddy. Daddy's got you." I didn't know if I believed it, but I needed him to hear it. I needed me to hear it.

Behind me, Amber was shouting into the phone, painting me as some kind of monster. I shouted back, trying to cut through the insanity, but it didn't matter. Once the word domestic hits a dispatcher's screen, the script is set. Somebody's getting cuffed. And let's be honest, it's usually the guy.

When she slammed the phone back in its cradle, I snatched it up and called my mom. I don't even remember exactly what I said, just a blur of words and panic, but she got it.

"I'm on my way," she said.

Amber, not to be outdone, called Taylor. We each rallied our own backup like opposing legal teams gearing up for trial.

The cops showed up within minutes. Two of them. One took Amber outside, past the crunching glass on the porch, to get her story. The other came inside and spoke to me while I sat on the couch with Cole clinging to me like a life raft. My voice shook as I told him everything, from the moment she left the night before, to the empty bed at dawn, to the mailbox and the shattering glass.

Then they switched. The one who'd listened to her came in to hear my version. The one who'd listened to me went out to hear hers. Same questions. Same answers. Just replayed for a different audience.

They stepped outside to talk on the front step, radios crackling quietly.

That's when my mom pulled up.

Taylor had gotten there moments before and was standing with Amber near the van. Mom didn't even look their way. She walked straight across the yard, up to the front door, introduced herself to the officers, and they stepped aside to let her in.

She came inside and saw me pacing, Cole on my chest, his tiny fingers gripping my shirt like he was afraid I might let go. She didn't say much. Just reached out, rubbed my arm with one hand, and touched Cole's head with the other.

The look she gave him was apologetic and furious and heartbroken all at once. It was the look of a grandmother silently saying, *I'm so sorry you're in the middle of this shitstorm.*

A moment later, the female officer opened the door and stepped back into the house. With her hands resting on her duty belt, posture firm but face soft, she walked over to us.

Her voice was calm. Almost gentle. But her words hit like thunder.

They were arresting Amber for domestic violence and child endangerment.

I stood there in my living room, glass on the floor, my son on my chest, and those words just hung in the air. It was poetic justice in the darkest possible way. She called the police on me, and they were taking her.

But I didn't feel victorious. There was no "gotcha" moment of satisfaction. This wasn't a movie where the villain gets hauled off and the hero stands in the doorway in slow motion. This was my wife. The mother of my child. Watching her in handcuffs didn't feel like I won anything.

It felt like we both lost something we couldn't get back.

I was relieved, yeah. The instant the squad car pulled away, the noise stopped. The immediate threat was gone. For the first time that morning, I knew Cole was safe. But it still broke my heart.

Mom held Cole for a while so I could talk to the officer and find out what would happen next. Where they were taking Amber, how long she might be there, what this meant for custody in the short term. All the normal questions, I guess, for a husband whose wife just got arrested for attacking a front door and showering their baby in glass.

The officer handed me her card and told me to call if I needed anything else. I thanked her, already knowing that card would probably end up in the trash as soon as my hands stopped shaking. After the squad car pulled away with Amber in the back, the other officer headed to her cruiser. The neighborhood went quiet again.

That's when Taylor stepped inside.

She didn't say a word at first. She just walked straight up to me and wrapped her arms around me. It wasn't some quick, polite hug. It was long and tight and full of about twelve different kinds of grief. I stood there holding the officer's business card in one hand and my sister-in-law with the other, completely unsure what that hug meant. *Was she mourning with me? Sorry for her sister? Grieving the whole mess? All of the above?* Probably.

She finally pulled back, wiped her eyes, and said she was heading to the police station to see what would happen next. Then she walked out, and the door clicked shut behind her.

That's when the thought hit me: *this might be the beginning of the end of my marriage.* Not because we had some epic love story that suddenly shattered. If I'm being honest, we probably never should've gotten married in the first place. But endings have a way of stirring up dust in corners you forgot were even there.

Because if the marriage ended, what else could I lose?

I might lose my son.

That realization hit harder than any punch I'd ever taken. Harder than Malik's fist. Harder than rejection at MEPS. Harder than watching every other plan for my life fall apart. I could live without a marriage that was built on shot glasses and orgasms. But I couldn't live without Cole.

That morning taught me something I didn't want to learn. Sometimes doing the right thing for your kid means admitting the whole structure is defective. Sometimes the person you had a baby with becomes the person you have to protect that baby from. It was the day "domestic violence" stopped being a headline and turned into the sound of glass shattering in my own living room. And it was the day I understood my love for my son would always outrun my loyalty to anyone else.

We didn't file for divorce right away. We did that thing couples do when everyone else already knows it's over, but they keep the show running a little longer anyway. We tried, one last time, to glue the pieces back together. From the outside, I'm sure it looked like progress. We were still in the same house, still sharing meals, still technically calling it a marriage. But underneath, we both knew it was over.

Still, I had to try. For Cole. For whatever was left of my conscience. I needed to be able to look him in the eyes someday, and look myself in the mirror, and say I gave it everything I had, even if the foundation had been cracked from the very beginning.

And then came the moment I knew I was done with all of it.

We were having dinner with her entire family at Monical's Pizza on Mattis Avenue. That place is burned into my memory now. Not because of the food, but because it's where something in me finally slammed shut. Silverware clinking on plates, kids shrieking, that low roar of a hundred different conversations layered on top of each other. We were wedged around a table, her whole family there.

The details blur now. Some comment was made. What exactly, I honestly couldn't tell you. But in the space of a breath, the mood changed. Suddenly, I felt like I was on trial. Like every head at that table turned toward me, and every mouth had an opinion, and none of them were kind. I felt ambushed. Surrounded. Cornered. That pressure that had been living in my chest for months doubled, like someone set a cinder block on my sternum.

And the worst part? Amber wasn't on my side.

She wasn't even neutral. She was right there with them. Whatever faith I still had in "us," in this idea that we could fix it, that maybe the counseling and the fights and the "we'll do better" talks would eventually mean something, all crumbled right there over a thin-crust pizza.

I stood up without a word, pulled the van keys from my pocket, tossed them on the table, and walked out. No dramatic speech, no final line. Just done.

Then I started walking. Almost three miles from Monical's to my parents' house. Each step felt heavier than the last, but somehow lighter the closer I got. Like I was carrying grief and setting it down at the same time. By the time I reached their doorstep, an hour later, I'd already made the decision.

That night, I closed the door on our marriage in my mind. Within a week, I officially filed for divorce.

On paper, it was simple. Two people who didn't belong together finally admitting it. Check the box, sign the line, file the form.

Custody, however, was a different story. Custody was war.

I asked for shared custody, but I wanted Cole to live with me. I had the steady job, the benefits, the roof, the routine. I'd never been in trouble with the law. I was the one working to provide for him every day. And she'd been arrested just a few months earlier for domestic violence and child endangerment.

I honestly believed there was no way a judge would look at that and hand him over to her. I believed that because I still believed in rules, fairness, and basic logic back then.

The court process dragged on. Continuance after continuance. My parents helped with legal fees because my Lowe's paycheck alone didn't stand a chance. Every hearing meant another day I couldn't work, another chunk of money I didn't have, another late bill I had to juggle. Rent. Food. Clothes for Cole. Diapers. Gas. Every dollar felt like it had to do the work of five.

I was drowning in responsibility and attorney fees.

Still, I showed up to every court date. Even the ones I wasn't technically required to attend. I needed that judge to see me. To see that I wasn't just some name on a case file. That I cared. That I was serious about fighting for my son.

Meanwhile, Amber would walk out of the courtroom laughing. Literally laughing. Like we'd just finished a sitcom instead of a custody hearing. It was a game to her. I don't even think she truly wanted custody. She just didn't want me to have it. It wasn't about parenting. It was about leverage. Control. Making sure I lost.

Those months of being in and out of the courthouse permanently crushed a part of me. The paperwork that never ended, the waiting around for someone to call your name, the constant knot in your stomach because your entire life is sitting in a folder on someone's desk. The sleepless nights were the worst, lying there doing the same mental loop over and over, wondering if you were about to lose your son because of a decision you couldn't control. It wasn't one big moment that broke me. It was a long stretch of small, steady hits that took piece after piece after piece.

Before all of that, I honestly believed the system worked. Not perfectly, but enough. I believed truth mattered. I believed intent mattered. I believed that if you showed up, did the right thing, kept your life clean, worked hard, and put your kid first, the court would see it. I wasn't expecting a trophy. I just thought there was a basic logic to it. Like if you did A and B, you'd get C. Like being the stable parent, the present parent, the one doing the actual work, would count for something.

Custody court doesn't work like that. It's not an equation. It's a minefield, and the rules change depending on who's talking, who's listening, and what someone decides sounds believable that day. Logic is usually the first thing to die.

People assume the worst part is the money, and don't get me wrong, it was brutal. Attorney fees, missed work, surprise expenses that hit when you're already stretched thin. It felt like getting bled out slowly. But the money wasn't what crushed me. The worst part was watching someone twist a story, change details, play innocent, and have it treated like it carried the same weight as the truth I'd been living every day.

Sitting on those hard benches, listening to her say things that weren't true, watching her posture and tone like she was performing, and realizing I couldn't just jump up and correct it the way you would in real life. You're stuck. You're told to keep your mouth shut. You're told to "let your attorney handle it." Meanwhile, she's out there acting confident, laughing in the hallway like this is all some game she knows how to win, and I'm sitting there with my stomach in my throat because my son is the prize in the middle of it. That kind of helplessness changes you permanently.

I came out of it less trusting. Not just of her, but of everything I used to lean on for comfort. People. Systems. Promises. The idea of fairness. I learned the world doesn't hand you justice just because you earned it. You can do everything "right" and still have your heart ripped out in under five minutes because someone else told a smoother story, or caught you on a bad day when you looked tired, stressed, or too emotional. It didn't feel like a process built to protect kids. It felt like a process built to manage conflict, and those aren't the same thing.

But the bitterness didn't get to drive. I let it teach me, not steer me.

Yeah, she changed me. The system changed me. That whole chapter burned off a lot of the naive faith I had about how the world works. It taught me how quickly things can turn, how careful you have to be, how being a good father isn't always enough on its own. You have to be able to prove it, document it, defend it, repeat it, and keep doing it even when you're exhausted.

It didn't destroy me, though. I still showed up. I still fought. And that fight gave me something I couldn't have gotten any other way: clarity.

I know exactly who I am as a father because I had to find out the hard way. I know what I can survive because I had to survive it while still changing diapers, showing up to work, and trying to keep my head on straight. And I know love, real love, isn't what you say when things are easy. It's what you do when you're scared, when you're tired, when you're being tested, and when it feels like the odds are against you.

So no, I don't believe in fairness the way I used to. I don't assume the right outcome just because you're the right person. But I do believe in showing up. I believe in staying present. I believe in being seen and being consistent when it would be easier to shut down. And sometimes, being the one who refused to disappear, being the one who kept coming back, kept standing there, kept fighting for his kid when it would've been simpler to break, that's its own small, stubborn kind of justice.

Leaving the courtroom on December 19th, I should've been thinking a thousand things at once. I should've been furious, arguing with myself, running through scenarios, plotting out the next step. But I don't remember any of that. I remember walking out and feeling like my brain had shut off. Like someone flipped a switch and everything went quiet.

I wasn't calm. I was numb. Hollowed out. The sadness, the anger, the disbelief, all came crashing in on me at once. It just smothered me.

The judge ruled that I'd get visitation every other weekend. Four days a month. That was it. Shared custody, child support, the whole package that probably looks "reasonable" if you don't know anything about the people involved. Someone could glance at it and say, "See? Balanced." Like it's a budget. Like it's splitting furniture in a divorce.

But I hadn't done anything wrong. Not one thing that justified this.

From the moment Cole was born, I poured myself into being his dad. It wasn't some side thing I squeezed in when I felt like it. It was the one thing that made me feel steady. I didn't have everything figured out, and I know I made mistakes because I was young and learning in real time, but I tried. Every day. Every late shift where I still came home and handled what needed handling. Every sacrifice. Every dollar that went to diapers, wipes, clothes, formula, toys, food. That was me trying to build a life for him that was better than what I grew up with. That was me trying to do it right.

And then, in a few short minutes, a man in a black robe told me I could only be a father four days out of thirty.

Four.

I remember that number more clearly than anything else from that day. Because once you hear it, you start doing the math without meaning to. Four days a month means twenty-six days where I'm not there. Twenty-six days where I don't get to put him to bed, don't get to be the one he runs to, don't get the normal moments that make you a parent. Doctor visits. Daycare stuff. The random little milestones you don't even realize are milestones until you miss them.

And I had this thought that made me feel sick: *what does that make me the other twenty-six days? Am I just nothing? Just a name on paperwork? A check in the mail? The "weekend dad?"*

I couldn't wrap my head around it. I couldn't accept that my role could be reduced to a schedule. That fatherhood could be chopped up into visits like I was some extended family member. I was his dad. That should've meant something.

Amber would be the one raising him day to day. She'd be the one making the calls and signing the forms and showing up to the doctor. She'd be the one there for the ordinary Tuesdays and Wednesdays where life actually happens. And I already knew what that meant, because everyone in my life knew how this usually goes. My family knew it. My friends knew it. Coworkers knew it. Nobody even had to say it out loud. People have seen the pattern enough times to recognize it.

I felt shortchanged. Robbed is closer to the truth. Not in some pitiful "poor me" way, but in a real, practical way where I was watching my life get taken apart in front of me, piece by piece, and there was nothing I could do to stop it.

Maybe the judge was old-school. Maybe he was one of those guys who automatically leans toward the mother because that's how he's always seen it done. Maybe he didn't care enough to dig into the details. Maybe he did care, but I was just another case in a stack and he had twenty more to get through before lunch. I'll never know. And that's part of what made it worse. There wasn't even a clear reason I could point to. No moment where someone could say, "This is why."

All I know is that when I walked out of that courtroom, my head went blank. But the next morning, the reality hit hard. I woke up and for a split second I forgot, and then it came rushing back. *Oh yeah. This is my life now.* I had just lost the biggest piece of my life, and not because I failed my son. That's what wrecked me.

Because I hadn't failed him.

And still, my brain did what it always does when something doesn't make sense. It started interrogating me. *Maybe the judge saw something in me I couldn't see. Maybe there was some flaw I wasn't aware of. Maybe I was missing something obvious. Did I come across wrong? Did I look unstable? Did I say something the wrong way? Did something about me read like, This man shouldn't be a father?*

No. I couldn't accept that. I wouldn't. Because it wasn't true.

I was a good father. I am a good father. And I tried every single day.

But life didn't pause just because I was an emotional wreck. It kept moving like it always does. I was still working at Lowe's, going through the motions because that's what you do when you don't know what else to do. Wake up. Work. Come home. Eat something. Sit on the couch. Stare at the TV without watching it. Sleep. Repeat.

I was living in that little triplex I moved into after Amber left. Simple place. Clean walls. New floors. Quiet neighbors. It wasn't a bad place. It was just empty in a way that made everything louder.

When you don't have your kid in the house, you notice everything. How quiet it is. How you catch yourself listening for sounds that aren't coming. How you look at the clock and realize there's nothing on the schedule because the person who gave your days meaning is somewhere else.

And I thought about it constantly. Too much, probably. I replayed the hearing in my head. I replayed everything I said and everything I should've said. I replayed old moments with Cole like I was trying to hold onto proof that I belonged in his daily life. I'd get angry, then I'd get sad, then I'd get angry again because the world kept going just fine while I was stuck.

But somewhere in that dull routine, between the anger and the questions and those empty weekends, something started to settle in. Not peace. Not a big inspirational turnaround. Just a tired, honest acceptance of a few things I didn't want to learn this way.

The system wasn't what I thought it was. People weren't always who they claimed to be. Fairness wasn't guaranteed, even when you were doing your best.

But I was still here.

I still loved my son.

And I was still going to show up for him, four days a month or thirty.

Losing faith in the system hurt. Losing faith in the idea of "fair" hurt even more. But I refused to lose faith in myself as his father. If the schedule was all I got, then I was going to make those days count. I was going to be consistent. I was going to be present. I was going to be the kind of dad he could count on, even if the calendar said I only existed every other weekend.

Because Cole didn't need me to be perfect. He needed me to be there. And I wasn't going anywhere. I made him that promise on his first day in the world and I meant it.

I made those weekends sacred. Even if the rest of my life felt like it had been fed through a wood chipper, those days were going to be different.

I couldn't control the court schedule. I couldn't control the child support. I couldn't control the fact that I went home to an empty place more often than not. But I could control this: when I had my son, he was going to know, without a doubt, that he mattered more than anything else in my world.

On my weekends, everything revolved around him.

Friday nights, I'd pull up to get him and the second he spotted me, his whole face lit up. That look alone could've dragged me through hell and back. Back at my place, we'd settle in front of my hand-me-down TV. Toy Story. The Lion King. Whatever phase he was in at the time, I was in it too.

I'd stretch out on the couch and he'd climb on me like I was a jungle gym, knees in my ribs, elbows in my stomach, zero awareness of how many bones a grown man actually has. Half the time he didn't even watch the movie. He watched me.

He'd stare at my face, trace my jawline with his little fingers, tap my nose, tug on my ears. Just checking. *Are you still here? Are you still mine? Daddy?* Every time his hand brushed my cheek, the answer settled in my chest: Yeah, buddy. I'm here. I'm not going anywhere.

I didn't have much money. Child support, rent, and bills chewed through most of my paycheck before I even got to pretend I had options. But those weekends taught me something I should've known: kids don't give a damn about the price tag. They don't care if you drive a beat-up car or have a flat-screen TV or live in a triplex that smells faintly like someone else's cooking. They care that you're there.

Not half-there. Not physically in the room while your brain is at work, or scrolling your phone, or spiraling into your own anxiety. Fully there. Knees-on-the-floor, eyes-on-them, heart-wide-open there.

I couldn't be there those other twenty-six days out of the month. The system made that call for me, stamped it, filed it, and charged me a fee for the privilege. But on my four days? On my four days, I belonged to him. Completely.

Was it enough? No. Of course it wasn't. What dad dreams about being an "every other weekend" bullet point in his own life story? No one grows up thinking, *Man, I hope I get to see my kid twice a month if the judge says it's okay.*

But it was what I had. And at that time, something had to be enough, or I was going to snap in half.

I won't pretend I handled it all with grace and zen-like acceptance. I didn't. There were nights, on the off weeks, where I sat alone in that small triplex, not even bothering to turn the TV on. Just staring at the blank screen, beer in hand, feeling the weight of the silence pressing down on me.

How do you go from being someone's entire world for forty-eight hours straight to not hearing their voice for days?

There were mornings I woke up and had to remind myself: *you're not playing house on those weekends. You're a dad. You have a son. He exists even when you can't see him.* And that sucked. It hurt.

There's a kind of grief in shared custody that people don't really talk about, and it isn't just the obvious stuff like birthdays and holidays. It's the quiet, everyday moments you don't even realize you're going to miss until they're gone. The Tuesday afternoons. The random Wednesday nights when they say something hilarious without meaning to, or they lose their first tooth, or they wake up one day obsessed with dinosaurs and suddenly your whole life is dinosaurs.

You don't get the call when it happens. You don't get to be there for the surprise. You just hear about it later, after the moment already passed, like you're getting an update on a life you're supposed to be living.

I grieved the version of fatherhood I thought I was signing up for. The normal version. The one where I tucked him in every night, packed his lunch in the morning, did the day-to-day stuff that doesn't look special from the outside but adds up to a whole childhood. I grieved the version where I was there for first days of school and scraped knees and science projects spread across the kitchen table. I thought that was the deal the day we stepped across that threshold and whispered, "Welcome home, buddy."

Instead, I got a highlight reel, like an Saturday afternoon ESPN special.

And I don't say that to sound dramatic. That's just what it felt like. Like I was getting the best parts, but not the full story. Like I was being handed these intense, beautiful little chunks of time and then sent back to my empty place to wait for the next one, trying not to miss too much in between.

But here's what I learned in that stretch of my life, in the months between the courthouse and what came next, when everything felt dark.

You don't need anyone else to validate you as a father.

You keep showing up when the system tells you you're only allowed four days. You keep showing up when your bank account is empty and your chest feels just as hollow. You keep showing up when it's unfair, when you're angry, when you're exhausted, when you're tired of fighting just to be present. You keep showing up when it would be easier to disappear. Not because you don't love them, but because the pain of being a part-time dad can make you want to shut down just to survive it.

You put gas in the car. You show up at 6 p.m. sharp at the designated drop-off point. You stand there waiting, trying to keep your face steady, and then you kneel down and open your arms and let a little boy run full force into you like you're the safest place in the whole world.

And then you build a life around that feeling. Not because it's enough. Not because it fixes what was taken from you. Because if he knows, deep in his bones, that you're not going anywhere, then the schedule doesn't get to rewrite what you are to him.

ROUND 18:
Leaving My Son to Become His Hero

I cherished every minute I had with Cole. Those weekends weren't "visitation" to me. They were my whole life compressed into a handful of hours. I'd count down to them. I'd plan every little detail, not because I needed a schedule, but because I couldn't stand the idea of wasting even one second. If I had him, I wanted him laughing, safe, fed, seen. I wanted him to feel like Dad was solid, like Dad was there.

But under all of that, there was this constant burn that never went away. The kind that sits behind your ribs and shows up in weird moments, standing in line, driving home, folding little shirts, hearing some random dad complain about having to "babysit" his own kid. I was furious at the system for looking right through me and deciding I didn't matter. Furious that I could show up, pay, play by the rules, and still be treated like a problem to manage instead of a father. Furious at Amber, too, especially those moments in court where she would laugh, like this was all some game and I was the punchline. It felt like everyone else got to act however they wanted, and I was the only one being measured, watched, judged.

And then there was the part I hated admitting even to myself. I was angry at me.

Because in my head, I had done everything "right," or at least what I believed "right" was supposed to look like. I showed up when I was told to show up. I followed the paperwork, the dates, the rules, the payments. I bit my tongue when I wanted to explode. I tried to be the reasonable one. The cooperative one. The guy who kept it together so nobody could point and say, "See? That's why he doesn't deserve more time." And somehow, after all of that effort, I still ended up with the kind of arrangement that made me feel like I was on weekend release. Like I had to earn the right to be in my own kid's life, and even then I was on a short leash.

What was worse than the anger was what was underneath it. This heavy, ugly sense of worthlessness that didn't just show up in the quiet moments. It followed me into the good ones, too. I could be sitting there with Cole eating donuts on a Saturday morning, and part of me would still be outside of myself watching it happen. I'd be holding his little hand walking into a gas station for snacks, trying to make it fun, trying to make it normal, and inside I'd be thinking, *You're not a real dad. You're just a guy visiting. You're playing house for a weekend and then you go back to your actual life.*

That judge's decision didn't just limit my time with Cole. It messed with how I saw myself as a man, as a father, as someone who had any value at all. It took the question I was already quietly afraid to ask and shoved it right in my face. *If I wasn't worthy of more than four days a month with my own son, what was I worthy of? Anything?* Because the way it felt in my body was brutal: worthless, useless, hopeless. And the scariest part wasn't the thought. It was how much of me started to believe it.

So, eventually the idea of the Marine Corps started creeping back in. Not in a heroic, chest-out, noble calling kind of way. More like this embarrassing little voice in the back of my head that kept showing up when I was tired, angry, and I couldn't sleep. The kind of thought you don't want to admit out loud because it feels like you're betraying something, or someone, just by thinking it.

But the Marine Corps started feeling like a reset button. Not because I was dreaming of glory. More because I was tired of making decisions and getting punished for them. Tired of trying to steer my own life when it felt like every road ended in the same place. The military, at least, was clear. No gray areas, no courtroom politics, no pretending you're fine while your insides rot out.

But this time, there was Cole. My son. And even if I only had him four days a month, those four days were the only time I felt like I wasn't a complete waste of space. Those weekends were the only place I could still feel love in a way that didn't feel complicated or conditional. It wasn't about how I performed or what I proved. It was just him, climbing on me, laughing, wanting me. For a little while, I could breathe.

And then the questions would hit, the same ones, over and over, like my brain was stuck on repeat and I couldn't shut it off.

If I left for boot camp, I wouldn't see him for months. No weekends. No snacks. No sitting on the couch with him watching The Lion King. It would be letters, if I could even figure out how to cram everything I wanted to say into a page. It would be a photo I'd stare at until I had every detail memorized, his cheeks, his eyes, the way his hair sat when it hadn't been brushed yet. And the part that hit hardest was the one I couldn't dodge: this time it wouldn't be the court taking him from me, or Amber calling the shots. It would be on me. I would be choosing to walk away from him, even if it was temporary, even if it had a bigger purpose.

That's when the guilt would come in loud and immediate. What kind of dad signs up to miss months of his kid's life? What kind of man agrees to not be there while his son is growing and changing, learning new words, doing new things, becoming someone new in real time? I'd be holding onto the little amount of time I did get with Cole like it was oxygen, and then I'd catch myself thinking about a version of me that wasn't constantly bracing for the next hit. I'd picture myself not being so tense all the time, not being so angry, not being so easily rattled. And the contradiction felt ugly. Not noble. Not "sacrifice." Just ugly. Like the fact that I wanted to become something better automatically made me a selfish piece of shit.

That was the loop I lived in, over and over, with no way out.

If I stayed, I got to be physically present in his life. I got to show up for the small stuff that was actually the big stuff, sitting on the floor with him, making him laugh, feeding him, changing him, playing with him until my back hurt, just being near him and feeling that calm that only he could give me. I could tell myself, at least I'm here. At least he knows my face. At least he knows my voice. But staying also meant swallowing the humiliation every time reality reminded me how temporary I was allowed to be. I wasn't "Dad" the way I thought I'd be. I was a visitor. A guy operating on someone else's schedule, following someone else's rules, trying not to step wrong because one wrong move could cost me time I couldn't afford to lose. And I could feel what that was doing to me. I'd be smiling and playing and acting normal around him, but inside I was getting smaller. More cautious. More desperate. Like I was slowly being trained to accept less than I deserved.

But if I left, I'd be choosing something for myself, and that felt dangerous in a different way. It felt like it would confirm everyone's worst assumptions about me. Like I really was selfish. Like I didn't love him enough. Like I was weak and trying to run from a situation I couldn't control. And then that same nasty whisper would show up, the one that always knew exactly where to find me: *you're not good enough anyway. Not as a father. Not as a man. Not for any of this.* It was there after court, driving home, sitting alone in my apartment, staring at the walls when the place got too quiet.

The Marine Corps wouldn't let me stay the same. That was the point.

I didn't want to join because I thought it would be some glorious movie moment. I wasn't imagining slow-motion salutes or some big inspirational transformation where everything magically makes sense. I was imagining a place where I couldn't spiral all day. A place where there was structure. Where expectations were clear. Where you didn't get to negotiate with your moods, or talk yourself out of doing hard things just because you were tired or depressed or pissed off. You got up, you did the work, you got stronger, you learned how to handle pressure without turning into a mess. I wanted that because I was exhausted. Not just tired. Exhausted from feeling like life had stripped me down and left me standing there with no plan and no confidence, just surviving from one hit to the next.

It also felt like my confidence had been getting chipped at for a long time, and this was just the worst version of it. I could trace it back to early stuff, like that middle school gym at a 7th grade dance, those moments where you start learning, quietly, that you don't measure up the way other people seem to. Then it got worse later, when I was in court trying to prove I wasn't the villain in my own story. It's hard to explain what it does to you when you keep showing up with your whole heart and you still get treated like you're guilty, and the best you can hope for is to be tolerated.

What I was craving wasn't a uniform. It was a way to look in the mirror and not hate what I saw. A way to stand up straight without it feeling like an act. A way to stop second-guessing myself every five seconds like I didn't have the right to trust my own judgment. The Marine Corps felt like a place where "man" wasn't just something you claimed because you hit a certain age. It was something you earned. Discipline. Accountability. Doing what you said you'd do even when you didn't feel like it. Not hiding behind excuses. Becoming someone other people could rely on, especially yourself.

And in my head, that mattered because I needed something solid to build the rest of my life on. I needed to believe I could become stable, steady, focused, reliable. Someone who didn't get pushed around by a courtroom, or a relationship, or his own emotions. Someone who could walk through something humiliating and still keep his dignity. Someone who could be under pressure and not fall apart later when nobody was watching. I didn't want a tough-guy image. I wanted an actual backbone. I wanted to feel like I could handle life without constantly getting kicked by it.

I kept coming back to this thought, and it wouldn't leave me alone: *what if becoming a Marine didn't take me away from being his dad. What if it was the only way I ever became the kind of dad he could actually look up to?*

Because I already loved him. That wasn't the question. The love part was easy. The trying part was constant. I was already doing "I love you and I'm trying" every day, in every way I could, with whatever access I had. But I didn't want to stay stuck as the guy fighting for scraps of time and hoping it would all work out. I wanted to be a man Cole could trust as he got older. A man with a plan. A man who didn't feel like he had to beg to be taken seriously. Someone he could point to one day and say, "That's my dad," and mean it with pride, not like it was a complicated sentence that needed extra context and a careful explanation.

And maybe that was the most honest part of it. I didn't just want to be better for him. I wanted to be better so I could finally respect *myself.*

By February 1999, I decided I was done with the wondering. I was going to find out for real, one last time, whether this was ever going to happen or if I needed to finally bury it for good.

434

I walked into the recruiting office on a freezing February morning and pulled open the same door I'd already walked through twice before. I didn't need help finding anything. I knew exactly where the Marine Corps desk was. The first time, I was eighteen and running on pure teenage adrenaline, convinced I was indestructible. The second time, I was twenty, still stubborn and still sure I could out-will whatever had stopped me. This time I was twenty-three, divorced, a dad, and honestly just tired of being told my future was decided by a stranger in a black robe.

The office itself felt like it was stuck in time. Same posters, same worn carpet, same smell of coffee and printer ink. Like the place hadn't moved an inch since the last time I'd been there. And I remember thinking, *yeah, everything's the same except me.*

The recruiter was new. Different face, same polished uniform. I sat down and told him everything. First attempt. Second attempt. The medical disqualifications. The chiropractor. The whole "two-year rule" thing I'd been told like it was some magic reset button. I explained it the way I'd rehearsed it in my head for years, like if I said it clearly enough, it would finally make sense to someone.

He listened, then shook his head like I'd just told him a story from a different decade.

"Times have changed," he said. "It's all digital now."

That was a slap to the face. I'd been walking around with this stupid little sliver of hope that at some point my file would just vanish. Like the system would forget about me, and I'd get to start over. But he told me it didn't work that way. My record wasn't "gone." It was basically permanent.

That's when I asked the question I'd been carrying for years, the one I always avoided because the answer scared me.

"Am I wasting my time going back to St. Louis again? Am I just setting myself up to get rejected like before?"

He leaned forward a little and shrugged like we were talking about something casual.

"Lie."

At first I thought I misheard him.

"Lie?" I asked.

"Yeah," he said, completely calm. "Downplay the back thing. Make it sound like nothing."

I just stared at him. I don't like lying. I don't like being accused of it, and I don't like signing up for it either. There's something in me that has always hated the idea of having to fake my way into being taken seriously.

But I was also exhausted. Exhausted from hearing "no" from people who didn't know me, from being reduced to paperwork, from feeling like I kept getting judged by a technicality instead of the person standing right in front of them.

I asked the obvious question because I had to.

"But won't they see my record? Won't they know I've been rejected before?"

"They'll see it," he said, like it didn't matter. "They'll ask why. And that's when you lie."

I sat there fighting with myself. Part of me wanted to stand up and walk out on principle. Another part of me, probably the part that had been getting punched in the face by life for a while, just wanted a clean shot. I knew my body was fine. I wasn't trying to slip in broken. I wasn't trying to cheat my way into something I couldn't handle. I was trying to get past one stupid label that had been following me around for five years like it knew me better than I knew myself.

"So… I just act like it wasn't a big deal?" I said.

"Exactly," he said. "Make it sound like you barely remember it."

And that's what I did.

The following week, I was back on a bus headed to St. Louis for processing. Same city. Same building. Same cattle-herd routine. The military has a way of moving people through a system that's both impressive and numb at the same time. No personality, no warmth, no room for nuance. It's all instructions and lines and waiting rooms and people calling your name like you're just another file to move from one pile to the next.

But I wasn't the same guy in that seat anymore. I kept thinking about my son, about the kind of man I wanted him to see when he looked at me. I needed something solid to hold onto when everything else in my life felt like it could get taken away with a signature.

Five years of effort led me right back to the same waiting chair, under the same fluorescent lights, with the same stack of forms. I watched other recruits get called in small groups, the oath room door closing behind them with that soft click every time. Every time it closed, it felt like it was closing on me too, like I was watching other people step into the life I'd been trying to earn for five years.

Then I heard my name. Not for the oath room. A doctor with a clipboard wanted to "talk."

He looked down at the paper, then up at me. No emotion. No curiosity. Just a question like he'd asked it a thousand times.

"What's this about a history of back problems?"

I felt my stomach drop. The recruiter's voice, *"Lie,"* popped right into my head, loud and clear. But right behind it was my conscience, the part of me that still wanted to be able to look at myself in the mirror and not feel like I'd sold my soul just to get what I wanted.

So I aimed for the gray area, the truth that had somehow gotten twisted into a permanent red flag.

"I'm not really sure, Doc," I said. "I went to a chiropractor when I was like seventeen. But every time I've tried to get in, it keeps coming up like it's some big deal."

He didn't even hesitate.

"If you've been treated by a chiropractor," he said, flat and clinical, "that means you have back problems. We can't take you if you've got back problems."

Something in me snapped, not in an angry, out-of-control way, but in a fed-up way. Like, *are you kidding me? This is really what's going to decide my life?*

"I didn't have back problems," I said. "I was at the mall with a friend. There was a new clinic with a kiosk offering free adjustments. I mean, it was free, so I tried it. That was it. One time. I never went back."

He stared at me for a long second. Not friendly. Not sympathetic. Just measuring me, like he was trying to decide if I was lying or if I was genuinely stupid enough to believe my own story.

"So why didn't you say that before?" he asked.

And that's when everything poured out. The truth.

"I tried to join right after that appointment," I said. "At eighteen. I didn't think it mattered. They disqualified me and told me to wait two years. So I did. I came back at twenty and didn't mention the chiropractor because it seemed irrelevant, and I still got turned away. Now I'm here again, five years later, still being punished for something that never even caused a problem in the first place."

I took a breath as he glanced back down at the paper on his clipboard.

"I've tried to do this three times," I said. "I keep coming back because I still want to be a Marine. I'm not trying to work the system. I'm just trying to get past something that shouldn't matter."

He watched me for what felt like forever. No reaction, no reassurance. Then he nodded once, like he'd made a decision and that was that.

"Alright," he said. "Let's get you through the physical."

Just like that, the door that had been slammed in my face twice finally peeked open. And once it slipped open, I didn't waste the opportunity.

I passed everything. Vision. Hearing. Blood work. All of it. The whole humiliating assembly line where you bend, turn, cough when they tell you to cough, and try not to think too hard about the fact that strangers in lab coats are deciding whether you qualify to have a future. Even the duck walk, squatting and waddling across the floor while someone watches your joints like they're inspecting a used car. I did it all without a hitch. No pain. No hesitation. No sign of this tragic "back problem" that had somehow become the headline of my entire file.

Finally, they circled **ACCEPTED** on my paperwork.

I got escorted into the oath room and stood shoulder-to-shoulder with a bunch of other recruits, all of us trying to look calm while our hearts fluttered with pride in unison. I raised my right hand, listened to the words, and swore to support and defend the Constitution of the United States against all enemies, foreign and domestic.

Five years of frustration, two rejections, and one carefully worded half-truth later, I was in.

Only two weeks from that moment, I'd be on a plane to San Diego for boot camp. I wasn't just heading into the unknown. I was walking toward the man I wanted my son to see when he looked at me.

For a long time, I honestly believed becoming a Marine would fix me. Like the uniform would scrub off the bad decisions, the weak moments, the half-finished attempts at being a man. I thought if I could just earn the title "Marine," it would cover everything I'd screwed up and make the whole mess look like it had a point.

But sitting in that freezing recruiting office, and then standing in that fluorescent hallway at MEPS for the third time, something hit me that I didn't expect. Transformation doesn't come from titles. It comes from conviction. What you're willing to do when nobody's clapping, and when it would be easier to stay the same.

And yeah, I did lie that day. Not proudly. Not casually. I've replayed that decision more times than I can count, and I still don't love it. But I also know what it was and what it wasn't. That little checkmark on a clipboard didn't define my honesty any more than it defined my spine. I wasn't hiding some dangerous condition so I could sneak my way in. I wasn't trying to scam my way into something I couldn't handle. I was refusing to let a system that only saw me as a file folder decide who I was allowed to become.

There's a difference, and I need to say that out loud because I didn't let myself say it back then. Back then, I either felt guilty or I felt angry. I didn't give myself the space to explain it in a way that was true.

At eighteen, and again at twenty, the Marines were about me. About proving something. About seeing if I could survive something hard and honorable and walk out the other side with a title no one could take away. I wanted something that felt earned, something I could point to when everything else felt shaky and say, "This is mine."

At twenty-three, it was still about all of that. I still wanted to prove I wasn't the guy who quits. I still wanted the discipline, the structure, the pride, the reset. But it wasn't just ego anymore. It wasn't just me trying to outrun my own disappointment.

It was Cole.

I wasn't running away from him. I was running toward the kind of man I wanted him to see when he looked at me. I wanted him to have a father who did something hard on purpose. A father who chose discipline instead of drifting. A father who didn't fold just because a judge, or a form, or a system told him "no" and expected him to accept it.

I needed that, too. I needed to believe I could still build something solid out of myself. Because if I couldn't trust me, then what was I supposed to give him?

I wish my parents had understood that. I really do.

Instead, the day I finally got accepted into the Marine Corps became, in their eyes, the start of a long disappointment. To them, it didn't look like conviction. It looked like abandonment. I'd just lost the custody battle, and now I was signing papers that meant leaving for months. To them, it looked terrible. To them, it looked like I was choosing the Corps over my son.

From the outside, I get it. I can admit that now without getting defensive about it. If my own son lost custody and then told me he was leaving for three or four months, I'd probably feel sick. I'd probably be furious. I'd probably say the same things that were said to me.

But here's the part that still sticks with me, even now. I wish, just once, they'd asked why I kept going back. Not with judgment already loaded in the question. Not as a trap. Just a real, honest, human "Why?" Like they actually wanted to understand me instead of correct me.

Because you don't try three times in five years, get rejected twice, and still show up again unless it means something deep. You don't keep walking into the same office, hearing the same doubts, dealing with the same humiliation, unless there's something on the other side you can't let go of. You don't keep climbing the same wall unless you're convinced there's a life up there you refuse to live without.

This wasn't a phase. It wasn't a whim. It wasn't me ducking responsibility. I wasn't chasing a fantasy. I was chasing a version of myself that felt real, stronger, cleaner, more grounded, and I wanted Cole to have that guy as his dad.

It was wired into me. It still is.

And for once in my life, I chose to trust that wiring, even if it meant being misunderstood. Even if it meant people assuming the worst. Even if it meant carrying the weight of the choice for the rest of my life.

Because the truth is, I wasn't trying to become a Marine so I could leave. I was trying to become someone who could finally stay, fully, steadily, with purpose, when it mattered most.

The ride to the airport with my parents was almost silent. The air in the car felt heavy, like every sentence we could've said was sitting there between us and nobody wanted to be the one to pick it up. I sat in the back seat like a kid getting dropped off for the first day of school. But there was no pep talk or hug. There was no "we're proud of you," no excitement, none of that.

At the terminal, we did that awkward little shuffle people do when everyone knows what's really happening but nobody wants to say it. We talked in scraps. Flight time. Where I needed to be. How long the check-in line looked. Just logistics and weather and anything else that didn't touch the real subject.

I kept catching myself looking around at other families, other goodbyes. Some people were laughing, some were crying openly, some were doing those long hugs that say, "I'm going to miss you but I'm proud." And it was hard not to notice how different ours was. We were standing next to each other, technically together, but emotionally we were miles apart.

When my group was finally called to board, I grabbed my bag and turned back one last time. That moment is stuck in my head because it was so clear without anyone saying a word.

My mom's eyes were wet, but she was holding it in. Jaw tight. Shoulders squared. Like she was physically forcing herself not to fall apart right there in front of me. My dad had his arm around her, but his face was locked somewhere between sadness, disappointment, and that tense "don't do this here" energy, like he was trying to keep the lid on a conversation he didn't trust himself to have in public.

They didn't need to say what they were thinking. I could feel it.

In their minds, I was walking away from my son. That's how it looked to them. I'd just lost in court, I'd just gotten handed this small, controlled version of fatherhood, and now I was getting on a plane to leave for months. To them it looked like I was choosing the Marine Corps instead of choosing Cole. Like I was turning my back on him at the exact moment I should've been doing the opposite.

And the worst part was, I understood why it looked that way. I didn't agree with it, but I understood it.

In my mind, it wasn't abandonment. In my mind, it was the only move I had left that felt like it could actually change my life. I wasn't doing this to escape being a dad. I was doing it because I wanted to come back as a different kind of dad. Someone steadier. Someone tougher. Someone with discipline and purpose instead of desperation and anger. I wanted Cole to have a father he could be proud of, not a guy who got steamrolled by the court and then just stayed on the ground. Not the guy who was pushed down on a middle school gym dance floor and then just watched everyone else from the bleachers.

But standing there at that gate, with my parents looking at me like I was doing something unforgivable, I didn't feel brave. I didn't feel noble. I didn't feel like a man making a strong decision.

I felt small.

I felt like I was fifteen again, being judged by the people who were supposed to understand me most, and realizing they didn't. Like whatever I was trying to become didn't matter to them because all they could see was what it cost. And I felt this ugly mix of things all at once, guilt, anger, sadness, and this stubborn little voice that still wouldn't back down.

Because even as I stood there taking their disappointment in the face, I still believed I was doing the right thing.

I just hated that it looked like the wrong one.

I'd seen the boot camp videos. The screaming. The games. The physical beatdowns. The loss of control. The stripping down of everything you think you are. And here I was, voluntarily walking right into it.

What if I can't hack it? What if I wash out? What if I just proved everyone right, that I make bad decisions and don't think things through?

But underneath all that fear and doubt, there was something else. Something quieter, but somehow more clear. A steady, stubborn sense that this was the door I had to walk through if I ever wanted to stop feeling stuck.

By the time my feet finally hit the floor in San Diego, it was late at night. I was braced for pandemonium. Drill Instructors waiting at the gate, screaming in our faces the second we took a step off the plane. That's how it looks in the videos. Hell, that's how it looked in my imagination.

Instead, nothing.

We waited. And waited. The Marine Corps wasn't in a hurry for anybody. They moved on their time.

When they'd collected enough of us, around fifty, they herded us onto this plain white school bus. For a second, if you ignored the uniforms and the tension, it almost looked like we were headed to church camp instead of government-sanctioned psychological and physical demolition.

I took a seat near the front on the left side.

My body was buzzing with nervous energy the second I stepped onto that bus, but my face was blank. I'd learned that look years earlier, fake calm, neutral expression, like if I looked steady on the outside maybe I wouldn't come apart on the inside. It was the same mask I wore in courtrooms.

Then a Marine Drill Instructor stomped up the bus steps and the whole atmosphere changed. He didn't just walk onto that bus. He took it over. The noise dropped. The air felt tighter. Even the guys who'd been whispering a second earlier went silent like they'd been caught doing something illegal.

He moved down the aisle with controlled aggression, no wasted motion, no friendliness, nothing soft anywhere. Not even his posture. Without saying a word to me first, he drove a folder straight into my chest so hard it knocked me back into the seat.

"Guard this with your life, RECRUIT!"

His voice hit like a punch. The folder wasn't heavy, but the message was. *You're mine now.*

Shit. Should've sat in the back.

As the bus pulled away from the airport, I tried to look out the window to catch a glimpse of California at night. City lights, highways, those palm trees you only see in movies. This was the farthest I'd ever been from home, and I wanted to remember it.

The novelty lasted about thirty seconds.

"HEADS DOWN!"

Fifty heads snapped down instantly, like we were all wired to the same switch. I folded forward, forehead angled toward my knees, eyes locked on the filthy rubber floor. It didn't feel like an instruction so much as a law of nature. My heart climbed right into my throat and stayed there.

The Marine walking the aisle wasn't just "in charge." He felt calm and dangerous, like he could ruin you without even raising his voice, but yelling was just the fun part. I could hear his boots on the aisle floor, slow and deliberate, stopping behind people for a second too long just to remind them he could.

As we started to slow down near the depot, I stole little glimpses through the window without lifting my head. Gates. Harsh lights. Rows of buildings lined up like everything had been measured with a ruler. It looked clean and crude at the same time, like the whole place was designed to expose weakness. We weren't arriving somewhere. We were being delivered.

I didn't know it yet, sitting there with my stomach tied in knots, but that depot would get etched into me. The smell. The lights. The way the air felt. The sound of boots on concrete. The way fear, pride, doubt, and adrenaline all piled into the same spot in my chest. That place was going to live in my head for a long time.

The bus lunged to a halt.

The Drill Instructor who'd been sitting across from me the whole ride, quiet as stone, suddenly exploded like he'd been holding his breath the entire time.

"When you get off this bus," he shouted, "you will move FAST. You will stand on the footprints. You will NOT speak. You will NOT look around. You will follow orders. You will NOT mess this up!"

And then came the line that officially ended my civilian life, whether I was ready or not.

"GET OFF MY BUS. NOW!"

I jumped up too fast, pure nerves doing the driving, and the folder slid off my lap like it was greased. It hit the floor and popped open. Papers went everywhere, skittering under boots and seats.

My stomach dropped straight through the bus.

Of course this happens to me.

For a split second I just froze, like my brain couldn't process that I'd already screwed up and I hadn't even stepped off the bus yet. Then I snapped into motion, scrambling on the floor like an idiot, grabbing papers with shaking hands while he lit me up. His voice was right there in my ear, and it felt like the entire bus was watching me.

I shoved everything back into the folder as fast as I could, not even sure it was in the right order, just trying to get it contained. I clutched it to my chest like it was a life raft and launched myself off the bus.

And the second feet hit the ground, I knew the truth I'd been trying not to think about all day. *There was no backing out now.*

Outside, the infamous yellow footprints waited, dozens of them painted onto the concrete, each pair angled at forty-five degrees. A Drill Instructor pointed and I moved without thinking, found an empty set, planted my feet where I was told, and snapped into the stiffest version of myself I could manage. Knees locked. Back straight. Eyes forward. My heart was pounding so hard it had to be visible through my t-shirt.

Right in front of us, on the building just to the left of the doors, were these huge red signs with big yellow lettering. Marine Corps colors I'd obsessed over for years, but now I couldn't even process the words. I caught enough to understand the theme: rules, consequences, and a pretty detailed explanation of how quickly your life could become miserable if you decided to be cute and test boundaries.

Then more Drill Instructors came flying out of the building like they'd been waiting behind the door with nothing but caffeine and bad intentions. They hit the rows fast, stalking up and down the lines, snapping their heads around, zeroing in on tiny mistakes like they were getting paid per correction.

"HEELS ON THE LINE!"
"TOES AT A FORTY-FIVE!"
"EYES STRAIGHT AHEAD!"
"NO TALKING!"
"QUIT BREATHING SO LOUD, RECRUIT!"

It wasn't just yelling. It was organized pandemonium. The volume was the obvious part, but what really got me was how exact everything was. Every command had a specific standard behind it. I remember thinking, in this weird detached way, they weren't just trying to scare us. They were trying to get into our bodies, into our timing, our posture, our reflexes. They wanted the old "you" to panic and shut down so the new "you" would start listening.

After about a minute of that verbal carpet bombing, they told us to fix our eyes on one specific sign. That was our introduction to the UCMJ, the Uniform Code of Military Justice. Or, as one of them explained with a smile that wasn't a smile, "the law that now owns your ass."

They rattled off the greatest hits like a prosecutor reading charges, and they didn't say it like information. They said it like a warning.

Article 86. Absence Without Leave. AWOL. Leave your post without permission and you'd find out, quickly, what "consequences" really meant in this world.

Article 92. Failure to Obey an Order or Regulation. In normal life, you ignore instructions and maybe someone gets annoyed, maybe you get a lecture, maybe you get fired if you're consistent about it. Here, it's federally mandated punishment.

Article 134, the catch-all. All disorders and neglects to the prejudice of good order and discipline. Basically: if you mess with the system in any way, they'll find a way to charge you with something.

They even mentioned Article 15, non-judicial punishment, like it was a fun little feature. No courtroom drama, no jury, no argument. Your Drill Instructor decides you screwed up, and now your week belongs to him.

None of us remembered the legal language. We didn't need to. The message was clear: from this moment on, our lives weren't ours anymore. Our time wasn't ours. Our bodies weren't ours. Even our mistakes didn't feel like they belonged to us. Everything, every decision, every movement, every breath, was now something the Corps could control.

Standing there on those yellow footprints, clutching that stupid folder I'd already been warned to "guard with my life," it all hit me. I'd finally gotten what I'd been chasing for five years. The thing I'd obsessed over, the thing I'd told myself would fix me, prove something about me, make me into the man I wanted to be.

And I had never been more scared in my life.

They had us. Completely. The yelling, the precision, the way every order hit like a hammer, everything about it did exactly what it was meant to do. I looked down the line and it was obvious: they had successfully scared every single one of us absolutely, unequivocally, shitless.

Guys were trying to look tough, trying to look blank, but you could see it in their throats when they swallowed. In the way they stood just a little too rigid. In how nobody wanted to be the one who moved wrong and drew attention to themselves. You know, like dropping the Drill Instructor's paperwork all over a school bus floor like an idiot.

We were herded single file into a building and marched into this room lined with tiny desks and waist-high podiums, each one barely big enough for a single recruit to stand at without bumping into something. The lighting was harsh, the air smelled like Pine-Sol, and everything about the setup felt intentional. Clean, sterile, and designed to make you forget what comfort even is. Everything about it was cold and as far from comfortable as possible.

They ordered us to empty our pockets, open our wallets, and lay everything out in front of us. Not "place your items here," not "set your things down." More like: put your whole life on display, and we'll decide what you're allowed to keep. It wasn't just a check for contraband. It felt like an inspection of who you were trying to bring with you.

Anything that didn't fit their approved list went straight into a gray metal trash can. No hesitation. No conversation. No "Are you sure?" No "You can mail that home." Just a dull thunk and it was gone, like it never mattered in the first place.

Photos. Notes. Little sentimental things guys brought because they needed something familiar in their pocket, something they could touch later and remember, *I'm still me, I still have people, I still have a reason to get through this.* I watched a couple of them stare at the trash can like they wanted to argue, like they wanted to reach in and take their stuff back, and you could see the fight happening behind their eyes.

Then they didn't do it. They swallowed it, tightened their jaw, and went quiet.

That was the first real lesson for me. Out here, what mattered to you did not matter to them. Not even a little. If it didn't serve the training, it was clutter. If it gave you comfort, it was a liability. They weren't interested in preserving who you were. They were interested in making sure you didn't have anything to lean on besides the rules and the next order.

Once that was done, whatever survived got shoved into a white mesh bag. Those bags would eventually hold our civilian clothes too, locked away in storage until graduation day. That was the deal, even if nobody said it out loud in a friendly way: you'd get your old life back only if you earned the new one.

Then came the phone call.

We were marched into another room lined with old telephones, the kind that looked like they'd been pulled from a movie set in the seventies. Above each phone was a paper taped to the wall with a script printed in giant block letters.

No room for personality. No room for love. No "Hey, Mom." No "I'm here." No "I love you." No "I'm scared as hell."

Just the script.

We were ordered to read it exactly, word for word, loud and fast, and then hang up. No questions. No replies. No goodbye beyond the one they put in your mouth. It wasn't a call the way a normal person thinks of a call. It was proof of arrival. A receipt.

It was 11:30 p.m. in California, which meant it was 2:30 in the morning back home in Illinois. I picked up the phone and punched in my parents' number with hands that didn't feel like my hands anymore. My mom answered groggy and confused, and before she could even get my name out, I was already spitting the words out like I was afraid someone would rip the phone away if I slowed down.

"This is Recruit Sawyer. I have arrived safely at Marine Corps Recruit Depot San Diego. I will contact you again in 3 to 5 days by letter. Do not send food or bulky items. Thank you for your support. Goodbye."

Click.

Just like that, the line went dead.

I hated that call. I hated how cold and robotic my own voice sounded, like I'd already been turned into someone else in the span of a few hours. I hated that I couldn't soften it. Couldn't say, "Mom, it's me." Couldn't ask how she was doing. Couldn't give her anything that sounded like her son.

And the more I thought about it, the worse I felt for her on the other end. Imagine being jolted awake at 2:30 in the morning and hearing your kid talk like a stranger reading off a hostage note, then the line cuts before you can even say, "Are you okay?" That has to be its own special kind of hell. Confusing, terrifying, and completely powerless.

I tried not to picture her face in that moment. Tried to block it out and focus on the process, the noise, the fact that I'd made this choice and now I needed to stand in it. I failed. Her face was right there in my mind, eyes wet, confused, probably a little angry because that's what fear can look like.

A few guys had it worse, though. When their turn came to call home, nobody picked up. You could see it in their faces the second the line went dead, like their brain couldn't accept it at first. They'd hang up, redial, try again, and the longer it went on, the quieter the room got.

Even the guys who'd been trying to act tough a few minutes earlier suddenly looked like little kids on the first day of school, pretending they didn't care while their stomachs were doing cartwheels.

After that, they shoved us back into formation. Chest to back, packed so tight I could feel the guy behind me breathing on the back of my neck. No one talked. No one even turned their head too much. You could tell everyone was scared of drawing attention, like eye contact alone might get you singled out.

The air was heavy with that nervous sweat smell that's the same everywhere, whether it's a courthouse hallway or a locker room before a big game. Everybody was swallowing whatever panic tried to crawl up their throat.

Standing there, I had a moment of clarity. I'd wanted this for so long that I'd rehearsed it in my head a hundred different ways. I'd pictured pride. Purpose. That rush of "I made it." What I got instead was the blunt reality that the Marine Corps wasn't interested in who I thought I was. It wasn't going to ask. It was going to decide.

The only question was whether I could take the fear, take the loss of control, take how fast it was already cutting me off from anything familiar, and still keep moving without coming apart in front of everyone.

Then they marched us to the barbershop.

In the Marine Corps, no one asks what kind of haircut you want. There's no menu, no "just a little off the top," no polite conversation about how you usually wear it. There's a chair, clippers, and a line that keeps moving.

We funneled into this tiny room where it felt like everything was happening at once. Shoes shuffling. Guys trying not to look freaked out. This one barber working like he'd done it a million times. The floor was already covered in hair. Not just a little. A full-on pile.

He wasn't rushing in a sloppy way, either. It was efficient. Sit. Buzz. Next. Over and over, like we were just another task on a checklist that needed to be completed before the real punishment started.

I remember him clearly. Dark eyes, dark skin, maybe Italian. Not mean, not friendly, just hard and focused. Like a guy who'd learned a long time ago that emotions slow you down. Before each recruit sat in the chair, he asked the same question in the same flat tone, without even looking up like it mattered whether you said yes or no.

"Any moles or bumps I need to know about?"

I figured they didn't want anyone bleeding on night one because a clipper caught something it shouldn't at full speed. Even that thought hit me weird. This is how they're thinking about us already. Not as people. As procedure.

When it was my turn, I sat down and said, "No," and stared straight ahead. I could feel the clippers vibrating in his hand before they even touched my head. Then they hit my scalp and it was just bzzz. Hair slid down my shoulders and into my lap. Fifteen seconds later, he was done, and he was already turning his attention to the next guy.

I'd never had long hair, so it wasn't some huge identity crisis for me. But some of the guys in that line? Different story. Ponytails. Shoulder-length hair. That whole rock-band thing like they'd spent years building a look and a personality around it.

And I couldn't stop thinking: *why didn't they cut it before they came?*

For me, that haircut was the moment everything stopped being theory. You can talk about joining all day. Watch the videos. Sign the papers. Act confident around your friends. But the second those clippers touch your head, it's different. Something flips.

The kid who walked in isn't standing there anymore. You're not a Marine yet, not even close, but you're not who you were either. You're this weird in-between version of yourself, new, exposed, and suddenly aware you have no idea how you're going to handle what comes next.

From the barbershop, we didn't "go" anywhere so much as shuffle where we were told. Supply was next, and it was the same theme: speed, control, no questions. Just a guy behind a counter eyeballing your height and weight and loading your arms like a grocery cart.

Cammies. Boots. Covers. Green T-shirts. Socks. Skivvies. Belt. Everything in a hurry, everything in bulk, and the whole time you're trying to keep up without dropping anything. You didn't pick sizes. You didn't ask for a different pair. You didn't even have time to think about what you were holding. You took what you were handed and moved along because your opinion wasn't part of the process.

Eventually we got marched into the squad bay that was going to be our temporary home. Two long rows of metal racks with thin mattresses and footlockers at the ends. More bodies than floor space. Everything metal, everything hard.

But for the first time in what felt like days, things slowed down just a little. Not enough to relax, not enough to breathe easy, but enough that you could finally look around and take it all in.

It was somewhere around three or four in the morning. None of us knew for sure. We had no watches, and there weren't any clocks in sight. That was another quiet little trick they played on you right away. Time stopped being something you tracked. It became something that happened to you.

You didn't "check the time" anymore. You just got moved from one thing to the next until your body started guessing what hour it had to be based on how bad your eyes burned.

I sat on my rack with my new running shoes planted on the cold floor, uniform still stiff in my hands, and just took in the room. I was twenty-three, which made me one of the "old guys," which caught me a bit off-guard. Most of the recruits around me looked seventeen, eighteen at most. Baby faces. Some of them still had that high school look, like they should've been worrying about prom pictures, not learning how to fold government-issued underwear into perfect rectangles.

And I kept thinking, *how are you even doing this?* I couldn't imagine walking into this place at their age. I couldn't imagine leaving home, leaving whatever life they had, and just handing themselves over to this machine.

Then the next thought was worse. I wasn't entirely sure I could do it at my age either. I'd made it here, sure, but that didn't mean I was built for it. It just meant I'd gotten through the front door.

Whatever I thought this was going to be back home, it was already something else. It was bigger than the videos. More real than anything I'd let myself picture. Sitting there in that squad bay, exhausted and holding a stack of stiff uniforms, I finally understood that I wasn't just watching my life change anymore. I was actually doing it.

We still weren't allowed to sleep. Not for another eighteen hours. We'd already been up all day traveling, then the bus ride, the shark-attack welcome, the haircut, the gear issue, the phone call. Now the sky was starting to lighten, and instead of a rack, we got our first trip to the chow hall.

For some reason, that moment is burned in me deeper than almost anything else from that first week. I can't pin it to one thing. It might've been the exhaustion finally catching up. It might've been the adrenaline dropping just enough for my brain to come back online. It might've been the first quiet second where there was actually room for a real thought.

Whatever it was, I remember the exact point where my mind cut through the routine and I asked myself, plain and direct: *what have you done?*

We went into the chow hall on autopilot. Heads down. Eyes half-open. Everything about the process was designed to keep you moving and keep you from thinking. Grab a tray, slide down the rail, keep the line tight.

Food hit the tray with no choice and no pause, eggs, potatoes, a biscuit, syrup that didn't belong to anything. Fill the cup under the orange-juice spout, don't spill, don't hesitate, don't create a problem.

It wasn't just breakfast. It was a system.

We sat at long tables and ate like we were being graded on speed. Nobody tasted anything. Nobody talked. You shoveled, swallowed, and kept your eyes where they were supposed to be.

Even if a Drill Instructor wasn't directly behind you, you could feel the pressure of him being somewhere close, watching for someone to get sloppy. Every movement felt monitored. Every second felt borrowed.

And somewhere in the middle of eating, six or seven swallows in, I looked up. In the chrome side of a napkin dispenser, I caught my own reflection. Buzzed head. Pale face. Dark circles under my eyes like bruises. The uniform looked stiff and wrong on me, like I was wearing someone else's life.

And the question hit again, harder: *what the hell did you do? What have you gotten yourself into?*

Right behind that came Cole's face. Not as a distant memory, but him in the backseat, looking up at me, laughing at some stupid thing I said. I had left him. I had chosen this. I was sitting in a chow hall in a place that was designed to break people down, and my kid was somewhere else living a life I wasn't part of.

My throat tightened. Homesickness hit like a punch to my chest. My eyes stung, and there was a quick flash of panic. *Don't do this here. Not in front of everyone. Not when you're surrounded by Drill Instructors who live for weakness they can smell.*

But there wasn't time to process anything. That was the point. You weren't there to feel. You weren't there to reflect. You were there to follow instructions and keep moving.

A Drill Instructor snapped at me that I was done. I forced down one last swallow, stood up, and got back in line with everyone else, carrying it all like it didn't exist because that's what the moment required.

The rest of that day blurred into one long sequence: more gear, more lines, more shouting, more "motivational" pain disguised as training. We were issued seabags and crammed all our new uniforms inside. They handed out sewing kits and rubber stamps with our last names so we could mark every single thing we owned.

Everything we touched became government property with our name on it.

We filed into a massive classroom with five other platoons, packed into rows of plastic chairs that dug into the backs of our legs. Above us, four giant monitors hung from the ceiling in a square, like a sports arena scoreboard watching all of us at once.

In the middle of the room, an instructor paced and barked out the basics. Rank structure. Expectations. "Core values."

Honor.
Courage.
Commitment.

Small words they said would define us, even though half of us were still trying to remember where to put our hands when we stood at attention.

Lunch was the same as breakfast. Fast, forgettable, functional. Still no clue what time it was. There were no clocks, no watches, no "almost noon" or "late afternoon." Time became something we guessed at by watching the angle of the sun through whatever window we passed. For the next three months, time didn't belong to us at all.

Then dinner. Then, finally, back to the squad bay.

We were running on fumes. We tried to square away our footlockers, folding things, rolling socks, lining up every item in perfect rows like tiny museum exhibits of our new lives. None of us really knew what we were doing. We just copied the guy next to us and hoped he wasn't as clueless as we were.

All I wanted was sleep. Real sleep. The kind where you actually disappear for a while. I wanted to close my eyes and not think about chow halls or yellow footprints or chrome dispensers that reflected back a version of me I didn't even recognize.

But there was one more thing: fire watch.

They wrote names for the rotation. Every hour, two recruits would stand post in the bay and guard the door. From what, I had no idea. But this was the Marine Corps. Somebody was always on duty, even if nothing was happening.

I got lucky that night, if you can call anything that happened that day "lucky." My name didn't get called, which meant I could actually get a full nights sleep without being woken up in the middle of the night to stand a post at the squad bay doors.

When I finally crawled into my rack, those scratchy wool blankets felt like the softest thing I'd ever touched. I pulled them over me, closed my eyes, and just disappeared for a while.

There would've been a thousand more stories from those weeks if I wanted to sit here and list them out. More fear. More pressure. More moments where my brain got loud and started replaying every decision that put me on that bus in the first place.

I could tell you about the constant confusion, the sleep deprivation, the way time stopped making sense, or the little moments that hit you out of nowhere and made you realize you weren't in charge of your life anymore. All of it is real. All of it mattered.

But those first days weren't about deep lessons or big speeches. They were about getting through the next ten minutes without doing something stupid.

My goal was simple, and honestly kind of pathetic in how small it was: disappear into the middle. Don't stand out. Don't get noticed. Don't be the guy who can't keep up, but don't be the guy they decide to use as a punching bag either.

Don't crack jokes. Don't look confused. Don't look scared. Don't ask questions. Just do what the person in front of you does, move when you're told to move, shut up when you're told to shut up, and try to blend into the mass of bodies so nobody has a reason to single you out.

What messed with me was how familiar that strategy felt. Because outside of boot camp, I'd spent years feeling invisible in a totally different way. Depressed. Quiet. In my own head. Feeling like I was watching my own life from a few feet back while everyone else moved forward.

Back then, being "unseen" hurt. It felt like I didn't matter, like I could disappear and no one would even notice. Now I was trying to do it on purpose. Trying to be invisible because it might keep me alive in this new world. That was the irony that kept popping up in my head when I had a second to think.

I'd spent so much of my life angry and ashamed about feeling unseen, and now I was hoping, almost begging, to be exactly that. Not because I wanted to be forgotten, but because being noticed came with consequences. Being noticed meant attention, and attention meant pain.

And life didn't care what I wanted. It didn't care about my plan, or my mental script, or the careful little rules I was making for myself. I could try to hide in the middle all I wanted, but I learned quickly that you don't get to negotiate with that place.

If they decided they saw you, they saw you. If they decided today was your day to get tested, corrected, pushed, embarrassed, whatever, you were up. No appeal. No "not me." Just your name, your face, and a whole lot of pressure that didn't care if you were ready or not.

ROUND 19:
Eagle Dreams and Penguin Knees

By the second or third week of boot camp, I was already in physical agony. The slow, grinding kind that starts before you even get dressed and makes you dread tying your boots because you know what's coming. It wasn't some sudden pain where you can point to one moment and say, "That's when it happened." It was a slow tally of sharp needles stabbing the inside of my kneecaps.

I'd never been a runner. In middle school I could knock out the fifty-yard dash in the top five, but distance running was always the thing I avoided. I didn't have the lungs for it, I didn't like it, and I never built myself into someone who could grind out miles without thinking about it. Boot camp didn't care about any of that. Boot camp was basically one long reminder that your preferences don't matter.

We ran constantly. Formation runs. PT runs. Sprints. "Fun" runs that weren't fun for anybody, especially not the guy whose knees were already on fire and screaming. A mile and a half. Two miles. Three miles. More than that sometimes. The worst part wasn't even the distance. It was the lack of recovery. You'd do something that should've earned you a day to heal, and instead you got another round. No mercy. Just the sound of hundreds of soles slapping pavement and your lungs trying to keep up while the cadence echoed in your head.

At first, I tried to hide it. That's what you do. You grit your teeth, lock your face down, and act like you're fine because everyone is hurting and no one wants to be the weak link. Pain was part of the deal, right? I wasn't about to be the guy limping to sickbay every morning, begging for a note, getting labeled as a hack. I told myself: *everybody hurts. This is just my version of it. Push through.*

But there's only so long you can fake "normal" when your joints are basically asking for a ceasefire.

Our third hat noticed before anybody else did. Staff Sergeant Martinez.

He was short and stocky, maybe five-four, five-five, not big at all, but he carried himself like he could pick up the whole platoon and throw it. Everything about him was compressed intensity. The kind of guy who could stare at you for two seconds and you'd start questioning whether you were standing correctly, breathing correctly, or even existing correctly.

One morning he watched me during a march. I wasn't full-on limping yet, more like a half-limp, half-waddle that I thought I was hiding. Apparently I wasn't. He saw it immediately.

"PENGUIN!" he roared across the formation.

And that was it. One word, and I stopped being "Sawyer" and became a joke.

Most guys imagine they'll get some cool nickname in the Corps. Something that sounds like you earned it in combat or at least did something impressive. Maverick. Reaper. Ghostfire. Something you could repeat later without wanting to punch yourself in the face. Not me. Penguin. Because I waddled in pain.

From that point on, everything got harder. Not just the running, but the attention. Every time my foot landed wrong, he saw it. Every lag, every little grimace, every moment where I tried to adjust my stride to protect my knee, he saw it. I'd been trying to disappear into the middle, and instead my knees and Staff Sergeant Martinez put me under a spotlight.

As the pain got worse, I kept doing the mental math that desperate people do. Just get through this one run. Just get through this one exercise. Just get through today. Tomorrow it'll calm down.

It didn't. Because there was never just one run. Never just one day.

One morning we'd just left the chow hall and were headed toward the PT field. The pain in my left knee was so sharp I could barely keep pace on the march, and the thought of running felt almost stupid. Every step was a warning shot. It wasn't soreness anymore. It was something else. Something unstable that felt like the joint could give up at any second.

We lined up for another formation run. I took my spot, clenched my fists, and tried to lock in. The guide took off, and the platoon surged forward into that "easy" rhythm that only feels easy when your body isn't betraying you.

My knee answered with a very clear no.

A sharp, stabbing hit went straight through the joint, and before I even understood what had happened, my leg folded. I went down hard into the dirt like somebody yanked my feet out from under me. Not a slow collapse. A drop. The kind that makes everyone around you react even if they try not to.

Immediately there was a Drill Instructor over me. Boots, shadow, voice.

"GET UP, PENGUIN! GET OFF MY DECK! MOVE!"

Adrenaline snapped me upright because fear will do that, but my leg didn't come with me. I tried to stand and it felt like my knee was made of wet cardboard. No strength. No stability. I couldn't put real weight on it without that tearing sensation that turns your stomach.

He leaned in, eyes narrow, and for a split second the screaming stopped and something else came through. He could tell the difference between "I'm hurting" and "I'm broken." They all could. They might not care about your comfort, but they knew what it looked like when something was genuinely off.

"Do you need to see the corpsman, recruit?"

That question hit me harder than the fall. Because it meant admitting it. Saying out loud I couldn't just will my way through it. Risking getting labeled, risking getting set back, risking getting dropped. Facing the thing I didn't want to face: my body might actually take this away from me.

I swallowed what was left of my pride.

"Yes, Sir! This recruit needs to see the corpsman, Sir!"

"Then get off my field. Now."

"Aye, Sir!"

I hobbled away, and every step felt like a small war between stubbornness and reality. By the time I got to Medical, I was sweaty, shaky, and furious. Furious at my knees, furious at myself, furious that after everything it took to get there, my own body might be the thing that votes me off the island. And it was my knees, not my back. The universe has a sick sense of humor.

I explained it to the corpsman: the slow build, how it had been getting worse, how it finally dropped me in front of the entire platoon. I didn't say the part about humiliation, but it was there. I didn't say the part about fear, fear of being forced out, fear of failing, fear of going home without the title, but I'm sure it was written all over my face.

They'd seen it all before. Recruits with real injuries. Recruits faking it. Recruits who just wanted out. I could feel them trying to place me in one of those categories without even saying it. There was this unspoken question in the air: which one are you?

They handed me a bottle of ibuprofen, the famous 800mg horse pills, and told me to take them with food at breakfast so they'd kick in before PT. No scans. No X-rays. No real diagnosis. Just Motrin and "we'll see."

Motrin is basically the Marine Corps cure for everything. Headache? Motrin. Rolled ankle? Motrin. Your leg fell off? Take two, hydrate, and stop being dramatic. It wasn't comforting. It was dismissive, and it made me feel stupid for even coming in.

I took the bottle, nodded like I was grateful, and limped back out into the sun.

By the time I made it back to the platoon, the run was already over. Nobody asked how I was. Nobody said, "You good?" Nobody said my name. I just slid back into line and kept moving like nothing had happened and nothing had changed, even though I knew it had.

I'd been singled out. I'd hit the deck in front of everyone. I'd gone to Medical. I'd come back with a bottle of pills and a problem that wasn't going away.

And I remember thinking, calm and clear: *this is where it starts. This is the part where you find out if your body is going to let you finish what your mind already committed to.*

From that day forward, every movement had a cost. Some days I could grit through it. Some days it took everything I had just to walk without showing the limp. My trips to the corpsman became more frequent, which led to the last thing any recruit wants stamped on their forehead: light duty.

Once you're on light duty, you're marked. People notice. You are not doing all the exercises. You sit out certain drills. While everyone else is running, you are "recovering." It doesn't matter if you are legitimately injured. It feels like you're betraying the tribe.

In the Marine Corps, nothing is just about you. If one recruit falls behind, somebody else carries the weight. If one person gets a break, everyone else sees it. And you see the resentment.

Even then, with the pain, the pills, and the limp that never really went away, no one ever gave me a real diagnosis. No, "Here's what's wrong." Just, "Take more Motrin. Don't run today. Come back if it gets worse."

It got worse.

It always got worse.

I can still feel that mix of intimidation and defeat, standing there in my sweaty cammies, clutching a bottle of ibuprofen like it was going to save my career, already suspecting the truth I didn't want to say out loud: my body was tapping out long before my pride.

Late at night, when the squad bay finally went quiet and the only sound was seventy-two guys trying to out-snore each other, I'd find myself on fire watch again.

Under the dim red glow from my flashlight, the metal racks, the green wool blankets, the concrete floor, it all took on this faded, almost underwater look. Like the whole world was on low battery.

I'd stand near the door or sit at the duty desk and pull out whatever scrap of time I had and turn it into letters. To my parents. To Katarina.

She technically wasn't my girlfriend again. We'd only reconnected a few months before I left for San Diego. But she was the one I wrote the most. There's always that one person you write to when you're not sure who else would really get it. She went through Army National Guard basic training the year before, so she understood the physical battle I was going through, and she knew me well enough to understand my emotional breakdowns.

I tried to explain the pain. On paper, it sounded almost reasonable. "My knees hurt," "we ran a lot today," "I'm pretty banged up." But that wasn't it. Not really. I wasn't just keeping them updated. I was trying to convince myself this all made sense. Trying to pin down something that felt bigger than words.

There's a big difference between remembering what you did in boot camp and remembering how it felt.

The pain wasn't surface-level. It wasn't a sore muscle you could stretch or a bruise that would fade. It lived deeper. Right in the center of the joint, like somebody tucked a slow, steady fire and a needle inside my knees.

My left knee was worse, but both of them ached all the time. Throbbing when I stood still. Stabbing when I ran. Burning even when I tried to rest. There was no "off." Just different intensities of the same misery.

Every step whispered the same question in the back of my mind, like a broken record: *What if your body quits before your will does?*

Boot camp hit me from every angle.

Some guys in my platoon had played sports their whole lives. Football, wrestling, soccer. They complained about how "easy" the physical stuff was, like the Marine Corps had personally let them down by not making it harder. For them, the real challenge was the mental grind. No sleep, no control, no privacy, no space that was truly theirs.

Other guys just glided. They never seemed rattled. They ran like machines, remembered every instruction, passed every exam. It was like they'd been built in a factory labeled "MILITARY ISSUE" and shipped straight to San Diego.

Me? I got the full package deal.

My body hurt in ways I didn't know was even possible back in the civilian world. My knees screamed every time I moved, and my brain wouldn't stop running its own miserable "fun run." *What if I get dropped? What if they decide I'm a liability? What if they send me home and that's it, no second chance, no redemption story, just me walking back into my old life with nothing to show for it except a limp and a bunch of excuses?*

That worry lived in the back of my mind all day, every day. It wasn't always loud, but it was always there. My emotions sat on this low simmer that didn't cool down. I'd get hit with nostalgia for home at random times, usually when I was exhausted and everything felt too quiet in my head.

Then it would flip into frustration with my own body, because I was doing everything I could to hold it together and it still felt like it was betraying me. Underneath all of that was this unbearable emptiness without my son that I didn't know how to explain. I just knew it was there, sitting in my chest like a weight I carried around without telling anyone.

But even with all of that, I never once let myself seriously consider quitting. Not once.

I couldn't afford to. The second I admitted it, even privately, even as a thought I didn't share with anyone, it would've felt like I cracked the door open. And in that place, a cracked door doesn't stay cracked. It swings wide. If I gave quitting a seat at the table, it would start talking louder than everything else. It would start making sense. It would start offering relief. And relief was dangerous.

So I didn't let it in.

I did what I've always done when things get too heavy. I kept moving. I kept hurting. I kept the mask on.

And at night, when we finally had a few minutes that belonged to us, I wrote. Not like some noble journal entry meant for the future. More like my way of getting all those messy feelings and fears I couldn't say out loud out of my head and onto paper. I wanted it out of sight. I wanted it gone.

I refused to let the word quit have a place in the story, even when my body was breaking down and my mind was trying to write its own ending for me.

The rifle range was the first place in boot camp where I felt like I belonged.

Everything else up to that point had been survival. Keeping up, keeping quiet, trying not to get noticed for the wrong reasons, trying to get my body through things it clearly didn't want to do. On the range, it was different. It wasn't about who could suffer the loudest. It was about doing something correctly, on purpose, over and over, with no room for excuses. Precision.

We were training on the M16A2, and from day one I made a decision: I wasn't just going to just qualify. I wanted that Expert badge. Not because I needed to impress anyone, but because I needed a win that was mine. Something measurable. Something that didn't rely on whether my knees decided to cooperate that day. It reminded me of that handwriting contest in first grade, the same part of my brain lighting up. Pick a target and obsess until you hit it.

So I drilled the fundamentals like they were a religion. Sight picture. Breath control. Trigger squeeze. Natural point of aim. I paid attention to details other guys brushed off because they were tired or distracted or just trying to get through it. At night, when we were finally under those itchy wool blankets and the squad bay settled into that exhausted quiet, I'd lie there and run through it in my head. Where my elbows went. How my cheek sat on the stock. How the front sight post looked when it was right. When to inhale, when to pause, when to let the shot break without forcing it.

By qualification day, I wasn't nervous the way I'd been for other things. I was focused, like my mind finally had something to do other than spiral. When we got on the line, I locked in and tuned out everything else. The noise, the heat, the yelling, the pressure of being watched. All I cared about was the next shot. Center mass.

The weird part was the further the target got, the calmer I felt. Close stuff is where people think it should be easiest, but long distance is where you can't fake it. Every little mistake shows up downrange. At 500 yards, five football fields away, something clicked. That's the distance where most guys started to come apart, where you'd hear the frustration, the rushed shots, the little panic creeping in.

For me, it was the opposite. I got steadier. The whole world narrowed down to a front sight post, a controlled breath, and a clean squeeze.

Out of ten shots at that distance, seven landed in the black. I knew it as it was happening. This quiet certainty that I was doing what I was supposed to be doing, and it was working. Not luck. Not a fluke. Just fundamentals and focus finally paying off.

Final score: 328. Expert.

For a minute, I felt ten feet tall. For once, I wasn't just getting through the day. I actually did something I came there to do.

Then a Marine came up to me and told me to report to the corpsman.

No explanation. No "good job." No hint that this was anything other than routine. Just a quick order and that look people give you when they already know the ending and don't feel like babysitting you through the middle.

The next phase of training was on deck. "Field Week." Longer movements, heavier loads, more running, more time on your feet, more everything. The part everyone talks about when they talk about earning the title. And my knee wasn't getting better. It wasn't even holding steady. It was the same sharp, stubborn pain every single day, and the only plan anyone seemed to have was to keep feeding me those giant ibuprofen pills like some generic version of a medical strategy.

So they made the decision I'd been trying not to make in my own head, and they didn't dress it up. I wasn't fit to continue. That was it. No long talk about potential. No pep talk. No "we'll get you back out there." Just a clean cut from the one thing I was finally starting to feel competent at.

One minute I was part of a platoon, miserable, exhausted, stressed, but moving forward like everyone else. The next minute I was separated and sent to MRP: Medical Rehabilitation Platoon.

It didn't feel like a temporary detour. It felt like a sentence.

MRP was advertised as rest. That word sounds gentle until you live it. It wasn't rest like recovery. It was rest like isolation. No drill instructors in your face every second, no range days, no sense of progress. The days weren't structured in a way that made you feel like you were earning anything. You were just there, a room full of guys who were injured or stuck or marked, in one way or another, as not currently useful.

And that label sticks. Even if nobody says it out loud, you can feel it in the air.

The place had its own energy, and it wasn't good. You could look around and see the same expression on different faces. The blank stare. Guys trying to act like they weren't scared. Everyone had a story, and the stories sounded different but meant the same thing: something happened to my body, and now my whole future is on hold.

Some guys had stress fractures. Some had back issues. Some had shin splints so bad they walked like old men. A few were clearly gaming the system, and everyone knew it, which made it worse because it put this extra stink on the rest of us, like we had to prove we weren't full of shit on top of being in pain.

We cleaned constantly. It was like cleaning was the replacement for training, like if we kept scrubbing and polishing and wiping things down, we could pretend we were still earning our spot. Floors, toilets, sinks, showers, railings, door handles, anything you could touch, we cleaned. Then we cleaned it again. And when there wasn't something in your hands, there was time. Too much time. The kind of time you can't hide from.

We sat around telling and retelling the same details, not because we loved our own stories, but because talking was better than thinking. Who got hurt and how. How long they'd been there. Who was improving and who wasn't. Who had a date to be reevaluated. Who had been waiting on paperwork for weeks. Who had already been threatened with being dropped.

You could feel people doing the math in their heads even when nobody said it out loud. What are my odds? Am I ever going to get out of here?

In regular training, you're under pressure, but you're also being dragged forward by the machine. You don't have time to sit and stare at your own thoughts because there's always some next thing you have to do. In MRP, the pressure came from inside. You were alone with your own inner doubts, and mine were brutal.

They weren't motivational. They were constant, personal, and loud. And the longer it went on, the more I could feel myself changing, like my brain was quietly building a case against me while I stood there cleaning a sink for the fourth time that day.

If you were stronger, you'd be with your platoon. If you weren't so weak, your knee wouldn't be the thing that stopped you. Everybody else is hurting too, so why are you the one sitting here?

And it wasn't just me. You could see it happening around the room in real time. Guys would show up with some fight left in them, still talking like they were just on a pit stop, still joking, still acting like they'd be back in training any day now. Then a week goes by. Ten days. Two weeks. The jokes get thinner. The conversations get shorter. The laughing turns into these little forced bursts that die fast.

More staring at walls. More staring at nothing. More snapping at each other over stupid things, like someone breathing too loud or taking too long at the sink.

When you're training, pain feels like a shared price. You limp together, you suffer together, you get screamed at together, and somehow that makes it feel almost normal. In MRP, pain feels like a label. Like you're not a recruit anymore, you're an excuse. You start wondering if you were ever cut out for it, or if you were just living a lie.

I hate admitting how much I leaned into the self-pity, but I did. At least it gave me something to feel. It was easier to be angry at my knee, angry at the system, angry at bad luck, than to sit with the idea that I might get sent home and have to face my life again with yet one more failure.

In my head, it wasn't just an injury. It was evidence. *See? You're _not_ good enough.* Proof that I didn't belong. Proof that everyone back home was right about me. That old, familiar voice didn't even have to get creative. It just stacked the same arguments it always had and waited for me to give in and agree.

By the time I really let myself see how deep I'd gone into that hole, the fire in me wasn't gone, but it was close. And in that place, with that much quiet and that much time, it didn't take much for it to feel like it could burn out completely.

About ten days into MRP, something in me transformed, but not the way it usually did. I was sitting on my rack, staring at the floor, feeling my brain do that familiar thing where everything starts to go numb. That quiet little mental collapse where you start believing every ugly thought you've ever had about yourself because there's nothing else to distract you from it.

And then, out of nowhere, one clean thought cut through the noise: *This is not how my story ends. Not this time.* Like a switch got flipped and I was suddenly sick of hearing my mind talk.

I hadn't spent five years fighting to get here just to get pulled off the line and quietly disappear into a rehab holding pattern. I wasn't about to let my Marine Corps story turn into, "Yeah, he almost made it." Are you kidding? That failure, that feeling of being almost great, would've haunted me forever.

If I was getting out of MRP, it wasn't going to be because somebody felt generous or decided I was a nice enough guy to give a second chance. It was going to be because I made it happen on my own terms.

I finally realized right there that the only way back to Cole is graduation. Period. So graduation became my new "Handwriting Award," the thing I could lock onto and obsess over when everything else felt shaky.

Physical therapy became my whole world. Not the kind of work you brag about, either. No heavy lifts. No swagger. No tough-guy nonsense. They'd send us to the gym and the pool for slow, controlled rehab. Small movements, boring routines, stretching, icing, stuff that looked like it should be happening to somebody's grandpa after a knee replacement.

And honestly, that messed with my head at first. You're surrounded by this culture of pushing through pain, and then suddenly your mission is controlled leg raises and ice packs? Seriously?

But it wasn't optional if you wanted out of there, and it was the only path back to training. So I treated it like training. I did the reps the way they told me to do them, not the way my ego wanted to do them. I paid attention to the little cues I would've ignored before, because in my head there was only one real exit from boot camp, and it wasn't some medical discharge with my tail tucked.

The only way out was graduation.

Then, finally, an actual diagnosis: patellofemoral syndrome. A fancy way of saying my kneecap wasn't tracking the way it was supposed to. Every time I bent my knee, it should've been sliding cleanly in a groove of my femur. Mine drifted outward and rubbed bone against bone.

So that grinding, stabbing pressure I'd been trying to explain wasn't me being dramatic or weak or imagining things. It was real, and now it had a name. And strange as it may sound, that helped. I didn't love hearing I was broken, but at least now I knew what I was fighting. And more importantly, it wasn't just all in my head.

It was a mechanical problem. A skeletal problem.

The solution wasn't glamorous, either. No miracle procedure. No intense "recover like a warrior" plan. It was basically: strengthen the inner quad, the part that helps pull the kneecap where it belongs. And of course you can't do that with some macho, impressive movement that makes you feel like an athlete. You know what works?

Walking in the pool.

So that's what I did. Every day. Lap after lap around the shallow end. Slow, steady steps with water pushing back just enough to make it suck, without the impact of running. I stretched and iced like it was a religion. I paid attention to every little improvement and treated my legs like they were the only thing standing between me and the one thing I refused to lose.

And over a short time, things started to shift. The pain didn't magically vanish, but it changed. It got more manageable. The joint felt less like it was trying to grind itself apart every time I moved. My body started to come back, but the bigger change was in my head.

MRP wasn't just a place where your knee healed or didn't. It was a place that messed with your head. It was where motivation went to die if you let it. Guys would show up hurt, angry, embarrassed, still talking like this was a temporary setback, and then slowly turn into ghosts. You could watch it happen right in front of you, hour by hour. Their shoulders would drop. Their voices would get quieter. They'd stop cracking jokes. They'd stop moving with any kind of purpose.

And the eyes. That was the real giveaway. Not looking at you, not looking past you, just looking through walls like they were already packing their seabags in their head. Like they'd accepted the ending and were just waiting for the paperwork.

That's when I understood the real threat wasn't my knee. It was MRP trying to convince me that this was the new me now. The broken guy. The sidelined guy. The almost Marine.

I couldn't live with that. Almost felt like a brand on my forehead, like it would follow me home and sit on my shoulders for the rest of my life whispering, *see, told you.* So I started intentionally getting involved. I volunteered for anything I could. I stayed in therapy longer than I needed to. I did the boring rehab stuff even when nobody was watching, because the whole point was to not turn into one of those zombies staring at the wall.

I helped other guys too. Nothing heroic. Just being the one who didn't let them get lost in their own heads. If someone was spiraling, I'd pull them into a conversation. If someone was quitting in their mind, I'd get them moving. Half the time it was just, "Get up. Come with me." Not inspirational, just practical. Sometimes that's all you can manage.

Eventually the drill instructors noticed, which is a weird feeling because you spend most of boot camp trying not to be noticed at all. Regular training teaches you that being visible usually means you're about to have a very bad day. But this was different. This wasn't getting noticed for screwing up. This was getting noticed because I was showing effort and consistency and leadership in a place where a lot of guys were barely motivated enough to wake up.

They promoted me to Squad Leader. Then, briefly, to Guide.

That part still makes me laugh, because it happened in the most Marine Corps way possible. The current Guide pissed off a DI, and there wasn't some leadership evaluation or a meeting or an inspiring speech about merit. The DI just looked around and pointed at me because I was standing closest.

"You! You're the Guide now!"

That was it.

It only lasted maybe six hours before they put the original Guide back in place, but I took it seriously for the six hours I was given. I didn't treat it like a joke, even if it kind of was intended to be a slap in the face to get the original Guide to step up. For me it wasn't about the title. It was about responsibility, and I took it as a signal that I wasn't invisible. That I still belonged in the conversation.

You can still lead. You're still in this.

When it finally came time to test out of MRP, it all came down to the PFT, the Physical Fitness Test. No shortcuts. No sympathy. No "he's been through a lot." Just standards and numbers on a sheet.

Three-mile run under 28 minutes. At least 60 crunches in two minutes. Minimum eight pull-ups.

I wasn't aiming to squeak by. I wanted it clean. I wanted it loud. Not for the drill instructors, not for the other recruits, but for me. I needed to know that after getting pulled out of my platoon, after the pool, after the endless doubt, I could still perform. I could still earn my way back.

Test day came and I wasn't thinking about motivational speeches or how inspiring this was supposed to be. I was thinking about pain and pacing and not letting my brain talk me out of effort.

I got on the bar and knocked out eighteen pull-ups. Then eighty-eight crunches. Then the run, three miles in 24:10, the best time I'd ever hit.

Crossing that finish line, I felt two things at the exact same time: pure pride and pure fear. Pride because I'd done what I said I was going to do. Fear because I knew my knees were going to make me pay for it later, like they were already writing up the invoice while I was still trying to catch my breath.

They held just long enough to get me through. It felt like a temporary truce, and I didn't trust it for a second.

That night, I got cleared. Just like that and I was told I was being scheduled to drop back into a training platoon.

I remember sitting there afterward and realizing how close I'd come to quietly disappearing. How easy it would've been to let MRP turn into my ending. Instead, I'd dragged myself back out the only way I knew how. By refusing to accept "almost," even when my body was giving me every reason to settle for it.

And yeah, I was proud. But I was also scared, because I knew what came next. Regular training didn't care about my little comeback story. The machine was still running, and I was about to step back into it.

By the next morning, I was in pieces again.

That one run wiped out three weeks of careful rebuilding. All that slow progress, all those controlled movements, every boring rehab exercise, it all got erased in twenty-four minutes of me trying to prove I belonged there with all those other guys, still pushing through. My knees went right back to that familiar deep, angry ache.

And the worst part was the timing. There was no going back to MRP now. That door had been locked and dead-bolted. You wanted back in, you got back in. Congratulations. Now deal with it.

I was going forward, ready or not.

I'd missed too much time with my original platoon to rejoin them. They were already past the phase I'd been pulled from and were closing in on graduation. They were finishing the story I was supposed to be in, and I was watching it from the outside like some idiot who showed up late and still expected a seat.

Instead, I got dropped into a new platoon late in the game, like I'd been parachuted into a movie halfway through. Just standing there like, *Hey guys, sorry to interrupt your suffering, mind if I suffer with you now?*

That was its own kind of hell.

With my first platoon, we'd become brothers the hard way. We'd been smoked together, frozen together, laughed and suffered and been humiliated together. They'd seen me show up day after day, even when my knees were already screaming before the day started. They knew I hadn't quit. They'd watched me trying not to limp. Hiding the pain and pushing through it. Trying not to look weak. They respected the effort. They admired my heart.

This new platoon didn't know me at all. And they didn't care.

From where they stood, I was "that guy." The one from medical. The guy who got an extra break, extra attention, extra time, and then showed back up when the hard part was already rolling. The broken toy somebody dropped into their box like it was no big deal. The outsider. The late arrival who hadn't earned the sand in his boots the way they had.

And they didn't bother hiding it. The teasing. The cold shoulders. The little side comments. The quick glances that said, Who the hell is this piece of shit? It wasn't subtle.

Honestly, I got it. If I'd been in their position, I might've looked at me the same way. I probably would've told myself the same story about some random recruit showing up from medical like he got a free pass. And that's the part that pissed me off the most, because I didn't even have a clean argument against it. What was I going to say, "You don't understand, I've done everything you have. Just with a different set of guys?"

Understanding it didn't make it suck any less.

All I wanted was to disappear into the middle of the formation. To be a nameless, faceless recruit lost somewhere in the pack. No attention, no spotlight, no labels. Just another body trying to finish what he started. Just someone who could keep his head down, do what he was told, and stop feeling like a walking exception.

But blending in wasn't an option anymore. Not here. Not this late in the game.

Because now I wasn't just fighting my knees. I was fighting the room. I was fighting the looks. I was fighting the feeling that I'd shown up with an invisible stamp on my forehead that said MEDICAL and everyone could see it. And every time my knees flared up, every time I moved a little stiff, every time I had to swallow that instinct to baby the pain, it felt like I was handing them proof.

See? Knew it!

Our senior drill instructor in that platoon was different. Not soft, never soft, but there was something a little more human about him. At that stage of boot camp, after the rifle range, heading into the final phase, the tone transitioned just a hair. Less rabid fury, more controlled pressure. Every now and then, you'd catch a joke. A half-smile you weren't supposed to see. We were inching from recruit toward Marine, and they treated us just differently enough that we could feel it.

He had a little classroom in the back of the squad bay, like all senior DIs did. That was where the screaming turned into something that almost resembled teaching. Talks about integrity, leadership, responsibility.

He'd come in, and the four squad leaders would scramble to stack footlockers into a makeshift throne. He'd sit down like a king addressing his court, and we'd sit cross-legged on the deck in front of him. Backs straight. Hands on knees.

One night, out of nowhere, he called me and the two shortest guys up to the front.

"Lollipop Guild," he said.

We knew exactly what he meant.

So there we were, three undersized recruits, bobbing up and down and singing in high-pitched voices:

> *"We represent the Lollipop Guild, the Lollipop Guild, the Lollipop Guild, And in the name of the Lollipop Guild, we'd like to welcome you to Munchkinland!"*

The platoon lost it. Even some of the drill instructors cracked. Our senior DI's lip twitched, fighting a smile. For half a second, he almost looked like a real person instead of a machine built out of hate and starched cammies.

That kind of mocking? I could live with. It was stupid, harmless, honestly kind of fun. If they were laughing with me or at me, I didn't really care. For a brief moment, it felt like I was part of something again.

But when the laughter died down, the isolation remained.

When the new platoon went to Camp Pendleton for combat training, the exact phase I'd been told was "too physical" for me the first time around, my knees were already catching fire again. The three-mile PFT I'd run just to escape MRP had stirred everything back up, like poking a hornet's nest with a stick and then acting surprised when you got stung.

Still, I pushed. The hikes, the obstacles, the field exercises, none of it was comfortable, but I hadn't signed up for comfort. I expected pain. I expected misery. I expected to feel like my joints were filled with shards of glass. Those things didn't scare me anymore.

What scared me was the idea that my body might quit again before my will did.

I had my tricks for the runs. I'd break the three miles into TV episodes in my head, tell myself I just had to get through the length of one sitcom. I'd sing songs silently in my mind and count them off like mile markers. If each song was about four minutes, five or six would get me through.

Because here's the thing about running in pain, or getting through boot camp, or surviving those stretches of life where everything feels like it's collapsing at once: the battle is almost never in your legs, or your lungs, or your muscles.

The battle is in your head.

The second you start obsessing over how much your knees hurt, how hot your lungs are, how tight your chest feels, you're done. The run doesn't beat you. Your own thoughts do.

If you focus too hard on your breathing, you start choking on it, like you're trying to pull air through a straw. Same with fear. Same with grief. Same with heartbreak. The more you stare at the pain, the bigger it gets.

You either learn to lead your mind, or it leads you.

By then, I'd been dropped, sidelined, rehabbing, and reinserted. I'd been the outsider, the broken one, the punch line, the Lollipop Guild recruit. My body was hanging on with duct tape, stubbornness, and Motrin, but my mind was more focused than it had ever been.

And standing there, surrounded by a platoon that didn't claim me, fighting knees that didn't want to hold me, I knew one thing for sure:

I was outnumbered. I was unwanted. But I was still moving. And I was going to need every ounce of that mental grit just to keep putting one foot in front of the other.

But my biggest mistake in boot camp was waiting for me, right on the edge of the Crucible.

The night before we stepped off, we packed our gear like our lives depended on it, because they kind of did. Every strap cinched tight, every pouch stuffed, every little required item in its exact, inspected place. Once it was all loaded, those packs turned into monsters, close to fifty pounds chewing on your shoulders and grinding down your spine.

I knew what was coming. Thirty-six obstacles. Fifty-four hours. Eight hours of sleep total. Two and a half MREs. The Crucible wasn't a hike. It was the culmination of character building and execution.

And my knees were already stinging with that familiar, stabbing pain just thinking about it.

So I made a decision.

I was going to carry as little extra weight as humanly possible. Every ounce mattered. I made sure to pack one thing in bulk: Motrin. The Marine Corps magic beans. I knew I'd be chewing those things like Skittles.

One of our required items was this heavy, thick, issued coat. Not crazy heavy by itself, maybe two or three pounds, but when you're already hauling the weight of a small human on your back, even a pound feels like concrete. The coat was built for cold and rain, not for desert heat.

So I made what I thought was a clever call.

Everyone else packed theirs.

I didn't.

We were in the desert. It was hot. I figured I'd sweat more than I'd ever freeze so if I could shave off even a little weight, maybe, just maybe, my knees would make it through the next two and a half days without completely giving up on me.

It didn't feel like cheating. It felt like survival.

Nothing bonds people faster than shared misery, and nothing makes you famous faster than making it worse.

That night, after hours of marching, we finally stopped long enough to throw up our tents. "Sleep" is a generous word for what we did. It was two, maybe three hours of closing your eyes and trying not to die, wedged into the sand with gear digging into you and your mind still marching even when your body stopped.

The sun went down and the temperature dropped fast. All the sweat we'd soaked into our cammies cooled down, and the uniforms that had been miserable all day turned into cold, wet rags clinging to your skin.

Then the order came.

"Put on your coats."

Here's the thing about training: there is no you. There is only all. If one person gets permission, everyone gets permission. If one person screws up, everyone pays. That's the ecosystem. That's the rule.

All around me, guys started digging into their packs, pulling out those big coats, wrapping themselves in instant warmth. You could hear the relief. That little involuntary sigh when heat finally hits frozen skin. It wasn't comfort, but it was something.

I just stood there.

Arms at my sides. Heart pounding. Stomach sinking. My brain went straight into panic mode. *How do I disappear? Maybe no one will notice.*

That was adorable.

A drill instructor from another platoon came pacing past, eyes sweeping the formation like a shark. He stopped. Turned. Locked onto me like he'd been looking for this exact moment all night.

"Recruit, why aren't you wearing your coat?"

There was this tiny window where I could've lied. I could've said I lost it. Said it fell off the truck. Said someone else grabbed it by mistake. I'd already cut one corner. Lying would've finished the job.

But even freezing and exhausted, I knew I couldn't do that. Not there. Not with everything already hanging by a thread.

"I didn't pack it, Sir."

He stared at me for a beat, then raised his voice so everyone in earshot, and that was a lot of people, could hear every word.

"Recruit Sawyer decided not to pack his coat so his pack would be lighter and the Crucible would be easier for him. Since Recruit Sawyer isn't wearing his coat, none of you will wear yours either. Take them off. Put them back in your packs."

Have you ever felt five hundred people hate you at the same time?

I have.

It rolled through the formation immediately. Groans. Swearing under breath. Heads shaking. Coats getting ripped back off and stuffed back into packs with this loud, resentful energy.

We were all already cold. Now everyone was angry and cold, and I was the reason.

And the worst part was how fast it happened. They'd just had it. They'd just felt warmth on their skin for a few seconds. They'd tasted relief. Then, because of me, it got yanked away like someone snatched food out of a starving person's hand. If I had to design a punishment that created instant hatred, it would've been that.

I wanted the ground to open up and swallow me. I could feel eyes on me from every direction, like spotlights. There was nowhere to go, nowhere to hide. Just me, my stupid decision, and five hundred cold, exhausted recruits not-so-silently asking the same question:

What the hell is wrong with you?

At some point, the drill instructors must've huddled up and realized that letting hundreds of sleep-deprived, calorie-deprived, half-broken recruits freeze in the middle of nowhere probably didn't look great on a safety report, because the order got reversed.

They were allowed to put their coats back on.

Of course, I wasn't.

That part was fair. I was the one who made the decision, so I was the one who paid for it. I stood there shaking in my wet cammies, trying to pretend my teeth weren't chattering, trying to keep my face neutral while my body went into full survival mode. *Don't look weak. Just stand there and take it.*

But knowing I'd dragged my brothers into it, even for a few miserable minutes, that's what burned.

That night drove in a lesson I've never forgotten: in the Marines, and honestly in life, your decisions are never just yours. One person cuts a corner, everyone pays. I forgot that. I never forgot it again.

The next morning, we packed up for the final push: the nine-mile, 700-foot climb to the top of Grim Reaper Mountain.

The air was a mess of excitement and dread. We were almost done. Almost Marines. All that stood between us and the title was one more long, brutal walk and one fierce, body-destroying climb.

The first five miles were slow, steady grinding. Packs chewing on our shoulders, knees complaining with every step, feet feeling less like feet and more like bruised meat. The incline got steeper as we approached the base. We all knew what was waiting for us up there. The last quarter mile was notoriously steep. Not a hill. A wall. The Reaper.

We finally got a short break at the bottom. Packs dropped. Rifles leaned against them. Some guys dug into whatever was left of their MREs, scraping the last crumbs of caloric energy.

I tossed back the last three Motrin pills I had saved to get me through the pain of this last push, praying that 2,400 milligrams of ibuprofen would give me the superhuman strength I would need to make it to the top.

After about fifteen minutes, we were ordered back on our feet. Packs on. Rifles shouldered.

Then the dizziness hit.

The edges of my vision blurred. The ground slanted. I blinked hard, squinted, tried to clear it. Everything went tight and yellow and far away. I stared at the dirt, locked onto my boots, like I could will them to keep moving.

Then everything went black.

The next thing I knew, I was on my side on the ground, and a drill instructor was crouched over me, screaming.

"STAND UP! GET UP NOW! GET OFF THE DECK!"

I had no idea how I got there. One minute I was upright, trying to tough it out, the next minute I was part of the landscape. A fellow recruit grabbed my arm and helped me sit up. Someone stripped my pack off, and the relief was instant.

Three 800-milligram Motrins on an empty stomach, almost no sleep, and over fifty miles of marching. Not exactly a masterclass in judgment.

I leaned back against my pack while the DI rummaged in his own. Without a word, he pulled out an MRE brownie and shoved it into my hand.

"Eat. Now."

He made me drink an entire canteen of water with it. One bite, one gulp. That brownie was so dry it felt like eating compressed dust, but I choked it down.

Two minutes later, I was back on my feet. No discussion, no sympathy, no out. Pack on. Rifle slung over my shoulder. Marching again.

Every single step hurt. My stomach lurched. My knees were lit up. My left one felt like somebody jammed a screwdriver under the kneecap and gave it a casual twist with every step.

But stopping wasn't an option. I locked my eyes on the boots in front of me and narrowed my entire world down to one thing:

Left. Right. Left. Right.

Then we rounded a bend and I saw it.

The final climb.

It wasn't long, just 700 feet, but it went straight up. The dirt was shredded from the boots ahead of us. Guys in front of me were literally on all fours, clawing their way up. I'm short, so I leaned forward and used the weight of my pack to keep from falling backward.

Every step felt like a debate between gravity and what was left of my pride.

All around me was the sound of exhausted bodies: labored breathing, grunts, groans, a few muffled curses. And even though we were front to back, jammed together on that narrow strip of ground, I felt completely alone. Like I was the only idiot who'd managed to nearly freeze his platoon and then drop himself on the side of a mountain in the same twelve-hour window.

And then, just as suddenly as it started, it leveled out.

Flat ground.

I'd made it.

The pack that had felt like it was loaded with bricks suddenly didn't feel like it was trying to kill me anymore. Around me, guys lifted their heads. Spines straightened. The pace picked up. You could feel this weird little wave of relief moving through the line, like, *holy shit, we're actually here!*

Then I saw something I wasn't prepared for.

The guys in front of me started raising their right hands in salute.

So I raised mine too, because at that point you're not thinking. You're surviving and copying the nearest functional human.

Standing maybe three feet in front of me and to the left of the formation was the Commandant of the Marine Corps. Four stars on his collar. The top dog. The kind of person you don't expect to see in real life, let alone when you're drenched in sweat, half-dead, and praying your knees don't fold in half leaving you in the dirt. He returned our salute, then started applauding as we passed.

A few steps later, we formed up at the top. Drill instructors in front of us, officers and staff NCOs nearby, everyone looking locked in and serious, but you could feel something different in the air.

The Reaper was behind us, the drop-off and the world below spread out like confirmation of survival. We climbed that. We dragged our bodies up that thing together, and nobody carried us.

Over the loudspeakers played "God Bless the USA" by Lee Greenwood. Over and over. Same song, same chorus, same lines, repeating until it stopped being background noise and started landing in places it hadn't hit before.

> *"And I'm proud to be an American*
> *Where at least I know I'm free*
> *And I won't forget the men who died*
> *Who gave that right to me..."*

Then the drill instructors started moving down the line, one by one, stopping in front of each of us. No yelling. No games. Just that quiet, controlled intensity they always had, except now it felt different. Like the blade was still there, but it wasn't being swung at your throat anymore.

One Marine at a time, they placed the Eagle, Globe, and Anchor into each outstretched hand.

We weren't recruits anymore.

We were Marines.

The sound up there is burned into me, not because it was loud, but because it wasn't. There was no cheering. No big celebration. No movie speeches. It was quiet sobbing. Shaky exhales. Guys turning their faces away like they could hide it. The kind of crying that doesn't come from one bad moment, but from months of holding your breath and pretending you're fine because you have to be.

And then, for the first time in a long time, your body realizes you're not in immediate danger anymore. You made it. You can finally let go.

That's what surprised me the most, how fast it hit. One second we're still grinding forward, doing what we've been doing all along. One foot in front of the other. No thinking, no feeling, just surviving. Then it's like the whole group hits an invisible wall where the fight stops. Not because the drill instructors told us to stop, but because we reached the place we'd been chasing. The pressure lifted, and everything that had been stuffed down for weeks came rushing up.

I remember standing there and knowing the tears weren't only about being tired. They weren't only about pain or lack of sleep or heat or cold or whatever misery was on the menu that day. It was relief, sure, but it was also vindication. We'd been pushed, doubted, broken down, corrected, screamed at, and told in a hundred different ways that we weren't enough yet. And there we were at the top, still standing.

And I had my own version of that running in the background. I wasn't just proud I made it up there. I was proud that I didn't quit on myself. That I didn't take the easy exit my brain kept offering when things got hard. I didn't do it perfectly. I didn't feel brave the whole time. I felt scared plenty of times. I felt angry. I felt small. I had moments where I wanted to disappear.

But I kept pushing anyway, even when I didn't trust my own body, even when I didn't trust my own head.

That's the part I keep coming back to. It wasn't some flashy, heroic triumph. It was messy. It was ugly crying and guys trying to swallow it back down. It was people shaking from exhaustion and emotion and not even knowing which was which. But it was genuine. We weren't just relieved. We were emptied out. And somehow we were filled up again at the same time.

I know that sounds dramatic, but I don't have a sophisticated way to say it. What else do you call it when you feel completely dismantled, and yet you're standing there with this weird, undeniable sense that something in you just shifted? Like you walked in as one version of yourself and you walked out as another. Still exhausted. Still beat up. Still human. But not the same.

By the time my senior drill instructor stepped in front of me, my legs were shaking so hard I still don't know how I stayed standing. My knees were on fire and balancing myself was becoming a fight of its own. But I pulled it together. I locked in, got my posture as straight as I could manage, and held out my hand because I wasn't about to get sloppy on the one moment I'd been grinding toward for almost four months.

He gently placed the Eagle, Globe and Anchor emblem into my palm. The same outline I'd traced with my thumb when the lights were out and I couldn't sleep, like touching it could keep me focused when everything else felt unstable. I'd wanted it since I was eighteen. Even during the years I acted like I didn't care, or told myself it wasn't realistic, or tried to bury it under "adult life." It was still there. It never left.

He looked me dead in the face and said, "Congratulations, Marine. Your son will be very proud of you."

That was it. One sentence. And it hit me harder than anything else that happened in San Diego.

I felt myself come apart, quietly, right there where I stood. The air left my lungs. My throat cinched. My eyes burned and then it was happening whether I wanted it to or not.

I'd been telling myself this was about earning the title. About proving I could finish something hard. About becoming a Marine. And it was all of that. But underneath it, the whole time, was something I didn't fully admit until that moment. I was also trying to become someone my son could be proud of. Someone I could look at in the mirror and respect again. Someone who didn't quit on himself.

Hearing my drill instructor say it out loud, my son, turned it from an internal argument into something real. It connected everything. Every time I'd limped through a day I wasn't sure I'd finish. Every time I'd been embarrassed, singled out, reshuffled, pushed aside, or treated like the weak link. Every time I'd had to swallow my pride and keep moving.

All of it suddenly had a name and a reason, and it broke me wide open.

I only hoped he was right. I hoped my son would understand it someday, not as some tough-guy story, but as proof that his dad didn't quit when it counted. But standing there with that emblem in my hand, I also knew something else for sure.

I made it.

Not the way I pictured it. There was nothing polished about my route through boot camp. I got dropped. I got sidelined. I got medically benched. I dealt with the resentment, other people's and my own. There were days I felt frozen in place, physically and mentally, and days I was sure I'd pushed my luck too far and it was all about to end.

I didn't glide through boot camp. I fought my way through it. I adapted. I got humbled. I rebuilt myself. I learned how to keep going even when my body was fighting me and my head was worse.

And I finished.

That's what I come back to now when I think about that moment. Not how it looked from the outside. Not whether it was impressive or messy. Not the stumbles or the bad days. Just the simple fact that I kept getting back up. I stayed in the fight. And I earned that emblem the hard way.

When I look back on those months in San Diego, it feels like the most concentrated version of real life I've ever lived. The pressure, the uncertainty, the highs and lows, the constant demand to perform even when you're not at your best, none of that is exclusive to the Marine Corps. The difference is that regular life spreads it out. Life gives you the same tests, just slower, quieter, with more room to pretend you're fine.

Boot camp doesn't let you hide from yourself. It takes a lifetime's worth of stress and doubt and growth and shoves it into thirteen weeks, then dares you to come out the other side without getting changed by it.

And standing there with that emblem in my palm, hearing "your son will be proud of you," I knew that was the point. Not just earning the title.

Becoming someone worth being proud of.

The descent on the back side of Grim Reaper felt like walking with someone else's legs, like my body had given everything it had and was still somehow moving on momentum and pride alone. We eventually reached a clearing, the promised land you hear about in every Crucible story: The Warriors Breakfast.

After two and a half days without real food or sleep, stumbling through miles of dirt and obstacles on fumes, that breakfast felt like an apology.

Steak and eggs.

In reality, it was probably pretty average. But in that moment? It tasted like heaven. The smell alone, grease, eggs, meat, almost made me cry all over again. I took my time. Small bites. Slow chewing.

I didn't gorge, and most of us didn't. We knew our stomachs were held together by willpower and MRE crackers. A few guys couldn't resist, went all in, and paid for it on the way back.

After that, the next six days blurred into logistics. Gear turn-ins, checklists, more lines than you'd think could exist in one place. The rifles, flak jackets, helmets, everything we had lived in and sweated into for months got scrubbed, inspected, and lined up for the next wave of scared kids who thought they knew what they were signing up for.

Eventually, we made it to the storage building where our civilian lives had been sitting in cardboard boxes and net bags, collecting dust while we got broken down and rebuilt. When I opened mine, it was like cracking open a time capsule from some other lifetime. Wallet. Clothes. Random little pieces of the "before" version of me.

When I'd stepped off that bus on day one, I weighed 111 pounds. Skin, bones, nerves, and a chip on my shoulder.

At my final weigh-in?

136 pounds.

Twenty-five pounds of muscle and misery. The Marine Corps doesn't leave much softness behind.

My knees were wrecked, but by that point the pain had faded into background noise. My mind had already moved on to something bigger: my son, and my parents, and the look on their faces when they finally saw me.

I kept picturing myself standing there in dress Charlies with the brass polished, the collar stiff, everything squared away, and hoping they'd see more than the uniform. Hoping they'd see the man I was trying to become underneath it.

At the same time, I knew there was a line they'd never be able to cross with me, no matter how proud they were. They could love it. They could cheer. They could tell people about it for the rest of their lives. But they'd never fully understand what I'd just lived through. Not in a disrespectful way. Just in the way reality works.

You can't explain the kind of sleep deprivation that makes you forget what day it is. You can't translate fear that sits in your stomach for weeks. You can't describe pain that becomes normal. And you definitely can't package brotherhood in a way they can fully understand if they've never felt it.

Only Marines understand Marines.

Before all of that, I thought strength meant never flinching. Never asking for help. Just grinding forward no matter what, staying quiet while you suffered, pretending you were fine until you weren't. That's what I thought being a man looked like. Tight jaw. Shut mouth. Carry it alone.

Boot camp, especially the Crucible, taught me something different.

Courage isn't never going down. Courage is standing up in front of people who might judge you and admitting, I'm hurt. I need help. And then showing up again the next day anyway, knowing you might get embarrassed again, knowing you might get sidelined again, knowing your pride is going to take another hit.

The pain stripped my ego down and forced me to separate pride from perseverance. It made me ask why I was really there. Not just to earn a title, not just to wear a uniform, but to become someone my son could genuinely look up to.

Not the dad who pretended to be bulletproof. But the dad who kept going, even when he clearly wasn't.

Being removed from training and sent to Medical Rehab gutted me. For a long time, all I could see in it was failure. Sitting on the sidelines while the platoon moved on without me felt like being erased. It was humiliating.

I told myself it was temporary. I told myself it didn't matter. But I felt it in my gut every day.

With some distance, I can see it for what it really was: a turning point.

It forced me to learn how to live inside disappointment without letting it define me. It forced me to learn how to lead in a room full of guys who were hurt, frustrated, angry, and embarrassed. Guys everyone quietly labeled as broken.

And I realized maybe we weren't broken at all. Maybe we were just being trained in a different kind of strength.

Struggling doesn't disqualify you. Hurting doesn't mean you don't belong. The only thing that really counts against you is quitting on yourself because you bought into the lie that pain means you're not enough.

I didn't quit.

Every day, even when my knees screamed and my pride felt like it was bleeding out, I still kept pushing. I did what I could. I took the next step. I stayed in the fight.

And in the end, that's what made all the difference.

Graduation came fast, which is weird to say after boot camp because most of the time it feels like the calendar is broken. You spend weeks convinced the finish line is some made-up concept drill instructors use to keep you moving. And then one day you blink and you're being told what to wear, where to stand, and how to act like this is all normal.

Visitors' Thursday was surreal in a way I still have a hard time explaining. You're standing there in your best uniform, pressed and squared away, trying to look like you belong in it. But inside, you're back in that old place, quietly checking the bleachers, scanning faces.

And for a couple hours, you're allowed to be human again. Not fully, not like real life, but enough to feel nostalgic. You walk your family around the depot and show them pieces of this world you've been living in. You point at a building and say, "This is where we got smoked," and expect them to understand your new language.

You point at the squad bay and you don't even know how to summarize it, because it wasn't just where you slept. It's where you learned how tired a person can be and still keep moving. It's where you learned what it feels like to be watched, corrected, yelled at, and then expected to perform like nothing touched you.

You want to tell them everything, but you also don't want them to see the parts that still feel raw. You're proud you made it that far, but you're also aware of the cost and you don't want to hand that weight to anyone else.

Then they're gone. The time ends, they disappear back through those gates, and it's like someone shut the door on the one soft moment you were allowed to have. You snap right back into training mode because you don't have a choice. There's still one last stretch before they present you as what you came here to be.

Friday morning, we left the squad bay for the last time. The racks, the footlockers, the usual routine, it all disappeared behind us as we formed up and moved out.

The same place that had been our whole world became something we weren't going back to, and even though I was exhausted, I remember feeling strikingly clear-headed. Like my body was running on fumes, but my brain was fully awake for it.

We marched to the parade deck and it wasn't the same kind of marching we'd done for the drill instructors. This was presentation. This was the public-facing version. No constant screaming in your ear, no humiliation layered on top of every correction. It was still strict, still controlled, but the purpose was different.

We weren't there to be broken down anymore. We were there to be presented.

And for the first time in a long time, it didn't feel like we were moving out of fear. It felt like we were moving out of pride. The kind that sits in your throat because you've spent months being told you're nothing, and now the whole point is to stand there and let people see that you are now **someone**.

Then the command came: "Dismissed."

We stepped back together, hit the about-face, and barked "Aye, sir!" like we'd done a thousand times. Only this time, it wasn't leading into another round of getting lit up. It was the end. Just like that.

I watched a lot of the new Marines turn toward their drill instructors. Handshakes, back slaps, that awkward mix of respect, gratitude, and relief. A few guys even hugged them. People were laughing, calling out nicknames, acting like cousins at a reunion. Guys were swapping phone numbers and talking about keeping in touch, saying the kind of stuff you say when you've been through something intense together. Relief, exhaustion, disbelief, pride, all stacked on top of each other.

But that wasn't me.

I didn't have that bond with this platoon. I hadn't grown with them. I'd been dropped, recycled, and stitched into the middle of their story. I wasn't the guy they suffered beside from day one. I wasn't part of their inside jokes or their shared memories. I was the add-on, the replacement part who showed up late and did what he had to do.

I didn't blame them for not caring that much about me, and I didn't expect them to act like we'd all built something together. We hadn't.

They weren't my brothers. They were the group I needed to stand inside so I could finish.

So when it ended, I did my about-face, gave my final "Aye, sir," and walked straight off the parade deck toward the bleachers where my parents were waiting. No lingering. No long goodbye. No emotional wrap-up with guys I wasn't close to.

Graduation came and went quietly.

I know if I'd graduated with my original platoon it would've been different. Those guys knew my story because they were with me every step of the way. They would've understood what it meant for me to still be standing there after getting dropped, after the knee issues, after all the time in limbo.

We would've earned things together in a way you can't recreate after the fact. I think there would've been real celebration in it. Real laughs. Real emotion. Maybe even the kind of pride that feels uncomplicated for once.

But that's not the version I got.

I got the version where my body betrayed me, my timeline got pushed back, and I finished the race surrounded by strangers. And I don't say that for pity. I say it because it matters.

People like to talk about making it, finishing, earning it, and I did. I earned the title. I wore the uniform. I stood on the parade deck like everyone else. Still, it didn't feel the way I'd told myself it would.

I wish I could say I felt nothing but pride, because pride would be the easiest emotion to carry. Instead, it hit that old familiar nerve of being on the outside. Tolerated. Technically included. Not really claimed.

I was a Marine, but there was a quiet part of me that didn't feel as proud as I wanted to be, because the moment I built up in my head didn't match what happened in real life.

For a long time, I thought becoming a Marine would be the chapter where everything finally clicked. The clean break from my past. The moment I could stop feeling like I was always trying to prove something and just finally belong somewhere.

In my head, graduation was supposed to come with this built-in payoff: brothers beside me, shared history, that feeling of, "we did this together."

What I got wasn't that.

What I got was lonely.

I walked away from graduation not with a group of friends, but with aching knees, a uniform that didn't magically fix anything, and a realization that success doesn't always feel the way you think it will. That day shattered one of the biggest illusions I'd been holding onto: that if you accomplish something hard enough, it erases the part of you that's always felt out of place.

I thought the achievement would patch that. I thought the title would silence it.

Instead, I learned something even more true. Transformation doesn't always come with applause, and the big moment doesn't always feel big when you're the one living it. Sometimes the biggest victories are quiet, and sometimes you're the only one who fully understands what it took. You can be surrounded by people and still feel like you're carrying the whole thing alone.

Graduation taught me to stop expecting fulfillment to show up exactly the way I pictured it. Life doesn't hand out emotional closure just because you suffered for something. Sometimes the only thing you walk away with is the fact that you didn't quit.

No crowd can measure that. No one can really validate it for you, because they weren't inside your head when you wanted to fold, felt invisible, and had to keep going anyway.

I used to think pride came from being seen. Approved. Celebrated. Validated. Welcomed into the group.

Now I know it comes from endurance. From staying in it when it stops being inspiring and when it's just you versus your own doubts, your own pain, and the part of you that wants an excuse to step out of line. Even when you're standing in formation, surrounded by people, and you still feel completely alone.

I didn't get the version of graduation I wanted, but I got through it. And that part is still mine.

Then came the moment that shut all of that noise off, for a little while anyway.

Amber flew out to San Diego with my mom and dad, and she brought Cole with her. He was a few months from turning two by then. Just big enough to run around and get into everything, but still small enough to sit on my lap.

I had played out a hundred versions of that reunion in my head. Him crying. Him staring at me like I was a stranger. Him clinging to Amber and refusing to let me touch him.

But that's not what happened.

He ran to me like he'd been waiting for me to show back up. He threw his little arms around me, and his head dropped onto my shoulder like it had never left.

That simple little weight broke me open.

He didn't pull back to study my face. He didn't act confused by the haircut or the uniform or the fact that I looked like a completely different version of myself. He didn't treat me like someone who'd disappeared. He just rested against me, calm and comfortable.

And that was everything.

That hug meant more than graduation ever could.

If someone came to me right now and said, "You can relive that exact moment every day for the rest of your life, but you have to go through four months of boot camp each time," I'd do it. Because that hug told me the one thing I didn't know how badly I needed to hear without words:

I was still his dad. He didn't feel like I'd abandoned him.

Love isn't always speeches and declarations. Sometimes it's a tired toddler melting into your chest like no time passed, saying everything you need to hear without saying anything at all.

That was the spine of the whole story for me. Not the uniform. Not the title. That hug.

After that emotional reunion, I took my parents, Amber, and Cole around the recruit depot. I didn't want to give them the sanitized version, the quick walk-and-point tour. I wanted them to understand what this place actually was. What it did to me. What it took from me. And what it gave me.

I wanted them to see the environment that had swallowed my life for months and then spit out a different, more improved version.

I showed them the squad bay where seventy-two of us slept. I showed them how everything had a place and how you could get lit up for something as small as a towel being folded wrong or a footlocker being off by an inch. I pointed out the showers, the part nobody back home really thinks about, how privacy just stops existing, how you learn to move through it without thinking, because if you stop and dwell on any of it, you're going to lose your mind.

I showed them the chow hall where we barely got down three bites before being herded back to the next thing. No talking. No lingering.

We walked by the obstacle course and I could still feel it in my body. The bruises. The scraped hands. The dirt ground into everything.

I pointed out the rappelling tower where I remember feeling confidence for the first time in boot camp. When we got there, I didn't just say, "That's where we rappelled." I told them, "I went down that thing three times. The first time I was scared out of my mind. The third time I didn't want it to end."

Every stop had a story. Every slab of concrete, every railing, every field had some piece of my life ground into it. I'd been so focused on surviving day to day that I hadn't really stepped back and noticed how much had changed in me while it was happening.

Walking them through it forced me to see it from the outside for the first time. Not as a recruit trying to make it through the next ten minutes, but as a person trying to understand what those months had actually done.

The squad bay taught me patience and discipline, and it also taught me how to live around other people in a way I'd never had to before. How to function inside a system where your mood doesn't matter and your comfort matters even less.

It taught me that brotherhood isn't always some warm, friendly thing. Sometimes it's just shared misery and shared standards and the understanding that everyone is getting dragged through the same hell.

The showers stripped away privacy. The chow hall taught speed and control and how to eat even when you're not hungry, because you don't know when you'll get the chance again. The tower taught me what it feels like to do something scary, then do it again and again until it becomes normal.

For the first time, I really saw the depot hadn't just changed my posture or my stamina. It had completely rewired how I dealt with discomfort and kept pushing when I didn't feel think I could.

It didn't turn me into someone else overnight, but it did force me to live differently.

The next morning we boarded our flight home. I had ten days of leave. After that it was back to California for Marine Combat Training, then straight to Aberdeen Proving Ground in Maryland for 8 weeks of MOS school. Refrigeration Mechanic. I kept telling myself I'd be home by October, like having a date on the calendar made everything feel more attainable.

That tour of the depot felt like the end of one version of me and the start of another. I didn't fully understand the new version yet, and I didn't trust it completely either. But I knew I wasn't the same kid who stepped off that bus just four months earlier.

And after holding my son, after walking my family through the place that reshaped me, I knew what I wanted next wasn't applause or a perfect ending.

I just wanted the strength to keep going.

ROUND 20:
Flirtations, Fractures, and Final Exams

After bootcamp graduation and finally getting back to Champaign, I won't pretend. I was really looking forward to seeing Katarina again.

Before I left, Katarina and I were back to trying to see if there was enough left of our past relationship, and new version of ourselves, that we could make a new one work. Right before boot camp we found our way back to each other, and those last little pockets of time felt easy again. Familiar.

There's a specific kind of comfort that comes from knowing there's someone back home who actually understands what you're going through. Katarina did. She'd been through Army basic training herself, so she wasn't romanticizing it or acting shocked when I described the exhaustion, the weird mental games, the constant hurry-up-and-wait. She also knew enough Marines to understand our boot camp hit different, and she respected it. And by extension, she respected me for choosing it.

During those thirteen weeks, sixteen if you count the MRP detour, she became my person. She was who I wrote to when I needed to say things I couldn't say out loud to anyone around me. She was the one I trusted with the softer parts, the parts that didn't fit the tough-guy Marine thing everyone expects you to be. Even when I tried to write like everything was fine, she could read between the lines. She could tell when I was hanging on by a thread versus when I actually felt proud of myself.

And yeah, the pictures helped.

Nothing inappropriate. You'd never get away with that. Drill instructors had this annoying, almost psychic ability to spot anything even slightly outside the rules. If you got a thick envelope, you didn't get to enjoy it privately like a normal human. They'd make you open it in front of everyone, flip through it, and you'd just stand there trying to act like you weren't sweating through your cammies because there might be something in there that got you smoked.

Katarina mostly sent normal photos. Her out with friends, smiling, looking like a person who slept in a real bed and ate real food. Living in daylight while I lived in sand and sweat. But there was one picture I basically etched into my mind. Her on the beach in a red, white, and blue bikini. She looked amazingly sexy. A nice distraction, to say the least.

So yes, I was beyond excited to see my son again. And I was glad to see my parents. That's not up for debate. But seeing your kid and your parents is a different kind of homecoming than seeing your girlfriend after months of deprivation, zero privacy, and living in a constant sea of dudes. I was human. I missed being wanted. I missed being touched. I missed feeling chosen by someone because they wanted me. Not because they had to. Not because we were family. Not because it was a duty.

But by the time I got home, I already knew something was different with Katarina.

In the beginning, during those first few weeks of boot camp, her letters came constantly. Almost a letter every day. They were like little slices of normal life I could hold in my hands. Even when she wasn't saying anything important, it still mattered. Her handwriting. The fact that she was thinking about me. The fact that I wasn't completely forgotten.

Then around week six or seven, it started to slow down. Two or three a week. Then one.

I'm not stupid. I knew what that meant.

She'd probably met someone else. Or at least let someone get close in the way people do when you're gone and life keeps moving. I didn't hate her for it. I wasn't sitting in a coffee shop writing poetry. I was getting smoked, getting broken down, living in a little fenced-off universe where time doesn't work like it does for normal people. Life doesn't pause for the people on the outside just because you're trapped inside the wire.

She still wrote, even when it got spaced out, and I honestly think part of that was because she knew I needed something steady to grab onto. So I didn't ask questions I already knew the answers to. I didn't want to force a confession, and I didn't want to hear the words out loud. I just kept writing back like I didn't notice the change, because pretending bought me a little more stability when I didn't have much.

When I got back, we reconnected. Physically, emotionally. After four months of being yelled at, told when to eat, told when to sleep, told when to speak, and basically trained to function like a robot, being close to her felt incredible in that simple, quiet way where your body finally unclenches and you remember you're a person. I tried to spend as much of my free time with her as I could.

My family did not approve.

My mom took it personally. Every time I had plans with Katarina it turned into guilt, tension, and some version of, "So I guess your family doesn't matter anymore." And once Mom got going, Dad would light up like a fuse. To him, me wanting to see Katarina meant I was selfish. That I was choosing a girl over my family and my son.

But it wasn't that simple. I wasn't running from my son. He was the biggest motivation I had those sixteen weeks of hell. I wasn't ditching my family. I was trying to cram multiple relationships into a window of time that felt way smaller than everyone else thought it was. I only had ten days of freedom before going back to the gates of hell and I wanted to make up for the last four months I was gone. With everyone I loved, not just the few they deemed worthy. I'd just come out of a world where nothing belonged to me, not my time, not my space, not my body. I was trying to get pieces of myself back, and part of that was being with the only person who understood what I just went through.

The truth is, my mom had always had something against Katarina. I never fully understood why. I still don't. It was like Katarina could walk into a room and automatically set off every alarm my mom had. My mom didn't need a reason. She had a feeling, and that feeling became truth to her. And once my mom decided someone wasn't good for me, it didn't matter what I thought. It didn't matter what Katarina did or didn't do. It was already decided.

One evening, it all boiled over.

I was getting ready to go see Katarina. Mom started in on me with the usual accusations, the same "after everything we've done for you" speech. Same script, new night. Then Dad stormed into the room, and I'll never forget what happened next. He raised his fist like he was about to hit me.

Let me just say this. Raising your fist at someone who just graduated from Marine Corps boot camp is one of the worst ideas you can have.

I had just spent four months being screamed at, pushed, tested, and trained to respond to aggression without hesitation. We weren't being taught to pause and process. We weren't being taught to explain ourselves. We were being trained to react instantly and decisively when something in front of us looked like a threat. Fight, not flight. Do not freeze. Do not back down. Kill, kill, kill was a mantra. We were trained to eliminate threats, not stand there and talk about our feelings.

So when his fist came up, mine did too.

It wasn't even a thought. It wasn't some planned act of rebellion or disrespect. It was muscle memory. It was my nervous system doing what it had been conditioned to do for the last four months.

We froze like that, both of us with fists raised, staring at each other in this split second that felt way longer than it probably was. I saw it in his face when he realized what he'd almost started. He stopped, but he didn't completely back down. His face went deep red and he started yelling, harder now, like the yelling could take the place of what he didn't do. He went straight into the same old routine. Selfish, ungrateful, choosing a girl over my own family.

I didn't stick around to hear the rest.

Not because I was scared. Not because I didn't have anything to say. I left because I didn't trust what would happen if I stayed. I didn't trust my own reaction if he took one more step toward me, or if he raised that fist again, or if the yelling turned into something physical. I'd just spent months learning how to respond to aggression, and the last thing I wanted was to find out, inside my parents' house, that the version of me they were dealing with now wasn't the same one who'd left.

So I walked out.

My parents had never supported my decision to join the Marines from the start. Not from the first recruiting office visit, not when I signed the contract, not even the day they dropped me off at the airport. They showed up, sure, but emotionally they were never with me on it. In their eyes, it wasn't sacrifice or strategy. It was abandonment. Me walking away from my son. Me ducking responsibility. Me choosing the military over being a dad.

And I get why it looked that way from the outside. A twenty-three-year-old leaving town to go play Marine while he had a toddler back home? If you ignore everything else, it's easy to slap a selfish label on it and call it a day. That's what they did. They stayed locked on the surface-level version of the story and refused to look any deeper.

What they couldn't see, or maybe didn't want to see, was that, in a big way, I was doing it for him.

I wasn't running away from responsibility. I was choking on it. When I left for boot camp I was twenty-three years old, broke, scared, and barely holding myself together. I had court drama hanging over my head, money stress I couldn't solve, just lost custody of my son and was told I could only be a dad four days out of a month, and this constant feeling that no matter how hard I tried, I was still one mistake away from losing everything. I didn't have a plan. I didn't have stability. I didn't have anything I trusted long-term. I had a kid I adored, and a life that felt like it could collapse if someone breathed on it wrong.

The Marines, in my mind, weren't an escape route. They were a way to build something solid under us. A foundation. Income. Benefits. Structure. Leverage. A path forward where I could stop improvising my life week to week and start becoming someone my son could actually depend on. I wasn't chasing a fantasy. I was trying to build a version of myself that could stand up straight and not feel like a fraud every time I said the words "I'm his dad."

They saw escape. I saw foundation.

So when I came home after those months of hell, I wasn't going to shrink myself down and act like I'd done something shameful. I wasn't going to apologize for making a hard choice that I'd already paid for. I'd earned the right to decide how to spend those ten days. I'd paid for that time with pain, exhaustion, injuries I was still dealing with, and everything it took to get through training without quitting.

And if they couldn't respect that, even if they didn't agree with it, then I didn't have much left to say. Because I didn't come home to be put back on trial. I came home trying to hold onto the small piece of freedom I had and figure out how to be a dad and a man at the same time, without being treated like either one was a betrayal of the other.

Those ten days of leave went by fast. I split myself between Cole, my family, and Katarina, constantly trying to keep everyone relatively appeased, fully aware that no matter how I divided myself, someone was going to feel cheated.

It was exhausting in a different way than boot camp. Boot camp was physical and loud and constant. This was quieter, but it got under my skin. Every choice had a consequence. If I spent extra time with Cole, someone else acted like I was neglecting them. If I made plans with Katarina, my mom treated it like a personal insult. If I tried to give my parents their "family time," I couldn't get my fix of physical closeness and intimacy that I had missed the last four months, and knew I wouldn't get again for three more.

I spent those days doing mental math. Hours, visits, car rides, who I'd disappointed, who I needed to reassure next. Trying to keep the peace instead of just being able to enjoy the time I had left to be a real person.

In their story, I was the selfish one. I was the one making choices that hurt people. I was the one who "changed." I was the one who came back and didn't automatically fall back into the role they wanted me in.

In mine, I was a twenty-four-year-old man trying to hold onto his sanity. Trying to be a present dad, a decent son, and still have some small piece of a personal life without it turning into a courtroom every night in my own house. I wasn't trying to punish anyone. I wasn't trying to choose one person to love and reject everyone else. I was trying to breathe.

But deep down, I already knew what was coming.

Once I went back for Marine Combat Training and then rolled straight into MOS school in Maryland, Katarina and I were going to be done. We both knew it. We didn't even need some big, dramatic "we need to talk" conversation, because the timeline had already said everything we needed to hear. Long distance, limited contact, training schedules, and two completely different worlds with two completely different priorities. It just wasn't realistic.

And it wasn't like this was a sudden surprise, either. We'd already started drifting while I was still in boot camp. The letters came slower. The gaps got longer. You could feel the energy change without either of us having to put it into words. Coming home didn't fix that. If anything, it just made it more obvious because now I could see the difference up close. Not just in what was said, but in what wasn't. Not in a cruel way. Just in that undeniable way where you realize you're not in the same place anymore.

If I'm being honest, I was okay with it.

What we had was real. I'm not going to rewrite it into something it wasn't, but I'm also not going to pretend it meant nothing. She helped steady me at a point in my life when I needed steadiness. She gave me something to hold onto that wasn't just commands and routines and getting through the day. She was a link to the outside world when I felt like I'd been stripped down to nothing but a recruit trying to survive the next minute. She gave me comfort when I didn't have it, and that matters. I'll always be grateful for that.

I wrote letters to my parents while I was in boot camp the same as I wrote to Katarina, but my parents had never stepped foot in a squad bay. They had never run through an obstacle course or stared at the ground, forty-seven feet in the air, from the top of a rappelling tower. They had never been screamed at by three drill instructors at the same time, and they had never been in the "pit" for hours at a time because someone made their bed wrong. They didn't understand what I was going through. Katarina did.

But I also knew it wasn't a forever thing. We weren't building a life together. We were getting through a season. She was there for that version of me, the one who was trying to pull himself together, trying to prove something to himself, trying to become someone different. And I could feel that version of me fading out as the next one took over. It didn't make the relationship fake. It made it useful. But it was also just temporary.

By the end of leave, I could feel it in a really clear, almost calm way. Not heartbreaking or not bitter. Like the next phase was already lined up and moving whether any of us were ready for it or not. The Marine Corps didn't pause for relationships, and my life wasn't going to pause either.

It was time to move on.

After just ten days of being "free," barely enough time to remember what it felt like to sleep without someone screaming at me, I was right back on a plane to California.

Destination: Camp Pendleton.
Mission: Marine Combat Training.
Duration: seventeen days.

Those seventeen days would end up being, without competition, the most physically miserable stretch of my entire life. Boot camp had already stripped me down to the studs. Pendleton looked at what was left and basically said, *Yeah, we can break that some more.*

When I left home, my knees had finally stopped screaming and settled into more into a pissed-off simmer. No more stabbing pain under the kneecaps, just that constant, hot ache, like someone had tucked a couple of burning coals behind them and walked away. Annoying, but survivable. Manageable. I let myself believe that was progress.

The second I stepped off the bus at Pendleton, strapped on the gear, and started humping those hills again, the pain came right back in full force.

I knew, instantly, this wasn't just going to be bad. This was going to be that chapter. The one you look back on and think, *Yeah, that's where I completely broke.*

The first couple of days tried to trick me. We were just issuing gear, getting briefed, trying to pretend the squad bay felt like home again. My knees throbbed, but it was just in the background. I even caught myself thinking, *okay, maybe this won't be as bad as I'm imagining. Maybe I overreacted.*

Then we hit the field.

From that moment on, it was the same miserable loop, over and over, like someone pressed repeat on suffering. Forced marches in full combat gear, pack, flak, rifle, miles of uneven ground. Every step turned into a fight between my mind and body. *Just one more. Just one more. Just one more.* And underneath that was an even louder fear of, *What if I can't?*

Being short in the Marine Corps is its own sick joke. Tall guys lead the formation; short guys get shoved in the back. A brisk walk for the front guys turns into a jog for the ones in the rear, especially when you're carrying around fifty pounds of gear. Uphill was brutal, but downhill was excruciating.

On the downhills, gravity took over and nobody cared how much it hurt to keep up. The guys up front eased into this light run, and the rest of us got dragged into a desperate, stumbling sprint just to stay attached to the formation. One loose rock, one bad step, and you were either rolling down the hill, blowing out an ankle, or getting flattened by thirty guys who didn't even have time to notice you'd gone down.

My glasses fogged up constantly. The straps from my pack dug so deep into my shoulders my arms started going numb, like my body was trying to check out one limb at a time. At one point my left arm just went completely dead. My rifle slipped, hit the dirt, and for half a second my heart just dropped. Losing your rifle doesn't feel like dropping equipment. It feels like dropping yourself.

I scrambled to sling it back on and sprinted to catch up, lungs on fire, heart punching the inside of my ribs. There was no sense of pride in pushing through it. Just the heavy, familiar feeling of, *Here we go again.* Trying not to fail in front of everyone.

Those seventeen days weren't about honor or courage or any of the recruiting slogans. They were about endurance in its ugliest form. No romance, no glory, just pain and forward motion and this gnawing fear that my body was going to hit its limit and abandon me in front of everyone. More than once, halfway up another hill, I was sure something was going to snap for good. That my knees would finally quit, that I'd end up right back in a rehab platoon, watching everyone else finish what I had started while I sat there on the sidelines, broken and useless.

But somehow, I made it.

And I wish I could say I walked out of Pendleton feeling proud, or strong, or transformed. I learned something about my limits, sure, but not in the motivational-poster kind of way.

I learned I could go past them. Way past them.

And there's a special kind of fear in realizing you're capable of surviving more than you ever wanted to. It doesn't make you feel invincible. It makes you wonder how much more you're going to be asked to endure before something finally, truly breaks.

Graduation from combat training was forgettable. No marching bands, no proud parents in the stands, no big speeches. After everything we'd done, it ended with a handshake, a nod, and a quiet, "Alright, you're done. Next."

That same day, I boarded another plane out of San Diego, just a fence and a runway away from the depot where I'd spent thirteen weeks being turned into a Marine. It felt strange to be so close to the beginning, already headed into the next chapter.

This time, I was bound for Aberdeen, Maryland.

A bus met us at the airport and carried us to Aberdeen Proving Ground, which would be home for the next couple of months. The energy shifted the second I stepped off that bus. The tension that had wrapped itself around my shoulders for months loosened just a little.

Aberdeen felt less like boot camp and more like a community college campus.

We lived in red-brick barracks that looked like basic apartment buildings. Inside, the layout was simple. A shared common room with mismatched couches, a couple of tables, and a TV that was always on but rarely watched. Guys would press uniforms while half-listening to whatever movie was playing, talking about hometowns, girlfriends, and the things we missed that didn't seem so important before we left.

Our rooms were twelve-by-twelve boxes with just enough room for two beds, two desks, and two wardrobes. Bare bones. My desk sat in front of the window, and from that spot I could see the base payphone.

That phone was everything. It was my lifeline to the outside world. I called home and even occasionally even got to hear Cole's voice. After months of only writing letters, being able to pick up a phone and actually hear a familiar voice was comforting.

Days fell into a comfortable rhythm. We went to class, learned refrigeration systems, took notes, did our labs. After chow each evening, we'd head back to the barracks to press uniforms and shine boots. But now it wasn't because someone was looming over our shoulder, but because that's just what you did. It was expected. It became ritual. Almost peaceful.

My knees finally had a chance to breathe a bit. They never fully stopped hurting, but I could walk without limping, and after Pendleton, that alone felt like luxury.

Weekends were where we got our sanity back. As soon as class let out on Fridays, we were released for the weekend, as long as we stayed within a fifty-mile radius. No one had a car, so the rec center was our go-to. Pool tables, movies, dances.

And then there was Joanne.

Joanne worked behind the counter at the rec center, the gatekeeper of Friday and Saturday nights. Her whole job, at least in my mind, was handing out billiard balls to a bunch of bored, horny Marines pretending we weren't one bad thought away from losing our minds.

She was nineteen, all girl-next-door with a twist. The kind of "good girl" look that made you feel safe and turned on at the exact same time. Green eyes that grabbed you and didn't let go, and a wide, easy smile that lit up the room. She had this bubbly personality and a little flirt in her walk that made it almost impossible not to stare.

So of course I flirted. That's what I did. It was practically my only skill set at that point.

But this time it didn't just bounce off and disappear into the background noise of a room full of Marines throwing out every line they'd ever heard in a movie. She actually flirted back. I couldn't wrap my head around that. She was surrounded by dudes in uniform every weekend, and I knew damn well I wasn't the only one taking a shot. There was no way

I was the best-looking or the smoothest. Half the time I could barely string a sentence together without sounding like a nervous idiot.

It took me two full weekends to grow a spine. All my little innuendos and throwaway jokes finally added up to one actual move. I asked her if she wanted to hang out sometime when she wasn't on the clock, fully prepared for the polite "aww, that's cute" brush-off.

Instead, she said yes. Just like that. Like it was the most natural thing in the world. And as if this sundae actually needed a cherry on top, she had a car and offered to pick me up for a night in Ocean City.

Game on.

We strolled the boardwalk like something out of a cheap romance movie, only it didn't feel cheap. It felt light. Free. We ate cotton candy, sticky fingers and all, and rode the huge Ferris wheel, the kind that makes the whole shore look like a postcard. I laughed. She laughed. I caught myself actually enjoying the moment instead of waiting for the other shoe to drop.

It was the most fun I'd had in almost six months.

Four months of getting screamed at through boot camp, ten days of leave back in Champaign that were way more complicated and stressful than restful, and the grind of combat training. All of it stacked on my shoulders, and then suddenly I was here. On a boardwalk at night with this ridiculously special girl I barely knew, and somehow it all felt worth it.

That night ended exactly the way the fairy tale version of my life would've written it. We ended up back at her mom's house, where she still lived, and we slept together for the first time. I don't have the perfect words for what that was like for me. Joanne was beautiful, obviously, but that wasn't the main thing. The real turn-on was how she made me feel.

She made me feel like I hadn't felt in a very, very long time.

Not even with Katarina. Not in those last few months when everything between us felt heavy and complicated. Katarina and I had history. We had stories and scars and old arguments that hung in the air like smoke. Joanne and I had none of that. We were new. A blank page.

With Joanne, I only felt what I felt right then. No regret from past screwups. No frustration from old fights. No ghosts hovering in the corner of the room. Just the two of us, tangled up in each other, living inside this one beautiful moment in time. For once, my brain wasn't sprinting ahead to worst-case scenarios or replaying old scenes in the background. It was quiet. I was there. With her.

From that night on, Joanne and I were a thing. Not forever. Life wasn't that generous. But for the next six weeks, she was my world. After that, my school would wrap up and I'd have to go back to Illinois, back to my son, a new job, and Marine Reserve drill weekends. Real life would come crashing back in.

But for right then, it was Joanne. Just Joanne. And I wanted to squeeze every second I could out of whatever this was.

One Friday evening, she picked me up for dinner at her house. Her mom was making crab cakes and had invited me to join them.

Crab cakes.

At that point in my life, she might as well have said, "Hey, come on over for sewer sandwiches," because that's about how I felt about seafood. I was a cheeseburger-and-fries kind of guy. But when a girl like Joanne invites you over for a special dinner her mom's cooking for you, you smile, rub your hands together like a kid on Christmas morning, and say you can't wait to dig in.

The crab cakes actually weren't bad. For someone who doesn't like seafood, that's high praise. I'm sure they were amazing to people who knew what they were talking about. To me, they were okay. Edible. Not a cheeseburger, but not punishment either.

But honestly, the food wasn't the point.

It was the way her mom talked to me like I belonged there. The easy conversation around the table. The laughter. The fact that I wasn't just some random Marine she was seeing. I was being invited in. I wasn't on the outside looking through a window for once. I was at the table.

I felt at home. I was comfortable. I was relaxed. I was happy. Truly, deeply happy in a way I hadn't realized I'd been missing until I felt it again. No arguments about spending my time with the wrong person. No raging court battles. No talk of child support. It was calm. Easy.

And I liked feeling that way. I liked it a lot.

My roommate, PFC Torres, and I had a routine. We'd stroll up to the rec center counter, sign out a tray of billiard balls, and play for hours, talking trash like we'd known each other for years instead of a few awkward weeks of forced proximity and government-issued furniture.

Now add a cast.

I had a cast on my right hand, and it was pure misery. Hot, itchy, and impossible to keep clean in the midsummer humidity. Sweat collected under it and every basic task turned into a slow-motion comedy bit. Writing, eating, tying boots, zipping pants, wiping my ass. You don't realize how much you rely on both hands until one of them is downgraded to plaster dead weight.

At this point, you're probably wondering, *Okay, genius, what did you do to earn the cast?* Fair question.

So here's the story.

My MOS class for refrigeration troubleshooting and repair had thirteen students. Three Marines and ten Army soldiers. The odds were already stacked against us in terms of brain cells and maturity levels.

There was one particular Army guy, a big dude with broad shoulders, thick neck, the whole "I peaked in high school" starter pack. And, as usual, I was the shortest one in the room, which automatically makes me the designated target for every unoriginal joke from the most insecure guy nearby.

Right on cue, he decided his life's mission was to be the first person in history to make a short joke that would change my world.

Spoiler: he failed.

For a twenty-four-year-old Marine who had been short his entire life and had heard at least one short joke every single day, you have to come up with something pretty damn clever to get a laugh out of me. This guy was not that guy. His best material was the classic, "How's the weather down there?" line, like he'd just written it himself and expected a standing ovation.

Nobody laughed. Not me, not the rest of the class. Just him, alone with his punchline.

After almost 9,000 days on this planet listening to the same bullshit, I was beyond over it.

I warned him. Multiple times. Calmly at first. I told him he wasn't funny, and if he kept it up, he was going to find himself picking his ass up off the floor. It wasn't a threat so much as a public-service announcement.

He tested the warning anyway.

One Tuesday morning, we were filing into the classroom like usual. I was minding my own business when he threw out yet another one of his empty little quips, and I snapped. Enough was enough. The Marine in me decided it was time to handle it. The intelligent adult in me apparently took the morning off.

I spun around, squared up, drew my right arm back, and launched my fist at his chest with everything I had. And that's when the universe decided to tell its favorite joke.

He instinctively brought his leg up to block, and instead of my fist slamming into his chest like I'd pictured, my knuckles crashed straight into his kneecap. Full force.

Pop!

Everybody heard it. That sickening, sharp crack that lets you know you've just done something incredibly stupid and irreversible. My hand lit up with pain, but I did what any prideful idiot would do. I pretended I was fine. I shrugged, turned away, and sat down like I'd just swatted a fly.

Inside, I was screaming.

The instructor walked in right then, so there was no follow up argument or fight. Just me sitting there with my hand throbbing, while this guy was probably thinking, *Did this moron just punch my knee?*

Over the next two days, my hand swelled up and started turning a nice shade of purple. It hurt so bad I had to use my left hand to turn doorknobs because any pressure on my right felt like someone was driving a nail through it. Eventually, I had to do the thing I hate most in the world. Admit I'd screwed up and ask for help.

I swallowed my pride and went to medical. A few X-rays later, the doc looked at me and told me I'd broken the ring finger metacarpal in my right hand.

Translation: I punched a guy's knee and broke my own hand. Hence, the cast.

Army kneecap: one. Big tough Marine: zero.

Those romantic Friday and Saturday nights in Joanne's backyard hot tub turned into something closer to a sketch comedy show starring me and my poor life choices. Instead of leaning back under the stars with both arms around the beautiful girl who inexplicably liked me, I had to sit there with my right arm propped up on the edge of the hot tub like I was signaling for a rescue helicopter. Half-submerged, half-awkward statue. Real smooth.

Somehow, I always found a way to ruin a good thing.

And because Maryland in the summer is basically a wet armpit, after about two weeks, the cast started to smell like something had crawled in there and died. It was a special kind of funk.

I knew the medics weren't going to swap it out just because it reeked. "It still works" is pretty much the military standard. So one night in the hot tub, staring at this nasty, sweat-soaked plaster prison, I made a decision.

I slowly lowered the cast into the water and let it soak. You could almost hear it sigh in defeat. Plaster and hot tub water mixed into this swampy, crumbling mess, and I just sat there pretending this was a brilliant plan and not the dumbest thing I'd done since, well, punching a kneecap.

The next morning, I walked into the clinic with my cast literally dripping, soft, and falling apart at the edges like a wet cardboard box. I put on my most innocent face, which, to be fair, was not very convincing.

The corpsman took one look at it and was not amused.

He gave me the full disappointed-dad speech.

"You have to keep it dry."
"You can't do this."
"You're risking infection."

I stood there nodding like a chastised teenager, thinking, *Yeah, yeah, Doc, I get it. Actions, consequences, all that. Can we just address the fact that my arm has smelled like a dead locker room for a week?* Reluctantly, he finally sighed, grabbed the saw, and cut it off. Then he wrapped my hand in a fresh, clean cast that didn't smell like death.

Small win. Temporary, obviously. But still. A win's a win.

The end of school snuck up on me faster than I expected, like everything else in that season of my life. One minute I was just trying to keep up, the next we were staring down the final exam.

I wasn't just trying to get through it. I wanted to prove something. To the instructors, sure, but mostly to myself. I wanted to confirm I hadn't gone through all of this for nothing, that I was actually learning something, not just enduring it.

I scored a 94 percent. Highest in the class.

For a short, beat-up Marine with a history of self-doubt and questionable decision-making, that achievement meant something to me. It felt like a small, solid piece of proof that I wasn't just a screw-up stumbling from one phase to the next. I could be good at something. I didn't have to be good at everything. I just needed to be good at something.

Then came the administrative circus.

Gear turn-ins. Paperwork. Hunting down signatures from offices scattered across base like a military-themed scavenger hunt. I checked off one office after another, one signature after another, feeling that strange mix of relief and impatience that comes when you're so close to being done.

I had one signature left. One office left. And my flight time was closing in behind me like a countdown clock.

Joanne came through for me again. She drove me to the last building, parked, and waited while I sprinted inside like my life depended on it. As soon as I had the signature, we were back in the car, racing across base so I could turn everything in at admin before the window closed.

There was just one problem. Technically, no one was supposed to be released from school while still wearing a cast. You were supposed to leave "whole." Healthy. Presentable. Like they were returning a fully functioning product to the civilian world.

Rules are rules. So I did what any determined, slightly reckless Marine with a plane to catch would do. I hid it.

I tucked my right arm behind my back, stood at parade rest, and tried to look as symmetrical and unbroken as humanly possible. Chin up, shoulders back, *nothing to see here.* The admin staff glanced at me, glanced at the papers, and signed off without a second thought.

The second the forms were in my hand, I turned and walked out of that office at a perfectly normal, nothing-weird-happening pace. Only after I cleared the doorway did I let out the breath I'd been holding. If they had noticed that cast, I would have been stuck there another month.

And honestly, another month with Joanne wouldn't have been the worst thing that ever happened to me. She had become a bright spot in a stretch of my life that was mostly made up of gray. But as much as a part of me wanted to stay, my head and my heart were already pointed home. Back to Illinois. Back to my son. Back to the life I was still trying to figure out.

I was done. And for once, I was leaving on a high note.

We barely made it to the airport in time. Joanne pulled up to the curb, the car idling as people rushed around us with bags and tickets. I grabbed my bag from the back seat, turned to her, and everything felt like it was moving too fast.

There was no long hug. No movie-scene kiss in the doorway with dramatic music swelling in the background. Just a quick goodbye, a rushed thank you, a small smile that was trying to hold more than it could, and the sound of the car door closing behind me.

After everything we had shared in those few weeks, the boardwalk, the hot tub nights, crab cakes at her mom's table, the feeling of being seen and included, that ending felt thin. Unfinished. Like I walked out of a movie ten minutes before the credits.

But I told myself there would be time to sort that out later.

There is always time, until there isn't.

Boot camp was a loud transformation. Pendleton was loud pain. Aberdeen was quiet renewal.

From the outside, none of it looked dramatic. There were no big speeches, no movie-moment turning point where everything clicked and my life suddenly made sense. If you'd watched it from a distance, it probably would have looked like I just moved from one duty station to another and kept going. But internally, it was so much more.

Boot camp taught me how to survive absolute chaos. It taught me how to keep moving when your brain is fried, your body hurts, and you're running on pure stubbornness. Pendleton reinforced that lesson with a different kind of intensity. Less "training environment," more "welcome to real consequences." Everything still felt intense, demanding, and physical. Every time I stood up too fast, every time I stepped wrong, there was this split-second calculation. *Is today the day my body waves the white flag?*

Aberdeen was different. It wasn't soft, but it was quieter. The structure was still there with the usual formations, expectations, and rules, but the volume was turned down. Nobody was screaming in your face every five seconds. Nobody was trying to break you down just to prove they could rebuild you. I was still a Marine, but for the first time in a long time, I wasn't living inside a nonstop pressure cooker.

And in that quieter space, I started noticing things I'd been too amped up to notice before. Routine didn't feel like punishment anymore. It felt like something that belonged to me. Simple stuff mattered in a way it never had. Pressing my uniform in a common room while talking with the other Marines. Straightening up my space because I wanted it clean, not because a drill instructor was going to tear it apart to make a point. Even the background noise changed. Some dumb movie playing in the rec room, guys half-watching it, half-arguing over nothing, and me just sitting there thinking, *this is what normal looks like now.*

I started paying attention to how good it felt to move without bracing for impact. The relief of standing up and not immediately feeling that jolt of panic in my knees. The weird gratitude of being able to walk somewhere and not spend the whole time accommodating pain. I didn't realize how much energy I'd been burning just constantly preparing myself for the next hit.

That's when I stopped waiting for life to announce itself in fireworks or big moments. I started finding it in the small stuff. The rec room, the payphone, the hot tub. Little moments that would've seemed pointless before. Laughing at something dumb. Sitting quietly without feeling guilty about it. Realizing I could just exist for a minute without performing for anyone.

That ended up being the real transformation. Learning when to exhale. Learning that survival isn't only white-knuckling your way through the worst of it. It's also figuring out how to come back to yourself when the worst part is over and nobody's there to tell you what you're supposed to feel next.

ROUND 21:
When the System Finally Saw Me

When my time at Aberdeen finally ended, I flew home a day earlier than my parents expected. I wanted it to be a surprise, so I gave them a later arrival date, then called my brother and let him in on it so I'd have a ride waiting at the airport.

My brother picked me up, and we drove back through streets I knew by heart. They felt slightly off, like I'd been gone just long enough to notice little changes. Or maybe I'd changed enough that I was seeing everything in a different way, for different reasons.

We pulled into the driveway, and I barely had time to unbuckle and grab my bag before the front door swung open. Mom and Dad came out fast, like they'd been posted up by the window. So much for sneaking in. They saw the car and did the math, and suddenly I was standing there getting wrapped up in those big, tight hugs that only a parent can give.

We did the quick version of catching up right there by the car. The flight. The base. The weather. How I was feeling. All the obvious questions that weren't really about information. My parents were taking inventory, making sure I was still me under whatever I'd brought home with me.

Then their eyes went straight to the black cast on my right arm.

I had to explain it and still somehow sound like a tough Marine. I tried to thread the needle, tell the truth without sounding pathetic, so I gave them the basics, downplayed the parts that felt embarrassing, and cracked a couple jokes. After the story and the laugh, I admitted I couldn't wait another minute to get that damn thing off my arm.

Then dad and I did the most predictable father-and-son thing imaginable. We headed straight for the garage.

I'd been living with that cast long enough to hate it in a way that's hard to explain if you've never had one. The itching you can't reach. The sweat trapped under it. The smell. The way it makes everything harder, showering, sleeping, getting dressed, doing anything normal. It wasn't just inconvenient. It made me feel stuck. And after months of being told what to do, where to be, how to move, how to act, the cast felt like one more layer of control strapped to my body.

Standing there in the garage with my arm out, it hit me how much that cast matched the way I'd been feeling for a long time. Boxed in. Restricted. Living inside rules that didn't fit me anymore. My old life had felt like that too, trying to be who I thought I was supposed to be, trying to hold things together, trying to act tough while quietly feeling trapped. You can function like that for a while, but eventually you start moving through life like you're wrapped in a hard shell. You show up, you work, you smile, and nothing feels loose or free.

Dad didn't argue. He didn't lecture me about waiting or following instructions. He just reached into the toolbox, pulled out the Dremel, and plugged it in.

When he fired it up, that high-pitched buzz filled the garage. The second he touched it to the cast, I felt the vibration run up my arm. Black dust started flaking off immediately and sprinkling onto the concrete like we were sanding drywall. A few passes, he'd stopped to pry and check, then went back at it again.

He didn't talk much. Neither did I. The sound of the tool said enough.

Then it finally came loose.

Dad pried it open, and the cast split and fell away. Taking it off meant I wasn't stuck anymore. Not held in place by what had happened, or by who I'd been before. The cast had a purpose. It protected what was injured while it healed, but after a while it stops feeling like protection and starts feeling like a cage.

That was my old self in a nutshell. A protective version of me built out of fear, insecurity, and straight survival. Useful at the time. Maybe even necessary. But not who I wanted to be anymore.

Because the truth was, there was a new me under there. Not a perfect one. Not a finished one. Just a version that had actually been through something painful and challenging and didn't surrender. The healing wasn't complete, but the process was real. I could see it. I could feel it.

I'm done being bound up.

I didn't stay with my parents long, two, maybe three months. Long enough to get my feet under me, but I needed my own space. A place that was mine. A place where Cole could feel comfortable.

I found an apartment a few blocks away, still in the same general neighborhood but a little deeper into the rougher area. Two buildings side by side, and one of them had a reputation for crime. It wasn't ideal, but it was cheap.

From the second I moved in, I set up the second bedroom for Cole. I didn't want it to be "a room he could sleep in." I wanted it to feel like his, like he had a permanent place in my life and not just a spot on the couch when it was my weekend.

I shoved my guilt, missing him, and regret into the background as much as I could and focused on the mission in front of me.

Get stable. Get ready. Get him.

I was able to have him for a week or two at a time, and I lived for those stretches. They didn't erase the months I'd been gone, but they helped. Little bricks in a bridge we were still building.

Then Amber came at me with child support.

Before I left for boot camp, I'd actually tried to do the right thing. I set it up so my mom would have access to my bank account and could write the checks every two weeks like clockwork, like I was still there. My military pay went in. The checks went out. Simple. Responsible.

According to Amber, she hadn't been getting everything she was owed. Something wasn't adding up.

I didn't want to be that guy, the deadbeat dad stereotype people whisper about. So I went straight to the courthouse and requested a ledger of every payment that had gone through the state. I wanted to see exactly what had been paid, when, and how much. If there were errors, of course I'd fix them.

When I saw the records, my jaw locked so tight I thought my teeth might crack. Not only had she been getting the correct amount, there were months she'd been getting double.

While my mom was faithfully mailing checks from my personal account, the state had also been automatically garnishing my military pay. Two separate streams of money, same destination. So instead of getting what the court had ordered, she was getting twice that.

The ledger didn't care about stories. It didn't care about tone of voice or hurt feelings or who said what. It was just dates and numbers in a column, and the numbers were clear. She hadn't been shorted. She'd been overpaid.

I didn't have extra money lying around. There wasn't some emergency stash tucked in a drawer. Nothing was magically "showing up" in my account to cover the gap. Every dollar already had an assignment before it even hit my hands. Rent. Food. Gas. Daycare. Whatever Cole needed.

And I wasn't trying to play games or cheat Amber out of anything. I just wanted it to make sense. I wanted it to be fair. That's it. Basic fairness.

So I did what I honestly thought was a reasonable compromise. For the next few months, I'd pay half of what the order said. Not because I was refusing to pay, but because I was trying to balance out the overage. She'd already received more than she was supposed to. In my head, I was just letting the scale tip back the other way, slowly, while still keeping money coming in on a consistent schedule.

For the next five or six months, that's exactly what I did. I made regular, bi-weekly half payments, thinking I was being logical. Responsible. Fair.

Yeah.

I look back at that version of me and shake my head, because I still thought doing the right thing would matter. I thought if you followed the rules, documented everything, kept your hands clean, and tried to be decent, the system would meet you somewhere in the middle.

I'd already started losing that belief the first time I sat in a courtroom and listened to strangers talk about my life like it was a scheduling problem. Apparently I needed the lesson again, in bigger letters, just to make sure it stuck. Because "fair" isn't always part of the equation. Not officially. Not in a way anyone is required to give a damn about.

And underneath all the numbers and payment schedules, there was another truth I didn't want to say out loud yet. It was never just about the money. The money was just the part you could point at. The part you could measure and argue over. The part you could turn into a spreadsheet, a court order, a weapon.

On paper, I was the "every other weekend" dad. Four days a month. That label got stamped on me like it was the whole story.

But real life wasn't doing that anymore. I had Cole most of the time. Sometimes one week. Sometimes two. Sometimes it turned into three or four weeks in a row. No formal transition. Just the reality of my kid being with me, day after day, because that's what was happening.

And it was a twisted kind of gift, because I got to be his everyday parent. The real stuff. Breakfasts. Bath time. Bedtime battles. Tiny shoes by the door. Laundry that never stopped. Tantrums and hugs and the little moments that make you feel like your heart is walking around outside your body.

It was exhausting but I loved it. I lived for it. It was exactly what I wanted, and it was exactly what Cole deserved to have.

But it also meant I was paying for most of his life out of my own pocket. Food, clothes, daycare, keeping a roof over his head when he was with me. And I was still sending full child support to Amber like nothing had changed.

So the paperwork said I was part-time. The reality said I was full-time.

On paper, I was the weekend dad. In real life, I was doing full-time work under a part-time label, and still getting charged full price for the privilege.

When it came to her designated pick-up time to take him back home at the end of my court-ordered weekend, she wouldn't show up. She was living with her mom and stepdad in Manito and I lived in Champaign, almost a two-hour drive. So, to shorten the drive for each of us, we chose a Burger King in Bloomington for the exchange. Neutral ground. Neutral parking lot. Simple, right?

Except it never was.

I'd load Cole into his car seat, pack a diaper bag or his little backpack, and drive to that Burger King like it was some kind of custody checkpoint. I'd park and sit there, watching the door, watching the road, scanning every car that pulled in, every person who walked out.

Sometimes she just never showed. No call. No notice. No, "Hey, I'm running late," or "I can't make it." Just nothing.

I'd sit there with our son, doing my best to keep him entertained while my anger climbed higher and higher. Then eventually I'd back out of the parking space and drive back home.

Other times she'd show up late, roll in like it was no big deal, grab him, and leave like she was picking up dry cleaning.

So I started covering my ass.

When I arrived at the exchange time, I'd go through the drive-thru and order a Coke. That receipt became my proof. Time. Place. Date. Evidence.

Sometimes, when the wait dragged on and I was still sitting there staring at an empty parking lot, I'd order a second one. I always waited a full hour. Receipts documenting the full span.

I wasn't just a dad anymore. I was my own court reporter.

This went on for months.

Sometimes I'd have Cole for two months straight and not hear a word from her. No calls. No "How's he doing?" No "Tell him I love him." Nothing. Just silence.

And during that whole stretch, I'd be doing the work, day in, day out, trying to give him something steady to stand on while the paperwork still labeled me the "every other weekend" dad.

What made it even harder to swallow was I was still paying child support like she was the one doing the daily parenting. Bi-weekly checks, right on time. Still covering child care expenses she wasn't even paying anymore, because Cole wasn't with her.

I was paying for childcare now. I was buying the food, the clothes, the diapers, the random little kid stuff that adds up faster than you can track it.

Meanwhile, the court order didn't care what was actually happening in real life. It cared what was printed on paper.

Then, out of nowhere, the phone would ring.

"Can you meet me at Burger King?"

No apology. No acknowledgment she'd been gone for eight weeks. Like nothing happened. Like I hadn't been the one doing baths and bedtime stories and breakfast and clean clothes and routine. Like I hadn't been scraping together dinners and keeping the lights on and building a stable rhythm for him.

And I always said yes. Not for her. For him.

Because as angry as I was, and I was angry, I didn't want him to feel punished for her choices. I didn't want him thinking, even for a second, that I was the reason he couldn't see his mom. I wanted him to have both parents, or at least the chance at that, even if I was the one carrying the weight in the meantime.

Not to mention, there was still an official court order with a judges signature on it that mandated Amber as the custodial parent. I didn't want to provide any reason, any excuse for the judge to amend the existing order that might negatively affect my time with Cole. So I played it by the book. I didn't have a choice. The courts made sure of that.

So I'd load him up, drive to Burger King, and do the handoff like it was a normal part of the week.

But every yes came with documentation.

Every handoff came with a timestamp. A receipt. A paper trail. I'd learned the hard way that if you didn't keep proof, it didn't happen. If it wasn't documented, it was just my word against hers, and the system loved acting like those two things were equal even when reality was screaming otherwise.

The inconsistency wrecked me. It wasn't just annoying. It wasn't just frustrating. It was terrifying.

Because I had no idea what I was sending him back into when she did decide to show up. I didn't know what kind of mood she'd be in. What kind of environment he was walking into. Whether there'd be food in the fridge. Whether anyone was sober. Whether there'd be a routine. Whether he'd be safe.

There was no structure. No stability. Just turmoil, mood swings, and attitude.

On paper, it was "shared custody." In real life, it felt like I was handing my son back into a storm and hoping he didn't get swallowed by it.

Eventually the whole mess exploded into a new wave of court dates. And court wasn't some clean process where you show up, tell the truth, and the obvious solution wins. It was delay after delay after delay.

She'd miss hearings, then reschedule, then show up with some half-baked excuse that pushed things out again.

Every continuance meant another bill from my attorney. Another day off work. Another explanation I had to give. Another knot tightening in my stomach while everyone else treated it like a scheduling conflict.

My focus never changed.

But this time around, I wanted sole custody. Not to punish her. Not to "win." I wasn't trying to rack up points or make her suffer. I wanted structure. I wanted consistency. I wanted Cole to have an actual home base.

One place where he knew what to expect. Where bedtime happened at bedtime. Where meals were meals. Where adults acted like adults. Where he didn't have to brace for the next mood swing or disappearance.

And if the roles had to flip, fine. Give her the every-other-weekend setup I'd been stuck with, while I did everything in real life. Let her show up consistently and prove she could handle it if she wanted more time.

I had the steady job. The stable home. The clean record. She had a domestic violence and child endangerment arrest and a track record of vanishing the second responsibility showed up.

In my head, it was a no-brainer. It felt like the kind of thing the court should solve in one hearing with one look at the facts. But in the court's head, it was still a multiple-choice question. Like there were a bunch of "valid perspectives" and we just needed to keep talking about it until everyone felt comfortable.

For a year and a half, it dragged on like that. She missed one court date, then another, then a third.

Every time, I walked in with this stupid little flicker of hope that maybe this would finally be the day we got clarity. Some decision. Some direction. Something that resembled justice.

And every time, it got punted further down the road.

Meanwhile, my parents' bank account was bleeding right alongside mine. Attorney fees, missed work, rescheduling, driving, filing. Death by a thousand bank withdrawals.

And my patience went with it. Drained out slowly while the system moved at its own pace, like this wasn't a kid's life hanging in the balance.

On the day that finally mattered, she didn't show up. Again.

But this time, her attorney didn't show either. No last-minute phone call. No frantic excuse. No "running late." Just two empty chairs on her side of the courtroom that said more than any story she could've cooked up.

My attorney and I walked up when the case was called, and the courtroom felt too bright and too quiet. The kind of quiet that makes you hyper-aware of everything. Your shoes on the floor. Papers shifting. Tiny sounds that shouldn't matter but suddenly do. The judge looked over at the empty side, then back at us like he was already annoyed before anyone spoke.

"Counselor, have you heard from the respondent or her attorney?"

"No, Your Honor."

The judge let out this long, irritated sigh, like he'd seen this exact thing a hundred times and he was done wasting court time on people who couldn't be bothered to show up for their own case.

"If she does not appear today, the case will default in favor of the petitioner."

My heart started pounding so hard I could feel it everywhere. Chest. Throat. Even my teeth. I stood there staring straight ahead, trying to look calm while internally I was pleading with God, *please let her stay gone this one last time.*

After all the times she'd popped up at the last second just to derail things and drag it out, it almost didn't feel real watching the minutes pass with that chair still empty. The longer it stayed that way, the more my brain kept waiting for the other shoe to drop. For some sudden entrance. Some excuse. Some reset button.

The judge called the case. Nothing from her side. Just me, my attorney, and that empty chair where a mother was supposed to be.

And then it happened fast. No speech. No drawn-out back and forth. Just a few sentences. The judge granted me 100% sole custody of Cole. She got visitation. She was ordered to pay child support, twenty percent of her wages, per state law.

On a court docket, it was legal wording and percentages. In my body, it felt like something unclenched that had been locked tight for a long time.

I didn't react the way you think you would. There wasn't some movie moment where I broke down crying in the middle of the courtroom. I think I just stood there trying to process the fact that I'd finally heard the words I'd been chasing for over two years.

My attorney was talking. The judge was already moving on. People were shifting around like it was just another case on the docket.

And I was standing there thinking, *wait... is this real? Is this actually over?*

For the first time in my life, I walked out of a courtroom feeling like the system saw me. It saw me as what I already knew I was: the parent who showed up, the one who stayed consistent, the one who did the unglamorous work when nobody was clapping.

And "showed up" wasn't a metaphor. It was literal.

I didn't have my son in that temporary, borrowed way anymore. Not "until she feels like coming back." Not "as long as nothing changes." Not with a legal label hanging over my head that could get yanked back whenever someone decided to make things difficult. There was no more "every other weekend" stamped on my forehead while my real life said something else.

He was home. My home. Our home. For real. For good.

I know from the outside it probably sounds like a standard custody story. Dad fights. Dad wins. Paperwork. End scene. But underneath all the legal language, the thick folders, and the months of stress, it changed how I saw myself. It proved I could take a hit, get dragged through something messy, and still come out standing if I stayed focused on what really mattered and didn't quit.

It told me: you fought for him. You didn't give up. You didn't get scared off. You didn't let the delays, the games, the money drain, or the exhaustion talk you into giving up.

Driving home with the custody papers sitting in the passenger seat felt unreal. I kept glancing over at them at stoplights like they might vanish if I looked away too long. It was just a stack of paper. It didn't look like much, but it held every late-night spiral, every sick feeling in my stomach, every time I stared at the ceiling wondering how long this would take and how much more it was going to cost, and every prayer I muttered under my breath when nobody was around.

And for the first time in a long time, doubt wasn't driving the car anymore.

I was.

And it wasn't just that I had my son. It was that, for the first time, I could feel that everyone else believed I deserved to have him. Not just hoped.

Not just crossed their fingers. They knew. The story finally got corrected in the one place that had been holding it hostage.

That's what got to me.

Because I'd spent so long feeling like I had to prove myself. Prove I wasn't the stereotype. Prove I wasn't the "young dad who couldn't get it together." Prove I was stable. Prove I was safe. Prove I was consistent. I'd been doing the work the whole time, but it's different when the people who love you most look at you and you can tell they're proud.

My brain flashed back to the garage and the Dremel tool. Dad standing there like it was just another Saturday project, cutting off my cast when I got home from MOS school. Back then it was simple. I was sick of the sweating and itching and feeling trapped in that hard shell, so we cut it off. Practical. Necessary. Overdue.

Sitting my car, driving to my parents house to share the news and pick my son back up, I saw it differently. That moment in the garage wasn't just about getting free of a cast. It was about taking off something that was technically "protecting" me, but also keeping me locked in place.

Back then it was fiberglass.

This time it was everything else. The label. The helplessness. The constant feeling that my life was being decided by people who didn't live it. For the first time, I wasn't just surviving the situation anymore.

I did the same thing with other areas of my life too. I cut off dead weight. I hacked away at the parts that were keeping me stuck: this role I'd been shoved into, this version of me that was always reacting, always defending, always bracing for the next hit.

Leaving that roach-infested apartment was another one of those Dremel moments for me.

That place was a nightmare. I'm a clean freak by nature. I don't just clean, I sanitize. Bleach once a week. Vacuum lines in the carpet. Counters wiped down. Floors done. Everything has a place. So living with roaches didn't just gross me out. It made me feel like I was trapped inside someone else's filth and paying rent for the privilege.

And it hit even harder because I had a toddler in the house. A kid who crawls, puts his hands on everything, drops snacks, picks them back up. The idea of bugs getting into his world, his toys, his blankets, his little bare feet on the floor, made my skin crawl. I was always on edge. Always checking corners and cabinets.

I tried everything you're supposed to try. I complained to the office. I called. I emailed. I let the exterminators in every time they scheduled it, even when it meant rearranging my day. I set off indoor foggers so often it started to feel like part of my daily routine, like taking out the trash. I'd bomb the place in the morning on my way out, come home, air it out, wipe everything down, and still, a few days later, there they were again.

No matter what I did, they kept coming.

At first, I told myself, *okay, we can manage this. It's disgusting, but we can stay on top of it.*

Then I realized you can't "stay on top" of an infestation when the source isn't even inside your unit. You're fighting what's living in the walls, in the building itself. You're cleaning your own space while the problem is baked into the place.

The breaking point came on a random afternoon.

I'd set off another fogger that morning, same as I'd done a dozen times before. I came home from work expecting the usual. Maybe a couple dead ones here and there. Then the clean-up. Then back to pretending we weren't living in a problem.

Instead, I walked in and froze.

The floor looked like a horror movie. Dead roaches everywhere. Not one or two. Dozens. Little bodies scattered across the floor like it had rained them while I was on my lunch break.

And the first thing that hit me wasn't even disgust. It was this sick thought: *if this is what's out in the open, what's still hiding?*

I didn't even think. I grabbed a big Subway cup, the kind you get with a fountain drink, and started scooping them up off the floor like I was picking up spilled ice. One by one, then faster, because once you start you can't stop.

By the time I was done, the cup was full. More than fifty dead roaches.

Fifty. In my home.

I remember standing there holding the cup thinking, *there's no way this is all of them. If I can collect that many in one afternoon, how many are still alive in the walls? How many are in the cabinets? How many walked across my son's toys?*

That was it. I marched straight down to the office, cup in hand. I didn't call first. I didn't knock politely. I walked in, went right up to the counter, and without saying a word, dumped the entire cup of dead roaches onto their desk.

They screamed. Full-on screamed. Jumped back. One of them started swatting at the desk like the roaches were still alive. Someone else yelled at me to get out.

Good.

Because now they knew what it felt like. Not for one second as a gross surprise on a countertop, but as a constant reality you're expected to tolerate. Something you're supposed to just live with like it's normal. Like it's acceptable.

In their office, the roaches were dead on a desk.

In my apartment, the roaches were alive in my son's room. In his toys. On his floors. In the place where he was supposed to be safe.

Once that landed, there was no "working with them" anymore. No "let's see what happens after the next treatment." There was only one answer left.

We were leaving.

I started looking for a new place immediately and found a small house on Garfield Avenue. Clean, older neighborhood. Big trees. Actual charm. I broke my lease at the apartment two months early and didn't lose a minute of sleep over it. I had documented everything. After years of court fights, I was damn good at documentation. The apartment complex never said a word.

The house on Garfield was perfect for us. Not fancy, not big, but ours. Safe and cozy. The kind of place that didn't impress anybody driving by, but felt right the second you stepped inside.

You walked into this big, simple living room first. It had that lived-in feel right away, like a room made for weekends and cartoons and half-folded laundry that never quite made it to the drawers. Nothing matched perfectly, and it didn't need to. It was the first space you hit when you came in, and it just felt cozy and lived in.

Off to the right, an arched doorway opened into a little dining room. I shoved the table up by the window so we could eat with sunlight coming in, even on days when everything else felt kind of gray. On the opposite wall, I wedged my computer desk in between a wall and a doorway that led to my bedroom, so the whole middle of the house felt connected. Living room, dining room, then straight into the parts of life nobody sees.

Right inside my bedroom door, the bathroom sat off to the right. Tight, basic, but right there. In the far corner was this big walk-in closet that I turned into Cole's bedroom.

That closet-bedroom still makes me smile.

It wasn't some Instagram-worthy themed nursery with hand-painted murals and custom furniture. It was a glorified closet with a toddler-sized bed, a dresser, a TV, his game system, and toys stacked wherever they'd fit. It was cramped and practical and a little ridiculous, but it worked. It was a tiny world carved out just for him, right off his dad's room. Practical, close, safe. I loved that setup more than any designer bedroom I've had since.

The only weird part was anyone who needed the bathroom had to walk through a corner of my bedroom first. A little awkward. But I wasn't hosting cocktail hours and formal dinners. Our social calendar was basically Cole, me, and whatever was on TV.

If you kept walking straight past the dining room, you hit the kitchen. It was a narrow little galley with the sink under a window on the right and the stove and fridge lined up on the left. You could stand in the middle and reach everything without moving your feet. Counter space was limited, and the cabinets were nothing special, but they held what we had. We didn't own many dishes, and I couldn't afford to stockpile food like some doomsday prepper anyway.

That kitchen saw a lot of boxed dinners, grilled cheese, and late-night cereal, and somehow it was always enough.

Off the back of the kitchen, a short set of stairs went down about five steps to the back door. Another five took you into the basement. The front half of the basement had two small rooms, probably meant for storage, with low ceilings. They felt like little chopped-up spaces where you had to duck your head to avoid a forehead bruise from a cast iron pipe hanging too low.

The back half was straight out of a low-budget horror movie. Old coal furnace from the 1940s, dirt floor, cobwebs. We didn't go back there much. I'm pretty sure even the spiders had boundaries.

A few years later, I turned those two rooms in the basement into bedrooms. It was makeshift and patched-together, but that's kind of how that whole season of life felt. Resourceful.

That gave me the chance to reclaim my old bedroom upstairs and turn it into something I'd never had before. A man cave.

I bought a small pool table from Walmart and somehow wedged it into the room like I was solving a life-size Tetris puzzle. The walk-in closet that used to be Cole's bedroom became my office. Not some mahogany-paneled, leather-chair situation. Just a simple desk in a converted closet with enough space for a computer and additional storage.

Most nights, after Cole was in bed and the house got quiet, I'd sit at that desk and disappear into early-2000s chat rooms, talking to strangers on a glowing screen. Not because I was trying to be mysterious or cool, but because I was a single dad home every night, and there wasn't exactly a line of social invitations forming at my front door.

In retrospect, that little house on Garfield was more than a rental with weird closets and a creepy basement. It was the first place where it felt like I was actually building a life with my son, even if that life was stitched together with Walmart furniture, hand-me-down dishes, and late-night conversations with people I'd never meet in person. And somehow, in that specific time of our lives, it was perfect for us.

It would be three long years before we heard from Amber again.

Not even her sister, who I stayed in touch with the whole time, knew where she was. No one did. It was like she fell off the face of the earth. No Christmas cards or birthday cards, no calls, no legal challenges. Just silence.

For three years, it was just me and Cole. In that quiet, something settled in me. The constant crisis mode eased up, and what replaced it was routine.

Every night, we had our ritual. It started back in the triplex apartment before I left for boot camp. I'd run his bath and sit there on the floor, watching him turn the tub into his own personal ocean. Water everywhere, toys crashing into each other, that high-pitched giggle that made the bathroom feel like the best place on earth. He was noisy, messy, and absolutely completely happy.

When he was done, I'd pull the plug, scoop him up, and wrap him in a towel, holding him against my chest for just a second longer than I needed to. Long enough to breathe him in. That warm, clean, just-bathed baby smell that should honestly be sold as a candle.

Then I'd lay him down on a soft blanket in the living room. Fresh diaper, clean skin, damp hair sticking up in little spikes. I'd stretch out beside him and run my fingertips gently up and down his back, barely any pressure, just a whisper of touch. It wasn't about some perfect bedtime routine from a parenting book. It was connection. Me saying, without words, *you're safe. You're loved. I'm here.*

Within ten or fifteen minutes, his breathing would slow. His little body would get heavier against the blanket, muscles unwinding one by one. Sometimes he'd fall asleep right there, pacifier hanging on for dear life. Other times he'd just go quiet, eyes half open, staring at me, completely at peace.

Those nights are burned into me. Just me, my son, a blanket on the floor, and this stupid amount of love I didn't know where to put.

As he got older, the routine may have changed a bit, but we still had one. By the time we moved into the Garfield house, Cole was three years old. Still my baby boy, but blanket time on the floor after a bath was replaced with a father-son dance in the living room. The living room was nothing special. Old hardwood floors, a bargain-bin entertainment center from Walmart, a basic stereo that had seen better days. But in those moments, it might as well have been a ballroom. It was our world.

I'd pop in a CD and skip straight to one song: "I Knew I Loved You (Before I Met You)" by Savage Garden. Cheesy? Absolutely. True? Even more absolutely.

Every time that opening played, it hit the same place in my chest. *I knew I loved you before I met you.* It felt like somebody had reached into my soul and turned it into a song.

I didn't know it back then, but I'd been carrying the shape of him around inside me for a long time. I just didn't know his name yet.

> *"... in your eyes, I see my future in an instant*
> *And there it goes, I think I've found my best friend...*
>
> *I knew I loved you before I met you*
> *I think I dreamed you into life..."*

I'd hold him against my chest, his head tucked into that perfect little corner of my neck, his tiny hands squished between us, and we'd sway. Slow, gentle rocking in the glow of a cheap lamp and a life I was trying my best not to screw up.

Sometimes we'd replay that song three, four, five times in a row. My arms would start to ache, my lower back would get tight, but I'd keep swaying. Every once in a while, he'd shift just a little, this tiny adjustment like he was telling me, *don't stop yet.*

So I didn't.

I know he won't remember those nights. Not the way I do. He won't remember the way his cheek felt against my neck, or how our reflection was displayed on the TV screen while we danced. But those nights are in him somewhere. Maybe not as a memory, but maybe as a feeling of safety. Warmth. Being wanted. Being chosen.

He may not remember. But I do. And I always will.

I remember all of it. The court battles. The roaches. The little house on Garfield. The bath-time back tracing. The slow dances before bed when the day finally turned down and it was just me and him.

On the surface, it probably looked like a guy trying to keep his head above water. Paying what I could. Dodging what I couldn't. Laying roach traps. Wiping counters. Folding tiny shirts. Nothing glamorous. Nothing you'd turn into a movie. Just the kind of life people walk past every day without realizing what it costs to keep standing.

But underneath all of that, something bigger was happening. I was becoming the father he needed. That's all it really was. Not just survival. It was a quiet, messy change happening in real time. Me learning how to show up for a little boy the way I always wished someone would show up for me. Not with big speeches or perfect moments, but with consistency and dependable routines.

You can't always control what shows up at your door. Judges. Roaches. Exes. Overdue notices. Knees that won't cooperate. Life doesn't ask permission before it drops something big in your lap and expects you to deal with it.

But you can control what you build inside your own walls.

You can decide you're done being walked on. You can stand up even when your legs are shaking. You can pack up and leave. You can start over in a place that isn't fancy but is safe and clean and yours. You can make your home stable even when the rest of your life is chaos. You can give your kid predictability with you, even if everything outside your front door stays unpredictable.

You can love your kid out loud, on purpose, every day. Not just when you feel strong. Not just when you have energy. Even when you're running on fumes. Even when it feels like life is closing in. Even when you're holding on by your fingernails and doing everything you can to not let him see it.

Life will hit you with things that feel completely unfair. You don't always get a vote in that. But you do get a say in what kind of person it creates.

I became a man who didn't just tell his son I'd be there. I became a man who actually was.

When he turned four, I enrolled him in preschool through the childcare program at my old high school, Central. No daycare bill. Just a structured place where he could burn off energy, learn how to share, and start figuring out how to be a tiny human around other tiny humans.

Walking back into that building as a dad was surreal. I used to drift through those halls as an uncertain, pissed-off teenager, hiding behind sarcasm. Now I was walking through them with a small backpack slung over one shoulder and a little hand wrapped around my fingers. Full-circle doesn't really cover it.

Every afternoon when I picked him up, his teachers had something good to say.

"He's so helpful."
"He's great with the other kids."
"He's such a little charmer."

It was like they were reading off a script I'd secretly hoped for but never dared to write.

By the end of the semester, they handed out fun little awards. Cole's?

"Little Romeo."

Of course it was. Those crystal blue eyes, those dimples, he had the teachers and the little girls wrapped around his tiny finger without even trying. I laughed when they told me, shrugged like, *yeah, that sounds about right,* but inside there was this quiet pride that hit me right in the chest.

He'd already been through so much, even if he had no clue. Court dates. Custody fights. Adults making decisions about his life in rooms he'd never see. And there he was, helpful, sweet, charming, and just... happy.

To see him not just getting by, but thriving? That was everything. That was the payoff for every sleepless night and every "am I screwing this up?" mess in my head.

The next semester was more of the same. Helpful. Kind. A tiny flirt. Every time I picked him up, I dragged my feet a little, stayed to talk with the teachers, watched him from the doorway as he cleaned up toys or hugged a friend goodbye.

Half of me was making small talk. The other half was just soaking it in. Watching him exist in a world I'd fought like hell to make steady for him.

For the first time in years, life didn't feel like one long emergency.

It felt steady. Not exciting. Not flashy. Just steady. And honestly, that felt like winning the lottery.

When preschool ended, he started kindergarten at Barkstall Elementary, a newer, shinier school on the better side of town. Upper-middle-class families. Polished hallways, fresh paint, a clean playground, nice cars in the pickup line. I remember looking around and thinking, *Good. Let him grow up around this. Let him see stability and structure.*

Barkstall required uniforms. Khaki pants or shorts and red, white, or blue polos. For a kid who seemed to grow a full size every three days, keeping him in clothes that actually fit was a financial juggling act. My parents helped, like they always did, and somehow we made it work.

And every time I saw him lined up with the other kids in his little uniform, shirt tucked in crooked, backpack hanging low, eyes bright, it made every dollar, every sacrifice, every compromise completely worth it.

We had finally landed in a life that felt calm.

Predictable.

Safe.

ROUND 22:
Good Intentions. Bad Moments.

There are a lot of memories from those early years that are warm and fuzzy in the way people mean when they talk about "the good stuff." Bath time mohawks. Slow dancing to Savage Garden in the living room. Wandering the mall with no real plan except to stay busy and maybe grab a pretzel. Those are the ones I pull out when I'm trying to reassure myself that, even in the middle of everything, I did okay as a dad.

And then there's this one.

My stomach still drops when it flashes across my mind. It isn't sweet. It isn't funny. It isn't "parenting is hard but beautiful." It's ugly. Really ugly. It's the kind of memory that makes you admit having a kid doesn't magically turn you into a patient person, or a mature person, or even a safe person in every moment. Sometimes it just exposes whatever you still haven't learned to control.

It happened at my best friend, and part-time roommate, Hailey's aunt's house. She had a swimming pool, and in the middle of a sticky Illinois summer that pool felt like the best thing on earth. That place became our little escape.

Cole was four or five then and the second we pulled into that driveway his whole mood would glow. He loved the water. He loved the excitement of it. He loved that it felt like a special day.

We'd go a couple times a month when it was warm. Hours in the pool. Splashing. Laughing. Me doing my best impression of a swim instructor with zero credentials. Just a dad trying to keep his kid afloat and help him learn. We worked on basics. Floating. Kicking. Putting his face in the water without panicking. Learning how to trust himself and how to trust me.

Every summer it played out the same way. Early on it was a lot of coaching and repetition. By August, you could see the progress. His arms would move with something that almost looked like rhythm. His legs would cooperate for more than a few seconds. His confidence would start to show up. I'd think, *maybe this is the year it really clicks.*

Then summer would end and the cooler months would erase half of what he learned. Next year we'd be right back at square one. "Blow your bubbles, buddy." "Kick-kick-kick." It became this seasonal loop we just accepted.

The part that haunts me doesn't happen in the pool.

It happens in the car.

We had to leave to go home, and Cole went into a full meltdown. Not normal whining. Not a slow pout. This was full-body heartbreak. Red face, shoulders shaking, hysterical sobbing. The kind of crying that doesn't stop because a kid can't stop it. It's not manipulation. It's grief at a level that only makes sense to someone who's five.

I wrestled him into his car seat. We were both wet, tired, sunburned, and running on fumes. I clicked the last buckle, checked it like I always did, and started driving. Hailey's aunt lived way out in the country, the kind of area where the road cuts through cornfields and you can go a long time without passing a house. No traffic. No people. Just open road and farmland.

We'd only been driving a few minutes, but his crying never let up. It stayed at this steady, piercing level that got under my skin. Between the noise, the heat, and my nerves being completely shot, I snapped.

I slammed on the brakes.

The car jerked. The seat belt locked across my chest. Dust kicked up behind us. I got out, went around, unbuckled him, and pulled him out of the car. He was tiny. Trembling. Hair still damp. Cheeks streaked with tears.

And then I did something I hate admitting, even now.

I set him down behind the car on that empty country road.

This little boy in swim trunks and sandals, standing there in the middle of nowhere, looking up at his dad. His dad, who was yelling at him.

"If you're going to keep crying like that," I said, loud and sharp, "then you can stay here and do it by yourself, because I am not listening to it anymore."

Then I got back in the car.

And I started to drive away.

Even writing that makes my throat hurt, because I can still feel the moment right after. The sudden silence. No more screaming. No more sobbing. Just the hum of the engine and my own breathing, too loud in the car. For a split second my brain tried to stay in the anger. Tried to justify it as discipline, as teaching him a lesson.

Then I looked in the rearview mirror.

There he was, exactly where I left him. Just standing on that long stretch of road, arms hanging at his sides, chest still heaving, watching my car move away from him.

That image cut straight through me.

What are you doing?
Who are you right now?

Ashamed, I hit the brakes again. I eased the car into reverse and backed up toward him. It couldn't have been far, fifty, sixty feet, but in my head it felt endless. Because in that short distance I had become the kind of father I never wanted to be, and I knew it.

He was exactly where I'd left him.

Still crying. Still alone.

I parked and got out. I tried to keep my face stern, because even in that moment some part of me was still clinging to this tired, misguided idea that I was "handling it." Like I could pretend it was a parenting tactic instead of what it really was. Me losing control and scaring my kid.

"Are you done crying so we can go home?" I asked, forcing my voice into something calmer.

He sniffed hard and tried to pull himself together the way only little kids do. That shaky, hiccupy breathing while they nod because they want the scary part to stop. We walked toward each other slowly. He didn't run. I didn't rush. We both moved like we weren't sure what the other person was going to do.

Then I picked him up.

And that's the part that makes me feel sick, too, because he came to me. He held onto me. He accepted me back. Like his little heart didn't even hesitate to forgive what he didn't deserve in the first place.

I buckled him back into his seat gently, checked the straps twice, got behind the wheel, and drove the rest of the way home in complete silence.

No music. No talking. Just me sitting in the consequences of what I'd done while my son sat behind me, quiet and small, still sniffling.

That moment still haunts me. Every. Single. Day. It sits there as a reminder that I'm capable of failing him if I'm not careful. It keeps me accountable, even years later, because I don't ever want to be that guy again.

Years later, when he was older and we could talk like actual people, I brought it up. I braced myself for it. I expected anger. Hurt. Distance. I expected him to confirm what I'd believed for years, that I carved something into him on that road and he carried it with him.

He looked at me. Blank. He didn't remember it at all.

I'm grateful for that in a way I can't fully explain, because I don't think I could live with myself if I knew he carried that moment the way I do. But I remember. I remember everything. The color of the sky, the heat in the air, the way the tires chirped when I hit the brakes, the way my stomach dropped when I saw him in the mirror.

It felt like the kind of thing that could break a kid. Make him feel abandoned. Disposable. Like love is conditional and can disappear the second you're "too much."

And I was the one who did it.

That's a heavy thing to live with. And I deserve the weight of it, because he deserved better than that version of me.

And that wasn't the only moment I wish I could erase.

When he was a baby, before words, before explanations, before he could point at something and grunt his way through what he wanted, there were nights when the crying just never stopped.

This was just after Amber and I split. Maybe a week or two after that tense night at Monicals Pizza. Just me and him in that quiet little place. I can still see it if I close my eyes. The dim lamp in the corner, the cheap rug, the squeak of the bedroom floor, the way his crib looked too big.

He was nine or ten months old. All cheeks and soft hair and those big, trusting eyes that hadn't learned yet that adults are a little bit of a mess.

No fever. No dirty diaper. No obvious reason I could point to. Just this raw, desperate, nonstop crying that came from somewhere way down in his tiny chest. The kind of cry that makes you feel helpless and trapped, especially when you're alone with it and you've already been running on empty for days.

I did all the usual things. I checked his diaper. Tried a bottle. Rocked him. Sang off-key lullabies I barely remembered the words to. Paced the floor in circles until my back hurt. Stood there bouncing him on my shoulder like maybe if I moved enough, his little nervous system would finally settle down.

Nothing worked.

The minutes dragged. An hour. Then another. Then another.

And I hit a breaking point.

At some point you stop feeling like a parent and start feeling like a cornered animal. You don't think in full sentences anymore. Your brain gets loud. Your chest gets tight. Your patience runs out and then keeps going into something darker. Panic. Anger. This weird fear that you're failing and you can't stop it.

I laid him in his crib and leaned over the rail, just staring at him for a second. My head felt too full, like there wasn't room for one more sound. My chest actually hurt. I could feel my heartbeat in my throat, pounding like my body was trying to climb out of itself.

Then I grabbed the side of the crib and shook it.

Not violently, not like I was trying to hurt him, but hard enough to rattle it. Hard enough to make the whole thing shudder. Hard enough that even as I was doing it, some part of me knew I was losing control.

"What do you want?!" I yelled.

At a baby.

A literal baby who had no words. No way to answer. No way to tell me, *I'm scared*, or *I'm lonely*, or *my stomach hurts*, or *the world is too big and I don't know how to exist in it without you.*

He didn't have language. He had one tool. Cry until somebody helps.

He didn't calm down. Of course he didn't. It scared him. His eyes went wide, the crying shot up another octave, and suddenly everything got louder and worse. My anger bounced off the walls and echoed back at me in that tiny room.

And I knew I'd crossed a line there, too.

Maybe not as dramatic as the day on that country road years later, but it was the start of a pattern. A weakness. A broken part of me showing up when I felt too overwhelmed.

That's what makes it hard to admit, because I wasn't some monster lurking in the dark. I wasn't abusive in the way people picture when they hear stories like this. I wasn't hitting him. I wasn't throwing him. I wasn't leaving bruises. I wasn't trying to hurt my child.

But I was out of control in a way that should scare any parent. And it scared me.

Because it wasn't about whether I meant to hurt him. It was about the fact that in that moment, I couldn't handle myself, and he was the one trapped in the room with me.

I was overwhelmed. Exhausted. Alone. And none of that excuses a damn thing. Because good intentions do not erase impact.

Looking back, I can see it clearly now. That moment in the crib didn't just scare him. It exposed something in me. It was one of the first times I learned you can shatter your own heart while you're trying to "parent" your way through someone else's emotions.

When I replay that country road in my head, I told myself I was teaching him something. About behavior. About "using his words." About consequences. All the stuff adults say to make it sound like they're being intentional and wise, when really they're just overwhelmed and losing their grip. I dressed it up as discipline because that felt better than admitting the truth. I was drowning, and I took it out on the smallest person in the room.

What I really learned was simpler and uglier.

If you don't deal with your own pain, it leaks all over the people you love most. Especially the small ones. The trusting ones. The ones who think you hung the moon and have no clue you're barely keeping the lights on.

That day on the road became a clear before-and-after line in my life as a dad, but the crib was the prequel. The warning. The early signal I didn't want to fully see yet. The whisper before the shout.

Before, I thought my job was control. To be obeyed. To "handle" tantrums. To prove I was in charge and he needed to fall in line. I thought if I kept the lid on tightly enough, everything would stay contained.

After, I started to understand that my real job was to be his safe place. To be the one person in the world who didn't blow up or disappear when his emotions got too big.

Kids don't come into this world knowing how to regulate themselves. They borrow calm from us until they learn how to make their own. They learn what to do with fear and sadness and frustration by watching what we do with ours.

And on those nights, in that small house, standing over that crib with my hands still shaking, I was not someone worth copying.

The crib moment. The road moment. And all the smaller ones in between, and those that would come later. The times my frustration came down harder than my patience, when my tone cut deeper than I meant it to, when my need for quiet mattered more than his need for comfort. It all kept pointing to the same truth, and it's not a fun truth to sit with.

Love isn't enough if you weaponize it with your temper.

You can mean well and still do damage. You can give everything you have and still make it worse. You can be trying your best and still be the one who hurts someone. That's the part nobody wants to say out loud, because it doesn't fit the "good dad" story. But it's true.

I've carried that guilt for years. Some days it's heavy and loud, sitting right on my chest. Other days it fades into the background, more like an ache than a punch. But it's always there. Like a shadow that follows me into quiet moments, reminding me not to forget what I'm capable of when I stop paying attention.

And as much as I hate admitting it, I've started to see that guilt as necessary. Not because what I did was okay, because it wasn't, and it never will be. The regret turned into a boundary. It became a line I refuse to cross again. It became an alarm I can feel now before I go too far.

Lower your voice.
Take a breath.
Put him down safely and step back.
Don't walk away to punish.
Don't weaponize their trust.

Your kid doesn't need a perfect parent.

They need a safe one. A present one. A human one who's willing to admit, *I messed up*, and then actually show up better next time. Not with big promises. But with different behavior. With restraint.

These days, when I dream about Cole, he's always somewhere between five and eight. That age range plays on repeat in my head like a looped home video. I've thought a lot about why. Part of me thinks that's the version of us my brain decided to freeze-frame. The sweet spot between tiny and grown. Old enough to talk and joke and have opinions. Young enough to still want to hold my hand.

Maybe it's because that's when things felt the most normal. Before life layered on more complications. Before distance. Before the kind of pain you can't fix with a bedtime story and a kiss on the forehead.

Some of my favorite memories live in that five-to-eight space. A lot of them take place at the mall.

On days when the weather was too miserable for the park, too cold, too wet, too "absolutely not today," we went to the mall. That was our spot. Our default adventure. Our little ritual.

It wasn't some big, glossy, high-end place. Just a regular four-wing, middle-America mall. We always parked by the food court, and the second we walked through those glass doors, we'd get hit with that familiar wall of smell. Grease, sugar, pretzels, popcorn, and the faint sound of carousel music floating through the air.

Painted horses frozen mid-gallop. Kids shrieking. Parents standing off to the side with that "I love you but I'm so tired" look on their faces.

We always ate first. Chinese or Subway, usually. Nothing fancy. Just two trays at a plastic table that rocked a little if you leaned on it wrong. We'd share bites back and forth, trade a piece of chicken for a chip, laugh when he'd get sauce on his cheek. It wasn't a big moment to anyone else, but to me, it was everything. Just me and my boy, tucked into our own little corner of the world.

Then we'd walk the mall.

Just "looking around." But we both knew we were headed to the kids' play area in the west wing. That was always the finish line. Still, we took our time getting there. Window-shopping. Pointing at random displays. Touching things we had no intention of buying. Letting the afternoon stretch out a little longer because neither of us was in a hurry to go home.

When we finally made it to the play area, he did the same thing every single time.

The place was bright and padded, the kind of setup where everything looked like it was made out of oversized foam. The sounds of kids laughing and squealing bounced off every surface. He'd stop right at the edge and hover there for a minute. Tiny jeans. Long-sleeve shirt. Hands fidgeting at his sides. Taking in all the other kids.

You could see it on his face. He wanted in so badly, but he wasn't quite sure how to jump.

It took everything in me not to reach down, give him a little push forward, and do it for him. Not to walk over and play social coordinator. "This is Cole. He's awesome. Let him in." But I knew he needed to figure that part out on his own. As much as it made my chest ache, I had to let him stand there on the fringe for a minute.

Almost every time, like clockwork, some kid would wander over and ask, "Do you wanna play?"

And just like that, he'd light up.

Those blue eyes, those dimples, his secret weapons. His whole face would open, the nervousness would melt, and off he'd go. Running. Climbing. Sliding. Laughing like he'd never been unsure at all.

But that's not the part that really got me.

What got me was what happened a little later. After he'd warmed up. After he'd found his footing.

Before long, he was the kid walking toward someone else standing on the edge. He was the one going up to the quiet kid, the one hanging back with their hands in their sleeves, and asking if they wanted to play. He was the one making room. Reaching out. Pulling someone out of their own little corner.

That meant something to me in a way I'm not sure he'll ever fully understand.

I didn't see him much during the day back then. He spent most of his weekdays at my mom's daycare while I was at work. I missed a lot of small moments. A lot of in-between time. So these mall trips were more than just a way to burn off energy indoors. They were my front-row seat to who he was becoming.

And what I saw was this.

He was kind.
He was gentle.
He was thoughtful.

He noticed the one kid standing alone and decided that wasn't okay. He didn't leave them there. He stepped toward them.

Those afternoons in that little mall are some of my favorite memories. Because every time I watched him run back to me, cheeks flushed, eyes bright, talking over himself to tell me what happened, I'd get this quiet, stubborn hope in my chest.

Okay, I'd think. *Maybe I'm not screwing this up completely.*

I loved that kid with everything I had. And somehow, despite all my flaws, that love was showing up in him.

But around that same age, maybe five, we had one of the hardest conversations of my life. The kind you don't forget, no matter how many years fall into the rearview.

By then, Amber had been gone for a while. Not the kind of gone where someone's "just busy" or "going through a lot." Gone-gone. No calls. No visits. Nothing. Not her parents. Not even Taylor, who I'd somehow stayed close with after the divorce, knew anything about her whereabouts. It was like she'd stepped off the planet and never bothered to leave a forwarding address.

That night, our routine was the same as always. Bath. Pajamas. Storytime. Sometimes it was The Three Little Pigs, sometimes one of those kids' Bible stories with the big-eyed cartoons and "moral of the story" endings. I'm not big on organized religion, but I believe in God, and I wanted him to grow up with the option to decide what he believed, not just inherit my confusion. So we read those stories, night after night, like any other dad and son trying to wind down after a long day.

I finished the story, snapped the book shut, and reached over to flip off the light.

"Goodnight, buddy," I said.

He sat up.

"Daddy?"

Something in his voice made my hand stop on the switch. It wasn't just a kid trying to stall bedtime. It had weight to it. I turned around and looked at him.

And then he asked it.

"Daddy… why doesn't Mommy want to see me? Why doesn't she want to spend time with me?"

There are questions that don't just hurt your feelings. They take the air right out of you, like that one did. I went numb, hand resting on the light switch like my brain needed something to hold onto so I didn't tip over. My stomach dropped. And my mind did that thing where it starts sprinting in five directions at once, trying to find an answer that won't hurt the person asking.

How do you answer that?

I could've gone with the raw version. The one that lived in the back of my throat for years.

I don't know where she is. I don't know if she's okay. She walked away. She chose herself over you. You deserve better than this.

Parts of that felt true. Parts of that probably were true. And some of it was just my anger trying to find a place to land. But none of it belonged in the ears of a five-year-old. Not when his whole world was already small and fragile.

Because every little kid deserves to believe their parents are good people for as long as they can. That's not naive. That's protective. The world will tear that belief out of them soon enough. I didn't want it to be me. I didn't want to be the one who planted a permanent idea in his head that his mom didn't want him.

So I did the only thing I knew how to do in that moment.

I lied.

"It's not that Mommy doesn't want to see you," I said, forcing my face into something calm and gentle, like I wasn't actually falling apart inside. "She loves you very much. She's just really busy with work right now, and it's hard for her to take time off. But she loves you, and you'll see her again soon."

The words came out smooth, like I'd rehearsed them. Like I'd been waiting for this question without admitting I was waiting for it. And the second they left my mouth, I knew what I was doing. I was building a little shelter for him out of something I couldn't guarantee. I was giving him a story he could live inside, even if it wasn't real.

Because the truth was, I didn't know anything.

It had already been years. I didn't know if she was alive. I didn't know if she was using. I didn't know if she was homeless. I didn't know if she was with someone new, or in jail, or somewhere pretending she didn't have a kid at all. I didn't know if she ever thought about him. I didn't know if he would ever see her again.

The only explanations my brain could come up with were drugs or death.

And at the time, drugs felt worse.

There was also this small, ugly corner of me I don't love admitting is there, but it was there. The part that didn't want her to come back at all. Not if she was going to blow in and out of his life like a storm, making promises and breaking them, tearing up the ground I'd spent years trying to make solid under his feet. It was easier without her. Cleaner. Less disappointment. Healthier for him, and honestly, healthier for me.

But even with that, I will never forgive her for putting me in that position. For making me sit on his bed and choose between two kinds of pain. Shattering him with the truth, or protecting him with a lie.

I lied.

I lied because I wanted his little heart to stay intact for just a little longer. I wanted him to fall asleep believing he was loved. I wanted him to feel chosen, even if the person who should've been choosing him wasn't there.

And then I turned off the light.

I stood there for a second longer than I needed to, because I didn't know how to walk out of that room carrying what he'd just handed me.

That's the part of parenthood nobody puts on Hallmark cards. It isn't just diapers and school plays and sports and college funds. Sometimes it's standing in a dark bedroom with your heart jammed in your throat, realizing you've become the filter between your kid and a truth they're not big enough to carry yet. Sometimes it's looking at your own child and knowing whatever you say next is going to hit somewhere deep, whether you mean it to or not.

I've made a lot of mistakes as a father. I've yelled when I should've listened. Walked away when I should've stayed close. Tried to "win" a moment instead of protect it. I shook a crib. I drove off on a dusty road. I've had nights where my patience ran out and my pride stepped in to fill the gap.

And that night, with my hand on the light switch and his eyes locked on mine, I added another one to the list. Not because I didn't love him. Not because I didn't care. Because I was trying to do something impossible. Protect his heart without destroying my own in the process.

I didn't know it then, but here's what I know now:

Trying your best doesn't mean you won't screw it up. Loving your kid doesn't mean you won't hurt them. Being a "good person" doesn't protect you from reacting badly when you're overwhelmed, scared, exhausted, or carrying your own old pain around.

The only thing you can really do is learn.

Let the regret burn a little. Not in a self-pity way, not in a "look how horrible I am" way. Just enough to keep it honest. Just enough to make sure you don't forget what it costs when you lose control. Let it mark the lines you won't cross again. Let it become that internal alarm that goes off sooner next time.

Then show up better in the next moment. And the one after that.

Because we don't get to rewrite those early chapters. They're ink. They're done.

But we do get to be different in the ones we're still writing.

It turned out Amber was still alive.

About six months after that night in Cole's room, the one where I lied straight to his face to protect his heart, I got a call from Taylor.

They'd finally heard from Amber. She was living only an hour away. And she had a new son.

I wish I could say I was shocked, but I wasn't. Not really. She'd been with the same guy for years, probably since right after our divorce was final. While Cole spent three years wondering why his mom disappeared, she'd been busy starting over. New life. New baby. New family.

And she left him behind.

But now there was this new reality sitting in my living room like an uninvited guest. Cole had a brother.

What was I supposed to do with that?

My brain went into overdrive. Not just anger or hurt, though there was plenty of both, but math. Moral math. Emotional math. The kind you can't write out on paper, that just spins around inside your chest until you feel sick.

Because here's the thing. I know what it means to have a "half" that never felt like half.

My brother and I are technically half-brothers. He came from my mom's first marriage. I didn't even know that until I was a teenager. Growing up, we were just brothers. We fought like brothers, broke stuff like brothers, got our asses chewed like brothers. When I found out we were "half," it didn't change a damn thing. He's still my brother. No asterisk. No fine print.

So who the hell was I to deny Cole that same experience?

I knew I had to tell him. That part settled itself pretty quickly. But I didn't feel any obligation to go chasing Amber down. I wasn't the one who vanished for three years. I wasn't the one who walked away from my kid and never called. She walked away. She left. She had another child. That made this her responsibility.

So why wasn't she picking up the phone?

Why wasn't she asking about her son?

Why was it always on me to fix the messes she made?

That's where the doubt crept in. I kept circling the same questions, over and over. *Was I doing right by him? Was I protecting him, or just trying to protect myself from her? Was I being noble, or selfish?*

Then the worst-case scenarios started playing out in my head. *What if she never called? What if I stayed quiet and, years later, they bumped into each other somewhere, or he found out by accident?*

"Oh yeah, you have a brother. Your dad knew. He just never told you."

He'd never trust me again.

And trust was all we had. How was I supposed to look him in the eye and say, "We always tell each other the truth," while sitting on something this big?

But then I'd swing hard in the other direction, because I also knew exactly what opening that door meant with Amber. She didn't walk through a doorway without trying to take the hinges, the frame, and whatever was inside the room. And if there was a legal angle she could play, she'd play it. I wasn't guessing. I'd lived it.

We were finally past the court stuff. Finally living like a real family instead of case numbers. Finally not having every month feel like a new crisis waiting to happen.

So it wasn't just a simple question like, *should Cole meet his brother?*

It was also: *am I willing to throw both of us back into the insanity to give him that chance? Am I willing to invite chaos back into our lives when I'd spent years trying to keep it out?*

I thought about it for a week. Every day. Not casually, either. The questions just sat in my chest. I'd be washing dishes and thinking about it. Driving to work and thinking about it. Laying in bed at night staring at the ceiling, replaying the same conversations that hadn't even happened yet.

I'd catch myself watching Cole, listening to him talk about school or a video game or whatever five-year-olds get obsessed with, and I'd feel that quiet panic in the background. *How do I tell him without breaking us?*

And nostalgia did what nostalgia always does. I'd think about my own childhood, my own brother, all the stupid fights and shared secrets and inside jokes that felt normal at the time and ended up being everything. I'd picture how empty it would've felt without him.

Then I'd get pulled right back into the same loop. *Am I protecting Cole from pain, or am I keeping him from something he might one day need?*

In the end, it came down to one thing I couldn't argue with. I couldn't be the reason he didn't know. If he grew up and found out I'd kept this from him, he'd have every right to look me straight in the eye and ask, "Why?"

So after seven days of pacing, second-guessing, and running the same scenarios in my head until I was sick of hearing my own thoughts, I did the one thing I knew might blow my life up all over again.

I reached out to Amber.

The night Cole asked about his mom was one of the most brutal moments of my life. I had to pick between honesty and protection, and I chose protection. I lied. Not to save myself, but to save him. To let him hold onto the idea that his mom was still a good person somewhere, doing her best.

The lie did what I needed it to do that night, but it took a chunk out of me in the process.

I realized afterward that even when you lie for "good reasons," part of you knows. You feel it. That crack sits there, waiting. Because the truth doesn't disappear just because you ask it to. It hangs back, patient, waiting to be dealt with.

Telling him about his brother was my way of drawing a line in the sand. Of saying, "I'm not doing that again." I couldn't control what Amber did, but I could control whether I became someone who hid things from my own son. I wasn't going to be the reason he found out late and felt betrayed twice.

So I chose the hard thing. I chose the messy truth over the safer silence.

And everything I was afraid of happened.

She took advantage of the situation to take me back to court. Again.

Not just to argue about child support this time. No, this time she wanted shared custody. She wanted to stroll back in after years of disappearing and act like she'd been there the entire time. Like the missed birthdays, the empty holidays, the nights he cried for her and she never called were just some minor scheduling error.

She wanted to rewrite her history.

I wasn't scared she'd win. Not for one second. She didn't have a leg to stand on. Her absence was her testimony. Every year she stayed gone was another exhibit against her. I didn't need to say much. The silence she left behind did all the talking.

The court saw it. Everybody saw it. It was obvious this wasn't about what was best for Cole. It never had been.

It was about her.

Her convenience. Her control. Her money. Her ego. She wanted her record cleaned up, her conscience washed, her image fixed. She wanted access without accountability. A title without the work. And most importantly, a way to get out of being held responsible for paying child support.

And still, even knowing we'd probably win, I dreaded every second of it. Because "winning" in court is a messed-up kind of victory. You walk out with a piece of paper that says you're right, sure, but you leave pieces of yourself scattered all over the courtroom floor.

You sit there while lawyers trade pieces of your life like they're arguing over a parking ticket. You listen to your kid's name get tossed around in sentences that sound like they were written by a robot that's never met him. You watch the person who bailed on him stand up straight and talk about "parental rights" like she hadn't forfeited them years ago.

In the end, she got nothing.

The judge gave her no changes. No shared custody. No relief.

In that courtroom, for me, for Cole, it was a win.

But it didn't feel like a celebration. It felt like walking out of a burning building, coughing, covered in soot, looking back at the wreckage and realizing the same thing you'd realized a hundred times before. She lit the match, and we were the ones who kept having to run through the flames.

In real life, it cost more than I could afford. Court doesn't just drain you emotionally. It empties your wallet, too. It turns every "next step" into a bill, every phone call into time you can't get back, every hearing into another day you have to beg off work and explain to people who don't really understand why you look like you haven't slept in a week.

My parents paid most of my legal fees. And I don't say that lightly. Every time they wrote another check, it wasn't just money leaving their account. It was goodwill. Patience. Understanding. And somewhere along the way, those started running out faster than the cash did.

My mom especially never let it go.

To this day, decades later, she still looks back at that time like it was some reckless, unnecessary disaster I chose to walk into because I "had nothing better to do." Like I woke up one morning, stretched, and thought, *You know what sounds fun? More court.* In her mind, because I wasn't the one physically signing the checks, I didn't care. Like it wasn't costing me anything.

And that's the part that still pisses me off, because she never asked why I made the choice. Not once. She never asked what it felt like to sit in that courtroom again and watch my life get reduced to lines in a file. She never asked what it did to me emotionally, how many nights I went home feeling like my insides had been wrung out, how often I had to swallow rage and fear and guilt just to keep functioning.

She saw the receipts, not the cost.

And that's where the fracture really started with my mom. The resentment settled in on her side and just stayed. Like dust in the corners nobody bothers to clean anymore. All these years later, that wall between us still feels real. It still sounds hollow when you tap on it. Like something never got repaired properly, just covered up and left to sit.

And the part that hurts is how difficult and heart wrenching it actually was for me.

I chose to do something I knew would be hard, something I genuinely believed was right, for my son. Not for me. Not for her. For him.

I regret what it did to our relationship. But I don't regret why I did it.

Because Cole got a relationship with his brother out of it. A real one. A good one. Sleepovers. Inside jokes. Actual shared history. Memories that belong to them. Not some awkward introduction at a funeral someday where everything feels too late and too heavy.

That part of the story turned out the way it should have.

If the price of that was my mother's permanent disapproval, I hate that. I really do. But I can live with it.

Because here's what that whole chapter taught me. Doing the right thing doesn't come with a round of applause. Sometimes doing the right thing is exactly what gets you judged. Misunderstood. Second-guessed. Sometimes it's what gets you quietly pushed to the edges of your own family. Sometimes the cost of your integrity is someone else's resentment.

You don't always get to control that.

What you do get to control is the intention behind your choices, and whether you can live with yourself afterward. I made that decision with a clear heart. I did it because I believed my son deserved to know his own blood, and I didn't want to be the person who kept that from him out of fear.

I've made peace with that. I had to.

I still hope, before it's too late, that my mom and I figure out how to meet somewhere in the middle. That one day she'll look past the dollar signs and see the kid who got a brother out of all of this. That she'll understand I wasn't chasing drama. I was trying to do something clean in a life that had been messy for too long.

But if we don't, I know this much. I didn't blow my life up for nothing. I did it so my son would never have to look back and wonder why nobody fought for his connection to his own family.

That fight didn't just test my patience. It tested my values. It forced me to decide whose approval I needed more, my mother's or my own. In the end, I chose mine.

ROUND 23:
Novocain by Night

I wish I could sit here and tell you I handled all that pain like some emotionally mature, self-aware adult. That I read the right books, had the right conversations, made peace with it all, and walked forward with my head high. But that's not what happened.

What happened is that over the next five years, I slid into what I can only describe as my reckless phase. At the time, I didn't call it that. I called it "living." I called it "getting my life back." I called it "freedom." If I'm being honest, a lot of it was me choosing to be numb on purpose.

I turned reckless promiscuity into a routine. I bounced from fling to fling, night to night. No planning for tomorrow. No "what are we?" talks. No depth. Not because I didn't understand real relationships, but because I didn't trust myself to survive one. I didn't want anything with weight, because weight is what crushes you when it drops.

So I kept it shallow. Just bodies and distractions. Loud and fun for a few hours, then dead quiet the second I was alone again. From the outside, it probably looked like I was thriving. Like I was finally free. Like I'd "moved on." Inside, it was hollow as hell. It was me grabbing at anything that could keep me from feeling what I kept dodging.

We'll get to that.

Because even while I was acting like I didn't need anything real, there was still one constant that kept yanking me back to center. The one thing I couldn't fake my way around. The one thing that made me stop, breathe, and remember who I was under all that noise.

Cole.

As he got older, I started noticing that "keeping him busy" wasn't the same as giving him what he actually needed. School was school. Mall trips were fun. Movie nights were our thing. But I could feel him shifting, like he needed something that built him up instead of just filling the time. Structure. Challenge.

And the Marine in me knew exactly where to look.

Martial arts.

He was around eight when I brought it up. To be fair, it was Taekwondo, but to him it might as well have been straight out of a movie. "Karate." That's what he called it, and the second I said it, his whole face changed. Eyes wide. Lit up. That was all I needed. If he wanted it, I was going to find a way.

I picked Taekwondo on purpose. It wasn't just about learning how to fight. It was discipline, respect, self-control, and defense. It was being taught how to handle power without turning into a little jerk. How to stand tall without hunting for trouble. That mattered to me. I wasn't trying to raise a kid who thought strength meant intimidation. I wanted him to learn control first, because control keeps you out of fights more than it wins them.

Money was tight back then though. Single dad, multiple jobs, more bills than breathing room. Monthly tuition was one thing, but belt tests were their own special kind of stress. Every new belt came with fees. Then there was gear, pads, gloves, uniforms, and those padded "weapons" that looked like toys but cost like they were made out of titanium.

But this felt important.

And I stayed. A lot of parents did the drop-off-and-run thing, and I get it. People are busy. But I didn't leave. I sat in those hard plastic chairs against the wall and watched every class. Not because I didn't trust anyone, but because I wanted him to look over and see me there. I wanted him to know I was paying attention. This wasn't just another activity I signed him up for. It was something we were doing together, in our own way.

He wasn't the kid who walked in and instantly smoked everyone. He wasn't the worst either. He hovered in that top-ten range. Focused and consistent. You could tell he was trying his ass off. What he didn't have in natural talent, he made up for with effort. That has always been what I respect most in anybody. Not the gifted one. The one with enough heart to keep grinding while the naturally talented kids stay a few steps ahead.

Every belt was a big deal to him, and he deserved to celebrate his accomplishments. But we couldn't celebrate in some big fancy way. Usually, it was simple. McDonald's. Ice cream. Something small. But it still felt huge. Like a little ceremony for the two of us. We've always celebrated the small wins, because the small wins prove you're moving forward.

Taekwondo did more for him than kicks and forms. He learned how to listen. How to take criticism and corrections without getting offended. How to lose without quitting. He learned what it feels like to mess up in front of everyone, feel embarrassed, and still get back in line and try again. He learned that confidence isn't pretending you're never scared. It's doing something in spite of fear.

Sitting there week after week, I learned something too. I watched him grow in real time. Not just physically, but mentally. And I'd have these quiet moments where I'd think, *man... for all the ways I've screwed up as a dad, for all the times I've questioned myself, this part? This part I'm getting right.*

Because there's no single thing that sums up fatherhood. There's no big speech where you say everything perfectly and it fixes the past. It's a thousand small choices. A thousand sacrifices nobody claps for. It's baths and bedtime back rubs. It's random slow dances in the living room. It's mall trips and movie nights. It's Chinese food at sticky food court tables. It's sitting in a folding chair watching your kid try to break a board while you act calm even though your stomach is doing flips.

Those are the pieces that make up my story as his dad. Not the rank. Not the court dates. Not the papers stamped and signed.

These moments, the good, the ugly, the ones that still wake me up at night, that's what I carry. That's what I'll take with me to the end. And if there's any proof I did something right somewhere along the way, it's him.

Then the internet happened.

Chat rooms were blowing up. Myspace turned into this weird little universe where you could build a digital version of yourself: your music, your pictures, your carefully chosen background that screamed, "I'm deep but I'm also fun, please validate me." For a guy always scanning the horizon for the next connection, the next distraction, the next something, it was perfect.

I got hooked fast.

I wasn't looking for love. I wasn't searching for a soulmate or some connection I could brag about later. I was hunting attention, plain and simple.

That truth is ugly, and I don't love admitting it, but I'm not dressing it up. I was almost at the point of having a different woman in my house every week. Not because I was some great catch or some misunderstood romantic, but because I couldn't stand being alone with myself. Silence felt like a threat. Alone time wasn't "peaceful." Alone time was where my brain started talking, and I didn't want to hear a word of what it had to say.

And I really didn't discriminate. Short, tall, curvy, thin. Redhead, blonde, brunette. White, Black, Asian. None of that mattered. If there was interest, if there was even a small spark, I was in. Some nights I'd juggle more than one at a time like it was some twisted little achievement. Looking back, that's one of the parts that makes me cringe the hardest, because I wasn't just doing it. I was proud of it.

At first it felt exciting. Then it stopped being exciting and turned into routine. Like brushing your teeth, except reckless and messy, built around avoiding my own head. Most of it was impulsive, short, careless. I didn't really notice how deep I was in until it didn't feel like a choice anymore. It was just what I did. One situation ended, and I was already looking for the next one. Like a junkie chasing a fix.

And the worst part? I was good at it.

I could talk. I could charm. I could make women feel wanted. Back then, I told myself I was being "responsibly irresponsible." Even writing that now makes me shake my head. But in my mind, I had rules. Boundaries. So I convinced myself it was controlled.

I was a dad first. Cole went to bed by 7:30 or 8:00 every night, no exceptions. That was our structure. Dinner, baths, bedtime, stories, the whole routine. Then, once he was asleep, my "free hours" started. Some nights it was just me and the couch. Other nights it was me, MSN chatrooms, Myspace, and an inbox moving faster than my common sense.

If someone came over, they never met my son. That was the line I refused to cross. He was always asleep before they arrived, and they were always gone before he woke up. Some stayed an hour, some stayed the night, but by morning they were out the door and he'd be at the table eating cereal, completely unaware of what happened while he slept. I used that as validation I was being a "good dad," even while I was playing with fire.

Looking back, I can't believe how reckless it all was. Not just for me, but for them. So many of these women drove to my house after only a handful of messages and maybe one phone call. We barely knew each other. If you put it in a movie, people would roll their eyes. But that's exactly what we were doing. All of us pretending it was normal. Pretending it wasn't risky. Pretending we weren't using each other for something we didn't want to say out loud.

At the time, I didn't ask myself many questions. I didn't want to. I just kept feeding the machine: attention, affection, validation, on demand. I told myself I was getting what I wanted. That I was in control. That this was just what single guys did after a divorce or a breakup or whatever label makes it sound more acceptable.

But I wasn't in control. Not even close.

All I was doing was numbing myself. It wasn't passion. It wasn't intimacy. It was me trying to shut off the noise in my chest for a few hours at a time. The relief never lasted. When it wore off, the emptiness didn't leave. It came back louder. So I chased the next message, the next flirt, the next hookup, hoping the next one would finally quiet it down.

It never did.

What's almost painful now is how obvious it was. None of it was about love. It wasn't even about real connection. It was about not being alone with my own thoughts. It was about being scared to sit still long enough to feel anything real. I wasn't running to people. I was running from myself.

And here's the part that hurts in a different way. Deep down, I did want

intimacy. Real intimacy. The kind where someone actually sees you, knows you, and stays. But I wasn't willing to risk being known, so I settled for being wanted. Being wanted is easier. It asks less. It's temporary. It doesn't require depth. It doesn't require me to open up parts of myself that even I didn't want to look at.

I wasn't handing my soul over to anyone. I barely wanted to admit I had one.

What stings the most now is realizing it wasn't just me I was playing with. These women weren't background characters in my story. They had their own history. Their own heartbreak. Their own reasons for being there. Some of them wanted more than a fun night and a quiet goodbye. It meant something, at least to some of them. That's where the shame shows up.

That's the thing about using people as distractions. Sooner or later, you realize you haven't just been dodging feelings. You've been dodging your own healing. You look back and see a trail of faces you barely remember, moments you can't even place on a timeline, and you don't get to hide behind "I didn't know better." You did. You just didn't want to deal with what knowing better would require.

What I know now is simple, even if it's hard to swallow. No amount of bodies in your bed fixes the broken thing in your chest. No amount of messages, flirty photos, or wild nights builds peace. Peace starts with self-awareness, self-respect, and the kind of honesty that feels ugly when you're doing it. You can't truly connect with someone else if you're still hiding from yourself, and back then I was hiding so hard I couldn't even see the damage I was doing.

Would I go back to that phase? No.

Would I erase it? Part of me wants to say yes, but I can't. It shaped me. It shoved lessons in my face that I clearly wasn't going to learn the easy way. It taught me the thrill of distraction is just that. A spike. A temporary high that always drops you.

Real growth doesn't show up when you're chasing the next hit. It shows up in the quiet, when you finally sit down with yourself and say, *seriously... what the hell am I doing?*

That was the moment I spent years avoiding.

What started as casual flirting and random late-night meetups slowly turned into something more intentional.

I turned it into a game.

The question stopped being, *Do we actually click?* and became, *Can I take this all the way?* Once I knew a woman was interested, it was like autopilot. Whether I was genuinely into her stopped mattering. What mattered was closing the loop. Proving I could.

After a while, they started to blur together. Not because they weren't real people, but because I was treating the nights like copies. Different faces, different stories, same script.

And yeah, it was thrilling. I'd be lying if I pretended it wasn't. There was a rush in the chase, a hit to the ego in knowing I could keep pulling it off. That's the part that makes me cringe the most now, that I enjoyed being good at something I'm honestly ashamed of.

But here's the twist that complicates it. It wasn't only about sex.

I actually liked talking to them. I liked hearing about their lives, their jobs, their kids, their exes, their dreams, their disappointments. Even if I never saw them again after that night, there was something oddly comforting about late-night conversations at my dining room table. Maybe because it reminded me I wasn't the only one trying to outrun something. Maybe it was because I just genuinely enjoyed having deep conversations with adults and it was an escape from the daily "single dad" and work routine.

Still, it all got organized in my head. Neat. Efficient. Optimized. The way the conversation started, the jokes, the drinks, the subtle shift from "hanging out" to "something more." It was muscle memory. Nothing looked planned, but it was.

Alcohol helped sell the illusion that everything "just happened."

"We were just drinking," became the built-in excuse the next morning, for them and for me.

Because I had Cole at home and couldn't disappear to bars every night, I started inviting women over to my house. Logistically, it made sense. Emotionally, it was a mess. Weirdly, it worked in my favor. "Single dad" sounds responsible and safe to a lot of women. Stable. Trustworthy.

Shamefully, I weaponized that.

Not in some "mua-haa-haaa" cartoon-villain way. Not with evil intentions. But I know it worked to my advantage, and that's where the shame makes yet another appearance. I used the image of being a good father as part of the soft sell, even if I never said it out loud.

We'd start at the dining room table or in the living room. Just talking. Laughing. Two adults pretending for a while that real life wasn't waiting right outside the door. Then, once things felt comfortable enough, I'd introduce the real stage: the man cave.

I built that thing with intention.

Pool table, stereo, dartboards, makeshift bar, low lighting. Not a nightclub, but cozy enough to feel intimate, careless enough to feel fun.

Then came the drinks.

For me, it was always the same combo. A bottle of Michelob Lager, and a full glass of my go-to Frankenstein cocktail. Jägermeister topped off with Red Bull. I'd sip that and chase it with beer.

Not classy. But effective.

If the energy felt stiff, I'd pull out the secret weapon, a relic of a board game I first bought back when Amber and I were first dating, called Pass Out.

It was designed to do exactly what it sounds like. The board was covered in colored spaces, penalty shots, "go to the bar" squares. The goal was to make ten laps. Nobody ever did. Halfway through, people were laughing too hard to count straight. It was ridiculous and stupid. But it worked.

Then there were the Pink Elephant cards. Every lap earned one. Each card had a tongue twister you had to read out loud. If you screwed it up, you drank. Five tries, and if you blew the last one, you still had to take that fifth shot, but then you could continue with the game. It was the kind of silly that lowers your guard before you notice it.

After an hour and a half, maybe two, the game would fizzle out. That's when I'd bring out the "Goody-Bag."

A simple, household Ziplock sandwich bag but inside were two more games: *Sip and Go Strip* and *Dirty Dice.*

Subtle, right?

Sip and Go Strip came first. Every card in that deck was some mix of "drink" and "remove or swap clothing." A sock here, a shirt there, underwear traded, someone wearing someone else's bra over a T-shirt. It was playful. It slowed down the pace in the best way. By the time the game ran its course, we were usually down to underwear or some combination of each other's clothes, laughing so hard we could barely breathe.

That's when the dice came out.

Four of them. Two with verbs. Two with body parts. Roll all four, pick your favorite combo, and suddenly the room got very small, very fast. It wasn't raw or graphic—it was teasing, suggestive. But it never stayed that way long. Within ten or fifteen minutes, the dice would be rolling themselves off the table, forgotten.

By then, we were past games.

Sometimes we ended up on the floor. Sometimes the couch. Occasionally the pool table. Once in a blue moon, we actually made it to my bedroom. But the location never mattered. The script was always the same.

Those games were basically a conveyor belt: drink, laugh, get looser, dare each other, blur the lines. We'd would be giggling and embarrassed and brave all at once, and by the time it ran its course, we were past pretending it was only about games.

Sometimes we ended up on the couch. Sometimes the floor. Occasionally the pool table. Once in a while, we made it to my bedroom. The location never mattered. The script did.

And here's the wild part. It worked. Every. Single. Time.

Not because I was some kind of wizard. Because I built a routine that walked the night from harmless to inevitable. It felt spontaneous. It wasn't.

It was a carefully constructed escape hatch from my life, from my feelings, from myself.

One of the first times I ran that whole routine start to finish was with my friend Hailey.

Hailey and I were really close friends. She lived with me for a while, so we were around each other constantly. We joked, teased, and had real chemistry. It hovered between friendship and something else, and we both knew it, even if neither of us said it out loud. But if we did, we'd call it "friends with benefits."

Somewhere in the middle of that, playing Pass Out a couple nights a week became our thing. Cards, shots, trash talk, inside jokes, and then hooking up. Casual. Easy. "Safe," at least by my definition back then. Safe meant we didn't have to talk about anything deeper than what we were doing that night.

Looking back, I probably put away more beer during that stretch than any other time in my life. At the time, it felt like fun. Like blowing off steam. Now it reads like avoidance.

One night, Hailey invited her friend Ariana to join us.

Ariana was stunning. There's really no other word. Dark hair, smooth skin, full lips, that quiet confidence that turns heads. The second she walked in, I knew exactly what part of my brain was going to try to run the show. But I had this little rule I clung to like it made me a decent guy: she's Hailey's friend. Don't do anything stupid.

Turns out, I didn't have to make the first move.

Ariana was skeptical about the game at first. She thought Pass Out sounded stupid, and honestly, she wasn't wrong. It is stupid. But we convinced her to sit down, take a few turns, and just go with it.

Thirty minutes later, we were all laughing our asses off because she kept landing on her own color over and over. The eye rolls disappeared. She went from unimpressed to fully committed, slurring through tongue twisters and trash talking like she'd invented the game.

By the end of the night, we were properly drunk and worn out. The kind of drunk where you're laughing at things that aren't even funny anymore, and you're dancing to music that isn't playing.

At some point, I got up from the table to release all of the beer I had been drinking. I cut through my bedroom on the way to the bathroom.

When I came back out, the view in my bedroom was unbelievable.

Hailey was on my bed, completely naked, laying on her back. Ariana was between her legs, in only her underwear, totally focused on what she was doing. No one jumped. No one panicked. No one scrambled to cover up or apologize or explain anything. They didn't even act surprised that I was standing there. The moment just sat there, calm and deliberate, like it had been happening for a while and my only job was to finally catch up.

And I did exactly what drunk, impulsive, emotionally stunted me did back then.

I joined in.

I didn't ask a single question. I didn't consider emotions or consequences or friendship or boundaries. I didn't think about what it might complicate once the alcohol wore off. I just followed the same instinct that had been running my life for years. Chase the next hit.

At the time, it felt surreal. Like something that happened to other people, or in some story you hear and don't really believe. It didn't feel like my real life. It reminded me of that night at Kayla's apartment with her boyfriend and Amber, that same excitement, that anticipation, that unexpected exploration of a woman I was extremely attracted to. Seeing, feeling, and tasting the women of my fantasies became an addictive drug, so that's exactly how I treated it afterward.

For a long time, I wore that night like a twisted badge of honor. It became a story I'd pull out whenever I wanted to prove I was the guy with the wild nights and the "you won't believe this" moments. I laughed about it. I bragged about it. I used it like evidence that I was winning some invisible game, instead of admitting I was unraveling.

That memory is burned into my brain in full color. I can still replay it. I can still remember the excitement of it. But now the nostalgia comes with a heavy, quieter shame. Not only because of what happened, but because of how automatic I was. How careless. How proud I was of something I should've at least handled with some respect, even if I wasn't ready to be honest about why I was doing any of it.

That whole era, the beers, the man cave, the drinking games, the revolving door, the threesomes that "just happened," looks different from where I'm standing now.

Back then, I sold myself a simple story. I was just having fun. Blowing off steam. Living life. Marine one weekend a month. Responsible single dad by day. Carefree guy by night. No harm, no foul.

Zoom out far enough and the picture changes. It stops looking like fun and starts looking like a guy working overtime not to feel anything real. Not to sit in silence. Not to let his brain catch up to what he'd been avoiding.

Because the truth is, I was lonely. I was hurting. I was carrying around regret about the Marine Corps, about my parents, about Amber, about all the ways I felt like I'd fallen short as a father and as a man. Instead of facing any of that, I did the easier thing. I numbed it. With attention. With alcohol. With a rehearsed routine that practically guaranteed I wouldn't fall asleep alone.

It took me a long time to admit this, but I would eventually learn that you can't sleep your way out of emptiness. You can't drink your way around your own reflection. And you can't build self-worth out of other people wanting you.

I tried. Hard. It doesn't work.

Under all that noise, I wanted real connection. The kind that doesn't need dim lights and party games to feel safe. The kind that's there even when you're not performing. The kind that doesn't disappear when the buzz wears off.

But that kind of connection costs something. Honesty. Vulnerability. Standing there without the armor, without the charm, without the sarcasm, without sex as a shortcut. None of that happens when your life is built around manufactured moments in a mancave bar you designed to distract yourself from you.

Do I judge the guy I was back then? A little. I'd be lying if I said I don't cringe when I replay certain nights. But mostly, I understand him. He was trying, desperately, clumsily. He didn't have the tools yet. He did what a lot of people do when they're hurting. He found a way to feel wanted, even if it was only for a few hours.

But you can't outrun yourself. You can fill your nights, your bed, and your calendar with people, but if you never stop long enough to sit with what's going on inside you, the emptiness doesn't leave. It just waits, and it gets louder the second the noise dies down.

I wouldn't recommend the path I took to anyone, especially not a single parent with a kid sleeping down the hall. But it's part of my story. A chapter I don't get to erase. One I've had to sit with, pick apart, and eventually make peace with.

So the best thing I can do now is tell the truth about it. Own it. Learn from it. Live differently than the man who honestly believed the next girl, the next game, the next night would finally make him feel whole.

But I didn't learn any of that until many, many years later. In the meantime, I kept driving down the same road.

Around that same stretch, I was working at a little kiosk in the mall, parked directly across from Bath & Body Works. That's where I met Sonia.

She was maybe five or six years older than me, with a son a few years older than Cole. Not the kind of "perfect tens" you see in movies, but she had something better: presence. She walked like she knew who she was. Confident. Put-together. Professional without being stiff. After so many late-teens and twenty-somethings still tripping over their own lives, being around a woman who paid her bills on time and knew what she wanted felt different.

It started small. A joke here. A comment there. Conversations leaning across the kiosk counter that lasted a little too long. Then lunch breaks together. Then a couple casual dates. Then nights at my place. I remember wondering if my usual charm would still work on a woman like her, someone with an actual career and real structure. Someone who wasn't impressed just because a guy had his own place and a car that started on the first try.

It did.

That was the thing back then. Whatever broken magnet I had in me still worked. The pattern didn't change much. Flirting, connection, drinks, the familiar dance. Sonia was steadier, more grounded, but even with her we didn't label it. We slid into a rhythm: lunches, late-night texts, random sleepovers. It wasn't exclusive, and I didn't pretend it was.

Because I didn't stop seeing other women.

There were so many random hookups in that season of my life that most of them are just static now. Flashes instead of full memories. A laugh. A car ride. A bedroom I barely remember. A face I'd probably walk right past today without even a flicker.

Honestly, I've probably forgotten more partners than most people will ever have.

That's not a flex. That's an indictment.

You can judge me. That's fine. I've done more than enough of that on my own.

Some stand out, though.

There's one that still makes me laugh a little, not because it was funny, but because of how long it lived in my head before it ever became real. A high school crush. The kind you daydream about in algebra when you're supposed to be solving for X, but you're really just staring at the clock and replaying some hallway moment like it matters more than your grade. She was a year ahead of me, older, cooler, and completely out of my league in that teenage way where you don't even consider making a move. You decide she's "never gonna happen" and file her away as a safe fantasy.

Then years later, life did what it does. We crossed paths again. Same face, same energy, but now we were adults and the context was different. That old charge hit fast and it caught me off guard. It wasn't only about who she was in that moment. It was what she represented. This unfinished thing from my past that never got touched.

She played it cool. She didn't make it easy. That made it worse in the best way. This wasn't like my usual situations where everything slid into place without effort. With her, I actually had to work. She had that energy like she knew what she was doing and wasn't impressed by my usual moves.

Eventually, it happened. We ended up in bed.

And here's the honest part. The sex wasn't mind-blowing. It wasn't some life-changing moment. It was just sex.

But there was still this weird, quiet satisfaction. Not because of how it felt, but because of what it did in my head. I got to touch something that used to feel untouchable. Like I reached back into that version of myself still sitting in class and proved the "never" wasn't permanent.

It didn't fix anything. It didn't change my life. It didn't turn into some love story.

But for a moment, it scratched a very specific itch. Proof that even the "never gonna happen" girl could happen.

Then there was the woman from the jewelry store across the mall.

By then, I was working shifts at the cookie shop.

Yes, I know. How many jobs did you have, dude? Apparently my commitment issues didn't stop with women.

It was one of those places that always smelled like warm sugar and butter. The smell clung to you. You'd leave work and still smell like cookies in your hair and on your shirt.

She started coming in on her lunch breaks. At first, it was normal customer stuff. A cookie, a soda, a little small talk while I rang her up. But it didn't stay normal. She lingered at the counter a little longer. Her smile held a little too long. Her eyes stayed on mine when they didn't have to. Conversations stretched like neither of us was in a hurry to end them.

She was cute. Friendly. Easy to talk to. The kind of woman you can joke with about nothing and somehow it still feels like something. And I liked the attention. I liked how effortless it was.

But she was married. Very married. Not in the vague "I think she has a husband" way. Married-married. Newly married. Less than a year in.

We flirted anyway, and we didn't half-ass it. The banter got blunt. The innuendos got less subtle. Those throwaway comments stopped sounding like jokes and started sounding like invitations neither of us pretended not to understand.

One slow afternoon, we ended up alone in the back room. No customers. No coworkers. Just the hum of the fridge and that thick, charged silence that shows up when two people have been circling something long enough and finally stop pretending.

The teasing went from words to hands in about three seconds.

We started making out like teenagers who found an empty hallway. Fast, sloppy, all urgency and no thought. I slid my hand into her jeans and felt her just melt into me like her body had been waiting for that exact moment. And for a few seconds, the world shrank down to nothing but heat and breath and the stupid thrill of doing something we both knew we shouldn't.

Then the front bell rang. A customer.

The spell snapped instantly.

I pulled back, breathing hard, stuck in this weird place between turned on and irritated that reality had the nerve to interrupt. I pulled my hand away, looked into her eyes, and tasted her from my fingers. Then I walked right back out front and helped the customer like nothing had happened.

The next day, we stopped pretending it was an accident.

We made a plan. Time, place, logistics. Like two people organizing a lunch meeting. And then we followed through. No drunken haze. No "it just happened" excuse. Just two people who knew exactly what they were walking into and chose it anyway.

That's what made it feel different from my usual routine. It wasn't random. It wasn't impulsive in the way I normally operated. It was deliberate. She knew what she was risking. So did I. And we did it anyway.

When it was over, that initial high faded fast and something heavier moved in behind it. Guilt.

Not just because she was married, but because she was newly married. Fresh vows. New husband. People probably still asking her how the honeymoon was. And there I was treating all of that like it was just another night in my rotation, like her life was some side mission in my story instead of her whole world.

We never did it again.

After that, the texts thinned out. Replies got slower. The flirting faded, then stopped. It didn't end with a blowup or some dramatic conversation.

It just dissolved. Like a weird dream we both agreed not to bring into daylight.

She stopped coming into the cookie shop as much too. When she did, it was quick. Order, polite smile, gone. No lingering. No extra talk. Just business. Like we both quietly decided the safest thing was to act like it never happened.

For a long time, I didn't know where to file it in my own head. It didn't fit under "fun." It didn't sit cleanly under "regret" either, not right away. It lived in that uncomfortable in-between space where you don't want to feel like a villain, but you also can't pretend you were innocent. You know you crossed a line, and you don't want to stare too hard at what that says about you.

Now, when I think about the cookie shop, I still smell the sugar. I can still picture her leaning on the counter, laughing at something I said like we were just two people killing time on a lunch break. And right alongside that nostalgia, there's a quiet, heavy shame that shows up every time.

Because I know exactly what I chose to be in that moment. And I can't pretend I didn't know better.

There were other encounters that stuck with me for stranger reasons, the kind that pop back into your head years later for no obvious reason.

It started the way those nights always started. Loud music, cheap drinks, that easy confidence you get when you've had enough to stop overthinking. We danced, flirted, laughed. Everything felt light in that way it only feels when you're not thinking about consequences, not thinking about tomorrow, not thinking about anything except the next ten minutes.

Next thing I know we're in their apartment, still joking, still wasted, still acting like we'd all known each other forever. And then we split off into separate rooms like it was planned. Like this was just what you did after enough drinks and enough flirting. No awkward pause, no "is this okay?" conversation. Just a smooth handoff into private spaces.

Halfway through, I suddenly just popped out of my drunken state.

It was like the alcohol drained out of my system in one breath. I didn't gradually sober up. I just suddenly felt awake. And when that happened, I really saw her for the first time. Not the version my beer-soaked brain had created in the dark bar, not the outline and the thrill of being wanted, but the actual person in front of me.

And I realized, bluntly, that I didn't feel anything for her. No attraction whatsoever. If I'd been sober, I wouldn't have even approached her in the first place. And that's not me trying to be cruel about her. It's me being honest about how much of my decision-making was being driven by alcohol and ego and the need to not end the night alone.

But there I was, already in it.

I didn't stop. I didn't say, "Hey, I'm not feeling this," like a normal, respectful adult. I just… pushed forward. And I remember how gross that felt internally, even while I was doing it. This weird, hollow determination, to finish what I started.

When it was done, I dressed as fast as I could. No cuddling, no hanging out. Just this immediate urgency to get out of there. I found my friend, we exchanged a look that said we both knew what this was, threw out a quick "later," and walked out.

And then there was the infamous Myspace girl.

She didn't have a profile picture, which should've been a giant warning sign even back then. But being bored, curious, and sexually charged is a dangerous combination, and I was loaded up on all three. She lived about forty-five minutes away in Bloomington. We messaged for a while, and we clicked in that shallow, flirty way that can feel like connection when you're just keeping everything surface level. Eventually I agreed to pick her up.

She had me meet her outside a bowling alley. Neutral territory.

We talked the whole drive back to my place. She was funny. Witty. Easy to be around. Under the dim glow of the car lights, everything felt fine, and I let my imagination fill in the blanks. I built the version of someone I expected to see when we got there.

Then we walked up to my front porch and stepped into the full blast of the outside light, and the whole encounter changed in a single second. Up close, her skin was bright red and angry-looking, especially around her neck and jaw. It wasn't a little flushed or "maybe she's sunburnt." It was inflamed and irritated. Pitted from acne scars.

From the neck down, she looked exactly like the fantasy version I created. But from the neck up, there was no amount of alcohol that was going to let me sit across from her and pretend I was still all-in after that porch-light reveal.

So I did what cowards do. I turned it into a performance.

I told her I needed to run downstairs to grab something from my bedroom. Instead, I called my buddy.

"Call me back in ten minutes," I said. "Make it sound like your life is on fire."

He laughed. "You got catfished, didn't you?"

Ten minutes later, my phone rang right on cue, and I put on the performance of my life. I paced. I swore. I played the part of the loyal friend dealing with a crisis. I made it sound like he'd been arrested over something ridiculous and needed me to come handle it immediately.

Then I turned to her with my best apology face and said, "I'm so sorry. I have to take you home. We'll have to do this another night. I might be gone for hours."

She said she'd wait. I told her she couldn't.

And we both knew exactly what was happening, even if we didn't say it out loud.

On the drive back, she went quiet. Her face lit up by her phone screen, thumbs moving. I didn't ask who she was texting, but I can guess. Probably a friend getting the play-by-play about the guy who picked her up, brought her back to his place, and then hit the emergency eject button the second he saw her under a porch light.

And then, about ten minutes from her place, the whole script flipped again. She leaned over and reached for the zipper of my jeans, like she was trying to salvage the night, or her pride, or maybe just take control of the situation in the only way she felt she could. By the time I pulled into her driveway, things had escalated further than they should've.

When we finished, she got out, looked at me and said, "Call me."

I never did.

I can try to spin that night now if I want to. I can tell myself we both knew what it was, we were both adults, it was transactional, nobody owed anybody anything. And sure, technically, that's all true. But I think we all know what it really was.

Disgusting.

Not all of it was awkward or ugly. Some of it was intense in ways I didn't see coming.

Like the girl from Subway.

This was before Amber, back when I worked at the Urbana store. She was gorgeous in this almost exaggerated way. Dark hair snapped into a tight ponytail, bright blue eyes, tanned skin, and a body... man, that body. Especially from behind.

She had a rough edge about her. This abrasive, hood-rat attitude that sat on top of everything else she did. You'd look at her and get pulled into those big blue eyes, and then she'd snap right back into that tough shell, like she couldn't afford to let anyone read her for too long. I don't know what she was trying to keep out, but she made it obvious she wasn't someone to be messed with.

That wasn't my style. It wasn't the type I normally chased. But I liked the tension of it. The thrill of trying to turn a girl that hard, soft. The idea that maybe if I pushed the right way, she'd let me past the walls and I'd get to see the real her behind those blue eyes.

And if I'm being honest, part of me wasn't just curious about her personality. I was curious about her body. Curious about what that tough mouth sounded like when it wasn't trying to scare someone off, what that edge looked like when it finally relaxed, what she'd do if she actually wanted me close instead of acting like she didn't.

So yeah, it felt like a challenge. Not just to get to know her, but to get under her skin. To see how much of that hardness was real, and how much of it was something she wore because she thought she had to.

We flirted at work, and eventually she invited me over. It didn't feel like some big plan, just one of those nights where the sexual tension that had been building between us might actually have an outlet. One thing led to another, and we ended up in bed. Well, more specifically, her living room couch.

She didn't play coy once we were alone. She told me what worked for her, what didn't, and what she needed from me to get where she wanted to go. Specific. Direct. Like she'd decided she wasn't going to waste time on guessing games.

And at some point, she steered things into territory most people either avoid or only talk about in jokes, like she wanted to see if I was all talk or if I could actually handle what she liked without getting weird about it. I didn't expect that kind of openness from her. But there it was, this surprising little pocket of vulnerability under all that edge.

Hearing someone with such a tough exterior like her say what she needed, and trust me with it, was a fresh turn-on.

We hung out for a week or two after that, then it fizzled like so many other almost-somethings in my life. No big blowup. No drama. Just a quiet fade.

And honestly, that was most of that era. Almost-somethings. Nights that started with excitement and ended in a blur. Conversations that could've gone deeper but never did, because depth wasn't what I was there for. Not really.

I met people I genuinely liked as humans, people I could've respected more, known better, maybe even built something real with if I'd let myself. But I kept it shallow on purpose. I kept it moving.

When I think about nights like that now, I feel two things at once. There's nostalgia for the era. The music, the late nights, the feeling that life was wide open and unsupervised, like consequences were something that happened to other people. It felt easy to believe I was just "living," just blowing off steam, just doing what single guys do. In real time, it even felt harmless. Like freedom.

And then there's the shame.

How often I treated people like props in my story instead of actual human beings with their own lives, their own bruises, their own reasons for being there. I was present enough to flirt, to charm, to chase the moment, but not present enough to actually care what it meant for the person across from me.

There were so many random hookups in that season of my life that most of them are just flashes instead of full memories now. A laugh that felt louder in the moment than it probably was. A car ride with music turned up. A bedroom I barely remember, a ceiling I stared at. Faces and names that, if I'm being honest, I'd probably walk right past today without even a flicker of recognition.

Not because they didn't matter as people, but because I didn't let them matter to me.

Back then, I wasn't willing to do that. And that's the part that sticks with me now. Not the sex, not the stories, not the wildness of it. The way I avoided connection while still taking everything that looked like it.

From the outside looking in, it probably sounds like I was living some twisted fantasy. Women at the mall, late-night hookups, wild threesomes, a man cave engineered for temptation. And sure, there were nights where I honestly believed I was living the dream. The drinks, the laughter, the half-naked people playing stupid games in my basement. It all looked like freedom.

But it wasn't. It was distraction.

Underneath the noise, adrenaline, and constant dopamine spikes, I was just running. From my parents' disappointment. From custody battles. From middle school gyms. From boot camp graduations with no follow-up handshakes or phone number exchanges. From a baby spoon on the front seat of a Ford Taurus. From a boot print stomped on my chest. From front seat rendezvous after work. From betrayal on a blanket next to a lake. From nights sitting on a floor listening to Tim McGraw and Toby

Keith songs on repeat. From unsaid good-byes at the airport. From all of the ways I'd failed as a partner, as a son, and as a man.

I built this careful, repeatable script because it gave me control. If I could guide the night from "Hi" to "your clothes on my floor" like a formula, then nothing unpredictable could happen. I couldn't get rejected in any meaningful way, because I wasn't actually offering anything meaningful.

Those nights didn't define me, but they did expose me. They showed me I was starving for connection and terrified of closeness at the exact same time. That I could make people feel wanted without ever really letting them know me. That I could stack bodies like sandbags around a heart I didn't trust anyone with.

Here's what I know now, after years of sifting through that wreckage: variety is not the same as connection. Being desired is not the same as being loved. Sharing a bed is not the same as sharing yourself.

You can't numb selectively. If you deaden yourself to pain, you deaden yourself to joy too. If you stay in the shallow end where nobody can really hurt you, you also never get to feel what it's like to be fully seen and chosen for who you actually are.

I don't sit in shame over that era anymore. Shame keeps you stuck. But I do sit in honesty about it. About the people I used, the people who used me, the nights that ended with me feeling lonelier than I'd been before anybody ever showed up.

That stretch of my life, eight, maybe ten years of turmoil and chemistry and carefully controlled detachment, didn't make me a monster. It made me a man who was hurting and didn't know how to say, "I'm hurting." So I performed instead. Like I always did.

You can build an entire world out of temporary highs, but it will never replace the quiet, steady peace that comes from being honest with yourself.

Real intimacy isn't something you manufacture with alcohol and games. It's something you sit still for. It's something you earn. It's something that starts the moment you stop running from your own reflection and finally say:

Here I am. All of me.

Sometimes those "one-night stands" lasted longer than a night. A few weeks here. A couple of months there. But the rules never changed.

From the very first conversation, I laid it out. No promises. No future tense. No "we" talk.

"Look," I'd say, "I'm not looking for anything serious. This is just fun. Casual. If that works for you, cool. If it doesn't, I respect that."

Nine times out of ten, they'd say the same thing back.

"That's perfect. That's all I want too."

And sometimes that was true. Sometimes it wasn't.

Every now and then, someone would be honest and say they couldn't do casual. I respected that. We didn't go on a "harmless" date just to see. We didn't "play it by ear." We just walked away before anyone got attached. No drama, no blocked numbers, no long sad text threads.

But more often, I got the version where their mouth said they were fine with casual, and their eyes, their questions, their little pauses between sentences said something completely different. I think some of them hoped that if they played along long enough, I'd change my mind. That one day I'd wake up and say, "You know what? Forget all that casual talk. Let's build a life together."

I never did. I couldn't.

Back then, I didn't have that gear. I was walled off. Guarded. Smiling, charming, present, but only up to a certain invisible line. I had my reasons. I'd been burned, and not lightly. Some of those burns were still blistered and raw under all the jokes and manufactured confidence. We'll get to that later.

For now, all you really need to know is this: I was chasing the rush, not the relationship.

It felt good to be wanted. It felt even better to know that, most of the time, I could make that feeling appear on demand. I'm not saying women were lined up around the block and I was out front with a clipboard and a waitlist, but I also wasn't exactly starving.

On average, I was seeing two or three different women a month. Sometimes there'd be a dry spell. Sometimes two overlapped. Some nights were wild; others were quiet and familiar, regulars I circled back to when I didn't want to be alone with my thoughts.

Most of them faded without leaving much behind.

But a few?

A few left scars.

ROUND 24:
The Doors I Wouldn't Close

At the time, my mom was running a daycare out of her house, partly as a business, partly to help me survive single fatherhood. I had full custody of Cole, and daycare costs are no joke. You basically work all week so you can afford to pay someone to watch your kid, so you can keep working. It's a treadmill that eats you alive. My mom stepping in kept me from falling flat on my face.

Shayla brought her son to Mom's daycare.

One afternoon, I was in the driveway waiting to pick up Cole when she pulled up. We started talking, the way parents do, a little small talk about kids, work, the weather.

She was beautiful in a way that made you lose your place mid-sentence. Soft curves, pale skin, strawberry blonde hair, big blue eyes. And her lips were the kind that made it hard to keep steady eye contact without feeling like you were staring. The first time I really took her in, she reminded me of Natalie Maines from the Dixie Chicks. Same face, same energy, that mix of sweet and confident that could flip into "don't test me" if needed. She even had a sleek little black sports car with custom plates and a blinged-out license plate frame.

We started talking more. Long phone calls that stretched past midnight. Dinners. Then more than dinners. It heated up fast. I liked her, a lot. There was an ease between us. It felt different than the usual hookups.

But even early on, something in my gut was off.

She had a handful of close male "friends" she spent a lot of time with. That alone didn't bother me. Some people just connect better with the opposite sex. I've been that friend for women more than once. The issue wasn't that they existed. The issue was that I wasn't allowed to meet them.

Any time I brought it up, "Hey, maybe we should all hang out sometime?" she'd shut it down.

"They just wouldn't be comfortable," she'd say. "You don't really know them."

That never sat right. If they were just friends, why the secrecy?

Eventually, after months of weird excuses and half-truths that didn't quite line up, I got my answer. She'd been cheating on me for most of the relationship, mainly with one of those "friends" she constantly talked about. The guy I'd suspected from day one. Turns out I was the extra the whole time.

And even though I'd had my suspicions for quite some time, it still stung. Not just because she cheated, but because I'd actually let myself picture something longer with her. Not necessarily forever, but more than the usual shelf life I'd gotten used to. I'd let myself relax. I'd let myself get attached. And then it died right around the seven-month mark.

Funny enough, seven months became a pattern for me. That was always the point where things either got real or fell apart. It was like a built-in deadline where people either stepped into something deeper or started looking for exits. And for me, if I wasn't all in by then, or if the relationship revealed it had been fake the whole time, I was out. No point dragging someone past the expiration date just because it was comfortable, or because starting over would be too exhausting.

Elena was beautiful. Smart. Funny. We clicked in that rare way where conversation felt effortless, like we'd known each other longer than we had. We had the same sense of humor, the same taste in shows, the same little reactions to things that made being around her feel easy. She wasn't just attractive, she was someone I actually enjoyed. Someone I could've pictured myself with if the timing had been different, and if the wiring inside my chest wasn't set up to run the second something started feeling real.

But every time things drifted toward the physical, she hesitated. It wasn't a hard "no." It wasn't her pushing me away. It was subtler than that. A quiet pause, a shift in energy, a gentle pullback like she was trying to slow the car down without slamming on the brakes.

Eventually she told me why.

She had herpes.

She didn't make it dramatic. No tears, no long buildup, no big confession. She just said it plainly, like an adult, because she wanted me to know before anything went further. I respected that. A lot. Her honesty actually made me like her more, because that kind of vulnerability is real. It's not sexy. It's not strategic. It's just human. She gave me a choice, and she did it in a way that said, *I'm not going to trick you, and I'm not going to hide from you either.*

So no, my instincts weren't twitching about the diagnosis itself. That's biology. That's life. People carry things. People deal with things. That part didn't scare me.

What started to get under my skin was everything around it, the little details in her stories that didn't fully line up. The "where I was" and "who I was with" stuff that altered depending on the day. The way certain nights didn't match what she'd told me earlier. It wasn't one smoking gun. It was that slow accumulation of moments where my brain would go, *wait... that's not what you said last time.*

I tried to ignore it at first because I wanted her to be who I thought she was. I wanted the easy connection to stay easy. I didn't want to be suspicious. I didn't want to be the guy interrogating timelines like I was building a case file. But the feeling didn't go away. It kept showing up, like a warning light I kept covering with my hand.

Then came the night it all came to a head.

She told me she was going to be at some bar across town with friends. And for whatever reason, instinct, bad luck, fate, call it whatever, my buddy and I ended up walking into a bar, in a completely different town, and seeing her with another guy. Not just standing near him. Not just chatting. She was wrapped up in him. Close enough that there wasn't any room left for interpretation. It wasn't "maybe." It wasn't "I'm overreacting." It was right there, in front of me.

And to make it even worse, she acted as if she didn't even know me. We made eye contact multiple times, and she would just look at me, bobbing her head to the music, this guy behind her with his arms wrapped around her waist, until she would eventually look away again. She acted as if I was just a fixture in the bar. Complete emotional detachment.

I don't remember much after that, other than drinking way too much.

And yeah. I've been lied to. Played. Betrayed. I don't say that to paint myself as a victim, or to justify the ways I handled things later. I'm not interested in building a courtroom case where I'm automatically innocent. I'm saying it because those moments helped build the version of me that came after. The one who kept it casual. The one who stayed emotionally unavailable. The one who clung to control.

Because if I kept things light, no one could claim I misled them. If I never promised more, no one could say I didn't follow through. If I stayed honest, technically honest, I could tell myself I wasn't doing anything wrong.

What I didn't see back then was that hiding behind "honesty" can still be a form of running. You can tell the truth and still keep your distance. You can be upfront and still be unavailable.

After things ended with Elena, I didn't suddenly evolve into this emotionally enlightened, self-aware version of myself. I didn't rise from the ashes. I didn't even smolder. I just slid right into something that looked a little healthier from the outside, but underneath, it had the same cracks running straight through the middle. Different girl, same broken guy.

That's when I met the girl from Davenport.

I met Jenna during on of my monthly drill weekends with the Marine Corps Reserves. She worked the front desk at the hotel where we always stayed, so before I even knew her name, she was already part of the regular monthly routine. Same place, same check-in, same little moment where you're standing there tired from the drive and trying to shift gears into "Marine weekend" mode, and she's right there behind the counter.

She had that girl-next-door look, pale skin, bright blue eyes, brown hair that somehow always sat right around her face, and this high-pitched laugh that carried across the lobby. She was my height, around 5'3", and at the time I took that as a sign.

And honestly, with a bunch of reservists cycling through the same hotel every month, I'm sure she'd heard every line from guys in uniform. I wasn't subtle about it either. I flirted with her like it was my second job. But she didn't look annoyed, and she didn't shut me down. If anything, she matched my energy, turning it into a fun, flirty exchange.

One drill weekend turned into a date, and the date turned into a routine. Before long, we were "together," as much as you can be when you live three hours apart and only really see each other a couple nights a month. But if I'm being honest now, it wasn't that clean. It wasn't some steady relationship building week by week. It was more like a scheduled thing we both slid into. We weren't really building anything day-to-day, and in the beginning we really didn't communicate much outside of those drill weekends. We were just filling gaps.

Those weekends had become predictable, and at the time I really looked forward to that. I'd roll in around eight on Friday night after the three-hour drive, tired and mentally fried, still half in dad mode and half in Marine mode. Same parking lot, same lobby smell, same check-in routine. If Jenna wasn't working, we'd end up at the bar downstairs, grabbing drinks and talking like we hadn't seen each other in months instead of weeks. If she was working, I'd do that thing where you hang around the desk way too long, pretending you have questions you don't actually have, just to keep the conversation going. And it didn't take much. Five minutes with her and whatever stress I'd been carrying around would quiet down, at least for the night.

The chemistry between us was intense. Physically, we clicked in a way that felt effortless, almost too effortless. There was no awkward warming up, no guessing games, no pretending we were shy about what we wanted. We were direct with each other, and that felt refreshing, like we'd skipped the part where people dance around the truth and went straight to the part where everything is honest.

We talked openly about what we liked, what we wanted, what we were curious about. The kind of conversations most people avoid early on because they're trying to look "normal" or play it safe. Jenna didn't play it safe. She had this fearless streak that was exciting. She rarely said no to anything, which made me feel different than I had with other women. Like I didn't have to hold anything back.

But there was another side to it too, and it took me longer to see it. When someone is that open, that ready to go along with anything, it can feel like real connection when you're in it. It can feel like you've found someone who "gets you."

Looking back, I can see how quickly I let intensity replace intimacy. How easily I confused being desired with being known. And how much I let slide because those weekends felt good and the rest of my life felt heavy. I didn't want to ask harder questions. I didn't want to slow it down and look too closely at what it actually was. I wanted the escape, and she fit perfectly into that.

One night, just to see if she'd actually do it, I dared her to strip down by the hotel sign near the road. I didn't think she would. It was one of those dumb, half-drunk dares you throw out when you're feeling bold and you want to see where the line is. More talk than anything.

But she didn't laugh it off. She didn't hesitate. She just did it. Clothes off, right there by the sign like it was no big deal, like the whole world could drive by and she'd just give them a wave and a show.

That was her. No fear, no shame.

But underneath all that spontaneity and fun, there was something else. She had a habit of telling stories that didn't feel real. Not the normal little exaggerations people toss in to sound more interesting. Bigger than that. Bigger people. Bigger drama.

The main one was this tennis player, Andy Roddick. She talked about him like he wasn't just some famous guy she'd watched on TV, but someone she actually knew. She swore they had this deep, personal connection. She said they talked on the phone, that he wrote to her, that they had this secret friendship that nobody else understood.

And I'm not saying I needed her to hand me a stack of evidence like I was a detective. But over time, it got harder to ignore that there was never anything concrete. No photos. No messages. No calls coming through where his name popped up. Nothing that ever accidentally slipped into view. It was always just her telling me, with total confidence, like the confidence itself was supposed to be the proof.

What made it worse was how the story grew. It started coming up more often, with more details, like she was trying to convince herself as much as she was trying to convince me. And I didn't know what to do with that. I never flat-out called her a liar to her face, but I also stopped playing along. I stopped nodding like it made sense. I'd go quiet, change the subject, or let it sit there between us in a way that made the room feel awkward.

That dynamic stayed with us for a long time, basically the whole relationship, a little over two years. A lot of good weekends, good sex, good laughs, and then this steady, irritating feeling in my gut that something was off. And instead of dealing with it, I kept pushing it to the side, because as long as the weekends were good, it felt easier not to make it a problem.

But Jenna stuck with me longer than the rest. When we were good, we were good. She even started driving down to visit me in Champaign sometimes, stretching our two-night weekends into something a little more real.

Eventually, we started experimenting together, bringing other women in. The first time we tried it was a disaster.

We found a girl online. She wasn't really my type. Not ugly, just not someone I would've chased on my own. Bigger girl, quiet energy. But at that point, we weren't trying to curate some perfect fantasy. We just wanted to say we'd done it. Check the box. Get the first awkward experience out of the way so it wouldn't feel like this big, mysterious thing anymore.

She came over and we did what we always did. Sat at the kitchen table, got drunk playing Pass-Out, acting like this was all casual and normal even though there was definitely that tension in the room. That mix of nerves and anticipation where everyone's laughing a little too loud and taking a little too long to finish a drink, because once you cross the line, you can't pretend it's just hanging out anymore.

Eventually, we ended up in bed. The "fun" happened. And that part went according to plan. Nobody freaked out, nobody backed out, nobody started crying or stormed off. It happened.

But once it was over and we were trying to sleep, she started farting. Loud. Constant. Relentless. The kind where you just keep thinking, *Okay, surely that's the last one,* and then another one hits like a punctuation mark. It was so comically awful it would've been funny if we weren't trapped in the same bed trying to pretend it wasn't happening.

Any leftover sexy vibe died right there. Jenna was quiet, I was quiet, and I just laid there staring at the ceiling, wide awake, thinking, *Well… that's enough of that.*

After that, things got better. Or at least more intentional. We learned pretty quickly that if we were going to do this again, it couldn't just be some random, half-drunk, "let's see what happens" set-up. It needed some thought, some boundaries, and at least a little bit of honesty about what we were actually looking for.

The next time we tried it, we invited my old roommate, Hailey, who I'd hooked up with plenty of times before. That one was easier right out of the gate. Familiar. Less pressure. There wasn't as much of that "what if this gets weird" feeling because I already knew her, and there was already history there. It didn't feel like we were forcing a fantasy. It felt like we were looping someone into something that already had a rhythm.

Then there was the girl from the department store. She wasn't the kind of woman you'd see walking through the mall and automatically do a double take. Not in that obvious, "everyone agrees she's hot" way. But for what we were chasing at the time, her body was perfect, and once you got her talking, the rest of it didn't even matter. She was fun. Funny. Smart. The kind of person who can make you relax even when you're doing something that was objectively weird. She didn't bring a bunch of tension into the room. She brought energy.

One night with her sticks out more than the others.

We started the night the usual way, drinks, flirting, testing the waters, everybody acting casual while also making it clear where things were heading. Then we ended up in bed. All three of us together, tangled up, figuring it out as we went. It was one of those nights where there's no script, no smooth transitions. Just a lot of trial and error and laughter mixed in with it.

About forty-five minutes in, I was done. Tapped out. I remember laying back, catching my breath, thinking that would be the natural end to the night. Most nights, that's the point where things slow down, everyone comes back to reality, and you start doing the post-game version of affection and small talk.

They didn't.

The two of them kept going. And going. And at some point, they slipped into their own world like I wasn't even there. Not in a mean way. Just in a way that was so locked in and self-contained it was almost funny. They were laughing, touching, exploring each other like they'd been waiting their whole lives for this exact night. Like the whole reason they were there was for that moment, and I was just in the background.

I laid there and watched for a while, not sure what to do with myself. Part of me was turned on, part of me was amused, and part of me was just genuinely tired. Eventually I stopped trying to make sense of it, rolled over a little, and drifted off like some exhausted extra in my own movie.

That was a first for me, falling asleep while my girlfriend was having the time of her life with another woman six inches away. I woke up later and it was still one of those moments where you have to blink a few times and go, *Did that really happen?* And then you remember, *yeah. It did.*

We had a few more nights like that with different women. Some were fun. Some were awkward. And then, like so many eras in my life, that chapter ended too.

In the end, the tennis fantasy wasn't even what broke us. That was always there in the background, annoying and confusing, but it wasn't the thing that finally snapped the whole relationship in half.

That part came from closer to home.

My "best friend."

He was the guy I went out with on the rare nights I actually got a break from being Dad. I didn't go out much. Most nights I was perfectly fine staying home with my son, keeping things simple, and if a girl came over after he went to bed, that was enough. But when I did decide to go out and be social, it was usually with him.

Turns out, while I was doing that, he was sliding into her messages behind my back. Asking her to get on webcam. Asking her to take her clothes off. I still don't know how far it went, and honestly, I don't think I ever will. They both swore it only happened once. And maybe that's true. But experience has taught me that "once" usually means "at least twice," and even if it really was only one time, the number didn't matter. One time was enough.

I was done.

On top of that, she started mentioning her ex more and more. At first it was casual, little comments, random details dropped into stories like they didn't mean anything. Then his name started showing up a lot. Enough that I noticed it. Enough that it started feeling like he was in the room with us even when he wasn't. She'd frame it like he was "just part of her past," but everything in my gut told me he was still very much part of her present.

He was local. I wasn't. That simple fact sat between us whether we admitted it or not. I was the guy who showed up for a couple nights a month. He was the guy who lived right there. So if she went back to him, it would've made perfect sense. Part of me wouldn't have even blamed her. Another part of me hated how easily I could see it coming, like I was already practicing the speech I'd give myself when she finally did it, trying to make it feel logical so it wouldn't hurt as much.

And here's the truth I didn't want to say out loud back then. I liked her. A lot. More than I wanted to admit. There were moments where I could see something real tucked inside all the escapades, and those moments messed with me because they made me want to believe in it.

But between the stories she told, the friend who betrayed me, and that constant, gnawing sense that I was never her first choice, there wasn't any solid ground left to stand on. I was trying to build something on weekends and chemistry, and it just wasn't enough. Not against real life.

Not against distance. Not against the parts of her I kept pretending weren't there.

Looking back, I do feel nostalgic for those weekends. For the escape. For the version of me who still believed attraction and excitement could patch over anything if it was strong enough. But right behind that nostalgia is the same familiar shame. Shame that I ignored the red flags. Shame that I stayed as long as I did. Shame that I called it a relationship when it was just another way to avoid being alone with myself, even on those short, two-days-a-month trips to Davenport for drill weekends.

Not long after that, during another drill weekend, I met someone else in the Quad Cities.

It was December and I had Toys for Tots duty, sorting Christmas gifts in a big warehouse full of Marines trying to look tough while handling teddy bears, board games, and Barbie dolls. It was loud, guys were cracking jokes, acting like it was just another task, but you could tell everyone was in a better mood than usual. There's something about seeing stacks of gifts meant for kids that turns the volume down in your head for a minute.

That's where I saw her.

She was stunning. I mean, breathtakingly beautiful. Dark brown hair, big brown eyes, lips that were distracting. She had a thin, almost athletic body. I remember thinking she looked like the type of woman who could walk into a room and already know she could leave with whoever she wanted.

She had four young kids. I remember that because she was wrestling big bags of toys, trying to juggle everything. And I was raised right, at least right enough that when I saw that, I walked over and offered to help carry everything to her car. Gentleman move. It was also an excuse to talk to her.

We got to her car, and I had that split-second moment where you can feel the choice sitting in your throat. I could just say, "Take care," and walk away like a normal person. Or I could shoot my shot and risk looking like an idiot in front of a woman who was way out of my league.

I was nervous as hell, but I leaned into the uniform and the moment.

"Some of us are going out for drinks later," I said. "You should come."

She didn't hesitate. She gave me her number and her address and told me to pick her up. Like it was the most normal thing in the world.

That night ended up being one of those nights where everything clicks. My buddies were definitely checking her out but she stayed glued to me. Hand on my leg under the table. Holding my hand. Laughing at my jokes. It felt like she was making it clear to everyone, including me, that she was there with me. Not because she had to be. Because she chose to be.

After that, we saw each other casually for about the next nine months or so whenever I was in town. Nothing official, just a few nights here and there. The distance was an issue, and I wasn't delusional enough to pretend I was ready at twenty-eight to step into a ready-made family with four kids. I liked her, but I knew myself. I knew what I could handle, and what I couldn't. Still, when we were together, it felt easy. Chill. Honest. Just two adults enjoying each other.

Eventually, she told me she'd started seeing someone closer to home. And I got it. No drama, no blow-ups. It had already been fading anyway. We were both grown enough to admit what it was.

One of the last nights we were out, she brought a friend with us to the bar. Her friend was gorgeous, and from the second she sat down, there was an instant energy and chemistry between us. Flirty. Teasing. It wasn't subtle, and it wasn't imagined. You can feel when someone is inviting you into something. I think we both knew we had this unspoken permission slip, because my situation with the first woman was already winding down and already in that gray area of endings.

The catch was the friend was very married.

That detail should've shut it down immediately. But it just became part of the thrill, which says something about where my head was at back then.

At some point we slipped out to my car for a few minutes. We told ourselves it was just a quick break, like we were stepping out for air, but we both knew what it was. The second the car doors shut, it turned into that kind of make out where you stop thinking and just react. It was intense, and it felt stupid and exciting at the same time. Before she got out, she slid off her underwear, pressed them into my hand, and told me to keep them.

"Think about me later," she said.

And I did.

I kept them in my pocket the rest of the night like some ridiculous teenage trophy, then threw them away when I got back to my room. Even now, I shake my head at that whole night, equal parts hot and pathetic. It wasn't romantic. It wasn't meaningful. It was just proof of how much I was living off impulse and attention, collecting moments instead of building anything real.

There was another woman around that time, too. Just a couple weekends in a row, nothing serious. I met her at the hotel bar where I stayed for drill. She was thin, a little rough around the edges, with that cute trailer-park vibe. She had that blunt, no-nonsense way about her that made it easy. We hooked up a few times, purely physical, no illusions of more. No "where is this going," no pretending it was deeper than it was.

It was what it was.

Until it wasn't.

Looking back, I can see the pattern so clearly it almost feels like a kick to the balls. It's like watching an old home video of myself and wanting to reach through the screen and grab that guy by the shoulders. The women, the hotel rooms, the long drives, the drinking games that turned into foreplay. It's not even the sex that sticks with me. It's the pattern.

I kept dropping myself into the same kind of situation over and over again. Exciting, intense, unstable. Tons of chemistry, not a lot of honesty. I told myself I was just "having fun," that I'd earned it, that I was single so none of it really mattered. But underneath all that justification, the truth was simpler and uglier. I was using chaos to distract myself from myself.

Davenport showed me what lies look like up close. The small ones people throw out like they're nothing, and the bigger ones they build entire personalities around. My so-called best friend showed me betrayal with a familiar face, the kind that messes with your head because it makes you question your judgment more than their character. The Toys for Tots woman and the married friend outside the bar showed me how easy it is to slide over lines you swear you'd never cross, then act like it "just happened." Like you didn't make a choice.

Jenna and all the threesomes showed me something else. How fast "adventure" turns into anesthesia. A distraction. Something flashy I could point to so I didn't have to admit how hollow things felt underneath.

The thing I should've learned a lot earlier, but finally started to get during that stretch, was that boundaries matter.

Not just the physical ones. Those are the obvious ones. Don't cheat. Don't force. Don't cross lines you'd be ashamed to say out loud. Basic decency. The harder ones are emotional boundaries. Standards. The lines you draw with yourself. The promises you keep when no one's watching and no one's holding you accountable.

I had to admit I'd been letting chemistry speak louder than my gut for years. I stayed in situations because the highs felt good, even when everything underneath was falling apart. I'd feel that uncomfortable twist in my chest, that sense that something was off, and instead of respecting it, I'd pour another drink, crack another joke, shift the attention somewhere else, and pretend it wasn't there.

I was proud of being "the honest one." I laid out the rules from the start so no one could ever say I misled them. No strings. No expectations. No broken promises. I told myself that made me decent, respectful, maybe even emotionally responsible. *See? I'm not the bad guy. I told you what this was.*

What I didn't understand back then was that you can be technically honest and still be completely emotionally unavailable. You can be crystal clear about what you won't offer and still have no idea what you actually need. Hiding behind honesty is still hiding.

Somewhere in the middle of all that, I started to understand a simple truth: If trust isn't there, real trust, built over time with consistency and honesty, then all the passion in the world is just noise. It's intense, it's addictive, it's exciting, and then it's over. And you're still you at the end of it. Still dealing with the same stuff you were trying to outrun.

What I really wanted, even if I couldn't bring myself to say it back then, was something different. Something quieter. Something grounded in respect, truth, and actual stability. I didn't just need the "right person." I needed to stop being the guy who kept choosing hysteria and calling it fate. I needed to become someone I could trust with my *own* life first.

That was the real turning point.

Not the night with multiple women. Not the stories that sound impressive in a locker room but feel empty when you're lying in bed afterward staring at the ceiling. The turning point was the quiet moment after all of it when I realized I was tired.

Tired of half-truths.
Tired of measuring my value against somebody else's dysfunction.
Tired of confusing instability with passion and calling that "love."

I didn't stop screwing up after that. I didn't suddenly turn into some enlightened relationship guru who made all the right choices. But for the first time, I started asking myself a different question. Not, "Can I pull this off?" or "Can I get away with this?"

Instead: "Does this line up with the man I want to be?"

And once that question showed up, I couldn't un-hear it. That, more than any wild story I could tell, is what actually started to change everything.

Another short relationship I had, short but serious, was with Selena. The woman I would marry and be divorced from in the time it takes most people to plan a wedding. Three months. A flash fire. It burned hot, burned fast, and left smoldering scars.

We met on Myspace. Yeah, that era. Glitter graphics, profile songs on autoplay, the drama of who made your Top 8 and who got bumped. I was scrolling one night, half bored, half lonely, and there she was. She lived in Tuscola, about twenty minutes south of Champaign, and the second her profile picture loaded, I felt that stupid little jolt in my chest.

She was twenty-five, I was thirty. Half Mexican on her dad's side. She had the kind of beauty that shuts your brain off. One second you're thinking about what you're going to say, and the next second you're just staring, hoping you don't actually drool. Flawless, sun-kissed skin. Long dark hair that fell in soft waves. Warm brown eyes, the kind you feel before you really see. And that smile, the kind of smile that could talk a cop out of writing a ticket. And her body. Let's just say it checked every box I knew I had and a few I didn't realize were on the list.

We messaged back and forth for a few days. That easy, nonstop kind of back-and-forth where you keep telling yourself you're going to put the phone down, and then there's another notification and you're right back in it. By that Friday night, we already had plans to meet at a bar my buddy and I frequented. I was jittery as hell, pretending to be relaxed, sipping my beer while my friend went to grab another round.

That's when I saw her walk by with her friend.

My stomach just dropped. It was that instant hot-cold rush, like my body couldn't decide if I should throw up or run. I couldn't tell if she'd seen me and decided to keep walking or if she had just not recognized me in person. That was the nightmare playing in my head. I stand up, say her name, and she hits me with the polite, "Ohhh… yeah, hi," smile that says, *Wow, your pictures were generous.*

I couldn't sit there and spiral. So I got up and followed them out to the beer garden, acting like I had way more confidence than I actually did.

She looked up, saw me, and smiled. Big, real, relieved. I hadn't even realized I'd been holding my breath until that exact second. The look on her face said, *Oh good, you're actually you*, and she looked genuinely happy to see me, and for a guy who never totally believes he belongs with a woman that beautiful, that look meant everything to me right then.

We spent the rest of the night totally into each other. Talking. Laughing. Leaning in closer and closer. Doing that thing where you pretend you're into the music or the crowd, but really you're just looking for excuses to touch each other's arms, shoulders, knees.

By the end of the night, I was at her apartment. And yeah, every ounce of tension and chemistry we'd built up online and at the bar showed up in real life. It was raw, intense, and exactly what I'd hoped it would be. It felt like confirmation. Like, *See? This is meant to be.*

We dated for about eleven months. Somewhere in there, I slid from "this is fun" into "this is my life now." She had two beautiful young daughters, five and three. They accepted me faster than I expected, and I slipped into this half-stepdad role I didn't even know I'd wanted until I was already in it.

My son, Cole, was eight at the time and I loved watching him step into big-brother mode. Sharing toys. Sharing snacks. Figuring out how to negotiate TV time without full-scale war breaking out in the living room. Sometimes I would just stand there and watch them all together, and this quiet thought would float through my head: *Maybe this is it.*

Some nights, Selena would go out with her friends and I'd stay home with the kids. I'd run bath water, get the towels ready, do the whole bedtime routine like I'd been doing it for years. Then it was pajamas, teeth brushed, little cups of water on the coffee table because someone always "needed" one last sip. We'd end up on the couch with a cartoon on low volume, and I'd sit there while they leaned against me.

I remember brushing their hair, one at a time, taking my time with it because I didn't want to pull too hard. Soft curls, little tangles, the quiet patience it takes to do something gently when you're tired. And that part still gets to me when I think about it now, because it felt real in a way I wasn't prepared for. I'd already done a lot of the "boy" side of parenting with Cole, roughhousing, video games, Legos everywhere. This was different. Pink towels and small pajamas and the serious, straightforward questions little girls ask at night, like whether the hallway light can stay on or if I can check under the bed one more time. It was special. It wasn't pretend, and it wasn't just "helping out." It felt like I was building something real.

And that's where the regret lives now. In the memory of how much I let myself believe in that version of life. I wasn't just dating Selena. I was investing in a routine, in the kids, in the feeling of being needed in a house that wasn't just mine. I let myself picture holidays, school mornings, all of it. I don't look back and think it was fake. I look back and realize how deeply I wanted it, how good it felt to have something that simple and real in my hands, and how hard it is to accept that wanting something doesn't automatically make you ready to keep it.

But there were cracks. And they weren't small.

Selena loved to go out. Not "once in a while to blow off steam" loved it. Not "occasional girls' night" loved it. This was random Wednesday night, full hair and makeup, tight jeans, heels, "I'll be back whenever" loved it. She worked a Monday through Friday secretary job at the University of Illinois. And then she would still roll in at one or two in the morning like we didn't have three kids sleeping down the hall.

We had the same fight on repeat.

"Why do you have to go out tonight?"
"I just want to have fun."
"You have to work in the morning."
"I'll be fine."

And then she'd go. Every time.

And I'd sit there on the couch, cartoons flickering on the TV, kids finally asleep in their beds, feeling less like a partner and more like free childcare. Like a live-in babysitter with romantic benefits and no say in how the household actually ran.

Back then, I told myself it was just a phase. That she'd grow out of it. That once we were more serious, once we got married, once life settled, she'd slow down. Be more of a family.

Now, looking back, I can see how hard I was trying to force that picture to fit. How much I wanted that family, that version of myself, that version of her. I miss those quiet nights with the kids. I miss the feeling of brushing their hair, lining up their little shoes by the door, hearing all three of them breathe softly in their sleep.

But what I really regret is how long I tried to build a life on top of cracks I could already see. Not because I didn't notice them. I did. I just didn't want them to be real. I wanted the story to work out more than I wanted to accept what the story actually was.

And somehow, even with all of that, even with the red flags waving right in my face, I proposed.

We decided to get married in Vegas. No big wedding, no flower arrangements to argue over, no endless guest list politics. We had both already done the traditional version in our first marriages. This time, we told ourselves we wanted something different. Something fun, easy, memorable. So in April 2005, we got on a plane and flew to Las Vegas.

The second we landed, I knew something was off. I couldn't tell if it was a bug, jet lag, bad airport food, or just my body trying to send me a warning I didn't want to hear. I felt this heavy, lingering nausea that wouldn't let up. First time in Vegas, supposed to be this big party weekend, getting married, and I was fighting the urge to throw up in the middle of the Strip.

We went to Margaritaville and I ordered the volcano nachos. When they hit the table, it looked like something off a TV food challenge, a ridiculous mountain of chips, cheese, jalapeños, the whole thing. I knew it was amazing. I just couldn't taste any of it through the nausea. I forced some down, pretending I was fine, trying to convince myself it was just travel catching up with me. Bit by bit, I started to feel better, and we were able to salvage the night.

Selena had a friend who lived in Vegas, so we got the full insider treatment. VIP access. The Playboy Club. Ghost. High-end lounges where you feel underdressed no matter what you put on. For a first trip to Vegas, it was incredible. Neon everywhere, music pounding. It had all the ingredients for one of those "best weekend of my life" memories.

But the moment that stands out isn't the club, the view, or the lights.

We were sitting in VIP at one of the clubs and her friend had drifted off somewhere, probably off talking to someone she knew. Selena excused herself to go to the restroom and I stayed behind with my drink, watching the Vegas craziness of all the club girls on the dance floor. Bodies moving, lights flashing. Something happening in every direction.

After about ten minutes, Selena came back to the table.

She slid into the seat all giggly and wide-eyed, with that mischievous look turned all the way up. Like she had a secret and couldn't wait to drop it in my lap.

"You'll never believe what I found in the bathroom," she said, leaning toward me like it was some funny story we'd laugh about later.

"What?" I asked.

"There was this white, powdery stuff just sitting on the back of the toilet," she said. "Like powdered sugar or something."

I remember just looking at her, waiting for the punchline.

"And I dipped my finger in it just to taste it to see what it was," she said, laughing like she'd just told me the most adorable, random thing.

I just stared at her. *Who does that? Who dips their finger into some random mystery powder on the back of a toilet in a Vegas nightclub and pops it in their mouth like it's a sample tray at Costco?*

No one. Absolutely no one.

She kept talking, still smiling, still playing it like she was this harmless, clueless girl who just wandered into a silly moment and couldn't help herself. It was so overdone it was insulting. It wasn't even close to believable. It was the kind of story you tell when you're trying to cover something you know you shouldn't be doing, and you're counting on the other person being too polite, or too emotionally invested, to call you out on it.

I knew exactly what really happened. She went into that bathroom and did coke. Probably with her friend. Maybe with someone else. I didn't need the details to understand the basic reality. Drugs were definitely involved, and then she came back to me with a ridiculous story designed to make me feel stupid for even questioning it.

It wasn't just the drugs. It was the lie. Not even a good lie, either. An almost comically bad one. The kind that says, "I don't respect you enough to tell the truth, and I think you'll believe whatever nonsense I tell you." It pissed me off, but I didn't want to have a fight in the middle of a crowded club the night before our wedding.

So I just sat there with my drink in my hand, listening, nodding, keeping my face neutral, because I could feel how close I was to snapping. I didn't want to make a scene. I didn't want to blow up the night or blow up our upcoming wedding. I did what I'd gotten good at doing back then.

I swallowed it. I played along. I acted like I wasn't furious, even though I was.

In my head, I was already running through the obvious answer. This should be it. This should be the moment I stand up, tell her I'm done, go back to the hotel room, pack my stuff, and book myself a solo flight home. Cut it clean. No more trying to make the version of her in my head match the version of her sitting right in front of me.

That should've been the moment I called it. But it wasn't.

I told myself we were already there. The trip was paid for, the wedding was planned, and our families back home were expecting it. They weren't just expecting it in a general way either. They were literally planning to watch the ceremony online, like this was some sweet modern twist on a real milestone. And instead of letting that reality sober me up, I used it as pressure. I twisted it around in my head until walking away felt like the bigger wrong, like I'd be the villain for pulling the plug, even if pulling the plug was the smartest thing I could've done.

That's one of my biggest regrets, not walking away in Vegas when I still had a way out. I didn't do it because I was scared of wasting money, scared of disappointing people, and if I'm being honest, scared of admitting yet one more massive failure and bad decision. I made it feel like calling it off was worse than living inside it. And once I made that choice, I stayed committed to it the way stubborn people do, by doubling down and pretending I didn't feel what I was feeling.

We pushed through the rest of the trip like nothing happened. Hoover Dam. More clubs. More "let's take a picture" moments. I smiled when the camera came out. I played the part. If you looked at the photos, you'd think I was having the time of my life. But I remember how forced it felt, like I was constantly trying to convince myself and everyone else that we were the perfect couple.

Then we ended up at the Little White Wedding Chapel for the quick Vegas-style ceremony, live-streamed back home. It wasn't very romantic. It wasn't even intimate. It was just efficient. No flowers, no aisle, no quiet moment where you look at each other and actually see your future in each other's eyes. It was basically, "Step here. Stand there. Okay, let's do this. Lights, camera, action."

The officiant didn't help. She looked like she'd done the same thing a hundred times already that day and hated every second of it. Cream-colored suit, flat voice, dead eyes, just going through the motions. "We are gathered here today…" came out in this lifeless drone. I honestly felt like she was borrowed help from a funeral home. And standing there, hearing her talk like that, it felt like an omen. A big, obvious one.

I wish I could say I took the hint. But I didn't. Always listen to your gut. I had that feeling, and I ignored it.

We'd paid for the photo package, so right after the ceremony they moved us outside like we were on an assembly line. Take this pose. Turn this way. Stand closer. Hold hands. Smile. Except the angles were awful, the lighting was worse, and everything about it looked cheap and forced. At the time, I was mostly irritated and embarrassed, because you want at least one decent wedding picture to put in a frame and hang on a wall at home.

Now, when I look back, those photos feel almost too accurate. They don't look like wedding day bliss. They look like two people trying to manufacture a moment. Ugly photos for an ugly mistake.

What happens in Vegas doesn't always stay in Vegas.

A few months into the marriage, on a Wednesday night, everything finally snapped.

The kids were already in bed, and I was on the couch with the news on, doing that half-zoned-out dad thing where you're technically awake, but you're already thinking about laying your head on the pillow and preparing for whatever the next day has in store.

Then Selena walked out of the bedroom.

She wasn't in sweatpants or a hoodie. She was dressed like it was a Saturday night. Hair done, makeup perfect, tight outfit, the whole look. The kind of effort you don't put in unless you're going somewhere you want to be seen. Not "I'm running to the store." Not "I'm meeting a friend for coffee." This was club-ready.

"Where are you going?" I asked.

She didn't hesitate. "Heading to Tuscola to meet up with the girls," she said casually, like she was telling me she was grabbing a snack from the kitchen.

I remember looking at the clock and then looking back at her, waiting for the rest of the sentence. Like maybe she was joking, or maybe I'd misheard the time.

"It's 10 o'clock at night," I said. "You're just now leaving?"

Tuscola wasn't around the corner. It was close to a thirty-minute drive each way. Even if she stayed for a couple hours, which already felt like a fantasy, she wasn't walking back in that door before one in the morning. And this wasn't a weekend where you can justify it with "we're both off tomorrow." This was a Wednesday. Real life. Work. Kids. Responsibilities.

She shrugged like none of that mattered. "I'll be fine. I just want to have some fun."

And that was it. Not because those words were shocking on their own, but because I'd heard that same message in a hundred different ways. It wasn't a discussion. It wasn't, "Is this okay with you?" or "Do we have anything going on tomorrow?" It was an announcement. The decision had already been made. My input wasn't part of it. I could be annoyed, I could be hurt, I could be sitting there realizing this was not what I signed up for, and it wouldn't change her next move at all.

My opinion was irrelevant. I was irrelevant.

When the door shut behind her, something in me finally broke. It was like a switch flipped, like a lock sliding into place inside my chest. Not anger in the "I'm going to explode" way. More like clarity in the "I'm done" way.

If she wanted to live like she was single, fine. But I wasn't going to keep volunteering to be the babysitter and butler at home holding everything together. I had let it slide when we were "just dating," because I kept telling myself the same comforting lie: Once we're married, it'll change. Once it's official, she'll take it seriously. Like a ring is some magic reset button that turns a person into a different version of themselves.

It doesn't.

And that part is on me. Not just marrying her, but ignoring myself the entire way there. Ignoring the red flags, ignoring the patterns, ignoring the fact that I kept explaining away the things that were already making me miserable. I made excuses because it was easier than admitting the truth. I was building a life with someone who didn't respect me, didn't commit to being a partner, and didn't care how her choices affected me.

We were married three months.

That is the whole story and somehow still not enough. Ninety days of legally binding bad judgment. Long enough to sign paperwork and take pictures, not nearly long enough to build anything real.

Our final fight was about the same thing we always fought about, her going out during the week like she didn't share a home, a life, and three kids with me. One more night of her walking out the door in full hair and makeup, one more déjà vu while I stood there feeling irrelevant.

I filed for divorce. No property to divide, no kids together, nothing to really argue about. Clean, quick, simple.

But she kept my last name.

That stung because it felt so unnecessary. We'd been married for what amounted to a blink, fifteen minutes in the grand scheme of things, and she held onto my name like it was something she'd earned.

My last name has always meant something to me. It isn't just letters on a license or a form you fill out. It's family. It's history. It's reputation. It's the thing you carry around your whole life, the thing people connect to you. I've always looked at it like something you protect. Something you build. Not something you grab during a quick Vegas ceremony and keep like a souvenir.

But legally, I'd handed it to her. I signed up for it. I made it official. And because of that, she had every right to keep it. That's the part that makes it even more frustrating, because there's no argument to win. There's no technicality. It's just a consequence of a decision I shouldn't have made.

And it's the symbolism that still crawls under my skin.

She got to walk away with the name and none of the work that's supposed to come with it. None of the effort, none of the loyalty, none of the partnership, none of the "we built this together" part that a shared name is supposed to represent. It felt like she got to take something that mattered to me and carry it around like it meant the same thing to her, even though she never treated the marriage, or me, like it mattered at all.

Then she took me to court and filed for an order of protection.

When things were ending, she kept "needing" to come back for "one last thing." It was never actually the last thing. Every time she left, there was suddenly something else she "forgot." A sweatshirt, a toothbrush, some random sentimental trinket that had apparently been sitting untouched in a closet until that exact moment. It didn't feel like a normal breakup where you split your stuff and move on. It felt like she was planting reasons to keep showing up, keeping a foot in the door.

All I wanted was a clean break. Take what you want, take what you need, and be gone. I wanted the house to feel like mine again. I wanted to stop having that constant tension in my body every time I heard a car door outside or a knock at the door, wondering if it was her again with another "quick" excuse.

Then one day she showed up again, saying she had to grab something else. And I decided enough was enough.

"You're not coming back in," I told her. "Last time you left was the last time."

She didn't take it well. She stayed on the other side of the screen door yelling, pointing, getting louder with every second. Her face was right up on the mesh, nose practically pressed into that flimsy grid, giving me hell through a piece of aluminum screen.

I was done. Not "I'm upset" done. Not "we'll talk later" done. Done in the way where you can feel there's nothing left to negotiate.

And in this stupid, tiny flash of irritation, more reaction than thought, I lifted my hand and flicked the screen right where her nose was. Not a punch. Not a shove. A flick. The same kind of motion you'd use if a cookie crumb was on your keyboard. It was petty, and it was impulsive, and it lasted half a second.

That half-second became an order of protection.

I never went to her house. Never showed up at her job. I didn't stalk her, didn't circle her neighborhood, didn't blow up her phone, didn't beg her to come back. I wasn't the one trying to force contact. If anything, I was trying to shut it down completely. She was the one finding reasons to keep showing up.

But on paper, I became the one who was "restricted" from going near her.

If it hadn't felt so pathetic, I probably would've laughed. This official document drawing a line I had already drawn for myself. Like the court had to step in and tell me not to do the thing I had no intention of doing anyway. It didn't change my plans. I had zero desire to see her. It just made it formal.

We were over. Really over.

Years went by and we just faded. No big blowout. No dramatic goodbye scene in the rain. Just two people slowly stepping in opposite directions until we were nothing but names in each other's phone. Every once in a while I'd think about her and feel that familiar twist in my chest, but mostly life moved on. Or at least it pretended to.

I finally bought my first house and signed those mortgage papers like I was finally leveling up in adulthood. I started a whole-house remodel project immediately after unlocking the front door. Drywall dust in the air, bare floors, exposed studs, half-painted walls. But still, it was my name on the deed. My future was hiding inside all that raw wood and torn-up carpet, waiting for me to get my shit together.

And for reasons I still can't fully explain, I wanted to show her.

Part of it was pride. *Look what I did. Look what I built without you.* Part of it was that stubborn, broken little part of me that refuses to completely shut a door, even when the house behind it is already on fire. Maybe I just wanted to see her alone, without the noise of everyone else's opinions, and figure out if there was anything real left between us, or if I was just hooked on the ghost of what I thought we used to be.

She agreed to come by on her lunch break. She had an hour total, which meant fifteen minutes to get there, fifteen to get back, and twenty, maybe thirty minutes in between. Twenty or thirty minutes in a half-gutted house with no furniture, no distractions, and way too much history echoing off the walls.

You don't need a wild imagination to figure out how that went.

We did exactly what we always did when words weren't enough and common sense didn't exist. We went straight back to the one thing we were consistently good at together. Old habits. Familiar hands. That same stupid rush that felt like love but never actually was.

Afterward, I stood there in my empty living room feeling less like a grown man starting a new chapter and more like a dog sprinting back to the same electric fence, acting shocked when it lit me up.

That was it. Our last time. Physically, emotionally, whatever you want to call it, that was the end. After that day, there was nothing left to drag out, nothing left to fix, nothing left to pretend. Nothing left to say.

Now when I think back on it, there's this strange, soft ache. A kind of nostalgia tangled up with embarrassment. I wanted so badly for that moment to mean something, for us to mean something, and instead I turned it into one more reminder that I didn't know how to let go.

I had the chance to walk away clean, to stand in that new house as a new version of myself, to close that chapter with at least a little bit of dignity. Instead, I opened the door and invited the past in one more time, just long enough for it to remind me exactly why it should've stayed out.

We talked a few more times in the years that followed. Nothing big. A random message here, a "Hey, how've you been?" there. Little check-ins that never grew into anything real. Just thin threads of conversation drifting between us like old smoke that never quite cleared.

The thing is, I've never been good at letting people go. I don't do clean exits. I don't block, delete, or pretend you never existed. If someone mattered to me once, some part of me feels this weird obligation to leave the door cracked, just in case, so every couple of years I'd send something small, something "harmless."

"Hope you're doing well."

"Happy birthday."

"A random meme that reminded me of you."

On the surface, they were just words. Underneath, they all said the same thing. I remember you. I haven't really put you down yet.

For a long time, I thought that meant I was a good guy. Loyal. Thoughtful. The kind of person who doesn't just erase people once the story changes. I liked that version of me. It felt noble.

But looking back, I can see what it really did. It wrecked things that hadn't even had a chance to grow yet.

All that "just checking in" sounds innocent, but it isn't. It stirs up old emotions that were finally starting to settle. You read a message, you hear their name, and suddenly your brain is right back to, *What if?*

What if we'd tried harder? Could we have fixed it? Did I walk away too soon? Did I screw this up more than I thought?

You start dragging ghosts into rooms they don't belong in, and then you wonder why your current relationship feels overcrowded. Spoiler: it's because you've set a place at the table for people who aren't even in your life anymore.

It's not fair. Not to the person you're with, and honestly, not to you either.

So if you're sitting there wondering whether you should keep tabs on your exes, whether you should keep that line open "just in case," here's my very unromantic answer.

Don't.

Just assume they're okay. Let them be okay without you knowing the details. Protect the life you're trying to build now instead of dragging old chapters into a book that's supposed to be moving forward. People from your past don't stop existing just because you stop reading their page.

But you don't have to keep flipping back to prove it.

I made that mistake for way too many years, pretending it was kindness when really it was fear, ego, and a complete inability to close a damn door.

Just stop.

Then there was Claire.

She owned a small pet boutique in the mall. She was about five years older than me, effortlessly beautiful, and carried herself like she'd already survived three lifetimes. She had that kind of laugh that pulled other people into it, even if they didn't know the joke. People noticed when she walked into a room, not just because of how she looked, but because she had this easy, unbothered confidence.

We connected fast.

Our conversations weren't about favorite bands or generic first date stuff. They were about business, brand image, sales strategies, customer psychology. I soaked it up. Owning a business had always been one of my pipe dreams, and here was someone actually living it. I'd sit across from her with a drink in my hand, listening, asking questions, trying to learn everything I could. The combination of intelligence and drive is unfairly attractive, and she had both.

She was such a polar opposite from Selena. The intellectual conversation and maturity was something I deeply craved after a complete lack of both during that fifteen month stretch with Selena. Selena was all about high heels and giggling. Claire was about spreadsheets and profit margin.

My gut, though, kept whispering the same warning.

Careful.

She'd just gotten out of a marriage. Fresh divorce. Raw edges. On some level, I always knew I was more rebound than real partner. She even introduced me to her friends as her "boy toy," with a laugh, like it was cute.

I laughed too. Pretended it didn't bother me. But it did. I wanted to be more than a prop in somebody else's "I still got it" phase. The problem is, I also really enjoyed being that prop.

She was honest in her own way. She wanted fun, distraction, adventure. And we definitely had that.

Looking back, I can see the disturbing resemblance between who she was at the time and the person I was five years earlier. I didn't see it then, but it's clear as day now. Damn.

Our weekends became a blur. Drinks, bars, late-night drives, and yeah, more than a few threesomes. Over the course of our time together, we ended up in bed with four or five different women. It felt unreal, like I'd accidentally walked into someone else's fantasy life.

There's one night I'll never forget.

The plan was simple. Get dressed up, hit the downtown bars, drink too much, and see what kind of trouble we could find. Claire told me she was bringing a friend. Then she clarified it in a way that made me pause.

"It's my son's girlfriend's mom," she said. "We've gotten close, and she's bringing a friend too."

I remember thinking, *okay, this is going to be awkward as hell.*

They showed up at my place before we headed out. The mom was adorable, about 5'1", curly brown hair, warm eyes, bubbly energy. Not the kind of woman who walks into a room and makes everyone stare, but she had that easy, naturally cute thing going on. The kind where you can tell she was comfortable in her own skin, and that alone made her attractive.

Her friend was a different story. She looked like she'd been built for attention. Tall, blonde, perfect skin, makeup that looked like a photo shoot for a magazine. Everything about her screamed "high maintenance," not in a bad way, just in a way that made you think she doesn't roll out of bed looking like that by accident. Curves that definitely didn't come standard.

We get to the bar, settle in, and we're barely ten minutes into the night when Claire leans in and drops it like she's telling me what the drink special is.

"They're trying to set up a foursome tonight," she says, casually sipping her drink.

I laughed because my brain assumed it had to be a joke. I almost choked, but then I realized she wasn't smiling like someone waiting for a reaction. She was smiling like someone who was waiting for a reply.

"Are you serious?" I asked.

She smirked. "You complaining?"

Nope. I definitely wasn't.

As the night went on, things split in a way that made it feel even more unreal. Claire ended up dancing with the blonde, and I was leaning against the bar with the mom. The music was loud enough that you weren't really talking so much as trading half-sentences and filling in the gaps with body language and eye contact. We were both a little buzzed, leaning closer than strangers usually do, laughing at things that weren't even that funny.

At some point, out of nowhere, she leaned her back into me and started moving to the beat. Slow. Deliberate. Not subtle. That kind of move that isn't an accident, and isn't a question. I remember glancing over at Claire, fully expecting a look, a comment, some kind of "okay, that's enough." Instead, she watched us, smiled, and went right back to dancing with the blonde like this was exactly how the night was scripted.

By the time the bars closed, we were all running on that mix of alcohol and adrenaline where everything feels like a good idea because you're not thinking about tomorrow yet. We headed toward Claire's house, stopping by mine first so they could grab their bags. And that's where the night went from wild to what is my life right now?

The blonde pulled out her phone and called her husband.

Yes, husband. Married. That detail would've been helpful earlier, but here we were.

At first, I assumed it was a quick check-in. The responsible version. "Hey, I'm safe, we're heading back, don't worry." Something like that. Except she didn't sound sneaky or nervous or even excited. She sounded calm. Casual.

"Hey," she says, "just letting you know we're heading to Carrie's for a foursome with her and her boyfriend."

I froze. Not because I was judging her, and not because I was suddenly clutching pearls. I froze because my brain couldn't make the tone match the words. It was delivered like she was updating him about the status of traffic.

Then she holds the phone out to me and says, "He wants to talk to you."

Of course he does.

I took the phone and put it to my ear, still trying to process what kind of marriage this was and what kind of night I had apparently wandered into.

"Those are some crazy girls, ain't they?" he says, laughing.

"Yeah," I managed. "They are."

"Treat 'em good," he says. "Make sure they're safe."

"I will," I said, because what else do you say to the husband of the woman who just laid out your sexual itinerary like it was a grocery list?

And I remember standing there with the phone in my hand and it hit me how fast my life had gone from trying to hold everything together to standing in my own living room getting "permission" from a stranger to do something that, in any other context, might've resulted in a trip to the Emergency Room.

When we got to Claire's house, she disappeared into the kitchen to make drinks while the rest of us settled into the living room. I sat on the floor and leaned back against the couch, still trying to catch up with what had just happened on that phone call just minutes earlier. My brain kept replaying the call like it was a prank.

Underneath that confusion was this giddy buzz in my chest, like I'd just been handed a hall pass by the universe.

Then, without any real warning, both women dropped down on either side of me. One of them kissed me. The other pressed her mouth against my neck. I swear my brain glitched. For a second I just sat there frozen, because suddenly the fantasy had hands and lips.

And my first instinct wasn't even excitement. It was this split-second panic, trying to figure out what category this was.

Am I cheating? Is this a test? Is Claire about to walk back in and blow up?

She came into the room, took one look at us, raised an eyebrow, and smirked. "Damn, you guys started without me."

No anger. No shock. No meltdown. Just that look on her face like she'd walked in and caught people eating before she'd sat down at the table.

She set the drinks down, peeled off her top like it was nothing, and joined in. And from there, the night stopped being a sequence of decisions and turned into something else entirely. More like fragments. Hands everywhere. Mouths. Laughter. Clothes disappearing into corners. That dizzy feeling where you lose track of what's happening first because it's all happening at once.

There's no clean, classy way to describe it without either overselling it or turning it into something cheap, and I don't want to do either. So I'll just say it plainly. It was the craziest, most amazing sexual experience of my life. Three beautiful women, one night, and a story that still sounds surreal even when I'm the one telling it.

It felt unreal, like I'd somehow landed in a situation that only happens in fantasies or late-night TV. Pure sexual sensory overload.

But even in the middle of all that pandemonium and pleasure, something familiar was still there, threading through the whole night. Jealousy.

Claire had sworn up and down she wouldn't care. "I'm fine," she'd said. "I don't get jealous." And maybe she believed that when she said it. But the more the night unfolded, the more I could feel the truth of it. If I spent too long kissing one of the others, if I focused on them a little too much, if my attention drifted away from Claire for more than a moment, she'd pull me back. Sometimes it was subtle, her hand on my shoulder, a kiss that wasn't sweet so much as possessive. Other times it was more obvious, like she was reminding everyone, including me, who the center of gravity was supposed to be.

At first, I won't lie, it felt flattering. Being wanted like that, being pulled in three directions, feeling like the prize. But eventually it started to feel tense. Like no matter how wild the night got, there was still an invisible boundary I couldn't cross without it becoming a problem later. And the crazy part was, I could feel that coming even while it was happening, like the fun had fine print attached to it.

That night became both the high point and the beginning of the end.

Because once the dust settled and the novelty wore off, I couldn't ignore what was underneath it anymore. For a few hours, it looked like freedom, like we'd somehow transcended all the usual rules and landed in this upgraded, evolved version of a relationship.

But we hadn't.

We were just two people using other people as props, trying to stretch the spark between us into something it was never built to be. The euphoria was real. I won't lie about that. It felt insane and electric and unforgettable.

But when it was over, when the room went quiet and the lights came back on, what we were left with wasn't liberation. It was the truth. We weren't actually built to go the distance.

And somewhere beneath the rush, I think both of us already knew it.

I didn't have a problem with Claire being wild when we were together. That was never the issue. I wasn't judging her for having a sexual side, or for being open, or for wanting to push boundaries. If anything, when we were on the same page, it was fun. It felt like we had this private world where we could be honest and adventurous without pretending to be something we weren't.

What I couldn't get past was what she did when I wasn't there.

I found out she'd been hooking up with other women behind my back. And I know how people try to play that down, like it's some technicality that doesn't count. "It's just a girl," "that's different," "it doesn't mean anything." Not to me. I don't care what's under somebody's clothes. If it's sexual, if it's behind closed doors, and I only find out after the fact, that's cheating. Period. It's not about gender. It's about honesty and exclusivity and what you agreed to, even if the agreement was never said out loud in some formal speech.

The weird part is, by that point, I wasn't asking for much. I'd already had my wild nights. That foursome, the threesomes, all the chaos and the stories, it wasn't some bucket list I was still chasing. That box had been checked. I wasn't looking for more "experiences."

What I wanted was her. Just her. Something steady. Something rooted. Something where I didn't have to wonder what the truth was every time she walked out the door. I wanted to feel like I was building toward something real instead of constantly negotiating the terms of the relationship in my head.

To her credit, she didn't lie about it. When it came down to it, she told me straight that she wasn't in that place. Not with me. Not yet. And maybe not ever. There was no dramatic denial, no gaslighting, no long performance. Just a blunt kind of honesty that left me with nothing to argue against, because the truth was clear. We wanted different things, and I wasn't going to be able to talk her into wanting what I wanted.

So that was it. We were done. And that sucked, because she really was an incredible woman.

She eventually got re-married and moved on with her life, and genuinely, I'm happy for her. She found what she wanted. It just wasn't going to be with me. And as much as that hurt at the time, it was also one of the first moments I can remember choosing the truth over the fantasy, choosing what I needed instead of trying to force someone into a version of love they didn't have to give.

Being upfront is a good thing. Being guarded is understandable. Real connection is always going to demand risk. It's going to require vulnerability, honesty that goes deeper than the disclaimer at the beginning, and a willingness to accept that someone might hurt you a little. Or a lot.

As wild as some of those nights were, as much as they would have sounded like the dream to a younger version of me who thought more was always better, those weren't the moments where I found myself. Those were the years where I lost myself in other people's beds and my own bravado. And buried inside all of that bravado, underneath the jokes and the "no strings" speeches, was the quiet realization that I finally wanted something more.

Shayla and Elena showed me that even when I tried to get closer, I ended up burned. Claire showed me that even the wild, movie-level nights, the ones that would have sounded like a fantasy to a younger version of me, couldn't touch the stuff that was broken underneath. None of it fixed anything. If anything, it just gave me better distractions from what I didn't want to feel.

Somewhere in all that noise, I learned that building walls does protect you from certain kinds of pain, and I clung to that. But those same walls also keep out the possibility of something real, something that might actually matter. You don't get to filter what comes through. You block it all or you risk it all.

I didn't walk away from those years hating women. I didn't even walk away hating myself, not really. What I walked away with was caution, and a clearer view of just how committed I'd been to staying in the shallow end and calling it "safety."

My gut was rarely wrong. I just found it easier to ignore it. It was easier to point to the fine print than admit I was scared to actually show up for anyone, including myself.

At first, that whole chapter with Claire felt like the excitement of the early, single, flirtatious years, but with the stability of the relationship I had hoped to get with Selena. When I met Claire, I was drawn to her ambition more than anything. That entrepreneurial fire in her chest lit something in mine. She made me want more for myself. She made me think bigger than the next paycheck and the next hookup.

That kind of inspiration is powerful. But just because someone inspires you doesn't mean they're meant to stay.

You can be absolutely captivated by someone and still not belong together. You can admire the hell out of them and still know, deep down, that you can't trust them, or yourself, with them. My gut had been screaming from the start, and I kept shoving a drink in its hand and telling it to calm down.

I confused stimulation with connection. The late-night talks about business, the mental sparring, the shared fire, that felt like intimacy. It wasn't. She wanted fun. I wanted fuel. I turned it into something deeper in my head because it felt better than admitting I was still running from real vulnerability.

And I learned something else too. When you don't know your own worth, you'll settle for being whatever fits into someone else's story. Boy toy, backup plan, side character in their "wild phase." That's all I was to her. And that's all I allowed myself to be.

She taught me that. Not by what she gave me, but by what she couldn't.

ROUND 25:
Hits Taken, Lessons Mistaken

As Cole got older, football quickly became his thing, our thing, really.

I've always loved the game. But I'm not that guy who can rattle off stats or argue draft picks like it's a second language. And I don't live on ESPN, or know every roster. But I can sit on the couch and watch two teams I don't care about beat the hell out of each other for three straight hours and still call it a good day.

Growing up in Illinois, I was a Bears fan by default, which feels more like a lifelong medical condition than a choice. But the truth? I never really cared who won. I just loved the game itself. The movement. The violence. The quiet, tense seconds between the snap and the whistle. The story it tells one play at a time.

So when Cole strapped on pads for the first time at ten years old, I was thrilled, and terrified.

That's the split-screen of being a dad. One half of you wants to wrap your kid in bubble wrap, the other half wants to throw him straight into the deep end and watch him learn to swim. Football is perfect for that. It's not just a sport, it's a crash course in life: how to take a hit, how to get back up, how to keep going when every muscle in your body is screaming quit. Stallone said it best:

"It's not about how hard you hit, it's about how hard you can get hit and keep moving forward. That's how winning is done!"

It teaches discipline. Accountability. That brutal little truth that your effort, or your laziness, doesn't just affect you. One missed block, one lazy tackle, one second of hesitation, and the whole team pays the price. That kind of pressure either breaks you or builds you. And when it builds you, it builds men.

Now, genetically, we didn't exactly breed a linebacker. I'm 5'3", his mom's 5'4", nobody was holding out hope for a D1 scholarship here. But what he lacked in size, he made up for in heart. And I'll take heart over height any day.

He was fast. Aggressive. Relentless. He played anything they'd let him play: offense, defense, special teams. One week he was at running back, then linebacker, then quarterback. If there was a way to be on the field, he was out there. I used to wonder when he'd run out of gas. He never did.

And I was always there too, camera in hand like some over-caffeinated, underpaid ESPN crew.

I had one of those big Canon digital cameras hanging from my neck every game. My memory has always been spotty, and photos help glue things together for me. Half the time I don't remember a specific play until I see the picture, and then I'm back there again: the smell of grass, the crushing thud of helmets colliding, the whistle cutting the air.

But I never wanted to be that dad who only saw his kid through a lens. So I'd shoot a few plays, then drop the camera to my lap and just watch. Not as a cameraman. As a dad. As *his* dad.

Some games I'd haul a video camera up to the top of the bleachers and set it on a tripod so I could capture the full field. From up there, you can see everything: the holes opening, the broken tackles, the breakaway runs. And Cole gave us plenty of those. Every Saturday felt like I was watching my own son's personal highlight reel.

But the games were only half of it.

I showed up for practice, too.

I didn't have to. Most parents didn't. But I got into this routine without even thinking about it: clock out, pick him up, drive straight to the field, grab my chair, and set up on the sideline like it was part of the schedule. Not because I thought I was earning some "dad points," and definitely not because I had anything to prove to the other parents. I just wanted to be there.

And I wasn't there to be a problem. No yelling at the coach. No trying to coach from the sideline. No play-by-play commentary. I stayed quiet and watched. I watched him run sprints until his face went red. I watched him miss stuff and get frustrated. I watched him get corrected, try again, mess up again, and then finally get it right. I watched the parts nobody posts online and nobody claps for: the repetition, the boredom, the moments where you can tell a kid is deciding whether he's going to push through or shut down.

A lot of practices weren't exciting. Some days the weather was miserable. Some days the energy was low and everyone looked like they'd rather be anywhere else. There were days he'd climb in the car afterward and barely talk, either because he was tired or because something didn't go his way. And I'd just let that be what it was. I didn't need him to perform for me. I didn't need to squeeze a lesson out of every ride home. I wanted him to feel support, not pressure.

Because what I wanted him to see was that I cared about the unglamorous part. Not just the games. Not just the moments where the stands are watching. I cared about the work it took to get there, and I cared about who he was becoming while he was doing it. The effort. The discipline. The decision to keep showing up when it's not fun and nobody's clapping. That's what I wanted to reinforce, whether football stayed in his life forever or not.

But there's one game I'll never forget.

His second season. He was eleven or twelve, that in-between age where they're still just kids but trying so damn hard not to look like it. We were playing an away game in Mahomet. Cool air, metal bleachers, that dusty grass smell that clings to everything.

On one play, he took a helmet straight into the hip. Dropped him like a rock.

I watched him crumple and every instinct in me started screaming, *Go. Run out there. Scoop him up. Get your kid.* That's the dad reflex, the part of you that doesn't care who's watching, you just want your kid out of the line of fire. But I stayed put.

He didn't need his dad sprinting across the field in front of his friends like some panicked rescue mission. He needed space to hurt, to catch his breath, and then decide what he was going to do about it.

They helped him off the field. He lay on his back on the sideline, one knee bent, hands over his face so nobody could see the tears. It hurt. Bad. You could see it in the way his chest rose and fell, that tight, shaky breathing kids do when they're trying to hold it together and it's not working.

The trainer knelt down beside him, rotated his leg, pressed into the bruised spot on his hip while I watched from a few yards away, absolutely useless. That's one of the worst parts of being a parent, by the way. Those moments when all you can do is stand there and feel it with them. You can't tag in. You can't take the hit for them. You just stand there and die a little while someone in khakis and a whistle makes the call.

And then Cole did what Cole always does.

He got mad at the pain.

He wiped his face, sat up, and then stood. Slow. Stiff. Limping. But upright. Determined. The stubborn spark in his eyes kicked back on, and I could practically hear the shift from *This hurts* to *I'm not done yet.*

A few minutes later, he was on his feet at the sideline, still favoring that leg but insisting he was ready to go back in. Inside me, it was a full-on collision: half pure fear, half ridiculous pride. The dad in me wanted to tell him, *Sit your ass down, ice it, live to fight another day.* But he wasn't built to watch from the sideline. Not that day. Not right then.

He looked at his coach and yelled, "Put me in!"

I finally stepped up beside him, slid my arm around his back, my hand resting on his shoulder pad. We stood there together at the edge of the field, waiting for the call. Someone behind us snapped a picture right then. You can't see our faces in it, just two figures from the back, standing shoulder to shoulder, looking straight out at the field.

It's one of my favorite photos on this planet.

Because to me, that picture is our relationship. Not father towering over son. Not son clinging to father. Just a father and son, side by side, facing whatever's coming next. Him, ready to limp back into the game. Me, ready to let him. Both of us scared. Both of us proud.

If I could freeze time anywhere, that might be where I'd hit pause.

Right there, I wasn't just his father. I was his teammate. His support. His quiet witness standing on the edge of the field while he chose courage over comfort.

And God, I love that kid more than I will ever find the right words for.

As he crept up on the teenage years, the change came in slow, like fog rolling in over a field. One day he's this kid asking if we can stop for ice cream after practice, shoes untied, grass stains on his knees… and then somehow, almost without me noticing, he's this quiet, closed-off, headphone-wearing stranger in a hoodie.

The biggest change came when girls entered the picture.

Not "dating" like we grew up with, where you picked someone up at their house and awkwardly met their parents in the doorway. This was middle school dating. Marathon phone calls, text messages until two in the morning, talking through headsets on Xbox while they shot each other in whatever game they were playing. Half relationship, half WiFi connection.

Around that same time, his music started changing too. This emo-punk edge started creeping into his playlists. Songs that were basically built out of heartbreak and anger and all these big, messy feelings kids don't really know what to do with yet. He didn't talk about it much, but you could tell it was doing something for him. He would play "21 Guns" from Green Day like it matched whatever was going on under the surface.

> *"… When you're at the end of the road*
> *And you lost all sense of control*
> *And your thoughts have taken their toll*
> *When your mind breaks the spirit of your soul*

It took me straight back to middle school, me in my own head, using music like a hiding place. Back then it was sad Chicago songs, Foreigner, whatever I could find that made me feel. I wasn't "processing" anything. I was just trying to feel something on purpose, because everything else felt too loud or too confusing or too out of my control.

Seeing him do his version of that was a grim reminder. Not because the music was "bad," and not because I wanted to police what he listened to. It was recognizing the pattern. The way a kid can be surrounded by people and still feel alone. The way music can become the safest place to put emotions when you don't know where else they're supposed to go.

I saw me in him. Different decade. Different songs. Same outcome.

Underneath all of that, he was carrying so much anger toward his mom. So much hurt. So many questions with no real answers. That emotional gap, her absence, slowly turned into something heavier: resentment, mistrust, isolation. That quiet belief that he was unwanted. He never said those words out loud, but I could feel it coming off him in waves.

And here's the part that still guts me: even with how close we'd always been, when he needed someone the most, I wasn't as present as I should've been.

I was in the house. I was technically "there." But he was in his room, in his own little universe, and I didn't push hard enough to step inside it. I told myself he needed space. I told myself it was just teenage stuff, just hormones, just a phase. I told myself a lot of things, honestly, because it was easier than admitting I was distracted too, and maybe a little afraid of what I'd find if I pushed that door open.

Because the truth is, I had my own life going on. I was working, trying to keep the bills handled, trying to keep the house functioning, trying to date and pretend I was normal. I was juggling my own emotions and my own mess, trying to glue myself back together while also being the steady parent. And somewhere in that, I started leaning on the idea that he was "fine." That he was strong. That because we were close, he automatically felt supported, even if we weren't actually talking the way we needed to be talking.

I was wrong.

He didn't want to talk to his dad about what he was feeling. Of course he didn't. Most teenage boys would rather chew glass than sit down and say, "Hey, I feel abandoned and angry and kind of broken." I wish we'd been the kind of family where that kind of conversation was normal. We weren't. We had love, we had loyalty, we had shared history, but we didn't always have the language, or the comfort, to sit in the hard stuff and actually say it out loud.

So he stayed in his room. He stayed in his head. And I stayed busy, telling myself I was giving him space, when what he really needed was me choosing to be more present than "in the same house."

But thankfully, he found his own way to let it out.

He started writing.

Just like I did at his age.

Seventh grade, right before thirteen, he began putting his feelings on paper. Poems, lyrics, little fragments of thoughts that read like X-rays of his heart. He scribbled them into notebooks and on loose sheets of paper, like he was trying to bleed some of the pain out of his chest and onto the page.

One day, he finally got brave enough to hand some of them to me.

I didn't expect much. A few angsty lines, maybe a forced rhyme or two about heartbreak and darkness and whatever band he was obsessed with that week.

Instead, I got punched in the heart.

His words were raw and honest and so much deeper than I was prepared for. The pain, the confusion, the way he described feeling unsafe, unseen, unwanted, it was all there. No filter. No performance. Just truth.

I sat there reading my twelve-year-old son's handwriting and I broke a little. The kind of breaking where your heart just folds in on itself because you suddenly see everything you've been missing.

I could see how much he'd been holding in. How much I'd mistaken for "normal teenage moodiness." How often I'd walked past his closed door, telling myself he was fine when clearly, he wasn't. He wasn't remotely close to being fine.

I wanted to grab him and never let go. I wanted to fix everything right there, with one hug and one long talk at the kitchen table. But some things don't work like that. Some things you can't fix with a speech and a pat on the back. Some things you just have to sit inside with them, even when it's uncomfortable, even when it hurts to hear.

I always believed keeping distance between him and his mother was the right call. For his safety. For his stability. For his sanity. But I never knew how to say that out loud without sounding like I was just trashing her or forcing him to choose sides. I didn't want him growing up thinking I was the one keeping her away.

So I stayed vague. I let him think it was mostly her choice. Or his. I told myself I was protecting him from the ugly side of the truth.

I don't know if that was the right move. I still don't.

What I do know is that if he hadn't started writing, I might never have known how scared he felt at her house. How much her husband's presence freaked him out. To this day, I don't know if that man was intentionally intimidating or just completely clueless. Maybe he thought he was being funny. Maybe he thought he was being "tough."

But to Cole, he wasn't funny. He was terrifying. And that fear dug in deep.

That's why I decided to include some of Cole's early writing in this book.

I could sit here and try to explain how powerful it was, how much it opened my eyes, how clearly it showed me the storm he was walking through... but I don't think my words can do him justice. His writing is where I first heard the version of my son I'd been missing. The one who didn't know how to talk, but knew exactly how to write.

And as his dad, reading those words, I didn't just see his pain. I saw myself in it too.

So I'm going to let his voice speak for itself.

Just like it did the day he handed me this:

"Name: 'Mom'

I found myself in my room thinking
What if I had a mom that was actually worth seeing
She never called me when I was little
That's the reason why I'm so bitter
She never comes to any football game I have
Doesn't support me and never has
I thought about throwin' the glass
When I had a stepdad scare me to death
But never scare my brother
The reason is because I was some other
Kid
And I wasn't his
I hid under my bed
Just to see his head poke under and grab me
Pull me out and have me screaming
Basically you are double teaming
Just stay away and don't come back
This will finally show you the facts
You always ask me why I act so depressed
Because without you I'd be blessed
I finally found a person who's a mother to me
And that's who I want it to be
Savannah.

-Cole"

At the time, Savannah and I had only been together five or six months.

She's my wife now, but back then, I had no idea where we were going. If history had taught me anything, it was this: around the seven-month mark, something always cracked. Someone, usually me, got spooked and bailed. That was my pattern. My expiration date.

So when I read those words from Cole, his heartbreak, his anger, his depression, and then, in the very same poem, the way he wrote about Savannah as this soft place of safety, it knocked the wind out of me.

To him, she wasn't just "Dad's new girlfriend."

She was comfort. She was safety. She was the person sitting in the dark with him when I didn't even realize the lights were off.

I didn't show Savannah the poem right away. Part of me wanted to run straight to her with it, like, *Look what you mean to him. Look what you mean to us.* But I didn't want to drop that kind of weight on her without thinking it through. She hadn't signed up to be anybody's savior. She'd just been kind. Present. Herself.

So I held onto it.

I typed every one of his poems, printed them out, and put them in a binder. Backed them up in the cloud like they were family heirlooms. Because they are. Those pages are a record of who he was at twelve years old, and who I was failing to be.

I think it's important that he can go back to them someday. To remember how he felt, what he carried, how far he's come… or how far he drifted. Sometimes you read something you wrote years ago and it hits you again, like an old version of you clearing its throat. Sometimes it reminds you of a dream you dropped. Either way, it wakes something up. It reminds you your voice counts.

Words count. Way more than that stupid childhood rhyme ever admitted.

"Sticks and stones may break my bones, but words will never hurt me."

Yeah, right.

Bones heal. Bruises fade. But there are sentences I've heard once that still echo. Words can hurt worse than any punch, and the worst part is, once they're out, you don't get a do-over. You can apologize. You can take responsibility. But you can't un-say them.

And yet, sitting there with my son's poem in my hands, I had nothing. No speech. No "teachable moment." Just silence. He had all the words I didn't.

Twelve years old, and he could say his pain out loud on paper better than I could as a grown man.

That was a turbulent time for him. He was dealing with the emotional fallout from his mom, the intensity of first "love," that pre-teen obsession that feels like life or death when you're in it. His early girlfriends held way more power over his identity than I realized. I watched him start to shape-shift to match them.

He started wearing white tank tops. Grew his bangs out to hang over his eyes. The emo look. On the surface, it just seemed like a style phase. I told myself, *It's fine. He's expressing himself.* And I meant that. I didn't care what he wore.

What I missed was that it wasn't just fashion.

It was armor.

He was trying to wear his pain. Give it a shape. Let the world know, without saying a word, that something hurt.

And I didn't see it. Maybe I was afraid of what I'd find. Maybe nothing I did would've changed anything. Maybe he still would've shut me out like most teenagers do. But at least I could've tried harder. I didn't. And that's on me.

There was one girl in particular who really wrecked him. Manipulative as hell, in my opinion. When that relationship ended, he was shattered. He talked about her for a year.

You don't forget your first heartbreak. It feels like the ground drops out. At that age, you don't know you can survive it. You don't know that "not being enough for someone" doesn't mean you're not enough. It just means they weren't your person.

You only learn that after a few crashes.

I had to go through a lot of wrong people before I understood what a right one might even look like. And even then, it wasn't like a neon sign lit up over their head. Half the time, I only realized someone wasn't right once my heart, time, and trust were already on the table.

Dating is hard as an adult. As a teenager, it's war with no armor and no training. Watching your kid go through it is brutal. You want to bubble-wrap their heart. You want to pull them out of the fire. But you also know some pain is part of growing up. You can't keep them from every hit. You can only try to stand close while they take it.

I didn't always manage that. Not well enough. Not consistently enough.

Cole did learn something powerful, though, even back then. He learned how to walk away from people who hurt him. That doesn't mean it didn't destroy him at the time. It did. But he walked. He didn't stay and let someone keep cutting pieces out of him.

Sometimes we chase what feels familiar, even when the familiar hurts. I did. Maybe he did too. But he also inherited that stubborn part of me that eventually says, Enough.

Still, I catch myself wondering: *if he'd had a more emotionally present dad, a real safe place to unload all of that, would it have cut as deep? Lasted as long? Could I have carried some of it with him instead of watching him drag it alone?*

I'll never know. That's the part that haunts me.

There are moments that don't look like anything special while they're happening. You only see what they were later, when you're looking back and realizing how much time disappeared.

For me, some of those moments were the tiniest ones with Cole.

Bath nights. That soft, damp warmth when I'd wrap him in a towel and carry him to the couch, his little body loose against mine. Running my fingertips down his back in slow lines, feeling him settle. Those quiet songs in the living room, dancing to the same track on repeat while he rested his head on my shoulder. Saturday afternoons at the mall, watching him edge his way out of his shyness and into the chaos of the kids' play area, then turn around and invite the next shy kid.

Back then, I thought being a father was mostly the big stuff: provide, protect, teach right from wrong. The obvious parts. The parts you can point at and say, See? That's parenting.

But those small, ordinary moments were everything.

Holding him after a bath taught me a different language, one made of touch and safety instead of lectures and rules. It taught me how much you can say to a kid without opening your mouth. How steady your own heart can feel when you choose gentle, even when everything else in your life is unstable.

Those slow dances in the living room, just me, him, and some random song on repeat, showed me that vulnerability doesn't need an audience. Sometimes it's you in old sweatpants, rocking side to side with a kid who trusts you completely. Just being there.

Watching him at the mall, seeing him go from the kid on the edge to the kid who walked up to other kids on the edge, reminded me that part of being a father isn't just keeping your own kid safe. It's helping them become the kind of person who makes space for other people.

Putting him in Taekwondo was supposed to be simple: give him structure, a physical outlet, discipline. But it turned into something else too. It reminded me that growth comes from the stuff you don't want to do: the stretches that hurt, the drills that suck, the repetition that feels pointless until one day it isn't.

And then adolescence hit, and it wasn't just his turning point. It was mine too.

For the first time, I had to look at my limitations, not just as a dad but as a man. I started to see how much I'd missed by living half in my own madness and half in his world, instead of being fully present in either.

Up to that point, I saw myself as the fixer. I was the guy with duct tape, advice, a plan. But this wasn't something I could fix with a lecture or a checklist. This needed things I wasn't naturally good at: patience, empathy, sitting in discomfort without trying to hurry past it.

Reading his poem broke my heart. His honesty, his hurt, the gratitude he showed toward Savannah, it cut straight through me and forced me to admit I'd missed things. A lot of things.

I learned that "being there" isn't just sharing an address or paying bills on time. Emotional availability doesn't come free with the title Father. You have to choose it. Especially when it's inconvenient. Especially when you feel clueless.

I couldn't rewrite the past. I couldn't go back and be the perfect dad for his younger self. But I could decide who I was going to be now. I could dive in instead of drifting. I could be the door that stays open.

That "emo armor" he wore wasn't just rebellion. It was a language. A way of saying, "I'm not okay," without having to actually say it. Learning to read that language took time. More listening than talking. More awkward, uncomfortable conversations than I wanted.

His words, those poems, weren't just sad lines on paper. They were a bridge. An invitation. "Here I am. If you actually want to see me, start here."

Regret is a really heavy burden to carry. It can crush you, or it can sit there and nag you into doing better with whatever time you've got left. I'm trying to let mine do the second one.

You can't give your kid a perfect parent. But you can give them an honest one. Someone who owns his mistakes, stays engaged, and doesn't pretend he has it all figured out.

Sometimes love means backing up a step so your kid can stand on their own. It never means disappearing. It means staying close enough that when they finally reach out, they don't grab empty air.

When Savannah and I first started dating, I had no idea she'd be the same woman holding me together years later while I ugly-cried over my son. Back then, she wasn't my safe place. She was this beautifully terrifying dream I didn't think I deserved.

She was almost seven years older than me, and it showed in all the ways that made me feel insignificant. She was polished and steady, like an adult brochure brought to life. Master's degree. Stable teaching career.

Beautiful house in a quiet neighborhood. Two kids. A pantry that looked like a commercial for a new grocery store in town.

Then there was me.

Twice divorced. Single dad. Juggling bills like it was an Olympic sport. Living in a neighborhood where sirens were just part of the ambience. I felt like a half-finished project someone abandoned in the middle of the garage.

I'd lie there at night, staring at the ceiling, and ask myself the same pathetic question on repeat: *What do I actually bring to her life that she doesn't already have?*

Every time things between us started to feel serious, the panic would creep in. I could see it play out in my head like a scene from a movie. Her, waking up one morning, rolling over, looking at me, and finally deciding she deserved "better." Better usually meaning taller, richer, more educated, fewer divorces, no antidepressants, and not quite so... me.

So I did what felt safest.

I broke up with her.

Then I did it again.

And again.

Three separate times, for the exact same reason: I thought I could outsmart rejection. I thought if I walked away first, it would hurt less than waiting for the moment she realized I was a downgrade and left me.

Spoiler: it still hurt like hell.

Every time I left, I missed her. I missed her voice in the morning, the way she laughed with her whole face, the way we'd lock eyes in the middle of a crowd and it felt like we were sharing the same thought. I missed the stupid little rituals that had already started to casually feel like home.

The third breakup is where everything broke loose.

I woke up alone in my bed and felt this heavy, sinking realization that I'd just thrown away the exact thing I used to pray for. I finally had a woman who challenged me, cared about me, pushed me, and actually believed I could be more than the mess I was. And I shoved her away because I didn't believe it myself.

My insecurities were just too numerous and too overwhelming. She had a master's degree. I had dropped classes. She had a beautiful newly-built house. I had a remodeled dwelling in the ghetto. I had just lost my job, and even though she told me it didn't matter, I knew it did. How couldn't it?

And then there were my antidepressants.

I don't hide the fact that I've needed medication. It's not a secret. I'm not ashamed of that. The problem wasn't the pills. It was how they suddenly became ammunition.

Any time I got angry, frustrated, or stood my ground a little too firmly, here it came: "Did you forget to take your pill today?"

There is nothing like having your emotions written off as a side effect. If I was upset, it couldn't be because something was actually wrong. It had to be because I was "off my meds." It was like she had a shortcut to shut down any feeling she didn't want to deal with.

Nothing makes you feel more insane than someone suggesting you might just be imagining your own pain.

My self-doubt shot through the roof. I couldn't tell what was valid and what was "chemically imbalanced," because she kept slapping that label on everything. I wasn't just arguing with her, I was arguing with my own mind. *Was I overreacting, or was I finally standing up for myself?*

During our second breakup, I tried to explain all of this instead of disappearing into my usual mix of silence and sarcasm. I wrote her a letter. Long, messy, overly honest. I was never one to censor myself to sound calm and reasonable.

I told her how small I felt when she dismissed the things that hurt me and steered the conversation back to my missing degree or the fact that I was temporarily unemployed, as if those bullet points automatically made her right and me wrong.

I wrote about the house. My house. The first one I had ever bought on my own. The one I poured myself into, room by room, scraping old paint, fixing what I could afford to fix, slowly turning it into a real home.

She wanted me to sell it and move into her house, the one she'd shared with her ex. Her town. Her friends. Her history. She wanted us to start "our future" in a place built on someone else's past.

I asked her if she had really thought about what that meant for me. For my son. For the tiny, fragile sense of pride I'd finally scraped together. I'd be giving up my neighborhood, my routine, my son's familiarity, and the one thing I had that was just mine. It wasn't just real estate. It was a piece of my identity.

I told her I didn't care that I didn't have my degree yet. I was enrolled in school again. I was trying to finish what I started. Losing my job shoved me back into school, and yeah, in the long run it was probably a blessing. None of that meant I was less of a man. It just meant I was rebuilding.

But it felt like every time we argued, she reached for the easy hits. My education, my paycheck, my pills.

I told her the hardest thing for me to admit: I didn't feel heard.

She wanted my life to fuse neatly into hers. My child in her school district, in her town, sleeping under her roof. Me at her table, on her couch, blending into her world. And in all of that, I didn't see much room for what I needed. For what my son needed. For the life I had been clawing together while everyone else's looked so easy.

I even called out things I knew she didn't want to look at, like the way her boys treated her. The eye rolls. The disrespect. The names. If I'd been their full-time stepdad, I would've shut that down real quick. Pull the plug on the electronics, set real consequences, something. She always said you could tell what kind of man a guy is by how he treats his mother, and I watched her sons treat her with complete disregard and disrespect. I couldn't understand why that rule didn't seem to apply in her own house.

I didn't pretend I was innocent, either. I know I can be blunt. I walk a thin line between honest and harsh. She'd tell me not to sugarcoat things, but when I didn't, she'd say I was too intense. I was trying to find the middle ground with her, but I never quite got it right.

I didn't write that letter to make her the villain and me the hero. I just told it the way I saw it. We were two people in completely different places of our lives, and it felt like trying to fit a square peg into a round hole.

She was forty-one, with a fourteen-year marriage behind her. Financially steady. Structured.

I was thirty-four. Two divorces. Unemployed at the moment. Walking back onto a community college campus like a man hitting reset halfway through the game. I was still trying to figure out who the hell I was supposed to be. We weren't starting from the same line, no matter how badly we wanted the same finish.

Then New Year's Eve showed up.

I invited Jenna over, an old fling turned good friend I knew would say yes. I told Savannah, and I was honest, but that was the line for her. Door slammed. No more almosts. No more "maybe later." That was it.

We were done.

I desperately tried to slip back into the old version of my life, the one with casual hookups, emotional distance, and nobody expecting much from me. The life where I could pretend I was fine as long as I kept everything shallow.

But the truth was, she had changed me, and I hated that I couldn't un-feel what I'd felt with her. I just didn't want to be with anyone but Savannah.

She took her laugh, her presence, the light she brought into every room, the soft moments, all of it. And I was left staring at a quieter version of my life that suddenly felt too big and too empty.

Looking back now, I can see it clearly. I was in love with Savannah, sure. But I was just as tangled up in my own shame. Shame about what I wasn't yet. Shame about what I thought she deserved. Shame about the way I kept breaking the heart of the same woman who someday would be the one holding me while I fell apart.

I had no idea then how much I would need her. I only knew how much I didn't feel worthy of being needed back.

And those fights about my job, my degree, my meds, they weren't really about any of those things. Not at the core. On my side, they were about this constant, gnawing fear that I wasn't enough. On her side, I think they were about her fear that she was signing up to carry more than she wanted to. More emotion, more confusion, more rebuilding than she ever imagined when she pictured "starting over." Like going backwards rather than moving forward.

She shouldn't have turned my soft spots into weapons. That part still stings. But I also handed those soft spots over.

I kept waiting for her to make me feel secure, to tell me I was worthy, to pat me on the head and say, "You're doing okay, you're not a screwup," instead of learning how to stand in that truth on my own. I wanted her stamp of approval on my life because I didn't quite know how to give it to myself.

Writing that letter was the first time I really said it out loud, to her and to me at the same time.

My life matters too.
My kid matters.
My dreams are not optional.

I am not some supporting character wandering onto the stage of someone else's perfectly curated life.

Real love doesn't ask one person to shrink so the other can stay comfortable. That's not partnership. Compromise is not the same thing as surrender. You shouldn't have to erase your own life just to fit more neatly into someone else's story.

And no degree, no salary, no three-bedroom house in a polished subdivision magically makes you more worthy of love. Those things can make life easier, sure. They can make you look more "put together" from the outside. But they don't rewrite whatever is already in you.

Losing Savannah taught me that.

It was brutal. It felt like someone took a spotlight to every insecurity I had and then walked away, leaving me alone with them. But it forced me to draw a line I had never drawn before.

I will not trade away the parts of me I just fought to rebuild.

Not for a woman.
Not for the fantasy of a picture-perfect life.
Not for the illusion of stability that can disappear the minute someone changes their mind.

In the end, I walked away bruised, but still on my feet. My son still had his home base. I still had this little physical reminder that I could build and hold something on my own, even when everything in me screamed that I wasn't capable.

But the real win was understanding that I deserve a kind of love where I don't have to make myself small just to keep the peace. A love where I don't have to apologize for having needs, emotions, dreams, or history.

And when love came back around later, the real kind, the kind that fit like something I didn't have to squeeze myself into, I was finally ready. Not perfect, not fixed, not magically healed. Just ready to let it fit me too, instead of breaking myself down to fit it.

As it turns out, there was a next time.

ROUND 26:
Need You Now. Need You Forever.

I can still see myself sitting alone in my living room, phone in my hand like it was life support. Call. Don't call. Text. Erase. Type again. "Seen." Nothing. Every time I reached out to Savannah, it felt like tossing a message in a bottle into a storm I made. On the rare occasion she did respond, it was shrewd little phrases that burned.

"Leave me alone."

And still, I didn't. I couldn't. Some part of me refused to accept that this was how our story ended.

Admitting I still wanted her back felt like walking right up to the edge of a cliff I'd already fallen off three times. I was the one who broke her heart, splintered it, walked out, then tried to come back like a revolving door. Any sane woman would have locked it, deadbolted it, shoved a dresser in front of it, then lit a match for good measure.

And the truth is, she had much bigger things to worry about than me.

Her fourteen-year marriage hadn't just ended. It exploded. Her ex-husband wasn't just some selfish guy or your standard run-of-the-mill cheater. He got arrested for child exploitation. One day he was "going down to the basement to tinker," and the next he was in handcuffs for things she never could have imagined. Her whole reality blew up overnight.

While I was stumbling in and out of her life, dragging my commitment issues, abandonment issues, and whatever other issues along for the ride, she was trying to keep her kids safe and her sanity intact. Meanwhile, the town turned her life into a sideshow. Every hearing, every court date, every tiny update about his sentence, all of it felt public. Her house became the backdrop for the nightly local news.

People whispered at the grocery store, at school pickup, in the hallways, probably right there in the damn produce aisle. They didn't whisper about him. They whispered about her. Like she should have known. Like the stain was somehow hers to wear.

And who was I in the middle of all that?

I was the guy who had already broken her heart three times. The last thing she needed was my bullshit insecurities parking on her front step again. I knew that. I could see it in plain daylight, even if I didn't always act like it.

But underneath the guilt, underneath the shame, there was something in me that refused to let go. Something stubborn. Something hopeful. Something that felt a lot like love that just wouldn't quietly die.

I believed, down deep, we were supposed to be together. That we weren't finished.

Her ex was just days away from sentencing when I decided to call her. Great timing, right? I knew exactly what would happen. Four rings, voicemail. But I called anyway.

My voice cracked as I left the message.

"I know you probably don't want to hear from me, but I just want to talk. I know your ex is going away soon, and I just want to be here for you. If I don't hear back, I'll come over. But please call me back."

It was naïve, I know that now. I was trying to turn my life into a movie. The kind where the guy shows up at the airport or in the rain, and somehow that erases the damage. I had this stupid little picture in my head of her seeing me, running into my arms, and everything snapping right back into place.

Real life doesn't work like that. Real life barely works at all some days.

She did call back, but not because she was sitting around missing me. It sounded more like damage control.

Her voice was cold. She told me not to come over. She repeated it. "Do not come to my house." But the fact that she called at all was enough for me to grab onto. I poured out everything in one breath. I'd made a mistake. I was sorry. I wanted her back. I loved her.

She cut straight through all of it.

"You can't have me back. You let me go. That's what you wanted."

I tried the classic line, "I didn't know what I wanted until it was gone," but it bounced right off. Her world was still burning down, and there I was, standing at the edge with a bouquet of apologies, hoping it would put out the fire.

She asked me why now. Why this moment. What changed.

So I told her.

A few days earlier, my mom and dad had stopped by the house. Dad noticed the picture of Savannah and me still stuck on my fridge. He paused, really looked at it, and said quietly, almost to himself, "I miss Savannah."

My dad doesn't say things like that. Feelings aren't his native language. Hearing that from him hit me right in the chest.

I missed her too.

I told her that story. I told her nothing happened with my ex on New Year's Eve, that it was just my insecurity and my old pattern of blowing up the best things in my life. She wasn't moved.

"You made your choice," she said. "I gave up."

When she hung up, it felt like swallowing a rock. Heavy. Lodged in my throat. I sat there staring at my phone like I'd just watched the last good thing in my life drift away, and I knew I was the one who cut the rope.

I didn't have a big circle of people I confided in, but I did have Alana, my buddy's wife. She never sugar-coated anything. I called her and let it all spill out. My dad's comment. Savannah's ex. My guilt. My regret. My love for her that just wouldn't die. And then I asked her the question I was scared to say out loud.

"Should I even try? Or should I just give up?"

"If you really love her," she said, "and you believe she might still love you, then you owe it to both of you to show her. And if she doesn't take you back, you live with it. But at least you'll know you gave it everything."

Those words burned inside me. The part of me that always quit early, always cut and run, got called out. If I really loved Savannah the way I said I did, then I needed to prove it. Not with promises. With actions. With determination.

And like fate was making a routine delivery to my radio, I heard "One Last Try" by Stevie Hoang on the radio:

> *"Let me start by saying baby I've been such a fool*
> *since we've been apart I've realized I'm needing you*
> *now I don't blame you if you choose to turn and walk away*
> *but girl I think that what we have is worth another day*
>
> *I know I made a mistake when I pushed you away..."*

So I decided to try. One last time. I knew exactly what I was risking. I knew it might make things worse, might be the final nail in the coffin, but I also knew I couldn't live with myself if I didn't at least show up in the one way I still could.

The day her ex was sentenced, I kept thinking about her, and I wanted her to know I was thinking about her. That I cared. That I was on her side, even if I'd been the one who walked away before things were fully settled between us.

So I sent her a text.

I told her I knew she was upset, and I just wanted to be there for her. I said I had something to give her and asked if I could come by after the hearing.

Her reply hit exactly like I knew it might.

She told me she didn't need me. Didn't want me anywhere near her.

I stared at the screen for a long second, feeling that sting spread through my chest. It wasn't surprising, but it still hurt. And even knowing that, I texted back anyway. I apologized. I told her I'd just leave it for her.

The drive to her house was just under an hour, but it felt like an eternity. I spent the whole time arguing with myself. Going over every memory we had, every fight, every soft moment in between. Replaying it all like there was going to be a clean answer hiding in the details. Part of me knew I was driving straight into rejection, and part of me was still hoping for some sign that I hadn't lost her completely.

I stopped at a store on the way and wandered the aisles like a guy trying to turn a feeling into something you could hold. Something that could say what I couldn't say without making it worse.

I ended up buying a teddy bear.

Nothing expensive or over the top. Just soft, small enough to hold. I found a toddler-sized University of Illinois football jersey and put it on the bear, white with pink numbers, the same quarterback number from the games we used to watch together on the couch. I sprayed it with my cologne so it smelled like me. A few days before, I burned a CD with Bon Jovi songs because she'd always been a sucker for Jon Bon Jovi's voice.

Was it cheesy? Yeah. I knew it was cheesy while I was doing it. But it wasn't about trying to impress her or win points. I wasn't trying to be clever. I just wanted her to feel seen. Like someone was still paying attention to the details, even if I'd failed her in the bigger ways.

When I pulled into her driveway, my heart was pounding so hard I swear I could hear it over the engine. I walked up to the garage and set everything down by the door. The bear. The card. The CD. Some candy tucked alongside it.

I stood there for a second just looking at it, letting myself picture her coming home and finding it. Maybe getting one small, quiet breath before the weight of everything crashed back down on her.

Then I got back in my truck and headed home.

I kept imagining her reaction. I kept wanting the story to end differently than it probably would. I kept thinking about how easy it is to hurt someone and how hard it is to try to undo it.

She found it all, the bear, the card, the CD, the candy. She smelled the cologne. She read the note where I told her I would always be there for her, that I loved her, and that I was sorry.

And I think part of her felt something. I think there was a pull back toward me, even if it was small and brief. But the wounds I'd left, layered on top of the trauma she was already living through, were deeper than anything a stuffed bear could patch. Her heart might have tugged in my direction, but her brain yanked it right back. Self-protection wins when the cost has been a broken heart three times over.

After that, life kept moving, because it always does. I worked. I raised Cole. And for once, I didn't run back to my old patterns to fill the empty space. No flings. No meaningless hookups. No trying to distract myself with warm bodies and shallow attention.

I didn't want anyone else. It was her or nothing, and I chose nothing over pretending.

I heard she went on dates. Tried to move forward. Tried to convince herself there was a world where I wasn't part of her story anymore. I understood it. I even respected it. But I also knew, deep down, she was still carrying me the same way I was carrying her. Some connections don't fade just because you decide they should. They quietly hang around, impossible to fully turn off.

Then one day her name popped up in my Facebook messages.

Just seeing it hit me right in the chest. I opened it and just stared for a second before I even read the words, because her name alone was enough to drag me right back into everything.

Her message was short.

"I can be your friend. That's it."

I didn't want friendship. I wanted her, completely, the way I'd always wanted her. But at that point, any piece of her felt like more than I deserved, and I knew it. I also knew she wasn't offering friendship because she suddenly forgot what happened. She was offering it because that was the only place she could meet me without betraying herself.

So I took what she offered.

I asked if she got what I'd left for her. She said yes and that it was sweet, but that I shouldn't have wasted my money.

I told her I didn't care about the money. I told her I just needed her to know that even after everything, after all my screwups and all her pain, I was still here. That I still loved her. That I'd still do anything for her.

And I knew how it probably sounded. Big words from the guy who already proved he could hurt her. But I meant it. I meant it even if it had to stay outside whatever boundary she'd drawn. If she was telling me "friend" and nothing else, then "friend" was what I was going to be. Even if it killed me.

We started texting again. At first it was surface-level stuff, safe conversations. Weather. Work. Kids. Small jokes. But underneath all of that, it felt like finally getting air after holding my breath way too long.

Even the boring messages mattered, because it meant I wasn't shut out anymore. It meant she was letting me exist in her world again, even if it was in the smallest way.

And then, of course, I couldn't keep my mouth shut. I never can.

I told her I loved her. Again. It didn't come out smooth or poetic. It just came out, like it had been sitting in my throat for months waiting for the slightest opening. I told her I'd never hurt her like that again. I promised her I'd be different. I promised her I'd protect her heart this time.

She gave me exactly what I deserved to hear. She told me there was nothing left to fix. That the damage was already done.

And she wasn't wrong.

But I kept promising anyway, because I didn't know what else to do. I didn't have some perfect speech that could undo the past. I didn't have a time machine. All I had was the truth of how I felt, and the choice to keep showing her, over and over, that I wasn't going anywhere. That I was willing to take whatever role she'd allow.

Eventually, I asked her to dinner, fully expecting a hard no, because that would've been the smart answer.

But she said yes.

When she walked into the restaurant, I stood up to hug her, but it was careful and stiff, more like I was asking permission than actually hugging her. It wasn't like the old hugs, the ones that felt automatic, like we didn't have to think about where our hands went or how long we held on. This time there was distance and caution. I could feel it. I didn't know if she felt it too, but I'm sure she did.

We sat across from each other and did the polite small talk thing for a minute. Work. How things had been. The kind of conversation you have when there's a volcano under the table and you're both pretending you don't feel the heat yet. I tried to play it normal, to be calm, but I've never been good at that with her.

And eventually I did the one thing I've always been consistent about.

I dumped my feelings right out on the table. No garnish.

I told her I was sorry. Not the "sorry" you say because you got caught or because you want the tension to stop. The kind of deep regret that burns a hole in your chest. I told her I understood what I'd done. I hated that I'd added pain to a life that already had enough. I told her I would do whatever it took to make it right.

She didn't make it easy.

She told me her family hated me. Her friends hated me. They had every reason to feel that way after everything I had done to her, after all of the pain I caused her.

I told her I'd look every one of them in the eye and apologize. Not to earn forgiveness on the spot, but because I owed it to them, to her. I told her I would walk into any living room, any kitchen, any circle of folded arms and crossed legs and take it. Own it.

If she needed to see me uncomfortable, good. I probably needed to see me uncomfortable too. I didn't want to talk my way out of the consequences. I wanted to face them and fix anything I could.

But she told me she couldn't promise me anything. And I didn't blame her. I didn't even try to argue. I just told her I was still going to try. That I was going to find a way to bring it back, even if it took time, and that I'd prove it with actions instead of just words.

When dinner ended, neither of us was ready to go home yet. We were always terrible at leaving each other, even when leaving was the responsible thing to do. So we hopped in my truck and drove to the mall like we used to, like we could pretend our way into some old, comfortable version of ourselves.

We wandered around, killing time on purpose, stretching the night out because neither of us wanted to be the one to end it.

It wasn't some big romantic evening, just simple stuff. She tried on sunglasses and I made stupid faces to vote yes or no. We teased each other. And for a little while, it felt like the old us showed up again. Not fully, but enough to remind me how easy it used to be. Like our hearts remembered even while our brains were still stuck in the wreckage.

Eventually we had to admit it was time. I drove her back to her car, still parked at the restaurant. The whole ride felt tense and restricted, like we were both thinking about a hundred things and saying almost none of them.

We hugged again, quick and polite, like we were both trying to act like this wasn't ripping us open. My heart was slamming around in my chest the entire time, and I couldn't tell if she was guarded, or if she was just as shattered as I was, or both.

I just knew I didn't want to let her go, because letting go felt like risking that this might be the last time I got to hold her at all.

I don't remember much of the forty-five minute drive back home. Just the mix of hopeful ache in my chest and that quiet, suffocating fear that I might still find a way to screw this up again.

We kept texting after that night. Most of it was normal, light stuff. Safe topics that didn't ask too much from either of us. But every now and then, the serious things would slip through, usually late at night when the world goes quiet but your heart is at full volume.

One of those nights, somewhere past midnight, she sent a message that stopped me cold.

"You've dated so many women. How do you know it's me you really want?"

It was a simple question, but I could feel what was underneath it. She was asking if she was about to sign herself up for the same kind of pain again. She was asking if she was going to spend the whole relationship looking over her shoulder, waiting for me to get restless, to start drifting, or decide she wasn't enough.

And I could picture it. Every ghost of every woman I'd ever been with standing behind her in her head, whispering the same thing. *He moves on. That's what he does.*

I stared at the screen for a second, because I knew I could answer it a hundred different ways in a text and none of them would mean what I really wanted to say. Some questions deserve a voice, not a blue bubble.

So I called her.

When she picked up, I didn't try to sound smooth. I didn't try to sell her on anything. I just told her the truth that had been sitting in my chest for a while.

"You know what's crazy? I've been thinking the exact same thing, but backwards. Why me? With everything you've been through, with every option you have, why would you even want me?"

And I meant every word.

Because I wasn't sitting there feeling entitled to her trust. I wasn't confused about why she'd question me. If anything, I was shocked she was even still talking to me at all. I knew what I'd done. I knew what I'd added to her life. And I knew what I'd taken away. I knew how easy it would've been for her to shut the door and never open it back up again.

So when she asked me how I knew it was her, what I heard was fear. And what I felt on my end was the same fear, just pointed the other direction.

Not fear that I'd miss out on someone else. Fear that I'd finally found the person I actually wanted, and I'd already proven I was more than capable of screwing it up.

I had been alone for a long time. I'd wrecked more relationships than I like to admit. I was used to being the guy who bailed before the house burned down. Most of the time, I was the one playing with the matches. Being genuinely happy with someone scared me. I didn't know how to stay in love without waiting for something to explode.

Her voice softened. She admitted fears of her own. She told me she hadn't dated much after her ex, that she didn't have the long list of relationships I had, but she knew the same fear. The fear of never being enough. The fear of never having solid ground under her feet again.

We talked for hours. Just two exhausted people letting their guard down for a while. We finally said the quiet parts out loud. That we were both scared, both insecure, both completely crushed by each other in a way we couldn't shake.

While we were talking, Lady Antebellum's "Need You Now" came on the radio in the background. She told me that song always reminded her of us. All those nights we both sat there staring at our phones, trying to be "strong," pretending we didn't need each other while every part of us wanted to cave.

Right then, I decided that was our song. A little broken, a little desperate, but honest. Just like us.

> *"Picture-perfect memories scattered all around the floor*
> *Reachin' for the phone 'cause I can't fight it anymore...*
> *...And I wonder if I ever cross your mind*
> *For me, it happens all the time*
> *I just need you now..."*

The butterflies came back hard after that. The next time I saw her, kissing her felt like the first time all over again. Awkward and absolutely perfect. We stood in the half-dark, pressed close, breathing each other in like we'd both been holding our breath for months and finally remembered how to exhale again.

I told her I loved her.

I didn't plan it. It wasn't some timed line I'd rehearsed. It just slipped out because it had been sitting there for a long time, waiting for the smallest opening.

As we went upstairs, between kisses, I remember begging her to say it back. Not in some macho, demanding way. More like a kid who finally made it back home and needed to hear the door wasn't going to slam this time.

She whispered it with tears in her eyes.

"I love you too."

Everything else went quiet for a second. The past was still there. The pain, the mistakes, the wreckage. But so was this stubborn truth. I loved her. She loved me. And for the first time in a long time, I was determined not to run from that. To stay. To actually build something with the woman who'd already owned my heart for years.

We started over. Carefully. More aware of the landmines. More aware of what it cost us the first time we blew everything up. We went back to the familiar things. Dinners, movies, late-night drives with no real destination. Just headlights on back roads and music turned up a little too loud.

But everything felt different now. Softer. Brighter. My whole life had this warm, golden tint around the edges whenever she was near. Even standing in line at the grocery store, I'd catch myself drifting off, thinking about her laugh or the way she tilted her head when she was really listening, and suddenly the rest of life didn't feel so harsh.

I was all in. Completely. No backup plan. No exit strategy. No half-hearted toe in the water. This time, I wanted the whole ocean.

Her family and friends didn't exactly throw me a welcome party. No banners. No balloons. If anything, I got the emotional version of airport security. Honestly, I couldn't blame them. If I were in their shoes, I wouldn't have trusted me either.

The difference was, for the first time in my life, I didn't get defensive. I didn't puff up. I didn't start listing reasons they were wrong about me. I kept my head down, stayed consistent, and did the work. Determined.

While we were rebuilding us, the rest of her life was still unraveling in slow motion. Without her ex's income, she couldn't hold onto her house. Having to sell it broke her heart. That place had been her safe spot, even with all the ghosts in the corners. Watching her lose it felt like watching her lose one more piece of herself. All I wanted was to step in front of the hit and take it for her.

If we were serious about building a life together, I knew my house had to be on the line too. Once upon a time, she'd asked me to move into her place, and I just couldn't do it. That house felt like a museum of a life I hadn't lived with her. Memories I wasn't part of. I couldn't sleep in rooms that had watched another man hang his coat on the same chair.

We needed fresh walls. A neutral starting line. Somewhere that belonged to us.

Even picking a town turned into its own little battlefield. I loved Champaign. It was the only place I'd ever really known. A mid-sized city with just enough spirit and just enough opportunity. A place where I imagined my son growing up seeing different kinds of people, different kinds of lives. Savannah's hometown, on the other hand, had maybe five thousand people if you counted the squirrels and stray cats. Too small for me. Too quiet. Too many judgmental eyes that already knew too much of her past.

To her, Champaign felt loud and chaotic. To me, her town felt suffocating.

So we did what grown-ups are supposedly meant to do. We compromised. We picked Monticello. Bigger than her town, smaller than mine, somewhere in between. Somewhere we could start over together on equal footing. Nobody's "home turf."

Even with that decision made, my old fears still crept in like they always did. Looking at home prices, I felt that familiar knot in my stomach. *Can I really do this? Am I enough to build this life with her? Or am I just playing house again, waiting to fail?* The doubts were loud, but for once, my determination was louder.

One day we were walking by the lake, fingers laced together, talking about nothing and everything. Out of nowhere I asked, "Wouldn't it be nice to just wake up to a beach and walk along the water like this any time we wanted?"

Her whole face lit up. She started talking about the ocean, the salt in the air, the palm trees at sunset. As she described it, I could almost feel the warm breeze myself. I told her I'd always loved the water too. Something in me loosens near it, like my whole body finally drops its shoulders.

That simple question opened a door.

Why were we only talking about starting over in places we already knew? Why not go somewhere we actually wanted to be?

Neither of us was chained down. My parents were healthy. My brother could help if they ever needed it. Savannah already felt cut off by her town. Judged. Pinned to her ex's crimes like she'd committed them herself. She could teach anywhere. We didn't have to stay in Illinois.

Once we got back to her house, just for shits and giggles, we got online and checked out Hawaii. We pulled up the cost of living and laughed so hard the dream died in about four seconds. Beautiful idea. Brutal math.

So I said, "What about Florida?"

I'd only been there once, back in '90 on a high school marching band trip, but I remembered the heat, the palms, the way the sky looked bigger somehow. Savannah had been many times and loved it. The more we talked about it, the more it made sense.

We started looking at teaching jobs for her in Florida. There were plenty. The 2008 housing crash had knocked prices down, and suddenly we were seeing beautiful homes going for way less than they should've. For the first time, the idea of palm trees instead of cornfields felt reachable.

She applied to a school in Kissimmee and got an interview, and we decided to treat it like more than just a work trip. We booked flights and called it a mini vacation together. We walked around town, toured the school, and did that dangerous thing where you start imagining a life before it actually exists. Palm trees in the background instead of flat fields. Warm air instead of ice on a windshield.

For a few days, it honestly felt like we were already halfway there. Not because everything was perfect, but because we could picture it. We could see ourselves living it. And once you can see it, staying put starts to feel like you're choosing the wrong thing on purpose.

Then they didn't hire her.

That phone call sucked the air out of both of us. The fun evaporated and it was like gravity came back all at once. But this time, we didn't let the idea die. We'd tasted possibility, and something in both of us was too stubborn to pretend we hadn't. We didn't talk about it like a fantasy anymore. We talked about it like a plan that just hit a small snag.

Not long after that, she got an offer from a school in Alva.

We were ecstatic. Not cautiously hopeful. Ecstatic. It felt like the universe took something away and then handed it back with an apology.

And like magic, both of our houses actually sold on the same day, and once that happened, things started moving fast. She put her notice in at the school in Illinois where she was a language arts teacher, and we started doing that thing where your brain is always half packing even when you're still living your regular life. Making lists. Measuring furniture. Mentally sorting what stays and what goes. Imagining what the kids will be like in a new place. What we'll be like in a new place.

Then the school called. Hiring freeze.

I still remember that moment because it was so sudden. One minute we were building our future, and the next it felt like someone yanked the floor out from under us. She was furious. Scared. Confused. And I was right there with her, trying to keep my voice steady while my stomach dropped.

We had just pushed all our chips onto the table. Houses sold. Job quit. Everything in motion. And now it felt like someone in a school administration office in Florida was about to decide our fate. They'd already given us this whole new life and then snatched it right back.

For a few hours, everything just hung there, all that hope and momentum suspended while we waited for a call back. You don't realize how fragile a "new beginning" can be until it's sitting in limbo like that.

A few tense hours later, they called again. The freeze wouldn't affect her. She'd already been officially hired before it went into place.

We both exhaled like we'd been holding our breath for days.

A few months before, I picked up a temporary job at a convenience store just to keep the lights on while everything shifted around us. It wasn't glamorous, but it was steady, and we needed steady. I didn't say a word about Florida to any of my bosses or anyone else at work. I needed that paycheck, and I didn't trust anything until it was actually happening. As far as they knew, I was committed to a career in management. In my head, I was already somewhere near the Gulf.

Two weeks before Christmas, I handed in my notice.

And on December 26th, 2010, the day after Christmas, we loaded everything we owned into a rented moving truck and pointed it south toward Cape Coral, Florida. Just the two of us, three kids, three dogs, a truck full of stuff, and a ridiculous amount of hope.

My dad drove the moving truck. He'd been a cement truck driver for forty-three years, so handing him the keys to a big rental truck felt like the safest decision we could've made. My mom rode up front with him in the cab like it was just another long haul, except this time it was our entire life bouncing around in the back.

I drove my Chevy Blazer, packed to the ceiling. The only real open space was the back seat, just enough room for the dogs to curl up and ride. I can still remember glancing in the rearview mirror and seeing fur, noses, and nervous eyes.

Savannah followed close behind in her Pontiac G6 with the boys, all of us keeping eyes on each other, making sure nobody got separated.

We were smiling like idiots. There's no other way to say it. We were tired, stressed, probably running on too little sleep and too much adrenaline, but we couldn't stop smiling. In our heads, we were already there. Already breathing salty air. Already talking about beaches.

Already imagining what it would feel like to wake up somewhere that didn't look anything like the life we were leaving behind.

The crazy part is, we hadn't even seen the rental house in person. Just photos and faith. Just a few phone calls, a lease, and the idea that it would all work out once we got there.

But it didn't matter. We weren't looking for perfect. We were looking for a new home. A new classroom for Savannah. A fresh start for me. A whole new chapter for us, with enough space for all the parts of our lives that finally felt like they were lining up.

For the first time in my life, I wasn't running from love. I was chasing it with my eyes wide open, hands on the wheel, determined not to let go this time.

For years, I honestly believed love could be salvaged with small gestures. Midnight voicemails. Novel-length text messages. Showing up with teddy bears sprayed in my cologne and leaving them on a doorstep. I really thought if I just found the right words, or timed the apology perfectly, she'd come running back and we could pretend nothing had been broken.

But life doesn't follow a script, and real love isn't rebuilding your image. It's rebuilding trust. It's becoming someone worth staying for in the first place.

It took losing Savannah over and over for that to finally sink in. Slammed doors. Unanswered calls. Those short, bitter texts that felt like she was building a wall between us. That's what made it clear. I wasn't cursed. I wasn't unlucky. I was the architect of my own heartbreak.

I was the one who kept breaking her heart and then acting shocked when she finally boarded it up from the inside. "I'm confused." "I need space." "It's not you, it's me." Like I was doing her a favor by not committing, by keeping one foot out the door.

So when I finally woke up and realized I didn't just want her back, I *needed* her, I had to swallow the fact that she didn't owe me a damn thing. Not forgiveness. Not a second chance. Not even the courtesy of texting me back. Underneath all of that was another truth I'd been dodging for years, too. I didn't just fear losing Savannah. I was terrified I'd never been worthy of her in the first place.

When we started talking again, slowly and carefully, testing old scars and trying not to step on landmines, something finally clicked. Wanting someone back isn't enough. You don't get credit for regret. You don't get rewarded just because you're finally scared of losing what you took for granted. I couldn't just say I'd changed. I had to actually change.

In the end, "starting over" didn't just mean patching things up with her. It meant tearing down the version of me that kept reaching for excuses. It meant leaving the city that held all my old patterns, leaving the comfort zones I hid inside, packing my life into a rented truck, and driving away with Savannah as a man finally choosing her on purpose.

This time, I wasn't just hoping she'd believe in me. For the first time, I was starting to believe in myself.

If I learned anything from all of that, it's that love isn't a second chance you're owed. It's a chance you earn, over and over, through a hundred small, boring choices that prove you're not who you used to be. Sometimes the most loving thing you can do is let someone walk away and do the work to become the kind of person they might want to walk back to.

I'm not proud of the pain I caused her. But I am proud I finally faced it. I owned it. And I let it build me into the man I'd been pretending to be for years.

ROUND 27:
The Night Tough Love Broke Me

The last time I really cried, the ugly kind, the kind that comes from way down in the place you don't let anyone touch, my son was seventeen. That night sits inside me like shrapnel. I can still feel it.

It wasn't one big explosion that got us there. It was a slow leak. Little fires everywhere. Eye rolls at the dinner table. Doors shut a little too hard. Half-truths that turned into full-blown lies. Disappointments that stopped feeling like "mistakes" and started feeling like, This is who he's turning into and I don't recognize this kid.

And then I did the one thing I'd always sworn I could never do. I told him to leave. I kicked my seventeen-year-old son out of the house.

It still sounds brutal when I say it out loud. Heartless. Cold. The kind of thing you judge other parents for when you're on the outside looking in. But it didn't feel like a choice. It felt like the last card in the deck. I told myself I was doing it to save him. If I'm honest, I was trying to save myself too. My sanity. My marriage. My family.

At that age, he was a firecracker. Charismatic as hell, funny, magnetic. People just gravitated toward him. But that same spark came with a reckless streak that scared the shit out of me.

He started sneaking girls into the house at night, like we were all idiots who couldn't hear a second set of footsteps. He stopped helping with anything. Dishes, trash, his own laundry, forget it. He barely acknowledged my wife or his stepbrothers. He'd walk through the kitchen, grab food, and disappear to his room like we were strangers renting space from him.

It was like he was living in our house while refusing to be part of our family.

I could feel the resentment coming off him like heat. Toward Savannah. Toward me. Toward our whole new family dynamic.

For years, it had just been him and me. Our little two-man team. Me and my boy against the world. Then suddenly, in his eyes, he had to share me with her, and with two other boys.

To me, it looked like, "Hey, Dad finally has a partner. We all have a family now." To him, it probably felt like getting demoted. Like I'd let somebody else move into a spot he'd held alone his whole life.

He didn't have the words for any of that, so it came out as attitude and distance and petty defiance. Silent protests. Smart-ass comments. That dead-eyed look teenagers get when they want you to know they don't give a shit.

Things escalated. I sat at the table one night and seriously considered military school. Not because he was on drugs or running with gangs or getting arrested, but because he was drifting. Irresponsible. Disrespectful.

And the lying. God, the lying.

About everything. Where he was. Who he was with. Whether he'd gone to work, done his homework, taken out the trash, you name it. Big things, small things, pointless things. He'd lie like it was his first language.

That's where the disgust started to really dig in. Not just with him, but with myself.

How did we get here? How did I raise a kid who can look me straight in the eye and feed me bullshit without blinking?

The final straw came on a night that still plays in my head in slow motion.

At the time, he'd just gotten a job at a local diner. A few evenings a week, nothing major. Just enough to give him some money and some independence. That night he was heading out the door like it was any other shift. Shoes half-tied, keys in hand, already halfway out of the room. He told me he was going to work.

And something in my gut immediately said, *No, he's not.*

It wasn't logical. There wasn't a detail I could point to. It was just that familiar internal alarm I'd ignored too many times because it was easier to believe him than deal with what it might mean if he was lying.

But that night I couldn't ignore it. Not again.

Something in me clicked into this calm, locked-in focus. Not an explosion. Not panic. More like a switch flipping from "idle" to "not today."

So I waited until he pulled out of the driveway, paced the house for about fifteen minutes, then I grabbed my keys, slipped on my shoes, got in the car, and drove over there. Quiet. Controlled. That pissed-off calm that feels almost worse than yelling, because it's so focused.

When I pulled into the diner's lot, his car wasn't there.

I drove through once, slow. Then again, like maybe I was somehow wrong, like maybe he parked in some weird corner or I'd missed it the first time. But no. The lot was what it was, and his car wasn't in it.

So I parked toward the back, turned off my lights, and just sat there in the dark.

I watched through the windows.

Waitresses moving between tables. A couple of regulars at the counter. The cook behind the line. The whole place looked normal. I watched the front door. I watched the kitchen entrance. I watched the back area like he might appear from behind the counter. I checked the lot again like it was going to magically show up if I stared long enough.

He wasn't there.

And I already knew that the second I didn't see his car, but I needed to know for sure that this wasn't a misunderstanding. It wasn't a mix-up. He didn't forget. He didn't get sent home early.

When I got home, I didn't come in hot. I wasn't yelling. I wasn't pacing the house or slamming cabinets. I didn't even feel like I had the energy for that. I was empty.

Because it wasn't just about where he went. It was that he could lie so easily. And what it meant that I'd gotten to the point where I had to follow my own kid just to find the truth.

Later that night, around nine, he came strolling back in like it was any other night. Phone in his hand, scrolling. Like he hadn't just blown a hole in whatever trust we still had left.

I was sitting in the living room with the lights low and the TV on mute, not watching anything, just waiting. I asked him if he'd been at work. One last chance to tell the truth.

He looked me dead in the eye and lied. Effortless. Casual.

That's when I snapped.

Not the way people imagine when they hear that word. I wasn't throwing things or screaming right away. Something just broke loose in me. Months of frustration, worry, and helplessness I'd been cramming down because I didn't know what else to do with it.

I'd been trying to keep the peace. Trying to be patient. Trying to choose the right moment, the right approach. And in that one second, with him lying right to my face again, I was done.

I told him to go.

And this time I didn't backpedal. I didn't do the usual thing where you say, "If you don't like my rules, you can leave," and then spend the next hour walking it back and handing out a hundred more chances. He'd already burned through all of those.

This time, I followed through.

My voice stayed calm at first, until it didn't. And then there was this finality in it that surprised even me.

The worst part is, he didn't have anywhere to go. No mother to run to. No close family right down the street. No backup parent waiting in the wings to soften the landing. I knew that. I knew exactly what I was doing, and that's the part that still turns my stomach.

He called a friend and the friend's mom took him in. To this day, I'm grateful to her in a way I don't even know how to properly explain. And at the same time, there's a part of me that still gets angry and ashamed when I remember that a stranger's house was where my son landed after I threw him out of his own.

Both of those feelings are true. I've never been able to make them cancel each other out.

When the front door closed behind him, something inside me went with him.

The house went quiet. No footsteps in the hallway. No cabinet doors opening and closing. No background noise of him just existing in the next room. Just this heavy silence pressing in from every direction.

I stood there in the entryway with my hand still on the knob, not moving, not thinking clearly, just getting hit with everything at once. Rage and betrayal that he could lie to me that easily, over and over. And this brutal, sharp grief because I'd just crossed a line I never thought I'd cross.

I'd just become the kind of father I swore I would never be.

I knew I'd made a decision that was going to change his life. I didn't know if it would wake him up or push him even further out of reach. Either way, it was my hand on the knob.

What haunted me most wasn't just what might happen to him. It was what might happen to us.

He'd been my best friend.

From the minute he was born, my whole world orbited around him. It was just… us. We were always together. We laughed, wrestled in the living room, had those long wandering talks about everything and absolutely nothing. I loved being his dad. I loved that I was his safe place, the one he could crash into when life hit too hard.

And now I was the one he needed to be safe from.

That thought made me sick.

I was pissed at him for putting me in that position. For pushing so hard. For tearing at the fabric of the life I'd tried so damn hard to build. But now my marriage was stretched thin and my home was tense. Every room felt like a minefield, something unsaid sitting in every corner, waiting to blow. And he was always the fuse.

I couldn't keep living like that, even for him.

That night, I crawled into bed next to my wife and everything finally caught up with me.

The pain hit full force. My throat felt like I was trying to swallow a fist. I curled into her, buried my face in her chest, and I cried. Not a couple of silent man-tears rolling down my cheek.

I completely lost it.

My whole body shook. I soaked her shirt. My chest felt like it caved in on itself. It didn't even feel like crying as much as it felt like something inside me finally splitting open, like all the fear and guilt and anger I'd been carrying had nowhere left to go.

I don't remember making much sound. Just those choked, broken breaths that happen when you're trying to breathe through it and you can't. No yelling. No dramatic wailing. Just this silent, shaking collapse that went on for what felt like forever. An hour. Maybe longer. Time stopped meaning anything.

She didn't say much. She didn't try to fix it. She didn't hit me with advice or try to talk me out of it. She just held me.

Fingers in my hair. A hand on my back. Staying steady while I broke.

She didn't fully understand. How could she? She wasn't inside my history with him, and she wasn't inside that moment the way I was. But she held me. And right then, that was enough. That was everything.

Because for me, that level of vulnerability feels humiliating. It feels like being exposed in a way I can't control. I've always had this fear that once someone sees me like that, raw, cracked open, not holding it together, they'll never be able to *un*see it.

I'm supposed to be the strong one. The steady one. The guy who keeps the roof from caving in. I can handle problems. I can take hits. I can keep moving.

I can't stand the idea of someone seeing me curled up and broken.

And that's part of why real intimacy has always been hard for me. Not sex. Sex is easy. Sex is mechanics and distraction and performance. It's a place I can stay in control.

It's the being seen that terrifies me.

I grew up with a father who was strong and quiet. Stoic to a fault. The kind of man who could walk into a room and settle it without saying much of anything. I saw him cry once in my entire life.

It was Memorial Day, and we were at the cemetery visiting his grandmother's grave, the woman who raised him. The sun was out, and the place had that familiar Memorial Day feel. People moving between headstones, flags planted in the ground, folding chairs, small talk. That mix of respect and routine.

I remember looking over and catching him in a moment he probably didn't even realize he was showing. Tears sliding down his face. No sound. No wiping them away. Just a few runaway tears on a man doing everything he could not to come apart.

That image never left me. It's still burned into my brain.

Then I joined the Marine Corps, and whatever softness I had left got stamped down even further. Don't cry, don't complain, don't feel. Emotions were treated like a liability. Tears were unforgivable. The safest thing you could be was numb.

And I got good at it, because you do what you have to do to survive the environment you're in.

But I can't blame the Marines. Or my dad.

I've made my own choices. I own my screw-ups, my anger, the times I've blown it and then doubled down instead of backing off. People did things that hurt me, sure. That's life. But I'm the one who chose how to respond, and I'm the one who has to live with the fallout when I chose wrong. That part is on me.

And for the record, I wouldn't change my childhood.

It wasn't perfect. There were days I felt like the universe handed me the short end of every stick and then snapped that stick in half just to be cruel about it. But as an adult, I can see how hard my parents worked. They didn't have much, but they gave us what they could. They loved us. They kept the lights on and the wheels turning.

They did the unglamorous, exhausting work of being steady even when life wasn't. That's more than a lot of people ever get.

So this part is for them. Thank you. You did enough. More than enough.

You gave me the tools to be tough, and eventually you gave me the perspective to understand that being tough doesn't mean never breaking. It means learning how to come back from the breaks without pretending they didn't happen.

That night, with my son's empty room down the hall, broke me.

But it also rebuilt me.

For most of my life, I'd defined strength as control. Control over myself, over my home, over my emotions, over outcomes. If I could manage everything tightly enough, nothing would fall apart. If I could hold on hard enough, I wouldn't lose anyone.

That was the lie.

When I kicked Cole out, I couldn't control any of it. Not him. Not his choices. Not the fallout. I couldn't even control my own damn heart. It did whatever it wanted. It ached, it panicked, it cracked open, and there was nothing "Marine tough" about any of it.

That night showed me how thin the line really is between love and pain. How a parent's "tough love" can look like pure betrayal from the other side. How the hardest thing you ever do for someone can feel like the cruelest thing you've ever done to them.

From my side, I was trying to draw a line. From his side, I'm sure it looked like I shoved him off a cliff.

I didn't feel brave. I felt like a failure. A coward. A fraud of a father who spent years trying to be the safe place and ended up being the one who slammed the door.

But looking back now, I see it differently.

Those tears didn't come from weakness. They came from love so deep it scared me.

I cried because I finally accepted I couldn't save him by holding on tighter. I cried because I had to let go of the fantasy that I could fix him if I just said the right thing or punished him the right way.

I cried because loving him meant giving him room to fall, even if that fall took him further away from me.

That was the night I started to understand what strength actually is.

It isn't rigid. It isn't a clenched jaw and a dry face. It isn't measured in how much shit you can swallow without flinching. That's just emotional constipation dressed up as toughness.

Real strength is soft. It's honest. It's standing in the wreckage of what you thought parenthood would look like and admitting you don't know what the hell you're doing, but you're still trying. It's letting yourself feel the full weight of what you've done and not running from it.

Sometimes love demands that we break our own hearts. Sometimes strength is letting go when every instinct in you is screaming to hold on.

And sometimes, the night you finally fall apart, is the night you finally tell yourself the truth.

ROUND 28:
The Unfinished Chapter

In high school and through my twenties, I poured everything I had into being romantic. That was my thing. My one reliable move. I didn't have money or status or some impressive career path I could point to. I had a basement, a half-functioning kitchen, and a heart that hadn't been bruised into silence yet.

When I was sixteen, I'd cook these "fancy" dinners for my girlfriend in my parents' house like I was auditioning for some low-budget cooking show. I'd follow recipes scribbled on scraps of paper, boil spaghetti, heat up jarred sauce, and act like I'd just pulled off a culinary miracle. I'd steal my mom's candles, dig out whatever plates I could find, drag a folding table into the basement, and turn that half-finished cave into my own version of a candlelit restaurant.

Yeah, it was cheaper than taking someone out. But that wasn't the point. I wanted the girl sitting across from me to feel like I'd built a little world just for us, even if that world still smelled like laundry detergent and an old couch. I wanted her to feel chosen. Not casually liked. Chosen. Worth the effort. Worth the time.

And honestly, those nights taught me intimacy isn't built on money. It's built on intention. On effort. On the quiet message underneath it all: *I thought about you. I planned this. You matter to me.*

Back then, romance felt easy. Automatic. It was my way of proving I was worth loving, even though I didn't really believe I brought much else to the table. No degree. No career. No stability. Just creativity, time, and this stubborn belief that if I loved hard enough, it would cover up everything I thought I lacked.

Now? After years of marriage, that effort isn't automatic. Not because the love is gone, but because life has crawled into every empty space where spontaneity used to live. Work deadlines. Kids. Bills. Exhaustion. All the tiny, relentless responsibilities that choke out the big gestures, and if you're not careful, even the small ones.

Some nights I'm just too tired. Some nights I'm too checked out. And if I'm being brutally honest, some nights I sell myself a lie: that the payoff won't be the same, that the effort won't mean what it used to, so why bother. Why set the table if no one's hungry?

Part of me wonders if she'd even want it anymore. And I know that might not be fair. It might just be a shield, because I don't want to risk feeling rejected. Because underneath that, if I'm really honest, I crave the simple stuff more than ever.

I don't need roses. I don't need some movie moment on a mountaintop. Give me a blanket on the sand, a cheap bottle of wine we pretend is expensive, and the sound of the waves folding onto the shore while we lie under the stars and talk. For me, conversation has always been the most intimate thing. Hearing her thoughts, her fears, her weird ideas at one in the morning, that's what pulls me closest. That's what makes me feel like we're on the same side.

These days, it feels like all of that is buried under noise. Screens. Notifications. Her scrolling. Me scrolling. Two people in the same room, living in different worlds.

We sit on the couch at night side by side, lit up by whatever our phones are feeding us, half-watching a show neither of us is really invested in. By the time we drift to bed, the only thing between us is exhaustion and blue light. The window for connection closes and we don't even notice it was open.

And then weeks pass.

When too much time goes by without us touching, really touching, I stop feeling like her husband and start feeling like a roommate with shared bills. We still run the logistics of life together, errands, calendars, groceries, but that undercurrent of you and me against the world quietly shifts into you and me, passing in the hallway. We're still a team, but emotionally it feels like we're running two different playbooks.

The worst part is knowing I've helped build that distance. My head runs so loud some nights I can't shut it off long enough to actually be present. There were nights she reached for me and I turned away, not because I didn't want her, but because I didn't know how to climb out of my own mind and into the moment. I wonder how many of those small rejections still echo inside her. How many of them replay in the back of her mind the way my own regrets replay in mine.

I wish I could say it cleanly, without tripping over my own fear: sometimes all I need is you lying against me. Your head on my chest. Your hand in mine. That's what quiets my brain. But every time I try, the words jam up. I don't want her to feel like I'm begging. I don't want her to feel like closeness is another obligation, another box to check on an already overloaded list.

We've been at this for seventeen years now, a record by any standard in my life. Maybe the routine, the silence, the dull ache of wanting more than either of us is saying out loud, maybe that's normal. Maybe most couples hit this point. But knowing that doesn't make it suck any less.

I miss the version of us who couldn't wait to be alone together. I miss being pulled in by her laugh, by the way she'd look at me like I was still worth getting dressed up for. I miss the nights we talked ourselves to sleep and woke up halfway through the night still tangled around each other like we were afraid to let go.

When you spend years stuffing your needs down because you're afraid of sounding needy, eventually you forget how to say them at all. You convince yourself your desires are burdens. So you go quiet. You hope your partner can somehow "feel" what you never say.

So I stay quiet.

I tell myself she can sense it, that she knows I still want her. I tell myself that one night we'll both put our phones down at the same time and fall back into a conversation that keeps us up too late on a Tuesday, like it used to.

That's part of why I'm writing this. Because I can't seem to get the words out of my mouth when she's sitting three feet away from me.

I want her to see that the kid who turned a basement into a restaurant is still here. He's just buried under overdue notices, work stress, teenage attitudes, and a brain that never goes quiet. I want her to know I still want her, her body, yes, but also her thoughts, her weird jokes, her stories from school, the way her laugh sounds in the dark when she remembers a punchline.

I want her to know that when we're lying there in bed and it feels like there's a canyon between us, my mind isn't saying, *I don't care.* It's saying, *I don't know how to bridge this without sounding like I'm begging for something I don't deserve.*

I want her to know my distance isn't rejection, and my silence isn't indifference. Every time I failed to plan something special, it wasn't because I didn't care. It was because I was afraid it wouldn't be received. Afraid it would just spotlight how far we've drifted instead of pulling us closer.

I remember every time I turned away. Every time she reached out and I only met her halfway instead of all the way. If I could rewind and fix those moments, I would. I'd roll over. I'd pull her in. I'd choose us over my restless mind.

So if she ever reads these words, really reads them, I hope she sees the spark that's still there under all the tired nights and busy days. I'm not asking for pity. I'm not looking for a gold star for "trying."

I just want her. Real. Soft. Present. The way she was when we first found each other. The way, deep down, I still believe we can be again.

Maybe one night soon, we'll both set our phones down on the nightstand at the same time. Maybe we'll sit outside and look up at the stars instead of down at a screen. Maybe we'll remember how easy it used to be to talk about nothing and somehow end up talking about everything.

And if that night comes, I'll be ready, with a blanket, a cheap bottle of wine, and the same simple truth I've been carrying all along:

She is still worth every candle, every effort, every long conversation in the dark.

And after all these years, I still want nothing more than her.

674

ROUND 29:
LIVING Behind Blue Eyes

If you've made it this far, you've basically walked through my whole life with me, hand in hand with the kid I used to be, the man I tried to be, and the mess I actually was most of the time.

You've seen behind the highlight reel. Behind the jokes. Behind the blue eyes.

And if there's one thing I hope you've picked up along the way, it's that none of this is a clean redemption story. There's no neat bow at the end of this book. No "and then he figured everything out and never screwed up again."

You've seen too much of me to buy that anyway.

What you've read is a trail of moments. Good ones, ugly ones, sacred ones, and a lot of really stupid ones. Strung together by a guy who spent most of his life trying to earn love, control love, or outrun it. Sometimes all three in the same week. I wish I could tell you there was a single turning point where everything snapped into place, but the truth is it's been more like a long, awkward stumble toward myself.

So if you're waiting for a tidy ending, this is your warning: you're not getting one.

What you're getting is the truest thing I know how to offer.

When I zoom out on all of this, I don't just see a bunch of random, chaotic stories. I see a scared kid who turned his whole life into an audition. The boy in the basement with dollar-store candles and spaghetti dinners wasn't just being romantic, he was saying, Pick me. I can be worth it.

Then the Marines handed me a new script: feelings are a liability. So I tried to be both things at once. The guy who'd do anything to make you feel special, and the guy who needed nothing in return. That's how you end up with a man who can pull off grand gestures but panics when it's time to sit still and be honest.

The sex, the games, the man cave routines, that wasn't freedom. It was control. I engineered nights so they would end exactly how I wanted, with women who never stayed long enough to see the cracks. If everything was temporary and scripted, no one could really reject me. They could only say, "That was fun," and leave. I told myself I was being "responsibly irresponsible," but the truth is I was hiding. Control kept me safe from the one thing I feared most: being seen and then walked away from.

The relationships followed the same pattern. Wildness dressed up pretty. Shayla, Elena, Jenna, Claire. Different faces, same seven-month curse. That was always the point where things either went deeper or blew up, and I kept choosing the explosion so I could say, I left first. On the outside I looked steady. On the inside I was a landmine waiting for the moment things got too real.

Through all of it, there was Cole. My son is both my favorite picture and my hardest mirror. The baths, the mall trips, the football game where we stood shoulder to shoulder, that's us at our best. But there's also the poem he wrote at twelve about pain I didn't see, the emo hair and late-night texts I dismissed as a phase, and the night I kicked him out at seventeen. That night broke me. I can call it tough love, and some of it was, but it left scars on both of us.

And then there's Savannah, the eye of the storm I kept walking in and out of until I finally understood what losing her would actually mean. We were two people who both secretly believed we were the least lovable one in the room, circling each other with the same fear: Why would you choose me?

Choosing her, moving to Florida, building a life from scratch, that wasn't a clean slate or a magic fix. Seventeen years in, we still lose each other on opposite ends of the couch. But I don't run at seven months anymore. I'm scared, I feel small, I hear the same old voice saying, I'm not enough, but I don't let it drive.

Underneath all of this runs a quieter thread: sacrifice and loneliness. Being the dependable one. The fixer. The guy who shows up for everyone else while ignoring his own check engine light. I don't help people for applause, but when you finally say "I can't" and suddenly you're the selfish one, it hollows you out.

I've had plenty of sex, plenty of "wild" nights, but very little of the kind of intimacy where you can completely fall apart and know the person next to you won't leave. The closest I've come was that night I cried over Cole and Savannah just held me. No fixing. No speeches. Just staying.

If there's anything I've learned, it's that you can't numb pain without numbing joy. Control isn't safety if it costs you connection. Walls keep out the hurt, but they keep out the possibility too. Being a good provider doesn't mean a damn thing if you're emotionally vacant.

I'm not the worst thing I've done or the best. I'm the sum of all of it, plus whatever I choose from here. My story doesn't excuse me, but it does explain me. And if there's any redemption in a life like this, it starts right where I'm standing now. Telling the truth about who I've been, owning the damage I've done, and trying, however imperfectly, to become someone who doesn't keep running from his own heart.

So where am I, as I write this?

I'm not the wild twenty-something in the man cave anymore. I'm not the thirty-year-old chasing long-distance flings across state lines. I'm not the freshly divorced guy leaving Vegas with a last name he regrets giving away.

I'm older now. Softer in some ways. More stubborn in others.

I'm a husband who still screws up but doesn't quit. A father who carries both pride and regret in the same chest. A man who still has trouble crying, but doesn't confuse tears with weakness anymore.

I'm still that boy with blue eyes that people have always said they loved. But now, when someone compliments them, I don't just smile and say thanks. I think about everything they've seen.

They've seen rage and lust and fear and shame.

They've seen my son being born. They've seen him walk away with a duffel bag over his shoulder.

They've seen ex-wives in wedding dresses and in courtrooms.

They've seen beer-soaked bar nights and quiet beach sunsets.

They've seen the moment I almost ruined my life. And the moment I decided I didn't want to keep living that way.

Behind these blue eyes, there is a whole universe of mistakes and miracles.

You've been in there now.

You've walked through the wreckage and the rebuilds. You've met the versions of me I'm proud of and the ones I'd rather keep locked in a basement somewhere with the old board games and empty bottles.

And you're still here.

So here's what I want to leave you with:

If you see yourself in any of this, even the parts that make you cringe, know this: you are not beyond redemption. Not the churchy version. The real version. The "I finally tell the truth about who I've been and who I want to be, and I start living like those truths matter" kind.

If you're a parent who has screwed it up, you're not alone. You will never get it perfect. Try for present instead. That's the thing your kids will remember.

If you're someone who keeps chasing chaos instead of connection, ask yourself who you're trying to outrun. My guess? It's not your ex. It's you.

If you're with someone right now and you've been holding yourself back out of fear, say the thing. Ask for the blanket on the beach. Turn off the TV. Put your phone down first. Reach out.

If you've hurt people, own it. Don't decorate it. Don't drown in it. Own it and start doing better. Quietly. Consistently. Without an audience.

And if you're someone who has built a whole identity around being strong, capable, put-together, do yourself a favor and let yourself fall apart at least once where someone can actually see you.

You might be surprised who stays.

Behind blue eyes, there has always been a boy who just wanted to be seen, held, and told, "You're enough. As you are. Not as a performance."

I spent decades chasing that statement in all the wrong places.

I'm not chasing it anymore.

Now I'm trying to live like it's true, even on the days when I don't feel it.

That's why I wrote this. Not to defend myself. But to tell the truth, the whole truth, about who I've been and how I got here.

So if you're still with me at the end of all this, here's what I'll say:

Thank you.

For listening. For watching the movie of my life without walking out of the theater halfway through. For looking behind the blue eyes instead of just complimenting them and moving on.

I don't know how my story ends. I'm still in it.

But now, at least, I'm not hiding from it.

And if there's anything worth passing on, to my son, to my wife, to anyone who's ever looked in the mirror and winced, it's this:

You don't get to rewrite your past. But you do get to decide what kind of person walks out of it.

I'm still deciding that every day.

Maybe you are too.

If so, pull up a chair…

… and take me behind your eyes.